# Stephen R. Mallory:
## CONFEDERATE NAVY CHIEF

# *Stephen R. Mallory:*
## CONFEDERATE NAVY CHIEF

BY

## Joseph T. Durkin, S.J.

1954

THE UNIVERSITY OF NORTH CAROLINA PRESS

*Chapel Hill*

*Manufactured in the United States of America*
*by The Seeman Printery, Inc., Durham, N. C.*

# *Preface*

THIS is the first published biography of the Secretary of the Navy of the Confederate States of America. It is the life story of Stephen Russell Mallory, one of the leading actors in that momentous episode of American history, the Civil War.

The documentary sources for a study of Mallory are not easy to find. On the day when the Confederate Government evacuated Richmond, as Mallory himself tells us, several boxes of official records were deliberately destroyed. Later, at her husband's instructions, Mrs. Mallory burned bundles of the Secretary's private papers, as well as other official documents in his files.

The most extensive work on Mallory, previous to the present book, is the unpublished Master's thesis of Miss Occie Clubbs, completed at the University of Florida. Miss Clubbs, in the preface of her excellent study, cites the opinions of several authorities on Southern history as to the paucity of materials concerning the Confederate Navy Secretary.[1]

The present author, however, has been fortunate in discovering—largely through the generous cooperation of Mallory's descendants—some new materials which, he trusts, constitute an ample documentary basis for a biography of Mallory. He is confident that he has at least found all the important Mallory sources that are or will be in the future available.

1. Among the scholars testifying to the lack of Mallory documents are the following: Dr. E. Merton Coulter, Dr. Ulrich B. Phillips, Capt. Dudley W. Knox, U.S.N. (Ret.), Dr. J. G. de Roulhac Hamilton, W. T. Cash, and many others.

# Contents

# *Introduction*

THE story of Stephen Mallory, Confederate Navy Chief, is only a chapter in the tragic history of the American Civil War, but it is also the portrait of one of the most human personalities produced by the conflict. The Navy Secretary was an important official of the Confederate Government, and hence he made history. But he was, above all, a man of warm feelings, of fears and faults and human charm, and of mingled strength and weakness. It is the aim of the present study to reveal this side of the hitherto most neglected member of the Confederate Cabinet.

If it were possible to summarize briefly Mallory's character, one might say, in the first place, that he was a man of heart. His love for his wife and children often bordered on extravagance, and his letters to them amply illustrate this keen tenderness of feeling. His messages to Mrs. Clement Claiborne Clay and to her sister and his communications with such intimate associates as John Reagan, Benjamin Hill, and C. C. Clay testify to his intensity of sentiment toward his friends.

In another sense, too, he had heart. He was, in every crisis that he was ever called on to face, a fighter. Most of his big battles he lost, for he was usually on the weaker side; but in none of his battles did he quit, and in none did he lose his capacity for laughing gently at himself and at others.

Furthermore, he was a person who found immense pleasure in using his mind. From his early boyhood days, he revelled in study. He had an intellect which was everlastingly thirsty for new knowledge, and which luxuriated in the toils of any mental problem. His intellectual curiosity was often, indeed, immoderate, and led him sometimes into hasty and disordered conclusions. But there is something essentially healthy and refreshing in his insatiable delight in anything that required the exercise of serious thought, especially on a topic that was new to him.

Mallory was not one of the great statesmen of the nation, but he possessed a quality which often raises the mediocre politician to a dignity of his own, if not to greatness. He was a public servant of sincere, unblemished, and irreproachable integrity—no trivial claim to present to the judgment of history.

His position in history depends ultimately, of course, on his work as chief naval administrator of the Confederacy. What should be the final verdict on his prosecution of the naval war?

In the first place, he conceived, with vision and imagination, a strategy of offense—the destruction of Northern sea-borne commerce by raiding cruisers—which was fundamentally sound. The decision to expend so much effort on the attack against Northern ocean trade was in accord with all the primary exigencies of the inferior naval condition of the South, and harmonized neatly with what were necessarily the basic political objectives of the Richmond war government.

As Mallory said so often, the South, ship for ship, could not match the North; therefore it was wise not to essay the impossible but rather to concentrate the attack on the North's one vulnerable side, her unprotected merchant marine. Serious injury to the latter would produce in the North economic, political, and psychological effects highly detrimental to a vigorous prosecution of the war by the Lincoln administration.[1] Northern industry and the structure of Northern finance would be impaired by considerable losses of cargoes at sea; the confidence of the Northern people in their government would be lessened; encouragement would be given to those groups in the North which had been cool toward the war from the beginning. Mallory's perception of the likelihood of these results of a commerce-destroying campaign, and his attempt to effect them, showed a wise intermeshing of strategic with large political policy.[2]

Furthermore, it is difficult to praise Mallory too much for his inspiration of genius which led to the creation of the first ironclad vessel of war capable of actual combat. Whatever the outcome of the war, the South, by producing the *Virginia* and her sister ships, revolutionized naval science. This

1. Cf. the ideas of Clausewitz on the relation between military strategy and political policy in Sir Frederick Maurice, *Governments and War: A Study of the Conduct of War* (London, 1926), 151-52.

2. It is interesting to note that the Nazis, after November, 1937, planned against Great Britain the same kind of naval war Mallory did against the North. Cf. Anthony Martienssen, *Hitler and His Admirals* (New York, 1949), 12: "U-boats and battleships predominated [in the German naval construction plans]. The idea of the 'balanced fleet' was postponed, for Raeder had decided that though there was not time to equal the British Fleet, there was time to build a number of independent units which would be strong enough to wage a successful war against Britain's long sea communications. Raeder's conception of naval war against England was to aim at avoiding major Fleet actions, and to concentrate on attacks against British merchant shipping. U-boats and fast powerful surface ships acting independently or with aircraft carriers were envisaged as the best means of carrying out this policy."

is undoubtedly the Confederate Navy Department's chief claim to fame, and, indeed, it may be enough.

To borrow the winged phrase of Winston Churchill, the Confederates, in the field of naval affairs, did very much with very little. Perhaps the greatest tribute to Mallory's energy and ingenuity in creating a navy from almost nothing came from a Federal admiral. Said David Dixon Porter: "We believe that all the [Confederate] iron-clads that finally got afloat or were burned on the stocks were calculated for before the war, the places of building them decided upon, . . . the material required for their construction [determined], . . . and the officers and artisans who were to be employed in the work selected. The Confederates could never, with all their energy and determination to win, have achieved such work as they performed in the building of an iron-clad navy without having had preconceived plans.[3]

The Confederate navy, it is true, did not succeed in breaking the blockade or in defending the coastal and river communications of the South. The arguments of those who held that both these things might have been done if Mallory had paid more attention to them will be presented repeatedly in this study. The careful critic cannot help perceiving considerable weight in these arguments. Mallory may indeed have somewhat slighted the needs of Atlantic, Gulf, and inland waters defense. On the other hand, it is doubtful that even five times as many gunboats could have permanently held the Union navy at bay, and Mallory could only do what seemed at the time to be most vital and urgent. Thus he staked the fortunes of the Confederacy and his own place in history on the theory that to hurt the North seriously in her sea-going commerce was to hurt the North seriously at home.

The story of Stephen Mallory takes us from Key West and Pensacola to Washington and Richmond. It was a long road, and he walked it honestly and firmly, as well as he could. And, to tell the truth, he seems to have enjoyed most of it.

3. David Dixon Porter, *The Naval History of the Civil War* (New York, 1886), 356.

# Stephen R. Mallory:
## CONFEDERATE NAVY CHIEF

# CHAPTER ONE

# Key West Prelude

K EY WEST is a dumbbell-shaped coral island
three and a half miles long and one mile wide, set low in the Gulf about
a hundred miles southwest of the tip of Florida. It was called by the
Spaniards *Cayo Hueso,* or Island of Skulls, on the strength of a legend concerning the early Indian dwellers of the region. Internecine war among the
savages, so runs the story, drove a small body of them in desperate retreat
southward from key to key. At the last island they made their final stand,
and were massacred to a man. Years later the Spanish explorers, finding
the spot adorned with a neat pile of skulls, gave the grim name to the key.[1]

In the early modern era the island was, for awhile, handed around like
a piece of attractive merchandise. Juan Pablo Salas, a Spanish soldier with
the Royal Artillery Corps stationed in Florida, received it from the Governor in 1815 as a reward for services rendered to that official.[2] In January,
1822, over a table in a bar in Havana, Salas transferred his little bit of
Florida to the American, John W. Simonton, for two thousand dollars.[3]
The latter sold undivided quarters of the island to John Whitehead[4] and
John W. C. Fleeming.[5] Soon after, other investors acquired part interests

1. Walter C. Maloney, *A Sketch of the History of Key West, Florida* (Newark, N. J.,
1876), 4-5.

2. Jefferson B. Browne, *Key West, the Old and the New* (St. Augustine, Fla., 1912), 7.

3. Simonton was a native of New Jersey who migrated to Mobile with an eye to turning
an honest penny in various types of speculation. Cf. Browne, *op. cit.,* 7.

4. He was the son of William Whitehead, who was cashier of the Newark Banking and
Insurance Company, the first bank chartered in New Jersey. John Whitehead subsequently
entered a mercantile firm in New York and finally emigrated to Mobile. He was a member
of the firm of P. C. Greene and Company. He died in New York in 1864, while vice-president of one of the largest insurance companies of that city. Cf. Browne, *op. cit.,* 199.

5. He was a personal friend of John W. Simonton and was engaged in a mercantile business in Mobile when the purchase and settlement of Key West was first thought of. After
visiting the island briefly in 1822 he returned in 1832 with the intention of developing the
Salt Pond there. He died suddenly in that year and was buried at Key West. Cf.
Browne, *op. cit.,* 199-200.

in what was now being called Key West.[6] By the year 1828 it was partly owned by the mercantile firm of P. C. Greene and Company.[7]

Two months after Simonton had made his rather momentous purchase, Lieutenant Matthew C. Perry sailed into Key West harbor and took formal possession of the island in the name of the United States.[8] He renamed the key Thompson's Island, in honor of the then Secretary of the Navy, Smith Thompson. The harbor was christened Port Rodgers, for Commodore John Rodgers, at that time president of the naval board.[9]

Key West was really a superb deep-water harbor with a spit of tawdry land tacked onto it. The topographical features of the latter are easily described. Along part of the ocean side and most of the Gulf shore of the island ran a low ridge, sloping back to shallow ponds and lagoons; behind these were stretches of stunted brush. The town extended backward from the ridge about a quarter of a mile. Across the largest of the lagoons at the southwest end of the island was a narrow foot bridge, a continuation of one of the town's main streets. As late as 1832 the total number of buildings in Key West was eighty-one.[10] The amount of taxes collected on real property was $329.61.[11]

It was perceived at once that the place was potentially an ideal naval depot and base of naval operations. Secretary Thompson pointed out that Key West would be highly important strategically in time of war between the United States and any European power having West Indian possessions.[12] The Secretary declared, in unconscious prophecy of a situation that would become almost a reality in 1862; "An enemy with a superior naval force occupying this position, could completely intercept the whole trade between those parts of our country lying north and east of it, and those to the west, and seal up all our ports within the Gulf of Mexico."[13] Nature, asserted Commodore Rodgers, had made Key West the advance post from which to watch and guard our commerce passing to and from the Mississippi. The port could control the Cuban and entire Gulf trade.[14]

But the most extended and most enthusiastic eulogy of the harbor and island as a naval and military station came from Commodore David Dixon Porter[15] in 1829: "The harbor of Key West, in my opinion, is the best harbor within the limits of the United States, to the south of the Chesa-

6. Maloney, op. cit., 6-7.                    7. Browne, op. cit., 210.
8. Maloney, op. cit., 8.                      9. Ibid.
10. Browne, op. cit., 52.                     11. Ibid., 51-52.
12. Ibid., 70-71.                             13. Ibid.
14. Ibid.
15. In the War Between the States Porter was one of the outstanding Federal naval officers, and the vigorous collaborator of General Grant.

peake. For the establishment of a naval yard, it has most decidedly the advantage over Pensacola and every other place south of the Chesapeake."[16]

The advantages of its location as a military and naval post, Porter continued, had no equal except Gibraltar. It commanded the outlet of all the trade from Jamaica, the Caribbean Sea, the Bay of Honduras and the Gulf of Mexico, and the whole western country of Louisiana and Florida. It "held in subjection" the trade of Cuba. It was to Cuba what Gibraltar was to Ceuta. It was to the Gulf of Mexico what Gibraltar was to the Mediterranean.[17]

It was not long before Key West was used as a base for a specific naval operation. In the very first year of its occupancy by United States forces it was the headquarters of Commodore Porter's "mosquito" squadron of small light-draught schooners and twenty-oared barges, engaged in hunting down the pirates who at the time were infesting the coastal waters of Florida.[18] For a boy who would soon come to the island, it was most appropriate that Key West was important from the viewpoint of the United States Navy.

Key West, though an outpost of civilization, was not uncivilized. There was some justification in the assertion of an old resident that "probably few new cities have ever started out with as high a class of population."[19] The same observer was correct when he said that "nearly all who came here had some means, and were people of culture and refinement."[20] The town was a small snug settlement of middle-class merchants and lawyers, associating amicably with a sprinkling of moderately well-to-do English civil servants from the Bahamas. They had made for themselves on the island a cozy bourgeois haven, retaining, though on a frontier, the due degree of bourgeois propriety and even, at times, stuffiness.

They lived in wide-verandaed, friendly looking houses of substantial timber, built on an architectural plan that was a blend of New England, West Indian, and Creole style. Atop some of the dwellings was the small poop veranda called the "widow's walk," from which anxious eyes could strain for a first glimpse of returning sails. Wide-spreading gumbo-limbo or sapodilla trees surrounded the houses, providing coolness and shade.

Within these homes was solid and comfortable furniture of mahogany, cedar, or pine. (Much excellent timber came to grief on the Key West reefs

16. Browne, *op. cit.*, 212.                   17. *Ibid.*, 213.
18. *Ibid.*, 73. For this campaign Porter had abandoned the use of the large frigates which could not follow the small pirate craft into narrow shallow waters. The "mosquito" boats bore such appropriate names as *Midge, Gallinipper, Gnat,* and *Sandfly* (*ibid.*, 73).
19. *Ibid.*, 13.                   20. *Ibid.*

in ships from the four corners of the earth.) Massive silver services and rich china were not unusual adornments of dining-room tables. Parlors were, normally, overstuffed with flouncing couches, great-grandfather chairs, multitudinous crockery creations, family portraits, and other assorted gew-gaws. It may have been all rather Bloomsbury comfort, but it was enjoyed with a vast complacency by all, in the slumbrous semitropical climate which permitted concentrated bursts of energy in the field of business between the hours of 11:00 A.M. to noon, and from about 3:00 P.M. to eight o'clock in the evening.[21]

Mingled, it is true, with this bourgeois atmosphere was a lingering Spanish tone. Some—although not the majority nor the most important—of the people of the island still clung to the cultural tradition of old Spain; and the influence of that tradition was far out of proportion to the number of its adherents. If, on a soft moonlit evening, a young blade serenaded his lady, it was usually a Spanish air that he played, on a Spanish guitar. On Sundays and holidays, along the breeze-swept promenade, a touch of old-world grace was added by the mantillas, large ornate combs, and Spanish shawls of the women.[22]

The town had, in 1827, a population of about three hundred souls, and it was one of the most isolated spots in the Western Hemisphere. There was not a church or a school on the island, nor, at that time, a court of law or even a magistrate within four hundred miles.[23] Contact with the outside world was maintained chiefly by means of the ships that called at the port, and especially the monthly steamer from Charleston.[24]

21. For the social and cultural atmosphere of early Key West, cf. Maloney, *op. cit.*, 17, 79-80; Browne, *op. cit.*, 13-15, 51, 174; Anon., "Key West and Salvage in 1850," *Florida Historical Society Quarterly*, VIII (July, 1929), reprinted from *Hunt's Merchants' Magazine*, January, 1852; Marie L. Cappick, Island Pageant: A History of Key West (unpublished manuscript; Key West, 1935); Occie Clubbs, The Life of Stephen Russell Mallory the Elder (unpublished Master's thesis; Gainesville: University of Florida, 1936); Simon P. Richardson, *Lights and Shadows of Itinerant Life: An Autobiography* (Nashville, 1901); Ernest Hemingway, *To Have and Have Not* (London, 1937); *Florida, A Guide to the Southernmost State* (Federal Writers' Project, W. P. A.; New York, 1939); *Key West, Florida: Photogravures*, ed. H. Crain (Key West, 1896); also, paintings of Key West scenes by Winslow Homer.

22. For the Spanish cultural influence in Florida, cf.: Caroline M. Brevard, *A History of Florida from the Treaty of 1763 to Our Times* (2 vols.; Deland, Fla., 1924), II, 31; Cappick, *op. cit.*, 6; Richard L. Campbell, *Historical Sketches of Colonial Florida* (Cleveland, 1892); George W. Cable, *Old Creole Days* (New York, 1918).

23. The first court at Key West was the Superior Court of the Southern Judicial District of the Territory of Florida. It was established in 1828. In 1847 was set up the District Court of the United States for the Southern District of Florida (Browne, *op. cit.*, 64).

24. The first mail steamer to Key West after the establishment of the post office in 1829 was named *The Post Boy*. She made, from Charleston, monthly trips which frequently lengthened out to fifty days. About 1848 she was superseded by the steamer *Isabel* (Maloney, *op. cit.*, 28-29).

The degree to which Key West was cut off from the rest of the world was revealed as late as 1835 in the complaints of the town journal regarding the mail service. On August 15, the islanders were still waiting for New York newspapers issued on May 28 and June 4. At the then prevailing rate of mail transmission, grumbled the editor, Key West would receive but four or five "half mails" yearly, for, to accentuate the inconvenience, half the mail was sometimes lost in transit. It is rumored, reports the Key West *Enquirer* on February 21, 1835, that the mail boat has gone on a turtling voyage, and it was said that this business would better suit her than that of a United States mail boat.

One might suppose that the bundles of newspapers, when they finally arrived, would be eagerly perused for news of the great world outside. Doubtless this was so; yet we must not underrate the force of Key West provincialism. Although the turbulent events of Jackson's second administration and numerous other happenings of national import would naturally loom large in the mind of the urban North, there were special local concerns in the little island town that tended to outweigh in popular estimation the larger affairs of the United States. This explains why the *Enquirer* could make such announcements as the following, scarcely complimentary to the journalism of the largest city in the country: "Nov. 22, 1834. . . . We have received New York papers as late as the 5th instant. They contain no news of importance. . . ." And "Nov. 29, 1834. We are favored with N. Y. papers as late as the 15th inst. They contain nothing of importance."

There were, it must be said, some unpleasant factors that were likely periodically to disturb the opaline tranquillity of the island. Hurricanes, sudden and fierce, sometimes leveled scores of buildings in a few minutes. The great storm of 1846 was to sweep away the lighthouse and drown every one of the seven persons dwelling within it.[25] In at least one instance a substantial house had been lifted from its foundations by the raging wind and carried bodily out to sea.[26] Even the corpses, long buried in the cemetery, were, in the storm of 1846, blasted out of their resting places and strewn around the streets.[27] A large box of muskets and a grindstone, says a reliable historian, were blown by the gale for a distance of nearly half a mile.[28]

There was also the recurring menace from the Seminole Indians. In 1840 more than fifteen families on Indian Key, fifty miles from Key West,

25. *Ibid.*, 41.     26. Browne, *op. cit.*, 158.
27. Cf. Stephen Mallory's description of the hurricane of 1846, in *New York Herald*, November 6, 1846.
28. Maloney, *op. cit.*, 61.

would be barbarously murdered by these savages. Because of further threatened attacks, Cape Florida lighthouse would be abandoned in 1836.[29] A punitive expedition sent from Tampa (Fort Brooke) in 1835 under Major Francis L. Dade of the United States Army would be ambushed on the march and massacred.[30] When this news reached Key West the citizens were badly frightened, although the scene of the massacre was hundreds of miles away. The *Enquirer* burst out in panicky headlines: "The Indians! Horrible Intelligence from the Seat of War!"[31] It was reported that refugees were hastening southward.[32] The island's volunteer militia was called out for guard duty. Patrols on land and water were maintained nightly, and a fast vessel was despatched to Havana to request the protection of any American man-of-war that might be in that harbor.[33] Such uncomfortable reminders never permitted the dwellers on Key West to forget that they were, with all their transplanted civilization, still on a frontier.

These disadvantages were, however, counterbalanced in the minds of the inhabitants by the consideration of cold cash returns from the two chief occupations of the settlement—commerce and the business of wrecking and salvage. Key West, despite its isolated position in some respects, was, as Commodore Rodgers remarked, "the most certain key to the commerce of Havana, [and] to that of the whole Gulf of Mexico."[34] It was one of the chief ports of call for merchantmen in the southern coastal waters of the United States, and the most important depot for the Caribbean and Gulf trade. The business of supplying and trading with the ships that paused so frequently at the Key West wharves kept the waterfront of the island pleasantly active. There was, on the part of the local ship chandlers and merchants, no undue hurrying or bustling, which, in view of the blanket of humidity that usually prevailed during the daytime, would have been

29. This is the present Cape Florida Light at Biscayne Bay, modern Miami.

30. Tampa was, of course, hundreds of miles from Key West; but the citizens of the latter place were not completely reassured by this fact. Dade, a native of Virginia, had served with distinction in the War of 1812. At the time of his fatal expedition he was in command of the Army post at Key West. Cf. Rowland H. Rerick, *Memoirs of Florida, embracing a general history of the province, territory, and State ...*, ed. Francis P. Fleming (2 vols.; Atlanta, 1902), I, 181, 201; "The Dade Massacre," *Florida Historical Society Quarterly*, V (January 1927), 125-38; W. T. Cash, *The Story of Florida*, (4 vols.; New York, 1938), I, 294-95.

31. January 10, 1836.

32. *Ibid.*

33. *Ibid.*, January 16, 1836.

34. Report of Commodore John Rodgers, November 24, 1823, in Browne, *op. cit.*, 71. Minor industries of Key West in its early period were sponge raising, fishing for the Havana market, and the manufacture of salt (Maloney, *op. cit.*, 58). Not until the era of the Cuban revolutions did cigar making become one of the leading economic activities of the island.

certainly inappropriate and possibly unhealthy; yet enough business was done to bring a comfortable profit to the coffers of the islanders.[35]

A more important circumstance from the viewpoint of possible economic gain was the fact that Key West was the nearest haven along a hundred-mile stretch of the most perilous reefs on the Atlantic and Gulf coasts. This dangerous shore line meant that many ships would run aground and imperil their cargoes, thus providing opportunity for the wreckers and salvors who operated their fast, tough vessels out of the island harbor; and it meant juicy profits for the merchants who, on extremely advantageous terms, bid for the salvaged goods at the Key West auctions.[36]

The colorful wrecking industry has been, at times, misrepresented. It may have been true, as the historian of Key West remarks, that, "to some extent, before it [the wrecking business] was regulated . . . it was a species of relentless piracy."[37] There are ominous hints—though no considerable proof—of unholy collaborations in the early days between wreckers and lighthouse keepers, who, for the accommodation of dishonest wreckers, would furnish false light signals, or no lights at all, on stormy nights, thus luring merchantmen onto the rocks.

Whatever the truth of these allegations, it is certain that by 1828 (the date of the establishment of the admiralty court at Key West) wrecking was a legitimate business, carried on in accord with strict rules of law. William Marvin, first judge of the Superior Court of the Southern Judicial District of Florida, was the author of many of these rules for the twenty or more wrecking vessels in the Key West area.[38] In case after case involving wrecking and salvage claims, he hammered out a code of procedure for wreckers and ships' masters and underwriters, and placed the activities of the former on a legal basis which assured equity to all parties.[39]

35. Cf. the following from the *Key West Enquirer,* September 19, 1831: "Our coming winter bids fair to be brisk and stirring. Five vessels bound to southern ports have passed through our harbor within a week, thus considerably shortening their voyage, avoiding the Gulf Stream, Tortugas shoals and southerly winds; and we have no doubt that when the last change in our pilotage law becomes more generally known, a majority of the southern traders, drawing less than twelve feet water, will avail themselves of the N. W. Pass. This will afford a ready and economical opportunity for supplying our merchants, and by furnishing a more frequent interchange of letters and newspapers, will add a few links to the chain which is yet to connect us with our northern friends."

36. Cf., in regard to wrecking industry: William Marvin, *A Treatise on the Law of Wreck and Salvage* (Boston, 1858), 338-41 ("Rules of Wrecking"); "Key West and Salvage," *supra cit.;* Kathryn T. Abbey, *Florida, Land of Change* (Chapel Hill, N. C., 1941), 184; *St. Augustine Examiner,* March 24, 1860; "Wrecks, Wrecking, Wreckers, and Wreckees on the Florida Reef," *Hunt's Merchants' Magazine,* April, 1842; Browne, *op. cit.,* 162.

37. Maloney, *op. cit.,* 53.

38. Browne, *op. cit.,* 166.

39. Marvin, *op. cit.,* 4-5, 6-27, 28-45, 105-80.

The laws governing wrecking were very detailed. In the first place, no ship or ship master could engage in the industry without previously securing a license from the court. Before any specific wrecking operations could begin, the consent of the master of the imperiled vessel must be obtained. The first wrecker to arrive at the scene of a wreck had full control of the procedure to be followed in saving the vessel and her cargo. This first comer could ask for the assistance of any other wreckers who might be near by or present, and, if the latter accepted the invitation, they became subject to the orders of the first wrecker and would, of course, receive their due share of the salvage profits. The respective powers of the wrecking master and those of the master of the imperiled vessel during the rescue operations were carefully prescribed and delimited.

The reward claimable by the wreckers was to be ascertained by the admiralty court's verdict on questions such as the following: How much of the cargo was saved by the wreckers? How much of it would have been saved even without the aid of the wreckers? What was the amount of labor and danger undergone by the wreckers in saving the ship or/and the cargo? How efficient were the wreckers in the operation as a whole? The amount—in money or goods—decreed by the court to the wreckers as compensation for their labors usually averaged about one-sixth of the value of the saved property. The remainder of the rescued goods was to be sold at auction at Key West.[40]

The wreckers' occupation was not without its perils. Sometimes the rescuing vessel itself would be damaged seriously or even disabled while engaged in its work. Often, in order to save cargoes, some of the wrecking crews would be obliged to dive in their bare skins deep down through waters impregnated with spilled dyes from broken bales of dry goods.[41] Sometimes it was necessary to swim through flooded ships' holds filled with thick quantities of floating spices injurious to the tissue of the human eye.[42]

40. Ibid., 89-104. A traditional Key West story (not fully documented) is that of Brother Eagan, who combined his occupation as a wrecker with the profession of preacher. One day, while addressing his congregation, he descried through the window of the church a vessel just run aground on the reefs. He knew the rush toward the wharves that would immediately follow the cry of "Wreck a-shore!" and he was determined to be first in the race. At the moment he was commenting on the text of St. Paul which begins, "Not all those who engage in the race receive the prize." Never pausing in his sermon, he walked slowly toward the door. When he reached the entrance he cried suddenly, "Wreck!" and dashed unceremoniously toward the water front, followed by half the male portion of the worshipers.

41. Browne, op. cit., 166-67, in re rescue of brig Isaac Allerton.

42. See the tribute to the wreckers written by the subject of this biography, Key West Enquirer (October 3, 1835).

It might justly be supposed that a boy growing up at Key West at this period would be much fascinated by the sea and the ships—merchantmen, vessels of war, and wreckers—and by the dreams that the sea and the ships would evoke in a young and fresh imagination.

In 1820 John and Ellen Mallory, after brief residences in New York and Mobile, settled down at Key West with their two sons, John, Jr., aged twelve, and Stephen, aged nine.[43] Ellen was Irish born. Sent as a child to the island of Trinidad to live with her two planter uncles, she had there eventually married John Mallory, a construction engineer from Connecticut.[44]

When the family came to Key West, Ellen was the only white woman on the island. She possessed, by all accounts, much charm and sweetness of character. "I hear her musical voice today," later recalled one of the old inhabitants, "as she was wont to speak, standing at the bedside of the sick and dying. Catholic by rites of baptism, Oh! how truly catholic, in the better and non-sectarian use of that term, was her life, devoted as it was to acts of kindness. With many opportunities of becoming rich, she died comparatively poor. Her mortal remains . . . [are] respected of all men. She left no enemy on earth."[45]

Naturally, Ellen Mallory was an important influence in her son Stephen's life. Despite her amiability there was also in her character, apparently, a tendency toward sternness. In his diary written years later, Stephen recalled that she "was passionate, and punished me severely and unreasonably at times; and this, from my peculiarly sensitive appreciation of wrong, rankled and festered in my heart, and was never entirely rooted out until after her death." Yet he attests that she spared no sacrifice to care for his upbringing, nor does he fail to add that she won his deep love, although he feels that he failed to show his affection as he should have done. He adds that "she was never severe save when angry."[46]

There was much to intrigue a boy's imagination in the romantic asso-

43. There is some doubt as to the year of Stephen Mallory's birth. It was certainly 1810 or 1811. The latter date, it would seem, is the more probable, since Mallory says in his diary that he began school at a spot near Mobile at the age of nine shortly after the family's arrival at Key West (cf. his diary, quoted on p. 12, *infra*).

44. Mallory to his son Buddy, from Fort Lafayette, New York Harbor, September 27, 1865. This letter, of considerable length, includes a review of Mallory's boyhood and youth. It was recopied by Mallory in his Diary and Reminiscences, the original copy of which is in the Southern Historical Collection, University of North Carolina Library, Chapel Hill, N. C. The Library of Congress has an authenticated typescript copy of the diary. The present author has used this copy and checked all references against the original.

45. Maloney, *op. cit.*, 61-62.

46. Mallory, letter to Buddy, *supra cit.*

ciations of the Florida Keys. Old men would tell stories of the famous pirate José Caspar, who stole the crown jewels from the king's palace and
hid them in a galleon. They were still there, it was solemnly believed, in
an old cannon of the *Renunciar,* lying five fathoms deep somewhere off
Indian Key. Caspar, it was said, had also sunk thirty million dollars in
a longboat near the island that bore his name. Or an old sailor might show
the boy an ancient map with its dimly marked sailing instructions for the
king's ships: "The galleons and fleet usually lying at Habana and the
whole Spanish Armada sail for Spain by this line."[47]

The sea and ships loomed large in the thoughts and lives of the people
of the island that was such a tiny speck dropped into the heart of the sea.
The great ocean that could be so tender and beautiful one moment, and so
fierce and terrible the next, meant to them life or death. They were tight
and deep in its embrace; it was their sole tie with the rest of the world;
it could keep them alive and prosperous, or it could, in a few moments,
wipe them into oblivion. The sea and the ships that rode the sea so that
three hundred people on Key West could work and play and raise their
families and fashion their individual destinies were, to the islanders, of
supreme and urgent importance. A boy's sensitive feelings would be aware
of much of this.

At the age of nine, Stephen was sent to the home of a friend of the
Mallorys at "The Village," below the town of Blakely, opposite Mobile, to
attend a country school in the neighborhood. The boy's new surroundings
were even more strongly pervaded by the romance and mysterious spell of
Spanish Florida. Some said that they could still hear in the woods, when the
moon was up, the far-off dying echoes of the bugles of the French crusaders.
The dashing ghost of Galvez, the Spanish cavalier who "looked too young
to be a general," though he was one, returned at times, it was said, to fight
again his hopeless, brilliant battle at Spanish Fort. The silent and shadowy
chieftains of the Alabamas, Choctaws, and Creeks would reassemble near
by, according to the legend, to gaze again with great longing at the land
that once was theirs.[48] There was mystery in the swamps, the rivers, the
bayous, the inlets, and the still lakes; there was a spell in the gloom of the
sandy, sparkling beaches; memories of French and Spanish and English
searchers for empire lurked in every prairie, bay, ancient oak, and coquina
ruin.[49]

47. Cappick, *op. cit.,* 548.
48. Marie L. Cappick, conversation with the author.
49. Alfred J. Hanna, "Florida's Mysterious Personality," *Florida Historical Society Quarterly,*
VIII (April, 1930), 221.

The headmaster of the school at "The Village" was an old Scotchman of doubtful pedagogical attainments, with a fondness for the hickory stick and good whiskey. Most of the scholars were grown young men—Stephen later called them "cow boys"—whose studies of reading and writing were interrupted every few days by a fight with the master, resulting always in a holiday the next day. Stephen was far younger than his schoolmates, and, although he says they were kind enough to him, he was driven a good deal to amuse himself with his own society, a necessity which, he felt, added to his strength of character and induced in him a habit of thinking for himself and of acting on his own conclusions.[50]

During his brief stay of six months or a year at the school, Mallory tells us, he learned to read, but very little else, save how to ride, shoot, and swim; for he spent most of his time in the pine woods and on the beach, nominally at school but in reality "kicking up his heels in a healthy country and acquiring a good constitution, a knowledge of birds and beasts and crabs and fishes." Once, for a brief moment, at this early period, Stephen Mallory saw history ride by. Andrew Jackson, on his way to repeat his capture of Pensacola, passed through "The Village." It is likely that the boys at the school ran out to see the troops; certainly Stephen did not realize how the event was bound up with his own future.[51]

Mallory always held that his character had been permanently influenced by an incident that occurred during these school days. One Saturday he was taken along by the larger boys on a hunting party. They had in the group but one old-fashioned single-barrel shotgun, which was used by each of the boys in turn. Suddenly Stephen found himself with the gun in his hand, facing what he thought was a coon, treed by their dog. He tremblingly took aim and fired. He was so small that in order to shoot the gun he had to hold the stock under his arm and receive the recoil on his cheek and nose; so that "whenever I shot her off I was prepared to cry."[52]

Down from the tree, badly wounded but still bitterly fighting, crashed not a coon, but a wildcat about four feet long, "with an enormous head, large claws, and upon the whole an ugly customer." The dog and this monster engaged in a vicious struggle, terminated in the best tradition by Stephen's beating the big cat senseless with a club. The young hero, with the tears still in his eyes from the gun's kick, had won from the incident a

50. Mallory, letter to Buddy, *supra cit.*

51. *Ibid.* As regards General Jackson's passage through "The Village," cf.: H. H. Holmes, "The Village," in *A Brief History of Baldwin County,* compiled by L. J. Comings and Martha M. Albers (Fairhope, Ala., 1928).

52. Mallory, letter to Buddy, *supra cit.*

self-reliance and confidence in himself which, he says, deeply affected his whole life afterward.[53]

Stephen's sojourn at Blakely was ended by his father's death and the boy's subsequent recall by his mother to Key West. John, the older son, also died at about this time. In order to support herself and Stephen, Mrs. Mallory now opened a boarding house for seamen. Shortly afterward, about 1826, for reasons still obscure, Stephen was sent for further schooling to the academy of the Moravians at Nazareth, Pennsylvania.

He had indeed entered a different world.[54] The Moravian settlement in Northampton County reproduced, in many respects, quaint and sober Protestant Bohemia of the seventeenth century. It was a lush and comfortable land, peopled by a gentle, pious, and industrious folk. The countryside was gently rolling, the very streams and brooklets spoke softly, the wheat fields breathed slowly and contentedly in the sun, the vineyards and orchards were a rich-spangled odorous quietness. The people worked hard, but serenely. They were a very simple people, in their manners and views. They were marked by a slow and unostentatious charm. German Pietism elsewhere had had its aberrations; here it flowered rationally and beautifully.

In Nazareth one walked through cobbled streets along which stood high-gabled, hood-chimneyed, tile-roofed houses with dormer windows of red-, blue-, and yellow-studded panes. Gardens were everywhere, even edging out into the middle of the narrow sidewalks. Stephen boarded and studied in the fortress-like limestone Nazareth Hall, with its ponderous rafters of heart-of-oak that spoke of the dim, deep German forests. In adjacent Whitefield House he attended divine services, an important feature of which was sacred music and the robust singing of hymns. The Moravians were justly celebrated for their organists, trombone choir, and orchestra. In addition, the Lord was praised with becoming dignity and fervor with mandolin, flute, cittern, viola, and harpsichord.

It was here at Nazareth, most probably, that Stephen imbibed a love of music which never left him. He learned to sing well, and to play the violin. He received also an elementary training in Latin and Greek, in accordance with the excellent pedagogical methods of the Moravians.[55] He must have been influenced, furthermore, by the atmosphere of tender

53. *Ibid.*

54. Clubbs, *op. cit.*, 13-31, gives a particularly good account of the whole of Mallory's Moravian period. For further details of the school and the locality, cf.: Levine T. Reichel, *The Early History of the Church of the United Brethren (Unitas Fratrum), Commonly Called Moravians in North America, A. D. 1734-1784* (Nazareth, Pa., 1888), 198 and *passim.*

55. Mallory, letter to Buddy, *supra cit.*

piety pervading the school. The "dear little ones," as the pupils were affectionately described by one of their teachers, were trained from their earliest years in the practice of a rather precocious though apparently un-affected religious devotion. Five or six of the eight- or ten-year-olds would often sit solemnly together on a bench and have a prayer meeting or, as they were taught to term it, a "love feast." They would sing hymns, then one of them would "tell of the Saviour's blood, how many wounds He had, etc."[56]

In somewhat dramatic fashion Stephen displayed, during these school days, a trait that would mark him throughout his life: a delicate sense of chivalry toward the fair sex. He became much smitten by the charms of a Dutch girl of Nazareth named Arabella Stout, whom he later described as being some six years his senior and "about three times my weight." When one of his fellow students referred to her as "a fat overgrown Dutch-man," Stephen's fists flew until he made the mocker admit that Arabella was not a Dutchman and that she was really very good looking.[57]

After about three years at Nazareth he was withdrawn from the school by his mother, because she could no longer pay his tuition. He had finished the only period of formal education he would ever have.

The fall of 1829 found him again at Key West, where his mother, single-handed, was still maintaining her lodging house. He helped her in every way possible by writing her business letters for her, running errands, and performing other similar chores, and, while not thus employed, he enjoyed himself in strenuous open-air activity. Every once in a while he would steal over to Cuba for a brief visit, or go hunting on the islands adjoining Key West. He mingled by preference with the rougher elements among his male associates, and learned to ride, fence, box, row, and shoot. Nor did he neglect the more polite acquisitions. He took up dancing, learned to play the flute, and studied French and Spanish sufficiently to read in those languages.

For a time he tried his hand at pioneering. He went with a friend to assist in establishing a plantation at New River, on the Florida coast, and spent a year in hunting, fishing, and learning woodcraft from Indian com-panions. After spending whole weeks in the forests and swamps he became so enchanted with the life of a hunter in such a genial climate that he seriously debated with himself the advisability of remaining there per-manently. From this momentary attachment to a vigorous outdoor life he

56. Reichel, *op. cit.,* 198.
57. Letter to Buddy, *supra cit.*

was, however, diverted in 1830, when he accepted the not very important post of Inspector of Customs at Key West.[58]

It was in the spring of 1830 that Angela Moreno, with her swift, imperious tread, walked into Stephen Mallory's life. Writing to his son, Buddy, years later, he thus described the story of that first meeting: "In 1830, early on a pleasant spring morning, sitting upon a wharf at Key West, I first saw your mother. She was dressed, I remember, all in white . . . [and had] then just [come] from Pensacola, and with two other young ladies, [was] on her way to Bridgeport to school. She spent a day at Key West, and my attention was very strongly attracted by her; so strongly that I never forgot her, but on the contrary thought of her much and often."[59]

Angela, the daughter of Francesco and Josepha Lopez Moreno, wealthy residents of Pensacola, was then about sixteen. She was Spanish to her finger tips, and could not at this time speak a word of English. She was not notably beautiful. A brunette of medium height, inclined to plumpness, her chief charm seems to have been a pertness and independence of spirit which, in some inexplicable way, magnetized people. She was, apparently, all feeling—swift-changing, shifting feeling—and her emotional vibrancy immediately won everybody's affection. She was a very complex person. She looked rather like one of Murillo's plainer and less thrilling Madonnas, and she had a temperament like that of Becky Sharp. She could be gay as a child one moment, and deep in despondency the next. She could be sweet and brave today, and bitter, jealous, or cowardly tomorrow, and always remained very much of a charming and unpredictable child. Raised and sheltered in luxury, and considerably spoiled, yet, paradoxically, she was amazingly unaffected.

At this first encounter Stephen saw her only for a few moments and did not speak to her. But he never forgot her, and he at once determined, in his naïvely egotistical way, to have her for his wife. Her own later comment on this crucial first meeting with her future husband was: "I remember that he was the only well-dressed young gentleman I saw, and he was very handsome. But no thought of him and the future entered my mind then."[60]

Meanwhile Stephen was much occupied. He had, quite calmly and confidently, taken another resolution: "I . . . at once made up my mind to study law, become a lawyer, and at some day to go to Congress."[61] It was

58. *Ibid.*                                    59. *Ibid.*
60. Interview with Mrs. Mallory in *New Orleans Times Picayune*, January 12, 1898.
61. Mallory, letter to Buddy, *supra cit.*

typical of him that he never envisaged the slightest possibility of his failing to achieve this rather elaborate ambition. He was, however, aware of much deficiency in his previous schooling. He determined therefore to complete his education by his own unaided efforts, a project he at once undertook much in the manner of an army storming a stockade.

Without a teacher or friend to advise him, he lost much time in reading useless as well as useful books, poring over anything and everything that came his way. Night was his favorite time for study. Locked in his room with a hot towel around his head to keep him awake, he fought his books and toiled over his notes grimly, doggedly. He admitted later that he was not immune to a weakness which sometimes accompanies such efforts: he began to develop a sense of superiority to those around him who were not similarly improving themselves. He became more and more retiring, sensitive, proud, and self-willed; and, if the truth must be told, a bit of a bore in conversation. To the end of his life he could never fully resist the temptation to wear his learning on his sleeve. More serious as a defect was his disorderly, confused method of study. If in later years his thinking and writing were marked by wide variety of topics and a versatility of illustration, rather than by clarity and a sense of synthesis, the reason lies probably in the chaotic character of his early intellectual preparation.

The list of the books he devoured during these years is somewhat incredible. It included works on the use and training of carrier pigeons; on the origin of political nicknames, such as Whig, Tory, Croppy, White Boy; on the theories of generation, the belief in ghosts, lunar rainbows, and the execution of Madame Roland; on the Koran; on the moral apothegms of Dr. Johnson; on the sayings of Sancho Panza; on the stones found in the ancient quarries of Palmyra; and much more of such awe-inspiring miscellany. His self-evolved system of study was marked by an almost insatiable passion for taking notes. By keeping a sheet of paper in every book while he was perusing it and noting briefly what seemed to be new and worthy of memorizing or an old established and interesting truth presented in a new light, and by then keeping these sheets and binding them together, he preserved an epitome of the ground over which he had traveled in his reading. In later life, he testified, this collection of notes was of great service, for often the sight of a single page of his scribblings would recall much of the book to which they referred.

Stephen's chief purpose, it would appear, in compiling such cumbrous rosaries of quotations was to provide for himself a ready means of spicing his conversation. In his letter of instruction to his son Buddy, written many years later, he elaborated on the benefits of having always at hand an apt quotation from the poets, or an interesting anecdote from the great novelists, or a relevant incident from history.

During this period he paid much attention also to the formation of good moral habits. A set of resolutions, in part originated by himself and in part selected from the writings of moralists, he carefully copied out and placed in a conspicuous part of his room, so that he could not avoid seeing them many times daily. He neither smoked nor drank, and on one point he seems to have been particularly earnest: he held women in deepest respect, and enjoyed their company as being one of the surest refining influences on his character. He recognized the fact, also, that "they, more than men, determine a young gentleman's status in society."

He declared later, looking back on this stage of his life, that a chivalrous, unselfish regard for women guided him in his relations with them, and that its consequences were purifying and refining. It mattered not, he declared, whether she whom he might invest with merit possessed it or not; the salutary effect upon him was the same. He recalls how Cervantes makes his hero fall in love with a rude country wench, and then shows us throughout the story that the effect of this love upon the hero himself was precisely what it would have been if she had been in fact the lovely princess he deemed her to be. It was sometimes far better, he observed, to love an ideal, with Dante and Don Quixote, than a reality with Henry VIII.

He set himself a high ideal in the matter of sincerity and truthfulness in words. Here, too, he was thinking particularly of his intercourse with the other sex. He felt that especially among women was the virtue of truth and the merit of sincerity appreciated. A man, he thought, might be "as homely as a stone fence, his foot might be obtrusively large, his eyes might squint, his gait and manner be awkward, and his figure ungainly"; but, if women know that they may rely upon every word and every act of his, he will command their respect, and might secure their affection. This circumstance, Stephen decided, arose simply from the fact—although few women thought enough of the point to know it—that it was precisely from the want of truth and sincerity in man toward them that their misfortunes had chiefly come.[62]

His reverence for womanhood was illustrated by an article that he wrote for the *Enquirer* in answer to the charge that "woman is only a necessary mechanical agent in the hands of men," and that "the distinguishing

62. *Ibid.*

characteristics of the sex are inordinate vanity and fugacity." He had a fictitious "Lucy" speak the following sentiments, which reveal much of his attitude toward the sex: "How my soul has sickened at observing a man of intelligence placing us upon a par with the inanimated productions from a sculptor's chisel, and deriving all his gratification from an exercise of the eye alone. Oh! could he appreciate our exalted sense of right, and scorn of wrong, our careful watchfulness over the feelings, and our anxious sympathy for the woes of those around us, our refined sensibilities, and our aspirations for all that is excellent, he would no longer accommodate his course to the adventitious circumstances in which we happen to be placed, or worship the trappings by which we happen to be adorned."[63]

The first church to be opened in Key West was under Protestant Episcopal auspices, and Stephen was among its charter members. His adherence to this religious body seems, at first, rather surprising since, being by birth and upbringing a Roman Catholic, he was, by the tenets of his faith, forbidden to participate in the organized services of other creeds. However, before 1845 a Roman Catholic priest rarely came to the island, and there was no established Roman Catholic congregation there. It is probable that Stephen felt that under such circumstances it was permissible to connect himself with the only available organization of Christian worshipers.[64]

While carrying on his routine of private study during the years 1830-1834 Mallory, in accordance with his resolution, was also learning law in the office of William Marvin. The Judge, as has already been mentioned, was the recognized authority on the jurisprudence of wreck and salvage. From daily association with such a master in a highly specialized field, Stephen himself, in all probability, acquired no small competence in the subject. From his fellow lawyers, generally, he could learn much. The enthusiastic historian is probably not exaggerating when he declares that few cities of larger population could have boasted of a bar superior to that of Key West in those days when its citizenry numbered less than a thousand.[65] The *Register* might make a flippant comment on the arrival of a vessel in 1828 with "an assorted cargo and seven lawyers";[66] but the profession in the

63. *Key West Enquirer*, March 7, 1835.

64. In 1834, says Maloney, *op. cit.*, 31, all the religious-minded people of the town "united for purposes of public devotion under the name of the Protestant Episcopal Church." The *Resolutions* of the citizens of Key West by which the congregation was established was dated March 7, 1831 (Browne, *op. cit.*, 79-80). Cf. also *ibid.*, Appendix G, 202-3, for letter of Key West citizens to Bishop Onderdonk of New York, requesting that an Episcopal minister be sent to take charge of the new church. Cf. *Key West Gazette*, March 21, 1831.

65. Browne, *op. cit.*, 64-65.                    66. Maloney, *op. cit.*, 12, n. ii.

island town was adorned by men of integrity and real ability. The young
student's work as inspector of customs, too, involved much practical application of the laws of revenue. Thus he was early led into the sphere of
maritime affairs.

Also at this time (1832) Stephen made a modest entry into the ranks
of local officialdom. He was elected town marshal—as a second choice,
incidentally, when the candidate first appointed had been disqualified. The
duties of the office were not burdensome. The marshal was bound to enforce the law of curfew, which required the ringing of the town bell at
9:30 P.M., after which it was strictly prescribed that "negroes, whether free
or not, were not permitted to play the fiddle, beat a drum, or make any
other kind of noise . . . without written permission from the mayor or an
alderman"; nor were stores allowed to be open.[67]

But, for Stephen, all was not work. Judge Marvin has recalled that
nothing pleased his young assistant better than to take his flute, get one
or two friends and Roberts, a Negro man with a fiddle, to join him, and
go out into the beautiful moonlit night to serenade some lady or ladies.
The Judge named Stephen as one of the "young men about town—a well-
behaved and orderly set of young gentlemen."[68]

He must have taken part in the form of entertainment known as a
"candy pull," at which square dances and Virginia reels were indulged in
while a pot of sugar was boiling on the fire. When the candy was sufficiently cooked it was "pulled" by men and maids, then cut into small portions and eaten by all. He would probably not have missed the afternoon
teas aboard visiting United States Navy ships, nor the dances that followed
on brightly illuminated decks. He was certainly prominent in the tennis
games which brought together the young men and the more active of the
young ladies on the excellent court at Fort Taylor. He would attend, with
gusto, the social event of the year, the Masonic Ball, where gowns from
Paris, brought by way of Havana in devoted parents' or sweethearts' sailing-
ships, were not unknown.[69]

The story of his participation in a civic movement begun in 1835 has
some interest for those who would form a picture of the young man as he
was at that time.

67. Browne, *op. cit.*, 51.
68. *Ibid.*, 12. Cf. also Mallory's own account of one of these evenings of serenade: Mallory
to his cousin (unnamed), from Key West, October 1, 1835 (Mallory-Kennedy Collection. For
further details regarding the nature of this collection, cf. *infra*, p. 44, n. 30).
69. Cappick, *op. cit.*, 517-18.

In that year it was proposed to rehabilitate the volunteer fire department of Key West. The need for such a reorganization had been strikingly impressed on all by a blaze which, without the slightest interference on the part of the fire fighters, had consumed several outbuildings on the grounds of prominent citizen Judge Webb.[70] The campaign for reform was inaugurated by an announcement in the *Enquirer* that a meeting of the Lafayette Fire Company would be held "on the 12th instant, at the Engine House, at candle-light," for the purpose of securing new and more energetic members.[71] To prospective recruits was offered a bait in the form of a new fire engine which had recently been purchased at public expense. On the front of this handsome apparatus was engraved the motto, "Where duty calls, there you will find us."[72] Doubtless, all at Key West hoped that the company would take this injunction seriously.

The revamped Volunteers elected Stephen Mallory as their director. His new duties gave him at least an opportunity to practice literary composition in a serio-comic vein on the occasion of the new company's first essay at putting out a fire: "At a few vigorous blasts from the [director's] trumpet, accompanied by a long, protracted cry of 'fire,' the company, including many contributors [to the *Enquirer*], was assembled; but such a regular irregularity of uniform was, perhaps, never exhibited since Falstaff's Regiment marched thru Coventry. I observed on this occasion that several firemen neglected their *hose,* owing, no doubt, to the rapidity of their movements. The cause of excitement was, happily for us, trifling; and although our appearance is brought to mind by 'The King of France with forty thousand men Marched up the hill and then marched down again,' still it is pleasing to reflect that if any real danger had existed, the same readiness to meet it would have been exhibited. Some disappointment was expressed at the insignificance of such a fire."[73]

Patriotic celebrations were frequent at Key West. At the Washington Centenary banquet of 1832 the future Secretary of the Confederate Navy offered a glowing toast to Daniel Webster, who, almost at that very moment, in the national capital, was delivering one of his great speeches in glorification of a strong central government. The toast was followed by an

70. *Key West Enquirer,* January 10, 1835. James Webb was the first judge of the Supreme Court for the Southern Judicial District of the Territory of Florida, established in 1828. He retired from this post in 1838, moved to Texas, and was for a time Secretary of State of the Texas Republic before its admission to the Union (Maloney, *op. cit.,* 13).

71. *Key West Enquirer,* January 10, 1835.

72. *Ibid.,* October 22, 1834.

73. *Ibid.,* January 24, 1835. Italics Mallory's.

address in Mallory's most rotund style, extolling the blessings of the Union. Other toasts seem to have been strangely prophetic; for instance, "The Union: An Inheritance to us from Washington; let no trifling cause burst the holy band"; and "The Progress of Improvement; the womb of time is pregnant with events beyond conception great."[74]

In 1834, Angela Moreno was again at Key West, on a visit to her friend Lydia McIntosh. She had grown to charming womanhood since the day four years before when she had first been seen by Stephen. She had spent two years at a school in Bridgeport, Connecticut, and then returned to Pensacola to make her debut in the society of that gay seaport town. She was one of the most sought-after belles of the day, and apparently found her chief delight in flicking her admirers with the whip of her caustic wit, deftly withdrawing in none too gentle mockery when they dared to become her suitors.[75]

Lydia McIntosh was Stephen Mallory's cousin. One evening he dropped in at the McIntosh home, ostensibly to pay his respects to his relative, but really to meet Miss Moreno. The visit was not a success. Angela, cool and mildly sarcastic, "talked down" to Stephen, treating him with amused tolerance. Stephen thought she was vain, too self-assured, and more fascinating than ever. "I could see by your face that you did not like my cousin," observed Lydia to her guest after Stephen had left. "I suppose," said Angela calmly, "that I showed by my eyes, which always speak the truth, that I did not like his looks." At about the same moment Stephen was writing in his diary: "I have formed an ideal of the woman I shall marry, and she comes up to it. She is a Catholic, speaks French, Spanish, and English, and is musical. She has a great deal else besides."

He decided to launch his attack in earnest. He was at his cousin's home one evening, at a party given in Angela's honor. At nine o'clock, when Mrs. McIntosh and her children rose to retire, Stephen requested Angela to remain alone with him, and announced that he would read to her. They sat down at opposite sides of the parlor table, with no great display of enthusiasm on Angela's part.

After reading aloud for a few moments, he laid down the book and, much in the manner of a lawyer addressing a jury, made a long proposal of marriage. He recounted "very seriously and formally," as he said later, how he had selected her for his wife the first time he had seen her. He told her

74. Browne, op. cit., 201-202.
75. Mallory, letter to Buddy, supra cit.

that she measured up to his idea of what his wife should be, that his love for her had steadily increased during her four years' absence, and that he could see no reason why she should not reciprocate his feelings.

To Angela, obviously, all this was a distinct shock. On the table at her elbow was her bedroom candlestick. She picked it up "with a very demonstrative manner," informed Stephen that, if she had suspected his purpose she never would have remained with him, and accused him sharply of deceiving her. He, in his turn, was indignant. As he expressed it later, he had dreamed of her, and of no one else, night and day since he had first seen her; and to be thus waved off in what he regarded as a most heartless and contemptuous manner, was more than he could digest.

Angela, candlestick in hand, rose to leave the room. Stephen jumped to the door, locked it, and put the key in his pocket. She stood in mute amazement and, finding retreat cut off, "looked," he admitted, "as if about to hurl the candlestick at my head."

He proceeded to tell her, quite calmly, that he wished to say to her what he had never before said to any human being; that he was, with his soul upon his lips, in the most respectful manner, paying her a greater compliment than he ever could pay to another; that, in brief, she must listen to him. She said, "Well, sir, I shall hear you." He then ordered her to sit down and refused to continue his speech until she had done so.

Apologizing for his seeming rudeness, he further described the intensity of his feelings. Angela sat rigid and spoke not a word. He concluded by telling her that he desired no answer at that time, but that after two years he would renew his suit, at which time he would expect nothing but favorable results.

He then walked over and unlocked the door, indicating that the interview was over. Angela was trembling and flushed. "You need never renew your offer," she said decisively, "for I will never listen to it again." She did not answer his "good night," refused to shake hands with him, flew upstairs, and returned to Pensacola the next morning.[76]

After this setback Stephen again took up his routine existence. As he checked long inventories at the Customs House, or copied out briefs in Judge Marvin's office, he kept dreaming of his charming "ideal."

It was, perhaps, his unrequited passion that inspired some verses of doubtful merit but great sincerity which, at this time, he began to contribute to the *Key West Enquirer*. These effusions were plentifully sprinkled

76. *Ibid.*

with references to a "silent sorrow" and to a grief that he would "ne'er impart," but which consumed his heart. His pain, he confided, was a "cherished woe" and a "loved despair"; and, in the true romantic tradition, he desired that the pangs he bore should never be known by the one who had inflicted them.[77]

Since the *Enquirer* was apparently willing to take more of this, Stephen reappeared in verse the next week to recall sadly how, when first he met her gay and young there shone such truth about her, and on her lips such promise hung that he did not dare to doubt her. He saw her change toward him—which was a rather glaring understatement—yet, he averred, he still clung with hope the fonder that, though false to all besides, from him she could'st not wander. But wander she did, and Stephen summarized his feelings in the twice-repeated refrain:

> But go, deceiver, go! The heart whose hopes could make it
> Trust one so false, so low,
> Deserves that thou should'st break it.[78]

In the next issue, in eight stanzas weighted with pathos and extra poetic feet, he gave instructions for his burial in virgin earth in some secluded spot on which the swallow and the fawn might securely play. He had become a faded flower, and his form was wasted.[79]

The most interesting of these metrical efforts were two characterizations of fair ladies written by Stephen a few months later. One was dedicated to "J***" and the other to "A***." It may not be too wild a surmise to say that, when he wrote them, he was trying to describe Angela's tantalizing and complex self. The descriptions agree rather closely with what we know from other sources about her character.

### TO J***

> She hath an eye so kindly mild and blue,
>     So sweetly eloquent and shy,
> So soft, yet fraught with ev'ry wile, that few
>     Who meet its glance e'er wish to fly.
> She hath a lip that would a stoic warm,
>     E'en make Diogenes his tub foreswear;
> Its very silence o'er us throws a charm
>     No other lip, when eloquent, could wear.
> Her tiny foot, so fairylike in form,
>     Seems proudly conscious of its grace;

77. *Enquirer*, November 8, 1834.
78. *Ibid.*, November 16, 1834.
79. *Ibid.*, November 29, 1834.

Yet shuns our eye with modest, sweet alarm,
    And seeks its native hiding place.
Yet, shun her timid blush and sunny smile,
    The witch'ry of her deep blue eye;
In every modest glance there lurks a wile,
    In every feature mischief sly.[80]

### TO A***

She is not beautiful[!], but ease and grace
In every thought she utters seem combined,
And when she speaks, her sweet expressive face
Proclaims unconsciously her dignity of mind;
And Midas-like, of whom the fable's told,
All themes by her discourse are turned to gold.[81]

To the disappointed lover's credit it must be said, however, that his sense
of humor and balance did not at this critical period desert him. In February, 1835, he composed a letter to the *Enquirer* in defense of an amusement
which at the time was very popular in Key West. The practice of dancing
had been condemned by some unnamed "stiff unbending knights" and
"aristocratic gentlemen whose pride it is to deviate as little as possible from
the beaten track of their ancestors." Stephen undertook to show from faith,
reason, and history that "this delightful accomplishment has been sanc-
tioned and practiced by eminent men of every age," and that "there are a
thousand good reasons for learning to dance, and scarcely a single fair
objection can be urged against it." David danced before the ark, and with
the Jews, Egyptians, and various primitive peoples, dancing was symbolical
of devotion. Stephen inserted here an important qualification: "We must
be understood to advocate only a just medium in this particular, and by no
means to sanction the activity of the modern sect of *jumpers,* who seem to
fancy that he who leaps highest draws nearest towards heaven."[82]

A century ago, he reminded his readers, the proportion of time spent
by a Frenchman between heaven and earth afforded matter of serious calculation for mathematicians. In those days it was nothing for a gentleman
to "send one foot on a pirouetting voyage of discovery, entangle it in the
flounces of a ladie's [*sic*] dress, twirl them up in a snarl before his impetuous
revolutions could be restrained, and then, by a dexterous counter-move-
ment, unravel himself without omitting a single curve or injuring a thread
of the muslin, *redress* the wrong done, then jump up like a sturgeon, cross
his legs six times, cut a figure which a Pithagoras [*sic*] could not demon-

80. *Ibid.,* January 17, 1835.                81. *Ibid.,* June 6, 1835.
82. *Ibid.,* February 14, 1835. Italics Mallory's.

strate, and end this wonderful display by quivering his left leg as a cat does her paw when it is accidently dipped in cold water."[83]

Thanks to the march of improvement, wrote Stephen, such violent exertions were neither practiced nor expected in 1835. The current dance was a "slow, graceful movement, tempered by dignity and ease," and could be learned by anyone.[84]

This was rather vivid writing. And no wonder! A large part of the piece was lifted almost bodily, and without credit to the original authors, from one of the *Salmagundi Papers* of William and Washington Irving and James K. Paulding, published twenty-eight years before.[85]

The fall of 1835 witnessed Stephen Mallory's first recorded political fight. Neither the issue nor his role in the conflict was important from the larger standpoint; but the affair has its interest as evoking from him an early statement of his views on democratic government.

First, it might be remarked that the concept of democracy dominant in Key West at this time appears to have been something short of pure Jacksonianism. Although one of the town's two newspapers, presumably speaking for the "best" citizens, proclaimed loudly that "We go for Jackson," the same journal, in the same issue, quoted with approval the following declaration which could have been endorsed in toto by Chancellor Kent of New York or by the staunchest patroons of the Hudson Valley:

"The right of suffrage is one of the dearest privileges guaranteed by the Constitution to a freeman, and whilst it would be the height of oppression and tyranny to deprive the individual of his legal right to a vote, it would on the other hand be equally an act of injustice to the community to permit men who have neither interest or property at stake (and who, consequently, cannot be affected by their acts) to appoint Legislators over the liberties and property of that community. If ever the liberties of our Country should perish, it will be by the perverted suffrages of such individuals."[86]

83. *Ibid.*, Italics Mallory's.

84. *Ibid*

85. Cf. *Salmagundi Papers*, "The New York Assembly." Stephen was obviously enjoying himself in his capacity of free-lance contributor to the *Enquirer*. He seems, however, to have made some unwarranted boasts which called forth from the editor this curt paragraph, placed at the top of column one, page one: "We have understood that some young gentleman in town named S. R. Mallory is claiming the honor of being an Associate Editor of the *Enquirer*. As we do not recognize this Knight of the Quill to be such, we are somewhat anxious to undeceive the public, promising them that before we leave our present state of single blessedness, (if ever we do so), the banns shall be properly published" (October 17, 1835).

86. *Key West Gazette*, June 8, 1831.

This is scarcely simon-pure democratic theory. For an understanding of Mallory's position in the debate to be described below, it is important to realize that he very probably agreed with these sentiments of his economic and social class.

In January, 1835, the Legislative Council of the Territory of Florida abolished the corporate charter of the city of Key West. The reasons behind the act were somewhat questionable. The law abrogating the charter provided for fines and other penalties against the members of the now extinct corporation unless they would pay over to a justice of the peace—and hence, ultimately, to the Territorial Council—all the taxes that had been raised since the incorporation of the city three years before. This, affirmed the interested parties at Key West, was transparent confiscation and tyranny as flagrant as the Boston Port Bill of 1774.[87] There was another and perhaps better founded charge leveled against the repealers. The charter, established in 1832, had imposed, for the first time in the town's history, a tax on real property. It was loudly declared in Key West that the rich local land holders had used the weapon of repeal in order to escape the burden of this taxation.

In mid-October the local party favoring repeal won a narrow victory in the election held to choose a delegate for the Legislative Council. The *Enquirer* claimed that the election result did not reflect the will of the mass of the citizens of Key West, all of whom wished the renewal of the charter of 1832.[88]

The next week the journal published a letter from a reader designated by the editor as anonymous, but who was, as events proved, Stephen Russell Mallory.[89] In this communication Mallory aligned himself firmly with the repealers. He did not deny that a majority of the citizens desired *some* type of charter; but he believed that it would be undemocratic and unjust to permit them to restore the charter of 1832. He insisted on the necessity of securing a charter which "will best subserve the interests of the community at large." The charter which had just been abolished was not such an instrument. Mallory's reasons for so thinking are suggested by one of his concluding phrases: "Let every citizen . . . who will be taxed, and subjected to its [the charter's] ordinances, express his views as to what amount the different kinds of property, and the different vocations, will be taxed, the salaries of officers, and the qualifications of voters."[90]

87. *Key West Enquirer*, June 6, 1835. Cf. also *ibid.*, July 25, 1835.
88. *Ibid.*, October 17, 1835.                    89. *Ibid.*, October 24, 1835.
90. *Ibid.*

This sounds like good old-fashioned republicanism of the vintage of Webster and Clay. It was salted, however, by a more truly democratic sentiment evoked by what Mallory regarded as the *Enquirer* editor's apparent aversion to having public issues thrashed out in general meetings of the citizenry. The editor had urged the citizens to have "no part nor lot" in any meeting or discussion regarding the formulation of an entirely new charter. This, declared Mallory, was undemocratic to the highest degree. This was how they had got the last one! A charter can indeed be drawn up without a public meeting of the citizens for whom the charter is made, and "so can any body of people be governed by laws made without their consent or approval, but in direct violation of both." It was Mallory's conviction that every citizen should have a voice in formulating the provisions of the charter which, once in force, he was bound to obey.[91] He wished to see Key West governed by men acting "rigidly" and efficiently; but experience proves that such men must be supported by the voice of the people; and will not the people support more enthusiastically a charter in the making of which they have had a part? He proposed therefore that a meeting of all the citizens be called in order to deliberate on the provisions of a new charter.[92] This, in fact, is what was done later. It is not clear to what extent Mallory's urgings contributed to the final equitable result.

The year 1836 came. Stephen, according to his promise, wrote to Angela a "very sensible letter" renewing his proposal of marriage.[93] He announced that, if she gave him no hope, he would enlist in the army to fight the Indians. Angela wrote back that she thought this an excellent idea. Her rejection seemed to him to be couched in slightly more polite terms, but it was equally as firm as the first.

With her letter in his pocket, he started out as a member of an expedition against the Seminoles in South Florida.[94] For the next two years he appears to have enjoyed himself thoroughly, in command of a fine body of seamen in his own centerboard schooner-rigged whaleboat, beating up the Indian quarters on the inland streams, in the Everglades, and up and down the coast. His boat he named *Angela*.

At the close of the campaign in April, 1838, he returned to the charge. His command, whether by accident or design, was to be mustered out at Pensacola, Angela's home. He determined to make another trial for her

91. *Ibid.*, October 31, 1835.  92. *Ibid.*

93. The following account is based on Mallory's narration as given in his letter to Buddy, *supra cit.*, with references to the four additional sources as noted *infra*, nn. 94 and 95.

94. In regard to Indian troubles at this time, cf. the following items from the *Key West Enquirer*: January 10, 16, 23, 1836.

heart. If he could have read that heart he would have approached the citadel this time with greater confidence. "Somehow," she confided later, "his fidelity and devotion touched me, and, as the years went by, I began to relent."[95]

In this new effort he adopted a more subtle tactic. With a fellow officer he took up quarters at a hotel directly opposite the Moreno residence. On the first morning of his arrival he ordered horses for himself and his companion and kept them waiting on the hotel plaza. Angela, he noted carefully, was on her piazza, observing all. He ostentatiously pretended not to notice her, and managed to consume a great deal of time in altering and arranging his saddle and stirrups. Then, from behind the Venetian blinds of the Moreno parlor, came the strains of a guitar, playing Stephen's favorite air. It was a command performance, by Angela's sister, at Angela's instigation.

But Stephen, without giving her a glance, rode off to visit Mrs. McIntosh, who was now living in Pensacola. He told the latter that he had come to Pensacola to see Angela, but that he would not call on her unless he could learn beforehand that his chances had improved. "What," he asked his cousin, "do you think of my chances?" Mrs. McIntosh replied that she thought he had better go and see for himself. He construed this response as favorable, leaped on his horse, and was off toward town at a full canter.

As he neared Angela's home, he was rehearsing to himself a "very sensible, frank, feeling, and manly address of about two minutes' length." He described it later as "a sort of 'You see I am here again, but this is the last time, better take me now, etc. etc.' speech."

He reached the Moreno mansion, announced himself to the servant, and was ushered into the parlor. He walked nervously up and down in the cool, dimly lit room with the closed blinds, wondering how she would receive him. He had stopped to look at a picture on the wall when suddenly he heard behind him a "voice at his very heart" say, "So, sir, you have come at last, have you?—after not even looking at me this morning?" It was Angela, looking very pert and—to Stephen—very lovely.

He at once forgot his prepared speech. He felt dizzy. Would she take a brief walk with him in the open air? He had, he explained, been living outdoors so much recently that he found a warm room very oppressive. She saw no reason why they should not. She picked up her bonnet and led the way.

95. Interview with Mrs. S. R. Mallory, in *New Orleans Times-Picayune*, January 12, 1898.

"What in the world has brought you here?" she asked in her cool way as they reached the street. "You have," he replied. "I came to see you alone. Refuse me and I go back at once; but not to give you up, for I am determined to marry you in spite of your teeth!" Angela showed no surprise, but said in a matter-of-fact tone, "I had determined to accept your offer if you ever renewed it. Why don't you kiss me, Stephen?"

They were married in the following July, 1838, and took up their residence at Key West. There can be no doubt that the match was a success, substantially. Toward his wife Stephen never lost the fresh, deep, yet boyish love of his courtship days. He regarded her as the "most truthful and most honorable being" he had ever met. He testified years later that her duty to God and her love and devotion to her husband and children constituted the mainspring of her life.

Yet he would have his difficult moments. It was clear that Angela loved him, and that she was a tender and dutiful mother. It is certain, too, that, as the years passed, she impressed all who knew her as a most gracious and attractive matron. She was gentle, womanly, and a polished lady of the world. Yet there seems to have been something lacking—precisely what, it is difficult to say—in her feeling toward Stephen. That he occupied an exclusive place in her affections, that she loved him intensely, is completely beyond doubt. The idea of any other man in her life is utterly inconceivable. Yet she never fully succeeded in keeping him, in her thoughts and acts, quite on a level with herself. She frequently treated him as she would treat one of her grown-up children. She was too likely to be disillusioned at his faults. She appears never to have been able to maintain full confidence in his judgment, nor in the constancy of his love for her. She was always demanding of him high and impossible evidences of a greatness and perfection of character which he simply did not possess. They must be looked upon as a firmly and essentially happily wedded couple; yet she was always Angela Moreno, sweet and good, but willful, mettlesome, and dazzlingly swift in her changes of mood. It may have been true that she was the stronger and more brilliant personality, and could not forget it.

By 1846 they had been blessed with four children, but had lost two by pathetically early deaths. In the cemetery at Key West are two small tombstones inscribed: "Ellen Josephine Mallory, died . . . April 18, 1843, aged 3 yrs., 7 mos."; and "Francis Moreno Mallory, died . . . Sept. 6, 1846, aged 2 yrs., 4 mos." To his remaining son, Stephen, Jr., and to his daughter, Margaret, Stephen was not only a father but a companion. He went hunting and fishing and swimming with the boy, taught him to box, and played games with him. When later he had another son and another daughter he would often throw himself on the floor beside them, turn out all the lights, and tell stories of "instructive legends."[96]

He now had a private legal practice, and was regarded by at least one of his older contemporaries as being the best lawyer of his age in the state.[97] With one or two others, he pleaded wrecking and salvage cases before Judge Marvin's admiralty court. Many of these adjudications are of special interest as revealing both the canons that guided the judgments of the admiralty court and the ability of Mallory as a trial lawyer.

In the case of *James Packer* [a wrecker] *et al*. vs. *Brig Horace and cargo*,[98] Mallory defended the master of the latter vessel against a salvage claim of the wreckers who had saved the ship and cargo from destruction on the reefs. The salvors had been awarded $950 for their services on behalf of a brig and cargo appraised at $3,634. They had pulled the vessel off the reef, but she had again grounded, and they had been obliged to extricate her once more. They were demanding compensation for this additional labor.

Mallory claimed that the second accident had been due entirely to the clumsiness of the wreckers, as well as to their failure to heed the advice of the ship's master. Practically all the damages sustained by the vessel were a result of this unnecessary grounding. The wreckers had adduced, as a reason for further reward, the fact that their rescue operations had been carried out in the face of rough seas, high winds, and some severe squalls. Mallory denied flatly, and backed his denial by referring to the weather reports, that, on the date in question, the seas were rough, or the winds high, or that there had been any squalls. He asserted also that there was on board the *Horace* a hawser (which the wreckers had declared was not there), and that without the wreckers' help the master could have got his ship off the shoals much more easily and with much less damage to her. He further charged that the first wrecker to board the ship had deliberately

96. Cf. *infra*, p. 116.

97. James D. Wescott [Westcott?], Jr., to Hon. W. Meredith, Secretary of the Treasury, from Washington, D. C., March 10, 1849 (Treasury Department Records, the National Archives, Washington, D. C.). James Diament Wescott (sometimes spelled Westcott) was a prominent lawyer and statesman of Florida. During 1830-34 he was Secretary of the Territory of Florida, and for a while in 1832 was Acting Governor. In 1834-36 he was Attorney-General for the middle district of Florida. He represented Florida in the United States Senate, as a Democrat, from December 1, 1845, until March 3, 1849.

98. Admiralty Records, United States District Court, Southern District of Florida, Key West, Vol. III. *James Packer et al.* vs. *Brig Horace and cargo*, Andrew Scott, Respondent (case filed in Superior Court, Southern District of Florida, May 24, 1842).

delayed beginning the rescue work—with consequent added injury to the vessel—until the other salvors, obviously his friends, could draw near. Despite these apparently valid arguments, the case was decided by Judge Marvin in favor of the wreckers.[99]

Another case found Mallory on the side of the wreckers. The ship York had been caught on the reefs, and her crew had chosen this moment to mutiny. Wrecker William Pent and his partners had clearly done a good piece of work, both in saving the vessel and a large part of her cargo and in helping the skipper to quell the mutiny. Judge Marvin, in granting to the wreckers a generous reward of $13,500 on the ship's assessed value (with cargo) of $95,000, laid down, at the same time, an admonitory rule of the court: salvors' compensations were to be held to a reasonable minimum, lest too high rewards would entice so many into the business as to create damaging competition for all. The Judge also castigated the mutineers severely, and decreed that they should receive no pay.[100]

Mallory's reputation for professional fairness was shown by the fact of his appointment in 1848 as arbitrator in a case involving a conflict of property rights between the Federal government and the Franciscan Order of priests. The circumstance that he himself was a Catholic was not regarded as a bar to his selection for this delicate and important task, and, in fact, his award favored for the most part the claims of the United States.[101]

Along with these varied professional interests, Mallory amused himself by acting as Key West correspondent for the *New York Tribune*. His most valuable production in this capacity was his description of one of the worst natural disasters in all Florida history, the hurricane of 1846. His account of the tragedy, published in two installments, was a combination of good narrative, bombast, and an appeal for funds to lighten the burdens of the victims.[102]

Mallory was also at this time acting as Collector of Customs, while retaining a considerable portion of the law practice of the district.[103] As col-

99. *Ibid.*

100. *Ibid.*, case filed March 20, 1846.

101. Report of the Solicitor of the Treasury, with documents, in relation to the claim of the Catholic Church at St. Augustine, to certain property held by the United States at that place, 1849, the P. K. Yonge Library of Florida History, University of Florida, Gainesville, Fla. Cf. also: "St. Francis Barracks at St. Augustine: the Franciscans in Florida," *Florida Historical Society Quarterly*, VII (January, 1929), 214-33. This legal suit was instituted by the government before the Catholic bishop had been appointed, and before it was known that he would be appointed (*Florida News*, September 8, 1858, quoting *Journal of Commerce*, n.d.).

102. From the *New York Tribune*, November 1, 1846.

103. Browne, *op. cit.*, 38-39.

lector, he made for himself an enviable reputation.[104] On the testimony of
Jackson Morton, a Whig opponent, he displayed in the discharge of the
duties of his office "honesty, capacity, and fidelity in an eminent degree."[105]
Since his assumption of the office of collector, wrote Morton, Mallory had
not interfered in politics or influenced votes through his official station. At
the Treasury Department he was regarded as a prompt, vigilant, and efficient officer. As far as could be ascertained from influential and respectable
Whigs residing in Key West, no considerable portion of that party desired
his removal.[106]

There were other tributes in the same vein. The chief fear of the Whigs
seems to have been that a candidate of their own, if he succeeded Mallory,
would greatly suffer by comparison. Therefore, they argued, they would
benefit more by Mallory's retention of the post.[107]

He had at this time, apparently, no desire for higher public office,
though he was an active member of the Democratic party in the county.
He refused all offers to run for a post in the state legislature, but worked
hard in the campaign for the party's candidates. Although a Democrat,
he professed himself to be a conservative. Although he believed in secession
as a right resulting from the history and theory of our government, he
deemed it hazardous as a remedy, and was thus held to be a "Union
man."[108] It is possible that this conservatism may at times have become
timidity. The view that Mallory, although a man of ability, was not as-
sertive enough to direct public sentiment is not lightly to be dismissed.[109]

Yet, in a letter written by a Whig during the period of Mallory's col-
lectorship there is a statement which contradicts the supposition that the
future Navy Secretary was not already a power in the politics of at least
the southern part of the state. This political opponent strongly urged Mallory's removal, on the grounds of his interference in politics. Mallory, he
declared, was rated by common consent of the Democrats as one of their
chiefs. He had been nominated as a delegate to the last Democratic convention at Baltimore and was being universally spoken of by his party as
their candidate for Congress.

104. As evidence of Mallory's zeal in performing his duty as Collector of Customs, cf.
Secretary of the Treasury R. J. Walker to Mallory, May 18, 1847, "Collectors of Small Ports,"
Set G, Vol. XI (Treasury Department Records, National Archives, Washington, D. C.). Also,
in same Treasury Department Records, Mallory to Secretary Walker, from Key West, September 21, 1845.

105. Jackson Morton to Hon. W. M. Meredith, Secretary of the Treasury, from Washington,
D. C., April 13, 1849 (Treasury Department Records, National Archives).

106. Ibid.                                    107. Ibid.

108. Mallory, letter to Buddy, supra cit.       109. Cf. W. T. Cash, op. cit., I, 424.

The removal of Mr. Mallory, the letter continued, was called for by the united voice of the Whigs of Florida, who saw in him a man who had availed himself of his official position to defeat their efforts to establish Whig principles in the state. The Governor and leading Whigs from every part of the country were united in this demand. Mallory's removal was being hotly opposed by the Democrats. The zeal which they were manifesting in this respect sufficiently indicated that he was a "chosen one of Israel."[110]

Into what type of man was Stephen Mallory developing during those years from 1845 to 1851? Was he constantly growing in his intellectual powers, acquiring greater skill and judgment as a lawyer and man of business, and becoming an increasingly competent public servant? We may safely believe that this was so. It seems certain that he was, at Key West, successful in practically everything that he undertook as a lawyer, land owner, dealer in real estate, and political leader. Significantly, he was the legal adviser of John W. Simonton, the original proprietor of the island.[111] He maintained intimate business relations with some of the most prominent of his fellow citizens. On at least one occasion he held power of attorney for the prosperous and influential Asa F. Tift.[112] With the important mercantile house of Tift and Company he was joint owner of a plot of land.[113] In the May term of the circuit court in 1842 he represented Asa Tift and John H. Geiger, also a leading citizen, in a tax case.[114] At the same session he defended Walter Smith, another outstanding figure of the town, in a civil suit against the equally prominent Fielding A. Browne.[115] With four other "first" citizens he went bond for the new United States Marshal, Joseph B. Browne.[116] The tributes he received for his incumbency of the Federal office of Collector of Customs and for his activities as state political leader have been noted above.

It is clear, therefore, that he had proven himself to be an able lawyer, businessman, and politician. One observation, however, may here be made.

110. W. G. M. Davis to unnamed, from Washington, D. C., August 8, no year [but most probably 1849] (Treasury Department Records, National Archives). In the same vein, cf. John Foreman [Whig] to Secretary of Treasury Meredith, from Washington, D. C., July 20, 1849 (ibid.).

111. Power of attorney given by Simonton to Mallory, April 21, 1851, Deed Records, Book E, p. 244, Monroe County Court House, Key West. Cf. also Maloney, op. cit., 51.

112. Given on July 27, 1845, Deed Records, Book D, p. 48, Monroe Co. Court House.

113. Deed Records, Book D, pp. 141-43, Monroe Co. Court House (joint sale of land to Philip Sawyer by S. R. Mallory and A. F. Tift, for himself, Tift, and A. C. Tift & Co.).

114. Minute Book, Vol. A, Circuit Court, Monroe Co., pp. 110-111.

115. Ibid., p. 112.

116. Ibid., p. 20.

The successes of Stephen Mallory up to this time had been achieved on a very restricted stage. Accomplishments in such a narrow theater were no sure guarantee that he had qualities of mind and will sufficient to carry him to similar victories in a larger national arena.[117] A leader at Key West could, conceivably, be tragically out of his depth at, for instance, Washington. But it may be said of Mallory that one of his finest traits was his capacity for mental and moral growth. For the larger problems that he would be called upon to face eight or ten years later, he was not yet prepared; but he was "coming along."

A characteristic which everyone noted in Mallory was his robust love of a "good time."[118] He was never intemperate, nor a carouser, but *joie de vivre* was strong in his make-up, along with his more sober qualities of industry, integrity, and attention to professional detail. He felt that life was, for the most part, good, and he was determined to enjoy it as much as possible.

Some held that this attitude inclined him at times to "ease up" in the midst of difficult problems, and caused him to lack that impatient earnestness which keeps really great men driving ahead with little attention to the softer, more pleasant aspects of existence. Others believed that his humane love of the amenities was a source of strength as he grappled with hard situations. They said that because he knew how to relax he could work—and, if necessary, fight—more effectively. As he himself was so fond of remarking, *nous verrons*.

117. In 1852 the population of Key West was 3,000. At this time it was the largest town in Florida. It contained 650 houses, 26 stores, 10 warehouses, 11 wharves, and 4 churches ("Key West and Salvage," 51-52). For a fuller description of the town at this period, cf. *Florida Republican*, Jacksonville, May 27, 1852, reprinted from the *New York Tribune* and possibly written by Mallory, since at this time he was still, in all probability, the *Tribune's* correspondent at Key West.

118. Anon., "Rummaging Through Rebeldom: Nineteenth Rummage," *New York Citizen*, August 10, 1867. Cf. also T. C. DeLeon, *Belles, Beaux, and Brains of the 60's* (New York, 1907), 85-86.

# CHAPTER TWO

## *United States Senator*

In 1850 men were striving desperately to brace up a structure that was—though they would not admit it—doomed to fall. Two opposed ways of life in the American Union were fighting for survival— the Northern Way and the Way of the South. One system was based on a social-economic institution called slavery, deemed by its defenders an absolute essential for white supremacy below the Mason and Dixon line. The other way was that of a free labor economy with social features antithetical, in many fundamental respects, to the ideals of the South. One way included a concept of state sovereignty which in some essential respects subordinated the Union to the states. The other way of regarding the Federal government was the outgrowth of the theories of high centralization of John Marshall, Story, and Webster. The opposition was further pointed by a great and resounding denial spoken by the North: Slavery shall not be extended into the Territories!

To Southerners that denial was a mortal blow at their social and economic security, an attack on their very homes. The South, therefore, was deeply, frantically alarmed. From that moment, she considered seriously the question, Can we remain part of a government which has such designs against us? Yet the South loved the Union, as the North did; the South had fought for the Union. So Southern men, with their Northern fellow-citizens, tried to heal the breach by means of a method which has often, in the course of history, solved such problems. The method was that of compromise, the Compromise of 1850.

By this device of statesmanship the slavery-extension issue was not settled, but merely postponed. It was not a definitive solution, but it was a step in that direction, for it represented a victory for the moderates of both sides. The South was still frightened and suspicious, the North was still determined to stop slavery. But a peaceful and final agreement was a real possibility when leaders of both sections could speak as they did in this year of good portent.

Governor Thomas Brown, of Florida, speaking against the Nashville Convention project, castigated that assembly as being "revolutionary in its tendency, and directly against the spirit if not the letter of the Constitution of the United States." He regretted that it should have been deemed expedient at this time by Southern members of Congress to countenance the calling together of a Southern convention before any overt act of aggression on Southern rights and institutions had been committed.[1]

On the other hand, Daniel Webster, in his famous Seventh of March speech, declared: "I put it to all the sober and sound minds at the North as a question of morals and a question of conscience. What right have they . . . to endeavor to get round this Constitution, or to embarrass the free exercise of the rights secured by the Constitution to the persons whose slaves escape from them? I repeat therefore, Sir, that here is a well-founded ground of complaint against the North. . . ."[2]

Political alignments in Florida at this time were the same as those in the South generally. The state was practically controlled by the Whigs, although in 1850 the Democrats won a majority in the state house and senate. Within the latter party was a radical or "fire-eater" group, who desired no compromise, but complete surrender on the part of the North. If the North should refuse these terms, the radicals counseled immediate secession. On the other hand, there were the moderates who stood with Clay and Webster. They would strive for a solution within the Union, they would trust something to Northern sense of justice, to Northern prudence, and to the healing and sobering effects of time. Which of the two groups was stronger was an open question, a question that must soon be solved.[3]

The state's senators at Washington in 1850 were Jackson Morton and David Yulee. Morton, whose chief claim to distinction lies, apparently, in the fact that he was Florida's only Whig senator, was a rather colorless figure with more than a touch of what Lord Acton termed a "safe sterility" of mind. Yulee, on the contrary, was a shrewd and courageous politician who later became a capable and energetic promoter of Florida railroads. At this mid-point of the century, he was a staunch follower of Calhoun. He had thrown in his lot openly with the fire-eaters on a program of full co-

1. Governor Brown to Hon. Messrs. Yulee, Morton, and Cabell, from Tallahassee, February 22, 1850, in the *Tallahassee Sentinel*, reprinted in the *Pensacola Gazette*, March 9, 1850.

2. Webster, *Works*, 6 vols. (Boston, 1851), V, 355.

3. The planters of Florida were usually conservative Whigs. Cf. Cash, *op. cit.*, I, 427.

operation with the Nashville Convention, summoned by Calhoun for the following June to consider immediate secession.

A grave decision was therefore imposed on the Democratic party in Florida. Yulee, his first term expiring in March, was running for re-election. Would the moderates who, for the moment, held the balance of power disavow him, at least for this time? Would they take their stand on the compromise, and accept the logical corollary—rejection of the Nashville Convention? Would they drop the radical Yulee[4] and select a "safer" candidate?

What the Florida Democrats decided to do with regard to this question is not clear even now. They certainly withdrew their support from Yulee, but in his place they picked a man who, on his own repeated declarations, endorsed every important principle held by Yulee. Stephen Russell Mallory of Key West was the Democrats' choice, and it is difficult to see what attractions he could have had for an anti-Yulee faction.[5]

In a communication regarding his previous appointment as alternate to the Nashville Convention, Mallory had stated his political position plainly, and that position could hardly be considered conservative.[6] He had expressed his gratification at being chosen for that post. He regarded his selection as evidence that his fellow citizens believed in his attachment to the South, an attachment to which all others, even the most holy and cherished, must be subservient. He frankly admitted that he did not look hopefully to the efficacy of the convention: but if it could harmonize to any considerable extent the discordant opinions of the South and induce union of sentiment on one or more prominent measures, such as Southern rights in the Territories or the recovery of fugitive slaves, or a definition of the bounds of Southern forbearance on these questions, it would accomplish a work of vital importance. The North, he was convinced, was firmly united against

4. For evidence of Yulee's very "advanced" position, see his correspondence with Calhoun, American Historical Association *Annual Reports*, 1929, 516 and *passim*.

5. Note the following testimonies: "The other gentlemen spoken of in connection with the office of Senator, approve Mr. Yulee's course on the Southern question. Mr. Mallory . . . says, 'I am with him [Yulee] even unto the end'" (*Floridian and Journal*, December 21, 1850). The *Florida Republican* (March 20, 1851) referred to Mallory as ". . . a talented Locofoco, claimed here to be everything required on the great questions of the day, and who accords in sentiment with the umpire [?] of the contest." See *ibid.*, in same sense, January 23, 1850. The Whig paper, the *Florida Sentinel* (February 4, 1851), declared that the Whigs voted for Mallory not because they thought that he held Whig doctrines, but because they regarded him as a lesser evil than Yulee. In fact, concluded this journal, few persons knew what Mallory's political opinions really were.

6. Mallory to B. M. Pearson, Esq., from Key West, June 8, 1850, reprinted in *Floridian and Journal*, February 8, 1851, from *Florida Republican*, January 30, 1851. Bird M. Pearson was a Democrat of radical tendencies and one time justice of the Florida Supreme Court.

the South.[7] The South must therefore prescribe the limits of her forbearance, and stand equally united upon that platform. "By every incentive," he declared, "by the soil we tread, by the air we breathe, by a thousand ties binding the heart, by the glorious past, by the critical present, we are called upon to unite for the preservation of our honor and our political rights." He did not doubt that the convention would be directed toward effecting such united action by the South. Its members had not assembled to discuss Southern rights, or to ascertain to what extent those rights had been invaded; upon those points public opinion in the South was settled. Men were beginning seriously to regard the moment for action as near at hand, and were facing squarely the probable consequences of resistance to the political aggressions of which the South complained. They were displaying that "solicitude for their political welfare which [evinced] a preparation for a political convulsion."

The North, he warned, did not believe the South to be in earnest, an opinion somewhat justified "not only by the writings and conversations of the many northern abolitionists and free-soilers domiciled amongst us, but by the extraordinary spectacle occasionally exhibited of some leading Southern man's advocacy of the doctrine which elicits and entitles him to the commendations of our Northern *friends*."

Mallory assured his correspondent that "nothing but important pre-engagements could have prevented [him] from accepting [the invitation to attend the convention]." It was his earnest hope that the labors of the convention would tend to avert the threatening perils. He was sure that, "should the evil hour come upon us, the people of our State will, at whatever sacrifice, stand squarely up to the great interest of the South."[8]

The *Floridian and Journal,* reprinting the above communication, commented: "Mr. Mallory has not swerved, so far as we know, from the views expressed in this letter, nor from the advocacy of any other movement tending to a union among the people. We have before remarked, and we repeat the remark, that he has given to the course of his predecessor, Mr. Yulee, on all the questions which have been under discussion, a hearty and unequivocal approval."[9]

Although Stephen Mallory did not go to the Nashville Convention, there came, soon afterward, his first chance for real political advancement. He was notified that his nomination for United States senator would go to the state legislature, and his friends felt that a solid majority of the party would

7. *Ibid.*                              8. *Ibid.* Italics Mallory's.
9. February 8, 1851.

support his candidacy. His immediate reaction was rather unexpected. In the face of his great opportunity he very sincerely demurred. He expressed his fears that the bringing forward of his name might "distract and divide the members of the Democratic party, and . . . impair those kindly and generous feelings which ought to exist among them."[10] Lamentable indeed would be the case, he felt, if support of his cause should result in a stifling of the deliberate voice of the majority, and thus evoke dissension within the party. He deemed it the duty of every good citizen to perform, to the best of his ability, the duties of any post to which the people might call him. But he did not feel justified in even seeming to sanction by his silence the use of his name in opposition to Yulee, "or any other good democrat who may enjoy the confidence of the party." He did not desire, nor was he willing to "assume the appearance of an aspirant" for political distinction at the expense of the harmony of the Democratic party; on the contrary, he desired it to be understood most unequivocally that he would ever strive, at any sacrifice compatible with honor, to maintain the party's unity and ascendancy. "If I have any influence," he wrote, "I shall be happy to exert it for the election of any other sound Democrat, who can be relied upon to battle for our great Southern interests, and the rights of our State. If I were the choice of the party, I would not feel at liberty to decline serving the State . . . but I cannot consent to the use of my name if discord is to result when a thorough union [within the party] is so manifestly important."[11]

These scruples were finally overcome. But not without foundation were Mallory's doubts that he was the uncontested choice of the party. The balloting in the state legislature developed into a bitter fight between the supporters of Yulee and those of the entry from Key West. After numerous repetitions of voting, Yulee was found to have received a majority of the ballots actually cast, but, since many of the members had submitted "blanks," he did not receive a majority of the votes of the whole number of electors. Finally, the legislature elected Mallory, but Yulee's friends maintained a vigorous protest.

Mallory's supporters pointed to the "invariable precedent" of the legislature in requiring for the election of a senator a majority of the whole

10. Mallory to J. T. Archer, Esq., from Key West, December 7, 1850, reprinted in Appendix of *Reply of Mr. Mallory, of Florida, to the supplemental argument of Mr. Yulee, claiming his seat in the Senate of the United States,* n.p. (rare pamphlet; Library of Congress, 1851). This correspondent of Mallory's is probably James J. Archer, of Maryland. He was a leading lawyer of that state, and was made a brigadier general in the Confederate army in 1862. His "Archer's Brigade" made a brilliant record in the campaigns of northern Virginia in 1862-1863.

11. *Ibid.*

number of electors, and in regarding blank votes as being cast against the candidate who was seeking re-election. The Mallory side further reminded their opponents that it was Yulee himself who in his previous election to the Senate had established this precedent. If the rule had not been followed in that former instance, Yulee would not have been senator even once.

Yulee appealed to the "people's law," the cold and concrete fact that the ballots, as actually counted, gave him a majority. According to immemorial English precedent, he held, this elected him; and it was, he declared, the more democratic method.[12]

Yulee threatened to carry his case to the United States Senate itself. The Mallory forces at once made capital of this fact.—"A more glaring contravention of State privilege, of which Mr. Yulee is [presumably] a zealous advocate, could hardly be conceived than that involved in the act which he now invokes the Senate to commit."[13] Florida had established her own election laws and had chosen her candidate according to those laws. Was the verdict of the sovereign State to be reversed by the Federal Congress? Mr. Yulee could hardly wish to be other than the representative of the sentiments of his state in Congress. That he had heretofore not represented these sentiments, and could not do so unless he changed his opinions and course in regard to the disputed election, there had been abundant developments to prove.[14]

The Florida press, for the most part, took sides with Mallory. The *Republican* remarked that "the analogies quoted by Mr. Mallory in support of his right are chiefly drawn from precedents in our own Legislature, and are therefore immediately in point, and should have far more weight than the numerous English and less pertinent cases cited by Mr. Yulee."[15]

Mr. Mallory, declared the *Floridian and Journal,* was totally guiltless of conniving at the divisions which resulted in the defeat of Mr. Yulee, or of courting the votes of the opposition.[16] Mr. Mallory's bearing during the whole struggle had been that of a high-minded, honorable gentleman. This

12. The chief documents relevant to this disputed election are in printed form in a pamphlet in the P. K. Yonge Library of Florida History, the University of Florida, under the title "Election of Senator of the United States by the General Assembly of Florida, for the term commencing 4th March, 1851." A similar though somewhat abridged collection is in the Library of Congress under title of *Reply of Mr. Mallory to the supplementary argument of Mr. Yulee* (cf. note 11, *supra*).

13. *Florida Republican,* Jacksonville, December 4, 1851.

14. *Ibid.*

15. December 25, 1851. Cf. also *ibid.,* December 4, 1851, for Yulee's complete presentation of his case, with editor's humorous complaint at its length. For Mallory's complete defense, cf. *Floridian and Journal,* February 15, 1851.

16. February 15, 1851.

attitude acquitted him of all blame and rendered the acceptance of the office tendered him a duty from which it was hoped he would not shrink. The action of those who voted against Mallory was not due to any opposition toward him, but because they conceived it to be a high duty to sustain Mr. Yulee.[17]

The Whig *Florida Sentinel* took occasion to poke fun at their rivals' family row. The Democrats, the journal recalled, had traditionally exhibited, in holding onto official positions, a tenacity that would challenge the admiration of an eel or a tortoise. "But this is the first case in which they have sought to try it upon each other."[18]

The *Richmond Times* ridiculed both claimants for what it termed "prudery" and "coquetry." Yulee had expressed "vociferously" his desire to withdraw from public life, but this protestation had been reversed as soon as he saw a chance of being re-elected. Mallory, on the other hand, had declared that he was "unwilling to be the instrument of Mr. Yulee's defeat," but "determines to make sure work of the defeat which he so much regretted." One can hardly tell, said the editor caustically, which to admire most,—"Mr. Mallory's reluctance to accept the office until his right to it was questioned; his wailings over Mr. Yulee's defeat until he found that Mr. Yulee did not consider himself defeated; or, on the other hand, Mr. Yulee's Caesarean opposition to the purple until he found that the electors would not give it to him, and then his disposition to have it, whether or no."[19]

"One feature of the case," observed the *New York Herald,* "is extremely unfortunate for Mr. Yulee. He is claiming the seat against the decided and expressed opposition of an unequivocal majority of the Legislature of Florida. This should not be. The elevated and proud position of Senator for the United States should never be sought under such circumstances."[20] Whatever his initial hesitations, Mallory was clearly determined to hold onto the senatorial seat which he believed he had fairly won. On March 25, 1851, he notified Governor Brown of his acceptance of the "exalted trust." While he was all too sensible of his deficiencies, he said he would undertake the high post "with the earnest hope that a disinterested devotion of all my energies to the interest of the State, may evince my sense of its generous confidence, and prove not wholly barren of public benefits."[21]

17. *Ibid.*
18. March 25, 1851. In the same sense, see *ibid.*, November 25, 1851, February 17, 1852.
19. *Florida Sentinel* (Tallahassee), April 1, 1851, reprinting editorial from *Richmond Times*, n.d.
20. Quoted in *Florida Sentinel*, April 1, 1851.
21. *Florida Sentinel*, April 8, 1851.

The *Sentinel* observed that this communication was "calculated . . . to dissipate . . . verdant doubts about his acceptance, which seem to have sprung from the numerous letters of his friends, who were a great deal more nice than wise, [and] who, in their efforts to place him properly before the world as a gentleman of much delicacy, and a politician without reproach, have certainly thrown a shade of the ridiculous upon his introduction into public life."[22] Mallory, the *Sentinel* thought, had "a fair share of sense, and [was] in every point of view, an estimable man."[23]

Yulee did carry his fight to the floor of the United States Senate, and Mallory was obliged to defend his own claim there. But in the meantime, as he prepared to leave for Washington at this real beginning of his public career, Stephen Mallory must have paused to take stock of himself.

One observer described him in 1867 as a ". . . stumpy, 'roly-poly' little fellow . . . ; for all the world like one of the squat 'gentleman farmers' you find in the south of England. . . . He looks and talks like a 'fine old English gentleman' of the squireen order. . . ."[24] His face was a bit plump, his complexion ruddy. His eyes were large and blue, with an attractive air of semi-puzzlement about them; his nose had a little tilt which the ladies of Washington and Richmond thought quite charming. He was a perfect host—"socially, a most estimable fellow . . ."[25]—and he was marked by a special gentleness of manner which almost everybody noticed immediately. He was an "assiduous worker, though endowed with little brilliancy; . . . painstaking and plodding, most scrupulous in all his dealings as a public or private man; in lieu of dashing abilities, he had much calm common sense, great patience, and more than ordinary penetration."[26] He had a streak of boyish playfulness, displayed in composing a recipe in verse for a newly wed friend,[27] or in catching his little nieces with long words in an informal spelling bee,[28] or in teasing his wife about one of her old admirers.[29]

He was also a man of extremely tender sensibilities, shown most clearly in his correspondence with his wife. "I long, my darling wife," he wrote in the midst of his greatest battle, ". . . to be in your arms again . . . ; I never before felt your absence so much; and, as years advance, like the bark

22. *Ibid.*
23. *Ibid.* Cf. also *Florida Sentinel*, December 23, 1851, analyzing and summarizing Mallory's reply to Yulee, and approving that reply; and *ibid.*, February 3, 1852.
24. "Rummaging Through Rebeldom: Nineteenth Rummage," *loc. cit.*
25. *Ibid.*                                    26. *Ibid.*
27. Mallory, Diary, "Recipe For Gumbo."
28. From conversation of the author with Mrs. O. H. Smith, half-sister of Angela Mallory.
29. Cf. *infra*, pp. 218-19.

of the oak that hardens and clasps more firmly all within, my affection for you becomes more and more the characteristic of my life. Love to the children . . . and a thousand kisses to yourself. God bless you."[30] He referred to her as ". . . the one woman of all this world who has ever controlled my heart, and soul and life."[31] He was won over at once to anyone who did her a kindness: "I feel, sometimes . . . that, in defense of a principle I conceived to be right, I could resist all the temptations of life save one; and I am forced to confess that any man or woman can enslave my heart and control my action by kindness to you."[32]

He was a man of courage, but not of the hard and tough courage that is often so difficult to distinguish from brutality. He had a certain delicacy of feeling which may account for his enemies' charge that he was soft; but he was a superb fighter, incapable, no matter what the pressure, of shirking a duty or a cause to which he had given his devotion.

His views on important subjects were usually sound and careful, but they frequently lacked sweep, range, and depth. He was not the type of man to whom come inspirations of genius or sudden instinctive revelations of truth. He was competent, in a routine way; reliable but never great.

Angela Moreno Mallory was an imperious, temperamental Spanish grande dame whose quick temper was always being checked by her instinctive gentleness. In her nature was a dash of mischievousness; she was unduly jealous of the affections of those whom she loved, but she was essentially a gracious woman and a valiant mother.

When she married Stephen she was already a cultivated young woman of the world. She sang well, was an accomplished pianist, and spoke French and Spanish to perfection. As a hostess she was poised and charming, and she became a sincerely beloved favorite in every society in which she moved. "Mrs. Johnston sends her love to you," wrote Stephen to his wife in 1862, "and she charmed me by saying that you were more beloved . . . by the ladies of Richmond than any stranger who had come here."[33] Again he wrote to her: ". . . I find that wherever you are known well, you have, with what Mr. Mantellini calls your 'dear, dern'd delightful ways,' contrived to

---

30. Mallory to Angela, from Richmond, August 31, 1862. (All letters of Mallory to his wife or children have been taken by the present author from the Mallory-Kennedy Collection in the possession of Mrs. Thomas Kennedy, Mr. Thomas Kennedy, Jr., and Miss Cora Mallory. all three of whom are residents of Pensacola, Florida. Miss Cora Mallory is a great-grand-daughter of the subject of this study, while the Kennedys are related to Mallory through the marriage of his daughter Ruby.)

31. Mallory to Angela, from La Grange, Ga., July 6, 1866.

32. Mallory to Angela, from Richmond, June 4, 1862.

33. *Ibid.*

make people love you."[34] One of these "delightful ways" was a frankness of speech which caused several mild sensations in Washington society. Confronted with some impetuous remark of her own, Angela would close the matter with a brusque, "I'm sorry, but it is true."[35] Her comment to a gentleman friend, who boasted that he had been married twenty-five years without having had a single angry word with his wife, was, "You must have had a d—— dull time!"[36] She complained once that Stephen talked too much when he accompanied her to funerals, and never let her enjoy them.[37] Whatever her idiosyncrasies, she had completely captured her husband's affections, and to the end of his life he worshiped her.

He was now starting out on a very long journey—a far more momentous and more spectacular journey than he dreamed of. Many a time he had sat on the wharf at Key West and watched the ships leave for distant ports. He had always been fascinated by ships. They would be very much in his life during the next fifteen years. They would greatly change his life, and almost break it.

34. Mallory to Angela, from Cedar Hill, June 22, 1866. "Mr. Mantellini" was a friend of the Morenos at Pensacola.

35. Clubbs, *op. cit.*, 328.

36. Conversation of author with Mr. F. M. Blount, Mallory's half great-nephew, Pensacola, Fla.

37. Conversation of author with Mrs. Scarritt Moreno, a daughter of Angela's half sister, Victoria, Pensacola, Fla.

# CHAPTER THREE

# Breaking In At Washington

WASHINGTON, that gawky, unkempt, dusty, unfinished, charcoal sketch of a capital, was, in the winter of 1851-1852, the scene of a social life sparkling and recklessly gay. The capital, wrote one of its fair adornments, is "an augmenting round of dinners, . . . receptions, and balls."[1] Belles and beaux made brilliant the matinee dances at the home of the lovely Parisian bride of John Slidell. The old-fashioned quadrille and cotillion were still in vogue, with an occasional waltz number; the more spirited German was being introduced. At the French Legation the Countess Sartiges was attempting, with some success, an American Versailles. Levees at the White House were thronged, and the solid gold spoons handed down by James Monroe were laid out again and again for state dinners.

The weekly Marine Band concerts on the White House lawn were fashion promenades brightened by the latest gowns and bonnets from Paris and London. Landaus and smaller rigs clattered up and down the avenue, bearing senatorial wives on formal calls or other errands of *politesse*. Debates in Congress and Supreme Court sessions were also social events, graced by society's leaders. There were numerous gaudy suppers like those of Mr. Corcoran,[2] who was said to have dined half of the Congress during a session.

Yet, despite the glitter of diamonds and rustle of silk and the ostentatious amenities, there was evident at times a note of immaturity and lack of final polish in this society. Washington, despite her flamboyant front, was still, from the social aspect, a provincial capital. Every once in awhile the veneer wore thin, as, for instance, at an inaugural ball, when the managers forgot to heat the ballroom and there was a very impolite stampede of the guests, male and female, to the cloak room, where wraps and coats were piled on

1. Mrs. Clement Claiborne Clay, *A Belle of the Fifties*, ed. Ada Sterling (New York, 1904), 29.

2. William Wilson Corcoran, noted Washington philanthropist.

the floor in wild confusion.[3] Washington was still a bit awkward, still somewhat adolescent.[4]

With all its imperfections, however, it was the beginning of the golden era of Washington society. The era did not last long, but meanwhile the world of fashion went by in color and gaiety, a senator's wife could spend $75,000 a year on entertainment and clothes, and it was exciting, with a touch of grandeur. Halfway through that decade in Washington Adelina Patti made her debut in *La Traviata,* and was toasted afterward by Baron de Stoeckl at Mrs. Riggs's.[5] Washington was captivated by Charlotte Cushman in *Meg Merrilies,* and applauded Brougham and Mrs. Gilbert and, above all, Jenny Lind. William Makepeace Thackeray recited "Lord Lovel" at the National. Even the austere Emerson permitted himself to be lionized, with due propriety, at a soirée.

Probably the most gorgeous ball in American history up to that time was provided during this era by the wives of Southern senators in honor of an English ambassador.[6] The White House was graced for awhile by perhaps its most charming hostess since Dolly Madison—the blonde and queenly and unaffected Harriet Lane. Lillian, the future second Duchess of Marlborough, was introduced, as a slip of a girl, to her first ball. And, a part of all this, and deeply relishing most of it, the statesmen of the nation— North and South—added a touch of splendor to a society that was at least beginning to bear the traits of a high civilization.

This was the bright surface of life at the capital. But there were deeper currents underneath, and, regarding them, a man's face would grow grave. As early as 1853 the sensitive Mrs. Clay remarked the constantly widening division between the Northern and Southern elements in the government city. This could be detected, she wrote, in social as in political gatherings.[7] During the first half of the Pierce administration, though feeling ran high in Congress, the surface of social life was smiling and peaceful. But gradually the two parties grew apart, and seldom met except in general assemblies.

3. Mary C. Ames, *Ten Years in Washington: Life and Scenes in the National Capital as a Woman Sees Them* (Hartford, Conn., 1875), 278-80.

4. For social background of Washington in the fifties: "The Grand Ball," *New York Herald,* February 12, 1855 (a very colorful description); "Ladies Oust Pressmen from Senate," *ibid.,* February 9, 1854; "Unfavorable Comments on Washington Society by New Yorkers," *ibid.,* February 14, 1854, February 22, 1854, February 15, 1855; "Spring Fashions," *ibid.,* March 21, 1856, March 23, 1856.

5. Baron de Stoeckl was the Russian minister to the United States with whom Secretary Seward negotiated for the purchase of Alaska. Mrs. Janet Madeleine Cecilia Shedden Riggs was the wife of George Washington Riggs, the Washington banker and philanthropist.

6. Clay, *op. cit.,* 118. The ball was given in honor of the Napiers.

7. *Ibid.,* 26.

In sending out invitations, even to purely social affairs, this circumstance had to be carefully considered.[8]

The truth was that the Compromise of 1850 had been nothing more than an armed truce. What a recent observer writes concerning the end of the decade was already beginning to be realized: ". . . War was the product, not so much of sectional differences as of emotions developed about differences, which by 1861 made it impossible longer to reason, to trust, or to compromise. Both sides believed the other to be composed of persons who could only be handled by force. . . . The North could say that it was fighting to save a Union which God had established as a great experiment in democracy. . . . The South . . . could say that it was fighting to save the original Constitution. . . . Higher ideals and purposes have never actuated two belligerents. Worse qualities have never been attributed to enemies."[9]

The credentials of the new member from Florida were presented to the Senate by Jackson Morton on December 13, 1851, and on that same day Mallory was sworn in. His first act in the national legislature was to defend his right to be there. Yulee's supporters were still contesting their rival's right to his seat and had mobilized some allies in the upper chamber. Mallory, in an exchange of open letters with Yulee, stated his position plainly: "Now although I am ready to bow to the paramount authority of conscientious convictions of duty, and although I know no championship more glorious than that of the 'people's law' [invoked by Yulee], as it is here styled, I would suggest that the championship in this instance is self-constituted; and that the gauge of battle is a seat in the United States Senate. I will state broadly the ground which I deem conclusive of the question. First, then, unless I can sustain the sovereign and existing right of the State to elect her United States Senators in her own manner; unless I can retain the seat on the high ground that, in the absence of congressional pre-regulation, any manner which the Legislature of my State may think proper to adopt is conclusive upon the Federal Senate, I do not desire to retain it at all. At this hour of the contest between centralization and State sovereignties, I am not disposed, should I be enabled to retain it, to exhibit in my own person the remotest approximation to an acquiescence in the doctrine that the Federal Senate may, under existing laws, rightfully exercise the power of annulling the deliberate choice of a sovereign State, manifested and sustained by its legislation and executive action."[10]

8. *Ibid.*, 27.

9. Avery Craven, *The Repressible Conflict, 1830-1861* (Baton Rouge, La., 1939), 64-65.

10. *Floridian and Journal*, February 21, 1852; in this same issue are reprinted most of the relevant documents in the contested election.

It was, interestingly enough, the aged and enfeebled Henry Clay who, in the last speech he made in the Senate, finally convinced that body that the new member from Florida should be confirmed in his seat. The Great Compromiser called attention to the fact that Mr. Yulee's claim had been presented to a congressional committee and rejected by the same. He could therefore see no reason why Mallory's status in the Senate should any longer be questioned.[11]

That Clay's interest in Mallory's fortunes may have been based on something more than a mere respect for congressional electoral procedure is suggested by a remark of the *Florida Sentinel* some months before: "We understand that Mr. Mallory happened to be in Havana during Mr. Clay's late visit to the island, and in response to the hope expressed by the latter, that Florida had been fortunate in her change of Senators, in securing one who would stand by the Union of the States, Mr. Mallory declared himself a Democrat and a friend of the Union, upon the basis of the Compromise."[12]

This statement raises the puzzling question as to how Mallory could be, in early 1851, in agreement with Yulee,[13] and, at practically the same time, an advocate of the compromise and a Unionist of the school of Henry Clay. The riddle is deepened by a further observation of the *Sentinel*: "This is a good beginning; and, indeed, it will be greatly Mr. Mallory's own fault, if, with the lights before him, unpledged, and in position for a free choice, he takes any other course than that so fully indicated by the people of Florida themselves in the last Congressional election."[14]

Where was Mallory standing at the time of his election—or was he standing on two opposite platforms at one and the same time? And how could the people of Florida elect Mallory on the grounds that he thought with Yulee, and yet indicate by their votes that they wished him to stand on Clay's compromise?

One fact seems certain: Clay's speech did much to get Mallory into the Senate. As a Whig journal of Georgia said, with some pettishness: "Mr. Mallory should and would never have been admitted to a seat, had it not

---

11. Clay said, in part: "Feeble as I am, I cannot refrain from making a few additional observations. There is no doubt of the duty and the right of this body to determine all questions of elections of its members. The question is as to the method of doing this, and that question has been settled, I believe, by every deliberative body upon earth. It is this: If there is a contest by two claiming the same seat, and the other party presents his petition claiming it, that petition is reported to a committee; it is reported upon by a committee and acted upon by the body" (32 Cong., 1 Sess., December 1, 1851 [*Congressional Globe*, 4]). Cf. also *ibid.*, 2. Yulee was re-elected to the Senate in 1855.

12. April 8, 1851.                           13. Cf. *supra*, p. 38, n. 5.
14. April 8, 1851.

been for the officiousness of Mr. Clay, who came out of a sick bed to secure that boon for him. He [Clay] has not been in the Senate chamber since."[15]

During the first several months of his stay in the capital, Mallory resided at the National Hotel, the fashionable headquarters popular with Southern statesmen, while his family remained at Key West. By the spring of 1854 his loved ones had joined him in Washington, and henceforth apparently spent part of each year at Washington and part at Key West. The Northern winters were difficult for the Mallory children, bred in the gentle climate of Florida; but Angela spent enough of her time in the capital to make herself generally known as a gracious and charming hostess, for the Mallorys entertained frequently in their Washington home. Angela won universal esteem and love. "I saw . . . night before last," her husband wrote to her in 1858, ". . . many of your friends, all of whom speak in terms of you that almost bring tears of affection in my eyes."[16] And later: "All your lady friends here inquire most affectionately for you, and no woman who ever came to Washington made more friends or a better impression than yourself. You are greatly admired, and I am frequently congratulated on having the most delightful wife that can be found in the Senate."[17]

The Senate of which Stephen Mallory was now a part would have been a distinguished body in any age.

There was Stephen Douglas, of Dantonesque audacity and almost womanly charm, with his "massive head covered with rich brown hair, a high forehead and deep-set eyes that were dark and full of fire."[18] He was smooth-shaven, with a clean-cut mouth, square chin, and facial lines that gave him an expression of sadness. He had an effervescent, affectionate nature. He could throw his arms around dignified Beverley Tucker of Virginia and say, "Bev, old boy, I love you!"[19]

15. Savannah *Georgian*, n. d. The extract from the *Georgian* is reprinted in the Florida *Sentinel* of February 3, 1852; the *Georgian's* article is from its Washington correspondent who writes under date of January 22, 1852. The *Florida Republican* rejoiced that Mallory was "in," and paid high tribute to his political character (July 2, 1852; August 26, 1852).

16. Mallory to Angela, from Washington, December 24, 1858.

17. Mallory to Angela, from Senate Chamber, January 10, 1859. "Mrs. Mallory," said another witness, "was universally beloved. If to be one of the most amiable, and the sweetest looking of matrons, entitled Mrs. M. to such popularity, she most richly deserved it. I am sure she could not speak or do evil to any one. Most thoroughly was she a lady, with one of those winning countenances and with those . . . black eyes for which her Spanish fatherland is . . . famous. Forever trying to do good in some way to someone, and often struggling to undo the mischief made by the social or other malice of the strongminded of her sex, she was naturally beloved" ("Rummaging Through Rebeldom," *supra cit.*).

18. Christian F. Eckloff, *Memoirs of a Senate Page 1855-1859*, ed. P. Melbourne (New York, 1909), 73.

19. *Ibid.*, 74.

Opposite the Southerners was Charles Sumner, built physically and intellectually on the classical model, with a Boston tie-wig Federalist background. Someone remarked during one of Sumner's violent anti-slavery speeches in the Senate, "The man may be a fool, but he has pluck. He knows they [the Southern radicals] would like to tear him limb from limb."[20]

Robert Toombs, of Georgia, was one of the most forceful speakers on that historic floor. He has been described as a "lion both in appearance and in actions."[21] Fearless, bold, and powerfully built, with a voice of thunder, he reminded people, it was said, of Edwin Forrest in the character of Jack Cade. He eschewed ornate language, choosing rather to strike sledge-hammer blows, shaking his great head the while, and pounding with his clenched fists upon his desk. He had also a habit, while speaking, of rising on his toes and then striking his heels hard upon the floor. He could speak for several hours without the least sign of fatigue, and the Senate always gave him undivided attention.

In the Senate during Mallory's second term, there was Jefferson Davis, austere, proud, select, polished, "with the bearing of a soldier and the tread of an Indian brave."[22] His frame was said to be more delicate than strong. He seemed always absorbed in matters above the common level. Considered a cold man, he was rarely seen to smile.

There was Seward, perhaps the most capable diplomat in that whole body. An unimpressive speaker, lacking the skills of the true orator, he nevertheless held great influence over the Senate, and he had the attractive power of the natural-born leader of men. Some called him the greatest political negotiator since Henry Clay. The South knew that he was dangerous.

There were others of lesser importance, such as John Crittenden of Kentucky, broadminded, generous, and brave, a natural moderate and an advocate of compromise, who said that "he had not come to the Senate to act as a partisan"; or Henry S. Foote, from Mississippi, an "eccentric, quarrelsome man, who talked fustian and indulged in personalities at every opportunity";[23] or Pierre Soulé, who was "more like a Castilian—picturesque, daring, eloquent, eager for conquests and fame beyond the horizon."[24]

20. *Ibid.*
21. *Ibid.*, 213.
22. *Ibid.* Davis was Secretary of War under President Pierce.
23. Frederic Bancroft, *The Life of William H. Seward* (2 vols.; New York, 1900), I, 212.
24. *Ibid.* It is not necessary to accept at its face value the following unfavorable estimate of the Senate of the fifties, from an obviously disgruntled observer: "What do . . . the people

Mallory had not been long in the Senate when he found himself in the midst of a debate on a matter relating to the navy. By an act of 1850, corporal punishment as a disciplinary measure on shipboard had been abolished. Now, two years later, a movement was on foot in Congress to restore this method of maintaining order and efficiency on vessels of war. Senator Stockton of New Jersey strongly opposed the renewal of what he and many others considered a "barbarous" practice. To the mild surprise of the Senate, doubtless, the opposite view was vigorously upheld by the new Senator from Florida.

This was really Mallory's maiden speech, except for the address given when his senatorial status was still in doubt. He began it modestly, being "not insensible to the hardihood of differing in opinion with that gentleman [former Commodore, then Senator, Stockton] on a subject so peculiarly his own."[25] But, said Mallory, we must deal not merely with opinions, but with facts—"I ask for any figures on the subject, but figures of speech." He felt, with due modesty, that he himself possessed some qualifications for the discussion of this problem. For twenty years he had been more or less familiar with shipping and seamen, and the views which he was here advancing had been derived from observation and conversation with seamen of every grade both in and out of the service. They were not hasty views; they had not been hastily adopted; they would certainly not be hastily abandoned.

The real question at issue was, Shall we have a navy? The question of corporal punishment struck at the very existence of the navy.[26]

He then developed a very effective *ad hominem* argument: Senator Stockton had been a great naval commander largely because he had employed corporal punishment to maintain discipline on his ship.[27] During

---

think of the U. S. Senate, so often said to be the most dignified body in the world? It has been turned into an arena for political blackguards, backed up with bowie knives and Pistols." (Hannibal Hamlin to [undecipherable], from Washington, April 22, 1850 [Hamlin Papers, Library of Congress]). Hamlin was a Senator from Maine. He had switched from the Democratic to the Republican Party in 1856, and later served as Vice-President under Lincoln. A probably exceptional indication of squeamishness in the Senate was the case of the clerk who insisted on softening the reading of Senator Hamilton Fish's "Hellgate" to "Hurlgate." This, said Fish, was an evidence of a reprehensible New England Puritanism (Fish to J. R. Brodhead, May 15, 1856 [Fish Papers, Letter Book, Library of Congress]).

25. *Speech of Mr. Mallory, of Florida, in the Senate of the United States, January 14, and 15, 1852, on the Restoration of Corporal Punishment in the Navy* (Pamphlet, Rare Book Division, Library of Congress), 1.

26. *Ibid.*, 1-2.

27. Commodore Stockton, in 1850, had explicitly and vigorously argued *against* the abolition of flogging. "Despite Commodore Stockton's powerful pleas against the disuse of the whip, the vote [abolishing corporal punishment in the navy] was carried [in 1850]" (William Elliot Griffis, *Millard Fillmore* . . . [Ithaca, N. Y., 1915], 92).

the time he had commanded the *Congress* for about twenty-one months in 1845-47, Stockton had approved the administering of 1,800 lashes. This was by no means unjustifiable or unusual, Mallory said. "I will venture to say that in this body the Senate—but no, I will not say anything personal; but take the other branch of Congress; I venture to say that there is not a member of that House who has been well raised who has not received a greater proportion of lashes from the rod than were inflicted by Com. Stockton on board the *Congress;* and that if there be one exception, you may pick him out and know him from his words and manners at this very hour."[28]

The American sailor, continued Mallory, had, until very recent times, been a superior seaman, largely because of the institution of corporal punishment in the navy.[29] The state of deterioration in naval personnel was due mainly to the abolition of that mode of maintaining discipline.[30] When the act of September 28, 1850, was passed, abolishing corporal punishment, our navy occupied the first rank among the navies of the world. The act caused immediate disorganization. The seamen commenced at once to exhibit a spirit inconsistent with proper discipline, and that spirit had been progressing to the verge of complete loss of morale.[31] "Unless some remedy shall be supplied to the officers of the Navy to enable them to control their crews, in the very first contest in which we shall ever be engaged, you will find that . . . proud banner . . . will be disgraced."[32]

Corporal punishment had been practiced in all navies since the beginning of naval history.[33] It was mere sentimentalism to say that this method of discipline "degraded" sailors, who, themselves, did not regard it in this light.[34]

Mallory attacked the manner in which the act of 1850 had been passed —". . . tacked on to the end of an appropriation bill . . . , passed by the smallest possible majority, at the very end of the session; [did] the prohibition exist any longer than the appropriation?"[35]

28. *Speech of Mr. Mallory . . . on the Restoration of Corporal Punishment . . .* , 4-5.
29. *Ibid.*, 2.　　　　　　　　　　30. *Ibid.*, 9-11.
31. *Ibid.*, 9.
32. *Ibid.*, 22.　　　　　　　　　　33. *Ibid.*, 2-5.
34. He shows by quotations from official English naval sources that British sailors, when they mutinied, never did so on account of any grievance with regard to flogging. When the mutineers of the *Nore* had possession of our ships, they themselves inflicted the punishment of flogging on some of their own number. In an instance where a surgeon failed to do his duty and it was desired really to debase him, the seamen would not flog him, as they wished a truly disgraceful punishment for him, so they tarred and feathered him (*ibid.*, 18).
35. *Ibid.*, 9.

In the last part of his speech he gave the basic reason for his earnest advocacy of a restoration of corporal punishment: the American navy must be rendered invincible by means of firm discipline. Most noteworthy, perhaps, was the additional reason which he developed to support this statement. The American people, he declared, were "the most military people on earth." Their military spirit was evinced not in the maintenance of standing armies or large war establishments, for their reliance on their own invincible prowess had taught them that such precautions were as unnecessary as they were unwise. But this aggressive *élan* was manifested in that cordial and hearty appreciation of military merit which had borne three successful and distinguished soldiers to the presidential chair. Every war in which we should ever be engaged would, in all probability, produce a soldier president. Since the War of 1812 the navy had become the idol of the nation, and the naval officer felt that the American people demanded imperiously that he should always conquer in any contest where the odds were in any way even. He was proud of his profession because his country honored it.[36]

The application of all this to the matter of the abolition of corporal punishment in the navy was evident. The fighting spirit of the naval officer could be destroyed in a single breath. If he felt that he could no longer render his profession efficient and successful, and that he was cut off from the path of honorable distinction, he would conclude that the country was indifferent to his success. If he was sent forth to fight battles and yet deprived of the means of enforcing discipline, his very commission would become the passport to defeat and degradation—"a mockery, a delusion, and a snare."[37] Mallory concluded with a glowing tribute to the character of the American naval officer. It was an idea he would insist on more than once during his years in the Senate.

In the present instance his implication was that such men could safely be trusted with the administration of corporal punishment. Who, he asked, were these officers who were being represented in certain quarters as satraps of cruelty? They were "of the chivalric spirits of the land, sifted from every grade of life by the most honorable impulse which prompts the hearts of freemen,—the impulse to devote life and all its holiest hopes to their country's service."[38] Obedient to the same impulses which ennoble human nature in other walks of life, their noble profession had taught them to love as brothers all who were true to its standards. The associations which home,

36. *Ibid.*, 20.                    37. *Ibid.*
38. *Ibid.*

kindred, and friends clustered around the heart, subduing it to the holiest sympathies and charities, guided and governed the wanderer upon the deep in all their strength and beauty. As a class, these men were indeed a credit to the nation; and "our . . . history, in recording their deeds of heroism and martyrdom, has devoted no line to their dishonor."[39]

Mallory failed to secure a restoration of the practice which he deemed so necessary for the efficiency of the Navy. The act of 1850 was not repealed, but two years later an article in the *New York Herald* might have brought to mind his stand on the matter: "The House of Representatives yesterday [February 13] was occupied [with] naval matters. The bill providing for more efficient discipline in the navy was taken up and passed. *The abolition of the 'cat' in 1850, and the neglect of Congress to provide a salutary substitute for that unusually effective though brutal mode of punishment, has led to a laxity of discipline detrimental to the public service.*"[40]

When we try to understand how the normally genial and gentle Mallory could have been the defender of a custom which to most people today seems barbarous, we can only conclude that his passionate concern with the development of a well-disciplined United States Navy overcame his natural aversion to the practice. A large section of the Northern press attacked the stand of the new Senator from Florida and coined for Mallory the sobriquet "Cat-o-Nine-Tails." The *Florida Sentinel* admitted that its own instincts were against the practice but noted that the partial abolition of the punishment was said to have already occasioned some difficulty in the navy. The editor was willing to assume that Senator Mallory had been influenced by the advice and representations of naval officers. "We have no sort of sympathy," said the *Sentinel*, "with that kind of morbid . . . philanthropy which is becoming so common; but it strikes us [that] some other effective penalty might be substituted for the Cat."[41]

The new Senator had, on the whole, made a good impression during his first months at the capital.[42] The Washington correspondent of the *Floridian and Journal* defended him from charges published a short time before in the *Savannah Georgian*. The general feeling in Washington, wrote the *Floridian's* observer, was that the Key West representative would ride out

39. *Ibid.*

40. February 14, 1855. Italics added by author.

41. *Florida Sentinel*, February 3, 1852. Cf. also *Pensacola Gazette*, October 5, 1850; November 16, 1850. The latter item is an argument against flogging.

42. "We notice . . . Senator Mallory, who seems to occupy a very respectable position in the Senate, and to have made generally a favorable impression. . . ." (*Florida Sentinel*, February 3, 1852).

the squall raised by the Yulee faction, and that "he is safely moored for six years in a position where he will do great credit to himself and honor to the State he has thus far so ably represented. Mr. Mallory's brief career as a Senator has gained for him a reputation as a ready and intelligent debater. Upon every question [on] which his mind has been brought to bear he has exhibited a profundity of thought remarked by the generality of observers. He enters upon his duties familiar with the general history of his country and the local wants of his State both with a moral and a manner which will reflect credit upon his constituency and give a character to the State in the Councils of the Nation."[43]

Mallory's initial Senatorial activities were concerned almost exclusively with Florida problems. Declaring his belief that railroad building was "of the first importance to the prosperity of the State,"[44] he petitioned the Senate Committee on Public Lands that a grant of land be awarded to the Atlantic and Gulf Railroad Company for the extension of its lines through Florida. The committee refused to give the lands directly to the company but recommended that they be handed over to the state, to be disposed of according to the state's determination. Mallory introduced into the Senate a bill to this effect, which passed that body but was defeated in the House.[45]

He also sponsored a resolution providing for the sale of the "large military and injudicious live oak reservations maintained by the Federal Government within the State, exempt from sale and taxation. . . , useless to the country and injurious to our [State] interests." Although voted by the Senate, the resolution failed in the House "because," as Mallory reported, "the engrossed bill itself was mislaid by a clerk or messenger and could not be found in the closing hours of the session."[46]

The interests of Key West were not forgotten by her representative. He secured the passage of a bill authorizing twenty thousand dollars for a naval establishment at the place. He pushed through measures by which "certain Spanish subjects, residents of Key West and New Orleans," were reimbursed for "their losses in the somewhat violent demonstrations of indignation at those places in 1851, excited by the barbarous conduct of the Cuban authorities."[47]

43. *Floridian and Journal*, February 21, 1852, from its Washington correspondent, writing under date of February 7, 1852, rebutting charges made by the Washington correspondent of the Savannah *Georgian*, and published in the latter journal's issue of January 29, 1852.
44. Letter of Mallory to his constituents, in the *Floridian and Journal*, September 9, 1854.
45. *Ibid*.
46. *Ibid*.
47. *Ibid*. It is possible that Mallory's interest in this matter was stimulated by his father-in-law, Francesco Moreno.

He moved a "Resolution of Inquiry" as to the best route for a canal across the isthmus of Florida, and secured an appropriation of twenty thousand dollars for a survey to be undertaken for this purpose. He extracted a grant of ten thousand dollars for the improvement of St. John's Bar, and another of three thousand dollars for leveling the ground behind the sea wall at St. Augustine. He introduced bills for the establishment of marine hospitals at St. Mark's and at Apalachicola, and obtained the Navy Department's recommendation for another at Pensacola. The hospitals at St. Mark's and at Pensacola would certainly be erected; he was still hopeful about the one proposed for Apalachicola.

He brought about the creation of a new Land District for South Florida, with its office at Tampa. This measure, he felt, would speed the surveying and settlement of state lands. He guided a bill through both houses making Palatka on the St. John's river and Bayport on the Gulf "ports of delivery." He obtained an appropriation of ten thousand dollars for carrying the mails between Charleston, Key West, and Havana, during August and September, by steamers instead of sailing vessels—"a measure of great interest to the people of Key West."[48]

Perhaps Mallory's most important work for Florida during this first period of his congressional activity was in connection with the question of Indian removal. He tried persistently and earnestly to secure Federal aid in expelling from the state the remnants of the Indians; he sought compensation for damages sustained by Floridians as a consequence of their depredations; and he demanded reimbursement for expenses incurred by the state in largely fruitless efforts to defend her citizens against Indian attacks.

It is difficult to over-estimate the uneasiness and, at times, the real fear felt by the Floridians with regard to the Indian peril. As late as 1840 the dwellers on the Florida Keys had been subjected to attacks by the Seminoles; massacres had occurred, and bloody battles had been fought. Immigration into the northern part of the state had been temporarily halted in 1835, owing to fear of Seminole incursions.[49] In January, 1836, armed Key West citizens were awaiting an expected Indian attack from the northward.[50]

48. *Ibid.* Later (in early 1853) he secured from Congress for Samuel Green a $26,000 per annum contract for carrying the mails between New Orleans and Key West (*Florida Republican*, April 21, 1853). Cf. also Mallory's letter to the editor of the *Floridian and Journal*, from Washington, April 4, 1853, reprinted in the issue of April 16, 1853, describing the nature and importance of this grant to Green.

49. *Key West Enquirer*, January 10, 1836.

50. *Ibid.*, January 16, 1836, January 23, 1836.

The first danger from the Seminoles had passed, but in the fifties a new outbreak of Indian troubles occurred. The savages, organized under the capable leadership of a half-breed named Billy Bowlegs, were again constituting a danger to the inhabitants of Florida; and the fact that the red men were only a few hundred in numbers did not to any great extent console the anxious citizens of the state.

Mallory's predecessor in the Senate, Yulee, had begun the campaign to secure Federal aid against the aborigines, but he had won no notable success. An unsympathetic Maryland journal ridiculed Yulee's assertion that he would not be content with the "crumbs" of appropriations for Indian removal that the North "was willing to throw at [the South]." The grant of several hundred thousand dollars asked for by Yulee, observed the editor, was certainly no crumb. It was to be hoped that Florida would remain faithful to the Union as long as she had an Indian to get an appropriation for, and as long as there was enough money in the United States Treasury to pay for him. "Without Florida," remarked the caustic Maryland publicist, "this Union would indeed be miserable; only think of the American everglades, and the silver swamps, with bullfrogs for nightingales, to say nothing of reptiles."[51]

Yulee's program was carried on vigorously by Mallory in three distinct though interrelated ways. In December, 1851, he introduced a resolution of inquiry into the depredations committed by the Indians against citizens of Florida since December, 1835. The object of this inquiry was, of course, to ascertain the amount of recompense reasonably owed to those citizens by the Federal government, on account of the damages sustained. In the same session of Congress he pushed through a "Joint Resolution directing the Treasury officers to pay to the State of Florida all moneys disbursed by her in suppressing Indian hostilities."[52]

But the new Senator's most important moves in regard to the Indian issue were in the form of letters addressed to high officials of the government. In a communication to the Commissioner of Public Lands he urged a specific plan for removal of the savages from Florida—immediate and complete surveying of the Indian lands, as a peaceful but effective means of forcing the aborigines out of those territories by enticing white settlers to come in. In the Senate, also, Mallory pressed this plan with special zeal.[53]

51. Pensacola Gazette, May 25, 1850, quoting "Correspondence of the Baltimore Sun, from Washington, May 16, 1850." The Gazette adds no comment.

52. Mallory, letter to his constituents, September 9, 1854, supra cit.

53. For an extended description of this proposal, and warm praise accorded it, cf. Florida Republican, June 30, 1853. Cf. also ibid., August 18, 1853, for Mallory's defense of the plan in the Senate.

When neither the Senate nor the administration seemed eager to relieve these distresses of the people of Florida, Mallory penned a sharp protest to the Secretary of the Interior, reminding him that a month had passed since the communication had been sent to the Commissioner of Public Lands. Moreover, a fortnight previously Mr. Cabell, Florida Representative in the House, and Mr. Mallory had conferred with the Secretary of the Interior and with the Commissioner of Indian Affairs, and, in a letter addressed to the Secretary of the Interior by the entire Florida delegation to Congress, the Secretary had been made aware of the excitement existing in Florida with regard to this matter. To neither of these communications, so far as Mallory knew, had any response been made. "Under ordinary circumstances this omission to reply to representations thus formally made would seem remarkable; and in view of the well founded apprehension entertained in Florida of a renewal of Indian hostilities . . . any further delay on the part of the Government to adopt measures for their immediate removal may be productive of lamentable results."[54]

That the Federal government was pledged to remove these Indians, said Mallory, did not admit of a doubt. Further evidence confirming this claim had been for two years on file in the Secretary's office.[55] Recent accounts from Florida averred that the Indians were again straying beyond their limits and committing depredations against the property of Florida citizens, and any attempt to restrain them or to recover from them any stolen property would inevitably lead to bloodshed and violence. He deemed it his duty earnestly to admonish the government that nothing but the removal of these Indians from the state, and that speedily, could prevent the most disastrous consequences.

The people of Florida were determined that these marauders should not remain there. A treaty, solemnly ratified by the Senate, stipulated that the savages should be removed by the Federal government. That treaty had never been cancelled, but it had been disregarded by the officers of the army who had been entrusted with the management of Indian affairs in Florida, and that disregard had been countenanced by the Federal government for several years. Agreements inconsistent with and in opposition to the treaty

54. Mallory to Secretary of Interior (A. H. H. Stuart), from Washington, March 2, 1852, reprinted in *Floridian and Journal,* March 13, 1852. Some of the evidence attested that the Florida Indians were not all bad; many of them resisted removal on the grounds that they earnestly wished to become United States citizens and remain within the State (*Floridian and Journal,* February 5, 1859).

55. Letter to the Secretary from Messrs. Thompson and Whitner, Commissioners from State of Florida, written "about two years ago," i.e., some time in 1850 or 1851.

had, without the sanction of the Senate, been considered paramount to the treaty.[56]

Mallory earnestly urged that this treaty, which was part of the "Supreme Law of the Land," be faithfully executed by the Federal government in order to "avert the necessity and the duty to themselves of the people of Florida adopting measures for their self preservation."[57] Reports had reached Washington, he said, that troops were now in the field, and that the border settlers were looking to the safety of their families.[58]

In the Senate, Mallory sought to push through a bill authorizing the President to employ the volunteer military forces of Florida against the Indians. In support of this measure the Florida delegation brought personal pressure on the Secretary of War, Jefferson Davis, who apparently sympathized with them and promised an early and favorable statement on the matter. "The people of the State," declared the *Floridian and Journal*, "will thank our Senators, and particularly Mr. Mallory, for their ready and zealous defence of the State from the insinuations of her traducers, and for their efforts to induce Congress to move in the matter."[59]

But the Indians could, for some time yet, feel fairly secure from any Federal coercion. Mallory's efforts of 1853 were not crowned with any considerable success, although they aired the Indian question thoroughly and must have made some impression on the administration and Congress. But the administration and Congress, if impressed, were in no hurry to move. Although Mallory was confident in June of 1853 that the government would "make an immediate move towards removal of the Indians in our State,"[60] his hopes were still unrealized as late as 1858. In that year an opponent of the removal measure remarked, to applause, that $250,000—the amount sought by Florida—was a very large sum of money for removing 160 Indians.[61]

56. Mallory to Secretary of the Interior, from Washington, March 2, 1852, reprinted in *Floridian and Journal*, March 13, 1852.

57. *Ibid.*

58. *Ibid.* Cf. also Mallory's follow-up letter to the Secretary of Interior, urging strong military measures against the Indians, reprinted in the *Florida News*, Jacksonville, January 29, 1853.

59. March 26, 1853.

60. *Florida Republican*, June 30, 1853.

61. Mallory to Charles E. Dyke, from Bridgeport, Conn., August 9, 1853, reprinted in the *Florida News*, Fernandina, August 25, 1858. Dyke was one of the great journalists of the prewar South. He attained his chief successes as editor of the *Floridian and Journal*, of Tallahassee.

# CHAPTER FOUR

# Naval Affairs

It was in the spring of 1853 that Mallory began his most important activity in Congress. He was appointed chairman of the Naval Affairs Committee of the Senate, a post which foreshadowed his future duties during the Civil War. He was pleased with the responsibility. Naval matters had always fascinated him, and he took his duties as head of the committee very seriously. Day after day would find him in the Library of Congress poring over naval histories and naval year books. And his gregarious bent made him very ready to talk with naval men concerning their specialties.

Certainly, at this time, there was nothing in his words or actions to suggest a lack of aggressiveness in protecting the interests of the Union against all comers, and particularly against Great Britain, which he described as occupying "from the Oroncos [Orinoco?] to Yucatan, and then to the Bahamas, almost every . . . important point where a gun can be planted or a standard reared."[1] At the Bermudas, he said, she had an active naval station. From these commanding watch towers she looked out upon the passing wealth of the United States; and, "should she ever acquire a naval position on the north side of Cuba, in the present defenceless condition of the Florida straits, and our pitiful naval force, the outlet of the Mississippi with all the commerce and navigation of the Gulf, would be as effectually sealed as if a convulsion of nature had reared up a mountain barrier before it."[2]

The United States Navy was at this period in a sad state of deterioration. Its power and efficiency had steadily declined until, in 1853, it possessed not one vessel that could have given battle with prospect of victory against any first-class warship of the major European powers. The ascendance of the

1. 32 Cong., 2 Sess., January 26, 1853 (*Congressional Globe,* Appendix, 130).
2. *Ibid.*

Democratic agrarians in the national councils during most of the preceding two decades had contributed to this neglect of our defenses on the sea. Concentration, also, on burning domestic issues had relegated to the background any sustained consideration of the needs of the navy. The Pierce administration, however, inaugurated a new policy which was clearly linked with the wider program of the Southern Democrats in defense of slavery. A cardinal concern of that program was that the peculiar economic institution of the South should be extended as widely as possible. Such an aim involved as a corollary a maximum of national territorial expansion, preferably southward into the Caribbean area, with special designs on Cuba. This in turn meant certain collision with British imperialistic ambitions in the same area, and the consequent need for a stronger United States Navy.[3]

In the opening session of the Thirty-third Congress, in December 1853, Pierce's Secretary of the Navy, Dobbin, outlined an extensive program for the modernization of the country's fighting forces on the sea and for the rehabilitation of coast defenses. He urged legislation authorizing sweeping reforms in personnel and immediate construction of six first-class, screw-driven steam frigates. The measure was rushed through the Senate without debate and, after meeting with some opposition in the House, was finally passed by that body by a vote of 112 to 43.

No one at the time, of course, sensed the dramatic irony of the situation. In May, 1854, a new and serious turn would be given to the slavery dispute by the passage of the Kansas-Nebraska Act. The same year would witness the birth of the Republican Party, the "sectional party" of the North. Anger in the South was on the rise as Northern legislatures continued to pass measures blocking the administration of the Fugitive Slave Law. At Peoria, in the fall of 1854, an obscure lawyer named Abraham Lincoln would make a speech destined to become a policy for the forces opposed to the extension of slavery. And, amid all this, the Southern leaders in Congress were unwittingly building up the Navy that would one day throttle them.

In the campaign for a more modern navy Senator Mallory's participation was not unimportant. As chairman of the Senate Naval Affairs Committee he worked, throughout the decade, toward strengthening the navy by the addition of more ships of the most effective design and size, and—his most weighty contribution—as sponsor of the Naval Reform Act and the Naval Retiring Board. The future head of the Confederate Navy lost no time in displaying his progressive outlook in the matter of ship design. The most

3. It is only fair to note that the expansionist program of the Pierce administration was not exclusively Southern, but was concurred in by many from the North.

advanced proposal for the construction of ships of war before 1861 was that of James Stevens, who, in 1842, had secured from Congress an appropriation of $250,000 for work on what may have been the first ironclad warship ever authorized for any navy. Work on this "Stevens Battery," as the vessel came to be called, dragged along from year to year and finally came to a stop. In 1853 the Senate took under consideration the advisability of granting another appropriation for further experiments on the ironclad. The proposal was vehemently attacked, particularly by Senator Pearce of Maryland.

In the debate which followed, Mallory argued strongly in favor of the appropriation and stressed the importance of continuing the experiments on the new type of warship. The position he thus assumed is significant for two reasons: he was one of the few members of Congress who perceived the potentialities of the new model, and he was defending a type of fighting vessel upon which, nine years later, he would stake the naval fortunes of the Confederacy. The virtue of the Stevens Battery, as Mallory showed, was twofold: it provided a movable defense for New York harbor, and its iron armor, of more than nine-inch thickness, made the vessel practically impregnable to gunfire. Such a movable defense was required, since the guns of our fortifications at Forts Lafayette and Hamilton had proved their inefficiency against ships entering the harbor.

The invulnerability of the ironclad was demonstrated by letters in Mallory's possession. We had progressed, he argued, two-thirds of the way toward the completion of this work; were we to stop now and have the shell of the work on our hands in this experiment? He conceded that it was only an experiment; but, he urged, it would be wiser to appropriate the balance of the money for the forwarding of even a more risky experiment rather than to leave our harbor defenses in their present doubtful state. He did not claim that he was entirely satisfied with regard to the feasibility of the experiment; but he did know that Mr. Stevens had been convinced that it would succeed—and Stevens had devoted a lifetime to such investigation. If success should come, the appropriation would be nothing in comparison with the results achieved. Other nations, including Britain and France, had never attempted experiments of this kind. They were watching the work on the Stevens Battery with keen interest. After going as far as we had in the matter, the rest of the money would be wisely expended even in proving the project untenable—if it was such, which he did not believe.

The Stevens Battery did not receive an extension of its appropriation; but Senator Mallory had stated some very forward-looking principles in naval design, and had exhibited a liberal receptivity to new ideas in the field. He deserves additional praise from the fact that in so thinking he was distinctly in the minority. Furthermore, there was a sequel to the story of the abortive Stevens Battery. In the winter of 1862 the Confederate Naval Secretary outlined a plan for attacking New York harbor by means of an ironclad vessel of the same basic type as the Stevens ship. Naval men of the North, realizing the inadequacy of New York's stationary defenses, were seriously concerned.

In other and more comprehensive ways Mallory was striving for a rehabilitation of the navy. It is clear that he had a deep love and enthusiasm for this branch of the armed services. He reminded the Senate that, "from the war of 1812 to the present moment, there is no sea on the globe visited by our commerce that has not witnessed the services of our naval officers in the protection of the life and property of our people; . . . and, sir, at this very moment [June, 1854], intelligence is reaching us that another energetic officer [Perry], in the execution of a most important and peaceful mission, has impressed our national character upon the rulers of Japan, and opened to American enterprise a trade for which the Old World has struggled for two centuries."[4] He recalled that the gallant spirits who composed our navy at the beginning of the century curbed the barbarous princes of Northern Africa, "and drew from the then existing Pope the declaration that infant America had done more for Christianity in one year than Europe had done in a century."[5] He reminded the Senate that our navy, "feeble in ships, arms, and men; feeble as it was in everything but character, courage, discipline, and devotion, was the first that ever dispelled the charm of British invincibility upon the sea."[6]

In the latter part of 1853 the future Secretary of the Confederate Navy had reported back favorably to the Senate from the Naval Affairs Committee a bill providing for six new steam frigates and for further basic reforms in the service. In June, 1854, Bocock, chairman of the Naval Affairs Committee of the House, presented a bill which, said the *New York Herald,* differed "in detail, though not in principle," from Mallory's measure; the newspaper urged the passage of Bocock's bill, which appeared (in the editor's view) "to go very much in detail upon all the subjects connected

4. 33 Cong., 1 Sess., June 22, 1854 (*Cong. Globe,* 1457, 1458).
5. *Ibid.,* 1456-57.
6. *Ibid.*

with the reorganization of the broken down and dilapidated institution [the Navy!]."[7] On June 20, 1854, the same journal announced that Mr. Mallory would press his naval bill in the Senate on the following day.[8]

In his speeches in the Senate on behalf of this measure, Mallory revealed some of his ideas on naval affairs. In the first place, he laid down the axiom which, a few years later, became the directing principle in the construction of ships for the Confederate Navy: "Naval strength (or weakness), from the character and design of the service, is altogether relative, and must ever be measured by that of its probable adversaries."[9] Therefore, he urged, if England built frigates, we must do likewise; if England built gunboats, we must do the same.[10]

He showed his alertness to new advances in naval design and ordnance. Having noted the success of the British in attaining greater speed in their vessels by means of "applying the screw to the ordinary ship of the line," he reminded the Senate that "the subject is fruitful in suggestions of the gravest national consequence."[11] He called attention to the work that was being done by Lieutenant John Dahlgren in developing improved ordnance: ". . . Under his zealous and scientific researches and attention our naval ordnance at this time is unsurpassed by any in the world."[12] He showed his appreciation of the importance of personnel problems by recommending a new method of selecting the candidates for the grade of midshipmen.[13] He favored the rule of appointment to the Naval Academy by congressional representatives rather than by the President.[14]

Mallory's perception of the value of the pioneer work in naval construction of John Ericsson was shown by his vigorous espousal of that in-

7. *New York Herald*, June 19, 1854. Cf. also *ibid.*, March 29, 1854.

8. *Ibid.*, June 20, 1854.

9. 33 Cong., 1 Sess., June 22, 1854 (*Cong. Globe*, 1456).

10. *Ibid.*  11. *Ibid.*, Appendix 2, 1457.

12. 33 Cong., 1 Sess., June 20, 1854 (*Cong. Globe*, Appendix 2, 1459). John Adolph Dahlgren became one of the outstanding Federal naval officers during the War Between the States, and has a secure place in the history of the development of American naval ordnance.

13. His proposal was that the Secretary of the Navy should choose these candidates annually from the grades of "petty officer, seaman, ordinary seaman, and boy." The point was that he desired midshipmen to be chosen from the ranks of existing experienced personnel (33 Cong., 1 Sess., June 19, 1854 [*Cong. Globe*, Appendix 2, 1436]).

14. "I did not believe that the power of appointment to the Academy could rightfully be taken from the Executive. I do not believe it now. But it seems that a large majority in the House of Representatives favors this state of things; and upon reflection I have considered that, as the Representative of the district is the organ through which its people may best make their wishes known, we have a chance, perhaps, of getting a better class of youths in the service by permitting the Representatives to appoint them than we should have if the appointment were intrusted to the Executive patronage at large" (33 Cong., 1 Sess., June 21, 1854 [*Cong. Globe*, Appendix 2, 1462]).

ventor's long unrecognized claims to reimbursement. For eight years
Ericsson's bill for his important services on the *Princeton* had gone unpaid.
On March 26, 1856, the Senate ordered the case to be submitted to the
Court of Claims, which awarded Ericsson $13,930. In the Senate on May
14, 1858, Mallory made an "earnest speech" in support of this award, which,
incidentally, was never paid.[15]

The Naval Reform Bill was passed by both houses of Congress in February, 1855. The *New York Herald* referred to it as "Mr. Mallory's bill providing for reforms in the personnel of the naval service."[16] The journal
praised the measure, noted its passage in the Senate by an unanimous vote
and in the House by a vote of 116 to 46, and declared that the bill "seemed
to be quite popular with many officers . . . in Washington."[17] It is worth
while noting these compliments, in view of the bitter debates that the carrying out of some portions of the act caused in the Senate during the following year.[18]

Naval affairs, although important, were not, of course, the chief preoccupation of the United States Senate in 1854. By the end of May Congress had passed the Kansas-Nebraska Act. Mallory, standing firmly with
his party, had voted for the measure, despite a trick executed against him
by Senator Sam Houston, the great Texan hero.[19]

It was becoming increasingly clear that the slavery issue was getting out
of hand. When the news of the passage of Douglas' bill reached a small
town in Illinois, a tall and gangling man named Lincoln sat up all night in
a tavern talking about it with his friends and repeating solemnly that the
country could not remain half slave and half free.

15. William C. Church, *The Life of John Ericsson* (New York, 1911), 148-50.

16. February 3, 1855.        17. February 6, 1855; cf. also *ibid.*, February 14, 1855.

18. Mallory took a strong stand against the proposal to extend the contract made by the
government with the Collins mail-steamer line, whose officials argued that these vessels were
readily convertible into ships of war and should therefore be subsidized by Congress. The
Collins steamers, he felt, were unfit for war purposes. They would be "exposed to utter annihilation by a single shot." Their side-wheels, shafts, boilers, and machinery were defenseless.
Along with Jefferson Davis, Secretary of War, and Senator Hunter, he opposed vigorously
(though not successfully) a pro-Collins congressional bloc which, it would seem, was not wholly
free from private pecuniary interests in the matter (cf. 33 Cong., 2 Sess., February 27, 1855
[*Cong. Globe*, Appendix, 353-55]). In regard to the Collins contracts, cf. *New York Herald*,
February 16, 1855, for account of the hot debate in the House over the renewal of the Collins
mail-steamer contract, with sharp aspersions cast on the Collins Line and its supporters in
Congress; cf. also *ibid.*, February 19, 1855, June 21, 1858.

19. "It is due to Mr. Mallory, of Florida," said the *New York Herald*, "that it should be
distinctly understood he left the city under the idea that General Houston had agreed to pair
off with him; and that this was General Houston's understanding is evidenced by the fact that
he, on Friday, asserted, in open session, he was paired off with Mr. Mallory. Notwithstanding this agreement, General Houston voted against the bill this morning" (March 5, 1854).

For Mallory the Kansas-Nebraska Act was the occasion of a spirited tilt between himself and one of the arch-opponents of the South. In discussing the various angles of the slavery problem, the Senate's attention had turned to the Fugitive Slave Law. The following blunt question had been presented to Senator Charles Sumner of Massachusetts: Would Massachusetts, if all her "personal liberty" laws should be declared unconstitutional, deliver up, on demand of the master, a slave who had escaped into her territory? Sumner was understood to have replied, "I recognize no such obligation."[20] It was at this point that Mallory entered the lists, and the following exchange took place:

"Mallory: When that honorable Senator here in the face of the country, in the presence of this Senate, within these hallowed walls, which have so often responded to the eloquence and patriotism of his own State; when he at the foot of this altar, upon which he pledged his fidelity to his country, upon which he called upon God to witness that he would defend and sustain her Constitution—when he rises in his place and tells the American Senate that he does not recognize the obligation of that Constitution, what does he expect at the hands of the Senator?

"Sumner: I call the Senator to order.

"The Presiding Officer: The Senator will state his point of order.

"Sumner: The Senator places in my mouth words and sentiments which have never fallen from me.

"Mallory: I should be unwilling to place in the mouth of a dog sentiments which were unbecoming to him, and will therefore ask the Senator, with all proper respect, to state what he did say; for that, I presume, is the understanding of the Senate.

"Sumner: I stated that I would never render any personal assistance in returning or reducing a fellow man to slavery.

"Mallory: Mr. President—

"C. C. Clay: When I hear the Senator from Massachusetts, with unblushing presumption and insolence, (Order!) without shame, without contrition or repentance, contumaciously repeating that he had said only that he would not reduce a fellow man to bondage—

"Sumner: Return.

"Clay: Return a fellow man to bondage—

"Sumner: Or reduce, which is the same thing.

"Mallory: Mr. President, when I gave way to my friend from Alabama [Clay], I had remarked that the Senator from Massachusetts, who sits near

20. 33 Cong., 1 Sess., June 29, 1854 (*Cong. Globe*, Appendix 3, 1558).

me, had here, in the face of the country, in the presence of the Senate at the foot of that altar whereon he had pledged his fidelity to his country, and sworn to maintain and defend her Constitution, I was interrupted by the Senator, who said that I had put words into his mouth which he did not utter. Sir, I deny it! I acknowledge that I heard the declaration with equal regret and indignation; and, as unwilling as I am to say anything which the rules of the Senate do not justify, or the occasion demand, I am still more unwilling to stand here and permit such language to pass without some note of condemnation. Sir, I heard the honorable Senator say, in open Senate, 'I recognize no such obligation'; whether that appears in the report or not, I have not examined.

"Sumner: It is true, and I repeat it now.

"Mallory: Sir, if the Senator will examine the Constitution, he will find it there written that a fugitive from service or labor 'shall be delivered up.' If he recognizes no such obligation, I leave it to himself to explain the consistency between the oath which he has taken and the sentiments which he disavows. Sir, can he rise in his place and say here that a Senator shall be permitted to make mental reservations? Is *that* the explanation? That he is at liberty to exempt himself from those obligations which bind the humblest citizen?"[21]

Mallory is listed by the biographer of Judah P. Benjamin as being one of the "more radical Southerners" who were willing to embroil the United States in a war with Spain in order to acquire Cuba as a slave territory. On May 17, 1854, the Floridian introduced a Senate resolution stating that there was a settled design to throw Cuba into the hands of its Negro population and thus to revive the scenes of the San Domingo revolution. A week later Benjamin presented to the Senate resolutions somewhat similar to Mallory's. The leader whose policy in regard to Cuba Mallory was following—and even, it would seem, anticipating—is described as being "a leader of the extreme Southern party in the Senate, . . . one of the ablest . . . defenders of the Southern point of view on slavery and States' rights," though no secessionist before December, 1860.[22] However a contradictory testimony to Mallory's aggressive political stand on the issue of states' rights was his close friendship with Zachariah Chandler, a Northern "fire-eater." A really radical states' rights man could scarcely have won the intimacy with Chandler which the Floridian enjoyed.[23]

21. *Ibid.*, 1552-54.
22. Robert D. Meade, *Judah P. Benjamin, Confederate Statesman* (New York, 1943), 92. Cf., *in re* the "Cuban plot," *National Intelligencer*, May 18, 1854.
23. Cf. Wilmer C. Harris, *Public Life of Zachariah Chandler* (dissertation, private edition

Mallory also found time to attend to more local and particular interests. He complained of what he termed "discrimination" against Florida in the matter of appropriations for the improvements of rivers and harbors. In the recent bill only one grant had been awarded to Florida, and that was a mere five thousand dollars for the improvement of the "haulover" between two streams. If, declared Mallory, the Senate had searched throughout the entire state for a point where money could be appropriated with the least possible advantage to the state at large, the Senate might have selected this very spot. On the other hand, the harbor of Apalachicola, which loaded seventy square-rigged vessels a year and shipped one hundred and sixty thousand bales of cotton from Georgia and other states, and which had a channel that had been surveyed by the United States authorities, was left without a dollar of appropriation.[24]

"Why," he inquired, "am I asked without consideration to vote money for places which I never heard of in my life, some of which I have no doubt it would be difficult to find on any map in the country, and which certainly never sent a return to the Treasury Department of a single ton of foreign merchandise and never saw a foreign flag?"[25]

He tried unsuccessfully to secure a money grant for a small waterway to the Indian river and the Mosquito lagoon at the "haulover." The opposition to the appropriation was based on the argument that Florida already possessed a sufficient number of canals. Mallory denied that the proposed improvement was a canal, and was challenged on the point by Stephen Douglas:

"Douglas: I . . . should infer there was a water-course running one way [at the haulover], and another running the other; and this is what they call a portage between them.

"Mallory: That is it.

"Douglas: This work, then, is a canal in the State of Florida, to connect these two water-courses.

"Mallory: I will not admit it is a canal. It is to turn water where it does not pass now, by making this improvement. (Laughter.)"[26]

distributed by the University of Chicago Libraries; regular edition published by the Michigan Historical Commission, 1917). Chandler was a Radical Republican, for many years the party boss of Michigan. He succeeded Lewis Cass in the Senate in 1857, and held his seat until 1875. Through trade, banking, and speculation he became one of the wealthiest men in his state. He approved of the Reconstruction Acts, although he felt that in some respects they were too lax. For evidence of Mallory's friendship with Chandler, cf. infra, p. 357.

24. 33 Cong., 1 Sess., June 29, 1854 (Cong. Globe, Appendix 3, 1167).
25. Ibid.                              26. Ibid.

He tried to have his old mentor Judge Marvin appointed as District Attorney for Southern Florida.[27] He was instrumental in having some lands at Key West conveyed to the United States Government.[28] His loyalty to the members of his own religious faith was displayed in a long speech in the Senate in May, 1854, defending Catholics against charges of un-Americanism.[29]

Mallory's Naval Retiring Board set off the fireworks in September, 1855.[30] Matthew Fontaine Maury, world-famous oceanographer and pioneer in the science of hydrography, was removed by the Board from active duty and placed on the "Reserve List."[31]

Maury's friends were indignant. The Board, it was charged, had committed a "grievous error, a large public wrong," and was attempting to "smother if not suppress altogether the hydrographical office of the Navy. . . ."[32] Maury himself protested bitterly. He had, for no cause, so he declared, been made to suffer a grievous wrong. He appealed to his friends to help him to right it. He had been in the service, he reminded his accusers, upward of thirty years. During that time no complaint of duty neglected, no charges against him for any cause had ever reached the Navy Department. Yet he had now been brought into official disgrace on what grounds he knew not. The thing had been done by a board of navy officers sitting in secret and acting mischievously.[33]

27. Mallory to Attorney-General Caleb Cushing, January 3, 1855 (Cushing Papers, Library of Congress).

28. Mallory to Cushing, February 14, 1854 (*ibid.*). He says that as he is going to Key West in a few days it will be "a feather in my cap" to conclude the business.

29. 33 Cong., 1 Sess., May 16, 1854 (*Cong. Globe,* 1194-95). It was during this debate that Salmon P. Chase paid the following tribute to Mallory: "There is no Senator upon this floor to whose action I should be more unwilling to take any exception than to that honorable Senator" (33 Cong., 1 Sess., May 10, 1854 [*Cong. Globe,* 1200]). For a defense of the Catholic position in answer to the un-American charge, and for a gentle criticism of Mallory's not completely successful rebuttal of the charge, see *Catholic Mirror* (Baltimore), May 20, June 3, 1854; also *New York Herald,* May 17, 1854.

30. The members of the Board when it first convened in June, 1855, were as follows: Captains Shubrick (S. C.), Perry (R. I.), McCauley (Pa.), Stribling (S. C.), Bigelow (Mass.); Commanders Pendergast (Ky.), Buchanan (Md.), Dupont (Del.), Barron (Va.), Page (Va.).

31. Cf. Secretary of the Navy James C. Dobbin to Maury, September 17, 1855; Maury Papers, IV, Library of Congress.

32. Anon. to Anon., from Naval Observatory, Washington, D. C., September 18, 1855 (*ibid.*).

33. Maury to Bishop J. H. Otey, from University of Georgia, September 21, 1855 (*ibid.*). James Hervey Otey was the first Protestant Episcopal bishop of Tennessee. Born in Bedford County, Virginia, he settled in Memphis in 1852. He was also an outstanding educator, and was one of the founders of the University of the South at Sewanee in 1858. He was an "old time" Whig, a staunch supporter of the Constitution as he understood it, and steadily opposed to war as a means of settlement of the sectional controversy.

The accusation that the Board was a secret inquisition which penalized officers without granting them an opportunity for defense was to be urged repeatedly. Maury grew eloquent on the point. The so-called "finding" had taken him by complete surprise, and was the clear result of envy. He inferred from the Secretary's letter in the *Intelligencer* that the Board had kept no record of its proceedings, had assigned no reason for its findings, and had published no account of its votes. If this were so, the Board was a "cowardly Inquisition, without precedent in this country."[34]

Not one member of the Board, complained Maury, had the least pretensions to any knowledge of science. The attack on himself had the effect of discouraging young naval officers from becoming proficient in naval science.[35] He would demand a court of inquiry, "and failing in that I shall ask to have the injunction of secrecy removed in my case, and each member of the Board left free to answer all questions."[36] He was aware that the Board would adduce his lameness as an excuse for their action.[37] But Nelson himself had but one arm, and, by the Board's ruling, General Scott might long ago have been retired from active service.[38] Most members of Congress, he believed, were more or less critical of the Board. He had heard of no Congressman besides Bocock, the father of the bill in the House, "and Mallory, its sponsor in the Senate," who were unqualifiedly in favor of the Board.[39]

In any study of the statesmanship of Stephen Mallory it is important to obtain a true estimate of the virtues and faults of the Naval Retiring Board.

34. Maury to William Blackford, from University of Virginia, September 23, 1855 (*ibid.*). William Matthews Blackford was a very competent scholar and editor and part owner of the Lynchburg *Virginian*. He married Mary Berkeley Minor, daughter of General John Minor.

35. *Ibid.* The Board's methods were thus described by the *New York Herald*: "It was the duty of this Board to pass in review nearly seven hundred officers, ascertain if they were competent to perform all their duties, afloat and ashore, and report the names to the department of those incompetent. A careful calculation shows that this Board gave about thirteen minutes to the case of each officer! The result of their session was that over two hundred officers were dropped, retired, or furloughed" (December 3, 1855).

36. Maury to William Blackford, September 23, 1855 (Maury Papers).

37. The following note is added to the letter indicated in note 36: "Up to this time he [Maury] never walked without the necessary support of a cane; now, however, he became so sensitive that he never used one, and on his return to W'ton. would frequently come home exhausted with a walk from the Navy Dep't." (This note is initialed by an unidentified "W. H. M.").

38. Maury to Blackford, September 23, 1855 (Maury Papers).

39. Maury to Frank Minor, from Washington, December 25, 1855 (Maury Papers). This correspondent of Mallory's is probably Francis Minor, b. August 15, 1820, d. February 19, 1892, son of Dabney Minor and Lucy Herndon. Cf. John B. Minor, *The Minor Family of Virginia* (Lynchburg, Va., 1923), 38.

It had been created by the bill of which he had been the chief sponsor in the Senate. Its ruthless "shelving" of officers judged to be incompetent for active service was largely an application of a reform for which he had fought strenuously for three years. In bitter debate he would defend the Board's actions as a whole. If the Board was what Maury and some others said it was, Mallory must share a great part of the blame.

The Board had its influential and vigorous defenders.

Hamilton Fish gently remonstrated with a friend for the latter's recriminations against the Board: "I cannot agree with you in the condemnation which you visit upon them." Their duty, he thought, was a delicate and (he doubted not) a very painful one, and was probably unsought by them. Many members of the Board had tried to escape the assignment. That they had made mistakes he did not question; but there probably would have been a strong disposition on the Board's part to correct those mistakes. If the issue were put to him to sustain the Board's action or to reverse it substantially, he felt that the interests of the service would require him to sustain the findings as they stood. If those who really had cause for complaint could show that errors had been committed, or that they had suffered injustice, he would take great pleasure in endeavoring to have such causes righted.[40]

"Two-thirds of that Furlough List," wrote Commander Thomas Turner to Fish, "ought to have been *dropped* [and not merely furloughed or retired], and that we *all* know."[41] He pointed to the "festered" condition of the Navy, wherein captains had been unemployed for twenty, or thirty, or forty years. "It was not to be expected that they [the Board] would do all they ought . . . for they had a vast deal to contend with, and it was a first effort, and the first duty of the kind we have ever been called to perform. There was no precedent . . . no antecedents to fall back upon. As you say, 'We must be thankful for small favors' just now. It will go far to purify the Navy and to build it up anew, and has given *new life* already to the remaining branches."[42]

As to the Board's alleged unfairness: they furloughed the son of one of their own members; they dropped the President's ward; they reserved Com-

---

40. Fish to Charles Morris, Esq., December 12, 1855 (Fish Papers, Letter Books, Library of Congress). Morris, a naval officer who had served with distinction with Decatur in the War of 1812, died the year following his writing of this letter.

41. Turner to Fish, from Philadelphia, September 21, 1855 (Fish Papers, Letter Files. Italics in original). Turner was in charge of the sloop *Saratoga* on the Home Squadron in 1858-60. He later commanded the *New Ironsides*.

42. *Ibid.* Italics in original.

modore Stewart, an uncle of one of the Board; they reserved an intimate friend of five members of the Board.[43]

The Board was defended by Senator Judah P. Benjamin of Louisiana. The fact, he argued, that they could not attain perfection, that they could not strike off from the list of officers "exactly such men as ought to be stricken out," did not make it any less their duty as faithful public servants to perform their disciplinary task.[44]

The fight against the "inquisitional tribunal" got under way early in 1856.

The fact that the Board had kept no record of its proceedings was made the basis of a vigorous attack by Senator Robert Toombs of Georgia. Since the Board was a court of special and limited jurisdiction, he thundered, it should have kept a record, and that record should have shown that each case on which its members acted was within the operation of the law. It could not be pretended that under the law they could strike a man from the rolls for whatever cause they thought proper. They were bound to confine themselves to the question of an officer's capacity to perform his duties on shore and at sea. If they went beyond that, their proceedings were null and void. Furthermore since, under the act constituting the Board, their proceedings should show that they had not exceeded their jurisdiction, those proceedings became void by not showing it. The Senator from Louisiana (Benjamin) had admitted that the Secretary of the Navy had made a mistake in conferring upon the Board, by means of his instructions, an authority which the law itself did not confer. By that admission the Board was clearly condemned. Moreover the Secretary, while conceding that the findings of the Board were in some cases wrong, had nonetheless confirmed their proceedings as a whole. That action was fatal to the whole procedure of the Board.[45]

43. *Ibid.* Commodore Charles Stewart commanded the *Constitution* in the War of 1812 and was himself referred to as "Old Ironsides." He was in charge of the Philadelphia Navy Yard from 1854 to 1861. In 1862 he was commissioned a rear admiral. He completed seventy-one years of naval service of one type or another. James Shedden Palmer, appointed commander in September, 1855, was the "intimate friend of five members of the Board." As a captain he led the advance in the passage of the Vicksburg batteries in the summer of 1862. He was commissioned a commodore in February, 1863, and at New Orleans and Mobile was Farragut's flag captain. He was popularly known as "Pie-crust" Palmer.

44. 34 Cong., 2 Sess., January 10, 1856 (*Cong. Globe*, 203); also *ibid.*, 388, 400-4. Says Meade, *op. cit.*, 99: "The American Navy was then burdened with a considerable number of incompetent officers who should have been retired from active service; but when a duly authorized board of naval officers sought to remove some of the unfit there was strong opposition from the men affected and their champions in the Senate."

45. Quoted in Ulrich B. Phillips, *The Life of Robert Toombs* (New York, 1913), 146; cf. also 34 Cong., 2 Sess., February 2, 1856 (*Cong. Globe*, 343-44).

Toombs aimed some of his shafts directly at Mallory, who, on the testimony of Maury, was the outstanding defender of the Board.[46] The Senator from Florida, said the Senator from Georgia, had declared that he supposed that Senators would hear the complaints of those who might have suffered from the action of the Board. Thank the Lord that such was the truth, that no injustice could be done to a great and distinguished body of public servants in this country without there being found willing ears to listen to it and to redress it in the American Senate! Even the Inquisition had brought its victims face to face with their accusers. This Board was charged with secretly accusing its victims, with secretly seeking informers to blast the fair names of their fellow-officers, and then concealing from them the nature of the alleged crimes and the names of the witnesses by whom the allegations were supported. All these despotic proceedings, declared Toombs sarcastically, Senator Mallory sought to excuse by proposing what he (Mallory) deemed excellent reasons for retiring old captains; and he kept the Senate amused with exploits of young heroes. It would seem from such recitals that we had many more captains than we had any use for. So what did Senator Mallory suggest? Since there was nothing for so many old captains to do, he deemed it expedient to help the situation by adding thirty-odd young and vigorous commanders to the list —in order, Toombs surmised, to help the old captains to do nothing! The real cause of these subterfuges, said the fiery Georgian, was—impatience for promotion.[47]

Maury informed a friend in late January of 1856 that ". . . Mallory . . . has already shifted the grounds from the leg[48] to the *want of sea service;* but if I can only get a good champion I shall beat them there, for their findings on that score are as inconsistent as the other. . . ."[49]

As an example of ". . . the spirit of fairness which I am to expect from the friends of the Board in the Senate . . . ," Maury cited the following action of Mallory: "To show that I had applied for this place [head of the Naval Observatory], Mr. Mallory produced a letter in the Senate last Monday written by me in February [18]42, stating that if a bill which was then

46. Cf. Maury to Professor John B. Minor, from Washington, January 28, 1856 (Maury Papers, V): "Mallory, who is their [the pro-Board group's] leader. . . ." John Barbee Minor, brother of Lucian Minor, was a teacher of law (for awhile at the University of Virginia) and author of legal works.

47. Phillips, *op. cit.,* 146-47.

48. For explanation of this reference to Maury's leg, cf. *infra,* p. 81.

49. Maury to Professor John B. Minor, from Washington, D. C., January 28, 1856 (Maury Papers, V. Italics Maury's).

before Congress for establishing a bureau of hydrography should become a law, and an officer of my rank should be eligible to it as chief, I wished to be considered as a candidate."[50] For so doing, Mallory was charged by Maury with a lack of ingenuousness, on the rather remarkable grounds that "no such bureau ever was established, and I have never been the chief of any Bureau; and at the time that letter was written the appropriation even, for building the Observatory, had not been made."[51] But Mallory's point was that Maury had, as a matter of fact, requested a shore office which, at the time of the request, Maury thought would be created.

This charge that Mallory was employing unfair tactics was, a few days later, repeated by Maury. He said that the former had attempted to frighten a Senator who opposed the Board by threatening to expose in open Senate the real reasons why the black-balled officers had been so treated. This veiled effort at polite blackmail, declared Maury, was linked with the well-understood attempt of some members of the Board to "concoct" reasons for their findings. "So you see," concluded the irate oceanographer, "there is another secret and irresponsible procedure which the Chairman of the Naval Committee in the Senate is using for a second trial of us in the dark. I wish some Senator would make him produce that spurious record in open Senate and demand to know what officers have dared to concoct it. . . ."[52]

The "report" which Mallory had promised to make to the Senate with regard to the Board would be, Maury forecast, "a white-washing affair."[53] The Senator from Florida had been "pursuing a course that . . . was very singular."[54] Commodore Perry, who was eager to testify in behalf of the demoted officers, had been refused the opportunity by the Board. The Naval Affairs Committee would, in Maury's judgment, recommend a board of revision, which he would regard as being unjust, for it would throw the onus of proof upon the "black-eyed boys."[55]

Up to this point we have been witnessing a stand-up fight between the Board and its defenders—with Mallory leading the latter—and the cashiered

50. Ibid.                                    51. Ibid.
52. Maury to Professor Lucian Minor, from Washington, D. C., February 4, 1856 (ibid.). Professor Minor, brother of John Barbee Minor, was at this time a teacher of law at the College of William and Mary. From 1828 to 1852 he had been Virginia's attorney for his native county, Louisa. He was also a noted temperance advocate. "Do you know," Maury wrote to Frank Minor on February 19, 1856, "that I thought Mallory was telling the truth when he was making that flourish about the number of times I sought to be relieved from service at sea." But on looking up his own records he found, he said, that Mallory was *not* telling the truth! (ibid.).
53. Maury to William Blackford, from Washington, D. C., February 21, 1856 (ibid.).
54. Ibid.                                    55. Ibid.

officers and their supporters.[56] Then, in late February, Mallory made what appeared to be a conciliatory gesture. He proposed a bill by which most of the retired and furloughed officers would be given a chance to have their cases reviewed. Maury thought that the move represented a distinct retreat on the part of the Floridian: "It [the bill] was drawn in concert with Dobbin and is . . . a regular 'give-in.' I saw him [Mallory or Dobbin?] today for a little while, and told him I thought it would do, with some alterations in details, in which he concurred, and he had me submit them as amendments. I also saw Bell today. He told me the [Senate Naval Affairs] committee were very desirous to know if the bill were satisfactory to me."[57]

Mallory did not stop here in his apparently very real "give in." Shubrick was requested by the Naval Affairs Committee to submit a full explanation of the Board's *modus operandi*—a request which was immediately complied with, in the shape of a eulogy of the Board.[58] On the heels of this, Mallory proposed on the floor of the Senate that Maury be reimbursed for his wind and sailing charts and sailing directions.[59] And, on the eve of the hot debate with regard to the Naval Retiring Board, the Chairman of the Senate Naval Affairs Committee personally presented to the Senate a formal petition for reinstatement from a demoted officer.[60]

Although he had entertained some lingering suspicions,[61] Maury was convinced by the end of March that Mallory's bill was a sincere attempt to reform the Board, as well as the officer personnel of the Navy. The oceanographer, apparently much mollified, regarded the bill "as yielding every-

56. The future General George B. McClellan was on the side of the Board. In a long letter to Senator Clayton of Delaware on the topic of national defense he said: "Free the Army from incumbrances, as you have already done to the Navy, by a retired list" (G. B. McClellan to Senator J. M. Clayton, from Strasburg, Germany, February 18, 1856 [Clayton Papers, Library of Congress]).

57. Maury to Frank Minor, from Washington, February 27, 1856 (Maury Papers, VI).

58. *New York Herald,* March 14, 1856.

59. 34 Cong., 1 Sess., March 18, 1856 (*Cong. Globe,* Appendix 245). The strongly partisan biography of Maury by his daughter asserts that Senators Mallory and Jefferson Davis both strongly opposed Maury's reinstatement when the bill praying for justice for those injured by the action of the Board was introduced into Congress. "Both," declares this not completely reliable source, "were inimical to Maury both before and after the Civil war" Diana Fontaine Maury Corbin, *A Life of Matthew Fontaine Maury* . . . (London, 1888), 112.

60. In this case of the demotion of Lieutenant L. Sartori the Board had undoubtedly erred. At the time he was retired, the Lieutenant was on actual combat duty in the Fiji Islands (*New York Herald,* March 22, 1856).

61. Only a week before: ". . . The Navy Bill and board business make but little headway in the Senate. I can't yet form any opinion about the scientific corps. Mallory has been *forced* to yield that much to me, and I reckon he will be in favor of tying [*sic*] up the corps as much as possible in order to curtail its usefulness" (Maury to Blackford, from Washington, March 24, 1856 [Maury Papers, VI. Italics Maury's]).

thing," and urged his friends to accept its principles. He felt that the administration was thus afforded an opportunity "to recover itself" by observing a liberal course towards the blackballed officers. He had learned from the Secretary of the Navy that some officers had already been selected for reinstatement, and that all the rest could have a court of inquiry. This, declared Maury, was a "considerable coming down" on the part of the pro-Board party.[62]

But it is questionable that Mallory had "come down" very far. In the spirited debate that began in the Senate in the early spring of 1856, he struck back hard at the opponents of the Naval Retiring Board, and fought for an acceptance of at least the essentials of the Reform Bill. This was perhaps the most extended and the most difficult contest in which he engaged during his whole career in Congress. If it is in the swift give-and-take of rough parliamentary discussion that a statesman reveals his real virtues and defects, this debate on the Naval Reform Bill and its Board is a valuable index to the political stature of Stephen Mallory.[63]

On May 15 the debate was in full swing. Mallory took the floor with a brief speech in defense of the general principle underlying the Retiring Board's actions. The chief reason for the alarming weakness of the Navy, he insisted, was the method of applying the seniority rule for promotions. He offered some rather sensational examples of the evils of this system. "Without going into detail," he stated, "I will say to the Senate that, by this rule of seniority, when this law [the Naval Reform Bill] was passed, we had 68 captains. . . . I will not undertake to say what was the age of the oldest; it might offend the sensibilities of gentlemen; but the youngest was fifty-six years of age. Be it remembered that, by special order in council, . . . Great Britain induces her captains to retire at the age of fifty-five, considering them no longer fit for duty. No captain could commence his novitiate when the law was passed, until he had reached the mature age of

62. Maury to Frank Minor, from Washington, April 1, 1856 (*ibid*).

63. Cf. the following favorable comments on the 1853 naval reorganization legislation: *New Orleans Picayune*, n. d., reprinted in *Pensacola Gazette*, February 19, 1853; *New York Herald*, February 6, February 14, 1855. The Naval Retiring Board was praised by Secretary of the Navy Toucey in his *Report* of December 3, 1855. Cf. also Commodore John Rodgers to Mallory, from Washington, October 15, 1857, enclosing pictures for Mallory "as a mark of thanks for the great interest you have ever shown in the Corps of which I am a member, and for the skill with which you have advocated in the Senate its advancement" (Mallory-Kennedy Collection). On the contrary, the *Washington Union*, March 19, 1853, protested against the drawing up of rules by the President's Naval Retiring Board without ratification of those rules by Congress. Only the latter body, argued the *Union*, had power to make rules for the navy.

seventy-four; whereas there was no hero in the last war who had not distinguished himself as a captain at the age of thirty-nine.[64]

In the British Navy, he noted, promotion was based not on seniority, but on merit. While, with characteristic moderation, he did not recommend abandonment of the rule of seniority, he would, by means of the Naval Retiring Act, scrutinize the corps thoroughly and frequently, purge it of incompetency, and thus make seniority a safe technique for advancement.[65]

In defense of the older officers of the Navy, Senator Butler of South Carolina referred to the *Iliad*. At the siege of Troy, he reminded the Senators, it was Nestor, who, with the trembling hands of age, buckled on his armor, and rebuked the youths for their cowardice. "Will you tell a man," asked Butler, "that because he is wounded, because he is feeble, that you have no use for him? Is this the way, in which you will use intellect? Do you regard merely legs and arms, and thews and sinews?"

Mallory had also read his Homer. He pointed out that Nestor, although he buckled on his armor, did not take actual part in the fighting, but stood back as a retired officer and confined his efforts to counseling the younger warriors. The naval profession afforded no exception to the rule, "old men for counsel, young men for war." He reminded Butler of David's remark that the days of our age were threescore years and ten. It was regrettable that so many Nestors had been put on the retired list by the Naval Board; but it was none the less true that a man could not be considered as efficient for the active and arduous service of the sea after the age of fourscore years.[66]

Another evil which the Retiring Board aimed to prevent was the frequent restoration to their commands, by political influence, of officers discharged for unfitness or even for criminal offenses. A glaring illustration of this was a case in which a post captain had been convicted by a court of his peers of official falsehood under the most aggravating circumstances. The court deprived him of command and suspended him for three years. A succeeding administration entirely relieved him from his suspension and gave him all his back pay, and, as a reward for his outraged feelings, placed him in command of one of the first squadrons of the country.[67]

The Board was frequently attacked for its insistence on good moral character as an indispensable element of an officer's general efficiency. (Senator Toombs had been particularly vehement against this policy.) Mal-

64. 34 Cong., 1 Sess., May 15, 1856 (*Cong. Globe,* Appendix, 573).
65. *Ibid.*                    66. *Ibid.,* 579.
67. *Ibid.,* 573-74.

lory urged strongly the thesis that one could not be a good officer unless he was also a good man. Character, he held, was not only essential to an officer, but it "lay at the very foundation of all his efficiency." To think otherwise was to take a very narrow view of an officer's duties, since some of the noblest triumphs of our naval men had been achieved in times of peace and by moral force alone. They had acted repeatedly as "pacificators," negotiators of treaties, and as representatives abroad of the country's character and honor, and as the guardians of the honor and rights and interests of their fellow-countrymen in foreign lands. Was the "efficiency" of a man for such duties consistent with infamy of character? On this point the Board was merely repeating the views of the founders of our navy, as expressed in the act of organization of 1800.[68]

This argument was ably countered by Crittenden of Kentucky, who charged that the Board was a "star-chamber tribunal on morals." There was, he held, a clear distinction between professional capacity and character. Whether an officer was capable of performing his duties was one question; whether, as a matter of fact, he actually performed them was another. No one could have doubted that the Duke of Marlborough was capable of performing his duty as captain and soldier; but he was, declared the Senator from Kentucky, the basest, the meanest, the falsest, and the most treacherous of men. What, asked Mr. Crittenden, would this Board have done with him as an officer, if morals were to be the decisive factor? What would the chairman of the Committee on Naval Affairs have done with such a man as that? Congress never contemplated that "vile inquisition, which, without specification, without charge, without a hearing, should, in private, and in secret, inquire into and determine upon every act of a man's lifetime." The Board, having secured a degree of power, had by construction expanded it into this wide, despotic, and unlimited authority.[69]

Mallory continued to repeat his view that an officer of bad character should not exist in our navy, while Crittenden, holding to his point that capacity was one thing and morals another, kept returning to the Duke of Marlborough. The question, he insisted, should be answered: Would the Senator from Florida have decided the Duke of Marlborough to be incapable? The Duke, replied Mallory, had already been so ably abused by Macaulay as to render further disparagement unnecessary. It must be said, however, that he was a very bad man, though one of the best soldiers in the

68. *Ibid.*, 578.
69. *Ibid.*, 585.

world. But it was to be noted that the question of his over-all efficiency had never been submitted to a board of examiners![70]

While Senator Crittenden was openly and elaborately congratulating himself on what he regarded as a victory in this exchange, Mr. Toombs interjected another historical character into the discussion:

"Toombs: How would Lord Nelson have been treated by the Board?

"Crittenden: He certainly would have been dismissed. The honorable Senator would have dismissed Lord Nelson.

"Toombs: On account of Lady Hamilton?

"Crittenden: Yes sir, he was of too amorous a temper."[71]

Mallory was quite at home in such verbal sword play, and was quick to retort. Nelson, he conceded, was an exception to the rule. Nelson, even if—in the words of the Senator from Georgia—he had been steeped in infamy and had committed all the sins of the Decalogue, would certainly have been retained in active service by the Naval Retiring Board. On that point the chairman wished to give his most unequivocal assurance. But the comparison, he added, was unfortunate. It was embarrassing for the officers who had been placed on the reserve list that any sort of parallel should have been attempted between Nelson and themselves. It was very unfortunate that a comparison had been drawn between them and a man who was posted at twenty-one years of age and died at a little over forty, after filling the world with his fame.[72]

Crittenden was in no way discouraged. He pressed his charge by ridiculing an inquiry that was at the moment being made by the Board—"not into the capacity of an officer, but whether he kept his accounts correctly in a mess bill when he was caterer ten years ago." The Board was much concerned, also, he said, by the same officer's sale of an Indian shawl to a lady for ten dollars, when it was worth only about seven.[73]

Mallory's reply to this shaft was not very strong. He confined himself to the statement that the Senator from Kentucky was not in possession of as many of the facts of the case as were known to the Board. This stage of the discussion closed with Crittenden's assurance that he did not mean to impugn the personal characters of the Board; he charitably supposed that they had acted under the influence of some strange hallucination, induced, possibly, by a sort of "pastoral letter" on the subject of morality addressed to them by the Secretary of the Navy. This instruction, he could not forbear

70. *Ibid.*
72. *Ibid.*
71. *Ibid.*
73. *Ibid.*, 586.

observing, would have become a Tillotson about as well as a Secretary of the Navy.[74]

A slightly different mode of attack was adopted by the ebullient Senator Sam Houston, possibly with his tongue in his cheek. The Board's retirement of Matthew F. Maury on the grounds that he had lost his "efficiency" because of a broken leg was unfair, Houston argued, since it was common knowledge that a member of the Retiring Board itself was still being retained on active duty despite the fact that he had broken his leg twice.[75]

Mallory had his retort ready. The Senator from Texas was referring to the case of Lieutenant Missroon, and the Senator was unaware of all the details. Lieutenant Missroon's leg had indeed been broken twice, but under what circumstances? He first suffered the accident while on active duty at sea; the leg was immediately set, and he performed two more years' active sea duty; then, finding that the operation had not been fully successful, and desiring to increase his efficiency, he left no stone unturned until he found surgeons in the United States—having threatened to go to France to find them—who were willing to perform the operation. He had his leg broken over again and reset; and on that leg he had already performed seven years' sea duty. His case was obviously not a parallel to that of Lieutenant Maury.[76]

The Board's action in retiring Maury evoked perhaps more opposition than any other of its moves. Bell of Tennessee delivered an extended defense of the shelved officer, stressing his high scientific attainments in the field of ocean cartography.[77]

In a long speech of May 15-16, Mallory replied to the Board's critics. He emphasized the point that the efficiency of our navy depended on a solid core of commanders whose competence was derived from actual experience in handling vessels at sea. The Senator from Tennessee had referred to the widespread reputation of Lieutenant Maury. Mallory did not deny the propriety of such praise. But, he urged, military rank should never be conferred for civilian reputation, no matter how great the latter. A fit and powerful navy was created by men who could handle vessels on the deep, not by men who were versed in whatsoever sciences on shore.[78]

There were, declared Mallory, far too many of our naval officers who had been on shore doing practically nothing for a period of years. The re-

74. *Ibid.*
75. *Ibid.*, March 18, 1856, 250.
76. *Ibid.*
77. 34 Cong., 1 Sess., April 1, 1856 (*Cong. Globe*, Appendix, 333-36).
78. 34 Cong., 1 Sess., May 15, 1856 (*ibid.*, 333-36).

cent report of the Senate Committee on Naval Affairs had given a detailed list of such officers. The difficulty was to get rid of these men. They resisted all urgings to performance of their duty. Some of them had come to be regarded by the oldest clerks in the department as being a sort of myth— "as the John Does and Richard Roes of the Navy." When these men came to the department to receive their pay, even the oldest clerks were startled. These officers' names were on the register, but they themselves had been away in the West or elsewhere, farming or attending to other business. The Retiring Board was doing its best, concluded Mallory sorrowfully, but it was extremely difficult to get these men out.[79]

The upshot of these spirited exchanges was that Mallory, by midsummer, 1856, pushed through the Senate a bill incorporating the essentials of his program for streamlining the personnel of the navy.[80] That Maury's estimate of the Floridian's "backing down" was premature is indicated by the comment of a contemporary. "I perceive," wrote W. W. Bartlett to Senator Crittenden in July, "that my worst fears are realized, and that Mr. Mallory has carried the main points of his bill, and for his promotions. I would not care for the promotions however if we could have security under the law; but will not Mr. Dobbin pack the Court of Inquiry to suit himself—and can it be made to act under oath? If so, we may have some hope yet."[81]

79. *Ibid.*, May 16, 1856, 584. Mallory attacked the rule of seniority which had left in the navy 197 midshipmen who, instead of being the "dear little midshipmen" one pictured, ranged in age from twenty-one to thirty-seven, who had to support their families on $750 per annum, and whose duty aboard was most menial. He pointed out the comparative youth of the great heroes of the American navy of the past. John Paul Jones was thirty-two at the time of the encounter off Flamborough Head; Hull was six years older when the *Guerrière* was captured; Decatur was twenty-seven when he blew up the *Philadelphia;* Perry was twenty-eight at Lake Erie; McDonough was thirty-two when he won his victory on Lake Champlain. Stewart was thirty-nine when he captured the *Syana* and *Levant,* and Bainbridge when he took the *Java* was thirty-one. The oldest captain of the War of 1812 was but two years older than the oldest midshipman of the navy of 1856. American war vessels sent abroad were commanded by men of seventy-four years of age, while the foreign captains whom they met were scarcely over fifty. This humiliation had led many naval officers to resign (*ibid.*, May 15, 1856, Appendix 2, 572-73). "We cannot give . . . military command, nor consign to the timid hearts and palsied hands of infirmity and age, the honor and interests of our flag upon the Deep" (*ibid.*, 572).

80. Cf. the following comments for and against Mallory's reform program: W. Gillis to Senator Clayton, from Wilmington, Del., August 2, 1856: "I feel it my duty to tender you my most hearty thanks for your generous noble and eloquent exertions in sustaining the action of the 'Naval Retiring Board.' . . ." (Clayton Papers, XII, Library of Congress). Maury to Frank Minor, September 7, 1856, enclosing following clipping from the Philadelphia *Public Ledger:* "Popularity of Our Navy. The United States steam frigate Merrimac, Captain G. J. Pendergast [one of the members of the Naval Retiring Board], sailed from Boston to New York. During her stay of three or four weeks at Boston, one hundred and ninety-four of her crew deserted,—unparalleled in the history of our navy . . ." (Maury Papers, VI).

81. W. W. Bartlett to John Crittenden, from New York, July 18, 1856 (Crittenden Papers, XIX, Library of Congress). It is to be noted, however, that an act passed in January, 1857,

The reforms advocated by the Southern congressmen are of no small importance in the history of the United States Navy. It seems safe to say that the measures so strongly urged by Mallory and by the Naval Retiring Board in the middle fifties formed the basis and model for the Federal Navy Department's reorganizational program of 1861-1865. This later legislation comprised, according to the historian of the navy, "measures for the amelioration and improvement of the service which had been agitated for many years."[82] The act of August 3, 1861, provided for a naval retired list and a naval retiring board of substantially the same type as that supported by Mallory in 1853-1855.[83] Other new regulations of the Navy Department under Lincoln bear a similarly strong resemblance to the Southern proposals of the Pierce and early Buchanan eras.[84] The high importance of these Civil War innovations, and their permanence, cannot be questioned, whatever inequities may or may not have been committed by the much-discussed Naval Retiring Board.[85]

provided for a board of inquiry to examine the claims of the cashiered officers who were petitioning for reinstatement. In case of a favorable finding, the officers were to be restored to their former rank (Phillips, op. cit., 148).

82. Charles O. Paullin, "A Half Century of Naval Administration in America, 1861-1911," United States Naval Institute Proceedings, XXXIX, 185.

83. Ibid., 187-88. Cf. also U. S. Statutes at Large, XII, 290-91; Annual Report of Secretary of the Navy, 1861, 18.

84. Cf. for example, the Retirement Rules of December 21, 1861, and the law of July 16, 1862, entitled "An Act to Establish and Equalize the Grade of Line Officers of the United States Navy." Concerning the latter law, cf.: U. S. Statutes at Large, XII, 329-30; the Navy Registers for 1863 and 1865; and Paullin, op. cit., 188-89. On July 22, 1862, the Secretary of the United States Navy appointed the first advisory board on promotions. On April 21, 1864, a law was passed providing for an examining board of three naval officers, concerning which board cf. Paullin, op. cit., 189-90; Annual Report of Secretary of the Navy, 1862, 40-41; and U. S. Statutes at Large, XIII, 53-54, 420.

85. "The Civil War effected profound changes in the personnel . . . of the navy. The legislation of this period respecting naval officers was the most important since 1798, and it still remains the basis of the organization of the navy" (Paullin, op. cit., 185).

# CHAPTER FIVE

# Problems: Domestic, Sectional, and International

T HERE WAS, of course, another side to Stephen Mallory's life at Washington during the administration of Franklin Pierce. While he was acting vigorously the part of a politician, he lived also as a very warm-hearted and society-loving human being.[1] The Mallory home, during the few months each year when Angela and the children were up from Florida, was the scene of frequent supper parties and soirées. The master and mistress of the house provided interesting contrasts. Angela presided with the easy dignity and polish of the old world social tradition.[2] The quality remarked in her husband on such occasions was a frank and boyish delight in playing host, and—it is curious how often the trait was spoken of—a very great gentleness of manner. His one not very serious social fault was a tendency to insert into his conversation, with inartistic regularity, quotations from literature—thus did his youthful zeal in note-taking return to haunt him. But Stephen, even in his oddities, retained a genuine simplicity and a sincerity that forestalled any unpleasant effect. Often, at their home entertainments, little Ruby would recite a piece for the guests, and rehearsing her for these appearances was one of her father's deepest pleasures.

The Mallorys were seen regularly at such glittering affairs as Mr. Corcoran's slightly rococo dinners, congressional and diplomatic balls—at which Angela's formal court dress à la Bourbon was an object of admiration—receptions at the White House, and theater parties at the National, where the social arbiters of the capital were laboriously creating the only diamond horseshoe south of Manhattan.

One evening in the summer of 1854 Stephen accompanied his small

1. For list of works useful for a description of social and political life in Washington of the fifties, cf. Bibliography, p. 422.

2. Cf. Mrs. C. C. Clay, *A Belle of the Fifties*, 55: "Mrs. Mallory . . . was particularly a favourite in the capital. . . ."

cousins, Genevieve and Ruby Senac (then pupils at the Georgetown Visitation Convent), to a party given in the girls' honor at the home of the British minister. Many notables attended, including President Pierce, Secretary Marcy, General Winfield Scott, and Jefferson Davis. For the occasion, greatness was willing to unbend. At the request of the Misses Senac the President obligingly rendered vocally "The Minstrel's Returned from the War," his first attempt at a song, as he told them, since returning from the Mexican War. The whole Cabinet, led by Governor Marcy, joined in the chorus, a variation on the spirited theme, "Damn his eyes."[3]

Mr. Marcy then sang "All around my hat I wears a green ribbon," with so much pathos that the "whole Cabinet and Company were bathed in tears."[4] (Mr. Marcy confided that this was his first vocal effort of the kind since the passage of the Nebraska Act.)

In the course of the evening President Pierce recited with much effect, "To be or not to be, that's the question," while Jefferson Davis, with perhaps more than a touch of the prophetic, spoke the impressive soliloquy, "Is this a dagger I see before me?" General Scott scored a distinct hit, "standing in the middle of the room and facing to the right, left and about, and waving his cocked hat [singing], in his most dashing style 'The bauld soldier boy' and 'Meine Faderland,' throwing in with fine effect the rich Irish brogue and the German accent." The party concluded with all of them "walking hand and hand, and General Scott flourishing his sword just as he did in Mexico," while they sang together, "We won't go home till morning."[5]

What were the deeper qualities of the man, the fiber of his character? A few years later these questions were answered, to some extent, in a letter from Mallory to his son. In giving "Buddy" instructions for good and useful living, he revealed unwittingly a great deal of his own heart and mind.

Openness and truthfulness, he believed, were cardinal virtues in a man. "With justice, and frankness, and truth as your guides in your intercourse with your fellows, you will rarely find them so unreasonable as to quarrel with you."[6] He was blessed with a fundamental optimism that never deserted him—a constitutional buoyancy of spirit that could never long be crushed under trials or pain, however severe. His enemies termed this quality weakness, or escapism, or a failure in realism; there may have been some

3. Ruby Senac to "our dear cousin Felix," from Georgetown Visitation Convent, June 11, 1854 (Mallory-Kennedy Collection).
4. *Ibid.*
5. *Ibid.*
6. Mallory, letter to Buddy, *supra cit.*

truth in the charges. Whatever defects the virtue implied, it meant that he never became soured or disillusioned at the faults of mankind, although he recognized their existence. "Human nature," he told Buddy, "is preeminently selfish, jealous and envious. I thank God that the ingratitude and selfishness of those whom I have ... served has not made me repent my conduct, or lessened my desire to do good to my fellows. Thank God for the Grace which enables me to say that I pretend not to judge of their motives, and do not condemn them."[7] He advised his son to avoid underrating men, but, at the same time, not to be governed solely by a reputation for greatness. "Men differ, to be sure, in capacity, but not half so much as the world supposes. The masses of men are pretty equal in this respect, and real greatness is rare. Many a man passes through life without the slightest claim to the high reputation for talent or genius with which he is credited."[8]

He was, without affectation, a kindly man—"Many hundreds of men, struggling with difficulties, I have most unselfishly helped, with open, generous, trusting confidence; without reward beyond the pleasure which my kindness to others ever brought to my soul. The sweetest pleasures of my whole life have been derived from my kindness to others."[9] He was deeply in love with his wife and children. "My love for my children and for their mother," he said, "is my rock of this earthly life."[10] He had a fierce family pride, and one of his chief objects in life was to leave to his children a "name which has never been tarnished or stained, but which . . . is above suspicion."[11]

Parallel with the discussions on naval affairs, the critical debates on the sectional issue continued during the Pierce and Buchanan administrations. Day after day the crowded galleries listened intently and anxiously as North and South fought out their differences on the floor of the Senate in an attempt to save the Union by the reconciliation of two sharply opposed sets of principles.

For both sides it was a losing fight, an earnest and sincere endeavor that failed; but there were moments when it seemed that the old method of compromise might succeed again in healing, at least temporarily, the breach. It was a solemn and crucial stage of the nation's history—the last great period of Southern statesmanship, and, under the strong leadership of Northern men, the beginning of the consolidated American Republic. Out of these bitter debates and out of the war to follow would be born in blood

7. *Ibid.*      8. *Ibid.*
9. *Ibid.*      10. *Ibid.*
11. *Ibid.*

and in tears a really new American nation. It was a momentous, pregnant time.

In March, 1856, while the fight over the Naval Reform Board was still under way, a diplomatic issue arose which tended to soften, at least temporarily, the bitter feeling between the sections. This was the "British threat." The evident designs of the British government with regard to Cuba, her apparent infidelities and deceptions in the matter of the agreements concerning the slave trade, her repeated forestalling of American efforts to secure coaling stations in various parts of the world, and numerous other actions interpreted as unfriendly by most Americans had engendered in the minds of the nation's legislators a real fear of war, and a determination to act firmly toward London in an effort to prevent war. For the Southern senators it was an opportunity to show where they stood with regard to the Union, with regard to the United States of America. Perhaps, in rallying with their Northern comrades against the common foreign foe, representatives of the slave states could convince the North that men below the Mason and Dixon line bowed to none in their love for the Union. Perhaps they could finally make the North see that the South sought only her rights, not separation.

Mallory did his share in stating to the Senate the Southern position in the Anglo-American crisis. He hoped that war with Britain would be averted, for he was convinced that war was the greatest calamity that a civilized nation could suffer. But he stressed the thought that was to be re-echoed again and again by Southern senators: ". . . Deeply as my own State would deplore hostilities, . . . I must declare, for her, that if we should unhappily be involved in a war with Great Britain or any other Power, whether the cause be a right one or a wrong one, there will be within her limits no recreant to the cause or to the country; nor will there be found upon her soil a man breathing any other than a determined spirit to see it out, honorably and successfully."[12]

The British would find that American parties, though split on many domestic issues, would always stand firmly together against any foreign foe. "Whenever an issue shall be made up with Britain or any other Power, these States,—'distinct as the waves, yet one as the sea'—will present a firm, calm, and united front. Many questions of a domestic nature will always more or less divide us, but a public enemy will ever unite us."[13]

12. 34 Cong., 1st Sess., March 13, 1856 (*Cong. Globe*, Appendix, 175).
13. *Ibid*.

In discussing the possibility of war, the Senator from Florida could not long remain away from his favorite field. He pointed out the inadequacy of our stationary harbor fortifications, and urged the view that sufficiently strengthened stationary defenses would be invulnerable to attack by warships, no matter how powerful. In support of this thesis he adduced the recent successful defense of Cronstadt and Sebastopol, in the face of the powerful gunfire of the attacking Allied war vessels.[14]

The war crisis with Britain passed,[15] but the sectional dispute did not. Out on the plains of Kansas, men on both sides were bringing nearer the Civil War. In accordance with the Kansas-Nebraska Act, the constitutional convention of Kansas, dominated by the Northern Democrats, had voted slavery out of the territory. A short time later, at Lecompton, the Southern party formulated another constitution which legalized slavery in Kansas. For the advocates of the North and of the South in Congress, these events provided new and bitter issues. All the old arguments for and against the extension of slavery into the territories were rehashed. The South spoke fiercely in defense of what she regarded as her most sacred rights; the North fought back with equal determination.[16] Time was running out. The chance for compromise was passing.

During the summer and fall of 1856 another vitally important matter preoccupied the minds of the Democrats in Congress. It was a presidential election year. Frémont, regarded by the South as being half Whig and half Black Republican, and Fillmore, standard bearer of the Know-Nothings, were running against Buchanan, the choice of the slavery interests. There was need of effective campaigning and of strong assertion of Southern claims if the Democrats were to retain their hold on the presidency.

In this crusade in defense of Southern rights Senator Mallory did his part. His speeches in support of the party nominee sound anything but timid or reserved. If he was, as later charged, too much of a Conservative Unionist to suit the South, his public utterances of this year cannot be adduced as evidence confirming the allegation.

At a Democratic ratification meeting at Washington in June, 1856, he gave an address made up of a rather remarkable mixture of bombast

14. 34 Cong., 1 Sess., March 13, 1856 (*Cong. Globe,* Appendix, 175).

15. Cf. Mallory's objections to the anti-American tone of the *London Times, ibid.,* 176.

16. The *New York Herald,* amid graver concerns, could not forego a quip at the Senate's expense in the course of this debate: "The United States Senate yesterday shook off its customary dullness, and indulged in a debate that partook somewhat of the exciting" (March 15, 1856). The debate referred to was that of Douglas versus Sumner and Trumbull. Trumbull, from Illinois, had been elected senator in 1855 with the aid of Abraham Lincoln's support.

and thoroughgoing Southern nationalism. The Democrats, he declared, had chosen from the altars of universal truth great principles of constitutional law, great elements of right, wisdom, and justice, and had woven them into a platform "upon which every man who loves his country more than he does his party may proudly stand and proudly conquer."[17] He saw the Northern movement against the South as a "black and portentous storm." Directing that storm were the North's misguided leaders, "moved by that mad ambition which taught the rebel angels rather to rule in hell than serve in Heaven." These Northern leaders "shout hosannahs to the Union, while they lay sacrilegious hands upon the constitution itself, the only bond by which the Union exists a day." Heedless of the great truth that "no degradation can be so humiliating to a free people as a constrained existence under a violated constitution," they "stoop to talk of coercing one portion of this confederacy into an ignominious subserviency to another, and to calculate the character and extent of our resistance."[18]

The Democrats, continued Mallory, stood on a platform asserting "the reserved rights of the States and the inherent powers of the people in the Territories." He could scarcely find words powerful enough to praise fittingly the Democratic party platform. To it "the pious Catholic mother, as she teaches her infant to lisp a thankful prayer to Heaven for the blessings we enjoy, will turn with tearful gratitude; for she sees inscribed upon its banner the cheering assurance of religious liberty; and she knows that as long as that proud banner floats, the hope of her future years may repeat the ritual a mother taught him, without political ostracism, in the land of his fathers."[19] The "stain of sectionalism" clung to every faction of the South's opponents, "as tenaciously as did the blood to the hands of Lady Macbeth."[20]

Another address of Mallory's given in October of that year before a "large and respectable audience of ladies and gentlemen at the Judson House" [Jacksonville or Washington?] won, said the *Florida News,* "golden opinions from all sorts of people. . . . Without the slightest attempt at rant or declamation," the newspaper continued, "he made a powerful argument in the most eloquent and convincing language." He depicted in "glowing but truthful terms," the dangers that threatened the South and the Union, and fixed the responsibility for this state of things on the right shoulders, to wit, the Black Republicans and their aids and abettors, the Know-Noth-

17. Reprinted in the *Florida News,* June 28, 1856.
18. *Florida News,* June 28, 1856.
19. *Ibid.*                              20. *Ibid.*

ing Party in the North. He compared the antecedents of Fillmore and Buchanan on the slavery question, and showed that whereas the former had always been against the South, the latter had been found consistently sustaining Southern rights and voting with the leading statesmen of the South.[21]

If Frémont were elected, he felt, "the South would be compelled to take measures for her own security," and he recommended that the South make herself economically independent of the North by discriminating against Northern commerce. (On this, however, the *News* disagreed with him.) Finally he took up the foreign and Catholic questions, and "so disposed of them as not to leave an inch of ground for the Know-Nothings to stand upon." "His effort agreeably surprised his friends," the *News* concluded.[22]

When it came to his own re-election as one of Florida's senators, Mallory had considerable opposition to face in his own state. His enemies were mostly Whigs and Know-Nothings. The Pensacola *Gazette,* one of his chief attackers, favored the Constitutional Union candidates in 1860.[23] There were two main charges brought against Mallory: neglect of the interests of the state outside of Key West, and favoritism to Democrats in the matter of patronage.

Mr. Mallory, complained the *Gazette,* had done nothing to secure ship-building contracts for the Warrington (Pensacola) navy yard.[24] "Beware," warned the journal, "how you [Secretary Dobbin and, by plain implication, Mallory] trifle with an insignificant populace; it is like a Serpent, it may sting when your heel is on its head."[25] The proposal to annex to Alabama all West Florida west of the Apalachicola[26] was the occasion for another blast of the *Gazette* against Mallory and Representative Augustus Maxwell. Why, asked the editor, was it proposed "by our party friends" to annex Pensacola and its county to Alabama? For no other reason than to deprive

21. October 11, 1856.

22. *Ibid.* See, in regard to the Know-Nothings, the *Florida News,* June 30, 1855: "Meeting at Key West Adopts Resolutions Against Know-Nothings, Mallory Participating"; *ibid.,* July 7, 1855, and July 14, 1855: "Know-Nothings Extend Their Attacks to Methodists!"

23. Dodd, *op. cit.,* 51 n.

24. Cf. *Pensacola Gazette,* April 12, 1856, September 16, 1856.

25. *Ibid.,* April 12, 1856.

26. In 1854 the Alabama legislature had proposed that all of Florida west of the Apalachicola be ceded to the former state. By 1859 so much favorable sentiment had come from West Florida that the General Assembly of Florida ordered a vote upon the subject (Rerick, *Memoirs of Florida,* I, 231-32). The cession would have left only the East Florida of Spanish days to bear the name of Florida. The previous plan, submitted by the Legislative Council in a memorial in 1844, had taken the Suwannee River as the dividing line and looked to the creation of two separate states (*ibid.,* I, 210).

the people of the region of their representation in both houses of Congress. Mallory and Maxwell had no interest in the welfare of the people of Pensacola and Escambia County, so long as those two politicians could count on the support of their constituents in the east. The two alleged representatives of West Florida in Congress "occasionally come over to us here, and after making . . . a number of soft cajoling speeches, in which are embraced a thousand unfulfilled promises, they leave us supposing them to be the very best men for our interests, when they, having the control, slight us in every instance."[27]

The *Gazette* further charged that Mallory induced United States war vessels to frequent Key West, to the detriment of Pensacola.[28] In brief: "We once thought . . . that our State had been extremely fortunate in having one of her Senators placed at the head of the Naval Committee; but, alas, . . . no man could have done us more injustice; he forgets his State and acts only for a section."[29]

The rather complicated relations of Mallory and Maxwell with a shifty local politician named O. B. Faulconer[30] were made the basis of another onslaught by the *Gazette*. Faulconer, a nominal Democrat, feeling himself snubbed by the two Florida congressmen in his earnest campaign for the post of overseer of the Pensacola navy yard, had written a public letter excoriating Mallory.[31] The latter, declared the disgruntled candidate, was consorting with Know-Nothings in order to win their votes, and was maintaining an alliance with Maxwell, "the resigned Republican and complete Know Nothing in Democratic pants."[32] (Mallory was indeed, it seems, for campaign purposes, making strange gestures of amity toward those not commonly regarded as his supporters. He attended the Methodist camp meeting held at Pensacola in September, and for this was reproved by the *Gazette*.)[33] This tirade of Faulconer's, remarked the *Gazette* significantly

27. April 12, 1856.
28. "It is a singular fact that of all the vessels in the Gulf but few show themselves here, and this the only place where is stored [*sic*] the provisions for the squadron. Why is this so? Is it not because there is a power behind the throne greater than the throne itself?" (*ibid.*).
29. *Ibid.*
30. Faulconer was variously termed a "transmorgrified plebian," a "Bug Bear of Political Intrigue," and an "unmitigated Humbug and Liar" by Henry Hilliard in a letter to the *Gazette* from Woolsey, Fla., September 16, 1856. Faulconer, strangely enough, was one of the trustees of the Pensacola Baptist Church of Christ (cf. Deed Book K, 400, March 9, 1852, Escambia Co. Court House) and, when an "arm" of that church was established at the navy yard, was ordained a deacon. He was also twice granted letters of dismission from the church (Minute Book of the Pensacola Baptist Church of Christ, 18, 19, 21, 25, 27, 29, 34, 35, 37, 79, 84, 89, 110).
31. *Gazette*, September 9, 1856; Faulconer's letter was dated February 16, 1856.
32. *Ibid.*                    33. September 23, 1856.

"must have brought him [Faulconer] into bad odor with his party associates who entertain sentiments of esteem and respect for Messrs. Mallory and Maxwell."[34]

Then occurred an incident which, to any one less versatile than Mr. Faulconer, would have proved to be highly embarrassing. Hardly had his letter been printed when announcement was made of his appointment as overseer of the Pensacola yard; and it was obvious that the favor had been won for him through the efforts of Messrs. Mallory and Maxwell. He at once wrote "a most disgusting and sycophantic and servile panegyric of Messrs. Mallory, Maxwell, and Yulee, which must have been thoroughly *nauseating* to those gentlemen themselves."[35] The *Gazette* admitted that it would have given much to know by what means Messrs. Mallory and Maxwell were reconciled to their protégé.[36]

All this may have been nothing more than routine political horse-trading; but, to the *Gazette,* every move of "Messrs. Mallory and Maxwell" was to be viewed with suspicion. The journal declared its intention of fighting Mallory vigorously in the forthcoming election, "while abstaining from all personalities."[37] The extent of its adherence to this last promise may be judged from its editorial on the eve of the voting day: "Prevent so far as your vote . . . is concerned, the re-election of the present *Incumberment,* and secure the election of some one who has *some interest* in common with the West [of Florida], and who will pay some attention to our interests. *Don't vote for Party and against your Pocket.* Examine the matter fairly and candidly, and see if there is not *one single* reason why any citizen of Escambia (unless he has been promised an office) should desire the reelection of Stephen R. Mallory; and even the promise of an office should be of no inducement, for he and his friends will have precious little influence with the Fillmore administration."[38]

In the election, the regular Democratic ticket triumphed. The *Gazette* was a hard loser. Never, declared the editor, had the city witnessed such a disgraceful spectacle. Money, clothing, whiskey, tobacco, and other necessaries were freely exchanged, in the most open and unblushing manner, for votes. In spite of all this, the Whigs and Know-Nothings could have elected their ticket had not the commodore of the navy yard, with his staff, taken

34. September 16, 1856.
35. *Ibid.* (italics in original).
36. *Ibid.,* September 9, 1856.
37. *Ibid.,* September 16, 1856. The journal expressed its desire for something more than a "resolution which may result in something for our children's children."
38. *Ibid.,* September 30, 1856 (italics in original).

the field on behalf of the Democrats. "We have on several former occasions," declared the irate manager of the *Gazette,* "defeated the Democrats *and foreigners,* and can do it any day in a *fair* contest; but backed as they have been this time by the United States Navy and Marine Corps, in addition to the $25,000 appropriation, we have been defeated by a small majority." Although overpowered by a spurious vote that should never have been admitted to the polls, the Whigs and Know-Nothings, the editor promised, would redeem themselves in November.[39]

The journal then concentrated its fire on the allegedly unfair discriminations practiced by Mallory's friends, at Mallory's instigation, at the navy yard. No member of the "American" (Know-Nothing) party could obtain work there. Forty or fifty "Americans" had been constantly applying for positions at the yard, and had invariably been told, "We are not employing hands now." But five Irishmen, landing at the yard one morning, were all employed there before nightfall.[40] Men who had labored in the yard faithfully since its foundation were suddenly dismissed; "yet, a Democrat, though he be a *convicted thief,* can get employment."[41]

In its issue of October 24, 1856, the *Gazette* published the affidavit of four members of the American Party who claimed that they had been refused employment at the navy yard because of their political affiliations. The chief engineer at the yard had told them that he was under instructions from Mallory and from Representative George S. Hawkins to engage no men who were opposed to the existing administration, and that Mallory had already secured the discharge of a master workman who had given employment to members of the Know-Nothing Party. The chief engineer had intimated that the four applicants might be accepted for employment at the yard if they joined the Democratic club of the district or obtained a recommendation from that organization.[42]

That Mallory was the chief culprit the *Gazette* had no doubt. Under a quadruple headline—"A Clincher! The Plot Unmasked! Prescription [Proscription?] by Authority! The Responsibility Fixed!"—the Senator from Key West was declared to be behind the "infamous transaction" at the navy yard. The commodore there was a man of straw, pulled this way and that by Mallory.[43]

39. October 11, 1856 (italics in original).     40. *Ibid.*
41. *Ibid.,* October 25, 1856 (italics in original).
42. Affidavit of Washington D. Austin, Clinton Trull, Samuel Hodges, and Lewis Favorite, Escambia Co. Court House, October 24, 1856, attested by Justice of the Peace George H. O'Neal, Escambia Co.
43. October 25, 1856.

Despite, however, this opposition from West Florida, Mallory was re-elected by the legislature to the Senate in 1856 and won some sincere compliments from a part, at least, of the Florida press. The *News* felt that he had been a "firm, untiring, and uncompromising advocate . . . and defender of Democratic principles," and that if consistency, earnestness, and long years of devotion to the principles and interests of the Democratic party constituted any claim to political preferment and honor, no man could urge such claims with purer motives than could Mallory. "He . . . ranks," declared the *News,* "at this day as one of the most effective speakers in the United States Senate."[44] Another tribute came from Henry A. Wise in the course of his speculations as to the composition of the Buchanan cabinet: "We navy men hope Mr. Mallory will get the Navy Department. He is every way qualified for the office."[45]

Despite his varied activities as senator and party politician, Stephen Mallory was never long disengaged from matters of ships and of the sea. In 1856 the Senate Naval Affairs Committee, led by their chairman, inspected at Secretary Dobbin's invitation a new gunboat anchored at Annapolis. The ship was named the *Merrimac.* Mallory looked it over with great interest, little suspecting that there would come a time when he would stake his own and far greater fortunes on that vessel.[46]

The following year, Senator Mallory exerted himself to defend the potentialities of Pensacola as a site for a United States Government ship yard. After describing the advantages of the Florida seaport as a ship-building

44. *Florida News,* January 3, 1857. The *Pensacola Gazette,* however, on learning of Mallory's re-election, came out with an article headlined: "Democracy Laid Out; The Mallory Faction Triumphant; Bring Out the Firecrackers and Whiskey!" (January 3, 1857). It warned the Democrats that now the time had come for paying off their "unwashed and hard-fisted" supporters, and that the Democrats would doubtless be embarrassed by the "difficulty which we foresaw and predicted long since, growing out of the characteristic practice of promising the same office to half a dozen different applicants." Says the *Gazette,* with a straight face, "Of course we are not in this cat fight, nor do we care much if it ends disastrously to all parties concerned." Clubbs, *op. cit.,* 173, makes the following comment on this election: "The victory of Mr. Mallory is the more pronounced when one finds that in an important county like Escambia in the Presidential election but eight years before, Taylor received 227 votes and Cass 155. Senator Yulee had remarked that Florida was the banner state of those who had voted for the Hero of Buena Vista."

45. Henry A. Wise to his cousin H. A. Wise, from Washington, D. C., November 24, 1856 (Henry A. Wise Papers, Library of Congress). Henry Alexander Wise represented his native state of Virginia in the House of Representatives from 1833 to 1844. Although at first a Democrat, he broke with President Jackson on the Bank question and became a Whig. He was Governor of Virginia from 1856 to 1860. In May 1861 he was made a brigadier-general in the army of the Confederacy.

46. Cf. J. C. Dobbin to Mallory, letter No. 13 (1856) of Letters to Congress, in Miscellaneous Letters to the Navy Department (National Archives).

center, he complained that "the prejudice of a few individuals who have more or less influenced the Navy Department when sloops were to be built, has hitherto succeeded in preventing the construction of a single ship at this yard." He offered the very pertinent observation that "it seems eminently proper that the advantages which such public works bestow should not always be confined to one section of the country." Not until a few years later would he, and others, realize the significance of his concluding remark that "Pensacola [is] the only yard we have south of Virginia."[47]

Another claim was made at a later date by Mallory on behalf of Pensacola. In the event of war between the United States and either of the naval powers of Europe, he believed, the Pensacola naval station would at once become a point of great interest, for in its immediate vicinity the first naval battles of the struggle would be fought; and he submitted that the best interests of the navy demanded that officers of the home squadron be required to familiarize themselves with the Pensacola Bar.[48]

All in all, Florida was very well pleased with her senator, particularly on account of his interest in naval affairs. The *News* termed him a "champion of the nation" and a "lover of his State." He was "emphatically a working-man," whose labors on the Naval Committee of the Senate had commanded the attention of other nations as well as of the United States. He was progressive, was always seeking the improvement of the navy, and was ever alert to any suggestion that promised greater efficiency to the naval service. And it was well known that his speeches were attractions in the Senate chamber.[49]

A few months after his re-election, Mallory broke a spear ostensibly on behalf of the laborers of Key West, but really in favor of their owners. These workers, some of them, interestingly enough, his own slaves, had been hired out by their owners for the construction project then under way at Fort Jefferson. It was charged by the Key Westers that white laborers at the fort were being paid higher wages than the slaves, while performing the

47. Mallory to Secretary of the Navy Isaac Toucey, from Washington, March 13, 1857, in Miscellaneous Letters to the Navy Department (National Archives). Cf. also "Report of the Secretary of the Navy . . . respecting the construction of a stone [dry-] dock at Pensacola," Navy Department, December 27, 1856, reprinted in the *Florida News,* January 24, 1857.

48. Mallory to Secretary Toucey, from Washington, March 22, 1858, reprinted in *The Florida News,* May 5, 1858. Cf. also, in *ibid.,* Toucey's reply to Mallory, dated April 2, 1858; and Mallory's further complaint at this time, in a letter to Toucey, regarding the failure of the *Wabash,* the flagship of the home squadron, to touch at Pensacola on her recent voyage (Mallory to Toucey, in Miscellaneous Letters to the Navy Department [National Archives], from Washington, March 22, 1858).

49. *Florida News,* January 24, 1857.

same duties.[50] Moreover the government, during the winter months, was in the habit of importing a large number of white workers from the North, thus displacing the Negroes, with consequent pecuniary loss to their owners.[51]

Mallory made a strong protest against both of these practices,[52] and secured a guarantee from the Secretary of War that "preference should in all cases be given to workmen belonging to the vicinity over those from a distance."[53] The alleged wage differential between whites and blacks was flatly denied by the commandant of the fort,[54] and Mallory expressed his satisfaction.[55]

In the Thirty-fifth Congress, opening in December 1857, the Southern Democrats continued their efforts to build up the United States Navy that was later to be their doom. Senator Mallory, as chairman of the Senate Committee on Naval Affairs, took frequent part in the debates.

In the light of the problems which he subsequently faced, in 1861 through 1865, it is interesting to note the earnestness of his view that, for an efficient navy, there was need of long and careful training of seamen. A navy, he reminded the Senate on June 7, 1858, is necessarily a work of years. A sailor is not the creation of a day; he requires long and careful training, and, once a sailor, he is good for nothing else. As to naval officers, it would be highly inadvisable to engage them for employment as we engage other types of workers, when we want them, and to induct them from the merchant service; in other words, to "have a navy on the spur of the moment, to fee a naval officer as you would a lawyer,—hire him for a special service."[56] The most opposite creature on earth to a sailor is a soldier. You cannot make sailors of soldiers,[57] nor can ships of war be built in the short time in which they could formerly. In a war with any first class naval power, our maritime cities would be destroyed and our commerce swept

50. Mallory to Captain D. P. Woodbury (commanding at Fort Jefferson), from Key West, November 10, 1857, Journal and Letter Book of Fort Jefferson (Federal Writers' Project Transcripts, Key West; courtesy of Judge Enrique Esquinaldo).

51. Mallory to Hon. W. Floyd, Secretary of War, from Key West, February 9, 1858, ibid.

52. Mallory to Hon. W. Floyd, February 9, 1858; also Mallory to Capt. Woodbury, November 10, 1857, ibid.

53. H. B. Wright (for Secretary of War) to Capt. Woodbury, from Washington, D. C., February 13, 1858, ibid.

54. Capt. Woodbury to Mallory, November 18, 1857, ibid.

55. Mallory to Capt. Woodbury, November 19, 1857, ibid.

56. 35 Cong., 1 Sess., June 7, 1858 (Cong. Globe, 2731 ff.).

57. This is practically what Mallory would sometimes be forced to attempt as Confederate Navy Secretary.

from the seas while we were desperately trying to build up a stronger navy.[58]

As a means of raising the quality of naval personnel he recommended higher wages for seamen on both ships of war and merchantmen, for he believed that "the merchant service of our country is the true nursery for seamen. It is the nursery because it gives them the highest rewards, it treats them best. . . ."[59]

The wage increases to merchant seamen, he urged, should not be given in the form of subsidies to ship owners. When money went into the hands of the owners, to be divided among the crews, the sailors usually lost out. The advances to the seamen would "always liquidate the amount to be advanced"—in other words, the pipes and tobacco they drew always counterbalanced any advance they were to receive. Mallory suggested to the representatives of the fishery interests that they "rise gracefully and . . . say, 'We want it [the bounty] no more; we have profited by it; but now we will agree to give the $300,000 a year we receive as fishing bounty as an addition to the wages of seamen in the merchant and naval service.' "[60]

Recruiting for the navy, he suggested further, should not be confined to Americans. A very large proportion of the men who served on our national war vessels were men picked up from all parts of the world. The true seaman was a cosmopolitan. He went where he could get the most wages and the best treatment. The very moment he became identified with a locality, he ceased to be a seaman; he would not go to sea if he could get money enough to buy a farm and stay on shore. The true seaman was a man who had no home but the sea; who sought the highest prize-money, the largest wages, and the best treatment all over the world. A poll of one of our ships of war revealed only 19 Americans out of a crew of 170. Mallory himself had had several vessels polled to prove this fact. Since the increase of our wage scale, the proportion of Americans on an American ship was about one in three.[61]

The keenest debate on naval affairs in the Thirty-fifth Congress centered about the question of what principle of design was the proper guide in building American ships of war. Should a few large ships be built, or many small ones? Should ironclads be favored, or "wooden walls?" What style of vessel was most desirable, in view of the special problems of defense and offense?

58. 35 Cong., 1 Sess., June 7, 1858 (*Cong. Globe*, 2737-39).
59. *Ibid.*
60. 35 Cong., 1 Sess., June 7, 1858 (*Cong. Globe*, 2731 ff.).
61. *Ibid.*

Two modern naval historians are very severe in their judgment on the policy of the Buchanan administration in these matters. American naval experts, say these two authorities, were far behind the times. While Britain and France were beginning to build ironclad vessels, we persistently refused to realize the value of such ships, and neglected to construct any. We placed our trust in smaller vessels of two types—steam frigates and sloops (the heavy and light cruisers of the day), and gunboats of narrow draft. In the principle, too, of our general strategic plan, it is charged, we were wrong; we adhered to the theory of the War of 1812, in which, as Mallory himself phrased it, "frigate was matched against frigate, sloop against sloop, and brig against brig."[62] Thus, it would seem, "American statesmen in the 'fifties were pointing their preparations toward the strategy which, in 1812, despite the subsequent legend of victory, destroyed the foreign commerce of the United States, disrupted its internal economy, and opened the way for armed invasion from the sea."[63]

It is interesting, in the face of these charges, to study Mallory's recommendations in the Senate debates of 1858-1859. While, it is true, he still held to the "ship-to-ship combat" theory of the War of 1812, he urged a further point which seems to absolve him of having been unprogressive or unwilling to follow the lead of Britain or France in constructing ironclads of considerable size *if* those powers should choose to build such.

He had looked abroad, he declared, where we must all look when we build ships, at the condition of other navies. In constructing our navy, we must unavoidably build our ships in reference to those navies with which we come in contact. He then laid down what he regarded as the cardinal rule: if we find Great Britain's frigates to be of a certain size, we should make sure that ours are no smaller.[64]

He then went on to show why, in his opinion, the government should concentrate on building small gunboats of shallow draft. Great Britain had recently launched 184 of such gunboats, of six-and-a-half-foot draft, and capable of entering the very smallest harbors of our country. Should we not build vessels to follow them? Only vessels as small as the British gunboats could do this; therefore, urged Mallory, let us build such ships, rather than men-of-war which would be incapable of getting near the British whippets inside American ports.[65]

62. *Ibid.*, 2732.
63. H. and M. Sprout, *Rise of American Naval Power, 1776-1918* (Princeton, N. J., 1939), 150.
64. 35 Cong., 1 Sess., June 7, 1858 (*Cong. Globe*, 2732).
65. *Ibid.* He quoted the report of the Secretary of the Navy Isaac Toucey (*Sen. Doc. No.*

Mallory insisted that he had no prejudices against large ships as such. But he felt that our primary standard for shipbuilding should be the contemporary practice of our chief rivals. "We are compelled," he warned, "to build . . . vessels as other nations do." If other nations build frigates of four thousand tons, we must put ours at four thousand. When we build a frigate, we must build her with reference to those with which she must contend.[66]

But, he continued, if we follow this norm we must build small gunboats, and not large or capital ships. For, "We find Great Britain and France have abandoned the idea of having many large vessels for special service and are building a smaller class."[67] These vessels could enter every American port from Galveston to Maine, while we had not a single vessel deserving of the name of man-of-war that could do the same thing.

Again, argued Mallory, the type of ship best suited for patrol operations against the slave trade on the African coast was not the large man-of-war but the small, light, fast sloop. It was well known, he said, that one small steam cruiser drawing seven and a half feet of water was worth all the fleet of larger vessels that might be sent there to protect our flag against infractions by slavers. Small steam cruisers were best adapted also for protecting our flag along the coast of Cuba. For such a task large frigates were impracticable.[68]

On June 7, Mallory moved an amendment providing for the construction of ten steam sloops of war. The amendment was defeated,[69] but the New York Herald warmly approved this effort to stiffen the naval bill.[70]

The charge that the Southern Democrats were secretly favoring the African slave trade was later to be denied by Mallory. He declared in 1860 that all Southerners were against such traffic in Negroes. But the South believed, he added, that the most effective means of thwarting the trade was

1, Ser. No. 977, p. 608, Report of Secretary of the Navy, December 6, 1858), stressing the need for small gunboats capable of entering shallow and narrow rivers on our own coast and abroad. The report stated that we had scarcely a vessel which could enter any of our Southern ports.

66. Ibid., 2738. That Mallory was not forgetful of local interests is suggested by a letter which he wrote to a Florida friend in early 1856: "I got my bill for ten War steamers passed through the Senate, and it is now before the House, and I have got the Secretary of the Navy's pledge to build one at Pensacola. This ought to have been done years ago, and would have been had its interests received the proper attention" (Florida News, April 19, 1856).

67. 35 Cong., 1 Sess., June 7, 1858 (Cong. Globe, 2738).

68. Ibid., June 12, 1858, 2980.

69. New York Herald, June 8, 1858.

70. Ibid., June 12, 1858.

not to lay laws against it, for such laws only provided England with opportunities to encourage the practice clandestinely.[71]

This was one of the most trying periods of Stephen Mallory's life. On a morning in March, 1858, he sat in his room at the National Hotel, pondering over three letters that lay on his table. One, from his wife, he regarded sadly. It was another of Angela's complaining epistles, finding fault with him for trifles, pouring out all the bad news from home and little of the good. It crushed and weakened him, as such letters from her always did. Yet, she was his darling Angela—"a more truthful being . . . and honorable I have never met in all my walks of life. Her duty to God, and her love and devotion to her husband and her children have constituted all the mainspring of her life."[72] Another note was from Governor Perry of his home state; it troubled him for far different reasons. The Democrats of Florida, wrote Perry, were losing confidence in Senator Mallory's capacity and will to defend their interests. They felt that his stand in the Senate against the supporters of Douglas was decidedly lacking in vigor. They felt that he was weak.

Stephen must have done some searching of his soul on that morning. No, he was not weak. He could not conscientiously accuse himself of being weak, or of being neglectful of Florida's interests. But he was trying to be fair to his opponents and fair to the Union; and he was enough of a moderate to fight to the last possible moment for the peaceful solution, the compromise satisfactory to both sides. His conscience was clear; but the accusation hurt him deeply.

He picked up again the third letter, from Ruby, his daughter, who was now five years old. He reread it for it was the one bright spot in the morning's experiences:

"My dear Pa: I thank you very much for the beautiful doll and fan you sent me. Ma put the fan away, but I play with the doll all day. I am very sorry to say that the shoes did not fit me. All are well and send love.

your little daughter,<br>RUBY MALLORY"[73]

But even the prattle of his beloved child could not completely console him at this moment. It was unfortunate that his day had begun thus, in discouragement; for, although there is no evidence that he guessed it, within

71. 36 Cong., 1 Sess., June 18, 1860 (*Cong. Globe*, 3102-3). Cf. also *ibid.*, June 16, 1860, 3063-70.

72. Mallory, letter to Buddy, *supra cit.*

73. Undated, from Mallory-Kennedy Collection.

a few hours he was to make what was probably his most effective speech in the Senate.

That afternoon the Senate galleries were packed with much of the non-official brains, and with more of the beauty and fashion of Washington. News had spread that the debate on the Kansas question would take a new and decisive turn. Southern senators, it was whispered in the Capitol halls, were in a fighting mood; and the advocates of the North were prepared to meet them toe to toe.

It was nearly four o'clock when Senator Preston King of New York finally sat down, after holding the Senate floor for two straight hours in a bitter attack on the Lecompton Constitution and against Southern policy in general. It had been a cold, almost brutal speech. In the galleries, Southern ladies sat rigid, with slow blushes mounting their cheeks. Mr. King had struck hard and had hurt.

"The Senator from Florida. . . ."

Mallory rose and stood by his desk. He had no notes, but he was going to speak. He was going to answer Senator King. He looked sick. Gout plagued him periodically, and spectators must have noticed his slight limp as he had entered the chamber. But he felt, as he wrote to Angela that night, that he must answer the Senator from New York. Everything that he had ever done or hoped to do drove him to answer that cruel attack on his homeland.

He began calmly, but, as he remarked later, with "ominous dignity." He reminded the Senate that hitherto during the debates on Kansas he had not opened his lips. Nor, he added, would he do so now, but for two facts: first, some pains were being taken in his own state to misrepresent him, and, secondly, he had been struck to the heart by Senator King's unfair attacks.[74] (It would have been interesting to watch Seward at this point. Was he smiling in his cold passionless way, or was he looking far ahead, speculatively, and with a deep uneasiness?)

After the exhibition they had just had, in which the history of Federalism, the Hartford Convention, and "modern Democracy" were so singularly mixed up with "border ruffianism" and the doings in Kansas, he did not suppose that any effort on his side of the chamber, short of a revelation from Heaven itself, could produce the slightest impression on the mind of

74. 35th Cong., 1st Sess., March 16, 1858 (*Cong. Globe*, 1136-40). Mallory had, as a matter of fact, participated to some extent previously in the debates on the Kansas question. Cf. *supra*, ch. IV, pp. 67-68.

the gentleman who had just spoken, or on the minds of those who thought with him. But he wished to remark that, if called upon to designate which speech he had heard, since he had occupied a seat in the Senate, was most calculated to awaken and cherish sectional excitement, and to produce discord throughout the Union, he would be forced to point to the speech of the honorable Senator from New York. That speech was not a broad, large, comprehensive view of facts, argued out to their legitimate conclusions and logical deductions without regard to where they might lead; it was, on the contrary, a cunning combination of fact and error, a web skilfully devised to bolster up the preconclusion at which the author's mind and the Senator's party had already arrived.

But, Mallory continued, the most disagreeable feature of the late speech was the "perfect barrenness" of the whole production, the want of light and life throughout. It reminded one of the cold northern blasts, of icy origin. The honorable Senator seemed to offer no solution save the subjugation of the Southern states. He told the South, in a manner half complacent and half triumphant, in effect, that "if we submitted gracefully to our fate we might, perhaps, die easily, but die we should." The speech, it must be said, was altogether a remarkable production; all he could say of it was that whatever in it was new, was not true; and whatever in it was true was not new.[75]

Mallory then took up the issue itself. The passage of the Kansas-Nebraska Act, he reminded his hearers, had inaugurated a period of political excitement which had thus far been characterized by such bitterness, such a spirit of rancor toward the Southern states as, in the judgment of judicious men everywhere, had not only weakened seriously the bonds of our social union, but had had a tendency to destroy the political Union itself. (There was a very audible murmur from the Republican side of the chamber. As Lord Brougham might have phrased it, Mallory was not meeting with complete agreement.) The obliteration of the Missouri Compromise line by the Kansas-Nebraska Act had righted a great national wrong, since, by the former measure, Southern economic institutions had been excluded from a vast expanse of American territory. Since the Kansas-Nebraska Act had been in effect, the South had been standing where she ever had stood—on the Constitution. She was demanding, in accord with the Constitution and the doctrine of the political equality of the states, the right to go with her property into the common territorial domain of the Union. The Lecompton

75. Ibid., 1136.

Constitution was nothing more than a fair application of the Kansas-Nebraska Act. It was logical, legal, and constitutional. There was cause for regret that Mr. Douglas, the sponsor of that act, had deserted his previous views, and could not see the matter in this light.[76]

At this point in Mallory's speech there came an interruption, the purpose of which the unemotional *Congressional Globe* does not make clear. Seward broke in to request Mr. Mallory to speak more loudly, so that the whole Senate might hear his "very interesting speech," to which, declared Seward, he was listening "with great pleasure." Mallory expressed his thanks for the compliment, but added that he could not expect to overcome all noises that might be made in the chamber. The presiding officer, Stuart, made a remark which suggests that the speech of the Senator from Florida was evoking other sentiments besides pleasure: "The Chair will endeavor to preserve as good order as can be maintained in the Chamber; and he submits to Senators that it is important, on account of the evident condition of the health of the Senator from Florida."[77]

It had been charged, Mallory continued, that the Lecompton Constitution was not submitted to the vote of the people, and that it did not reflect the will of the people of Kansas. His retort is reminiscent of Edmund Burke. Who, he asked, were the people of Kansas? The honorable Senator from New York had said that the people were the majority. Such a doctrine, Mallory held, had never been recognized in this country. He denied that "the people" necessarily meant a majority politically, or in any other sense. The only recognizable "people" of Kansas were the law-abiding inhabitants thereof, who, under the shadow of and by the power of law alone, had made their wishes and their wants known. These were the people of Kansas, whether they were the majority or minority. States had in the past conferred, and might at any future time confer their whole political power upon a minority. They had at times made disqualifications dependent upon the tenure of freehold estate, or upon the payment of tax, or upon militia duty, or upon the color of the skin; but, whomsoever the State chooses to confer her political authority upon, these are the people—the political people. It was of these political people that Mallory spoke, those people of Kansas who, clothed with the mantle and authority of law, had come in the persons of their representatives to the Senate to make their wishes known.[78]

76. *Ibid.*, 1136-37.
77. *Ibid.*, 1138.
78. *Ibid.*

The Senator from Florida paused and sat down, after signaling the Chair that he required but a brief intermission and was not relinquishing the floor. He kept his seat for a minute, breathing deeply. It is noteworthy that the Senate waited in silence. Then he continued. The South, he said, was looking boldly out on the dangers that faced her, and would, henceforth, in his judgment, take a new departure. She would be warned, nerved, invigorated, saddened, perhaps, but unintimidated by the past. She could not ignore the fact that her enemies were gathering in strength around her. She could not doubt that she would one day see a sectional party in power, with the South in the position of a doomed minority, still appealing to the Constitution. She would, however, never admit that her security and rights in the Union depended on an equality of slave and free state representatives. If she should be forced to admit it, he would counsel secession tomorrow. But he could not admit the dread possibility. The security and rights of the South depended on the Constitution. The continuance of the Union depended on the willingness of the Northern sectional party to observe the Constitution.[79]

The South had long governed the Union, but the reins of power were falling from her grasp. It was now to other hands that her destinies were committed. Mallory conceded the fact. He reminded the Senate that the genius of Southern men, their knowledge of government, and their constitutional conservative spirit had, from the beginning of the nation, put its mark unequivocally on the policy of cabinet and legislature, even as their valor had led every charge in defense of the nation.[80]

Seven presidents of the United States had been slaveholders; whenever the country had sought intellect, genius, or courage in her sons, she had found them among slaveholders. Under the guidance of Southern men, the country's progress in all that ennobles and elevates the race had been the marvel of mankind. There had been sectional discords, family jars; but, under the leadership of Southern men, all differences had been laid on the common altar of the Constitution and dissipated through a love for the Union. The South had dominated the government indeed; but such had been the fruits of her dominance.[81]

This was impassioned oratory. The Senate sensed it, even though more than half of the Senate stared at the speaker with cold hostility. Mallory,

79. *Ibid.*, 1139.                    80. *Ibid.*
81. *Ibid.*

a plain, unaggressive man, was speaking fighting words from the depths of his sincerity. The next paragraph was both an announcement of a retreat and a warning: "In withdrawing from her [i.e., from the "position of dominance" in the nation's councils, but not, of course, from the Union itself] . . . with all her banners aloft, with her fame established and her name unsullied, with placid seas beneath and smiling skies above her, freighted with the hearts, the hopes, and the liberties of mankind,—if we surrender her, we surrender the noblest trust that ever passed from the hands of man; and . . . if we do surrender her, great will be your responsibility, and great will be our honor. I only wish to remind you that, when we demand her back, as demand her we shall, let us see that no stripe of the glorious banner is erased, that no star of it is dimmed."[82]

The Senator from Florida had one last word to say. He would be brief. It became the South now, he said, while time for reflection and counsel still existed, to know what place she was to occupy in the Union. Conservative and hopeful as he was, hoping and believing, as he did, that the political skies were brightening, and that the darkest hour was just before the dawn, he yet trusted, nay, he knew for a certainty, that the South would never submit to that last degradation of free people—voluntary acquiescence under a violated Constitution.[83]

As Senator Mallory left the Capitol late that afternoon, feeling weary, probably, and not a little ill, he could indeed have said to himself that, on that day, he had spoken well for the South. He would not have many more opportunities to do so.

A few months before, Mallory had received one of the most important offers of his political career: Buchanan tendered to him the post of Minister to Madrid. The terms of the President's letter were flattering. After much thought "as to which of my fellow Citizens was most likely to accomplish the objects of the Government . . . as Minister to Spain," he had deemed it best for the public interest to offer the mission to Mallory. The mission was one of a highly honorable and responsible character; and if Mallory should fulfill it successfully he would "identify his name with one of the greatest events in our history." Even if he should fail, after an able and

82. *Ibid.*
83. *Ibid.* The address was praised by the *Florida News*, March 31, 1858: "The extracts [given in two full columns] . . . serve to strengthen the views expressed by Senator Hammond concerning the designs of the North and position of the South in the Union. The speech is eminently Southern in tone, and shows the pressure of that sectional animosity and aggression felt in Washington, which has forced Mr. Mallory to speak as he does."

earnest effort, this would still be an additional step toward the "accomplishment of an object which cannot much longer be delayed."[84]

These thinly veiled hints as to the government's designs with regard to Cuba were of course not lost on Mallory. But the honor must be declined. He expressed to the President his sincere gratitude for the tribute implied in the offer. He was moreover confident that the political condition of Spain was pointing to that change in our relations toward her to which we had so long looked. He felt that we might by prudence and firmness now expedite and effect it, and that those who might be instrumental in producing it would win enduring honor. But "circumstances of a domestic nature" constrained him to refuse the honorable distinction.[85]

Before the end came, Stephen Mallory had one more chance to play the part of the moderate statesman in support of the Federal government in the international field. The issue was Cuba. Since the beginning of the century Americans had had their eyes on the Caribbean island. In early 1859 the Cuban annexationist movement, stimulated and alarmed by evident British designs on the territory, assumed new vigor in Congress.

The Senator from Florida took an active part in the discussions of American policy with regard to the tempting bit of land. The Cuban question, Mallory felt, must be approached not from a sectional point of view but in its broadest national aspect.[86] It was, he claimed, not really a sectional issue. There were in the North as many in favor of acquiring the island as there were in the South. Southerners therefore should not be accused of desiring Cuba only in order to add another slave territory to the Union. While admitting that Spain, at the moment, was unwilling to part with Cuba, he hoped to show that "Spain may be induced, even now, in this very year, for a proper consideration . . . not as an enemy, but as a friend having mutual ties and mutual interests [with us], to part with Cuba, perhaps, upon terms creditable to both parties."[87]

Mallory leaned heavily on a rather convincing historical argument, based mainly on the very frank and forceful declarations of Jefferson and Clinton, showing that the acquisition of Cuba was a natural corollary of the purchase

84. President James Buchanan to Mallory, from Washington, D. C., July 7, 1858 (Buchanan Papers, Pennsylvania Historical Society, Philadelphia, Pa.).

85. Mallory to Buchanan, from Bridgeport, Conn., July 13, 1858, *ibid*. After Mallory's refusal of the honor, Benjamin was offered the Madrid post (Meade, *Judah P. Benjamin*, 113-14; cf. Buchanan to Benjamin, August 31, 1858 [Pickett Papers, Library of Congress]).

86. 35 Cong., 2 Sess., February 21, 1859 (*Cong. Globe*, Appendix, 294). Cf. the charges made by the Northern press to the effect that some Southern senators had, in 1850, secretly promoted Lopez' filibustering expeditions to Cuba (*Pensacola Gazette*, June 8, 1850).

87. 35 Cong., 2 Sess., February 21, 1859, (*Cong. Globe*, Appendix, 294).

of Louisiana. He stressed also the thesis that the island was strategically necessary for the defense of our southern coast line. Using Cuba as a base, any enemy possessing sea power could strike against us across the Gulf, force the gates of the Mississippi, and close that great waterway to our commerce.[88]

Hitherto our policy toward Cuba had been one of acquiescence in Spain's continued possession of the island; but we had consistently opposed its transfer to any other power besides ourselves. Now, however, Spain had become so weak that Cuba was at the mercy of any power with covetous designs. We could not afford to let any other power take Cuba.

Mallory was quite severe on the diplomatic policy of Britain and France. Spain's unwillingness to part with the island, he asserted, was being sustained by the active and unceasing influence of Great Britain and France, an influence prompted not by any special interests of those powers in the Western hemisphere, but by a "desire to thwart and embarrass the policy and progress of the United States." Britain, while she had persistently opposed our Cuban policy, and even interfered elsewhere to prevent our acquisition of coal deposits for our navy in other seas, had taken with a strong hand islands, countries, empires, and millions of people. On the South American continent, from the Orinoco River up along the Spainsh Main to the Caribbean islands, and out by the Bahamas to the distant Bermudas, she had seized upon salient and strategic points wherever a gun could be planted or a standard raised.[89]

He was for proclaiming to Britain and to the world that the question of Cuba was an American question, and that our government looked forward to the time, and that not a distant one, when the Gulf of Mexico should be a closed sea, as much under our jurisdiction and control as the Irish Channel was under the control of England; and that no foreign flag should then float upon its bosom but by the permission of the United States.[90]

He discussed frankly the question of the African slave trade in its bearing on Cuba. The South, he declared, was all in favor of abolishing this trade—a significant statement, running counter to many accusations of that day and of more recent times.[91] But the safest way of abolishing the trade was to annex Cuba to the United States. As long as Cuba remained in the

88. *Ibid.*, 295-96.                    89. *Ibid.*, 296.
90. *Ibid.*
91. Cf. H. and M. Sprout, *The Rise of American Naval Power*, 1776-1918 (Princeton, 1939), 148.

hands of Spain, Great Britain would continue her interference in the affairs of the island, under the pretext of suppressing the slave traffic. Finally Great Britain would secure the island, liberate the Negroes, and reduce them to the wretched condition of the blacks of Santo Domingo.[92]

He sponsored a proposal which displayed marks of real statesmanship: we should induce Spain to part with Cuba by conceding to Madrid generous commercial privileges. We should, in other words, give Spain a real bargain, make it worth her while to sell Cuba. He could not forbear, however, an addendum which suggests something more (or less) than statesmanship. When he reflected, he said, upon the geographical position of Cuba, upon its command of our commerce, upon its despotism, upon the claims of her people on the United States, upon its fertility and resources, but, above all, upon the repeated provocations which Spain had given us, he was reminded of the reply of Lord Clive, when called before the Parliamentary Committee to answer for his alleged spoliation of the Indian Princes: "By heaven, gentlemen, when I reflect upon the temptation, I am astonished at my own moderation."[93]

In the summer of 1859 occurred a minor event with ironic overtones. Margaret Mallory, Stephen's daughter, christened the new United States steam sloop *Pensacola* at the Warrington Navy Yard. It was one of the ten such vessels constructed in accordance with the bill which her father had done so much to make a reality. Less than three years later the ship led the Federal attack against New Orleans.

When, on an overcast damp morning in December, 1859, an Abolitionist fanatic led sixteen men against the arsenal at Harpers Ferry, the War between the States drew immeasurably nearer. The crack of John Brown's muskets was the prelude to the roar of the guns at Gettysburg; and there were those on both sides who sensed the fact. To the South the attempt appeared as part of a dastardly campaign to raise the blacks in bloody rebellion against their masters. For John Brown there was a perhaps unwarranted display of sympathy in the North.

92. 35 Cong., 2 Sess., February 21, 1859 (*Cong. Globe*, Appendix, 298-99). Mallory bitterly denounced what he termed the "cold-blooded and barbarous" policy of the British, particularly with regard to their program of "emancipation" of the Negroes (35 Cong., 2 Sess., *Cong. Globe*, Appendix, 294-302). For an example of the war feeling against England in the summer of 1858, cf. *New York Herald*, June 7, 1858, "The British Outrages," concerning the seizure of U. S. brig *Lillian* by a British man-of-war in United States waters.

93. 35 Cong., 2 Sess., February 25, 1859 (*Cong. Globe*, Appendix, 301). This speech won warm praise from the *Floridian and Journal*, March 19, 1859. The editor termed it the "able and interesting effort of our distinguished Senator," and "one of the very ablest speeches made in the Senate" in support of our Cuban policy.

In the Senate debates following the raid, Mallory took no leading part, but, in a short address on December 7, 1859, he spoke a solemn warning. Southern Senators, he declared, stood in that chamber under a consciousness of responsibility such as they had never before felt in the whole course of their lives. They represented constituencies moved, from the highest to the lowest individual, by the conviction that their safety in the Union was in peril, that they were no longer wanted in the Union, that their fellowship was not sought, but repudiated. This was no transient, no evanescent feeling. Gentlemen of the Opposition would gravely deceive themselves if they regarded it as such. He thought they were on the brink of a crisis such as the country had never seen before; and he therefore felt deeply.[94]

Mallory engaged in just one more critical debate—a brisk passage of arms with Senator Lafayette Sabine Foster of Connecticut, on the enforcement of the Fugitive Slave Law:

"Mallory: Before the Senator from Connecticut sits down, let me ask him—I presume he will answer frankly—whether he himself is in favor of carrying out, in good faith, that constitutional provision which provides for the return of fugitives from labor?

"Foster: I am perfectly free to answer the honorable Senator from Florida; and I say to him, with the utmost frankness, that I believe in carrying out every provision of the Constitution of the United States as its makers intended that it should be carried out. I would make not one exception. The gentleman may state the most obnoxious clause or the most attractive one; and I will say to him, in entire frankness, I believe in carrying out each and all.

"Mallory: The Senator from Connecticut doubtless intends to be frank and candid, but he has not answered the question.

"Foster: Then the gentleman will allow me to say that I did not understand it.

"Mallory: The Senator does not intend to be evasive, I know.

"Foster: I certainly do not.

"Mallory: Is he in favor of returning fugitive slaves from Georgia, when claimed by that State, to their owners?

"Foster: According to the provisions of the Constitution, I am. I trust that is sufficiently frank; if the gentleman desires it, I will be more specific, if I can find any words in the English language to make myself so.

"Mallory: The Senator from Connecticut is a good, sound lawyer; he

94. 36th Cong., 1st Sess., December 7, 1859 (*Cong. Globe*, 27).

knows that the fugitive slave law has been pronounced constitutional by every court which has had jurisdiction of it. Now, I ask him if he is in favor of carrying out that law so declared by the courts to be constitutional?

"Foster: I am in favor of carrying it out just so far as it is constitutional, to the utmost extent of its constitutionality.

"Mallory: That is the Senator's 'frank answer.' It is precisely the answer I expected.

"Foster: I am glad the Senator expected a frank one."[95]

Not all of Stephen Mallory's attention was occupied with questions of grave national or international import. Angela, at Pensacola, was again causing him trouble.[96] The enforced separation by distance was not good for either of them. Angela's affections, it is quite clear, were easily alarmed.

On New Year's Day, 1859, he had to reassure her with regard to an allegedly charming widow. He wrote to his "darling wife, my beloved Angela," that he had laughed heartily as he read her caution against the widow——. He had met the lady once momentarily, he recalled, and, in a letter to Angela, had mentioned her name twice. Whereupon love in Pensacola had taken alarm and pictured Mrs. —— as possessing all the arts of an Aspasia, planning the capture of his heart, while he pursued her with fiery youthful eagerness, forgetful of his wife at home.[97]

She need not worry. He must tell his charming Angela, privately and confidentially, that in this and similar matters she is "a —— [the dash is Stephen's] woman"; nevertheless if he had the remaking of her, he would not, he confessed, have her other than she was. But, for heaven's sake, when next she assumed the mantle of Mentor, and sought to guard a Telemachus against a Calypso, let her not permit her cautions to be wasted against a "rickety frame work of bones and muscles, . . . an anatomical preparation whose dangling skinny arms tell of corresponding legs, and whose little pumkin [sic] belly gives the lie to the hips which crinoline would seek to impose upon us." Let Angela's suspicions at least commend his taste by being directed against some "plump, pretty, charming, vivacious, bright and lovable bedfellow" like his own dear wife. How he wished that Mrs. —— knew Angela's suspicions of her, written as they were with numerous "!!!"!

There could be no real doubt as to where Stephen's heart lay. In this

95. *Ibid.*, January 26, 1860, 561-62.
96. For a description of the Mallorys' "magnificent new house" then being finished at Pensacola, cf. *Floridian and Journal*, April 9, 1859, quoting the *Observer*, n.d.
97. Mallory to Angela, January 1, 1859.

same letter he made the point clear. It was, he reminded Angela, the beginning of the new year; and, as his first act of 1859, he would assure her of his "measureless and unswerving affection" and his deep conviction of her own devotion, affection, and truth. He loved her more at that moment than ever before, if such were possible; and he swore that never for an instant since their marriage had his affection for her lapsed for an instant. He renewed his vows to her, not because he loved her more than previously, but because it gave him relief to repeat those solemn assurances, as, he was sure, she also did, to the Saviour of mankind. He frequently discriminated between women, extolling some or condemning others; but no feeling touching in the remotest degree his adoration for his dear wife, his first and only love, had ever dwelt for an instant in his heart, and never could. "I wish you were with me," he wrote, "and may the prayers of your . . . husband for your happiness prevail, for he is nothing without you."[98]

Angela, apparently, was not thoroughly convinced. A few weeks later Stephen complained that her letters were not only unaffectionate but infrequent, and that this had induced in him a bitterness of heart and a gnawing, crushed feeling of disgust with life. He begged her to write often and kindly to him; he would repay her with a thousand kisses for every letter.[99]

98. *Ibid.*
99. Mallory to Angela, February 10, 1859.

# CHAPTER SIX

# An End and A Beginning

THE YEAR 1859 WORE ON, and the North and South drew farther apart. In 1860, the two great parties prepared for the conventions that would choose the presidential nominees for that most crucial of national elections.

It was perhaps already too late for a compromise. What had happened by the spring of 1860 might be interpreted in this way: the "lawyer's argument" of the South had not been successfully answered by the North; the legal right to extend slavery into the territories and the legal right of a state to secede had nowhere, in the words and writings of Northerners, been really refuted. And the South was convinced that her very existence depended on holding fast to these two constitutional dogmas.

The Northern Republicans, on the other hand, believed that the United States was a nation and not a dissoluble compact. This argument, be it remarked, was not primarily a legal or constitutional argument. It was, rather, in the eyes of the North, a statement of existing conditions. It could not be proven with certainty by any appeals to the Constitution, or to general political theory. But, to the North of 1860, the oneness and indissolubility of the American Union, the result of a unique set of social, economic, and political factors, and the forging of history, was a fact so clear as to make all legal objections against it irrelevant. "Physically speaking," said Lincoln, "we cannot separate."

This was the tragic impasse of 1860-1861. The swift and pregnant events of the first months of 1860 were but the workings out of a fateful dialectic that perhaps could not, at that late date, be brought to a halt. In April the Democrats met in convention at Charleston, and split wide open. In the June reassemblings of the two blocs of the now crumbling party of Jefferson and Jackson, Douglas and Breckinridge were nominated for the presidency on separate tickets. To heighten the confusion, Bell of Tennessee was put into the running by a new political group.

Meanwhile, in May, at Chicago, the Republicans had nominated Abraham Lincoln. The lines were drawn.

It was a time when men on both sides were called upon to make a terrible choice between dread alternatives. The judgment of history must be charitable if there were some men who made mistakes in their choice.

As events moved swiftly and, perhaps, inevitably to a crisis, what was Stephen Mallory's political attitude? The question is important, because his own people later charged that, in those tense months preceding the outbreak of war, he had showed undue timidity in defense of Southern rights. He was, it was said, a Unionist whose Unionism overshadowed his devotion to the Southern land of his birth; he was lacking in vigor and courage at the moment when the Southern cause was most in need of those qualities in her sons.

After the war, while he was a political prisoner, Mallory, in a petition for pardon addressed to President Johnson explained what his political position had been through 1860. He insisted that "from the casting of his first vote until the secession of his State, his political life, as exemplified in faith, words, and acts, had been devoted to the maintenance of the Union." He had "never been a member of a convention nor of the legislature of his State, and had never advised nor counselled her secession." The record would show that no word of disloyalty to the Union had ever been uttered by Stephen Mallory.[1]

In the face of the Southern conviction, after the election of November, 1860, that the Republicans were bent on degrading the South, he had "dreaded the perils of secession, and had believed that ample remedies for all political wrongs would be more wisely and more advantageously secured within the Union than out of it." Whatever might be the arguments in favor of secession as a remedy consistent with the theory of the Constitution, he regarded it but as another name for revolution, justified only as a last resort from intolerable oppression.[2]

These affirmations might indeed appear to substantiate the allegations that Mallory was not a thoroughgoing fighter in defense of the South. Two points, however, must be remembered. In the first place, the letter to Johnson was intended by Mallory to be an apologia with a view to securing his

1. Mallory to President Johnson, from Fort Lafayette, June 21, 1865 (Mallory-Kennedy Collection).
2. Ibid.

freedom from a charge of treason. It would not be surprising—and not necessarily a proof of insincerity—if, in such a communication, he consciously or unconsciously "regularized" to some extent his political attitude of five years before.

Furthermore, the evidence of Mallory's senatorial career, up to the moment of his retirement from Congress, does not reveal him as a consistent conservative in the matter of Southern rights and Southern grievances. His speeches and letters written on sectional issues during the period 1856-1860 are not the utterances of a mild and timid statesman who is not "standing up" for the South. No man who thought with Yulee in 1850 could be called anything but a vigorous battler in furtherance of Southern demands; no orator fulminating as bitterly against the North as did Mallory at the Democratic ratification meeting of June, 1856, could be accused of lukewarmness in the Southern cause.

The most significant evidence, however, of a surprising strain of real radicalism was displayed by Mallory in the contest between Jefferson Davis and Albert Gallatin Brown in early 1860. In March of that year Davis had introduced and carried in the Democratic caucus a resolution affirming that there was no present necessity for Congress to enact specific legislation for the protection of slavery in the territories. The measure was regarded not as a retreat from the Southern position, but merely as a tactical move. It was, however, sharply challenged by Brown, who offered an amendment insisting on specific legislation regarding slavery. His position surprised no one, as he had always been regarded as a fire-eater of the fire-eaters.

Brown's amendment was put to a vote and decisively defeated, with only three favoring ballots. Of these, one was Brown's, one was Johnson's[3] of Arkansas, and the third, surprisingly enough, in the light of the usual estimates of his political character, was Senator Mallory's. It is difficult to see how the man who supported an extreme radical position in 1860, against an overwhelming majority of his party, could be considered a confirmed conservative in early 1861. It is significant, moreover, that one of the most consistent defenders of Mallory's naval administration during 1861-1865 was this radical Southern nationalist Albert Gallatin Brown.[4]

There were some in the South, certainly, who approved of Mallory's political record as his career in Congress drew to a close. The act providing

3. Senator Robert Ward Johnson was later a member of the Confederate Senate.
4. James B. Ranck, *Albert Gallatin Brown, Radical Southern Nationalist* (New York, 1937), 184-87. Cf. also: 36 Cong., 1 Sess., May 24, 1860 (*Cong. Globe*), 2324-25, and *ibid.*, May 25, 1860, 2347-50; Henry Wilson, *Rise and Fall of the Slave Power in America* (3 vols.; Boston, 1872-77), II, 657-60.

for a pay increase for officers in the navy was referred to by the *St. Augustine Examiner* as the "bill introduced by our distinguished Senator, Mr. Mallory, and managed by him with masterly ability."[5] Having been a close observer of the late congressional proceedings, continued this journal, it was proud to say that no member of that body had borne himself with more dignity and ability than Mallory. He had stood by the side of General Davis of Mississippi in support of the bill for the benefit of the widows whose husbands had fallen while engaged in the military service of their country. He had made able speeches on all the leading topics that had been discussed by the Congress.[6]

A domestic anxiety weighed on Mallory's spirits in the fall of 1860. His daughter Maggie at Bridgeport fell dangerously ill. Angela traveled up from Pensacola to nurse her, while Stephen returned south from Washington to take care of the children during her absence.

In a series of letters obviously designed to cheer both Angela and the patient, Stephen described persons and manners at Pensacola.[7] Angela's numerous sisters and sisters-in-law were apparently making the most of Stephen's hospitality. He reported that he was "getting along very well in his new capacity as hotel keeper."[8] Sue Moreno complained constantly of her health. "When it is good, it must be a dreadful thing. We have had to cook extra everything to meet the wants of her mouth, which, I confess it, has made upon me an impression of awe and respect, if not of apprehension. And whenever its slow, monotonous, but sure and insatiable open-

5. *St. Augustine Examiner*, April 28, 1860. Cf. also *ibid.*, March 30, 1860: "Hon. S. R. Mallory is not unmindful of his constituents in matters that have a bearing upon local interests and convenience, any more than he is in our greatest public interests."

6. *Ibid.*, April 28, 1860. Contemporaries have provided a few sidelights on political attitudes at Washington in the spring of 1860. "I have never seen such a den of noise, confusion, vulgarity, and corruption as in the House of Legislation," wrote a Southerner, "and unless men are bribed, there is only a remote chance for justice to private claims" (Senator John L. Manning to his wife, from Washington, May 14, 1860 [Williams-Manning-Chesnut Papers, Southern Collection, University of North Carolina]). The Japanese "good will" delegation had arrived, with a suite of seventy-two persons. "Com. Tattnall says it is a pity to have such genteel people demoralized by association with the heads of departments and Senators and Congressmen. They [the Japanese] are too modest to consent for the women to look at them. That, I suppose, will wear off before the impudence of these Washington belles. Everything is confusion as regards politics; nobody knows anything about anything" (*ibid.*). Concerning the persons whose papers constitute the valuable collection referred to in this footnote: James Chesnut, Jr., son of Colonel James Chesnut, was the husband of Mary Boykin Chesnut, the shrewd and vivacious lady whose diary has been recently re-edited by Ben Ames Williams. Mrs. David R. Williams was Mrs. Chesnut's sister "Kate." Senator John Laurence Manning was a political leader of South Carolina and one-time governor of the state.

7. Mallory to Angela, September 6, 1860.

8. *Ibid.*

ings and closings begin, I feel as if I were gazing on that terrible cave of Alfredo, into whose dark and portentous jaws many traces were seen to lead but none to come out."[9]

The outstanding trait of another of Angela's sisters, Maria, besides her "hilarity," was laziness. "She is the most pious and devoted being to her own peculiar god, Indolence, that I ever saw, and never lets an opportunity slip of doing nothing; and whether it be to obtain an appetite, to facilitate digestion, to improve the mind by reflecting or the body by exercise, she has but one resource; and lying flat on her back she awaits in sleep what Providence may provide her. A poppy and not a pappy must have presided at her birth, infused its spirit into her being, and made her an opiate for all time to come."[10]

There was always pleasant news about Ruby and Attie. One night, after he had told them a story about "bad Injuns" and they had gone to bed, Stephen gave them the good news that Maggie was improving. "Ruby jumped up, and with her peculiar shake of the head and enlargement of the eyes, said, 'Well, I prayed to God to make my sister well, and I knew all the time He would do it, too, because He can do it if He likes, and better than the Doctors with their old medicine, too.' "[11]

He gave them daily lessons in such subjects as Terrestrial and Celestial Geography with the Use of Globes. "After resorting to the Globe to show them where you and Buddy and Mag are, and where the Japanese have gone to, and the position of Key West, Ruby convinced me that she had received fully a quarter's instruction by asking me if people stood still and waited for the places to come around to them, or did they climb up in the cars on the outside of the globe? Attie at once pronounced her to be a dunce, and proceeded to explain and expatiate upon the solar and planetary system generally."[12] The wonders of the telegraph, as briefly sketched to them by Stephen, furnished another source of disagreement between his two pupils. Ruby insisted that the words came through the middle of the wire, where nobody could see them; Attie told her that she "didn't know anything about it, nor himself either."[13]

9. *Ibid.* In another letter he returned to the subject of Sue: "She is none of your soft headed shallowpated women,—not she; but one of those solid, substantial, deep, incomprehensible, mysterious and impenetrable beings who clothe their glowing thoughts in silence, and use their mouths, not for idle words, but for the legitimate purpose of satisfying and appeasing the demands of their truest friend, the one who is the last to desert them,—the Stomach" (Mallory to Angela, September 8, 1860).

10. Mallory to Angela, September 6, 1860.    11. *Ibid.*

12. Mallory to Angela, September 23, 1860.

13. Mallory to Angela, September 6, 1860.

On one very hot day, in order to keep them from playing in the sun, he enlisted their aid in building a "first rate dog house." They worked at it all day, and the result was "an elegant and private dog cottage." Ruby felt that her services in driving nails and holding boards to be sawed were amply rewarded by the permission granted to her pet Trump to sleep in one corner of the new dwelling.[14] Attie had morning and evening jobs at whitewashing and gardening. Ruby had set in order her mother's collection of seashells, a task that occupied her during an entire week. No children, he said, could be happier, and the servants were vying with one another in taking care of them.[15]

Stephen kept Angela posted on the more important of the town's social events. A gay bachelor named Spottswood "starts for New York two days hence to get a wife and some other drugs and medicines, much to the dissatisfaction of ancient maidens here, who think that, whether in medical or conjugal practice, domestic remedies are best."[16] The unique Maria had returned from a brief visit to the mainland, and again inspired his descriptive pen. She applied most religiously the apothegm of Angela's revered "Oncle," that "the day is made for rest and the night for sleep." She had no ambition, no desire to improve her mind, and, as her grandfather said, "no notting." She was also pre-eminently obstinate.[17]

Amid all this banter he did not forget his sick child at Bridgeport. "Poor thing," he wrote to Angela, "how I sympathize with her sufferings and how wretched they have made me. I trust to heaven that she is constantly improving. . . . You are worth more to her, and can do more for her, than all the medical faculty."[18] Nor was he unmindful of Angela's well being: "You do not say anything about your dresses, etc., which you thought I might express to you; if you want anything tell me in time, because if Mag's improvement should permit it I earnestly desire you to enjoy your visit to the utmost possible extent, and play the belle as much as you please."[19]

The trying episode had a happy ending. On September 20, Stephen wrote a gay note to Maggie. Her mother's letter, he told her, gave him the joyous assurance of his dear daughter's improvement. He had ever been accustomed to suppress any decided exhibitions of feeling; but nature, as she deals in balances, compensations, and equivalents, made him pay for the maintenance of an outward calm which covered his deep inward

14. Mallory to Angela, September 8, 1860.    15. *Ibid.*
16. *Ibid.*                                   17. *Ibid.*
18. *Ibid.*                                   19. *Ibid.*

concern: she "made a safety valve of one of my large toes, and let the grief out there terrifically." He conceded that no one had any sympathy for those suffering from gout, and one felt almost ashamed to complain of toe-ache; but he earnestly wished that every man had at least one attack of it per annum. All the servants of the house, he assured Maggie, had displayed the liveliest solicitude about her illness, and were eager to see her.[20]

The Christmas season of 1860 was a tense and anxious time. On December 20 the South Carolina State Convention adopted the Ordinance of Secession. Six days later the Federal garrison of Charleston harbor moved into Fort Sumter. Before the end of January, four more states, including Florida, would be out of the Union.

The President-elect seemed fumbling and unsure of himself. His cautious speeches since November had satisfied neither his own supporters nor the South. It was evident that he was still groping for a solution—and not finding one.

Buchanan, with no inconsiderable statesmanship, was trying earnestly to hold back the flood. While he scored the abolitionists for provoking the South, he spoke also to those who would use the weapon of secession: "This Government . . . is a great and powerful Government, invested with all the attributes of sovereignty. Its framers never intended to implant in its bosom the seeds of its own destruction."[21]

The Crittenden Compromise, proposed in mid-December, was having hard sledding. The tone of Southern feeling was well expressed in a statement of a group of Southern members of Congress: "The argument is exhausted. All hope of relief in the Union . . . is extinguished, and we trust the South will not be deceived by appearances or the pretence of new guarantees."[22]

On December 27 Mallory wrote to his friend James H. Hammond, analyzing the political prospects. Public affairs, he said, looked gloomy, and at Washington gloom was deepening into despondency. The Republicans, he felt, would not yield an inch, and nothing would be done by the current Congress either to prevent secession or to diminish the public excitement

20. Mallory to his daughter Maggie, September 20, 1860.

21. James D. Richardson, *A Compilation of the Messages and Papers of the Presidents 1789-1897* (6 vols.; Washington, D. C., 1896-97), V, 633.

22. Edward McPherson, *The Political History of the United States . . . during the Great Rebellion* (Washington, D. C., 1864), 37.

and fears. Lincoln and his party were determined to enforce the revenue laws, and to begin instantly upon his inauguration to use force to this end, if necessary. This program meant, of course, either the capture of Charleston harbor or the blockade of its coasts, as well as the capture or blockade of all Southern ports or coasts. The Republicans were infatuated in their incredulity as to the condition of the South, or they affected to be so.[23]

Mallory then made some pungent comments concerning pro-Southern feeling in the North. The masses of New England, "whose brains are being reached through their bellies, and whose stomachs begin to comprehend the true position of public affairs," were changing their views. Could they make themselves heard, they would overwhelm abolitionism and secure by constitutional guarantees all the just demands of the South. But the members of their state legislatures were already elected, and they could not be reached for some time. Every Northern man—save the Republican leaders—whom Mallory had met, admitted the justice of Southern complaints and affirmed the readiness of the Northern people to provide a remedy and this feeling was spreading.[24]

Nothing, however, declared Mallory, could or would be done in time to prevent Alabama, Georgia, Florida, or Mississippi from seceding, although the move would be embarrassed by the proposed convention of the border states advocated by Governor John Letcher of Virginia. No program could be wise which would tend to separate the border and cotton states.

Dispatches concerning Anderson's movement on Sumter were creating intense excitement in Washington. This probably would "disembarrass the Prest., who will at once order him off." The Republicans were determined on civil war, if they could bring it about in any form or by any means. They knew that the sight or smell of blood operates on men as it does on

23. *Mallory to Hon. James H. Hammond, from U. S. Senate Chamber, December 27, 1860* (Hammond Papers, Library of Congress). Hammond represented South Carolina in the Senate from 1857 to 1860. He was a strong secessionist and went so far as to advocate the death penalty for abolitionists. In August, 1860, Mallory had addressed a large Breckinridge and Lane ratification meeting at Pensacola (*Weekly East Floridian*, August 9, 1860).

24. Cf., for example: G. Bates to Hon. William Porcher Miles, from Boston, January 28, 1861 [*Porcher Miles Papers*, Southern Collection, University of North Carolina]. Miles represented South Carolina in the House of Representatives from 1857 to December, 1860. He was strongly pro-slavery and pro-secessionist and took a prominent part in the Washington phase of the negotiations concerning the status of the Charleston forts in early 1861. New Yorker George W. Cullum, writing to his friend Miles, declared that he had voted against the Republicans in the preceding November, but he was a firm Union man and would therefore oppose secession; however he insisted that two-thirds of the Northerners held their Southern brethren in warmest affection (Cullum to Miles, from New York, March 6, 1861, Miles Papers).

other animals, and with intensified effect—crushing out humanity, silencing argument, dethroning reason. They knew that if they could bring war about before the following fourth of March, and find it existing on their advent to power, they could carry it on with fire and sword. They wished to raise new regiments, to fill them with their starving thousands, and to send them to hold the posts in the north, south, east, and west, thus releasing their regular troops to march against the South. These, thought Mallory, were crude calculations, with hate supplying but poorly the place of judgment and logic.

If bloodshed could be staved off, he concluded, there would be a triumphant end of all the difficulties. But every hour indicated the danger of civil war. He trusted that Florida would make her "going out" dependent on the like action of Georgia and Alabama. All the Gulf States, he predicted, would have seceded by March 4. Everything looked gloomy, he repeated, and heaven only knew when the skies would brighten.[25]

Mallory's political associates during the critical days of December, 1860, were such sincere advocates of conciliation as Crittenden, Pugh, and Vallandigham.[26] Neither Mallory nor Yulee would join in a letter sent to constituents early in December, in which immediate secession was urged.[27] It was not until January, when the secession of Florida was but a matter of days, that the future Secretary of the Confederate Navy was found cooperating with those Southern senators who desired secession or had come to regard it as inevitable.[28] All Southern conservatives were at this time being pushed hard by the radical Southern press, pulpit, and politicians.[29] In the opinion of at least one observer, "The Senators from Florida were never regarded, however they seemed, as favorable to the secession movement; . . . but neither . . . exerted any considerable influence at Washington in the direction of disunion during the winter of 1860-1861."[30]

Whatever his hesitations and doubts, Mallory, early in January, added himself to the "happy unanimity" that existed among the senators from the still unseceded states. Together with Jefferson Davis and John Slidell he served on a steering committee appointed by these senators on January 6, 1861, which passed a resolution that, "as soon as may be," the rest of the

25. Mallory to Hammond, *supra cit.*

26. Dodd, *op. cit.*, 57-58.

27. Clubbs, *Life of Stephen Russell Mallory the Elder*, 211-12.

28. Dodd, *op. cit.*, 57-58.

29. *Ibid.*, 65-66.

30. S. S. Cox, *Union—Disunion—Reunion: Three Decades of Federal Legislation, 1855-1885* (Providence, R. I., 1885), 72.

Southern States should leave the Union.[31] It is not clear whether Yulee's report that he had "not been able to find Mr. Mallory this morning [January 7]"[32] was an indication of any sudden coolness shown by the latter with regard to the secession resolution of the group.[33]

The tragic moment came, finally, on a morning in February, 1861.

The Senate galleries were crowded, as they had frequently been during the past critical years; but the appearance and manner of the spectators were different today. They had come, most of them, knowing full well what to expect. They were there to attend a solemn departure ceremony, almost a solemn requiem. Southern men had dressed themselves carefully in their best clothes to sit in that gallery on that morning. Some of them wore uniforms of the United States Army, with wound stripes. Southern women were in formal visiting garb; never before had they looked so charming, and never had they looked more grave. They realized what this morning's events in the Senate chamber might mean to them. But there were some things, they knew, that were more precious than peace.

One after another, the Southern senators made brief farewell speeches, gathered up their papers from their desks, and walked from the chamber.[34] As they departed they were accompanied by no riotous cheers from that

31. Mallory to a friend in Florida whose name, according to J. Franklin Jameson, has been cut out of the MSS, from Montgomery, Ala., March 22, 1861, reprinted in *American Historical Review*, XII (October, 1906), 108.

32. Yulee to J. S. Finegan, January 7, 1861 (*The War of the Rebellion: A Compilation of the Official Records of the Union and Confederate Armies* (128 vols.; Washington, D. C.: The Department of War, 1880-1901, Ser. 1, Vol. I, 443). Henceforth, for references to this work, the abbreviation *O.R.A.* will be used. The abbreviation *O.R.* will be used in referring to *Official Records of the Union and Confederate Navies in the War of the Rebellion* (30 vols., Washington, D. C.: Navy Department, 1894-1922).

33. Cf. also Tate, *op. cit.*, 40; *St. Augustine Examiner*, December 15, 1860. The *American Annual Cyclopedia and Register of Important Events of the Year 1861*, 124-25, lists the members of the senatorial caucus above mentioned: Alabama, Benjamin Fitzpatrick and C. C. Clay, Jr.; Arkansas, R. W. Johnson and William E. Sebastian; Georgia, Robert Toombs and Alfred Iverson; Louisiana, J. P. Benjamin and John Slidell; Mississippi, Jefferson Davis and Albert G. Brown; Texas, John Hemphill and Louis Wigfall; Florida, David Yulee and S. R. Mallory.

34. It would appear, from contemporary evidence, that the so-called "leaders of secession" in the Senate were in an unsought-for and delicate position. The *New Orleans Delta*, January 19, 1861, sought to disabuse the North of the idea that secession had originated with the politicians: "There has been no ... movement in our political history with which the politicians have had so little and the people so much to do; men in high places and honors are not eager or prompt to engage in revolution." The *Charleston Mercury*, January 17, 1861, said with, of course, a degree of exaggeration stemming from its ultra-radical bias: "From the first to the last the Southern politicians have been stumbling blocks in the way of Southern advancement." With these sentiments the latest biographer of Judah P. Benjamin agrees. He believes that the secession movement everywhere in the South "certainly outran the politicians" (Meade, *op. cit.*, 150).

portion of the gallery where their friends and relatives sat. The South that day in the Senate was very firm, but it was also very sorrowful.

It was the turn of the senior Senator from Florida. Mallory addressed the chair in a speech not lacking in eloquence.

He concurred, he declared, with all that his colleague, Senator Yulee, had said; and he asked but a brief moment to add a few words more. In retiring from the Senate, he could not help feeling profound regret that existing causes imperatively impelled himself and his colleagues to make the great withdrawal. When reason and justice should have firmly asserted their ascendancy over party and passion, the causes of the Southern movement, demanded by considerations dear to freemen in every age, would stand proudly vindicated.

Throughout her long and patient endurance of insult and wrong, the South had clung to the Union with unfaltering fidelity, a fidelity which, while nourishing irritation in the hearts of her sons, had but served to nerve the arms of her adversaries.

Florida had come into the Union fifteen years before, upon a basis of equality with the original states, and their rights in the Union were equally her rights. She could not, if she would, separate her action from her Southern sisters; and, demanded as her action was by those considerations which a free people can never ignore, she would not if she could. From the Union governed by the Constitution as the Founding Fathers had made it, there breathed not a secessionist upon Florida soil; but a deep sense of injustice, inequality, and insecurity, produced by causes all too well known, had been brought home to the reason and patriotism of her people; and to secure and maintain these rights which the Constitution no longer afforded them, they had placed the state of Florida out of the Union.

In thus turning from the Union to the veiled and unknown future, the Southern people were neither ignorant nor reckless of the lions in their path. They knew that the prompt and peaceful organization of a practical republican government, securing liberty, equality, and justice to every citizen, was one of the most difficult as it was one of the most momentous duties devolving upon men; and nowhere perhaps on earth, except in America, could this great work be achieved.

But, so well were human rights and national liberty understood by the Southern people, so deeply were those people imbued with the spirit of freedom and with skill in government, that, "were this Republic utterly broken and destroyed, like the shattered vase of the poet, to whose very fragments the scent of the roses still clings, its very ruins breathing the true spirit of civil and religious liberty would plead for and demand a wise and noble reconstruction."

Whatever, then, might be the immediate results of the momentous crisis, let there be no fears for the freedom of the men of the South. "Nor," declared Mallory, "do I admit for a moment that the great American experiment of government has proven or can prove a failure; but I maintain, on the contrary, that passing events should inspire in the hearts of the patriot and statesman not only hope but confidence."

Five states had already dissolved their connection with the Union; and throughout the several stages by which their people, in their sovereign capacity, had reached secession, they had exhibited a calmness and deliberation which found no parallel in the history of mankind. This was entirely the result of the admirable system of state governments in the South. "And," added Mallory, ". . . were this Federal District, with President, Congress, Departments, and Courts, and all the machinery of Federal Government, suddenly sunk a thousand fathoms deep,—under the admirable working of these State governments the rights and liberties of their people would receive no shock or detriment."

In thus severing her connection with sister states, the South desired to go in peace, and to maintain toward those states an attitude not only of peace but, if possible, of kindness; and it was for them to determine whether the South should do so or not, and whether commerce, the great pacificator of the world, should connect the two sections as producers, manufacturers, and consumers, in future friendly relations. If, on the other hand, folly, wickedness, or pride should preclude the hope of peace, there would come that greatest of all calamities that can befall a nation—civil war.

"But, sir," continued the Floridian, "be our difficulties what they may, we stand forth a united people to grapple with and to conquer them. Our willingness to shed our blood for this cause is the highest proof we can offer of the sincerity of our convictions; and I warn, nay I implore you, not to repeat the fatal folly of the Bourbons, and mistake a nation for a faction; for the people of the South, as one man, declare that, sink or swim, live or die, they will not as freemen submit to the degradation of a constrained existence under a violated Constitution."

But the South desired to part from the North in peace. From the earliest establishment of the Anglo-Saxons upon the American continent until that hour they had never, as colonies or States, shed each other's blood; and it was to be trusted that they would never do so in the future. The South was saying to the North: "We seek not to war upon, or to conquer you; and we know that you cannot conquer us. Imbrue your hands in our blood, and the rains of a century will not wash from your hands the stain, while coming generations will weep for your wickedness and folly."

Mallory then spoke a paragraph for which he was severely rebuked by some of the more radical journals of the South: "In thus leaving the Senate, and returning to my own State, to pursue with unfaltering head and heart the path, be it gloomy or bright, to which her honor and interest may lead, . . . I cannot forbear the acknowledgment of the kindness and courtesy which I have ever received from many of the gentlemen of the Opposition; Senators to whom I am indebted for much that I shall cherish through life with pleasure, and toward whom I entertain none but sentiments of kindness and respect. And I trust, sirs, that when we next confront each other, whether at this bar or at that of the just God, who knows the hearts of all, our lips shall not have uttered a word, our hands shall not have committed an act, directed against the blood of our people."[35]

On the day after the Southern senators' formal leave-taking, Senator Fitch, of Indiana, moved that the President of the Senate "fill vacancies on the committees caused by the withdrawal of Senators Jefferson Davis, Yulee, Fitzpatrick, Clay, and Mallory." In the debate that followed, Senator Seward showed a spirit of generosity which might have accomplished much six months earlier. "I am utterly opposed," he declared, ". . . to this transaction. I am for leaving these seats here for those senators or for other Senators from the States which they represent, to be resumed at their own time and at their own pleasure."[36]

On March 14, 1861, the following resolution was adopted by the Senate: "Whereas, The seats of Senators Benjamin, of Louisiana, Brown and Davis, of Mississippi, Clay of Alabama, Toombs of Georgia, and Mallory of Florida, having become vacant, Therefore, Resolved, That the Secretary be directed to omit their names from the roll of the Senate."[37]

Before severing his communications completely from Washington, Mallory took part in a train of events which has been commonly denominated the "Pickens episode." His actions in the affair were roundly condemned

35. 36 Cong., 2 Sess., January 21, 1861 (*Cong. Globe,* 485-86).

36. 36 Cong., 2 Sess., January 22, 1861 (*Cong. Globe,* 501). In this same speech, Seward made an interesting (implicit) admission of the right of secession (cf. George P. Lathrop, "The Bailing of Jefferson Davis," in the *Century Magazine,* February 1887, 637, note).

37. 36 Cong., 2 Sess., March 14, 1861 (*Cong. Globe,* 1456).

in many Southern quarters, and it is not until very recently that his course has apparently been justified.

As the advent of war became almost certain, it was realized that Pensacola would be the military and naval key for the control of the Gulf region. Two days after the ordinance of secession was adopted by the Tallahassee convention, Florida troops took possession of the Pensacola navy yard, as well as Fort Barrancas and Fort McRea. Fort Pickens, however, across the bay, remained in Federal hands.[38]

Mallory has been accused of preventing the Florida authorities from seizing the latter vitally important point. He has been represented as timidly fleeing from the thought of offering armed resistance to the Federals at Pickens, and the loss of the fort has been laid at his door. His whole behavior in the affair was said to be cowardly, indecisive, and even disloyal to the South.

What really happened? In a long letter a few weeks afterward, Mallory told the story.

At first, he declared, he had urged the taking of Pickens by Major Chase, the state commandant at Pensacola.[39] But, in the meantime—certainly through no fault of Mallory's—the Federal troops had moved into the fort. Chase telegraphed to Mallory that the works could not be seized without an assault at an immense sacrifice of life and at the expense of the total annihilation of the garrison. Mallory showed the telegram to Yulee and to the senators of six other Southern states. It was "unanimously agreed upon full consideration" to inform the Florida commander "that the capture of the work was not worth in the then condition of affairs one drop of blood," and a telegram to this effect was signed by all the senators of Texas, Louisiana, Mississippi, Alabama, Georgia, Arkansas, and Florida, and sent to Chase. "Chase," Mallory believed, "had no idea of assaulting Pickens, believing it to be madness to do so."[40]

38. *The Pensacola Journal,* "Pensacola Might Give Them One Last Tribute," March 17, 1935.

39. Mallory to unknown, from Montgomery, March 22, 1861, *supra cit.*

40. *Ibid.,* 104-5. The following was the crucial series of telegrams: (a) To Governor Perry, signed by Jno. Slidell, J. P. Benjamin, A. Iverson, Jno. Hemphill, Louis T. Wigfall, C. C. Clay, Jr., Ben Fitzpatrick, Jeff. Davis, S. R. Mallory, from Washington, January 18, 1861: "We think no assault should be made. The possession of the fort is not worth one drop of blood to us. Measures pending unite us in this opinion. Bloodshed now may be fatal to our cause" (*O.R.A.,* Ser. I, Vol. I, p. 445). (b) C. C. Clay, Jr., and Benjamin Fitzpatrick to Governor Perry, from Washington, January 19, 1861: "Telegraph not to attack Fort Pickens. Florida Senators and friends think it unwise" (*ibid.*). (c) S. R. Mallory and D. L. Yulee to Governor Perry, from Washington, January 20, 1861: "The Southern Senators all agree that no assault on Fort Pickens should be made; that the fort is not worth one drop of blood at

The decision not to fight for Pickens was, therefore, not taken on Mallory's sole responsibility; it was concurred in by men whose devotion to the South could certainly not be questioned.

Mallory's next act was anything but timid. He learned that four warships were being sent to Pensacola harbor, to cooperate with Fort Pickens. Chase, he knew also, could not prevent their progress. What was to be done? "After full consideration with our Southern Senators," he wrote in a letter, "I exerted every argument with the President and Secretary to keep them [the warships] out at Sea, and at last by asserting boldly that we would raise said batteries and sink them at their anchors, that their coming in was a warlike menace, that I would man and fire the first gun myself, etc., etc., I got them to countermand their orders; and to render this secure I induced the Secretary to send Captain Barron, U. S. Navy, with me to Pensacola, who proceeded to every ship as she came in sight of the Port and warned her off. Thus they were kept out and we were not demoralized by their presence."[41]

Mallory's activity was not yet finished. On his way south he learned that the warship *Brooklyn* was headed for Fort Pickens with reinforcements for the fort. Chase admitted his complete inability to stop them. Mallory wired at once to Slidell and to some of the other Southern former Senators who were still at Washington. The *Brooklyn,* he warned, must not be allowed to go to Fort Pickens with reinforcements. Such an act would mean instant war. If the existing state of inactivity could only be preserved, "we will guarantee that no attack will be made upon [Pickens]." Slidell and his associates were to "impress this upon the President and urge that the inevitable tendency of reinforcements under present circumstances is . . . war." War was to be staved off if at all possible.[42]

---

this time, and desire us to invoke you to prevent bloodshed. First get the Southern Government in operation. The same advice has been given as to Charleston, and will no doubt be adopted there" (*ibid.*). Madison Perry was Governor of Florida from 1857 to 1861. During the war he was colonel of the Seventh Florida Regiment.

41. Mallory to unknown, from Montgomery, March 22, 1861, *supra cit.*

42. *Ibid.*, 105-6; also Mallory to Slidell *et al.,* from Pensacola, January 28, 1861 (Simon Gratz Autograph Collection, Pennsylvania Historical Society). Cf. also, *in re* Fort Pickens *O.R.*, Ser. I, Vol. IV, pp. 211-16. Stanton did not view Mallory's actions in the Pickens incident as in any way benefiting the Federal cause: "Senator Mallory . . . promised that Pickens should not be attacked if the President would agree not to reinforce it, and he [the President] agreed. As such a bargain was as advantageous, almost, as an actual surrender of the fort to the secessionists, Stanton 'earnestly opposed it.' He urged that the South was 'merely seeking time for more perfect war preparations; that if Pickens were not reinforced at once it could not be reinforced after hostilities had begun, and that the result would be the loss of the fort.' His argument was without effect, Buchanan ordering Secretaries Holt and Toucey . . . to send the instructions mentioned" (Frank A. Flower, *Edwin McMasters Stanton, the Autocrat of the Rebellion, Emancipation, and Reconstruction* [New York, 1905], 100).

The move had its effect. Upon Chase's assurance that he would not attack Pickens, the President ordered the soldiers to remain on board the *Brooklyn*. Mallory insists on the fact that Chase had no idea of making a move against the fort in any event, because of the clear insufficiency of his forces. A point had been gained by sheer threat and diplomacy which could never have been won by force.[43]

Thus, concluded Mallory, "my making a truce, as it is called, is the sheerest clap-trap ever uttered by a lying demagogue. What I did was to give the Administration a fright and induce them to propose terms to Chase to keep troops out."[44]

Certainly in the eyes of many Northern men Mallory was anything but a timid counter-revolutionist in early 1861. Joseph Holt, the United States Judge Advocate General, in a scathing communication of November, 1865, charged the former Secretary of the Confederate Navy with having been one of the prime inciters of the rebellion.[45] "Of the criminality of Mallory at that early period," declared Holt, "the evidence, though less full and significant [than in the cases of such others as Yulee, Slidell, Benjamin, or Davis] is perceived to be sufficiently positive to fix upon him beyond a question the character of one of the original conspirators against the Government."[46] The accusation was confirmed by Brevet Major General A. Asboth, in a letter to Stanton in December, 1865: "Instead of preventing disruption between the people of the South and the Government of the United States, and especially preventing the capture of Fort Pickens, he [Mallory] was actually urging both the secession of the South and the speedy occupation of the Pensacola forts."[47]

As evidence of Mallory's "traitorous animus," the following documents were adduced by Holt and Asboth.

On January 2, 1861, Mallory, with other Southern senators, asked the Secretary of War for information regarding "the numerical force of the troops now in garrison at the various posts in the State of Florida, and the amount of arms, heavy and small, and ammunition, . . . at the various forts

---

43. Mallory to unknown, from Montgomery, March 22, 1861, *supra cit.*

44. *Ibid.* In his letter to his son Buddy (*supra cit.*) four years later Mallory said: "Every man who ventures to climb morally, physically, or intellectually, makes himself a tempting mark for the shafts of envy, hatred, or malice to practice on. I have realized this perhaps neither more or less than thousands and have been as little deterred by it."

45. J. Holt to Hon. E. M. Stanton, November 23, 1865 (*O.R.A.*, Ser. II, Vol. VIII, pp. 862-66; with cross-references to Mallory's "treasonable despatches" in *ibid.*, Ser. I, Vol. I, pp. 349, 351, 442, 443).

46. Holt to Stanton, November 23, 1865, in *ibid.*, Ser. II, Vol. VIII, p. 865.

47. A. Asboth to Stanton, December 10, 1865, *ibid.*, 833.

and arsenals in that State."[48] The request was refused, for security reasons, by the Secretary of War *ad interim*, who happened to be the same J. Holt.[49] The reasons for the request were revealed in a letter of January 5, 1861, addressed by Senator Yulee to a correspondent in Tallahassee. From this communication, said Holt, it was clear that the Southern senators, including Mallory, were meditating a "gigantic conspiracy."[50]

The substance of what Yulee had written was that the "immediately important thing to be done" was the occupation of the forts and arsenals in Florida. The naval station and forts at Pensacola were first in consequence. For this purpose an armed force was necessary. Toombs had promised to use his good offices with Governor Brown of Georgia in order to raise a force sufficient to take the Pensacola navy yard and forts. The arsenal at Chattahoochee was to be looked to, to prevent the removal of arms. "What is advisable is *the earliest possible organization of a Southern Confederacy and of a Southern Army*" (italics Yulee's). The North was rapidly consolidating against the South on a plan of force. A strong Southern government, such as eight states would make, promptly organized, and a strong army, would bring the North to a reasonable sense of the gravity of the crisis. "I shall give the enemy a shot next week before retiring," Yulee concluded; "I say enemy! Yes, I am theirs, and they are mine. I am willing to be their masters, but not their brothers."[51]

On January 6, Mallory forwarded to the president of the Florida Convention the resolutions adopted by the Southern senators. These declarations of "open revolt and aggressive war," as Holt called them,[52] were promptly put into action. On January 7 Fort Marion and the arsenal at St. Augustine were seized by Florida and Alabama troops; on January 12 the important

48. This communication of the Southern senators to the Secretary of War is in *ibid.*, Ser. I, Vol. I, p. 349.

49. Holt to Southern Senators' Committee, January 9, 1861, in *ibid.*, 351.

50. Holt to Stanton, November 23, 1865, in *ibid.*, Ser. II, Vol. VIII, p. 863.

51. Yulee to Joseph S. Finegan, Esq., or to Colonel George W. Call, from Washington, January 5, 1861, in *ibid.*, Ser. I, Vol. I, pp. 442-43. General Joseph S. Finegan was later acting Confederate commander in East Florida. Major George W. Call is referred to as being of the Second Florida Regiment in 1862. He was killed in action in the battle of Fair Oaks, Va., May 31, 1862. Cf. Brigadier General Samuel Garland, C.S.A., commanding Third Brigade, Third Division, to Major J. W. Ratchford, June 3, 1862, in *ibid.*, Ser. I, Vol. XI, Part 1, p. 964. George W. Call is not to be confused with General Richard K. Call, Territorial Governor of Florida during most of the Seminole Wars, 1835-39 and 1841-44. Cf. Jefferson Davis' well-reasoned rebuttal of the charge that the Southern senators had formed a "plot" in 1860-61, *Rise and Fall of the Confederate Government*, I, 201-9.

52. Holt to Stanton, November 23, 1865 (*O.R.A.*, Ser. II, Vol. VIII, p. 863). The resolutions are in *ibid.*, Ser. I, Vol. I, pp. 443-44.

forts Barrancas and McRea and the navy yard at Pensacola were captured.[53] What Holt termed the "skulking treachery" of Yulee and Mallory did not stop here. On January 9 they sent the following telegram to Governor Perry of Florida: "Federal troops are said to be moving, or to move, on the Pensacola forts. Every hour is important. Georgia and Alabama if called will aid in the work, we think. The two seaboard forts are vacant of Federal defenders. Chase, at Pensacola, built and knows the works. [Signed] S. R. Mallory, George S. Hawkins, D. L. Yulee." On the next day Mallory wired to Chase: "All here look to you for Pickens and McRea."[54]

It is against this background that Mallory's subsequent reversal of his position must be judged. When, on January 18, he strongly urged that Pickens should not be attacked by Southern troops, and when he endorsed the phrase that was later used against him with such damaging effect by his Southern critics—"the fort is not worth one drop of blood at this time"— the military situation had radically changed. By the eighteenth the positions could have been taken only at a heavy cost to the Southern forces; and, perhaps more to the point, in recommending a "no attack" policy, Mallory was merely echoing the views of Benjamin, Slidell, Iverson, Hemphill, Wigfall, Fitzpatrick, C. C. Clay, and Jefferson Davis.[55]

In the light of the foregoing, the claims of both the enemies and friends of Mallory that he was "moderate" in January, 1861, should be reassessed. It is necessary to qualify considerably, for instance, such a statement as the following, which was made in his behalf during his imprisonment after the war: "I know the fact that at Montgomery he was one of the very few who avowed a willingness to go back into the Union on the basis of a satisfactory compromise. He lost his popularity in Florida at the beginning of secession because he aided to prevent an attack on Fort Pickens."[56]

53. Holt to Stanton, November 23, 1865, loc. cit.
54. Both these telegrams are in O.R.A., Ser. I, Vol. I, pp. 444-45. For the complete correspondence with regard to the "conspiracy," cf. ibid., Vol. LII, Part 2, pp. 9-16.
55. Cf. p. 125, n. 40.
56. Wm. W. Boyce to Seward, July 29, 1865 (O.R.A., Ser. II, Vol. VIII, p. 713).

# CHAPTER SEVEN

# *Wanted:*
# *A Navy and A Policy*

A BATCH OF TELEGRAMS sent from Montgomery in mid-February, 1861, marked a solemn moment in the lives of a few score officers in the United States Navy.[1] The provisional Confederate government was summoning to its temporary capital a select number of persons versed in sea warfare, for the purpose of forming a navy.

The invitation reached Raphael Semmes late on a Sunday afternoon as he sat in his Washington home in the midst of his family. At that time he was a commander in the navy of the United States and chairman of the important Lighthouse Board. His answer was sent at once: "Despatch received; I will be with you immediately."[2]

Semmes has described the feelings of men like himself who, in that crucial month, were called on to make a most difficult decision, to choose between their state and the country in whose naval service they had for years held commissions as officers. The dilemma was cruel. A naval officer's profession was his only fortune; he depended upon it for the support of himself and his family. If he remained where he was, there awaited him a competency for life, and promotion and honors; if he went with the South, a dark and uncertain future was before him. Furthermore, the emotional

---

1. For details of the social life and general atmosphere of official circles at Montgomery, cf. Eron Rowland, *Varina Howell, Wife of Jefferson Davis* (2 vols.; New York, 1931; also R. B. Rhett, "The Confederate Government at Montgomery," part I of *Battles and Leaders of the Civil War* (4 vols.; New York, 1884-87), I, 99-110. It is to be remembered that Rhett, editor of the *Charleston Mercury,* 1860-62, was bitterly unfriendly to the Davis administration.

2. Semmes to C. M. Conrad, from Washington, D. C., n.d., in Raphael Semmes, *Service Afloat: or, The Remarkable Career of the Confederate Cruisers "Sumter" and "Alabama" during the War between the States* (New York, 1893), 76. Lawyer and statesman Charles Magill Conrad, of Louisiana, served his state in the United States Senate from April, 1842, to March, 1843, and was a member of the Louisiana constitutional convention of 1844. He was Secretary of War under President Fillmore from August, 1850, to March, 1853. He was a member of the first and second Confederate Congresses, and, for a while, a brigadier general in the Confederate army.

associations growing out of long years of service together, and the sharing of the sacred traditions formed in midshipman days at Annapolis, made it extremely painful for the Southern officer to separate from his brothers in the service. The flag, too, as Semmes admitted, had a charm difficult to resist. The midshipman had trained and studied under its folds, and had dreamed of devoting his entire life to its defense and glory. He had gazed at it in some foreign port, as it waved proudly from the gaff-end of his ship, and from the sight he had drunk in new inspiration to do and dare for his country. Many bearded men, Semmes testified, were affected almost to tears as they saw this once hallowed emblem hauled down from the flagstaffs of Southern forts and arsenals.[3] They were like men who had been forced, in spite of themselves, to realize the perfidy of a friend, who must be now given up, as no longer worthy of confidence or affection.[4]

Love for their state was, for most of the Southern officers, the deciding factor. Robert E. Lee expressed the sentiments of many besides himself when he wrote: ". . . I had to meet the question whether I should take part against my native State. With all my devotion to the Union . . . I have not been able to make up my mind to raise my hand against my relations, my children, my home. I have therefore resigned my commission in the army."[5]

By the act of the Confederate Congress passed at Montgomery, February 21, 1861, the Confederate Navy was established. Almost immediately President Davis named, as head of the Navy Department, Stephen Russell Mallory.

There were several reasons for choosing the former Senator from Florida. Whether one of them was the (supposed) fact he was regarded by the President as being a conservative, moderate, and "safe" man, is doubtful on two counts. In the first place, as this study has sought to show, the political positions previously assumed by Mallory did not support the view that he was ultra-cautious and lacking in boldness. In the second place, it is not clear that Davis was meditating a "conservative" war, and that he was seeking therefore "weak" men for his cabinet.[6]

3. Cf. the following admission of a radical Southern politician as he proposed the old flag as a basis for the design of the new Confederate banner: "Although I have not much more veneration than you have for the stars and stripes, there are many who have, whose feelings, or fancies, have a right to be regarded" (M. E. Huger to Porcher Miles, from Savannah, Ga., February 7, 1861 [Miles Papers, Southern Historical Collection, University of North Carolina]).

4. Semmes. op cit., 72-73.

5. R. E. Lee to his sister, from Arlington, Va., April 20, 1861, in ibid., 74.

6. William Gilmore Simms wrote thus to Porcher Miles in the spring of 1861: "My own opinion is that the people of all the South are monstrously ahead of all their politicians. . . .

It might be observed in passing that many of the charges of "timidity" and "defensive-mindedness" leveled against the Davis administration were rash and ill considered. The South, because of her strategic position—and especially by reason of her strategic deficiencies—was committed to a defensive war, whether she liked it or not. But a defensive war did not necessarily imply a half-hearted war.[7]

If indeed the new Secretary of the Navy was a naturally timid politician it is difficult to understand how, throughout his term of office, he retained the consistent support of the radical Southern nationalist Albert Gallatin Brown. As chairman of the congressional Committee on Naval Affairs, Brown, as already remarked, worked harmoniously with Mallory, and he vigorously opposed the creation of the Naval Investigation Committee of 1862.[8] The fiery "ultra" was not the man to cooperate easily with reaction or timidity in any form.

Whatever Mallory's deficiencies, he was an excellent choice from one important point of view: he was a Floridian. A Northern journal afterward described caustically and not untruly how the Confederate cabinet was largely the outcome of the exigencies of political geography.[9] The blunt fact was that for harmony within the government each of the already seceded states had to be awarded representation in the President's council. Thus, Georgia got the chief post, South Carolina the next in importance, and Alabama the third. When the cabinet minister next in rank was to be decided upon, Florida was the state from which he had to come, since she stood next in grade of date, having seceded on the same day as Alabama, and two weeks before Louisiana.[10] If the method did not always bring to Montgomery the men best fitted for the posts, it at least gave an early assurance to states' rights sensibilities, which, as has long been recognized,

It is only the trading politicians that care about a President at all. The *people* of the South want their rights, not office. Those who want office scarcely can understand them" (Simms to Miles, from Woodlands, S. C., May 21, 1861 [Miles Papers]). Alfriend asserts that Davis believed that secession would mean war (Frank H. Alfriend, *The Life of Jefferson Davis* [Philadelphia, 1868], 286-87).

7. Cf. Percy S. Flippen, *Herschel V. Johnson of Georgia, State Rights Unionist* (Richmond, 1931), 209, 211. Cf. also Johnson's adverse criticism of the cabinet as a whole (*ibid.*, 212-14). The *Richmond Enquirer*, June 13, 1862, blamed the Confederate Government for not pursuing the tactic which, it declared, was most in accord with the Southern character, i.e., vigorous offensive. Cf. also, in regard to the alleged incompetence of the Confederate government, George Cary Eggleston, *A Rebel's Recollections* (New York, 1875), ch. VIII, "Red Tape." It is to be noted, however, that Eggleston was an intemperate and often jaundiced writer.

8. Ranck, *Albert Gallatin Brown*, 213-14; and *supra*, ch. VI, p. 114. Cf. also *Journal of Confederate Congress*, XI, 243.

9. *New York Citizen*, August 10, 1867.

10. *Ibid.*

were to prove repeatedly, in such ways as this, a serious obstacle to the Southern war effort.[11]

It would be unfair, of course, to deny that an important reason for Mallory's appointment lay in his considerable experience in naval affairs. The exact extent of his abilities in the field, however, is wrapped in some doubt, even at this late date.[12] It is true that from his earliest years he had been, in one capacity or another, associated with ships. As a young man he had had practical experience in the navigation of small vessels, and had commanded a longboat in the Seminole War. From his work as Collector of Customs he had learned a great deal about our merchant marine. At Key West he had been one of the few leading admiralty lawyers. He had, during his terms as chairman of the Senate Naval Affairs Committee, made an earnest study of the history and problems of our own and other navies. He had taken a special interest in innovations and improvements in ship design and ordnance.[13]

He possessed in regard to naval affairs a kind of impulsive progressivism, which, although it sometimes led him astray, enabled him in other instances to recognize and to develop with boldness sound new proposals.[14] He was by no means a great administrator, but he was a conscientious, methodical, and generally reliable one. A Northern critic believed that Davis had selected him because he was a quiet, easy-going man who would not grumble very loudly if a "higher power" saw fit to meddle, now and then, with the administration of the Navy Department.[15]

In some official quarters there was considerable opposition to Mallory's appointment. When President Davis submitted the Floridian's name to the Committee on Naval Affairs, the final vote on confirmation was thirty-six yeas, seven nays. In the minority were two out of the three Florida representatives on the committee.[16]

11. Burton J. Hendrick, *Statesmen of the Lost Cause: Jefferson Davis and His Cabinet* (New York, 1939), 10-11.

12. Cf. *St. Augustine Examiner*, Apr. 13, 1861, quoting *New Orleans Crescent*, n.d.

13. Madeleine Vinton Dahlgren, *Memoir of John A. Dahlgren, Rear-Admiral United States Navy* (Boston, 1882), 155-61.

14. Frank M. Bennett, *The Steam Navy of the United States: A History of the Growth of the Steam Vessel of War in the United States Navy, and of the Naval Engineer Corps* (Pittsburgh, 1896), 161-62. The appendix to this work is a satire on the "crackpot" invention of a marine engine by one Dickerson. The satire is entitled: "The Navy of the United States: an Exposure of Its Condition, and the Causes of Its Failure! Uncle Sam's Whistle and What It Costs; A Tale," 1864. Mallory, while chairman of the Senate Naval Affairs Committee, had been egregiously taken in by this half-baked proposal of Dickerson's.

15. *New York Citizen*, August 10, 1867.

16. *Journal of the [Confederate] Provisional Congress*, February 28, 1861; March 4, 1861. Cf. also *Journal of Confederate Congress* [to be carefully distinguished from the Provisional

General Jackson Morton and a Mr. Blount, two leaders of the Know-Nothing party of Saint Rosa County, Mallory charged, had sought to create the impression in Tallahassee that he was not sufficiently sound on the question of Southern rights. The basis of the allegation was the series of incidents relating to the surrender of Fort Pickens. Of his behavior in that affair, said Mallory, he was justly proud and in no way ashamed.

He had kept clear of Montgomery for the explicit purpose of avoiding any appearance of seeking official position, and had sincerely desired to remain in private life. Jefferson Davis, long a personal friend, had offered him a seat in the cabinet. He had resolved at once not to take it, and had come to the capital to say that, although he could not accept any public place, he would cheerfully give to the Secretary of the Navy all the aid in his power in the organization and conduct of the department.

Upon reaching Montgomery he had learned from the President that his nomination had already been sent to the Senate, and that it was being opposed by two of the Florida delegation. "Of course I could not carry out my purpose and withdraw in the face of unknown opposition." On the following day he had learned that these gentlemen—Patton Anderson, the other Florida representative, had not yet arrived—opposed him for the above-mentioned reasons and disclaimed all "personal grounds." The opposition of Jackson Morton needed but to be seen to be despised; with James Owens, Mallory was more favorably impressed. "I know he [Owens] only saw the matter as Morton presented it; but Morton, from mental and physical structure and from rancor long indulged toward me, . . . with that sort of chuckleheadedness which distinguishes all he says, could not do justice to a political adversary."

Anderson and Owens had since come over to his side. It was to be noted, said Mallory, that Morton had run as a Submissionist against the Secession candidate, and had been elected on the Submissionist ticket from one of the extreme western counties of Florida.[17]

---

Congress], I. 95-96; 105-6; also *ibid.,* II (Senate), 74. The vote was thirteen to six in favor of Mallory's confirmation as Secretary, March 18, 1862. John N. Maffitt, later one of the Confederacy's most successful cruiser commanders, regarded the appointment of Mallory as a grave mistake (Private Journal of Maffitt, under date of May 2, 1861, quoted in Emma Maffit, *The Life and Services of John Newland Maffitt* [New York, 1906], 221). On the other hand, the Florida legislature issued a glowing encomium of the new Secretary of the Navy ("Joint Resolution expressing the sentiments of the people of Florida toward the Confederate Government and her armies in the field," passed by House of Representatives and Senate and approved by the Governor [Milton], December 17, 1861 [*O.R.A.,* Ser. I, Vol. LIII, Supplement, 200]).

17. Mallory to unknown, from Montgomery, March 22, 1861, *supra cit.,* see note 31, p. 121. Concerning Jackson Morton, cf. *supra,* pp. 37, 48.

There were many, indeed, who felt that he had considerable capacities for the post. It was a minority view that was expressed by a Northern journal a few years later: "Mr. Mallory . . . had been in the habit of *seeing* some ships (especially those of war) at the navy yard, near his residence, and out in the bay; he also had (so it is said) a merchantman's and wrecker's experience for qualifications."[18]

Yet it must be remarked that the duties of administrative head and co-planner of strategy of the Navy Department were different from anything that Mallory had done before. The Confederate Navy Secretary would be called on to display qualities of the highest stamp in the art and science of organization and statesmanship, and in the formulation of high strategy. By 1861, he had acquired no more knowledge and skill in naval affairs than were sufficient to place him in the class of a clever amateur in the field. But he improved rapidly—he had always had a capacity for improving rapidly in any position to which he had been called.

It will be instructive to note, however, that every once in a while, he displayed a superficiality in his knowledge of naval matters. He once declared, for example, without reservation, that the Confederate banded rifles were "of a class never before made." This, as has been remarked by a recent authority, was a rather surprising statement, in view of the widespread use of guns of this type in Europe for several years before 1861.[19] In at least one instance during his congressional career, he had been badly fooled by a crazy scheme for revolutionizing marine engines.[20]

In brief, Stephen Mallory, in 1861, was a capable and earnest small-town official trying with no small degree of confidence to fill a post that a statesman of unique and pre-eminent qualities, with a thorough grasp of naval history and unusual administrative gifts, would have found a fair field for his powers. But he possessed one important quality that sometimes raises the average man to greatness—he was filled with a passion for learning his job. It was thought by some that Mallory was flattered by his appointment, and that he entered on his duties with relish and confidence.[21] More exact, probably, was the opinion of others, that he had not sought the post but,

18. *New York Citizen*, August 10, 1867, *loc. cit.* See also the *St. Augustine Examiner*, March 30, 1861.

19. J. P. Baxter, *Introduction of the Ironclad Warship* (Cambridge, Mass., 1933), 230, n. 2; cf. also Mallory's own statement in *O. R.*, Ser. II, Vol. II, p. 175, in his report of March 29, 1862.

20. Cf. *supra*, p. 133, n. 14.

21. "Rummaging Through Rebeldom: Nineteenth Rummage," *New York Citizen*, August 10, 1867.

once saddled with it, began, somewhat to his own surprise, to enjoy the challenges that it offered.

The local habitation of the Navy Department at Richmond was, in the words of the semi-official directory, on the "2nd story, right hand side," in the Mechanics' Institute, situated on Ninth Street, between Main and Franklin. The Chief Surgeon of the Navy, continues the directory, was to be found "in the 4th story of the Mechanics' Institute, No. 35." Visitors to the department were not to proceed without due observance of protocol. "Persons," warns the directory, "are notified not to enter any of the offices without addressing the messengers. Positively no persons, on or without business, will be received in the offices after 3 o'clock, P.M. Gentlemen will please read the signs on the doors."[22]

The administrative pattern of the department was, in broad outline, as follows.

The Secretary, with two chief aides, constituted the top controlling bureau. Here was the place of origin of general naval strategy, of broad administrative directives, and, often, of specific orders to officers and commanders afloat and ashore. While, theoretically, the President possessed a wide and undefined power to participate in and even to control the decisions of this "admiralty board," he usually refrained, as a matter of actual fact, from so doing. Assisting the Secretary and his two advisers was a clerical force which, in 1862, totaled four clerks and one "messenger."[23]

The more important of Mallory's pair of aides was Ed. Tidball of Winchester, Virginia, a handsome, dapper little robot, seldom guilty of an original thought, but a tireless and utterly reliable weaver of red tape. The other chief adviser was Commodore French Forrest, also of Virginia, a "fine, white-haired old blusterer of the real old-tar school."[24]

Subordinate to this supreme bureau were four operational departments,

22. Charles A. Vanfelson (one of the Navy Department messengers mentioned in this paragraph), *The Little Red Book or Department Directory, for the use of the public in the Confederate States of America* (Richmond: Tyler, Wise, and Allegre, Printers, Enquirer Job Office, 1861), 17-18. Cf. also *An Official Guide of the Confederate Government from 1861 to 1865 at Richmond; Showing the Location of the Public Buildings and Offices of the Confederate, State, and City Government, Residences of the Principal Officers, etc.* (Richmond, n.d.).

23. *Confederate States Navy Register for 1862* (Richmond: Enquirer Book and Job Press, 1862). The annual salaries of the Secretary and his immediate staff were as follows: the Secretary of the Navy, $6000; Tidball, the chief clerk, $2100; the "first clerk," $1500; the next two clerks, $1200 each; the fourth clerk, $1000; the messenger, $500 (*ibid.*).

24. *N. Y. Citizen*, August 10, 1867, *loc. cit.* Concerning the general administration of the Navy Department, see *Journal of Confederate Congress*, Vol. III (Senate), under titles (in index) "Navy of Confederate States" and "Committee on Naval Affairs"; also C. O. Paullin, *Proceedings of the United States Naval Institute*, XXXII-XL (1906-14).

the first of which, in order of importance, was the Office of Orders and Detail.[25] This was primarily a kind of placement and personnel bureau. It kept a careful up-to-the-minute record of the past tours of duty and present stations of all the officers of the navy; it made the routine assignments or re-assignments of officers to posts afloat or ashore; it determined rank and promotions; it handled generally what could be called problems of personnel.[26] It also, on no perceptible logical administrative grounds, managed the supplying of coal to the navy,[27] and supervised purchases of ship furniture;[28] it was, apparently, in charge of the ropewalk at Petersburg;[29] and it directed the recruiting service, and administered all courts martial and courts of inquiry.[30] There was no analogous sub-department in the United States naval organization, for, as is clear from the above description, the Confederate Office of Orders and Detail performed the functions of several bureaus of the older establishment.

Lawrence Rousseau of Louisiana, the oldest of the captains who had resigned from the navy of the United States to cast their lots with the Confederacy, was the first to head this bureau of rather scattered functions. He was in his late sixties, and had been regarded by some as a fit choice for the post of Navy Secretary—"fitter for that than for anything else," in the words of an observer slightly contemptuous both of Rousseau and of the highest Confederate Navy office.[31]

The Office of Orders and Detail kept a firm and assiduous hand on the persons and matters confided to its care. Its personnel register was to show the time that each officer had served, and in what grades, the length of his service in each grade, the station on which the service had been performed, the class of vessel, if any, to which the officer was attached, and the nature of his service.[32]

25. *Regulations for the Navy of the Confederate States* (Richmond: Macfarlane and Fergusson, 1862; Rare Books Division, Library of Congress), 151, hereafter cited as *Confederate Navy Regulations*.

26. *Ibid.*, 151-52.

27. "Report of Office of Orders and Detail," October 21, 1864, in *Report of the Secretary of the Navy, 1864*, 41-42; see also Franklin Buchanan (officer in charge of this office) to Commander John R. Tucker (commanding *Patrick Henry*), February 24, 1862 (*O.R.*, Ser. I, Vol. VI, p. 776).

28. "General Orders and Circulars," 85.

29. "Report of Office of Orders and Detail," *supra cit.*

30. "General Order of July 18, 1863," in "General Orders and Circulars" (Rare Books Division, Library of Congress), 87.

31. *N. Y. Citizen*, August 10, 1867.

32. *Confederate Navy Regulations*, 1862, 151. Original confirmation of naval officers to a specific grade was the privilege of the Congress. This apparently applied even to the appointment of officers of relatively minor commissioned rank. See: *Journal of Confederate*

Whenever it was ordered by the Secretary of the Navy that a vessel be prepared for service, the Office of Orders and Detail was to submit to the Secretary a list of officers for the vessel.[33] Ships having complements of over two hundred persons were to be commanded by captains; to a vessel of not less than seventy-five or more than two hundred complement a commander was to be assigned; all other vessels with crews not exceeding seventy-five persons were to be in charge of lieutenants.[34]

In making assignments the Office of Orders and Detail was supposed to equalize, as much as might be consistent with the public interest, the service of officers on the various stations and in the several classes of vessels.[35] There was to be maintained always an exact record of the services of each officer of the navy. This record should show the officer's applications for service; his assigned reasons for declining any service, if such refusal or refusals had occurred; if he had ever returned from foreign service before the completion of a cruise, his assigned reasons for so doing; if charges had been preferred, or complaints at any time made against him, the disposition made of such charges or complaints, and the results; and "any other facts which will aid the Department in forming a correct opinion of the availability of the officer."[36]

Commanding officers were frequently reminded of their obligation to render to the Office of Orders and Detail periodical reports regarding personnel under their charge. These reports were to be drawn up "in accordance with the prescribed forms to be found in the Appendix under their appropriate heads of punishments, enlistments, desertions, transfers, discharges and deaths."[37] From each commanding officer, afloat or ashore, the office demanded monthly statements of the number of each rating of his petty officers, seamen, second-class firemen, ordinary seamen, coal heavers, landsmen, and boys, with a description of any deficiencies or excesses in

---

*Congress,* I, 394, 407, 792, and II (Senate), 66-69. Also, as evidence of the dominant authority of the Congress with respect to determinations of grade, Secretary of War Benjamin to Major General Benjamin Huger, December 25, 1861: "Congress has passed a law authorizing the President to appoint to temporary rank in the army officers of the navy serving with troops ashore without prejudice to their rank or position in the navy" (*O.R.A.,* Ser. I, Vol. LI, part 2, Supplement, 426).

33. *Ibid.*
34. *Ibid.,* 1.
35. *Confederate Navy Regulations,* 1862, 151, article 2.
36. *Ibid.,* 152.
37. Circular of Office of Orders and Detail (John K. Mitchell, commander in charge), April 21, 1863, in "General Orders and Circulars," in *Register of the Commissioned and Warrant Officers of the Navy of the Confederate States to January 1, 1864* (Rare Books Division, Library of Congress), 85, hereafter cited as *Register of Confederate Navy Officers, 1864.*

the complements of their commands in each grade.[38] "It is important," commanders were warned, "that the returns required should be complete."[39]

Officers proceeding under orders were to certify the day on which they left their residence, from which day their pay would commence, "unless it shall appear that due diligence has not been observed by them in obedience to said orders."[40] Commanding officers were to endorse upon the orders of all officers the day they reported for duty; and, "if there has been any unusual delay in reporting, the facts are also to be stated by the officer receiving the report."[41]

Frequently recurring in Navy Department correspondence are evidences of the alert and meticulous administration of the Office of Orders and Detail. Whether laying down rules for acting midshipmen's examinations, or raising the rank of boatswains, carpenters, sailmakers and gunners of more than five years' service, or issuing directives for recruiting officers,[42] or meeting a request for repairs of a check-valve chest of a war vessel,[43] or determining, in collaboration with the War Department, the relative rankings of army and navy officers and the limits of jurisdiction of army and navy officers when serving together,[44] this very active bureau of the Confederate Navy did its part in maintaining the order and efficiency of the service. Nor were the elementary principles of sound economy neglected. Commanders were exhorted to "avoid all extravagance in the purchase of furniture, and to see to it that no articles be allowed that are not indispensable; all such articles provided for the navy must be plain and of the most economical kind."[45]

In recognition of the value of prudently decentralized administration, a branch of the Office of Orders and Detail was established at Wilmington, for the purpose of assigning pilots to the numerous blockade runners.[46] The move increased considerably the efficiency of that important service,[47]

38. *Ibid.*

39. *Ibid.*

40. *Ibid.*, 83.

41. *Ibid.*

42. *Ibid.*, 82-83.

43. Franklin Buchanan (in charge of Office of Orders and Detail) to Commander John R. Tucker (commanding *Patrick Henry*), February 24, 1862 (*O.R.*, Ser. I, Vol. VI, 776). See also, in *ibid.*, "you are authorized to give the bounty of $50 to all persons, except boys, who will enlist for three years or the war, . . . under the law you refer to."

44. See the memorandum of Buchanan in regard to relative rank and scope of command of army and navy officers when serving together (enclosure in letter from Mallory to Secretary of War, September 26, 1861 [*O.R.A.*, Ser. I, Vol. LI, Part 2, Supplement, 315-16]).

45. "General Orders and Circulars," *supra cit.*, 85.

46. Francis B. Bradlee, *Blockade Running During the Civil War and the Effect of Land and Water Transportation on the Confederacy* (Salem, Mass., 1925), 80.

47. *Ibid.*

although Mallory was criticized for not officially incorporating these pilots into the navy.[48]

The size of the establishment directed by the Office of Orders and Detail was not very large. The number of commissioned and warrant officers in the Confederate Navy totaled, in late 1864, a little less than seven hundred.[49] The total number of enlisted men at any given time was probably less than four thousand.[50] The four principal commerce-destroying cruisers were manned chiefly by foreign sailors.[51] The navy, at the zenith of its strength, had only a half dozen small squadrons, a dozen stations, and about forty vessels of all grades, from the powerful, swift *Alabama* to the little *Drewry* which ran between Richmond and the ironclad fleet off Dutch Gap.[52]

Next—or perhaps equal—in importance among the Navy Department bureaus was the Office of Ordnance and Hydrography. Its main work was the manufacture, purchase, and distribution of ordnance and munitions for the navy; but it took care also of all matters relating to nautical instruments, charts, maps, etc., as well as the construction and maintenance of docks and navy yards.[53] It had control of a procedure that was to be of high importance in the Confederate war tactics: the periodical exchange of guns between army and navy units.[54] It kept a careful history of every gun in the naval service, and for this purpose every commander was obliged to send to the Ordnance Office periodical accounts of the number of times his guns were fired, the amounts of the charges at each firing, the behavior of the gun, and other relevant details.[55]

48. *Ibid.*, 37; cf. also William H. Parker, *Recollections of a Naval Officer, 1841-1865* (New York, 1883), 284-85.

49. Register of *Confederate Navy Officers, 1864.* Cf. also: *New York Citizen,* August 10, 1867.

50. Soley, "The Union and Confederate Navies," in *Battles and Leaders of the Civil War,* Vol. I, part 2, p. 631. Cf. also S. S. Lee (Captain in charge of Office of Orders and Detail) to Mallory, October 21, 1864 (Report of the Office), in *Register of Confederate Navy Officers, 1864,* 41.

51. *Ibid.*

52. *New York Citizen,* August 10, 1867, *loc. cit.* Cf. also the *Confederate States Navy Register for 1862.*

53. *Confederate Navy Regulations,* 1862, 180; Vanfelson, *op. cit.,* under "Office of Ordnance and Hydrography"; "Report of Office of Ordnance and Hydrography," Nov. 4, 1864, in *Report of the Secretary of the Navy, 1864,* 43-46.

54. See Commander Brooke to Flag Officer W. W. Hunter, September 4, 1863: ". . . You are authorized to loan General Mercer, for the defense of Savannah, four guns of the *Georgia's* armament. It is to be distinctly understood, however, that these guns are to be returned when required for naval purposes. Please report to this office the calibre, numbers, and distinguishing marks on each gun loaned, and request General Mercer to cause a record to be kept of the number of discharges which may be made from each gun." (*O.R.,* Ser. I, Vol. XIV, p. 766).

55. *Ibid.*

At the head of this bureau was Commander John M. Brooke, one of the outstanding ordnance officers of American naval history. A veteran of eighteen years' service in the United States Navy, he was the inventor of the famous Brooke rifle, and had also prepared a deep-sea sounding chart of high importance. He was described as a "very dark looking man, who did not impress a stranger with being as great a genius as he really was."[56] The operations of the Office of Ordnance and Hydrography will be described in greater detail as this story progresses.

A third bureau of the Navy Department was the Office of Provisions and Clothing. Its main functions were to provide food, clothing, and "small stores" for all naval personnel. Its chief was a superannuated and none-too-brilliant veteran of forty-four years' service in the old navy—"old tottering John De Bree."[57] Supplies were sent from the bureau to ships or shore stations in answer to requisitions made by the local officers of supply (called paymasters or assistant paymasters), subject to the approval of the commanding officer of the vessel or station.[58]

The paymasters and assistant paymasters were both officers of the vessel or station to which they were attached and, at the same time, the real administrators of the Office of Provisions and Clothing.[59] They were under the orders of both the commander of their vessel or shore station, and the chief of the Office of Provisions and Clothing. However, since the latter bureau, a part of the Navy Department, outranked in authority even the highest local commander, and since the paymaster was under one aspect the bureau's agent, there was the possibility that the paymaster, by order of the bureau, might sometimes reject or modify a requisition made by the local commander. This subtle, if not somewhat confused, check-and-balance arrangement proved, in the main, to be in the interests of efficiency and economy, and was usually satisfactory to all concerned.

Care was taken to maintain the purity of the administrators of the Office of Provisions and Clothing. All persons employed in the navy, or for naval purposes, were strictly prohibited from having any interest in purchases or contracts for supplies of any kind for the navy. Neither could they legiti-

---

56. *N. Y. Citizen*, August 10, 1867, *loc. cit.* Cf. also *Ordnance Instructions for the Confederate States Navy relating to the Preparation of Vessels of War for Battle, to the Duties of Officers and Others when at Quarters, to Ordnance and Ordnance Stores, and to Gunnery* (3rd ed.; published by order of the [Confederate] Navy Dept.: London, 1864; Rare Books Division, Library of Congress).

57. *N. Y. Citizen*, August 10, 1867, *loc. cit.*

58. *Confederate Navy Regulations*, 1862, sub "Paymaster"; also, *ibid.*, 138.

59. In 1862 there were eleven paymasters, and fourteen assistant paymasters (*Confederate States Navy Register, 1862*).

mately "receive any emolument or gratuity of any kind from any contractor or other person furnishing supplies, either directly or indirectly, nor act as agent or attorney for any contractor on account of purchases, contracts, or works for the navy."[60] There is evidence, indeed, that the Navy Department as a whole was remarkably free from corruption. "It is only right," declared an outspoken critic of many features of the Confederate Government, "to add a word or two in regard to the Navy Department, which cannot be said to the credit of any other branch of the Government. There was never any occasion to dismiss any of its immediate officials. Not one of them was ever, during the war, found derelict in duty or a defaulter to the amount of a dollar."[61]

One of the early acts of the Confederate naval authorities was to repromulgate the United States Navy rule of 1800 regarding religious worship and good moral behavior on board ships. Commanders of vessels were strictly enjoined to "show in themselves a good example of virtue, honor, patriotism, and subordination, and be vigilant in inspecting the conduct of all such as are placed under their command, and to guard against and suppress all dissolute and immoral practices, and to correct all such as are guilty of them. . . ."[62] The commanders of all ships having chaplains on board "shall take care that Divine service be performed in a solemn, orderly, and reverent manner, twice a day and a sermon preached on Sunday," barring accidents or bad weather; and they were to "cause all, or as many of the ship's company as can be spared from duty, to attend at every performance of the worship of Almighty God."[63]

Officers and seamen alike were expected to live up to the canons of sound morality. Several reminders of this obligation were found in the navy rules, for example, the blunt declaration that ". . . if any person when brought on board [as a recruit] shall be so much intoxicated as to require restraint, he shall not be received until he becomes sober";[64] or the injunction that "no money shall be paid to any person in debt to the Confederate States. . . ."[65]

The other important bureau of the Navy Department was the Office of

60. *Confederate Navy Regulations*, 14-15.

61. *N. Y. Citizen*, August 10, 1867, *loc. cit.*

62. "An Act for the better government of the United States Navy," approved April 23, 1800, and repromulgated for the C. S. Navy in "General Orders and Circulars," 63.

63. *Ibid.*

64. *Confederate Navy Regulations*, 165.

65. *Ibid.*, 137. To this statement was added, "except for stopped spirits or rations," i.e., in the event of a stoppage of the daily ration of spirits a fixed sum of money was to be paid to each seaman as a compensation (*ibid.*, 136-37).

Medicine and Surgery, presided over by Dr. W. A. W. Spotswood, Virginia-born but a Floridian by adoption, a "brawny, gray-haired six-footer, rough and ready in ways and looks, but a gentle-hearted man."[66] He had seen twenty-five years' service in the United States Navy, thirteen of them at sea, and, until the end of the war, he administered his sub-department with fidelity and, for the most part, with efficiency. Under Spotswood were, in 1862, twenty-two surgeons, fifteen assistant surgeons, and nine "assistant surgeons for the war."[67] There were, besides the bureau's headquarters and its largest hospital at Richmond, medical stations and hospitals at Charleston, Wilmington, Savannah, and Mobile, a medical station (though not a hospital properly so called) at Selma, Alabama, and one in Florida. These medical centers were supplied directly from bureau headquarters with "medicines, medical stores, surgical instruments and appliances, hospital stores and furniture."[68] Some part of the required medicines and drugs were manufactured at Richmond by the bureau's three apothecaries and chemists, and part was smuggled in through the blockade.[69]

It is reasonable to suppose that the following tribute paid to the medical department of the Confederate army, by a Southern critic of no friendly bias toward the government, could be substantially applied to the naval medical service as well: ". . . The medical section of the War Department was not ill managed. At no time was the hygene [*sic*] of the Southern army inferior to that of the Northern, and at no time were there as many surgical incapables in the Confederate as in the Federal service,—allowing, of course, for the rule of proportion as to the bulk of both armies. Besides, the hospital system in the South, everything considered, was quite as perfect as that at the North. The rates of mortality in Dixie's forces will compare favorably with those in the sick lists of 'Yankland's' armies. There was always a dearth of medical supplies. . . .[70] There was a scarcity of surgical instruments, . . . of suitable stimulants . . . and a proper nutriment. Nevertheless, the Medical Bureau of the War Department surmounted these difficulties, and saved more lives and limbs in proportion, than did that of the North."[71]

66. *N. Y. Citizen,* August 10, 1867, *loc. cit.*

67. *Confederate States Navy Register, 1862.*

68. "Medical Purveyor's Department, C. S. N., Richmond, Nov. 1, 1864: Annual Report of Receipts and Expenditures . . . from October 1863 to October 1864," in "Report of Office of Medicine and Surgery, Nov. 1, 1864," in *Report of the Secretary of the Navy, 1864.*

69. *Ibid.*

70. This statement seems to be contradicted by the facts listed in the "Report of the Office of Medicine and Surgery, 1864," *supra cit.*

71. *N. Y. Citizen,* July 20, 1867, "Sixteenth Rummage."

A partial index of the efficiency of the Confederate naval hospitals may be had in the reports of these institutions with regard to admissions, discharges, and deaths. From October, 1863, to October, 1864, the Richmond hospital discharged 645 out of 842 admitted, and recorded 21 deaths; Charleston, out of 247 admitted, discharged 154 and recorded 18 deaths; Wilmington out of 135 admitted, discharged 90 and recorded 3 deaths; Savannah out of 394 admitted, discharged 270 and recorded 15 deaths; Mobile out of 372 admitted, discharged 251 and had 12 deaths.[72]

Medical methods in the early sixties were, of course, quite different from modern techniques, and some of the surgical instruments and other "hospital utensils" provided by the Confederate medical bureau would scarcely be found today. The dietary for the naval hospitals included such substantial items as beef, mutton, potatoes, barley, hominy, and veal, fish, and oysters.[73] An interesting example of an early theory of preventive medicine is Dr. Spotswood's admonition that "Attacks of fever will always occur, and there are no means of prevention except through the medium of strict attention, on the part of officers, to the comfort of the crews in regard to clothing, food, and regimen, that will strengthen and fortify the system against attacks. I would therefore suggest the issuing of a spirit ration, and allowing to the crews their breakfast with hot coffee, at an early hour every morning, before proceeding to scouring the decks, as a means of counteracting the effects of the damp and chilling draughts so prevalent on all fresh water courses and malarial regions at the dawn of day."[74]

Besides these four bureaus, there were a few specific services of the Navy Department which existed as semiautonomous administrative units. An example of such was the department of steam engineering, under the con-

72. "Abstract from the quarterly reports of sick at the hospitals on the different Stations ... from the 1st of October 1863 to the 1st of October 1864," in *Report of the Secretary of the Navy, 1864.*

73. *Instructions for the Guidance of the Medical Officers of the Navy of the Confederate States* (Richmond, 1864; Rare Books Division, Library of Congress). In this manual, cf. especially "Allowance Table" (Form A), 8-13; "Nomenclature of Diseases" (Form L), 24-26; "Dietary for the C. S. Naval Hospitals," 33.

74. "Report of Office of Medicine and Surgery," November 1, 1864, in *Report of the Secretary of the Navy, 1864.* Cf. Secretary Benjamin's vigorous protest against the practice of allowing spirits to some of the younger men of the army: "The deleterious effects of a ration of spirits, issued regularly to our volunteers, and many of whom are very young and totally unaccustomed to the use of liquor would in our opinion be very great." The deficiency in the coffee ration, he continued, might be partly supplied by tobacco, which "would go far to satisfying a large majority of the troops, and your experience will suggest to you other articles. But I have an invincible objection to issuing whiskey as proposed" (Meade, *op. cit.,* 193, based on War Department Letter-book, October 28, 1861, Benjamin to Col. Northrop, National Archives, Washington, D. C.).

trol of chief engineer William P. Williamson, who was styled engineer-in-chief of the navy.[75] The naval constructor, J. L. Porter, with his two assistants, seems to have been practically a semi-department in himself.[76] The Torpedo Bureau, established in 1862, became, because of its constantly growing importance, actually a fifth administrative department of the navy, equal in importance to any of the others. The Marine Corps was really a field unit, designed for a specialized combat service in cooperation with the navy, and it was therefore as a matter of convenience placed under the Navy Secretary's authority. It was allowed by law eight captains and twenty-nine lieutenants, but only nineteen of the latter were ever appointed. "Of these," said a severe critic of the Confederate government, "not one half were needed in that service."[77]

The funds required for inaugurating the activities of the Navy Department were appropriated by the Confederate Congress.[78] It is worth noting that these and all subsequent grants of money were made not directly to the Navy Department but to the Treasury, on which the Secretary of the Navy was obliged to draw.[79] This somewhat indirect method of financing his operations was frequently embarrassing to Mallory.

The total expenditures of the Confederate government from February, 1861, to August, 1862, were $347,272,958.58. Of this sum the Navy Department used only $14,605,777.86.[80] The Navy Department received less appropriation early in March, 1861, than any other department except the "executive mansion."[81]

From the outset of the war, the basically weak financial condition of the Confederate government was a serious handicap to the administrators of the Navy Department. It must be remembered that there were, at this time, no capitalists or monied men of any importance in the South.[82] The wealth of the Confederacy was frozen in land, slaves, and cotton, and was

75. C. S. Navy Register, 1862, 5.

76. Ibid., 10.

77. N. Y. Citizen, August 10, 1867, loc. cit.

78. See bill authorizing two additional clerks and a draftsman for Navy Department, passed January 14, 1862 (Journal of Confederate Congress, I, 547, 550, 606, 670).

79. See Mallory to Secretary of Treasury Memminger, December 26, 1861, transmitting Navy Department's estimate of amounts required for pay of additional seamen authorized by Act of Congress approved December 10, 1861, and for additional officers authorized by Act of December 24, 1861 (Rare Books Division, Library of Congress). See also Mallory to Memminger, November 26, 1864 (Rare Books Division, Library of Congress).

80. J. T. Scharf, History of the Confederate States Navy (New York, 1887), 32.

81. Ibid., 32, note 1.

82. W. J. Tenney (editor of the American Annual Cyclopedia), The Military and Naval History of the Rebellion in the United States (New York, 1865), 486-88.

not in the fluid and accessible form of currency.[83] The dollars the government could raise by taxation were definitely and fatally limited in amount. The proposal was made that the considerable supplies of cotton in private Southern hands should be bought or borrowed by the government and used as payment for the large purchases of ships, munitions, and other supplies that had to be made abroad. This plan was, to an extent, put in force, under considerable difficulties and disappointments.[84]

In anticipation, this much should be said: during the last eighteen months of the war, the financial condition of the Navy Department was remarkably sound. "Toward the end of the war—for the last year or two," said an apparently unbiased observer, "no Department in Dixie's government had anything in the way of credit that approached the credit and the means of meeting it which the Navy Department possessed. Time and again both the Treasury and War Departments borrowed hundreds of thousands from it."[85] Shortly before the final collapse of the Confederacy, Frazer, Trenholm,[86] and Company transferred, by order, to Captain Bulloch, the Confederate Navy's financial agent in Europe, about 250,000 pounds sterling. This was in addition to what was elsewhere to his credit, and apart from the money paid by the French government on account of the ironclads.[87]

One of the first problems to be solved by the new Navy Secretary was that of disposing of the plethora of officers who had flocked to the Confederate naval headquarters. In March, 1861, the Confederate Navy Department possessed twelve small ships and approximately two hundred officers of all ranks from commodore to chief gunner. Obviously the supply of these commissioned men was out of all proportion to the demand.

How was the Secretary to place to their own satisfaction the ten former United States commodores and captains, the twenty or so ex-commanders, the fifty or so ex-lieutenants, and the fifty or so of all other grades in "the line"? How was he to satisfy the thirty-odd former United States surgeons and assistant surgeons, as well as the many rival and politically influential

83. *Ibid.*

84. Walter Geer, *Campaigns of the Civil War* (New York, 1926), 446-47, and Appendix I, 460-61; Samuel B. Thompson, *Confederate Purchasing Operations Abroad* (Chapel Hill, N. C., 1935), 51-53, 82-102; Edward Channing, *A History of the United States* (6 vols.; New York, 1927-30), V, 332-42; *O.R.*, Ser. II, Vol. III, pp. 531-32.

85. *New York Citizen*, August 17, 1867, "Twentieth Rummage."

86. George A. Trenholm, of this firm, was Secretary of the Treasury of the Confederacy from July, 1864, to the end of the war.

87. *New York Citizen*, August 17, 1867, *loc. cit.*

applicants from civil life for such duty? How was he to dispose of the
half dozen former United States pursers, and the crowd of eager claimants
for these posts who came backed by the urgent entreaties of congressmen?
All of these, incidentally, were seeking assignments with ranks as high at
least as those they had held in the old service.[88]

Furthermore, the abilities and general fitness of many of these officers
were of very doubtful quality. It may have been uncharitable to term them
"old fogies," but undoubtedly there were many who, as Semmes said, had
come to Montgomery "bringing with them nothing but their patriotism and
their gray hairs."[89] There was a further circumstance which added to the
Navy Secretary's embarrassment: many of the older among these officers had
been, during the past five years, unceremoniously cashiered by Mallory's
Naval Retiring Board. Among the earliest arrivals at Montgomery, for
example, was Catesby ap R. Jones, dropped onto the retired list by the Board
in 1855. Some of these men it would be necessary to use in important
combat posts. Did the Secretary's former connection with the Retiring
Board reduce, to any degree, his influence with these officers with whom he
must now work so closely and harmoniously, for the success of the Confederate naval effort?[90]

It would seem that Mallory handled this difficult personnel problem with
considerable success. It was in such cases as these that his natural bon-
homie and cheery guilelessness of manner operated smoothly to attain his
ends. Apparently he was able, at least in most instances, to place the applicants at the proper post—or, what was more difficult, on the most convenient shelf—with a minimum of friction. He seems to have had a knack
of delivering a disagreeable order wrapped up in a soothing friendly conversation, laced with a few witticisms which, if they were sometimes obvious or awkward, at least served to soften refusals that might otherwise
have been sources of resentment.

It took two years for Mallory to solve fully the problem of rank and
promotion. In handling the problem, he kept steadily before him the prin-

88. *New York Citizen*, August 10, 1867, *loc. cit.* Cf. also Scharf, *op. cit.*, 33.

89. Semmes, *op. cit.*, 368.

90. Note the significant amendment proposed by Senator Ochiltree to the act fixing the size
of the navy's officer personnel: "No officers appointed under the provisions of this act shall
be finally dismissed from the service except upon the finding of a court martial or court of
inquiry after charges duly preferred. And when charges shall be preferred against an officer
he shall be furnished with a copy of the same, and shall have the right to appear before the
court martial or court of inquiry to answer the same, either by himself or by counsel" (*Journal of Confederate Congress*, I, 125, March 11, 1861).

ciples which he had advocated in the United States Senate during the era of the Naval Reform Acts.

His first move was to permit the officers to retain in the Confederate Navy the rank which they had held in the old service. This was mainly a bow to the exigencies of morale. His next step, embodied in an act of Congress of April 21, 1862, was to make promotion dependent solely on "gallant or meritorious conduct during the war." This was a shrewd means of pushing ahead the really competent officers, without hurting too much the sensibilities of the earnest but ineffectual graybeards. The Secretary agreed fully with the anonymous observer who held that a naval war could not be won on arthritis. The policy was further implemented by the Act of May, 1863, which established the "Provisional Confederate Navy," as distinct from the "Regular Navy." The former was officered by the younger and more active men who, by their transfer to the new division of the service, were awarded increased rank. The regular navy became thus a kind of retired list, but the feelings of the older officers were saved by the fact that they were not superseded by their juniors on the same list.[91]

As the war progressed, however, this double classification of naval personnel evoked some criticism which deserves attention. After more than a year's trial of the system, the chief of the Office of Orders and Detail complained that he had experienced some difficulty and confusion in the administration of the affairs of his bureau, because of the "two distinct organizations of the navy." He felt that the classification of officers under the headings of regular and provisional navies, with these officers' duties being confined strictly to their respective spheres, had operated to the prejudice of the service. The law of the provisional navy prevented officers of the regular navy from serving afloat unless they were transferred to the former organization by appointment. This arrangement militated, in some instances, against the prompt assignment of officers to vacant positions, since the number eligible for duty afloat was insufficient to meet the demands of the service, and those attached to the regular navy could not be employed without violating the law which created the new branch of the service. It might be advisable, thought the chief of the Office of Orders and Detail, to transfer the whole personnel of the navy to the provisional organization.[92]

The rule was rigidly followed, at least in the early period of the war, that no naval appointments would be made from civil life while resigned

91. Scharf, *op. cit.*, 27-52.

92. S. S. Lee (captain, in charge of Office of Orders and Detail) to Mallory, September 21, 1864, in *Report of Secretary of the Navy, 1864.*

officers of the old navy were available. "The number of Surgeons and Assistant Surgeons," wrote the Secretary, "is limited by law to five each, and appointments thus far have been confined to Officers of these grades who resigned from the U. S. Navy in consequence of the secession of the Confederate States."[93] As late as June, 1864, Mallory could say: "We are not making appointments of master's mates outside of those already in the [old] naval service."[94]

The Secretary faced another puzzle which, under other political circumstances, he would have been spared: the problem of centralizing at Montgomery, and later at Richmond, the control and administration of all the naval resources and naval operations of the Confederacy. In keeping with characteristic Southern political localism, most of the states boasted navies of their own. While, by the act of the Confederate Congress of March 15, 1861, these navies, together with all United States government ship yards, arsenals, and so forth, were to be handed over to the Confederate government, yet there was bound to be some difficulty in submitting the local units to the full control of the Davis administration. For example, although Virginia in April, 1861, agreed to place her naval operations under the "chief control and direction of the President of the Confederate States," yet, as late as June, 1861, Captain W. F. Lynch, of the Virginia navy, seems to have acted in entire independence of the Navy Department at Richmond.[95]

There was not much that Mallory could do about this situation. As the war progressed, the state navies, without completely losing their identity, merged themselves with the "provisional" navy; but it is worth asking to what extent, during the first two or three months of 1861, before the amalgamation had been completed, the consequent looseness in the general organizational arrangement retarded the Secretary's program.

Every other problem, however, paled into insignificance before that of securing ships of war. Concerning this all-important matter there were several questions that had to be answered by the Secretary.

If the Department was to construct its own ships, many obstacles were in the way. The deficiencies of the Confederacy in the matter of ship-

93. Mallory to H. [?] T. Elliot and Wm. S. Wilson, from Montgomery, April 22, 1861 (F. J. Dreer Collection, Pennsylvania Historical Society, Philadelphia).

94. Mallory to Hon. James M. Baker, from Richmond, June 2, 1864 (*ibid.*). Baker was a Senator from Florida in the first and second Confederate Congresses.

95. W. F. Lynch to Captain Samuel Barron, June 2, 1861, in Scharf, *op. cit.,* 96. The fall of Hatteras Inlet was ascribed, by the *Charleston Tri-Weekly Courier,* to the tardiness of North Carolina in turning over to the Confederate government the control of the state defenses (September 7, 1861).

building facilities were notorious. Semmes has described how the South had neither shipyards (save Norfolk, which was soon lost, and Pensacola, which was inadequate and also, finally, captured) nor workshops, steam mills or foundries, except on the most limited scale; while all her ports would be as good as hermetically sealed so far as the introduction of the heavy materials essential for the construction of ships was concerned. There was not, in the whole Confederacy, the means of turning out a complete steam engine of a size suitable for ships. The timber for the potential Confederate ships still stood in the forests; the iron required was still in the mines, and there were no smelters in sufficient number; the hemp required for ship ropes had actually to be grown and reaped, and ropewalks had to be built. There was not a rolling mill capable of turning out a two-and-a-half inch plate. There was not a sufficient force of skilled mechanics.[96]

It seemed clear, therefore, that the Confederate Navy must come into existence largely through the purchase of already completed ships or by means of ship construction instituted abroad. The most likely places for making such purchases or for having ships built were in England and France.[97] It was also possible, at least in the early months of the war, to pick up some vessels from Northern dealers whose devotion to the Union had not altogether submerged their business sense.

In this matter the Confederate government was active in several directions at once. In May, James Bulloch and James H. North were sent to England on a buying mission.[98] They were to try to secure ironclads, and, if possible, the great French ironclad *Gloire*. Before the end of March, Confederate agents had been despatched for the same general purpose to New York, Philadelphia, Baltimore, and Canadian points.

96. Scharf, *op. cit.*, 30-32; Semmes, *op. cit.*, 83. Cf. also *O.R.*, Ser. II, Vol. II, 149-54; and *Report from the Joint Select Committee to investigate the management of the Navy Department*, February 17, 1864 (Rare Books Division, Library of Congress). Cf. also the testimony of James R. Soley: "The South entered upon the war without any naval preparation, and with very limited resources by which its deficiencies could be properly supplied. Indeed, it would hardly be possible to imagine a great maritime country more destitute of the means for carrying on a naval war than the Confederate States in 1861. No naval vessels, properly speaking, came into their possession, except the *Fulton*, an old side-wheeler built in 1837, and at this time laid up at Pensacola, and the sunken and half-destroyed hulks at Norfolk, of which only one, the *Merrimac*, could be made available for service" (Soley), *op. cit.*, p. 624. Says Scharf, *op. cit.*, 46: "All the labor or materials requisite to complete and equip a war-vessel could not be commanded at any one point of the Confederacy."

97. S. B. Thompson, *op. cit.*, 7; cf. also Mallory to Bulloch, May 9, 1861 (*O.R.*, Ser. II, Vol. II. pp. 64-65).

98. For details of Bulloch's first interview with Mallory, cf. Bulloch, *The Secret Service of the Confederate States in Europe* (2 vols.; New York, 1884), I, 41-48; also Herbert H. Todd's pamphlet, *The Building of the Confederate States Navy in Europe* (private edition distributed by the Joint University Libraries; Nashville, Tenn., 1941).

Nevertheless, Mallory could not trust solely to the method of purchase from outside the Confederacy nor to the method of construction abroad. Despite all the deficiencies of the South in shipbuilding facilities, part of the Confederate navy had to be built at home. The necessity was met decisively, and without delay.

Between June, 1861, and December, 1862, the Navy Department closed thirty-two contracts for the construction of forty gunboats, floating batteries, and vessels of war, with firms or individuals at various points of the Confederacy. In addition, the Department had several vessels (exclusive of those that were being built abroad) in process of construction under the direction of its own officers.[99] For the completion and servicing of this fleet there had been erected, by the mid-point of the war, a powder mill capable of supplying all the powder required by the navy, a ropewalk, two engine-boiler and machine shops, five ordnance workshops, and shipyards to the number of eighteen.[100] By the end of 1863 the Department had in operation also a grist mill at Albany, Georgia,[101] several iron furnaces and rolling mills, and several nitre works.[102]

In some quarters the government was severely criticized for not employing a ship-purchasing method which, it was alleged, would have enabled the Confederacy to secure a much larger fleet than was ever in fact acquired. An appropriation of ten million dollars in bonds invested in cotton, it was claimed, would have made it possible for the government to obtain by purchase a sufficient number of first-class steamers for breaking the blockade. Such a proposition, in fact, was actually made to the Confederates by the East India Company, which had for sale a fleet of ten swift and stout steamers, built for armament and capable of long voyages. At the small cost of ten million dollars, covered by bonds for forty thousand bales of cotton, these ships, it was said, could have been equipped, manned, armed, and placed in American waters within six months after the formation of

99. Scharf, *op. cit.*, 44. Note the following testimony from a Northern historian: "They [the South] certainly far surpassed us . . . in the force, rapidity, and skill of the early operations and dispositions of the war" (James M. Hoppin, *Life of Andrew Hull Foote, Rear Admiral United States Navy* [New York, 1874] 169. Concerning the early commencement of the building of ironclads by the South on the Mississippi and the armoring of river steamers, see *ibid.*, 170.

100. Scharf, *op. cit.*, 46-47.

101. Message of President Davis to House of Representatives, January 4, 1865, enclosing letter of Mallory to the President, dated December 21, 1864 (Rare Books Division, Library of Congress).

102. Colonel I. M. St. John, chief of Bureau of Nitre and Mining, to Secretary of War Seddon, October 1, 1864 (*O.R.A.*, Ser. IV, Vol. III, pp. 695-702).

the Confederacy. The cotton crop of 1860 was good, and there were many planters who wished to cooperate with just such a project.[103]

The feasibility of this plan has, however, been vigorously questioned. It is not clear, says Schwab, where the government could have found ships to carry the cotton to Europe before the Federal fleet closed the Southern ports, nor is it likely that the Treasury Department could have obtained at such short notice the means with which to buy the cotton from the planters. "The Confederate Government," concludes this author, "could never have entered into such a gigantic scheme."[104] There are those who still believe, on the other hand, that the method might have been successfully applied.[105] In any case, the responsibility for accepting or rejecting the plan was not mainly Mallory's.

The soundest quality of the Confederate shipbuilding program was, as is well known, the emphasis that was placed on the construction or purchase of ironclads. In a report to Congress on May 8, 1861, Secretary Mallory had stated his intentions in this regard. The inequality between the batteries of ships and guns placed in regular or temporary military works on land, he declared, had frequently been demonstrated and long since acknowledged; and the leading military and naval minds of England and France had during the past few years been actively employed in the effort to establish an equation of strength between guns and forts. As a means to this end the foreign experts were trying to evolve a type of ironclad vessel that would withstand the gunfire of the most powerful shore battery. Mallory regarded the possession of a ship of this kind a matter of the first necessity for the Confederacy. Such a vessel, he felt, could, at the moment,

103. Alfred Roman, *The Military Operations of General Beauregard in the War between the States, 1861-1865* (2 vols; New York, 1884), II, 419-20. Cf. also *ibid.*, 423-24; Hamilton Basso, *Beauregard, The Great Creole,* New York, 1933, 104-5; Meade, *op. cit.*, 166; W. E. Dodd, *Jefferson Davis* (Philadelphia, 1907), 321.

104. John C. Schwab, *The Confederate States of America, 1861-1865: A Financial and Industrial History of the South during the Civil War* (New York, 1901, 233-34. Cf. Memminger's very complete description of the unworkableness of the plan, in Henry D. Capers, *The Life and Times of C. G. Memminger* (Richmond, 1893), 348-51, 352-55, 356-57. Cf. also Schwab's concurrence with Memminger's arguments: "His [Memminger's] arguments against the practicability of either [the government's] purchasing the entire cotton crop or making advances on a large part of it were convincing. Such a scheme involved the issue of from 100 to 175 millions in additional Treasury notes, and would wreck the government's finances by destroying its credit at the outset of what promised to be a gigantic war. The value of its currency would be doomed, and the government would be in no way benefited by holding the planter's note or his cotton, neither of which the government wanted" (Schwab, *op. cit.*, 16).

105. Cf., for instance, Bradlee, *op. cit.*, 7-8: He thinks that the plan could have been achieved in the early days of the war.

traverse the whole coast of the United States, prevent all blockades, and encounter with a fair prospect of success the entire Federal navy.[106]

The Secretary then laid down his master principle of strategy, in its relation to shipbuilding. If, he said, to cope with the enemy upon the sea we follow their example and build wooden ships, we shall be forced to build several at one time, for one or two of such wooden vessels would fall an easy prey to the enemy's comparatively numerous steam frigates. But inequality of numbers might be compensated for by invulnerability; therefore not only economy but strategic principle, as well, dictated the wisdom and expediency of fighting with iron against wood. Naval engagements between wooden frigates as they were then built and armed, he felt, were obsolete efforts, simply contests "in which the question, not of victory, but of who should go to the bottom of the sea first, [was] to be solved." He asked the Naval Affairs Committee for authorization to begin at once the construction of ironclad vessels.[107]

Early in the spring of 1861, discussions and experiments were instituted by the Navy Department to determine how floating batteries and naval rams could be best constructed and protected by iron plates. Mallory, while not neglecting the building of vessels of other types, kept insisting that he would pin his faith on a few powerful ironclads. He termed them, with some inaccuracy, a "class of vessels hitherto unknown to naval services."[108] This was indeed an application of the principle he had so often advocated in the Federal Congress: in constructing ships of war we must constantly keep in mind the qualities of the vessels they will be called upon to encounter. Referring, no doubt, to his years of experience as head of the United States Naval Affairs Committee of the Senate, he remarked that "the speed and power of the ships of the United States are definitely known."[109]

Mallory's keen realization of the utility of ironclads and his promptness in beginning to build them is perhaps his chief claim to praise. His farsightedness and energy in the matter stand out more clearly when one considers the quite different attitude of the Federal Navy Department with respect to the new type of vessel.

Admiral David D. Porter, of the United States Navy, asserts that at first

106. *Investigation of the Navy Department. Report of Evidence Taken Before a Joint Special Committee of Both Houses of the Confederate Congress to Investigate the Affairs of the Navy Department* (O.R., Ser. II, Vol. I, p. 742). Cf. also O.R., Ser. II, Vol. I, pp. 740-43; *Report of Secretary of Navy to Congress, July 18, 1861.*

107. *Ibid.,* p. 742.     108. *Ibid.,* II, 51.

109. *Ibid.* Cf. also Jefferson Davis, *The Rise and Fall of the Confederate Government,* II, 194-95.

neither the Federal Navy Department nor its ship constructors perceived the importance of ironclad vessels. When, to meet the threat of the reconstructed *Merrimac,* they began to build the *Monitor,* they still felt extremely doubtful of the worth of the new experiment.[110] The chief constructor of the Federal Navy Department, John Lenthall, at first condemned the *Monitor in toto,* and he was considered at that time, according to Porter, the ablest naval architect in any country.[111]

It is instructive to compare with Mallory's report of May 8, 1861, the statement on the same topic made by Gideon Welles almost two months later. In what Professor Soley calls "somewhat ponderous observations,"[112] the Federal Navy Secretary asked for nothing more than the creation of a board to inquire into the wisdom of building ironclads. It would be for Congress to decide whether, on a favorable report by this board, they would order one or more ironclad steamers.[113]

As a result of this recommendation, which, as Soley remarks, was hardly such as the urgency of the matter demanded,[114] the suggested board of inquiry was appointed a whole month later.[115] (Mallory had, without waiting for an appropriation, approved the plans for the *Virginia* or *Merrimac* on July 11.)[116] On September 18, 1861, more than two months after Mallory had approved the specific plans for the *Virginia,* and about four months after Mallory had sent Bulloch and North to Europe to buy ironclads, the board made its report.

Opinions differed among naval and scientific men, the officers declared, as to the wisdom of adopting iron armature for ships of war. (Mallory had asserted, four months before, that "the leading military and naval minds of England and France had during the past few years been actively employed in the effort . . . to evolve a type of ironclad vessel that would withstand the gunfire of the most powerful shore battery.")[117]

For coast and harbor defense, continued the board rather guardedly, ironclads were certainly formidable adjuncts to fortifications on land; but as cruising vessels their utility and the likelihood of their adoption by the world's navies was open to serious doubt. ("I consider," Mallory had declared four months before, "the possession of a ship of this kind a matter

110. Adm. David D. Porter, *The Naval History of the Civil War* (New York, 1886), 357.
111. *Ibid.,* 358.                          112. Soley, *op. cit.,* 616-17.
113. *Ibid.*                                114. *Ibid.,* 616.
115. *Ibid.*
116. William C. Church, *The Life of John Ericsson* (New York, 1911), I, 245-46.
117. *Report of the Secretary of the Navy to Congress, May 8, 1861.*

of the first necessity for the Confederacy.")[118] But, as long as other nations were endeavoring to perfect such vessels, the United States must not be behind in the race. However, said the board, as a parting shot, it should be remembered that no ship or floating battery, no matter how heavily plated, could cope successfully with a properly constructed fortification of masonry.[119]

In transmitting to Congress this combination of bad prophecy and decidedly qualified endorsement, the Secretary of the Federal Navy continued his "perfunctory" attitude in the matter of ironclads.[120] (Mallory, on the other hand, had had his ironclad building program actually under way as early as the preceding March.)

In planning the broad lines of Confederate naval strategy Mallory had, in some respects, no choice, while, in other respects he could select from alternative policies.

In the first place, it was the inescapable duty of the Confederate Navy to defend—sometimes in cooperation with the army and sometimes unaided —the whole coastline of the Southern states, including all important harbors, bays, inlets, and the inland rivers, the most important of which was, of course, the Mississippi. Protection of all these points was vital. It could be best effected, Mallory correctly saw, by means of steam gunboats of light draft, similar vessels of larger size and consequent greater gun power, and large ironclads such as the two great ships that were being built at New Orleans. In addition, the Department developed another means of defense— —the torpedo (the modern mine), one of the really great inventions of the war, and perhaps the most consistently successful of all Confederate weapons.

Another and equally imperative duty of the Confederate Navy was to strain every effort to break through, and to assist merchantmen to break through, the blockade that threatened to strangle the South. For this the Secretary depended primarily on the ironclads. Most of the blockading vessels were necessarily wooden; a few Confederate ships like the *Virginia* could scatter them or sink them, Mallory believed, and relieve Southern ports.[121]

Where Mallory had his free choice was in regard to the possibility of raiding the sea-borne commerce of the North. Fast cruisers of the type soon to be made famous by the *Sumter* and *Alabama* would, he thought, be extremely effective for this purpose. Privateers could also be used. There

118. *Ibid.*
120. *Ibid.*, 617.
119. Soley, *op. cit.*, 616-17.
121. Hendrick, *op. cit.*, 369-72.

would be two beneficial results of this strategy: it would strike an indirect but serious blow at Northern war industries, and it would, in all probability, force the Federals to divert some warships from service in maintaining the blockade.[122]

In early July, 1861, the converted screw steamer *Sumter*, with Raphael Semmes in command, began her depredations in the Caribbean. The *Florida*, and finally the *Alabama*, were soon to follow. In addition, privateers were being commissioned by the scores.

122. Note the following qualifications with regard to the importance of the cruisers. "Cruisers on the sea," says R. S. Henry, "a handful of them, and ports into which the swift ships of the blockade runners could slip, were but incidents. The cruisers might, as they did, drive the American carrying trade into neutral vessels, but still the trade went on. The United States had the world from which to draw men and supplies and arms and equipment of all sorts; the Confederacy, except for the little driblets that trickled through Mobile, Charleston, Galveston, far-away Brownsville, . . . and, most important of all, Wilmington, had itself alone" (*The Story of the Confederacy* [New York: New Home Library Edition, 1943], 238-39). Cf. a similar criticism from another authority: "Activity on the high seas was of secondary importance during the war, even though . . . it made stirring headlines" (Allan Westcott, ed., *American Sea Power Since 1775* [Philadelphia, 1947], 194). "However high their nuisance value, in the final analysis the raiders exerted only a negligible influence on the outcome of the war. And in the end the Federal Government's overall strategy to ignore the raiders and tighten the blockade appears to have justified itself" (*ibid.*, 205).

# CHAPTER EIGHT

# First Successes and Failures

Dᴜʀɪɴɢ ᴛʜᴇ ꜰɪʀsᴛ ᴡᴇᴇᴋs of the war, Mallory wrestled with the task of conjuring a navy and a naval administration out of almost nothing. Meawhile, events were moving rapidly.[1]

Lincoln's blockade of Southern ports began in April. Before the end of that month, Virginia had joined the Confederacy. On May 14 the English government issued its proclamation of neutrality, recognizing the Confederate States as lawful belligerents. The Federal armies were being built up. The great industrial system of the North was swinging into action for the prosecution of the war.

The lights in the Navy Department offices at Montgomery, and later at Richmond, burned late night after night as that sultry spring moved toward a hot summer.[2] Mallory's shipbuilding program was laboriously getting under way. Valuable time was unavoidably lost in creating almost literally out of the ground foundries and rolling mills such as those at Selma, Richmond, Atlanta, and Macon, smelting works at Petersburg, and a chemical factory at Charlotte. These had to be built before the ships could go under full construction. It was not a case of converting industry to war purposes; the industries were not there, and had to be made.

The only shipbuilding centers of any adequacy were at Norfolk, New Orleans, and Memphis. At Norfolk the keels of some of the new gunboats

1. Cf. Ben La Bree (ed.), *The Confederate Soldier in the Civil War, 1861-1865* (Louisville, Ky., 1897), "Comprehensive History of Confederate States Navy from Its First Organization to the End of the War," by Admiral Franklin Buchanan *et al*.

2. The atmosphere of Richmond at this time has been described by a Confederate observer: "Richmond . . . was in a state difficult to describe. The hotels were thronged, troops were coming in, messengers were riding to and fro, and everybody was in motion. I particularly noted this fact: even at the hotels, the seats were not occupied; no one could sit still; I suppose the great excitement accounted for this. Dispatches [were] coming in hourly, . . . reports spread from mouth to mouth." (Captain William H. Parker, *Recollections of a Naval Officer*, 205).

were laid,[3] and very shortly the *Virginia,* the strange, ill-starred ship that was to come so close to winning the whole naval war for the South, began to take shape out of the old *Merrimac.* Work began at Memphis in late August on the powerful ironclad rams *Arkansas* and *Tennessee.* At New Orleans were being planned the two most formidable vessels of the Confederacy, the *Louisiana* and the *Mississippi.* The river steamers of the Mississippi were being converted into tolerable ships of war. Bulloch had closed a contract in England for the construction of *"No. 290"* and some other cruisers. Neither he nor North, however, had succeeded in securing any ironclads by purchase.[4]

The defensive batteries on the Potomac, Rappahannock, and York rivers were being rushed to completion, and the rivers were sown with the extremely effective torpedoes. It was clear, from the first days of the war, that the safety of Richmond would depend largely on these measures.

There was always, of course, the urgent problem of securing funds to keep the Department operating and the ship workers paid. There was the imperative need of drafting more mechanics and other specialists.

The commissioning of privateers was not the direct responsibility of the Navy Department; but Mallory was doubtless aware, amid the encircling clamor of his own special theater of activity, that the applications for letters of marque had been gratifyingly numerous.[5] His sense of the ironic must have been stirred when he saw that many of the applicants were shipowners of New England, whalers of New Bedford, and other seagoing persons of the North who believed in salting their patriotism with a bit of realism.[6]

It is at least possible that this phase of the Confederate war effort was forwarded by some of Mallory's Spanish friends in Cuba and by the colorful Moreno at Pensacola. The Cuban, Manuel Crugat, in a letter to the Navy Secretary, urged that Señor Don Mariano Alvarez, former consul at Key

3. Cf. *Journal of Confederate Congress,* I, 578 (December 16, 1861): "The Chair laid before Congress a communication from the Secretary of the Navy, containing estimates 'for the construction of fifty additional gunboats.'" Also, concerning appropriations for gunboats, *ibid.,* 578, 606, 621; concerning purchase of gunboats or construction of same, *ibid.,* 132, 144, 151, 371, 390, 407, 410, 446, 565, 578, 587, 606, 620, 629; further details concerning construction of gunboats, *ibid.,* II (Senate), 94, 97, 107, 111, 112, 282, 298, 323, 338.

4. The Confederate "Volunteer Navy" was a source, alternately, of encouragement and embarrassment. Cf. Scharf, *History of the Confederate States Navy,* 91-92; also: Papers of Master B. J. Sage, C.S.N., of La., referring to Plan to Form a Confederate Volunteer Navy (CXLVI), in VN. 1861-1865, Confederate Navy, Organization and Reorganization of, National Archives.

5. Cf. list of applications for letters of marque, Pickett Papers, Library of Congress, No. 119. The standard work on the Confederate privateers is William M. Robinson, Jr., *The Confederate Privateers* (New Haven, 1928).

6. Scharf, *op. cit.,* 67, note 1.

West and more recently consul-general and chargé d'affaires at Santo
Domingo, and "an intimate friend of [Mallory's] brother-in-law Fernando,"
be appointed as diplomatic agent of Spain to the Confederate Government.
"Undoubtedly," wrote Crugat, "Spain naturally is destined to be the warmest friend of the South in Europe, as well as in America, if for nothing else
for the similarity of institutions in its West Indian colonies."[7]

Mallory's father-in-law, acting as Spanish consul at Pensacola, proposed
the intriguing theory that the town and harbor at that place constituted
a neutral area, a suggestion (reported the Federal commander of the district) "against which I politely protested."[8] The majority of the inhabitants
of Key West, although "continually watched with the strictest vigilance,"[9]
were in favor of the South. If, as a Confederate naval officer claimed,
"anarchy reigns rampant in [the] island," it is not improbable that an occasional privateer was given surreptitious aid and comfort there.[10]

The Confederate laws regulating the activities of the privateers were
rather remarkable for their scrupulous attention to the rights of neutrals, as
well as for their solicitude in safeguarding the rights of the enemy.

Non-contraband enemy property on neutral vessels was not to be subject
to seizure. United States vessels in Confederate ports, except those ships
actually (since April 5, 1861) in United States government service, were to
be allowed thirty days after the publication of the law of May 6, 1861, to
leave those ports and reach their destination. In case of any action taken
by a privateer against the vessels or property of neutrals, or of citizens of
the United States, the district courts of the Confederate States were to decree
damages and costs to the party injured, for which damages the owners and

7. Manuel D. Crugat to Mallory, from Havana, March 24, 1861 (*O.R.*, Ser. II, Vol. II,
p. 50).

8. Brig. Gen. Alexander Asboth, U.S.A., to Brig. Gen. Charles P. Stone, U.S.A., from
Barrancas, Fla., December 5, 1863 (*O.R.A.*, Ser. I, Vol. XXVI, part I, p. 834). Continued
General Asboth: ". . . he [Moreno] . . . has two sons in the rebel army; [and has] contrib-
uted $25,000 to Jeff. Davis' Cabinet."

9. A. Lilly (late of C. S. privateer *Beauregard*) to Secretary of War J. P. Benjamin, from
Key West, February 11, 1862 (*O.R.*, Ser. I, Vol. I, p. 821).

10. *Ibid.* Cf., concerning aid given to the Confederacy by foreign mercantile houses at New
Orleans, Major General Benjamin F. Butler to Secretary of War Stanton, from New Orleans,
October 27, 1862 (*O.R.A.*, Ser. III, Vol. II, pp. 689-90. There emerged, with the blessing (not
publicly proclaimed) of both governments, a brisk commerce between some of the Northern
and Southern traders. Cf. J. B. Jones, *A Rebel War Clerk's Diary at the Confederate Capital*,
ed. Harold Swiggett (2 vols.; New York, 1935), I, 180-81: "November, 1862. Mr. Randolph
says, in his letter to the President, that trading with ports in possession of the enemy is forbidden to citizens, and not to the government! He has granted a license to citizens in Mobile
to trade cotton in New Orleans for . . . supplies in exchange."

commanders of the vessels making such illegal captures, and also the vessels, were to be liable.[11]

Commanders of privateers were to "pay the strictest regard to the rights of the neutral vessels," which were to be given "as little molestation or interruption as will consist with the right of ascertaining their neutral character, and of detaining and bringing them in for regular adjudication in the proper cases." Commanders were to avoid particularly even the appearance of using force or seduction, with a view to depriving such vessels of their crews or passengers, other than persons in the military service of the enemy. Toward enemy vessels and their crews the commanders were to proceed, in exercising the rights of war, "with all the justice and humanity which characterize this [Confederate] government and its citizens."[12]

So Stephen Mallory fought his war from Montgomery and Richmond in those first few months of ebb and flow of Confederate fortunes. It was a warm, humid spring and early summer. "We are having terribly hot weather here," wrote an army officer to his wife, "and it does us good to think how it must toast the Yankees."[13]

The Navy Secretary was not too busy for an occasional few hours with his sister-in-law Pila Garnett at Hanover Junction, nor too preoccupied to note that "Pila's good looks were wonderfully preserved, she appears only about twenty four."[14] He resolved that he must do something for Theodore, her seventeen-year-old son, whose gentlemanly and respectful manners charmed him. Pila's daughter Ella wrote verses about ducks, chickens, pigs, sheep, horses, flowers, etc., thus reminding him of his own little Ruby's versifications, and making him feel a bit homesick. Colonel Garnett was, Stephen thought, "an odd but good man," who, in that critical summer for the Confederacy, was much perplexed as to how he should compose a letter of condolence to the bereaved husband of a lady whom he had once courted.[15]

On the evenings when he dined with the President and Mrs. Davis and a select group of "government ladies," he was quick to perceive and to be

11. Scharf, *op. cit.*, 53-55.

12. *Ibid.*, 68-69.

13. Edward Mason to his wife Bessie, from Richmond, June 4, 1861 (Alexander Papers, Southern Historical Collection, University of North Carolina).

14. Mallory, Diary, part II, p. 2.

15. *Ibid.*, 2, 4. Concerning amusements and social life in wartime Richmond, see Francis B. Simkins and James W. Patton, *The Women of the Confederacy* (Richmond and New York, 1936): "Gayety and Extravagance," 177-93; "Amusements and Social Diversions," 194-205; "Female Fashions," 155-58; "Bazaars and Amateur Theatricals," 200-3. Also Eron Rowland, *Varina Howell, Wife of Jefferson Davis*, 87-102, 134-45, 146-58, 281-88.

amused at a lesser war of feminine personalities. Mrs. Wigfall, he saw, was determined to snub Mrs. Davis and her sister Miss Howell. Mrs. W.'s manner was a "perpetual rebuke," and her air one of toleration and sufferance. But Mrs. Davis and Miss Howell were the last women in the world to take such an exhibition quietly; consequently there was a "perpetual cross fire of sharpshootings in an amicable way." Cutting things were said blandly, and "quiet smiles or . . . laughter convey and cover rifle balls."[16] It is pleasant to learn from a later entry in Stephen's diary, however, that Mrs. Davis and Mrs. Wigfall finally had a personal explanation and agreed upon a truce.[17]

He was forced to make some very pungent criticisms of the President's wife. Mrs. Davis, he regretted to say, lacked precisely those qualities on which she most plumed herself—refinement and judgment. Her attempts at mimicry, although they sometimes amused, were not only usually failures, but they presented her in a light at once undignified and undesirable. She was "ill-bred and under-bred." But, having said this of her, he must add also that she was a truthful, generous, and good woman! He designated, as one of her outstanding virtues, a perception of the ridiculous that was perfectly riotous in its manifestations.[18]

Maggie, Mrs. Davis's sister, came in for her share of rebuke. She was "kind and amiable when permitted to have her way." But usually she seemed to be in a morose and ill humor. She was "contrary, unyielding, and unamiable, though having a fair mind and pretty good sense." She would be surprised to be thought selfish, yet this vice was the "bane of her views of life." Stephen could not share in her ridicule of persons with whom he was daily associating, and was therefore condemned almost to constant silence at dinner. She annoyed the President terribly by her indiscreet, ill-timed, and tart remarks, but he conducted himself admirably under the pressure.[19]

The new Navy Secretary did not neglect the performance of the usual errands for Angela. He wrote sometime in May that he had already despatched to her the requested "provisions, flour, bacon, cheese, etc., and a box of potash for soap." He enclosed a "wonderful recipe for making soap." He sent also with his letter a note to be transmitted by Angela with all speed to General Bragg's headquarters at Pensacola.[20]

16. Mallory, Diary, part II, pp. 3, 6.        17. Ibid., 6.
18. Ibid. For details of the character of Mrs. Davis, see Eron Rowland, op. cit., II, 14-18, 303-9, 310-23. Concerning life in the White House of the Confederacy, ibid., 197-208.
19. Mallory, Diary, part II, p. 8.
20. Mallory to Angela, from Montgomery [?], May, 1861.

A few days after the fight at Bethel Church, Attila Mallory received from his father a description of how "the Virginia and N. Carolina troops gave the N. York Zouaves and other of Old Abe's men 'particular Tessie.'" The men of the South fought well and bravely, he reminded Attie, because their cause was just, and God would not permit "Old Abe's" soldiers to succeed against the Confederates.[21]

It is somewhat surprising that he did not picture for Attie the most colorful of the troops then in Richmond, a regiment of Zouaves just arrived from Pensacola, most of them originally "wharf rats" from New Orleans. They were "all muscular and athletic fellows with shaved heads, long moustaches, and goatees, red skull caps, gaiters and red zouave pants, and look wilder, and are usually drunker, than any Indians; they [were] the lions of the town . . . and cut out all the other uniforms."[22] Attie would have been interested also in the delegation of Creek and Choctaw Indians who came to Richmond to make an alliance with the Confederacy and to offer the Confederate armies 25,000 fighting redmen.[23]

Attie was instructed to be a good boy and to be obedient and kind to his mother. He must also save up all the manure he could for the garden which he and his father, God willing, would be able to make soon at home. Would he not try to learn to write to his father, if only a single line? He was to take good care of "Dear little Ruby"; and he must, above all, always tell the truth.[24]

An entry in Mallory's diary at this time indicated another preoccupation of his nonofficial thoughts. It suggested indeed the chief tragedy of his private life: "21 June. Wrote to my dear Angela today, and recd. a letter from her. She writes and feels very unequally, and makes me so wretched by her murmurs and complaints against me that I am unfit for business long after reading one of her bitter epistles. But I ought not to complain of anything she does. She is a noble, generous truthful and lovable woman, and God knows has my whole heart and soul."[25]

Why was Angela so acting? It is difficult to say, exactly. As there had been in Washington in 1858, there was another allegedly fascinating widow, this time at Richmond, to the consequent alarm of Angela's affections. A few weeks after writing the above, Stephen was obliged to record that he

21. Mallory to Attila, June 15, 1861.

22. Edward Mason to his wife Bessie, from Richmond, June 8, 1861 (Alexander Papers, Southern Historical Collection, University of North Carolina).

23. Same to same, June 6, 1861.

24. Mallory to Attila, June 15, 1861.

25. Mallory, Diary, part II, p. 5.

had received an "absurd letter from Angela about Mrs. ——, and her fears that Mrs. —— would come to Richmond." He wrote, he said, a "humorous note" in reply. He concluded this entry characteristically: "Angela, dear Angela, God bless her, for a noble minded whole souled, loving nature; I adore her for ever and ever."[26]

Hardly another week had elapsed when he received a new letter from his wife which, as he described it, "distressed me greatly, and has rendered me wretched." He found it more and more difficult to control his feelings under the "dire stress" that her letters caused him. When he opened them he did so with misgivings and fears that he would be again reproached. His mental strength and clearness of mind were being impaired by the sadness into which the letters cast him—"yet, I love her to adoration, and always shall, in spite of her inconsiderate course towards me." Nevertheless, he soliloquized, how little she realized what risks she was running in thus assailing him. Soon he would not have the courage to open her letters at all.[27]

But the trouble lay deeper than simple jealousy or the mere fact of separation. The fact is that Angela seemed, for a while, to have lost faith in her husband, chiefly on account of what she apparently had come to regard as his weakness and lack of spirit in the Pickens episode. Mixed with this feeling, apparently, was the beginning of a disgust on her part for everything connected with the war.

At one of the most critical moments of those first few months of the conflict, Stephen wrote to her that her letter of a few days before had quite crushed him, pressed down as he already was by the weight of official matters. He quoted the line which had struck him to the heart: "Never has one being been made to suffer more for the sins of another than I am for yours." What sins she meant, he knew not, for he could not believe that she was charging him with the "vague offences, political, that the low herd of cowardly dunces about Pensacola prate of." He had no regrets, he assured her, in regard to his actions in the crucial February of 1861. Though he had not been able to prevent the attack on Fort Pickens, he had argued against the act. He was proud of his conduct, which, he felt, had been approved by every candid and patriotic mind in the country. Upon that conduct, every word and act of it, he stood ready to challenge the country and to meet all men face to face. His detractors, he was sure, envious of his political distinction, and thinking that he stood in their way, desired to ele-

26. *Ibid.*, part II, p. 8 (July 1, 1862).
27. *Ibid.*, 9-10 (July 26, 1862).

vate themselves by pulling him down. But—"nous verrons." Then he ended the letter in the tone which he ever used in writing to his wife: "I want to see you day and night."[28]

We may speculate as to how much Angela's discouraging letters affected her husband's capacity to handle his important departmental work. Unfortunately, she frequently timed her complaints so that they reached him at moments of particular official stress. She was certainly at this time not helping him to think clearly and with coolness on matters of the highest importance to the Southern cause.

The summer and fall of 1861 witnessed a stream of successes for Mallory's hit-and-run commerce-raiding program. Semmes was roaming at will in the South Atlantic with his formidable *Sumter*. By the end of August Northern merchantmen were being gradually driven from the high seas. The Northern press was complaining loudly of the Federal navy's helplessness in the face of these depredations. The *New York Herald* declared that no Northern vessel could any longer secure a charter, or be insured for any reasonable rate. English bottoms, the journal asserted, were taking almost all American trade; the shipping interests of the Union were "literally ruined."[29]

But toward the end of this same summer, and during the fall, occurred a series of Confederate defeats which were ominous not only in their immediate results but also in their wider implications. On August 29 a Federal combined land and sea attack took Hatteras Inlet and Fort Hatteras, thus opening the way for further penetration into the waters of North Carolina.[30] In September, Ship Island fell, providing the Federals with a base for their operations against New Orleans. On November 7 came the crowning disaster of the year—Port Royal was lost.[31]

28. Mallory to Angela, September 25, 1861.

29. August 10, 1861. The total number of Northern vessels captured or destroyed by the Confederate cruisers is thus tabulated by John H. Reagan in his *Memoirs* (New York, 1906), 155: "49 ships, 18 brigs, 35 barks, 34 schooners, one steamer, one pilot boat; 138 in all." For further details with regard to the crippling of the Federal merchant marine by the Confederate cruisers, see Dudley W. Knox, *A History of the United States Navy* (New York, 1936), 285-95; H. W. Wilson, *Ironclads in Action: A Sketch of Naval Warfare from 1855 to 1895* . . . (2 vols.; London, 1896), I, 142-76.

30. The interesting report of a Federal naval officer, R. B. Lowry, five weeks after the seizure of Hatteras Inlet, said that the inlet, having been captured, proved to be of little benefit to the Federal forces. The Confederate naval units still in the sound were too strong to permit the Federals' use of Hatteras as an effective base. Water and weather conditions also contributed to this result (R. B. Lowry to H. S. Stell-Wagen, U.S.N., from Hatteras Inlet, October 10, 1861 [*O.R.*, Ser. I, Vol. VI, pp. 303-4). Cf. also Reports on fall of Hatteras Inlet, August 1861 (*ibid.*, 138-45).

31. Concerning the taking of Port Royal, see Report of Brig. Gen. T. W. Sherman to War

Even the pro-administration journal, the *Richmond Enquirer,* expressed
its restrained disappointment at the "surprise" accomplished by the Federals at Hatteras Inlet.[32] The fall of Port Royal, the *Charleston Mercury*
urged, proved the inefficacy of land batteries against steam-driven ships.[33]
The only effective defensive weapon against steamships or ironclads was
ironclads, said this newspaper, and the Navy Department, it was charged,
was not building enough of this type of vessel; at least it was not building
them fast enough.[34] This allegation, in view of what Mallory had already
done with respect to ironclads, would appear to be quite extreme.

Certainly Mallory himself appeared to have no doubt that his Department was doing its best. He was achieving good results with his commerce-
raiding plan, and he was directing the operations of the cruisers with skill,
sound appreciation of the human nature of his commanders, and great boldness of strategic conception. If he was at times somewhat theatrical in his
instructions, and gave the impression that he was rather enjoying the thrill
of the thing, it would be ungenerous to begrudge him this satisfaction.
Managing such a campaign was one of the tasks he was well equipped to
do, as is suggested by some of his orders.

In mid-July he directed John H. Tucker of the *Patrick Henry* to leave
the James River for a raiding cruise. He assured the Commander that the
Department was unwilling to limit him by any instructions as to the time
and manner of running the blockade, or as to his cruising ground, or as to
the duration of his voyage. The Department was trusting to Tucker's good
judgment, and desired him to realize the fact. It was evident, however,

Dept., from Port Royal, November 8, 1861 (*O.R.,* Ser. I., Vol. XII, pp. 288-90). Also *ibid.,*
292-93, 300-7, 295-298. (The last reference is a reprint of a detailed account of the action,
taken from the *Savannah Republican,* n. d.)

32. August 31, 1861. The *New Orleans Picayune,* September 8, 1861, insisted that the loss
of Hatteras Inlet could have been avoided by greater foresight on the part of the War and
Navy departments: "The leaving of a door open when it might have been closed, building
forts for the very purpose of having them taken, argues by no means vigilant patriotism."
Similarly, the *Charleston Tri-Weekly Mercury,* September 21, 1861: "To put a fort there,
without protection from shells . . . was to invite assault and sacrifice those who withstood it."

33. November 13, 1861. Note, incidentally, the *Mercury's* espousal of the exactly opposite
argument, issue of November 4, 1861. Cf. also *Richmond Enquirer,* February 20, 1862, supporting the *Mercury's* position of November 13, 1861.

34. "Our Navy is [yet] to be established; nor can we long defer the building of ships and
the providing of the means necessary for defending our coast" (*Richmond Enquirer,* September
13, 1861). Under the headline "Where is Mallory?" the *Charleston Mercury,* November 22,
1861, said: "Lieutenant Governor Montague . . . , despairing of Mr. Mallory, intends to urge
the [South Carolina] Convention to appropriate a million of dollars to build a State Navy."
Cf., in same sense, *ibid.,* October 16, 1861, "Our Nashville Correspondence," and November
1, 1861; the latter issue reprints adverse criticism of the Navy Department from the *New
Orleans Bulletin,* n. d.

that the success of the cruise would be greatly forwarded by an escape from the river without the enemy's knowledge. Should Tucker be doubtful at any moment as to the course of action to be pursued, he should remember that he was, "in accordance with the rules of Christian warfare," to "inflict upon the enemy the greatest injury in the shortest time."[35]

The Commander was to keep in mind the fact that the speed of the *Patrick Henry* surpassed that of any of the ships of the United States, and that the power of her battery enabled her to engage such vessels as the *Harriet Lane* and the chartered steamers of the enemy's navy generally. Tucker thus had the means of escaping from the enemy's first class ships in order to concentrate his attacks on those of the second rank. The seizure of one of the latter, with her signal book, might lead to the capture of some larger vessels.

Steam propellers were badly needed by the navy, as well as all ordnance and military stores; acquisitions of this nature Tucker was to endeavor to send safely into port. Should it be found impracticable for the *Patrick Henry* to leave the river, she was to cooperate with the military forces against the enemy, keeping watch day and night upon his movements, and attacking and annoying him as much as possible. If circumstances should dictate the landing of the crew, in order more efficiently to collaborate with the army, the ship was to be placed under the shelter of the Jamestown battery and kept ready for instant service.

Finally, Tucker was to impress upon his officers the importance of establishing and maintaining good discipline and of inciting every man to do his duty; and he was to report regularly and in detail to the Department the name, birthplace, age, character, and qualifications of every man on the ship whose good conduct, particularly in action or in moments of great peril or excitement, might merit commendation. The Commander was to keep the Department advised of his movements, and he was to endeavor to prevent the unauthorized advertisement of them.[36]

Mallory appreciated fully the warning expressed by Bulloch that efficient and loyal crews for the commerce raiders could not be had without the assurance of regular pay and the promise of prize money or ultimate reward from the government for good service at sea.[37] The improvised

---

35. Mallory to Commander John H. Tucker, from Richmond, July 13, 1861 (*O.R.*, Ser. I, Vol. V., 812-13).

36. *Ibid.*

37. James D. Bulloch to Mallory, from Liverpool, March 21, 1862 (*O.R.*, Ser. I, Vol. I, p. 755).

method of payment which the Secretary was by circumstances forced to adopt was evident from his instructions relative to keeping the *Sumter* supplied with money. From the public newspapers, he had learned that the vessel was at the Spanish port of San Roque, and that she was badly in need of repairs. He wrote to the Confederate Commissioner at London, James M. Mason, enclosing in favor of the *Sumter's* paymaster a letter of credit on the Liverpool banking house of Frazer and Trenholm, with the request that Mason transmit the said letter of credit to the paymaster "upon learning the port at which the steamer may be when you receive this letter, or inform him that you have in your possession the letter. . . ."[38]

The Secretary was sometimes called upon to give a reprimand. In the summer of 1863 he reminded one of his most capable lieutenants, John N. Maffitt, commanding the *Florida,* that the latter's recent report was the first received from him by the Department since the ship had left the Confederate States. Maffitt was requested to send frequent dispatches, in duplicate. The news of the deaths of two of the *Florida's* petty officers, the Secretary remarked drily, had been learned by the Department through the newspapers. In such cases, full details were to be sent at once to Richmond. The rebuke was softened by the information that Maffitt had been promoted to the grade of commander. The Department congratulated the master, officers, and crew of the *Florida* on the brilliant success of their cruise, and Maffitt was assured that he could have more men if he wished to fit out some of his prizes as cruisers.[39]

The streak of daring, and flair for the spectacular, in Mallory's administrative methods are indicated in his special orders to Acting Master Thomas Hogg, in charge of a boarding expedition in May, 1864. The party was to be started from Wilmington by the shortest and safest route to Panama, where they were to take passage on either of the two Federal screw steamers running between Panama and South American ports. Then came the laconic instruction: "After reaching the high seas you will consider upon and devise a means to capture the vessel in the name of the Confederate States, and effect the capture without fail."[40] After securing control of the steamer they were to organize their crew, hoist the flag of the Confederacy, arm the vessel, and proceed to cruise against the enemy in the Pacific.[41]

This was the type of swashbuckling tactic Mallory loved to plan. Often

38. Mallory to Hon. J. M. Mason, March 1, 1862 (*ibid.,* 670).
39. Mallory to Maffitt, August 7, 1863 (*ibid.,* II, 657-58).
40. Mallory to Acting Master Thomas E. Hogg, May 7, 1864 (*ibid.,* III, 356).
41. *Ibid.*

his highly colored conceptions along these lines were extravagant and bordered on the naïve. It is to be remarked, however, that the project described above was a complete success.

Implicit in the Secretary's orders was his conviction that even in war one must be a gentleman. He exhorted Hogg that his conduct toward the people of captured ships should be marked by "that spirit of humanity which ever characterizes the conduct of our naval officers."[42] Yet, surprisingly, he could sometimes adopt measures of considerable harshness toward prisoners of war. On being informed that a Confederate midshipman, captured by the enemy, was being treated not as a military prisoner, but as a criminal, and that he had been held in solitary confinement for more than two weeks, Mallory issued the following order to the Confederate army officer in charge of prisoners: "Painful as it is to resort to retaliatory measures the barbarity of the enemy leaves no alternative but to treat prisoners in our hands precisely as he treats our fellow-citizens, his prisoners of war, his refusal to provide for an exchange of prisoners and failure even to respond to a communication made under a flag for that purpose having closed against us the usual resort of civilized nations in like cases.

"You will therefore be pleased to provide two cells as nearly the size of that in which Mr. Hudgins [the Confederate midshipman in Federal hands] is confined as practicable and place in them Lieut. George L. Selden and Master Albert Kautz, officers of the U. S. Navy. The health of the prisoners will be duly provided for and they may be informed that the cruel treatment of Mr. Hudgins has constrained us to subject them to this severity."[43]

At the same time aware of the power of propaganda, Mallory urged his

42. *Ibid.*

43. Mallory to Brig. Gen. John H. Winder, C.S.A., August 15, 1861 (*O.R.A.*, Ser. II, Vol. III, pp. 703-4). It is interesting to compare in this connection the reaction of General Robert E. Lee to a similar and very much worse provocation later in the war: "I have the honor to acknowledge the receipt of your letter . . . relative to the murder by the enemy of Mr. Creigh and Captain White. As I have said before, if the guilty parties could be taken, either the officer who commands or the soldier who executes such atrocities, I should not hesitate to advise the infliction of the extreme punishment they deserve; but I cannot think it right or politic to make the innocent, after they have surrendered as prisoners of war, suffer for the guilty. I think, however, that something should be done, if possible, to put a stop to the barbarities of the enemy. I can see no remedy except in refusing to make prisoners of any soldiers belonging to commands in which these outrages are perpetrated. It is true the innocent may sometimes suffer by this course, but it will have a tendency to make those who do not approve the savage usages of their comrades exert all their influence to restrain them" (Gen. R. E. Lee to Secretary of War, July 18, 1864; *O.R.A.*, Ser. II, Vol. VII, p. 473).

commanders to seize every opportunity for placing the character of the war and Southern principles in "the proper light."[44]

A subject for self-congratulation by the Navy Department in the second half of the year 1861 was the success enjoyed by the blockade runners. One of Mallory's prime responsibilities was to keep open the South's essential life lines to Europe, and at this time, even without the aid of the still uncompleted ironclads, the job was being very adequately done. The long, black, rakish-looking, two funnelled hulls—frequently displaying with great ostentation the British flag—that swept quietly in and out of Wilmington, Charleston, and other ports, bound for the West Indies or Europe, were not entirely manned and managed by the Navy Department, but they were under its general supervision, and were frequently officered by naval personnel or protected by naval gunners on board. Often the Navy Department was called on for various intelligence services on behalf of the blockade runners, and also at times supplied pilots[45] or even an escort ship.[46]

The records of entrances and clearances of merchant ships at Southern ports during the first year of the war show the porous character—it would not always remain thus—of the mobile sea wall with which Lincoln was seeking to hem in and strangle the Confederacy.[47] But Mallory foresaw correctly that the blockade would, as the war progressed, tighten. Therefore, the *Alabama*, the *Sumter*, and their sister ships would have another aim besides that of weakening Northern industries. The raids of the cruisers against Northern commerce must be made so damaging that the Federal government would be forced to withdraw numerous ships from the blockading squadrons in order to pursue the "highwaymen of the sea."

The Napoleonic strategy of diversion did not succeed, for the Federal Navy Department was aware of the game that Mallory was playing. But

44. Mallory to Acting Master Hogg, May 7, 1864 (*O.R.*, Ser. I, Vol. III, p. 356. For a refutation of charges of cruelty practiced by Confederates against prisoners, see Morris Schaff, *Jefferson Davis, His Life and Personality* (Boston, 1922), 205-16.

45. Cf. request of a Confederate agent in London for the cooperation of the Secretary of the Navy in facilitating the entry of a blockade runner laden with arms, clothing, and powder, to be sent from England (Charles J. Helm to Secretary of State R. M. T. Hunter, from London, September 30, 1861; Pickett Papers, Vol. I, No. 48, Helm's despatch No. 1). (Robert Mercer Taliaferro Hunter became Secretary of State after the resignation of Toombs, and served in that post from July 25, 1861, to February 18, 1862, when he was succeeded by Judah P. Benjamin and became a member of the Confederate Senate. He participated in the abortive Hampton Roads peace conference of February 3, 1865.)

46. Helm to Secretary Hunter, from Havana, November 15, 1861 (Pickett Papers, Vol. I, No. 48, Helm's despatch No. 5).

47. Cf. "Entrances and Clearances of vessels in Southern ports [during the blockade] and correspondence relative to the blockade, etc." (Pickett Papers, Nos. 18, 30, 43, 78). Also "Confederate Navy, Record of vessels at Bermuda and Nassau, 1861-1865" (*ibid.*).

he cannot be condemned for trying. With a little more luck—and time— he might have been able to smash the blockade by another means, his iron-clads. As he said truly, the *Mississippi,* if completed in time, could have raised the blockade of every Gulf port in ten days. The tragedy lies in the phrase, "if completed in time."[48]

There was one aspect of anti-blockade warfare in 1861 that was not with-out an element of humor. The smuggling of goods in and out of Con-federate ports was being done mainly through the instrumentality of North-ern merchants.[49] Munitions of war for the Southern armies were being furnished in large quantities by the citizens of the United States to the enemies of the United States.[50] Horace Greeley denounced in a famous lament these Union patriots who could not forget that they were men of business.[51] They were called upon, indeed, to display no small ingenuity. Being fully aware that the blockade runners would have no dealing with anyone whom they knew to be a Yankee, and realizing also that the block-ade runners would always be attracted by European labels, the Northern merchants had recourse to a mild deceit. In the shops at Bermuda could be found bushels of Connecticut pins and cases of Massachusetts shoes marked "London," elegant felt hats from New York labeled "Paris," and good old Irish whiskey from New Jersey.[52]

There were also at this time difficulties and disappointments for the Navy Secretary. He was pushing ahead the shipbuilding program, espe-cially at Norfolk, New Orleans, and Memphis; but, in building ships, one of the great problems was how to secure enough iron. In May, Captain Duncan Ingraham, in charge of naval affairs in Alabama waters, had been ordered to obtain at any cost wrought-iron plates of two- to three-inch thick-ness and to rush them to New Orleans, where the new gunboats were being constructed. Ingraham had found that no iron works in Kentucky or Ten-

48. Mallory to Captain John K. Mitchell, commandant of naval station at New Orleans, March 15, 1862 (*O.R.*, Ser. II, Vol. I, p. 466).

49. Scharf, *op. cit.*, 626, quoting Judge Cowley's *Leaves from a Lawyer's Life Afloat and Ashore,* 112.

50. *Ibid.*

51. Cf. Scharf, *op. cit.*, 626-27. Cf. also the denunciation of these merchants by Judge Smalley, presiding in United States Circuit Court for New York, on January 14, 1861, in his charge to the grand jury for the term.

52. Charles Hallock, "Bermuda and the Blockade," in *Galaxy* (April, 1867) 897. The following significant item appeared in the *Charleston Mercury,* October 23, 1861: "[From Our Richmond Correspondence] Our dry goods men are rejoicing the eyes of the ladies with the sight of fresh prints and new patterns just imported from England. I hear that the statistics of the ships will show that the *Bermuda* brought over a cargo twice as large as the *Great Eastern* could contain."

nessee would run the risk of doing business with the Confederacy. There was an iron foundry at Atlanta that could be used, but it would require several months of reconversion and reconditioning before it would be ready for war work.

By midsummer, with the iron shortage seriously handicapping the shipbuilding program, Mallory was forced to bargain for the iron of already laid railroad tracks, to be melted and rerolled into coverings for war vessels. He urgently asked the Secretary of War for permission to remove for this purpose the rails of the Portsmouth and Welden or the Norfolk and Petersburg railroads.[53] The Secretary of War replied that orders had been given repeatedly to remove the iron of those roads and to hand it over to the Navy Department, but the pressure of the enemy had, up to that time, rendered the operation impracticable.[54] Again, Mallory wrote to Governor Vance of North Carolina, making the same request, and adding diplomatically that the iron would be used in armoring vessels destined for the defense of the waters of that state.[55]

But even more difficult to secure than iron or powder was the money required by the Navy Department for current expenditures.[56] In mid-September Howell, the navy agent supervising the shipbuilding projects at New Orleans, sent an urgent telegram to Secretary Mallory. In order to pay the workmen at the New Orleans yards and some others near by, four thousand dollars in specie had been borrowed from the Bank of America in that city. For the payment of this debt Mallory had sent to his agent Treasury notes, which were all that he could secure from Memminger's department, instead

53. Mallory to Hon. G. W. Randolph, October 28, 1862 (*O.R.*, Ser. I, Vol. VIII, p. 843).
54. Randolph to Mallory, October 29, 1862 (*ibid.*, 844).
55. *Ibid.* Cf. Governor Vance's favorable reply, *ibid.*, 849-50. Mallory and Vance were in communication with each other at frequent intervals until the end of the war. The correspondence was not always amicable. As late as November, 1863, Mallory was still having trouble in securing iron from the Governor (Vance to Mallory, November 28, 1863 [Vance Letter Book, Z. B. Vance Collection, North Carolina State Department of Archives and History, Raleigh, N. C.]). (The foregoing reference to the Vance Collection has been furnished by courtesy of Professor Frontis W. Johnston, of the Department of History of Davidson College, Davidson, N. C.)
56. Cf. Reports of the Secretary of the Treasury in Capers, *Memminger*, 417-88. Concerning the financial legislation of the Confederate Congress, cf. Schwab, *op. cit.*, 1-83. "The Confederate finances," says W. E. Dodd (*Jefferson Davis*, 320-21), "were from the beginning badly managed." Schwab (*op. cit.*, 69) says that the so-called funding act of February 17, 1864, "wrecked the Government's finances beyond the hope of saving them from utter ruin." For an opposite and very favorable view of this act, cf. Capers, *op. cit.*, 361-65. For a general defense of Memminger's financial administration, cf. *ibid.*, 347-48. Capers holds that Memminger's recommendations were sound, but that the Congress refused to carry them out and was unwilling also to grant to the Secretary of the Treasury the minimum executive powers that he required.

of specie. The bank, Howell reported, refused to accept anything but cash. The work on the ships would stop, he warned, unless the creditor's demands were met.[57] A week later came another wire from the harassed agent, enclosing a note written in the flowing hand of the bank president himself: "Dear Sir: The Cashier desires me to remind you of the Loan of $4000 which, in the many matters you have to attend to, may have escaped from your memory."[58]

Repeatedly, the Treasury Department filled Mallory's requisitions partly or largely in Confederate government bonds, instead of furnishing the total sum in cash or treasury notes. The Navy Department's creditors at New Orleans would not accept these bonds, which, therefore, had to be returned to Richmond to be cashed or exchanged for treasury notes and then transmitted again to New Orleans. This caused delays in shipbuilding operations and led in some cases to cancellation of contracts.[59]

A spirited though amicable exchange of letters between the Secretary of the Navy and the Secretary of the Treasury in early 1862 indicated the difficulties experienced by both Departments in this matter of disbursements.

Several of the Navy Department's recent requisitions, complained Memminger, as well as the Secretary of the Navy's last letter on the subject of treasury notes, implied that the Navy Department was unaware of the impediments which prevented the Treasury Department from paying out treasury notes. The Treasury Department had about two hundred and thirty one millions of treasury bonds, and about fifty millions of treasury notes; that is, about four and a half times as many bonds as treasury notes for the appropriations anticipated and made up to the following November 1.

The Secretary of the Navy was asked to believe that it did not depend on the mere will of the Secretary of the Treasury as to whether or not requisitions would be paid in treasury notes. A stern necessity compelled the bonds to be used wherever purchases were to be made, or, in fact, where any payment was to be made otherwise than for absolute cash demands. The Secretary of the Treasury had had constantly in view the fact that the Navy Department required cash "for pay and for mechanics' wages," and the record showed that whenever requisitions included such items they were

57. Flag Officer George N. Hollins to Mallory, September 13, 1861 ([Confederate] Treasury Department Records, National Archives).

58. Enclosure in letter of Mallory to Memminger, September 20, 1861 (ibid.).

59. Cf. Mallory to Memminger, February 22, 1862 (Treasury Department, C.S.A., Incoming Correspondence to Secretary of Treasury; National Archives). Cf. also Mallory to Memminger, February 22, 1862 (O.R., Ser. II, Vol. I, 714).

always supplied with a sufficient amount of treasury notes to pay the demands.

But when the requisitions were for coal or ordnance, or for such supplies as could be purchased, it became necessary to resort to bonds, which, in such instances, had been supplied to the Navy Department's disbursing officers, as they had been supplied also to the paymasters of the War Department. It was to be noted, incidentally, that the Navy Department had received proportionally far fewer of the unpopular bonds than had the War Department; for while the latter department had used upward of eleven million of bonds, the Navy Department had used less than one million. The Secretary of the Treasury urged his colleague the Secretary of the Navy to impress upon his disbursing officers the duty of making purchases at least in part with bonds, to the utmost extent of their power.[60]

In his reply to this letter, Mallory admitted the inability of the Treasury Department to pay all requisitions in treasury notes exclusively. But, he declared, the general character of the Navy Department's expenditures did not admit of the use of bonds to any great extent; these expenditures must be paid in notes or not paid at all. The Navy Department could pay out a small proportion only of bonds to notes, not more, generally, than one fifth. This fact Mallory had "so frequently and so earnestly urged, from the conviction that the credit of the Department and its ability to build and equip vessels and to conduct its operations generally have been crippled by the practice of the Treasury Department in sending to our disbursing officers bonds which they could not use, and to pay debts for which notes were specially required on the face of the requisitions."[61]

Memminger's suggestion that the naval disbursing officers be impressed with the necessity of making purchases at least in part with bonds had, of course, been anticipated. But, repeated Mallory, "the point is that the great mass of our expenditures will not admit of being paid in bonds. . . ."[62]

Concerning the alleged heavier burden placed upon the War Department in this matter, Mallory wrote: "You say that while the War Department has used upwards of eleven millions of bonds, this Department has

60. Memminger to Mallory, April 4, 1862, in *Correspondence with the Treasury Department of the Confederate States of America, 1861-1865,* compiled under the direction of Brevet Major General E. D. Townsend, Adjutant General, U. S. Army, by Raphael P. Thian, Chief Clerk, Adjutant General's Office (5 vols.; Washington, D. C., 1880), Appendix, Part IV, p. 279 (Duke University).

61. Mallory to Memminger, April 7, 1862, in *ibid.,* Appendix, Part V, pp. 509-10.

62. *Ibid.* Concerning the relative (and absolute) smallness of the Navy Department's expenditures during the war, see Reports of the Secretary of the Treasury in Capers, *op. cit.,* 417-88.

used less than one million. I know not, without reference to our files, what the proportion is; but, assuming your statement to be true, it shows that, while the War Department has used of bonds one cent in every seven and six-tenths of a cent of its expenditures . . . [the Navy Department has used in bonds] nearly twice the amount of the War Department in proportion to its [the Navy Department's] expenditures; and this, too, notwithstanding the expenditures of this Department do not admit of the use of bonds to the extent of those of the War Department."[63]

Navy Department requisitions, furthermore, were usually met by the Treasury only after long delays. Mallory later declared that his demands upon Memminger's funds to meet payments in New Orleans had been made usually within twenty-four hours after receiving the requests from the agents. But the Treasury's delay in paying had normally been from twenty-five to forty days. Then, frequently, the payment had been furnished in the form of the embarrassing Confederate bonds. The Navy Secretary cites the instance of a request made by agent Howell on December 24, 1861, for $42,000. On the sixth of February, 1862, Howell had received from the Treasury a draft, one half of it in bonds which he had to return to Richmond to be cashed. The balance of his requisition he received in currency on February 17, forty-eight days after his original request.[64]

The effect of all this on the Navy Department's undertakings at New Orleans was indeed serious. Captain Hollins later testified that the mechanics at the Gulf city knocked off work sometimes for two or three days at a time in the midst of important operations, because they were not being paid. It became proverbial, he asserted, that the Navy Department could not be trusted to pay.[65] General Lovell could not assemble a crew of workers to repair the raft below New Orleans until he could convince the men that he was not representing the Navy Department.[66] It was Hollins' belief that the blame for this financial mismanagement was not to be laid at the door of the Navy Department, but that the Treasury Department was at fault.[67]

It was charged that Mallory was too niggardly in supplying funds to his subordinates even when the funds were available. This accusation was

63. Thian, op. cit., Appendix, Part V, pp. 509-10.

64. Mallory to President Davis, March 8, 1862 (O.R., Ser. II, Vol. I, 714).

65. Testimony of Hollins before the Investigating Committee (O.R., Ser. II, Vol. I, p. 477).

66. Major General Mansfield Lovell, military commandant at New Orleans, to Secretary of State Judah Benjamin, from New Orleans, February 27, 1862 (O.R., Ser. II, Vol. I, p. 683). Cf. also the testimony of Governor Thomas O. Moore of Louisiana before the Investigating Committee, ibid., 608 ff.

67. Testimony of Hollins before Investigating Committee (O.R., Ser. II, Vol. I, p. 477).

elaborated especially by Beverly Kennon, the colorful and somewhat erratic ordnance officer at New Orleans. Kennon, if we may credit his own testimony, had achieved wonders in preparing, purchasing, and even inventing various types of guns, ammunition, and other war supplies. Yet, he complained, he was removed from his post on the grounds that he was spending money too lavishly. The Navy Department, he declared, had actually lost money by his recall. Block tin for which he had paid twenty-five cents the Department was forced to buy later at five dollars; flannel bought by him at thirty cents a yard had to be purchased later at two or three dollars; zinc bought by him at about twenty cents was bought later at sixty-eight or eighty-seven cents.[68]

The Navy Secretary rebutted these allegations with some solid arguments of his own. Kennon, he said bluntly, had been found to possess three faults: he was insubordinate, he was extravagant in his official expenditures, and he drank too much. (As to the first of these points, Kennon himself admitted that he had an aversion for making formal requisitions and for submitting reports, both of which operations, he declared, obstructed his work. As to the charge of intemperance, he conceded that he had taken a few glasses of beer.)

Mallory further submitted that there was good reason for the Navy Department's caution in endorsing money requests emanating from New Orleans. The expenditures at that point exceeded for every object and in every case all estimates and calculations of the Department. For example: Hollins had recommended the establishment of a laboratory and had declared that $5,000 would be sufficient for the purpose. The Department had given him the necessary authorization. What had happened? The completed project had cost about $146,000. The accounts presented for the fitting up of the *General Polk* showed that the vessel herself cost $8,000, while her repairs, alterations, etc., ran up a bill of $52,459.99. Hollins, without the knowledge or authorization of the Department, and in the absence of any appropriations for meeting the payment, had contracted for ordnance and ordnance stores totaling about $500,000. He was further reminded that he was, by naval regulations, entitled to the services of a clerk while on land, at a salary of $900 per year, but the Department was not aware that he had any right to a secretary, whom he had engaged without permission.[69]

68. *O.R.,* Ser. II, Vol. I, pp. 521-31.

69. Mallory to Flag Officer George N. Hollins, commanding at New Orleans, November 22, 1861 (*ibid.,* 515).

Lack of ready funds handicapped the Navy Department to an increasingly distressing degree as the war progressed. The difficulty was never fully solved. Within the administration itself, all was not going smoothly.

If we may trust Mallory's account, which, in truth, is rather inconsistent, there were already present signs of the fatal defect that would weaken the Confederate war effort at its most crucial stages—the deficiency of really great governmental leaders.

Jefferson Davis as an administrator, thought Mallory, had his serious faults. While none would deny the President's intense sincerity, industry, and unselfish devotion to the cause,[70] yet he was often dilatory in dispatching his work and in making decisions; and, according to Mallory, "he neither labored with method or celerity himself, nor permitted others to do so for him."[71] He permitted much of his time to be taken up with petty details, especially military details, for which he had a particular fondness; the consequence was that matters of higher and more pressing importance were often neglected.[72]

He apparently did not know how to run his Cabinet meetings in such a way as to facilitate, rather than block, the work of his colleagues. Mallory described the President's method in this way: "His [Cabinet] officers were in the habit, individually, of conferring with him almost daily, and he usually assembled them twice or three times a week for consultation. These meetings occupied from two to five hours, far longer than was required. . . . But from his uncontrollable tendency to digression,—to slide away from the chief points to episodical questions, the amount of business accomplished bore but little relation to the time consumed; and unfrequently [sic] a Cabinet meeting would exhaust four or five hours without determining anything; while the desk of every chief of a Department was covered with papers demanding his attention."[73]

70. Cf. the glowing tribute to Davis' honesty and "superb courage" in Dunbar Rowland, op. cit., X, 124).

71. Mallory, letter to Buddy, supra cit. Cf. a contrasting picture of Davis' mental ability, with an added compliment to his literary style: J. B. Price to Davis, from Jefferson City, Mo., September 1, 1889, in Rowland, op. cit., X, 133-35. Colonel James Barry Price, although a Virginian by birth, attained prominence as a public-spirited citizen successively in Tennessee, Louisiana, and Missouri. During the war he was active in the introduction of war munitions from foreign ports for the use of the Confederacy.

72. Mallory, letter to Buddy, supra cit. Concerning Davis' self-declared repugnance to his office as chief civil executive, and his preference for military action, cf. Dunbar Rowland, op. cit., VI, 346, Speech of President Davis at Montgomery, from Charleston Daily Courier, October 3, 1864.

73. Mallory, letter to Buddy, supra cit.

He was also, said Mallory, a perfectionist, in the sense of wishing to make no move unless it could be done without the shadow of a flaw, and this habit frequently paralyzed his activity.

In his dealings with members of Congress and with high military officers, Davis was, according to Mallory, often cold and haughty, at least in appearance, and in addition annoyed them by a glaring lack of punctuality in keeping his appointments. Before the war was a year old, he had alienated a lifelong friend, General Joseph Johnston, by going over the latter's head in appointing higher officers.[74]

Mallory had plenty of opportunity to watch his chief closely, and he left a detailed description of Davis' character and working methods. The President had the faculty, common in men of the world, of "being surprised at nothing." This defensive armor enabled him to "listen to the announcement of defeat, while expecting victory, or to a foreign dispatch destructive to hopes widely cherished, or to whispers that old friends were becoming cold or hostile, without exhibiting the slightest evidence of feeling beyond a change of color, a tell-tale which he could never entirely command; and yet his sensibilities are extremely acute."[75] Under such circumstances, "his language, temperate and bland, his voice calm and gentle, and his whole person at rest, he presented rather the appearance of a man wearied and worn by care and labor, listening to something that he knew all about, than of one receiving ruinous disclosures."[76]

He fully understood and appreciated the evils resulting from hasty conclusions, and, guided by a stern consciousness of this and schooled by long mental discipline, he rarely allowed his irascible and excitable nature to lead him into inconsiderate action. "Like an elegant, polished, highly finished, well poised and well charged dueling pistol, whose hair trigger responds to the slightest touch, he could be very readily fired, but he never went off half cocked. A look, a word,—nay, his own reflections,—may cause his color to change, his eyes to flash, and his form to straighten up rigidly; but his lips remain compressed until judgment opens them."[77]

74. *Ibid.* For a defense of Davis in regard to the removal of General Johnston, cf. James Lyons to W. T. Walthall, from Dagger's Springs, July 31, 1878, in Rowland, *op. cit.,* VIII, 215-16. Lyons was an ardent Whig who practiced law in Richmond. On the death of John Tyler in 1862 he was elected to the latter's place in the Confederate Congress and was later appointed a judge to try political prisoners. W. T. Walthall was, at the end of the war, a colonel in the Confederate army. Afterward he aided Jefferson Davis in the preparation of *The Rise and Fall of the Confederate Government.*

75. Mallory, Diary, part II, 2.

76. *Ibid.*

77. *Ibid.*

Although apparently cold and exclusive, Davis was naturally genial and social; few men proved to be more attractive in private society. No one delighted more to relieve his burdened heart and mind by pleasant conversation upon general subjects, a taste which the seclusion of a Cabinet meeting and the presence of trusted friends prompted him very frequently to gratify. Upon such occasions, aided by the inspiration of a good cigar, his conversation, rambling pleasantly over fields other than Confederate affairs, was extremely engaging.[78]

He was a good judge of men, in Mallory's opinion. From indications which often escaped the observation of others he could frequently determine the general designs of those with whom he was brought in contact, before they had time to become reserved. He possessed a remarkable knowledge of the habits of men in various walks of life. This enabled him to bring himself at once to the level of those with whom he was conversing—to use their own familiar phrases and figures of speech and to be thoroughly at ease with them, a species of flattery which was well calculated to make men communicative. He was a favorite with all children, whom he never failed to interest, and his own children regarded him as their pleasantest playmate.[79]

With regard to the President's difficulties with the Congress, Mallory had this to say: "Mr. Davis' relations with the members of the Congress from and after the first year of the war were not what they should have been, —certainly not what the interest of the country required. I do not intend to go into details upon this subject, for it is an unpleasant one. In justice to him it is proper to say that if coldness or misunderstandings and misrepresentations frequently followed his intercourse with them, it was not because he was not ardently urging the prosecution of the war with the utmost vigor. In a body as large as that composing both houses of Congress, there must necessarily be found some men in whom public was generally subordinated to private interest; and many whose real zeal for the public welfare was much mingled with selfish considerations. A wound to their self esteem affected their action in public affairs, and Mr. Davis' sins in this respect towards them, real or imaginary, were seen in their votes and speeches."[80]

78. Mallory, letter to Buddy, *supra cit.*
79. *Ibid.*
80. *Ibid.* Cf. the following criticism leveled against the general character of the Confederate Congress: "In justice to President Davis I must say that there never was in my opinion a body of men less fitted for the task which they had undertaken than the first Congress, and I am told the second was worse. Jealousy, selfish ambition, and consequent discord prevailed from

Davis' manner of receiving visitors left something to be desired, and would seem to be inconsistent with Mallory's previous observation that the President was "naturally genial and social." "Few men could be more chillingly, freezingly cold," Mallory wrote. "Those who came without special appointment usually found him engaged with a mass of papers before him, telling as plainly of his occupation as his formal and scanty [in his corrected copy of this passage, Mallory has erased the word "scanty"] courtesy did of the importance of his time and his sense of its interruption. There was no waste of words, no ignoring of his preoccupation, few generalities, and, in spite of any amount of self-complacency, sensible men soon felt . . . that it was wrong to engross his time if they could, while bores were convinced that they could not engross it if they would; and their stay was generally brief; his face yielding its only approach to a smile when he saw them depart."[81]

Toward all he wore his opinions very openly, and made few concessions to those necessary arts by which friends are drawn closer, enemies conciliated, and refusals softened. In rejecting proposals from members of Congress or from anyone else, "he rarely satisfied or convinced them simply because in his manner and language there was just an indescribable something which offended their self esteem and left their judgments room to find fault with him."[82] Some of his best friends left him at times with feelings bordering closely upon anger from this circumstance, and with a determination never to call upon him again. Many of those men, including some of the "most sensible, prudent, calm and patriotic . . . of both houses," were in this way permanently alienated from him.[83]

Vainly did his advisers urge him to adopt a more conciliatory manner toward those with whom he must work. "He could not do this; it was not in his nature; and his restless, manly, open and turbulent spirit turned from what to him seemed the feigned approach to seeking popularity; and he scorned to believe it necessary to coax men to do their duty in the then condition of their country."[84]

the commencement" (James Lyons to W. T. Walthall, from Dagger's Springs, July 31, 1878, in Dunbar Rowland, *op. cit.*, VIII, 214), Mr. Lyons is, obviously, something less than temperate in his expression of opinion. Cf. also the following typical observation of President Davis with regard to the attitude of Congress: "The notion that under our form of government an expression by the Legislative of want of confidence in the Executive Department is an appropriate exercise of constitutional power, and should cause a change in the Cabinet, is quite unfounded, and it is not difficult to see that it arises from a false analogy [with the government of Great Britain]" (Davis to Hon. J. A. Seddon, February 1, 1865, in *ibid.*, VI, 459).

81. Mallory, letter to Buddy, *supra cit.*    82. *Ibid.*
83. *Ibid.*                                    84. *Ibid.*

Davis seems to have had more confidence in Mallory than in any other member of his Cabinet, with the possible exception of Benjamin. Usually the President did not interfere in the administration of the Navy Department, as he sometimes did in other bureaus of the government. In almost every instance of disagreement between Mallory and others, and whenever Mallory was attacked, the President stood firmly on his Secretary's side.

By some it has been thought that Mallory was an influential adviser of Davis, second only to Benjamin.[85] Certainly he was regarded by contemporary criticism as being one of the leading formulators of administration policy. It would be illuminating to have a record of the conversations between Mallory and the President on the not infrequent occasions when they rode together along the battle front.[86]

As the summer changed into fall, it was clear that a strong bloc in the Congress was gunning for the President. Mallory thought that this opposition was instigated and nourished only by envy and ambition, but a chance remark in his diary hints at a possible deeper reason: he deemed it unwise that Cabinet meetings were now held so infrequently, since, as a result, many important events or measures transpired without the knowledge of the other chief officials.[87] This was an interesting reversal of Mallory's previous complaint regarding the frequency and length of Cabinet meetings;[88] but it suggested also that perhaps the Congress, as well as the members of the Cabinet, was being kept unnecessarily in the dark concerning matters of which it could have been safely informed.

The main charges against the administration were elaborated in some blasts from the tireless *Richmond Examiner,* which declared that the Cabinet was composed of "men of palliatives, expedients, and partial measures."[89] The President had "sought to play the political virtuoso, storing away in his cabinet articles of value to him only, because no one else could be induced to think them valuable."[90]

85. John A. Crago, Contemporary Confederate Criticism of President Davis (unpub. Master's thesis, University of Florida, Gainesville, Fla., 1940), 58.

86. Cf. Mallory, Diary, part I, 21-22: "28 June 1861—Accompanied the President during the last three days to the field of battle." For further descriptions of the character of Jefferson Davis, see Elisabeth Cutting, *Jefferson Davis, Political Soldier* (New York, 1930), ix-x; Armistead C. Gordon, *Jefferson Davis* (New York, 1918), 290-317; J. B. Jones, *op. cit.,* II, 372.

87. An army officer in Richmond defended the President on this point. Affairs were being so bungled, says, in effect, this witness, that the Confederacy needed, if not a despot, at least a strong and firm administrator (Edward Mason to his wife Bessie, from Richmond, June 4, 1861 [E. P. Alexander Papers, University of North Carolina]).

88. Cf. *supra,* p. 176.                    89. February 4, 1862.

90. February 27, 1862. Cf. the following attacks on Mallory in particular. Said the *Savannah Republican* (March 11, 1862): "Mr. Mallory had been nominated for the Naval

But Davis and his official advisers were not altogether without their defenders. "No disappointed ambition," declared the *Richmond Enquirer,* "no private griefs can warrant . . . attack on the Government which, even if true, could . . . weaken the great cause for which the patriots of the South are struggling, and give 'aid and comfort' to the enemy."[91] The same journal, in its lead editorial of March 7, 1862, presented a long review of Davis' policies and administrative acts, with the aim of providing proofs of his true and loyal statesmanship. A similar defense of the administration and of Davis himself was stressed in the *Enquirer* a few days later. "Davis," it was asserted, "had . . . uttered his defiance in the Washington senate and gone to his people, before the *Whig* [a prominent anti-administration journal] waked up. So of the Secretary of the Navy. No man can or does question these or any of the others mentioned by the *Whig*."[92] The charge of "despotism" leveled, rather inconsistently, at Davis was rebutted with vigor.[93]

A large and vocal group in the South would never cease to question the integrity of Mallory's position on the question of secession. He had been a strong pro-Union man before 1861, ran the charge; was he really and wholeheartedly in favor of the Southern revolution now? In a letter to Governor Milton, of Florida, Mallory struck back at his defamers. "I notice what you say about systematic opposition to me," he wrote, "and I thank you sincerely for your generous support which I shall ever remember. My whole course on the secession question has met my own approval at least, and so far from shunning investigation I court the closest scrutiny. I have written a letter [rebutting some general charges] . . . I feel that I have ren-

---

Bureau and unanimously rejected. He [Mr. Davis] cannot administer the government on the narrow basis on which he has set out." "There is considerable complaint of Mr. Mallory," declared the *Southern Confederacy* (March 20, 1862), "on account of his administration of the Naval Bureau." This journal criticized Mallory severely for his alleged failure to provide a sufficiency of ironclads (*ibid.,* March 21, 1862). "Won't somebody pinch Mr. Mallory," asked the editor, "and tell him to shake off his drowsy spell?" (*ibid.*).

91. *Richmond Enquirer,* March 8, 1862. "The statement [that two or three million dollars' worth of enemy shipping had been destroyed by Confederate cruisers] will show how unfounded the complaints have been that the Navy Department has been showing no energy in the matter" (*Daily New Orleans Picayune,* March 23, 1862). In similar vein, from the *Southern Confederacy* (January 31, 1862): "This feat of provisioning Fort Pulaski was one of the most brilliant of the war. All honor to our glorious little navy."

92. *Ibid.,* March 20, 1862. In the same sense, *ibid.,* June 26, 1862.

93. *Ibid.,* July 9, 1862, reprinting and commenting favorably on a letter of Senator Benjamin H. Hill, of Georgia, to the *Atlanta Confederacy,* defending the Davis administration. For an expression of the "despotism" charge against Davis, cf. *Richmond Examiner,* January 2, 1862. For another general defense of the administration, cf. *Georgia Constitutionalist,* n.d., quoted by *Richmond Enquirer,* February 27, 1862.

dered most valuable service to my State, and I certainly am prepared to stand upon and sustain my course; my only regret being that I may be compelled to speak more of myself, and [of] my action, to defend myself against my enemies, than my modesty would otherwise approve."[94]

Harmony was temporarily restored at Richmond by the general lifting of spirits consequent on the battle of Manassas. But, barely a month later, came the disaster at Hatteras Inlet, which, declared Mallory, was due to inexcusable inaction and inattention somewhere. The Secretary of the Navy had a long conference with the President concerning this naval loss, and came away from the meeting seriously alarmed at the state of the Chief Executive's health. Davis looked worn, feverish, and discouraged. He soon rallied, but the brief revelation of weakness had given Mallory a shock.[95]

A wholesome counter-irritant was, however, at hand, at least for the Secretary of the Navy. Whatever the failings of the Confederate government, he believed, the rulers at Washington were infinitely worse. He was convinced that the Republicans were rapidly fastening a monarchy upon the country. It was indeed, he conceded, their only salvation. An established church and a safe monarchy constituted their only chances of survival, for they had no fixed or sound views of really republican government. Already their Constitution had been used to sanction suspension of trial by jury and the disregard of habeas corpus, and personal liberty was being struck down. When the Northern troops came home, the Washington government, from motives of sheer self-preservation, would be forced to become a military despotism.[96]

This charge of despotism leveled by the South against the Federal government was further elaborated as the war progressed. In the fall of 1863 the visit of Russian warships to New York harbor moved Southern editors to the construction of a bitter analogy: "The sympathies and the interests of the two parties . . . run very much in the same channel. The two despots of the East and West sit, grimly regarding each other across the intervening world, and say God-speed to the glorious work of 'order' in which both are engaged. Certainly between the Empire of Russia and the so-called Republic of the United States there is the greatest identity of likes and dislikes. Both have an unlimited desire for territorial expansion; both have an utter antipathy for freedom of speech and of the press; both delight in enormous armaments; have the barbarian love for vastness and display, and despise

---

94. Mallory to Governor John Milton, from Richmond, October 13, 1861 (W. H. Milton Collection, Florida Historical Society Library, St. Augustine, Fla.).

95. Mallory, Diary, part I, 14.          96. *Ibid.*, 8-9.

the restraints of law or humanity when opposed to the gratification of their wishes. At present, too, they have an additional bond of union. Both are annoyed by rebellions. One is striving to crush the embryo independence of a free-born race while the other struggles to repress the efforts of a gallant people to shake off the yoke of the czars. There are other points of resemblance between these two nations. In both, a gloss of civilization covers the intrinsic savagery of nature. This, in the Russian boyard, takes the form of diplomatic refinement and courtesy; in the Yankee, it appears as a sham intellectual culture and pseudo-philanthropy. Each looks with nervous sensitiveness to the opinion of Europe. The Russ, recently emerging from Scythian rudeness, desires the applause of that civilization into which he is a newcomer, while the Yankee looks back with servile admiration and craving for praise to the society [England] in which he knows his progenitors held but a humble place. There is also a similarity of government. Both are now military despotisms, and have a common interest in the suppression of every struggle for liberty and the suffocation of every lofty aspiration."[97]

If Mallory is to be believed, the Northern administration also was suffering its due share of heckling from within. Southern spies in Washington, posing as good Republicans, were reporting that "cliques and parties, animated by mutual and deadly hostilities, exist among the officers of the Army, Navy, . . . and even in the Cabinet."[98] The "New York Committee," representing the bankers of that city, had recently gone to Washington to force McClellan to advance, demanding a victory and prophesying direful results if a victory were not speedily secured. Lincoln had sent for McClellan, Mallory wrote, and the General replied in substance that his army was not prepared to advance, and that if forced upon the point he would

97. *Richmond Examiner*, October 5, 1863. As part of the effort to enlist the enthusiasm of all classes in the prosecution of the war, Southern publicists offered to Catholics the argument that the South was fighting for the rights and freedom of members of that faith. Cf. *Richmond Enquirer*, May 10, May 18, 1861, the latter containing the letter of an Irish Catholic named Mark Downey to Henry A. Wise, and Wise's reply asserting the above claim. The *Richmond Whig* (October 11, 1861) spiced the argument with a bit of humor: "The best joke of the season is the arrest in New York of a stalwart son of Africa for delivering a vehement speech in favor of Secession. After he was taken to Court, he insisted on continuing his harangue and offered to prove to the satisfaction of the Court, that the Yankees were guilty of a monstrous crime and folly in insurrecting against their legitimate masters, the gentlemen of the South. We have been long convinced, that the negroes are a far superior race, far more high-toned and aristocratic and gentlemanly than the Yankees; and if the North country was fit for a civilized being to live in, we should be in favor of driving the present inhabitants into the Bay of Fundy, and giving it over bodily to the negroes."

98. Mallory to Governor John Milton of Florida, from Richmond, November 2, 1861 (Milton Letter Book, Florida Historical Society Library).

resign rather than incur the risk of another Bull Run. The Republican leaders then said that McClellan ought to resign, but Lincoln stood by him and told him to take his time.[99]

There was no doubt as to Mallory's vigorous Southern sentiments in this first winter of the war. "Strange as it may sound to us," he wrote to Governor John Milton, "the Republicans and even the Democrats in the North are still dreaming of a 'reconstruction of the Union,' and hug themselves with the belief that we would consent to a connection with them. I trust that those among us, and there are many here, who entertain such a dream, will soon awake to its utter unreality. Upon no terms, and under no circumstances should we consent again to go into any Union with them; and if we can silence grumblers for eighteen months more, there will not be found one man in one thousand among us who will not feel degraded by the proposition. We are a purer, nobler, braver and better people in all respects that they can ever become so long as the Puritan blood flows in their veins; and I know as well as I can know anything in the future that all mankind will so acknowledge us."[100]

Mallory was looking confidently for a speedy recognition of the Confederacy by the great powers of Europe.[101] The French emperor, he was assured, had determined to raise Lincoln's blockade, and would soon act alone if not joined by England. The latter power had come to the same conclusion, but, "as her cotton people are subscribing largely just now and . . . developing cotton in Maia and Africa, Lord Jno. Russell wishes to delay getting out cotton from the South for a short time, fearing that to raise the blockade now would be to arrest this cotton movement."[102]

In the midst of his deep concern for the naval interests of the whole Confederacy, Mallory did not forget the needs of his native state. He had four gunboats under construction in Florida for the defense of Florida.[103] He had sent several consignments of guns and ordnance to various key points of the state.[104] In October he wrote to Governor Milton the following reassuring report: "Two more VIII-inch guns left here for Fernandina a day or two since, with two rifled guns in field carriages, with 100 rounds of

99. *Ibid.*                                            100. *Ibid.*

101. *Ibid.*, November 19, 1861.

102. Mallory to Gov. John Milton, October 29, 1861 (W. H. Milton Coll.). Cf. also Mallory to Milton, November 2, 1861: "Lord Jno. Russell would recognise us at once, were it not that he fears he would thereby put a stop to the money movement now going on to develop new cotton supplies in Maia. So soon as the Manchester interest shall subscribe fully to this new movement, he will act in our case" (Milton Letter Book).

103. *Ibid.*, November 19, 1861.

104. *Ibid.* Cf. also Mallory to Milton, October 13, 1861 (W. H. Milton Coll.). Also *ibid.*, October 20, 1861.

ammunition. . . . These guns are designed for the vessel being built there, but will be very useful in the meantime. I have made a contract for building a vessel (propeller) on the Appalachicola, and she is commenced, and I write today . . . to ascertain what we can build on that river. If we can build a steamer there I will begin at once; and if not we may build a barge perhaps."[105]

Governor Milton was much distressed at what he termed the interference of the War Department with the affairs of the Florida militia. The state was bending all efforts to build up the militia for the purpose of incorporating it in the Confederate armies. But the War Department had repeatedly given authorization to private individuals (frequently from outside the state) to raise troops in Florida. This created confusion and seriously hindered the state's military effort. A recruiting officer of one such private company, said Milton, had recently passed through Pensacola, seeking men from Florida in order to defend the coasts of Alabama—"now, is there not something ludicrous in men being taken from Florida to defend the coast of Alabama?"[106] Mallory's action in response to Governor Milton's request that he do something about this unhappy situation is evident from his letter to Milton of November 19, 1861. General E. Kirby Smith was sent to Florida as a "trouble-shooter," and Mallory managed to dispatch a few more heavy guns to main defense points in the state.[107] It is possible— though it cannot be proved—that it was due to the representations of the Secretary of the Navy that Bragg's forces around Pensacola were not withdrawn into Virginia in that fall of 1861.[108]

105. *Ibid.* Cf. also Mallory to Secretary Walker, August 1, 1861: "Fernandina wants four guns. This Department can furnish them if you direct it. The people there apprehend that Fort Clinch, at that place, unarmed and nearly completed, will be taken by the enemy, and that with these guns they may prevent it. Please say whether this Department shall furnish guns, carriages, etc." (*O.R.A.*, Ser. I, Vol. LIII, 179). Secretary Walker to Mallory, August 1, 1861: "Your note of this morning, informing this Department that Fernandina was in want of guns and that your Department could furnish them, has been received. You are respectfully requested to furnish and forward these guns at your earliest opportunity, providing them also with gun carriages and equipments if it should be in your power" (*ibid.*, 179).

106. Milton to Mallory, November 2, 1861 (Milton Letter Book).

107. Cf. *supra*, pp. 181-82, n. 94.

108. At a conference held on October 1, 1861, near Manassas, a proposal for an invasion of the North was discussed by President Davis and Generals Joseph E. Johnston, P. G. T. Beauregard, and G. W. Smith. A requisite for such a movement was the mustering of reinforcements from other sections. "The President," says R. S. Henry, "advised that he could not furnish the reinforcements asked for, 'without a total disregard of the safety of other threatened positions.' The project was dropped and the policy of the dispersed defensive was continued, although it would seem that the Confederacy could better have sent some of the fine regiments that General Bragg was drilling and training about Pensacola, and de-

In a letter to Mallory at about this time Milton struck a more personal note in a brief but pregnant paragraph: "From recent indications I think a scheme of systematic opposition to you is designed by some men in our State, and permit me to say to you that under all circumstances you may rely upon my friendship. . . ."[109]

With the approach of Christmas, 1861, the Navy Department had some additional reverses to record. The Federals had consolidated their positions at Hatteras, at Ship Island, and especially at Port Royal, and were in virtual control of the upper Mississippi. Two Confederate attempts to recover the vital harbor defense position at Pensacola had failed.

From North Carolina waters Mallory was receiving ominous reports which foreshadowed the disaster to occur there before the next spring. Governor Clark[110] of that state informed the Secretary of the Navy on September 7 of an imminent attack on Fort Macon, and said that the garrison of the place had no gunners who could manage the guns. He urged Mallory to supply the place with officers who understood the use of artillery.[111] In reply, the Secretary of the Navy declared that he had sent all possible aid, in the form of men and guns, to North Carolina defensive positions, but that it was impossible to send any more at the present time.[112]

Commander Hunter, directing defensive operations off Roanoke Island, expressed his doubts concerning the loyalty of the troops defending that vital point. He believed the position would be safe only if garrisoned by more dependable forces from another state.[113] But the Secretary of the

tachments from other garrisons, to attempt a promising move" (*The Story of the Confederacy*, 76). Cf. also, as a complement to the foregoing: "Mallory . . . , next to Benjamin, was to have the most power as an adviser [to Davis], being on friendly terms with Davis" (Crago, *op. cit.*, 58).

109. Milton to Mallory, from Marianna, October 2, 1861 (*O.R.A.*, Ser. I, Vol. VI, p. 288).

110. Henry Toole Clark was Governor of North Carolina from July, 1861, to January 1, 1863. After the war he was elected a member of the famous North Carolina legislature of 1866.

111. H. T. Clark to Mallory, from Raleigh, September 7, 1861 (*O.R.*, Ser. I, Vol. VI, p. 725).

112. "We have sent from Norfolk to North Carolina, up to July 15, 203 guns; in addition, up to 2nd of October, 39; in all, 242 guns, including 6 rifled 32-pounders. We have rifled and banded 23 guns, 6 of which have gone to North Carolina, and we cannot send any more rifled guns at present, our vessels being in want of them. Two additional vessels were ordered yesterday to North Carolina" (Mallory to S. Cooper, Adjutant and Inspector General, C.S.A., enclosed in a letter of the latter to Brig. Gen. D. H. Hill, commanding at Goldsboro, N. C., from Richmond, October 3, 1861 [*ibid.*, p. 736]).

113. Commander Thomas T. Hunter to Mallory, from C.S.S. *Raleigh*, off Roanoke Island, September 10, 1861 (*ibid.*, p. 725). It is to be noted that the responsibility for the supplying of coastal defense positions with men and ordnance was not exclusively that of the Navy Department but was to be shared by the Army.

Navy was confident that he held an ace in the hole. At Norfolk, Memphis, and New Orleans he was building five formidable vessels which, he felt, would turn the tide of battle in favor of the South. Of these ships four were powerful ironclad rams—the two under construction at New Orleans were the largest of the type in the world—while the *Virginia,* the vessel being prepared at Norfolk, was an ironclad of smaller proportions but awesome potentialities. With these ships, Mallory believed, the Confederacy would not only be able to defend its own shores effectively, and break the blockade; it could also strike mortal blows at Northern ports and Northern war vessels.

The *Virginia* was Mallory's pet. Frequently, during the early winter of 1861, the experts in charge of the building of the ironclad came up to Richmond to report how the work was progressing. The ship, they promised, would be ready for action by March. Mallory called her a "novelty in naval construction, ... untried, and her powers unknown."[114] She was completely covered with iron plates of two-inch thickness, lay so low in the water that her prow was actually submerged, and was practically invulnerable to the heaviest gunfire.[115] She represented, perhaps, the boldest effort of Confederate naval design; and she would, in the following spring, engage in one of the most crucial battles of naval history.

But the *Virginia* was not all. At New Orleans was being constructed the *Mississippi,* later the recipient of such extravagant encomiums from Fed-

114. Cf. his description of the *Virginia* in his *Report of the Secretary of the Navy, March 29, 1862 (O.R.,* Ser. II, Vol. II, pp. 174-76). For Mallory's part in conceiving and forwarding the work on the *Virginia,* see John M. Brooke, "The *Virginia* or *Merrimac:* Her Real Projector," in *Southern Historical Society Papers,* XIX (1891), 1-34. Testimony of the same John M. Brooke in *O.R.,* Ser. II, Vol. I, p. 786: "The novelty of the hull [of the *Virginia*] consisted in submerging the ends, but no experiment could be made to determine how it would succeed. Everything connected with the ship, except the old hull, was novel, so far as practical application was concerned, and the difficulties were overcome as they presented themselves, by consultation, reflection, and study." Cf. the following praise of Mallory by a modern naval expert: "In introducing armored ships the Confederates showed much enterprise. Early in 1862 Mallory had several ironclads nearing completion" (Charles O. Paullin, "A Half Century of Naval Administration in America, 1861-1911," in *United States Naval Institute Proceedings,* XXXIX, 173). For an adverse criticism of the effectiveness of Mallory's ironclad gunboats, see Lt. J. Taylor Wood to Lt. Catesby ap R. Jones, from Richmond, March 24, 1863, in *O.R.,* Ser. I, Vol. VIII, pp. 862-63. For a defense of Mallory's casemate type of ironclad as compared with the Federal turreted monitors, cf. Scharf, *op. cit.,* 672-73. The Confederate type (casemate), says Scharf, grew out of the necessities of the South's unfavorable economic situation. Concerning Mallory's insistence on actual experiments for determining the resistant qualities of the *Virginia's* iron shield, see *O.R.,* Ser. II, Vol. I, pp. 785-88.

115. Cf. the more precise description of Scharf, *op. cit.,* 152: "The iron plating . . . was two inches thick. The underlayer being placed horizontal, and the upper laid up and down —the two [together] being four inches thick—were bolted through the woodwork, and clinched inside."

eral naval men. A recent critic of Northern sympathies has declared his opinion that the ship, when completed, would have been invulnerable to any guns that could have withstood the impact of her formidable ram. He regards as not unfounded the Confederate boast that she was the most wonderful warship in the world.[116] She, as well as the *Virginia*, was held by Confederate naval experts to be "entirely a new conception."[117] They were confident that she would be able to keep the Mississippi River clear of all blockade.[118]

It is much to the Secretary's credit that he drove ahead with his ironclad building program and gambled so heavily on the *Virginia*, in particular, despite the opposition of many of the leading officers of the Navy. Such prominent authorities as Matthew F. Maury, for instance, had little confidence in the new type of fighting ship and urged the construction of small wooden gunboats. So little was known about ironclads by Southern naval men generally, later declared Commander Brooke, that very few officers were willing to express an opinion with regard to the new type until the experiments with the ships had been made.[119] Mallory doggedly continued to believe in the ironclad, and was only too willing to make the experiments.[120]

116 Rear Admiral W. M. Parks, U.S.N., Retired, "Building a War Ship in the Southern Confederacy," *U. S. Naval Institute Proceedings,* IXL, 1301.

117. Testimony of Captain Arthur Sinclair (in charge of the building of the *Mississippi* at New Orleans) before Naval Investigating Committee, *O.R.,* Ser. II, Vol. I, p. 511; cf. also *ibid.,* 546-47.

118. "I am satisfied," declared Captain Sinclair, "that she could have . . . kept that river clear against the blockade" (*ibid.,* 511).

119. *Ibid.,* 785.

120. Cf. the meticulous experiments performed in order to ascertain the suitable thickness for the *Virginia's* iron plates (*ibid.,* 785-86).

# CHAPTER NINE

# The Virginia ... Norfolk ...
# New Orleans ... Richmond

F OR THE CONFEDERATES the year 1862 brought sober tidings. By mid-February three more vital defense points had fallen—Fort Henry on the Tennessee, Fort Donelson on the Cumberland,[1] and, perhaps the most severe blow of all, a Federal land and sea attack had captured the fortifications on Roanoke Island, North Carolina.

This position was the key to all the rear defenses of Norfolk. Its fall threw open to the enemy two sounds—Albemarle and Currituck—eight rivers, four canals, and two railroads. Norfolk's communications with Richmond were threatened, and General Huger's army was cut off from its chief source of supplies at the former city. The enemy was now lodged in a roomy harbor safe from the storms of Hatteras and commanded the sea from Oregon Inlet to Cape Henry.[2] Both the Army and Navy departments were bitterly criticized for having defended Roanoke Island too lightly.

For at least four and a half months before the tragedy at Roanoke Island, naval officers had been calling attention to the inadequacy of the arrangements for the defense of the coasts of North Carolina.[3] The chief

1. For details of the campaign against Fort Henry and for the important part taken by Foote's gunboats, cf. Hoppin, *Foote,* 190-207. Walter Geer, in *Campaigns of the Civil War* (New York, 1926), 62, says: "This [operation against Forts Henry and Donelson] was the first instance in the Civil War in which a river was used as the line of operations, and it furnished nearly the only successful instance in any modern campaign. The ease with which transports can be harassed by the enemy on shore renders the use of rivers as lines of operations very exceptional." He quotes also from Matthew F. Steele, *American Campaigns* (2 vols.; Washington, D. C., 1922), I, 167. Cf. also John C. Ropes, *The Story of the Civil War* (2 vols.; New York, 1933), II, 3-95.

2. Scharf, *History of the Confederate States Navy,* 393. The position should have been guarded, says this authority, by at least 20,000 men and several more vessels, rather than by the single brigade of General Wise and the little fleet of seven small ships under Captain Lynch. The Confederate squadrons in North Carolina waters were, in the very first action, dissipated and scattered. The enemy in his expeditions up the rivers of the state did not encounter a single armed vessel.

3. Cf. H. K. Burgwyn (a prominent citizen of North Carolina) to Mallory, from Goldsboro, N. C., September 4, 1861 (*O.R.,* Ser. I, Vol. VI, p. 721): "Fort Macon has not one

charges related to the alleged improper placing of the land forces on the beaches,[4] the poor morale of some of the troops,[5] and the unwillingness of the army to reinforce the naval units in North Carolina waters with men of previous naval experience who were then serving in the land forces.[6]

That the Navy Department had made its due contribution to the North Carolina defenses is fairly evident from a report of Mallory at the beginning of October, 1861. Up to that time, he said, the navy had sent from Norfolk to North Carolina 242 guns, including 6 rifled 32-pounders. The Department had rifled and banded 23 guns in all, of which 6 had gone to North Carolina. No more rifled guns could be sent there for awhile, since the navy's ships were in urgent need of them. Two more rifled guns had been sent to North Carolina the day before.[7] Flag Officer Lynch, at the end of his long report to Mallory in late January, 1862, after detailing what he believed to be the serious deficiencies of the army's preparations at Roanoke Island and Hatteras Inlet, concluded with the sentence: "I mention these things to protect in a very probable event the reputation of the Navy."[8]

A hint of a further possible and more basic cause of the fall of the North Carolina posts was contained in a complaint addressed by Brigadier General Henry Wise to Captain Lynch less than a month before the Roanoke disaster. Apparently it was not clear to all the officers immediately concerned whether the floating battery at Redstone Point, on Croatan Sound, was under naval or military command. A midshipman had been detailed to give gunnery instructions to the soldiers who were manning the battery. These men were certainly to some extent under the midshipman's control; but they were also commanded by their own captain. Lynch declared that the army authorities were not enforcing obedience to the naval instructor's orders. As a consequence, all was not going smoothly at the battery.[9] This

---

practical gunner; has only forty reliable fuzes, no rifled cannon, no ordnance officer, and only raw troops without proper supplies. It must fall. It should be supplied at once with a competent naval ordnance officer."

4. Flag officer William F. Lynch to Mallory, from C.S.S. *Sea Bird*, off Roanoke Island, January 22, 1862 (*O.R.A.*, Ser. I, Vol. IX, p. 147).

5. *Ibid*. Cf. also Commander Thomas T. Hunter to General Benjamin Huger, from C.S.S. *Raleigh*, off Roanoke Island, September 10, 1861 (*O.R.*, Ser. I, Vol. VI, p. 725).

6. Lynch to Mallory, *supra cit*. Cf. also Flag Officer F. Forrest (commandant of Norfolk station) to Flag Officer Lynch (commanding Virginia and North Carolina coast defenses, etc.), September 23, 1861 (*O.R.*, Ser. I, Vol. VI, p. 733).

7. Adjutant and Inspector General S. Cooper to Brig. Gen. D. H. Hill (commanding at Goldsboro, N. C.), from Richmond, October 3, 1861, enclosing communication from Mallory, n. d. (*ibid.*, 736).

8. Lynch to Mallory, *supra cit*.

9. Brig. Gen. Henry A. Wise to Captain W. F. Lynch, from C.S.S. *Sea Bird*, January 9, 1862 (*O.R.*, Ser. I, Vol. VI, pp. 754-55).

was an early example of a confusion and clash of administrations—military and naval—which may have had more to do with Confederate failures on land and sea than has been commonly recognized.

Under the caption "The Roanoke Island Disaster: The Inaction of the Navy Department," the *Norfolk Day Book* asserted that "criminal negligence is chargeable somewhere. . . ."[10] It had long been common knowledge, the journal declared, that the Burnside expedition was hovering off the Carolina coast. It had been equally patent that the Roanoke Island fortifications were not sufficiently manned. Yet nothing had been done for the further defense of the important point. The *Day Book* declared that twenty gunboats or more should have been stationed in the sound. Ten months had elapsed since the navy yard at Norfolk had come providentially into Southern hands, and fifty such gunboats might easily have been constructed there, armed, manned, and placed at the mouths of the numerous small streams in the sound and elsewhere. But not a single craft of this kind had been built. This, thought the journal, was a startling fact and evinced what the public regarded as culpable negligence. Although within a few hours' ride of this great depot of the Confederacy, Mr. Secretary Mallory had not once visited the navy yard at Norfolk "since he warmed his official seat," nor had he manifested the administrative energy in the matter of these gunboats which the time demanded of him.[11]

Mallory's opponents made much of the charge that the Navy Department had failed—culpably and ingloriously—to build a sufficient number of gunboats, the type of vessel pre-eminently fitted, it was claimed, for the defense of coastal and river positions. The pro-administration *Richmond Enquirer* endorsed the statement of one Harvey Brown that "in every river and harbor of the Gulf, a gunboat drawing six feet of water, and well armed with good rifled guns, can do more and better service than a forty gun ship such as the *Niagara* and the *Richmond*." One such gunboat in a river, thought the *Enquirer*, with a good shore battery to which it could retire for cover against a superior attack, would secure the shores of the river against depredating parties and against any demonstration of the

10. *Norfolk Day Book*, quoted, n.d., in *Richmond Enquirer*, February 14, 1862.
11. *Ibid.* Concerning the fall of Roanoke Island, cf. the mutual recriminations of Flag Officer William F. Lynch and Brig. Gen. Henry Wise, revealing a jarring lack of cooperation between army and navy units at Roanoke Island, and possible loose administration by the Navy Department: Major Gen. Benj. Huger to Brig. Gen. Henry Wise, with enclosure, from Norfolk, February 3, 1862 (*O.R.*, Ser. I, Vol. VI, pp. 760-62); Brig. Gen. Wise to Major Gen. Huger, from Great Bridge, Norfolk Co., February 17, 1862 (*ibid.*, 762-65).

enemy not made in large force. The small vessels would also greatly increase the difficulty of maintaining the blockade.[12]

It was alleged that Congress had made appropriations for a considerable fleet of gunboats. But, it was said, the Navy Department had as yet made no contracts for the construction of these vessels.[13]

The charges, while exaggerated, appear to have some weight. The fact was, at this time and throughout the war, that the Confederacy did not place in coastal and inland waters the number of small gunboats considered by many naval experts as the minimum requirement for the respectable defense of those waters. This is not to say that, in view of the Navy Department's already heavy commitments in other fields, this could have been done; it is merely to remark that it was not done.

The chorus of condemnation against the naval administration increased in volume during the following few weeks. Mallory was said to have displayed a "lack of energy and efficiency."[14] The Confederacy, grumbled the *Charleston Mercury* sarcastically, was handicapped by "inferior advantages, —and superior feebleness in the head of the Navy."[15] It was not to be doubted, admitted the usually sanguine *Richmond Enquirer*, "that the South, with those resources in the department of naval enterprise which she possessed in the beginning, could have achieved a brilliant career in naval warfare, if her measures had been conducted by able hands. She has thrown away by official incompetency a magnificent opportunity to carve out a brilliant history upon the ocean. That the South could have made a better fight on water than she did is a fact well known to ourselves and will be

12. *Richmond Enquirer*, January 14, 1862.

13. *Richmond Examiner*, January 13, 1862. Cf. also J. Alexander to President Davis, from Memphis, March 19, 1862 (*O.R.A.*, Ser. IV, Vol. I, p. 1009): "The Secretary [of the Navy] was entirely too slow in commencing to build gunboats, and he is now heartily cursed from one end of the country to the other. The property taken and destroyed by our enemies on the Tennessee and the Cumberland would have built gunboats sufficient to have protected all the rivers in the South. Now, should he [the enemy] get down the river, we lose all our boats." (The writer of this letter was apparently a cotton planter of Tennessee.)

14. *New Orleans Bee*, n. d., in *Charleston Mercury*, March 7, 1862.

15. *Charleston Mercury*, March 15, 1862. It is noteworthy, incidentally, that charges against naval officials were not confined to the Confederate side. At about this time the *New York Herald* delivered this barrage against Secretary Gideon Welles: "It turns out that the splendid preparations made to sink [the *Virginia*], of which the Department has given us such solemn assurance, consist of an invitation for her to come out and place herself in such a position that a ball from Fortress Monroe may destroy her. Until the rebels accept this invitation . . . the *Merrimac* and her consorts may capture as many schooners as they like, and keep our whole fleet and army at bay. If, in the meantime, the rebels would only send a gunboat or two up the Potomac, and throw a large shell directly into the sleeping apartment of the venerable head of the Navy Department, we will forgive them all the other damage they may do us in a year" (*New York Herald*, n. d., reprinted in *Richmond Enquirer*, April 24, 1862).

the subject of eternal shame to those at home through whose conduct it was not done."[16]

Furthermore, it was charged, there had been on the part of the Navy Department a marked want of intelligent stimulation of Southern manufacturing industry. The War Department, it seemed, was doing all it could in the way of indirect premiums and other encouragements to assist the development of the iron interests of the country. But this interest, which was equally important to the Navy Department, had received no intelligent assistance whatever from Mallory.[17]

To these various charges rebuttals were offered by the Navy Department's defenders. Mallory was being blamed for not having built enough gunboats; but had Congress made all the necessary appropriations?[18] A stronger, because largely unintended, vindication of the Navy Department with regard to the "gunboat charge," was presented by the normally anti-administration *Richmond Examiner* in rather surprising fashion later in the spring. "Indeed, when the history of this war is reviewed," the *Examiner* said, "it will be found that the chief service the enemy has gotten from his gunboats has been to frighten bad officers and worse troops into surrendering positions which they might have continued to hold. Nowhere have the gunboats effected either real damage or extensive slaughter. Port Royal was taken by the heaviest ships in the navy, coming up in deep water. At Donelson the gunboats were smashed; at Island No. 10 they did no harm; at Drury's they were beaten by three guns."[19]

This seems to leave the question of the usefulness of gunboats pretty much up in the air. The *Examiner's* consistency, of course, might be saved by the argument that gunboats, while ineffective in offensive movements, were highly valuable for the defense of small harbors. But even for this purpose such vessels would seem to be poor gambles if they were actually as defective as the *Examiner* claimed them to be. The truth, was, perhaps, that nobody—including Mallory and his critics—was quite sure as yet as to the powers and weaknesses of gunboats.

The most effective of the pro-Navy Department arguments were those of a more general character. "This is not the time," admonished a friend of the administration from Georgia, "to indulge in recriminations against the public authorities. They have done well, or as well as could be done under the peculiar circumstances by which they are surrounded."[20] The

16. *Richmond Enquirer*, May 14, 1862.    17. *Richmond Examiner*, January 13, 1862.
18. *Richmond Enquirer*, February 14, 1862, letter of "A Georgian" to the editor.
19. *Richmond Examiner*, May 19, 1862.    20. *Ibid.*

*Richmond Examiner* practically conceded the case to Mallory's Department by the following rather remarkable admission: "The enemy far outnumber us, and they have an equipment of artillery, shipping and machinery which must give them great advantages in all places where these instrumentalities can be fully employed. Along the water-side, whether at Roanoke Island or elsewhere, the chances are ten to one of their taking any positions they may bring their armaments to bear against. Along the great water courses of the interior, this same wealth in artillery, boats and men, must place us at a great disadvantage. It would be silly and weak to despond over accidents like these [the fall of Roanoke Island]. We have many more such events to meet and patiently digest. With their heavy force, it is not possible to prevent successes of the sort."[21]

The blame for the fall of Roanoke Island was probably allocated most justly by the investigating committee appointed by Congress to inquire into the causes of the disaster. It was the verdict of this Committee that the War (Army) Department had been negligent in garrisoning the island with far too few troops. The post had fallen not mainly by reason of the naval attack, but because the defending land forces had been too weak to repel an onslaught made from the land side by the enemy. The fact that in the report of the committee there was no complaint against the Navy Department was a fairly complete disavowal of any serious deficiency on the part of the Navy Department in the affair.[22]

In regard to one sector Mallory felt a particular anxiety. The shore batteries protecting Richmond, and the obstructions in the James, were that city's first lines of defense; they had to be held if the capital was to be safe. Every few days he would mount a horse and make a personal inspection of the key point of these defenses, Drewry's Bluff. There he had concentrated the best and most powerful of the Confederate naval ordnance; on the skill and courage of the men in charge of those great guns, acting in accord with the gunboats and, it was hoped, with the *Virginia*, the safety of Richmond would depend.[23] In addition, the James and York rivers had

21. *Ibid.*, February 11, 1862.

22. Cf., for reprint of and comment on the report, *Charleston Mercury*, April 17, 1882. Also following testimony of Lt. B. P. Loyall, C.S.N., before the committee: "It is my opinion and belief that the island, with the defenses and the forces upon it at the time of the attack, could not have been maintained against the force of the enemy" (*O.R.*, Ser. I., Vol. VI, p. 600).

23. Already the Federal squadrons had tried several times to breach the James River defenses, but had been in each instance repulsed. Cf. *O.R.*, Ser. I, Vol. VI, pp. 742, 733-34; Scharf, *op. cit.*, 94 sq. In the early summer of 1862 the *Stevens* attacked up the James, and created much alarm at Richmond (*O.R.*, Ser. I, Vol. VII, pp. 368-39).

been thickly sown with the deadly submarine mines which, before the end of the war, were to prove so effective.[24]

McClellan's plans in the Peninsular campaign were predicated on the hope that the Federal navy would maintain control of the James.[25] It became, therefore, the duty of the Confederate James River squadron and shore batteries to prove that this hope was visionary. The Confederate naval forces were doing rather well at the task, and, in addition, were cooperating in many helpful ways with the army. The C.S.S. *Teaser* was acting as an intelligence and liaison unit for Lee's troops on both shores of the river.[26] A substantial naval vessel had been completely transferred by the navy to the land forces for the purpose of transporting troops.[27] The shore batteries were manned largely by naval personnel.[28]

The navy's servicing of these crucial positions was, however, criticized adversely in some quarters. Not enough naval guns, it was charged, were being sent to the James River stations.[29] The Yorktown battery was in a state of disrepair.[30] The Navy Department was too grudging in supplying powder for the guns at Norfolk.[31] Too many naval officers and naval enlisted personnel were being shifted from the shore batteries to other less important posts.[32]

The Secretary's hopes were, of course, still resting heavily on the *Virginia*. Reports and instructions passed swiftly and urgently between Rich-

24. Cf. M. F. Maury's detailed description of the mines in the Potomac (*O.R.*, Ser. I, Vol. VII, pp. 544-46).

25. Geer, *op. cit.*, 87; Ropes, *op. cit.*, II, 99-212.

26. Mallory to Gen. R. E. Lee, June 17, 1861 (*O.R.*, Ser. I, Vol. V, p. 808).

27. Mallory to Secretary of War L. P. Walker, June 19, 1861 (*O.R.A.*, Ser. I, Vol. LI, part 2, supplement, p. 141).

28. Gen. Benj. Huger to Secretary Benjamin, from Norfolk, December 23, 1861 (*O.R.A.*, Ser. I, Vol. LI, part 2, supplement, p. 426); Secretary Benjamin to Gen. Huger, December 25, 1861 (*ibid.*, 426-27). Major General Huger had insisted on the indispensability of naval officers for commanding the shore batteries in the Norfolk area. Mallory had withdrawn three of these officers, but, at the earnest request of the army, had sent them back to the batteries.

29. Lt. I. N. Brown, C.S.N., to Maj. Gen. L. Polk, from Norfolk, August 2, 1861 (*O.R.*, Ser. I, Vol. XXII, p. 791).

30. Brig. Gen. J. B. Magruder to Mallory, from Williamsburg, Va., September 11, 1861 (*O.R.*, Ser. I, Vol. VI, p. 725). Cf. also Geo. Minor (commander, for chief of bureau of ordnance and hydrography), to Brig. Gen. John B. Magruder, September 21, 1861 (*O.R.A.*, Ser. I, Vol. LI, part 2, supplement, pp. 306-7).

31. Maj. Gen. Benj. Huger to Secretary of War, from Norfolk, December 10, 1861 (*O.R.A.*, Ser. I, Vol. LI, part 2, supplement, pp. 410-11).

32. *Ibid.* Cf. the following, indicating that the navy did not always receive all that it sought from the army. Mallory to Flag Officer F. Buchanan, March 2, 1862 (*O.R.*, Ser. I, Vol. VI, p. 779): "I am requested by the Adjutant-General to inform you that it will be impossible for General Magruder to act in concert with or render you any aid in the plans agreed upon to attack the enemy at Newport News, and you will therefore be governed accordingly, and for the present act independently."

mond and the Norfolk navy yard during the first two months of 1862.[33] By the beginning of March, Mallory knew that the ironclad was practically ready. It was none too soon. In those same last days of February, 1862, Nashville had been taken by the Federals, and the Confederate cruiser *Nashville* (by an ironic coincidence) destroyed. Grant was about to begin his concentration at Pittsburg Landing, and Johnston was grouping his forces to oppose the Federal General at Corinth. Time indeed was running out, and the tide of battle was none too favorable for the South.

Into the strategic balance, Mallory was confident, the new ironclad at Norfolk would throw a heavy and decisive weight. He sent a long instruction to Flag Officer Buchanan, who was to command the vessel. The *Virginia,* he felt it was unnecessary to remind his subordinate, was a novelty in naval construction. The Department would give no specific orders as to the manner of her attack upon the enemy. The ship's powers as a ram, even without guns, were deemed formidable, and it was hoped that Buchanan would have an opportunity to test them. Like the bayonet charge of infantry, this mode of attack would doubtless commend itself to the Captain in the present scarcity of ammunition, and it would be effective at night against enemy ships at anchor. If Buchanan could pass Old Point and make a dashing cruise on the Potomac as far as Washington, the effect upon the public mind would be immense. The depressed morale of the South, caused by recent military reverses, called for a sudden and bold blow by the navy. "Action, prompt and successful action," was the need of the hour.[34]

On March 6, Buchanan was getting ready to move the *Virginia* out into the river. On the seventh he received the following message from the Secretary: "I submit for your consideration the attack of New York by the *Virginia.* Can the *Virginia* steam to New York and attack and burn the city? She can, I doubt not, pass Old Point safely, and, in good weather and a smooth sea, could doubtless go to New York. Once in the bay, she could

33. For example, Mallory to Capt. S. S. Lee, commanding Norfolk navy yard, March 3, 1862: "You are specially requested to urge on the completion of the ironclad gunboat [*Virginia*] in course of construction. Advertise for mechanics in North Carolina, if you need them, and employ one hundred or a thousand or more if necessary, but push on the work. Stimulate your workers by every means in your power, and if you want more officers, or desire the detachment of any you have, for the good of the service, you are requested to suggest them. The Department wishes to do all in its power to develop the full powers of the Yard" (*O.R.,* Ser. I, Vol. VII, p. 753). Concerning the building of the *Virginia* and the debate as to who first originated the plans for her building, see *Southern Historical Society Papers*, XIX, 3 ff., in support of the claims of Brooke and Porter; *Asheville Times*, August 22, 1926, in support of the claim of Commander Gabriel Galt Williamson.

34. Mallory to Captain Buchanan, February 24, 1862 (*OR.,* Ser. I, Vol. VI, pp. 776-77).

shell and burn the city and the shipping. Such an event would eclipse all
the glories of the combats of the sea, would place every man in it pre-
eminently high, and would strike a blow from which the enemy could
never recover. Peace would inevitably follow. Bankers would withdraw
their capital from the city. The . . . navy yard and its magazines and all the
lower part of the city would be destroyed, and such an event, by a single
ship, would do more to achieve our immediate independence than would
the results of many campaigns."[35]

On the next morning—the eighth—the *Virginia* finally took her trial trip,
which turned out to be also her first combat. Escorted by two small gunboats, Buchanan steamed his awkward yet formidable craft down the Elizabeth River and into Hampton Roads, into the very midst of an enemy
squadron, the guns of which, together with Federal shore batteries, out-
numbered his own by about eleven to one. The *Virginia* could make but
five knots, and was so unresponsive to her rudder that it required thirty
to forty minutes to turn her. But she would wreak havoc that day, and
win for herself a significant place in the annals of naval warfare.

At Fort Monroe lay the Federal frigates *Minnesota,* with forty guns, the
*Roanoke,* forty guns, the *St. Lawrence,* fifty guns, and six gunboats. There
was a strong Federal land battery at Newport News, another on the land
side of Fort Monroe, and the "great gun" at the Rip-Raps. The big frigates
*Cumberland* and *Congress* also lay near by, their officers and crews in no
wise anticipating a battle.

At Sewell's Point Buchanan made his historic decision. He turned the
*Virginia* with her little escort toward Newport News, called his men to
stations, and, moving to within a mile of the *Cumberland,* began his engagement with that ship. The action soon became general, the big Federal
frigates and shore batteries concentrating their heaviest fire on the Confederates. Buchanan continues the story in his official report: "The *Virginia*
stood rapidly on toward the *Cumberland,* which ship I had determined to
sink with our prow, if possible. In about fifteen minutes after the action
commenced we ran into her on starboard bow; the crash below the water
was distinctly heard, and she commenced sinking, gallantly fighting her guns
as long as they were above water. She went down with her colors flying.
During this time the shore batteries, *Congress,* and gunboats kept up their
heavy concentrated fire upon us, doing us some injury. Our guns, however,

35. Mallory to Captain Buchanan, March 7, 1862 (*ibid.,* 780-81). This statement of Mallory's as to the potentialities of the *Virginia* is rather naïve. The vessel would have foundered
in the open sea. Cf. *infra,* p. 201, n. 49.

were not idle; their fire was very destructive, to the shore batteries and vessels."[36]

Reinforced by two frigates and by a gunboat under Commander John H. Tucker, Buchanan now turned his attention to the *Congress*. "We were some time in getting our proper position, in consequence of the shoalness of the water and the great difficulty of managing the ship when in or near the mud. To succeed in my object [of attacking the *Congress*] I was obliged to run the ship a short distance above the batteries on James River, in order to wind her. During all the time her keel was in the mud; of course she moved slowly. Thus we were subjected twice to the heavy guns of all the batteries in passing up and down the river. . . . [Finally] . . . we opened upon her. . . . The carnage, havoc, and dismay caused by our fire compelled them to haul down their colors and to hoist a white flag. . . ."[37]

During the rest of the afternoon the combat continued between the Confederates and the other Federal ships. At nightfall the firing ceased, and Buchanan anchored his squadron off Sewell's Point. The *Virginia* had sunk or completely disabled the two largest ships of the Federal fleet and, for five hours, had stood up under the combined fire of the Federal floating and shore batteries. The new vessel had proven beyond the shadow of a doubt that she possessed immense destructive power and an astonishing invulnerability to the heaviest gunfire.

Back in the Navy Department office at Richmond, Stephen Mallory, during that whole day, had stayed at his desk, receiving hourly reports of the battle. This day and the one following marked the single clean-cut triumph of his administration. For this moment he had planned, fought against opposition, and prayed. Even in his somewhat restrained announcement of the victory in his official report to the President, his elation revealed itself: ". . . The dashing courage and consummate professional ability of Flag-Officer Buchanan and his associates achieved the most remarkable victory which naval annals record."[38]

The significance of the victory was perhaps best expressed in Josiah Tattnall's congratulatory message to Buchanan: "That which I admire most in the whole affair is the bold confidence with which you undertook

36. Report of Capt. Buchanan to Navy Department, enclosure No. 2 in message of President Davis to Congress, April 10, 1862 (*O.R.*, Ser. I, Vol. VIII, p. 44).
37. Flag Officer Franklin Buchanan to Mallory, from Naval Hospital, Norfolk, March 27, 1862 (*ibid.*, 44-45).
38. Mallory to President Davis, April 7, 1862 (*ibid.*, 43).

an untried thing."[39] The compliment, in precisely these words, was due equally to Mallory.

The combat on the following day between the *Virginia* and the Federal ironclad *Monitor* was a further proof that the wooden fighting ship was obsolete. For several hours the two vessels pounded away at each other, while, during long periods, each was also subjected to the fire of shore batteries and of other ships in the Roads. The issue was a draw, neither ship being able to destroy the other.[40]

The *Monitor,* the Confederates were forced to admit, was a powerful vessel, scarcely inferior to the *Virginia;* and, the Confederates knew, there would be many others of the same model built in the North. The South had led the way in the new type of naval warfare; but the North, with her vastly superior ship-building facilities, would enjoy immense advantages in a race to construct the greatest possible number of ironclads.

However, despite these sober speculations, which must have occurred to thoughtful men of the South, the net result of the two days' conflict had been a victory for the Confederates. Against overwhelming odds, measured in terms of ships and guns, the South had seriously weakened the Federal blockading squadron at the mouth of the James, and had shown the awesome potentialities of the new type of warship.

The friends of the Navy Department made the most of the opportunity to say, "We told you so!" After describing rather lyrically the details of the *Virginia's* victories, the *Richmond Enquirer* declaimed: "As showing the amount of labor necessary for the full equipment of this unique vessel, it may be stated that twelve hundred men have been thus employed constantly for six months past. Much of the work was done in Richmond. This simple statement will show how unfounded have been the complaints that the Navy Department was showing no energy in the matter. The trumpets indeed were not sounded nor the bells rung at every step of the progress. The Department did not even stop to answer the allegations that the whole scheme was an expensive abortion; but, quietly, and with the energy we have described, it pressed forward the vast work."[41]

One of the few ungracious notes in the chorus of praise was emitted by the intransigent *Examiner.* "The success of the *Merrimac,*" said the journal, "however gratifying it may be, is in fact a severe reflection upon our sloth

39. Flag Officer Tattnall to Buchanan, from Savannah, March 12, 1862 (*ibid.,* 57-58).

40. Cf. Buchanan's report of the engagement (*O.R.A.,* Ser. I, Vol. IX, pp. 1-14).

41. March 11, 1862. For an account of the *Virginia-Monitor* battle and its political significance, see Commodore Foxhall A. Parker, U.S.N., "The 'Monitor' and the 'Merrimac,'" *U. S. Naval Institute Proceedings,* I (1874), 155-62.

and inactivity in naval preparation. It proves what we could have done in this department of our operations if we had employed the proper energy. There are several other hulks in the Portsmouth Navy Yard that may be rendered just as formidable to the enemy as the *Merrimac* herself; and fifty gunboats could have been also constructed to give these large war vessels aid and comfort."[42]

A few years later a persistent critic of Mallory asserted that the Navy Department, instead of contenting itself with one *Virginia,* could have had ten such ironclads, and could thereby have easily prevented the disasters at the North Carolina coast positions except, possibly, at Hatteras, "had the Secretary of the Navy . . . possessed the ability and zeal essential to his responsible position."[43]

The naval war, of course, was not yet won for the South. The urgent problem in the minds of the strategists in the days following the *Virginia's* victory was how to use the ironclad's vast potentialities most effectively. It must be remembered that McClellan was slowly but steadily forcing his way up the peninsula between the York and the James toward Richmond, thus flanking Norfolk. How could the *Virginia* best cooperate with the Confederate land forces in scotching this threat?

At the beginning of the second week in April, General R. E. Lee wished the ironclad to pass Fort Monroe by night and move into the York river, since he had received reports from General Magruder that the enemy was about to change its base of operations from the James to the York.[44] Four days later came a dispatch from Magruder declaring, in apparent contradiction to Lee's opinion, that the *Virginia* would be most useful "by remaining where she is."[45] Mallory, on April 16, transmitted to the Secretary of War the orders which had been just issued to Tattnall ". . . to keep himself informed of the enemy's movements in the Roads, to destroy his transports, to prevent him from crossing or ascending James River, and to render his squadron as destructive and formidable to the enemy as practicable."[46] If, added Mallory, the military operations on the peninsula could be better supported or assisted "by further or different orders," would the Secretary of

42. *Richmond Examiner,* March 20, 1862.

43. E. A. Pollard, *Southern History of the War* (2 vols.; New York: Chas. B. Richardson, 1866), I, 280.

44. R. E. Lee to Mallory, April 8, 1862 (*O.R.A.,* Ser. I, Vol. XI, part 3, pp. 429-30).

45. J. B. Magruder to Secretary of War Randolph, from Yorktown, April 12, 1862 (*ibid.,* 437).

46. Mallory to Secretary of War Randolph, April 16, 1862 (*ibid.,* Vol. LI, part 2, supplement, pp. 538-39).

War kindly indicate his views?[47] In endorsing the general sentiments of this communication, General Lee repeated his view that the *Virginia* should go into the York River.[48]

As is well known, the ironclad did not move into York River; she did no further damage to the enemy; and she was soon to be destroyed at her moorings by her own commander just before Norfolk fell. It is difficult, however, to detect any outstanding strategical error in the Navy Department's orders of March, April, and May regarding the vessel. Mallory's directions of April 16 seem to constitute as wise a disposition of the *Virginia* as any of the other plans proposed.[49]

Besides the employment of the *Virginia,* the Navy Department was cooperating in many other important ways with the army defending the approaches to Richmond, Norfolk, and Yorktown. Naval vessels on the Rappahannock were towing up boats loaded with grain and other supplies for the army commissary.[50] Lieutenant Lewis of the navy responded promptly to the appeal of Major General Gustavus W. Smith for aid in removing the guns and other public property from Fort Lowry to Fredericksburg.[51] At the request of Major General Theophilus H. Holmes preparations were made for sinking four heavily ballasted ships as obstructions across the Rappahannock.[52] The gunboats on the James were keeping the army informed of the enemy's movements in the river, were trying to disperse and destroy the Federal transports, and cooperating closely with the land batteries.[53]

47. *Ibid.*
48. *Ibid.* Concerning the proposed movements of the *Virginia* cf. *ibid.,* Vol. XI, part 3, pp. 476-78.
49. Said Parker, *op. cit.,* 268, referring to the other suggested adventures for the Virginia: "As to the *Merrimac* [*Virginia*] going to New York, she would have foundered as soon as she got outside of Cape Henry. She could not have lived in Hampton Roads in a moderate sea. She was buoyant enough to float when she had a few days' coal and water on board. A little more would have sent her to the bottom. When she rammed the *Cumberland* she dipped forward until the water nearly entered her bow port; had it done so she would have gone down. Perhaps it was fortunate for her that her prow did break off, otherwise she might not have extricated herself. The *Merrimac* with but a few days' stores on board drew 22½ feet of water. She could not have gone to Baltimore or Washington without lightening her very much. This would have brought her unarmored hull out of the water and then she would no longer have been an ironclad."
50. Mallory to Secretary of War Randolph, dated April 6, 1862 (*O.R.,* Ser. I, Vol. V, pp. 578-79, enclosing report of commanding Lieut. H. H. Lewis to Mallory, dated April 3, 1862, from Fredericksburg).
51. *Ibid.*
52. *Ibid.* Cf. also, concerning cooperation between the services in this area, *O.R.,* Ser. I, Vol. VII, pp. 765-803.
53. W. H. Taylor, Assistant Adjutant General, to Major General J. B. Magruder, April 3, 1862 (*O.R.A.,* Ser. I, Vol. XI, part 3, p. 418).

Apparently the teamwork between the two services in the area was good. General R. E. Lee supported the request of the Secretary of the Navy that six or eight nine-inch guns be transferred from a shore battery near Norfolk and used to arm the new gunboats.[54] Lee also urged his subordinate officers to lend army mechanics to the navy at need.[55] Army and navy officers worked well together, it would seem, at the batteries.[56] Occasionally, as in the case of the management of the obstructions in the James, there were conflicts of administration,[57] but such jarrings were apparently exceptional.

Whatever his deficiencies, Mallory, in those early days of 1862, was not inactive. He was urging Captain S. S. Lee, the commander at Norfolk, to get the ironclad *Richmond* finished at the earliest possible moment for the defense of Norfolk, Richmond, and the James. "The safety of Norfolk," he wrote to Lee on April 22, "depends, in my judgment, upon the immediate completion of the *Richmond*. The *Virginia* must soon be withdrawn, and the *Monitor* must be opposed by the *Richmond* or nothing."[58] Work on the vessel was to be pushed on day and night. Lee was to secure "every available mechanic," and the Secretary was sending to him in a day or so a hundred additional workmen.[59]

Two days later Mallory wrote to the Norfolk commander: "With an overwhelming force at your doors, and the prospect of losing Norfolk within twenty days distinctly before us, it will not do to limit the work upon this vessel [the *Richmond*] to one half this available time. I think you will be able to find lanterns and to organize a corps of men, boys, or girls even, to hold them [the lanterns] and thus enable the mechanics to work at night. If practicable it must be done."[60]

54. R. E. Lee to General Benjamin Huger, from Richmond, April 3, 1862 (*ibid.*, Vol. LI, part 2, supplement, p. 528).

55. *Ibid.*

56. Cf., for example, Mallory to Capt. Lee, C.S.N., May 15, 1862 (*O.R.*, Ser. I, Vol. VII, p. 800): "Proceed to Drewry's Bluff and take command of the naval defences of the James River, relieving Commander Farrand, who will remain there second in command. General Mahone has been assigned to the chief command, but the naval force is expected to fight all the batteries, complete the obstructions, and mount additional guns where you may deem them necessary. Consult freely with General Mahone and defend the river to the last extremity. Apply to me promptly for all and any aid I can afford you."

57. Cf. A. L. Rives, acting chief, engineer bureau, to Secretary of War Randolph, received at engineer bureau, Richmond, July 15, 1862 (*O.R.A.*, Ser. I, Vol. LI, part 2, supplement, p. 592).

58. Mallory to Capt. S. S. Lee, April 22, 1862 (*O.R.*, Ser. I, Vol. VII, pp. 772-74).

59. *Ibid.*

60. Mallory to Lee, April 24, 1862 (*ibid.*, 773-74). A routine order, typical of many sent by Mallory at this time, was the following to Lt. Wm. A. Webb, C.S.N. (commanding

This last dispatch was written on April 24, a day dark for the Confederacy for a reason entirely dissociated from Norfolk concerns. On this date Farragut ran past the forts which protected New Orleans. The incident marked the tragic failure of Confederate naval strategy in a sector far from the James and Richmond, but, as events proved, equally important.

While directing naval operations nearer home, Mallory had not for one moment forgotten the perilous condition of New Orleans. As he planned for the victory of Hampton Roads and later rejoiced over it; as he watched carefully over the defenses of the James, and sought to save Norfolk, he kept his eye with increasing concern on the great Gulf port. Commodore Laurence Rousseau[61] was instructed as early as July 9, 1861, to accept and equip for service whatever steamers Governor Moore of Louisiana might turn over to him, and which, in the naval officer's judgment, would be useful for the public service. Rousseau was ordered also to give to General Twiggs,[62] if the latter so desired, all the large guns made for the navy by the Tredegar works at Richmond and by the iron works at New Orleans. Eight hundred yards of the heaviest chain cable was sent to New Orleans on July 10, to be stretched across the river as an obstruction to any enemy vessels that might attempt an upward thrust from the Gulf.[63]

Confederate intelligence agents who had actually succeeded in securing jobs in the Federal shipyards at St. Louis kept sending reports of an imminent movement of the enemy in force down the Mississippi against New Orleans. In estimating the responsibility of the Secretary of the Navy for a mistake in judgment which contributed to the fall of the Gulf port, it is only fair to remember that the reports of these intelligence operatives at St. Louis provided considerable grounds for believing that the attack on New Orleans would come from the north. It is to be remarked also that many at New Orleans shared this view, or some modification of it. Lovell thought that the attack would be directed not against New Orleans but against Mobile.[64] As late as February 27 he wrote to Secretary Benjamin: ". . . I regard Butler's Ship Island expedition as a harmless menace so far

---

steamer *Teaser* in James River at City Point), April 20, 1862 (*ibid.*, 769): "With the vessel under your command you will tow to this city a vessel now in the James River about City Point loaded with timber for this Department. The timber is required for immediate use."

61. Concerning Rousseau, cf. *supra*, p. 137.

62. Major General D. E. Twiggs was in charge of Department No. 1, New Orleans.

63. Mallory to Secretary of War, July 10, 1861 (*O.R.A.*, Ser. I, Vol. LIII, supplement, pp. 707-8).

64. General Lovell to President Davis (*ibid.*, Vol. VI, p. 761); Lovell to Secretary Seddon (*ibid.*, 790).

as New Orleans is concerned."[65] There was, indeed, on the part of Farragut's own officers, the feeling that the New Orleans forts could not be passed.[66] Furthermore, the anticipation that the onslaught would come from up river was not without considerable grounds. The capture of Island No. 10 and the Federal operations around Fort Pillow suggested strongly that the threat to New Orleans from that quarter was the more formidable one.[67]

That the attack against the city would come from the north, Mallory never seems to have doubted. It was a miscalculation, an erroneous guess on his part, and was opposed to the view of some of his chief naval advisers, who urged that the thrust against New Orleans would come from the south. The only way to save the city, they argued, was to have a powerful defensive squadron on her southern flank. Mallory refused to be convinced. The blow, he was positive, would come from up the river. There was no need of sending more ships to the points below New Orleans; indeed, he argued, it would be dangerous to do so.

Although, as events proved, he was fatally wrong in this opinion, he was right on another point. The urgent need, he saw correctly, was to have completed, before the attack came, the two giant ironclads that were still under construction at New Orleans. To achieve this he spared no effort.[68] Telegrams and dispatches streamed from the navy office at Richmond to those in charge of the work on the *Mississippi* and *Louisiana*. Toward the end of February, despite his intense preoccupation with the *Virginia* at Norfolk, the Secretary wrote to Commander John K. Mitchell, in command of the New Orleans station, stressing the importance of having the ordnance and ordnance stores for the *Louisiana* ready on time. Mitchell was to "make all proper exertions" to have guns and carriages ready for the big ironclad.

---

65. Lovell to Benjamin (*ibid.*, 832).

66. Lewis, *op. cit.*, 47.

67. Hoppin, *op. cit.*, 294-303, 154-68. Foote wrote to Secretary Welles on April 17, 1862: "It is reported that Commodore Hollins left Fort Pillow on Sunday to bring up the heavy gun-boat *Louisiana*, now about completed at New Orleans. With the exception of this vessel, however, we have little to apprehend from the other rebel gun-boats..." (quoted in *ibid.*, 300). Knox, *History of the Navy*, 193, points out the fact that naval history before the Civil War had witnessed only rare instances of ships successfully attacking land fortifications such as those defending New Orleans. The same observation is made by Wilson, *op. cit.*, I, 40-42, 57-59.

68. A partial extenuation of Mallory's error concerning the direction of the attack against New Orleans may be found in the following statement concerning Benjamin's difficulties as Acting Secretary of War: "His problems were accentuated by the inadequate railroad, telegraph, and postal systems, and the wretched dirt roads. Sometimes it would be weeks before Benjamin would know what was happening in Texas or the Indian Territory, and there would often be anxious hours before he would even receive communications from nearby states" (Meade, *Benjamin*, 185).

If necessary, the contractors were to be urged to work gangs of men on the vessel at night. Mitchell was ordered to keep the Navy Department advised of "everything connected with the subject which you may deem of interest"; and he was assured that everything possible would be done at Richmond to facilitate the work on the *Louisiana*.[69]

At the same time the Secretary promised that the *Mississippi's* shaft, which was being made at the Tredegar iron works in Richmond, would be sent to New Orleans at the earliest possible moment.[70] Three weeks later he was forced to wire that the Tredegar works have "disappointed us terribly." The shaft was not ready and, although promised from day to day, might not be ready for another week. If the contractors could get another shaft at New Orleans, they were to do so at once. The Secretary added the injunction which, during this tense period, he so often repeated: "Work day and night to get your ship done, with no regard to expense."[71]

Mitchell was instructed to consult with General Lovell, the military commander at the Gulf port, and to take the *Louisiana* out of the hands of the contractors and to complete her himself, if, in his judgment, they were not doing everything practicable to complete her at the earliest possible moment. If Mitchell required more mechanics, and was otherwise unable to procure them, he was to ask General Lovell for details of men to work upon the *Mississippi*. He was also to adopt all means in his power to have rolling mills constructed and contracts made for iron armor.[72]

As the sultry days of early spring approached, and the defense problems of the James and Norfolk continued to tax the Secretary's mind and energies, the situation at New Orleans also grew increasingly tense. William C. Whittle, now the chief naval commander there, was becoming more and more worried, as indications pointed almost with certainty to a Federal naval concentration in the Gulf. The citizens' committee, and the people generally, of the threatened city were much dissatisfied with Mallory's handling of the problem of defense and were impatient at what they described as the tardiness of the work on the ironclads. On February 26 Gov-

69. Mallory to Mitchell, February 24, 1862 (*O.R.*, Ser. II, Vol. I, p. 466).

70. Mallory to the Tift Brothers (contractors), February 23, 1862 (*ibid.*, 605).

71. Mallory to Tift Brothers, March 15, 1862 (*ibid.*, 605-7).

72. Mallory to Mitchell, March 15, 1862 (*ibid.*, 466). Despite these evidences of activity on the part of the Navy Department, there were many at New Orleans who expressed their vigorous dissatisfaction with Mallory's plans for the defense of the city. The Navy Department, complained the *New Orleans Bee*, "has done nothing" for New Orleans (December 12, 1861). The same journal in its French edition of November 9, 1861, had urged support of a civic movement to raise $500,000 for the building of ironclads, which, said the editor, the Confederate Government was apparently not able to furnish to New Orleans.

ernor Moore of Louisiana, in a long telegram to President Davis, accused the Navy Department of "inefficiency and apathy . . . which was too painful and perilous to permit of any longer silence." The work on the *Mississippi*, the Governor complained, was not going ahead at any reasonable speed, and the Tift brothers, her builders, refused to accept the aid in men and money that was being lavishly offered by the local civil authorities.[73]

Lovell was now protesting against Mallory's insistence on weakening New Orleans' defenses in order to send more ships and batteries up the river for the purpose of blocking the attack which the Navy Secretary was expecting from the north.[74] Mallory seems to have placed too much confidence in the ability of the forts below the city to drive back any ships attempting to come up the river. He may be excused, to some extent, for so overstressing the defensive possibilities of these land positions. Whittle said that from his own conversation with General Lovell, as well as from observations which he saw daily in the New Orleans newspapers, he was led to believe that the military authorities were confident they had the power to prevent ships from passing the forts.[75] Captain Sinclair testified in the same vein. The passage of the forts, he agreed, was unexpected by the authorities at New Orleans, who showed their confidence in the city's southern defenses by refusing to move the municipal treasury further northward.[76]

At the end of the first week in April—while the threat to Norfolk was growing increasingly grave—began the strange tug-of-war between the Confederate Navy Department and the naval commanders at New Orleans and Fort Pillow, the puzzling contest of views and desires which had a great deal to do with the subsequent fall of the Gulf port. The sequence of events was as follows:

On April 6, Whittle, at New Orleans, became gravely alarmed. The enemy was in force at the mouth of the river and was preparing to move up.

73. Governor Thomas O. Moore to President Davis, February 26, 1862 (*O.R.,* Ser. II, Vol. I, pp. 608 ff).

74. Lovell to Benjamin, March 10, 1862 (*ibid.,* 687-88). C. L. Lewis, *op. cit.,* 42, writes: "Incredible as it may seem, as late as April 17 there was an exchange of telegrams between Governor Thomas O. Moore of Louisiana and President Jefferson Davis, concerning the *Louisiana* which had actually been ordered by Secretary of the Navy Mallory up the Mississippi to reinforce the squadron of Fort Pillow. This order . . . shows how completely out of touch the government in Richmond was with the real situation at New Orleans and with the impending disaster there. Indeed, the *Louisiana* could not have moved up the river against the current, even if obedience to the Secretary's order had been attempted." Cf., however, *supra,* pp. 203-4.

75. *O.R.,* Ser. II, Vol. I, p. 449.

76. *Ibid.,* 510 ff. Cf. also Governor Moore's testimony, *ibid.,* 612-613.

More ships were needed at once to block this attack; where could he get them? Whittle answered the question in irregular but decisive fashion. Hollins, he knew, was at Fort Pillow with a small but efficient squadron; to Hollins he wired directly—without consulting Richmond—asking the Commodore to come down to New Orleans with all his ships at once.[77]

Hollins wished to accede to this urgent request, but he seems to have desired also a confirmation from navy headquarters. He wired to Mallory on April 9, stating that the Federal ships had just passed below Island No. 10; that, with his own squadron he could do nothing to stop the enemy's further progress; and that, on the other hand, his vessels could render good service if sent below to New Orleans.[78] On the next day he received a wire from the Secretary informing him that "his proposition to quit the enemy and to go to the mouth of the Mississippi can not be entertained."[79] He was to stay where he was and "oppose his [the enemy's] descent of the river and his movement of vessels at every step."[80] Furthermore, the *Louisiana* and *Mississippi* would be sent up at once from New Orleans to join Hollins![81]

On the eleventh, while Richmond was feeling more and more apprehensive about Norfolk, Hollins repeated his request, informing the Secretary that he himself had already left for the Gulf port in order to confer with Whittle. Immediately, on the same day, came Mallory's reply, sent to meet the upriver commander at New Orleans: "Your dispatch received yesterday proposed to abandon opposition to the enemy's descent of the river by your fleet and to carry your fleet to the mouth of the river. This proposition is totally inadmissible; every effort that nautical skill, invention, and courage can put forth must be made to oppose the enemy's descent of the river, and at every hazard. You inform me that you have gone to New Orleans [without permission, the Secretary might have added!] at the urgent request of Captain Whittle. You will therefore send these orders to the senior in command of your squadron by telegraph. The *Louisiana* must join your squadron at the earliest practicable moment."[82]

General Lovell now entered the argument. "With forty [enemy] vessels in the lower river," he wrote to Randolph, the Secretary of War, "please

77. *Ibid.*, 520.
78. Hollins to Mallory, from Fort Pillow, April 9, 1862 (*ibid.*, 519-20). For series of Mallory-Hollins telegrams, see *ibid.*, Ser. I, Vol. XXII, pp. 839-41.
79. Mallory to Hollins, April 10, 1862 (*ibid.*, Ser. II, Vol. I, p. 519).
80. *Ibid.*
81. Mallory to Hollins, April 11, 1862 (*ibid.*).
82. *Ibid.*

protest in my name against sending the *Louisiana* up the river. . . ." He begged Randolph to try also to induce the Secretary of the Navy to permit Hollins to bring his ships down to New Orleans.[83]

Mallory, despite this added pressure, stuck to his original orders. For this he has been, after the fact, roundly condemned. The following questions might, however, be asked: What was the size of the force under Hollins? Could it have prevented the capture of New Orleans? Should Mallory have disregarded the reports of his intelligence agents upriver, who told him that all the signs pointed to an attack from above?

But the attack did not come from the north! After several days' bombardment of Forts St. Philip and Jackson the Federal fleet ran by them, and Farragut forced the surrender of New Orleans by threatening to fire on the city. On the twenty-fourth marines were landed at the Gulf port to raise the flag of the Union. The army under Butler followed quickly, and the unfinished *Mississippi* was burned by the Confederates.[84] All the key points on the river, save Vicksburg and Port Hudson, were now in the hands of the enemy.[85]

It was a stunning blow for Mallory. "The destruction of the Navy at New Orleans," he wrote in his diary, "was a sad, sad blow, and has affected me bitterly, bitterly, bitterly."[86] Two weeks later he wrote to his wife: "I do not know how you discovered that the naval losses on the Mississippi affected me; but the fact is (and I would not refer to it had you not done so) that they almost killed me, and I am ashamed to say that I have lain awake night after night with my heart depressed and sore, and my eyes filled with tears, in thinking over them. Our men fought splendidly, and merited by their gallantry the victory they had not the force to achieve. This has made me very weak, and neutralized the effect of all the medicine I have taken; but I am getting over it."[87]

83. Lovell to Randolph, April 11, 1862 (*ibid.*, 620). Cf. also Randolph's reply to Lovell, confessing his inability to change Mallory's views (*ibid.*, 695).

84. Mallory to the Tift brothers, May 24, 1862, on receipt of the news of the destruction of the *Mississippi:* "Deeply regretting the overwhelming necessity which seemed to dictate the destruction of the vessel constructed by you as the agents of this Department, you have the thanks of the Department for the patriotic and untiring zeal, energy, and industry displayed by you throughout the work" (*ibid.*, 607). Concerning the capture of New Orleans, cf. West, *Porter*, 113-41.

85. The expected bitter criticisms of the Navy Department were not long in appearing. Cf. *Charleston Mercury*, May 3, May 5, April 28, April 29, 1862.

86. Mallory, Diary, Part I, p. 19.

87. Mallory to his wife, May 11, 1862. Note the grim implications of the following item of a few weeks later in the *New Orleans Daily Delta:* "It appears from a report in one of the morning papers that the 'Union Association of New Orleans,' lately organized, has for its ob-

From all the discussions regarding the alleged shortcomings of both army and navy departments in the defense of New Orleans, there emerges a fact of more fundamental significance—a fact that was perhaps an important element in Confederate failures in other theatres of the war. As Major General Lovell testified, ". . . There were two separate and distinct organizations for the defense of Department No. 1, viz, that under the control of the Secretary of War, of which I was the senior officer, and that under the Secretary of the Navy, of which Commodore Hollins and afterwards Commander Whittle were the seniors."[88] The two administrations, declared Lovell, were "entirely independent of each other," although they were directed by their respective heads to "cooperate cordially" for the defense of the city. The General insisted, after the event, that "the best feeling existed [between the two services] and there was very seldom any difference of opinion between us as to what should be done."[89] Yet one is justified in asking whether this split administration was calculated to produce efficient and swift cooperative action at critical moments such as those that faced the Confederates at New Orleans in April 1862.

Lovell himself, more than three months before the fall of the city, had complained of the Navy Department's failure to carry out a strategic measure which the General regarded as essential to the protection of New Orleans, and which he had repeatedly urged on Commodore Hollins.[90] The measure involved the use of shallow-draft launches for the protection of navigable streams running up into the country, a tactic in accord with general strategic views expressed by Mallory himself several years before.[91] The launches had not been furnished. "I should have had [them] at numerous points along the coast," wrote Lovell to Secretary Benjamin, "had I not kept in view your expressed wish that all clashing, even in appearance, should be avoided between the two arms of the service. I hope that . . . you may be able to devise some plan by which either the entire matter

---

ject 'to reinstate in this city the Constitution of the United States and the State of Louisiana as they were previous to the act of secession.' This is well. Thousands have been anxiously waiting for some such movement on the part of prominent citizens before daring to come out and acknowledge their true sentiments. Thousands have chafed at the false and insolent statements [to the effect that there 'was no Union sentiment here to be developed'] which filled our daily papers for some days after the arrival of the army of deliverance" (June 7, 1862).

88. Testimony of Maj. Gen. Lovell at Court of Inquiry at Jackson, Miss., April 8, 1863 (*O.R.A.*, Ser. I, Vol. VI, p. 562).

89. *Ibid.*

90. Lovell to Secretary Benjamin, January 7, 1862 (*ibid.*, 798-99).

91. Cf. *supra*, pp. 97-99.

may be placed under my control or the naval officer in command may have orders to afford such aid as I may officially require of him."[92]

From the side of the navy also had come protests suggesting that the dual administration was causing serious inconvenience to defense preparations. Hollins had asserted in late March, 1862, that the army was hijacking guns sent to New Orleans specifically for naval purposes. He requested, rather stiffly, that the Navy Department inform him precisely what his authority was; for, he declared, "as it stands now, I have the mortification of seeing my orders countermanded by inferiors [of the army] and my officers threatened with imprisonment for attempting to carry them out."[93] It is only fair to add that Hollins, upon Mallory's protest and the prompt intervention of Secretary of War Randolph, received back his guns.[94] But the incident was another example of a conflict of aims and actions between the two arms of the Confederate service, and a confusion of administration which certainly did not make for effective results in the field and on the waters.[95]

It may well be the case that such clashings of army and navy aims and such vagueness as to the limits of the authority of army and naval officers constituted a larger factor in Confederate failures than has usually been realized. Nor were the disagreements and incidents of mixed jurisdiction confined to the New Orleans theater. At the Mobile station, marines (subject, of course, to the Navy Department) were serving with General Braxton Bragg's land forces; but, Bragg charged, groups of them were taken away periodically, without warning, by the Navy Department, thus embarrassing the army.[96] Moreover, the navy had made frequent requisitions on Bragg's ordnance supplies.[97] As a further indication of confused administration, there were in Mobile waters two steam gunboats commanded

92. Lovell to Secretary Benjamin, January 7, 1862 (*O.R.A.*, Ser. I, Vol. VI, pp. 798-99).

93. Geo. N. Hollins to Mallory, March 21, 1862 (*ibid.*, Vol. X, part 2, pp. 380-81).

94. Mallory to Secretary Randolph, April 1, 1862 (*ibid.*, 379-80), with Randolph's endorsement on this letter (*ibid.*, 380).

95. Cf. also the similar charges made by Gideon Welles: "August 10, 1862. Am sorry that better progress is not made in the war upon the Rebels. Our squadrons are paralyzed everywhere by the inactive and dilatory movements of the army. Vicksburg should have been taken by the first of June, but no adequate cooperating military force was furnished, and as a consequence our largest squadron in the Gulf and our flotilla in the Mississippi have been detained and injured" (*The Diary of Gideon Welles*, ed. John J. Morse, Jr. [3 vols.; Boston, 1911], I, 71-72). It might be added that if this lack of cooperation actually did exist between the arms of the Federal forces in the midsummer of 1862, it was certainly corrected shortly afterward, at least in the Vicksburg area.

96. Gen. Braxton Bragg to Adjutant General, C.S.A., from H.Q., army of Pensacola, November 29, 1861 (*O.R.A.*, Ser. I, Vol. VI, p. 772).

97. *Ibid.*

by landsmen.[98] The naval units in the area were cooperating poorly with the army, and Bragg and the ranking naval officer on the station were at daggers' points.[99]

At Galveston, the army officer in command was apparently ordering naval officers around, to the acute displeasure of the latter, and, over the objections of the naval commander, restaffing at least one vessel of the navy with army officer personnel.[100] Major General Leonidas Polk, at Columbus, Kentucky, had purchased a river steamer, made her into a gunboat, appointed a naval lieutenant to command her—and had then informed the Secretary of the Navy what had been done, and how much it would cost the Navy Department.[101] It is but just to add that the General said that he acted "under the pressing emergencies of the service on this river," and that he had previously confided his plans to the Navy Department; but the tenor of the correspondence between Polk and the Department suggests strongly that the masterful General was in no mood to be stopped by technicalities of protocol.

There was a confusion of command in September, 1861, in the case of the shore batteries on the James.[102] Many of these guns were manned by soldiers and commanded by naval officers who had no clear-cut authority over the members of the land forces.[103] Some guns sent by the Navy Department to one of its commanders on the James had been intercepted by Brigadier General Magruder and assigned elsewhere.[104] A minor climax of this administrative mélange occurred in the early summer of 1863, when a board of inquiry, composed entirely of army officers, placed naval officers on trial for alleged incompetence in defending New Orleans.[105]

98. *Ibid.*

99. Bragg to Adjutant General, from Mobile, December 29, 1861 (*ibid.*, 789-90); Mallory to Secretary Benjamin, January 9, 1862 (*ibid.*, 799-801).

100. Commander W. W. Hunter to Mallory, from Galveston, April 4, 1862 (*O.R.*, Ser. I, Vol. XVIII, pp. 838-40; *ibid.*, Vol. XIX, pp. 792-804).

101. Major General Leonidas Polk to Mallory, from Columbus, Ky., September 25, 1861 (*O.R.A.*, Ser. I, Vol. III, pp. 707-8, 716-17).

102. Captain Franklin Buchanan to Mallory, September 26, 1861 (*O.R.*, Ser. I, Vol. VI, p. 734).

103. *Ibid.*

104. Commander W. C. Whittle (commanding naval defenses in York River) to Captain D. N. Ingraham (in charge of Office of Ordnance and Hydrography, Richmond), from West Point, York River, July 12, 1861 (*ibid.*, Vol. V, p. 812).

105. Mallory protested to President Davis that the court of inquiry was "illegal and fraught with mischief to both branches of the military service." He reminded the President that the naval officer in command at New Orleans had already been subjected to a court of inquiry formed of his peers, and that all the operations of the Navy Department with respect to New Orleans had been investigated by a committee of the Congress (Mallory to President Davis, June 8, 1863 [*O.R.A.*, Ser. I, Vol. VI, pp. 629-30]).

In keeping with the tradition that troubles never come singly, Mallory, six days after the fall of New Orleans, was obliged to warn the naval commander at Norfolk to prepare for the evacuation of that post.[106]    The retreat of the Confederate army up Yorktown peninsula was rendering the great navy yard untenable. On May 3, with further news of the New Orleans debacle still pouring into Richmond, the Secretary of the Navy sent to Captain Lee the momentous order: "You have been informed by General [Joseph] Johnston of his contemplated movement [withdrawal] on the peninsula, and that Norfolk must consequently be abandoned."[107]    The supplies, as much as possible of them, were to be transported at once to "a safe place in North Carolina." All "ordnance stores and guns which cannot be saved" were to be destroyed.[108]

If Norfolk should fall, there was all the more need for defending the approaches to Richmond. On May 8, at the height of the crisis, General Robert E. Lee pressed Mallory for more naval gunners at Drewry's Bluff and for more obstructions in the river. At once Mallory sent to Commander Ebenezer Farrand, senior officer at the Bluff, the order: ". . . You will . . . make the best arrangement in your power to resist the enemy. Three of the enemy's gunboats and one of their ironclads, are in the James River, and they may be at Drewry's Bluff tomorrow morning. Ammunition for your battery is being sent to you tonight, and two companies of artillery. . . . Sink the *Jamestown* and any other of our gunboats that you deem proper to close the river. The enemy must not be permitted to pass, and your energy and ability are relied on to prevent them."[109]    The next day the Secretary reiterated his instructions: "You must lose not a moment of time in adopting and perfecting measures to prevent the enemy's vessels from passing the river. This duty is committed to the Navy, and you will establish your batteries, magazines, and defenses with all possible energy, working day and night, if you have men enough, until completed."[110]

These earnest precautions did indeed help much to save Richmond, although, by May 11, Norfolk was in Federal hands, and—an equally disastrous blow—the mighty *Virginia* had been destroyed by Tattnall to prevent her capture by the enemy.

As late as May 5, Mallory had been basing his hopes on the ironclad. "We look to the *Virginia* alone," he wrote to Tattnall on that date, "to

106. Mallory to Capt. S. S. Lee, April 30, 1862 (*O.R.,* Ser. I, Vol. VII, pp. 778-79).
107. Mallory to Lee, May 3, 1862 (*ibid.,* 783).
108. *Ibid.*
109. Mallory to Farrand, May 8, 1862 (*ibid.,* Ser. II, Vol. I, pp. 635-36).
110. Mallory to Farrand, May 9, 1862 (*ibid.,* 636).

prevent the enemy from ascending the James River. Her presence in the river is of vital importance. . . ."[111] Tattnall, however, without orders from Richmond, had placed her, by nightfall of May 11, hors de combat forever. His action was bitterly criticized. Mallory himself declared: "The destruction of the *Virginia* was premature. May God protect us and cure us of weakness and folly!"[112] Tattnall was later acquitted of blame by an investigating committee, but it is not clear that a more vigorous commander could not have saved the ship.[113]

As to the responsibility for the loss of Norfolk: Even the most consistent critics of the Secretary realized that the Navy Department had been gravely handicapped by the failure of the Confederate land forces to hold their positions on the peninsula. It was admitted by some that once the army had begun its retreat, Norfolk was doomed, no matter what the navy might do.

Angela had been at her husband's side during a part of these trying days, but had returned to Pensacola before Norfolk fell. On the very day on which he issued the order for the evacuation of that point, he wrote to her: "You have been gone a week, and it already seems to me an age since I heard the voices of yourself and my dear children. Everything is as quiet about the house as the grave. The table is so empty that I cannot endure to remain more than two minutes at it, and the bed is so large and desolate that I sit up reading nearly all night. We must all endure much suffering, my dear wife, ere we win our independence; and we must present to the foe an undying resolve to conquer or to die."[114]

The one bright spot in the picture was the successful defense of the capital. For this achievement the Navy Department could justly claim much of the credit. On the tenth of May, the day before the fall of Norfolk, the Drewry's Bluff fortifications were still unfinished; five days later, when the attack came from the river, they were ready. Three Federal ironclads, including the *Monitor*, and two wooden gunboats were driven back in a four-

111. Mallory to Tattnall, May 5, 1862 (*ibid.*, Ser. I, Vol. VII, p. 785).

112. Mallory, Diary, I, 19. Cf. "Findings and Proceedings of the Court of Inquiry *in re* the destruction of the *Virginia* on May 11, 1862, with allied documents, such as the pleas of the *Virginia's* crew for vindication," *O.R.*, Ser. I, Vol. VII, pp. 787-89. Commodore Porter believed that it was just as well from the Confederate viewpoint that the *Virginia* was destroyed, since she could not have faced Federal ships any longer (West, *op. cit.*, 132).

113. Cf. *O.R.*, Ser. II, Vol. I, pp. 626, 632 ff. For documents concerning the destruction of the *Virginia*, see *ibid.*, Ser. I, Vol. VII, pp. 787-99. Concerning the findings of the court of inquiry into Tattnall's action in destroying the ironclad, see *ibid.*, 765-803.

114. Mallory to his wife, May 3, 1862.

hour fight distinguished by the deadly work of Confederate naval sharp-shooters firing Enfield rifles from pits on shore.[115]

The Navy Secretary witnessed the battle. At its conclusion he sent a dispatch to Commander Farrand, in charge of the naval units at the Bluff: "The enemy has retired, but to return with a larger force; and the sacred duty of confronting and repelling his advance upon the river is devolved upon the navy. The country expects much from your command, and I feel assured that it will do its duty and nobly sustain the character of the navy."[116] A Confederate officer struck the day's keynote when he shouted after the retreating *Monitor*, "Tell Captain Jeffers that is not the way to Richmond!"[117] Several other attempts by the Federals to force the Drewry's Bluff block were beaten off during the next six weeks, until the sea-and-land offensive against Richmond was, for the time, dropped.

While he fought against his discouragement over the New Orleans defeat and strove to meet the threat on the James, the Secretary wrestled with other dark doubts and fears. The enemy, he confided to his diary, was strong and eager, and the Southern people were not as devoted to the cause as they should be. They did not comprehend sufficiently, he feared, the political degradation to which a union with the North would subject them, and the "gradual but inevitable inferiority and its stamp which would thereby be fixed upon them and their children."[118] The possible fate of his own wife and children was ever before his mind. What would become of them if he failed, and if the South were subjugated? If he should never see them again, let God watch over them, and reunite them to him in Heaven.[119]

But his spirit was far from broken. Indeed his gaiety at this time is sometimes remarkable. On May 11, the day of the fall of Norfolk and the burning of the *Virginia,* he found time to notify Angela that he had sent to her a box containing the mustard, oil, pickles, Attie's tool chest, and Ruby's harmonica. He could even summon up enough of his old-time spirit

---

115. The spirit of at least some of the Confederate naval officers under pressure was typified by the brief statement of Lieutenant John Maffitt on assuming command of the *Manassas*: "My difficulties are great, my ambition greater" (to Secretary of War G. W. Randolph, from Nassau, New Providence, May 21, 1862 [*O.R.,* Ser. I, Vol. I, p. 758]). Says Mrs. Putnam: "There never was a period of more alarming excitement than this in Richmond during the entire war, until the time of the ultimate evacuation of the city" (Mrs. Sallie A. B. Putnam, *Richmond During the War; Four Years of Personal Observation* [New York, 1867], 129). The same author gives a vivid description of the panic which affected some of the citizens at this time (*ibid.,* 129-31).

116. Scharf, *op. cit.,* 717.

117. *Ibid.,* 715.

118. Mallory, Diary, part II, p. 18.

119. *Ibid.*

to threaten to have a fist fight with Attie if that young man continued to eat green fruit; and Attie was to be sure that "though he may whip me I will try my best."[120]

On that same black day for the Confederacy he had made an observation trip to the batteries at Drewry's Bluff, and he described to Angela his visit. Expecting an attack on the river defenses, he "jumped upon a horse and went down like Mr. Gilpin"; and as the horse objected to his rider's umbrella, the rider arrived at the end of his eight-mile canter "as wet as a wash rag." Three iron ships and two wooden ones of the enemy came up, fired but one shot, then retired. The Secretary rode home "with a puddle of water in the small of my back and my boots full of whiskey . . . as stiff as a —— horse."[121]

Mallory was far from convinced that the war was lost. Though constantly anxious about the Drewry's Bluff defenses, and continually urging their further strengthening, he was able to report on May 15 the repulse of an enemy assault of two and a half hours' duration against them. There was no defeatist tone in his letter to his wife that night: "The enemy will do his best to get here [to Richmond], and we will do our best to keep him away; and we will not leave Richmond without a determined contest to hold it. If his boats ascend the river, I hope we shall have manhood enough left to fight with him at the wharves, and at the street corners, if necessary, to repel him. God bless you, my darling wife, and keep you in confidence in his mercy. . . . If you were as trustful in God as I am, you would think of our future as I do."[122]

Five days later he told Angela that the Confederate army had fallen back on Richmond, and McClellan was preparing to attack the city. "We are to have a fight for its possession, and will not abandon it so long as it can be

120. Mallory to his wife, May 11, 1862.
121. *Ibid.*
122. Mallory to Angela, May 15, 1862. Cf. Mallory's orders to Captain S. S. Lee, under date of May 15: "Proceed to Drewry's Bluff and take command of the naval defences of the James River, relieving Commander Farrand, who will remain there second in command. General Mahone has been assigned to the chief command, but the naval force is expected to fight all the batteries, complete the obstructions, and mount additional guns where you may deem them necessary. . . . Consult freely with General Mahone and defend the river to the last extremity. Apply to me promptly for all and any aid I can afford you" (*O.R.*, Ser I, Vol. VII, p. 800). Some wolves, as might be expected, were still howling. Said the *Atlanta Confederacy*, n. d.: "Inexcusable errors have been committed by those having management of our affairs. Why were the Cumberland and Tennessee rivers left open,—those highways to the heart of the Confederate States? Why were gunboats not built last summer, when we knew the enemy was building them?" (reprinted in *Richmond Examiner*, May 28, 1862).

held."[123] Even the women of the city preferred that it should be shelled rather than surrendered.[124]

In the last week of May, in another note to his wife, he described a trip on horseback to a point dangerously near the enemy lines. He rode to within fair range of their pickets and saw the "Yankeys" moving around in considerable numbers. Their pickets, he thought, must be afraid of Confederate sharpshooters, for they were continually shifting their positions, no sentinel standing still except when he was behind a tree. If only Mallory had had his "sharps" rifle with him, he would, he vowed, have gone out and taken at least a dozen good shots at the Yankees. A battle was daily expected, and the enemy would be given a good whipping. The river defenses had ceased to be a source of worry, he said. He had worked night and day over them, and they were now so strong that he was actually afraid the enemy would not make a second attempt to pass them. On their previous try, the Federals had been thrown back decisively.[125]

The state of Confederate morale in Richmond in May, 1862, was, therefore, good; but there were for Stephen Mallory other circumstances to try the heart. The Navy Secretary's time at home was "a solitude," he wrote to his wife. His heart would swell, and the tears come to his eyes, every time he entered the room which she had occupied during her stay in the capital. He felt that their affection for each other, based as it was on mutual esteem and free from any selfish alloy, was growing even stronger with age; and, "though I can never love you more than I have, . . . I can never love you less." This thought, he declared, was a solace to him for all the ills of life.[126]

Angela, however, after so loyally and bravely rallying to his support in the dark days after the fall of New Orleans, had had another relapse in morale. He had been "greatly saddened" by the "tone of complaint and

123. Mallory to Angela, May 20, 1862.
124. *Ibid.* The temper of the women of the South during the tense days of 1861-1862 is evinced by various contemporary testimonies. Edward Mason wrote to his wife Bessie, from Richmond, June 4, 1861, concerning a certain Jenny Gibbes, whose husband or sweetheart was in the fight at Charleston: "They say she stood it bravely while the fight was going on at Charleston, and watched from the battery, but nearly had hysterics when it was over" (Alexander Papers, University of North Carolina). Declared the *Richmond Examiner,* February 4, 1862: "The most efficient class to bring out the men and resources of the country in this war have been its women. In the great struggles of nations, like that in which we are engaged, they should have queens for their rulers; for it is woman alone who is proof against the persuasions of time-servers and the sin of backsliding. There has been but one Lot's wife in all the tide of time."
125. Mallory to Angela, May 27, 1862.
126. *Ibid.*

distress" of one of her communications late in May. And this letter had apparently been followed by another of even gloomier character. But, instead of discouraging him, her weakness seemed to have stiffened his dogged determination to fight it out with courage and hopefulness. He opened his heart to her in a letter of early June.

She must not think, he assured her, that he was "annoyed" (as she had feared) by the complaining tone of her letters. They made him sad, but they did not "annoy" him. He reminded her that his own disposition was naturally optimistic, while hers was of the opposite character. Where her mental vision could see nothing but a cloud, he could always detect that the cloud had a silver lining. On her account alone, and not on his own, was he saddened by her desponding tone; for, "having thrown away the scabbard determined never to sheathe the sword but with an honorable peace," he was buoyed up not more by hope than by duty and principle; and he thanked God that their enemies were powerless to weaken his exertion or to crush his hopes for the bright future of the country, and for "that independence without which life would be unworthy of us."[127]

He wished his dear Angela could have witnessed—from a safe distance —the glorious fight of the preceding Saturday. The sight, he was sure, would have raised her spirits. Mounted beside President Davis and staff he had watched the steady march of twenty thousand Confederates across an open plain in the face of withering fire. "I found myself . . . screaming . . . as exhilarated as if I had just swallowed a bottle of champagne; steadily, grandly, strongly, they moved on; scarcely a man wavered; . . . and even the wounded, as they dropped upon the ground, sent up shout after shout after their advancing comrades to charge the enemy."[128]

Even at the high point of the battle his sense of the ridiculous did not desert him. He had rocked with laughter—and drawn a surprised frown from the President—at a poor Confederate running disgracefully to the rear sans gun—and trousers. Such incidents, however, were exceptional. The Second Florida Regiment had "behaved splendidly and suffered greatly." Out of 430 men, 202 were killed or wounded. Only one officer of all the three highest grades escaped unscathed.[129]

So, courage, Angela! It was no time for weakness, when, in Richmond, the women were gallantly bolstering the morale of furloughed and wounded soldiers by means of "starvation parties"—entertainments at which, by

127. Mallory to Angela, June 4, 1862.
128. *Ibid*.
129. *Ibid*.

common consent, refreshments were banned. Materials of all kinds were so scarce that young girls took down the damask curtains of their parlors to make into dresses. Frequently the same girls with whom a young officer had danced on Sunday night would attend his funeral on Wednesday.

Perhaps what Angela lacked was precisely a sense of humor, and an appreciation of the ridiculous. Stephen tried to draw her smile by describing one of his frequent visitors, brother-in-law Garnett, who had a weakness for strong drink. Whiskey made Garnett pugnacious, but, if any of his "enemies" came into the room while he was declaiming against them, his native good humor and sociability would overcome his pugnacity and he would invite them to take a drink with him.[130] He spent night after night in Stephen's room, "puffing away at his pipe, uttering his words in jerks, like water from a demijohn; his eyes become as small and bright as an old coon's, and a little thin straight gash represents his mouth [reminding one of] . . . a choice old piece of China, perfect except for one little flaw." At the Arlington, Mrs. Fry[131] still "rises and subsides like a gentle snow flake, —as graceful and as cold." And, perhaps the touch most deftly calculated to cheer her up: "By the bye, I sent you by a careful hand last week the powder puff and powder you desired."[132]

But three weeks later Angela had become even more discouraged, and Stephen had recourse to mild irony. He had just received, he told her, her gloomy letter, in which she expressed the conviction that he would be doing his family a greater kindness by knocking their brains out than by sending them (as he was proposing to do) further south for safety. Angela had described at great length her condition of wretchedness, misery, etc. He supposed that he should thank her for this letter, as it was the only one he had had from her in some time. Its contents were so well designed to solace and aid him in his labors, so cheering in its assurances that all his efforts and anxieties for his family were properly appreciated, that he could not but congratulate her on its production.[133]

Perhaps she could be bantered out of her melancholy mood. He teased her about one of her old admirers, who had turned up in Richmond as a prisoner of war, "Major Whiting, your old beau, who . . . looks particularly contemptible, but, as I know that you retain a sneaking notion, a lurking

130. Mallory to Angela, June 12, 1862.
131. Probably Mrs. Birkett Davenport (Baker) Fry. Her husband was a wealthy lawyer and cotton manufacturer who became a colonel in the Confederate Army. They were residents of Georgia.
132. Mallory to Angela, June 12, 1862.
133. Mallory to Angela, June 28, 1862.

fondness for him,—and to enable you to maintain your old position with him when I shall be knocked on the head,—I have provided a room for him as your friend, and shall invite him in your name to occupy it." Whiting had apparently, in the distant past, presented Angela with an engagement ring, which had been instantly returned to him. Stephen assured her that she "will have another chance at that old diamond ring," and he trusted that she would retain it the next time. "Yours," concluded the letter, "in spite of your teeth!"[134]

Nor did the tactful husband neglect other possible ways of bolstering morale; Angela might freely ask him to send her anything "from a shoe to a chemise." (Evidently the blockade runners were bringing in more than ammunition.) If she asked for shoes, she was to mention the size in inches as well as in numbers. And, as a parting shot: "Do tell me what to say to Whiting. I know he will want a lock of your hair."

Angela, temporarily at least, fell in with Stephen's mood and replied in terms hardly complimentary to her former suitor. She told her husband to remind Whiting that she had not forgotten the latter's gift to her of an *unpaid-for* engagement ring. Whiting's excuse was that he had intended fraud neither upon her nor upon the jeweler; he had expressly informed the latter that he "took the ring as he expected to take 'Miss Meriner,'—upon speculation; that if he married her he was to pay for it, and if not he was to have the privilege of returning it." She was interested to know that he had been anxious to learn from Stephen the latter's opinion of her disposition; and she confessed that none of the little tendernesses, the natural and anticipated familiarities which usually follow an engagement ring, had fallen to his lot. (Whiting had confided to Stephen that whenever he had solicited such manifestations of regard he had found her looking at him "like a wild cat at bay," and that his ring had been as unproductive as his attentions.) "I could not help but sympathize with him," Stephen wrote, "and . . . told him that my acquaintance with 'Miss Meriner' had been intimate—in fact quite intimate—that we had long been bosom friends; and that my experience tallied with his exactly."[135]

Difficult as it was, at times, to manage Angela's feelings, it was far more of a task to satisfy the opposition press which continued to snipe at the Navy Department and at the administration as a whole. Congress had long realized, declared the *Montgomery Advertiser,* that Mr. Davis' secretaries were more bent on making a little reputation for economy than on supply-

134. *Ibid.*                    135. Mallory to his wife, July 10, 1862.

ing the sinews of war. It should be clear that "the navy would be a total failure unless Mr. Mallory should be set aside for a competent officer." His nomination had been at first rejected and then afterward confirmed by the Senate, at the dictation of the President. "Our navy, which started out under such brilliant prospects, and distinguished itself by some . . . gallant feats, is fast going to the bottom of the ocean in consequence of the persistent obstinacy of Mr. Davis' holding on to his Secretary against the wishes and interests of the country."[136]

Another journal deplored the "defensive complex" of the government. The war could be won only by vigorous offensive operations against the North. Such a policy, however, the present leaders of the South were too timid or too slothful to adopt.[137] And the *Richmond Examiner* further asserted that Davis was trying to set up a despotism.[138]

In late June of 1862, McClellan was closing in on Richmond, while the Federal squadrons were hammering insistently at the fortifications on the James. The peril was grave for the capital of the Confederacy. Jackson and Ewell were hurrying down with their forces from Winchester to hit the Federals in the rear. On the twenty-first, Stephen Mallory wrote in his diary: "We are looking for a battle before the city, in a few days. We have everything to fight for; God grant that we may be successful." He added, in this intimate record, that his life, if it could gain this victory, would be instantly offered. He would glory in the chance to sacrifice himself utterly for so great a result. The horizon, he conceded, looked dark; but he remembered that such had been the character of all great issues at times.[139]

But Richmond was not to fall—yet. Lee and Jackson struck savagely at McClellan's besieging army and stopped it in its tracks. Mallory's batteries at Drewry's Bluff and his gunboats and obstructions in the James beat off the attacking river squadron. By June 29 the Federal forces, on land and water, were in full retreat. To quote Mallory's way of expressing it—"Thus has this boastful and bullying horde of barbarians been driven from its strong-hold before Richmond." He added, without realizing the ominous significance of the statement, "Our loss in officers is heavy."[140]

On the day after the main battle, he rode through the enemy's abandoned works, which, he said, were so strong that only the Yankees' terror could have induced their abandonment. These positions, if defended, he

136. *Montgomery Advertiser,* June 7, 1862.
137. *Savannah Republican,* n.d., quoted in *Richmond Examiner,* May 14, 1862.
138. *Richmond Examiner,* April 15, June 28, 1862.
139. Mallory, Diary, part I, June 21, 1862.
140. Mallory to his wife, June 30, 1862.

believed, could have been taken only at the cost of thirty thousand Confederates. Scattered abroad in the woods and camps for miles were Yankee overcoats, blankets, flannel shirts, soda crackers, gingerbread, bayonets, broken guns, empty bottles and jars, tin cups, boots, newspapers, books, tracts, and other debris. The enemy was twenty miles away, in full retreat, with fifty thousand men in pursuit. Yankee prisoners reported their army as being demoralized and sick of the fight.[141]

The Confederates, Mallory wrote exultingly, fought like heroes. Indeed, nothing less than a "separate and distinct resolve of each man to take a foeman by the throat and drag him to the Earth" could have won the engagement. Lee's and Jackson's men had taken position after position, battery after battery, against all odds and despite every loss. In one place, one hundred Confederates were killed in a little space not a hundred feet square. But "we . . . drove the enemy step by step for twelve miles with musketry and artillery playing in their teeth at every step."[142]

The Yankee regulars, he admitted, fought well. Their discipline was far more thorough than that of the Confederates, and their charges, retreats, and other maneuvers were all creditably executed. Nevertheless "our men rushed at them, every man for himself, shouting curses and imprecations upon them, and with deadly intent visible in every movement. The Yankeys would not stand to grapple . . . but always fled in disorder when we got within a few yards of them"[143]—a somewhat contradictory statement.

By July, the immediate danger to Richmond was past. There would be a lull in the fighting, Mallory thought, though both parties were preparing to renew the struggle as soon as possible. He believed that the true character of McClellan's "strategic withdrawal" was dawning on the minds of the Northern people. As the wounded arrived in their cities by the boatloads, and the long lists of dead appeared in the daily papers, the people began to understand that the difference between a great defeat and a great "strategic move" was the difference between "tweedle dum and tweedle dee," and that the fancied quicksteps of "on to Richmond" were but funeral marches to the grave.[144]

In a letter to his friend Governor Milton of Florida, the Secretary showed his own fighting spirit. "The movement of our forces today [he was writing on July 4] terminates, for the present, military operations against McClellan . . . which . . . have resulted in the triumphant success of our arms. Broken, disorganized, and demoralized, he . . . has . . . lost . . . everything

141. *Ibid.*
142. *Ibid.*
143. *Ibid.*
144. Mallory to his wife, July 21, 1862.

—even his honor. His scattered forces this evening are collecting, it is alledged [*sic*] at Beverly, some thirty miles from Richmond. The brutality practiced by him evinces a savage and inhuman vindictiveness consequent upon his ignominious defeat, to which a parallel cannot be found in the annalls [*sic*] of civilized warfare. He has taken no heed of his killed or wounded from the first days of the fight, the 25th ulto., and while he has left them in our hands with his Surgeons he has destroyed purposely the medicines and medical instruments essential to their treatment. He has removed the fences from growing crops of wheat ready for the harvest, while at the same time he has destroyed the ... implements of husbandry, and has practised upon Citizens, guilty of no offence save an undying hatred of the North, cruelties at which the mind shudders. But a just and all wise God has brought home to them their guilt in a manner the most impressive. The unburied forms of thousands of Yankees, strewn throughout a line of nearly twenty miles, are eloquent though silent monitors of the justice of Heaven wrought through the instrumentality of a people whose Soil they came to conquer and polute [*sic*]."[145]

As yet, the Confederate losses had not been ascertained. "We know only that they are heavy." The Second Florida Regiment had behaved splendidly.[146]

The Navy Department now had the river so strongly protected that they wished the whole Yankee fleet would attempt its passage. In Richmond optimism was riding high. The effect of the recent Confederate victories on Europe, it was thought by many in the South, had been immense. Intervention and recognition of Southern independence by France and England seemed, even to normally less sanguine spirits, a real possibility. It was believed by not a few that Lincoln desired to make peace but had not the power to do so, and was compelled by party pressure to continue the war. The Navy Secretary feared not the final result, and was "ready to shoulder a gun at any moment and fight in the ranks before receding an inch from our demands."[147]

Even in these swift and crowded hours there was time for smaller things. A package was dispatched to Angela to prove that, "though Secretary of the Navy, etc., etc., my soul, where your wishes are concerned, is not above buttons." He had "taken the liberty" to send also two light dresses, which

145. Mallory to Governor John Milton of Florida, July 4, 1862 (Milton Letter Book). Florida Historical Society Library, St. Augustine, Fla.)
146. *Ibid.*
147. Mallory to Angela, July 21, 1862.

he begged that she would accept as a slight token of his regard. "May I," he asked, "take the further liberty of requesting that you will wear them? Perhaps then when they enfold all that my heart holds dear, your thoughts may turn to one who, the further he journeys from you, only drags like a fettered prisoner a greater length of chain, and who constantly cherishes the hope of a more intimate acquaintance with you?,—in fact, of becoming your bosom friend?" The common fan, he regretted to report, had become very scarce, as they had almost all been purchased for the use of hospitals; but he was sending her a few of these also, "to raise the wind."[148]

He trusted that she would excuse what might appear to her to be an unreasonably long letter. He had not deceived himself with the conceit that he could sustain her interest throughout such a long effort. But the pleasure of talking to her was so great that he could not forego it, and he risked "being regarded as dry and prosy by one whom I wish I could squeeze to death at this moment, and of whom I am happy to say that I am the happy and sole possessor and the devoted lover."[149]

148. *Ibid.*
149. *Ibid.*

# CHAPTER TEN

# The Naval Investigating Board

ALMOST BEFORE the victorious guns at the Bluff had ceased to smoke, the Navy Department came under fire from a new and unexpected quarter. A group in the Confederate Congress moved a resolution in mid-August, 1862, providing for an investigation of Mallory's administration. Great dissatisfaction was expressed at what was termed the "inadequacy" of the Navy Department. Bitter things were said about the Secretary, and the Southern press began to take sides.

Mallory felt deeply hurt. "I am as sick as I am disgusted," he wrote in his diary, "with the carpings and complaints of ignorance and presumption, that I have not built a navy! I feel confident of having done my whole duty, of having done all that any man could have done with the means at hand. I have my own approbation at least."[1]

His reply to his critics was swift and vigorous. Through his friends in the legislature he demanded an immediate investigation of the Navy Department. This, he was sure, would be the best means of refuting his enemies. A joint committee of members from each house of Congress was appointed and began its labors at once.

"Confident," he wrote to Angela, "that my administration of this Department must be triumphantly vindicated, I am perfectly satisfied with both committees, and glad that Foote[2] is at the head of the one in the

1. Mallory, Diary, part II, p. 21, June 24, 1862.
2. Henry Stuart Foote, perhaps Mallory's most bitter enemy, was born in Virginia, but removed to Jackson, Mississippi, in 1826, where he became prominent as an able criminal lawyer and politician. He was elected to the United States Senate on the Unionist ticket in 1847. He helped to frame the compromise measures of 1850 and was for a time chairman of the Senate committee on foreign affairs. He was chosen governor of Mississippi on a Unionist platform in the autumn of 1852, and served as governor until 1854, when he migrated to California. He returned to Mississippi in 1858 and practiced law in Vicksburg. He vigorously opposed secession in the Southern convention at Knoxville in May, 1859. He sat in the lower house of the Confederate Congress as a representative from Tennessee. He was a consistent and bitter opponent of President Davis throughout the war and was, indeed, averse to a continuance of the struggle.

House."[3] In a letter to the President he declared his determination, as chief of the Department, to "challenge and invite the most searching investigation of its conduct, that the triumphant vindication of its course must result." He felt that it was due no less to the government than to the people that such investigation should be promptly made.[4]

As usual, he opened his heart to his wife. There was, he told her, much to be proud of and nothing whatever to regret in his conduct of the naval war. His aims, he felt, had been "large and high." Knowing that the enemy could build a hundred ships to the South's one, his policy had been to make ships of such invulnerability as would compensate for the inequality of numbers—wherefore the *Merrimac, Arkansas, Mississippi, Louisiana,* and the others. He believed that he had "revolutionized the naval warfare of the world" and "astonished all people by showing what could be done." Yet the destruction of the great Confederate vessels by no fault of his, just as everybody saw their gigantic power, had brought upon his head the "rage of the ignorant, the rabble, and the prejudiced, who always constitute the majority of mankind."[5]

He honestly felt that he knew something of naval affairs, in the largest sense of the word. The condition and history of all the navies of the world were known to him. His time and study had been long turned to the subject; and, "be my knowledge and ability much or little, I have faithfully devoted them to the cause of my Country, and fear not the judgment of impartial men, or the verdict of history." He was resolved that the committee of the House should demand from Foote and his crony Conrad their charges, of which the latter gentlemen had been careful to specify none; and he would see to it that the whole history of the Navy Department would be known and vindicated. Rather than lose this chance for a full revelation of the Department's achievements, he would willingly make Foote and Conrad the whole committee and abide by their report of the facts. Conrad's hostility, he believed, was personal; Foote "is a fool and is crazy besides, and hates the Administration and the President with an intense hatred."[6]

What was actually Mallory's record at this point of the war? What were the real accomplishments of his Department, and what were its failures?

The commerce-raiding program had undoubtedly attained its imme-

3. Mallory to his wife, August 31, 1862.
4. Mallory to President Davis, August 27, 1862 (Davis Papers, Duke University).
5. Mallory to his wife, August 31, 1862.
6. *Ibid.* Concerning Conrad, cf. *supra,* p. 130, n. 2.

diate objective, although it had not realized its ultimate strategic aim. The merchant flag of the United States had been practically driven from the ocean,[7] but the hoped-for result had not followed: the Federal blockading vessels had not been lured from their stations off Southern ports.

In the all-important field of coastal and river defense, the Confederate Navy Department could point to a few very important victories but was forced to acknowledge several disastrous defeats. Richmond had been well served by the *Virginia,* by the shore batteries under naval command, and by the highly efficient mines and other obstructions in the James and York rivers. Charleston, Wilmington, Savannah, and Mobile were holding out doggedly, sometimes against powerful Federal attacks. In the case of the first three ports, the army—especially Beauregard's artillerists at Charleston—deserved a great share of the credit;[8] but the contribution of Mallory's department, particularly in the matter of mines and torpedo boats, had been indispensable and large.

The navy was not effectively holding the upper reaches of the Mississippi but was being slowly forced southward. There had been, it is true, a few brilliant counterattacks by the Confederates. In mid-July the ram *Arkansas* had fought her way through a whole Federal squadron above Vicksburg;[9] but the over-all situation in this sector was, for the South, not good. The loss of New Orleans, Hatteras Inlet, Roanoke Island, Ship Island, Port Royal, and other vital coastal and river points was a score against the Navy Department, although the army shared responsibility for these failures. The destruction of the two great ironclads at New Orleans had been a staggering blow.

Perhaps the most noteworthy achievement of the Navy Department had

7. While in 1860 two-thirds of the commerce of New York was carried on in American bottoms, by 1863 three-fourths would be handled in foreign vessels. (Scharf, *op. cit.,* 783). Immensely effective, too, had been the privateers. Their operations had boosted marine insurance rates on American ships to prohibitive heights. By the first August of the war, the privateers had captured nearly sixty Federal vessels. The *New York Herald* estimated the loss to American shipping at $20,000,000, a relatively huge sum in those days. "Our shipping interest," bemoaned the *Herald,* "is literally ruined" (*New York Herald,* October 10, 1861).

8. Since Beauregard left Charleston in 1861 and did not return until September, 1862, the gunners at Charleston in the summer of 1862 were not, of course, technically his.

9. Scharf, *History of the Confederate States Navy,* 310-26. For the official report of the run of the *Arkansas,* see I. N. Brown, Lieutenant commanding, to Flag Officer W. F. Lynch, from C.S.S. *Arkansas,* at Vicksburg, July 15, 1862 (*O.R.,* Ser. I, Vol. XIX, pp 68-69). Cf. also the observation of Secretary Gideon Welles: "The most disreputable naval affair of the War [from the Union standpoint] was the descent of the steam ram *Arkansas* through both squadrons till she hauled in under the batteries of Vicksburg. . . . I have written them [the Federal officers commanding in the theatre] . . . briefly, but expressively, on the subject of the ram *Arkansas*" (Welles, *Diary,* I, 72).

been in the field of progressive naval and ordnance design. The great significance of the *Virginia* from this aspect is too well known to require emphasis. In the matter of electric mines, torpedo boats, and submarine vessels, the accomplishments of the Confederacy were equally momentous. Of these more will be said later. It is enough to remark here that the pioneer work done by Mallory's officers in these three classes of offensive-defensive weapons constituted a major contribution to the modern science of naval warfare.

And what of Mallory himself, after one year and a half of war? Under stress of his high responsibilities, had he grown or decreased in stature? A partial answer to the question may be supplied by a study of his relations with the other leaders of the Confederacy.

One of the most significant sidelights on Mallory's character is provided by his intimacy with Judah P. Benjamin. There is much evidence to support the view that the latter was by far the most able figure in the Confederate Cabinet. The more one studies the man in action, listens to his words, or reads his letters, the more clearly does the conviction grow that here was an intellect and a will distinctly superior to those of the rest of the statesmen of the Confederacy. No one could doubt that he "saw through" men, that he was a shrewd and cold and accurate judge of men.

It is therefore suggestive that with none of his official associates was Benjamin on more intimate and sincerely friendly terms that he was with Stephen Mallory.[10] During their careers in the United States Senate, the two men had thought together on many issues.[11] During the period of the Confederacy they worked in close harmony on matters of finance, supply, and diplomacy,[12] and, as in the affair of the proposed seizure of distillers' corn by the Confederate government, they were frequently found on the same side in an equally divided Cabinet.[13] They were bracketed together as "dependents of favor" by journals opposed to the administration.[14]

10. Rembert Patrick calls Benjamin a "warm personal friend" of Mallory (*Jefferson Davis and His Cabinet* [Baton Rouge, 1944], 256) and says that Benjamin "did much to help him [Mallory] forget the unkind words [of critics of the Navy Department]" (*ibid.*, 269). The same author again says: "During the four years of the war he [Benjamin] was on terms of close friendship with . . . Mallory" (*ibid.*, 201). Clifford Dowdey refers to ". . . Benjamin's friend, Mallory" (*Experiment in Rebellion* [New York, 1947], 208).

11. For example, on the Cuban issue (Meade, *Benjamin*, 92), and on the question of Indian removal (*ibid.*, 138).

12. Cf. Dowdey, *op. cit.*, 208-9.

13. Cf. Meade, *op. cit.*, 231.

14. Cf. for example, *Charleston Mercury*, August 11, 1863.

They went on private excursions with each other.[15] These facts throw some light on Mallory's character, if we accept the very plausible supposition that Benjamin was not likely to throw himself away on mediocrities, dullards, or small men.

While the adage that a man may be judged by the intimate company he keeps may be pushed to extremes, it is again significant that the next most intimate friend of Mallory in the Cabinet was the one member of the Davis administration who attained any notable success in statesmanship after the war—John Reagan of Texas.[16] Reagan's regard for the Navy Secretary induced him to make a special trip to New York in 1865 in order to visit his "old associate," as he called him, in prison.[17] Mallory always spoke of him in terms of close intimacy and affection.[18]

To Toombs and Stephens, Mallory could scarcely be expected to be as warmly attached, nor could he work with them as smoothly and as readily, since, from the early days of the war, these two fiery souls were in almost constant opposition to the basic policies of the administration. In one entry in his diary, Mallory implied what may have been his normal feeling towards Toombs—a feeling of deep suspicion of the general motives of the Georgian.[19] And he could hardly have had a very different attitude toward Stephens, in view of the latter's persistent animus against Davis.[20]

With only one member of the Cabinet did Mallory have a serious disagreement. He could not work harmoniously with the incompetent Walker, whose inglorious tenure of the post of Secretary of War ended in the early fall of 1861. The latter, without informing his Cabinet colleagues, had asked Congress for $162,000 and 400,000 men. "If this course of separate action is pursued," wrote Mallory hotly in his diary, "I must leave the Cabinet, as it subjects me, with others, to misapprehension."[21]

15. ". . . Benjamin went off with the Navy Secretary on some little outing of their own down the river, for which they borrowed an army ambulance" (Dowdey, *op. cit.,* 359).

16. Reagan was Postmaster General of the Confederacy. After the war he served in the United States Senate and was one of the sponsors of the Interstate Commerce Act of 1887.

17. Reagan, *Memoirs,* 228.

18. Cf., for instance, Mallory to Reagan, from Bridgeport, April 11, 1866, *infra,* pp. 380-82.

19. "There is evidently a spirit of Opposition to the Prest. and administration growing up in Congress, instigated and nourished only by envy and ambition, and I think that the Cobbs of Geo. are engaged in it, and that Toombs' retirement from the Cabinet has something to do with it" (Mallory, Diary, part I, p. 12, August 11, 1861).

20. Concerning Stephens' opposition to administration policy, see Rudolph von Abele, *Alexander H. Stephens* (New York, 1946), 191-256.

21. Mallory, Diary, part I, p. 10, July 26, 1861. Cf. also *ibid.,* September 4, 1861: "We [the President, Benjamin, Memminger, and Mallory] all concurred in expressing a disbelief in the ability of Walker to perform the duties of that Department [of War], and the Prest. added that he did not think that any civilian could. From the whole tenor of the conversation I look for a speedy resignation of Genl. Walker."

Of Walker's successors, Randolph cooperated with Mallory in the most cordial and efficient manner and won the latter's esteem;[22] while Seddon, though not as helpful to the Navy Department, was on sufficiently good terms with the Secretary of the Navy to be invited to the Mallory home for "pea soup"—according to the "Rebel War Clerk," J. B. Jones.[23]

Among Mallory's many friends in the Congress, two men—C. C. Clay and Benjamin F. Hill—could be singled out as his special intimates. Hill later shared the Navy Secretary's postwar imprisonment, and the Hill and Mallory children were playmates of long standing. The Mallorys and the Clays were united in the bonds of close affection, and spent much time in visiting each other.

Of the military leaders, General Joseph E. Johnston seems to have been most familiar with Mallory. In the Navy Secretary's diary are at least two references to "my friend Genl. Johnston."[24] Mallory felt no hesitation in writing to the aggrieved field leader a personal and very frank letter containing the type of reprimand that one addresses only to one's close friends.[25] Mrs. Johnston was extremely fond of Mrs. Mallory, and had endeared herself to Mallory by the means that always won his heart—compliments to Angela.[26]

22. *Ibid.*, 28, November 19, 1862: "Resignation of Genl. Randolph as Secretary of War took place last Saturday, Nov. 15. I regret it, for he was a hard working Secretary and more familiar with the details of the office than any successor will probably be." Cf. also Patrick, *op. cit.*, 257: "Randolph cooperated with the Navy Department to a greater extent than did his successor Seddon."

23. It is not necessary to consider Jones's remark as too serious a reflection on Mallory's earnestness: "When the cat's away, the mice will play, is an old saying, and a true one. I saw a note of invitation today from Secretary Mallory to Secretary Seddon, inviting him to his house at 5 P.M. to partake of 'pea-soup' with Secretary Trenholm. His 'pea-soup' will be oysters and champagne, and every other delicacy relished by epicures. Mr. Mallory's red face, and his plethoric body, indicate the highest living; and his party will enjoy the dinner while so many of our brave men are languishing with wounds, or pining in a cruel captivity. Nay, they may feast, possibly, while the very pillars of the government are crumbling under the blows of the enemy" (*Rebel War Clerk's Diary*, II, 290).

24. Cf. Mallory, *Diary*, part I, p. 3, June 12, 1861: "The enemy is drawing his forces around Harpers Ferry, and I fear that my friend Genl. Johnston will be surrounded. . . ." *Ibid.*, p. 15, September 13, 1861: "My friend Genl. J. E. Johnston feels sore about being oversloughed [in the matter of the President's appointments of Cooper, Lee, and Sydney Johnston]."

25. Cf. *ibid.*, p. 16, September 16, 1861: "Cabinet meeting today. The Prest. shewed us a letter from Genl. Joe Johnston,—a protest against the apput. of Cooper, Lee, and Sydney Johnston over his head in the grade of Genl. It is an intemperate letter, written evidently under great excitement of feeling. The Prest's answer is short and abrupt, and thus terminates for a time, at least, a life long friendship. I must write to Johnston, but hardly know what to say under the circumstances." And, two days later: "Sent a letter to Genl. Johnston in which I endeavor to show him that he has treated the Prest. unjustly" (*ibid.*, p. 17).

26. Cf. Mallory to Angela, June 4, 1862: "Mrs. Johnston . . . charmed me by saying that you were more beloved here [in Richmond] by the ladies . . . and had more friends than any stranger who had come here."

The one general whom Mallory viewed with considerable displeasure was Beauregard—a feeling, incidentally, which seems to have been reciprocated. In one of the frankest of Mallory's diary observations is this estimate of the hero of First Manassas and Charleston: "21 June. [1861]. Interesting Cabinet meeting yesterday. President had ordered Bragg, who was 2nd in command at Corinth, [to Beauregard], to proceed to Mississippi and assume Command. Beauregard would not permit Bragg to go, but left Bragg in Command, and goes himself to Mobile for his health. Beauregard, with the finest army ever found upon this continent, about 100,000 strong, remained about six weeks after the battle of Shiloh inactive, with the enemy in his front, and then retreated without notice to the Prest. or War Dept., and up to this time no reason for his retreat is known, and now he abandons his army without leave or notice. My own idea is that his mind has given way under the weight of his command; and that, finding Bragg about to leave him, he ran away from an army that he could not manage. If a soldier were thus to go off without leave he would be tried for desertion and be probably shot, and an officer would be shot or cashiered. Beauregard has never voluntarily fought a battle, and never will."[27]

Toward the incomparable Lee, Mallory felt as he should have felt. There is no evidence that he ever opposed or disagreed with the greatest military leader of the war, and the official relations between them were always of the most harmonious nature. In this connection, one brief sentence in the Mallory diary is eloquent in its simplicity: "Genl. Lee inspires confidence as Commander in Chief."[28]

During September and early October, while Lee sparred with McClellan in Virginia and Maryland, and while Bragg was attempting a none too successful counteroffensive in the West, the Naval Investigating Committee held its sessions at Richmond. For an evaluation of the achievements and defects of Mallory's administration during the critical first year and a half of the war, and for a clearer understanding of some important aspects of his character, the proceedings of this body are of great value.[29]

The composition of the committee—it was really two committees merged into one—is interesting. The House members appointed for the investigation were Henry S. Foote of Tennessee, Ethelbert Barksdale of Mississippi,

27. Mallory, Diary, part I, pp. 19-20, June 21, 1862.
28. *Ibid.*, 20, June 24, 1862.
29. The following pages are based on *Investigation of Navy Department. Report of Evidence Taken before a Joint Special Committee of Both Houses of the Confederate Congress to Investigate the Affairs of the Navy Department, O.R.,* Ser. II, Vol. I, pp. 431-809.

James Lyons of Virginia, William W. Boyce of South Carolina, and Lucius J. Dupré of Louisiana. The Senate members were Clement C. Clay, Jr., of Alabama, Thomas J. Semmes of Louisiana, Augustus E. Maxwell of Florida, James Phelan of Mississippi, and Robert M. T. Hunter of Virginia.[30] During most of the sessions Clay acted as chairman.

Of these men, Foote was an inveterate enemy of Mallory's, while Clay, the chairman, who, by reason of his position, would be able to exert considerable influence in directing the course of the questions and in applying the committee's rules, was one of Mallory's warm personal friends. The other members of the committee could be said to be reasonably objective judges with respect to the Navy Department's activities. Certainly the committee was not, in its general composition, a group of Mallory's enemies. He could justifiably expect from it a fair deal.

At the investigators' first meeting on September 4, in one of the rooms of the Navy Department, general rules of procedure were laid down. Resolutions were submitted to the Secretary of the Navy, outlining the scope of the inquiry. He was invited to be present, at his own discretion, whenever a witness was being examined. He was informed also that the committee would always be glad to receive from him communications in writing regarding any matter whatsoever.[31]

Most of the investigation would focus on the recent misfortune at New Orleans and on the events leading up to it. The committee desired to know the answers to the following questions: (1) Had the Navy Department done, in general, everything possible to defend the Gulf city? (2) Had the Department exerted itself to the utmost to complete the *Louisiana* and the *Mississippi* at the earliest possible time? (3) Could the Department be fairly blamed for the loss of these two ships? (4) Had the Department erred gravely in refusing to allow Commander Hollins to bring his squadron down to New Orleans? On a few other points, too, besides those relating to New Orleans, the committee would seek enlightenment.

The first witness called by Clay was Captain W. C. Whittle, naval commandant at New Orleans from March 29, 1862. When he took charge at the Gulf port, the Captain testified, the "progress of things there . . . was as favorable as could under the circumstances be expected," although there

---

30. Hunter resigned from the committee and was replaced by Senator Robert L. Y. Peyton of Missouri.

31. For a complete preview of the ground to be covered in the investigation, cf. *O.R.*, Ser. II, Vol. I, pp. 431-33. For Mallory's letter communicating the requested documents and giving some very general answers to some of the questions, cf. *ibid.*, 433-34.

was great difficulty in securing labor and other requirements.[32] This general endorsement of the department's activity at New Orleans was later confirmed by other witnesses. Both Commodore Hollins and Captain Mitchell, for instance, with ample opportunity to observe the New Orleans situation at close range, testified that the government had done everything possible for the defense of the city.[33]

The most important part of Whittle's testimony concerned the peculiar relationship which had existed between the civilian contractors—the Tift brothers—and the *Mississippi,* and the bearing of this relationship on the subsequent loss of the ship. With regard to the building and disposition of the *Mississippi,* said Whittle, he had had no authority, on account of the "special nature" of the contract between the Navy Department and the Tifts. By the terms of this contract, the civilians were to be in full control of the vessel until she had been completed. No military or naval officer had been allowed to give any orders regarding the construction or movements of the *Mississippi* unless such orders were approved by the Tifts.

Therefore, Whittle continued, he himself had received no instructions from Richmond before April 24 as to what should be done with the uncompleted *Mississippi* if the enemy should pass the forts below New Orleans. Presumably the Navy Department was leaving all to the discretion of the Tifts. On the fatal twenty-fourth, he said, on hearing of the breaching of the southern defenses, and in the absence of any order from Richmond, he had taken it on himself to place Captain Sinclair in command of the *Mississippi* with instructions to "use every exertion . . . to get her up the river, and failing to do so, to destroy her." This measure, said Whittle, he did "on my own account," and "without regard to [i.e., in the absence of] telegraphs from here [Richmond] or anywhere else."[34]

At this point in the examination of Whittle came the first evidence that the case for the Navy Department would, in this investigation, be adequately defended. Senator Semmes, in order, as he said, to refresh Whittle's memory, produced a very interesting telegram. It was from Secretary Mal-

32. *Ibid.,* 435.

33. "Semmes: I asked you . . . whether everything had been done by the Navy Department for the purpose of defending the city of New Orleans that could be done in the construction or purchase of ships, etc. Hollins: I think they did everything they could have done" (*ibid.,* 477). "The Chair [to Mitchell]: Do you mean that the Government could not defend the city of New Orleans by the means then at command there, and that in order to defend it successfully it would be necessary to divert the means of defense from other places, at the risk of exposing them to capture by the enemy? Mitchell: That is what I mean" (*ibid.,* 471).

34. *Ibid.,* 438.

lory to Whittle, dated April 24, instructing the latter to take the *Mississippi* up the river in order to prevent her from being captured. Whittle said that he had never received the message.

The subsequent examination of the naval commandant turned on the crucial question: If he had been in control of the *Mississippi* would he have moved the vessel up the river earlier and thus, possibly, have saved her? Foote, in particular, was very eager to prove that Whittle would have done precisely this, and that he was prevented from doing so only by Mallory's highly imprudent conferring of authority in the matter upon the Tifts.

But Whittle was not so sure on the point; and he was obviously a very cautious witness. He admitted that he had thought that the forts below the city could not hold off the enemy's fleet, but, on the other hand, he had felt that the *Mississippi* would be in an even more dangerous position if he should move her up, since there was an equally formidable threat of an enemy attack from above.

Foote pressed his point hard. If Whittle, he asked, had been so convinced of the ability of gunboats to run past land batteries, would he not, if he had had control of the *Mississippi,* have carried her to some part of the river to have her finished, in preference to leaving her at New Orleans until it was too late to save her?

"If," Whittle answered carefully, "I had known any place where to have carried her, I would." The commandant insisted that he had believed that the ship was in danger from above as well as from below. Military men had been publishing dispatches, some of which appeared in the newspapers, asserting that the city was safe from below; the reports of an attack from above were, on the other hand, persisting; he had therefore become convinced that to take the ship farther northward would be equally as dangerous as to leave her where she was. "In this dilemma," he admitted, "I did not know, in the name of G——, what to do with her."

Foote, however, was determined to get the answer he wanted. "I will put the question," he said, "in another, and perhaps a plainer form. Entertaining the opinion that gunboats could pass a battery, if you had control of the vessel, would you not, in season, have launched her to some part of the river, to have her finished, in preference to leaving her there until it was too late to save her?"

"If I had known any place where to have carried her, I would," was Whittle's answer.[35]

35. *Ibid.,* 440.

'   As the investigation proceeded, Senator Foote tried hard to uncover something sinister in the admittedly unusual type of contract by which the Tifts had been hired for work on the *Mississippi* and *Louisiana*. In this effort he was joined by Senator Conrad,[36] who took no pains to conceal his belief that between Mallory and the Tifts there had existed some iniquitous arrangement of at least a semitreasonable character.

The examination of the pro-Mallory witness Senac provided Foote with an opportunity to press the point. This part of the investigation brought out clearly the fact that the whole procedure was a contest between a pro-Mallory and an anti-Mallory faction, rather than a cool objective, judicial probe. Senac, under cautious prompting from the pro-Mallory chair, affirmed that the Tifts had received for building the *Mississippi* nothing but their personal expenses; they had sought only the glory and prestige of constructing such a vessel. The witness further declared that he had known Asa Tift since 1847 and could vouch for his integrity and loyalty to the South. Was there, inquired the chair, any relationship of blood or of marriage between the Tifts and the Secretary of the Navy? None whatever, replied Senac.

At this point Senator Foote took over the questioning of the witness. It was evident that he was—or at least thought that he was—hot on the trail of something.

He presumed that Mr. Senac would not deny that the Tifts and Mallory were very intimate friends. The witness replied slowly that he believed that this was so. "Where," asked Foote, shifting the angle of his attack slightly, "are the Tifts from—where were they born?"

"Senac: I believe, in Mystic, Connecticut.

"Barksdale (interjecting himself into the discussion): How long have they resided in the South?

"Senac: I think, since they were ten years old; one of them I know had been a resident of Georgia for thirty years.

"Foote: Where are the estates of these gentlemen located?

"Senac: Mr. Nelson Tift owns a large property in Georgia. Mr. Asa Tift owns considerable property in Key West.

"Foote: That property is in the hands of the Federal Government, is it not?

"Senac: So I heard.

"Foote: Do you know that that property is under the special protection of that government, for his benefit?

36. Conrad was not a member of the committee but a witness for the prosecution.

"Senac: I have every reason to believe it is not. [Senac supported his statement by referring to a sum of money deposited by Asa Tift in the hands of Messrs. Maitland and Co., of New York City, which was paid over by that firm to the Federal government. This information, said Senac, he acquired 'by letters that I saw from Mr. Wall, of Key West.']

"Foote: How did this Mr. Wall know anything about them?

"Senac: There was an intimacy between Mr. Tift and Mr. Wall in business matters, and there was also an association between the principal merchants there, which had been called the 'Holy Alliance.' [Senac said that he had seen some descriptions of this Holy Alliance in a letter shown to him by Mr. Tift, and also in a newspaper.]

"Foote: Is Maitland a countryman of his?

"Senac: I don't understand you.

"Foote: Is Maitland a brother Yankee?

"Senac: I don't know where he was born."

Mr. Lyons broke in with the question, "What has been the general character of the Tifts in society since you have known them up to this time?" Senac responded, "They have always occupied the highest position that any men could occupy in the community."

"Lyons: Has either of them been engaged in political life?

"Senac: I think not. They have had their opinions in politics, however. Mr. Asa Tift was a member of the Florida convention and voted for secession.

"Foote: Is it, in your judgment, a conclusive proof of a man's being entirely a man of public and private integrity that he voted for secession?

"Senac: Not at all. I don't think it is conclusive of any such thing.

"Foote: Was Mr. Nelson Tift a supporter of Mr. Mallory?

"Senac: "I don't know.

"Foote: Has he any holy alliance with him, as you called this alliance of merchants a while ago?

"Senac: I don't know, sir."[37]

[There is considerable evidence to suggest that the Tifts were, at least during the first few months of the war, on surprisingly good terms with

37. Concerning previous business relations between Mallory and the Tifts, see J. C. Dobbin (Secretary of the Navy) to Mallory, August 16, 1856: "In reply to your letter of the 16th inst., desiring, in behalf of Mr. Tift of Key West a loan from the United States Coal Depot of one or two hundred tons of coal, the Department informs you that special permission will be given to let Mr. Tift have the coal upon his furnishing satisfactory security for its prompt return and of equal quantity" (Miscellaneous Letters of the Navy Department, National Archives).

some Yankee business firms—and with the Federal government itself. From their office at Key West the two brothers wrote, as late as May and June of 1861, several letters to New York commercial houses which are hardly the type of communication one might expect from the men who, less than four months later, would be employed by the Confederate Navy Department to build ironclads at New Orleans.

[On May 19, 1861, the Tifts urged Messrs. Benner and Deaker, of New York, to continue the trips of their freighter to Key West. Should the Federal government raise objections to this, an application to the Federal Secretary of the Treasury was recommended by the Tifts.[38] Less than two weeks later Asa Tift wrote the following to the same firm: "I hope you will be able to keep the *Kimball* and *Bogata* [*sic*] running to Key West. There will be Government freight, it is presumed, so they can be filled up regularly. Ours is a Union town. The panic has passed off, and those most watched now are, I think, the fellows who always try to get on the strong side. Quite a number of Patriots have gone away, and the officials appear to place confidence in those who remain."[39]

[On June 11, Asa sent two letters to New York. The first, to R. L. Maitland and Company, declared that "the policy of the [Federal] Government in permitting shipment of provisions to Key West is properly appreciated."[40] The second, to E. W. Barstrow [Barston?], reminded the latter that "no manufacturer or other person, North or South, has 'fared badly' with this correspondent, nor will they be likely to do so, unless his means shall first be arrested by *his Northern* correspondents,—and I will also say as much for every respectable merchant in this city. I will continue to sell your bills, if possible, and remit proceeds."[41] And, three days later, Asa Tift wrote to Benner and Deaker: "I hope the *Kimball* is with you and will get a good freight out. Send the coal, if possible. A representative from the commanding officer here has gone to the Secretary of the Treasury, asking permission that clearances may be freely granted to Key West."[42] Asa had written to Maitland and Company on May 16: "On the 14th inst. . . . I advised you of my draft @ 3 months sight . . . in

---

38. A. F. Tift and N. C. Tift to Messrs. Benner and Deaker, May 19, 1861 (Letter Book of Mallory Steamship Line, Key West Office, 825).

39. A. F. Tift (per C. Tift) to Messrs. Benner and Deaker, May 30, 1861 (*ibid.*, 834).

40. A. F. Tift (per C. Tift) to Messrs. R. L. Maitland and Company, June 11, 1861 (*ibid.*, 843).

41. A. F. Tift (per C. Tift) to E. W. Barstrow [Barston?], June 11, 1861 (*ibid.*, 841). Italics in original.

42. A. F. Tift and N. C. Tift to Messrs. Benner and Deaker, June 14, 1861 (*ibid.*, 848).

favor of C. and E. Horn for . . . fifteen hundred dollars. I also made a suggestion relative to my necessary affairs, but I must confidentially leave every thing pertaining to my interests in your hands, entirely [?], with your good discretion, knowing they will have the protection you have always extended over them."[43]]

Nelson Tift himself was called to the stand. By his testimony he seemed to clear himself rather conclusively with regard to all the points at issue. Foote did not succeed in his effort to extract from the shipbuilder some admission of previous business relations with Mallory.[44] Also the "special contract" made by Mallory with the Tifts appeared to have been above board and for the good of the cause. Tift denied that his arrangement with the Navy Department had been of an exclusive or monopolistic character. On the contrary, he asserted, Mr. Mallory had desired that whenever the Tifts should find any other persons who could construct ships, the Department should be informed so that these additional contractors should be set to work—"not under our [Tifts'] directions, however."[45]

The terms of the "special contract" were frankly and ingenuously described by the witness.[46] The objection that it had been unwise to have the shaft for the *Mississippi* manufactured at Richmond instead of at some point nearer to New Orleans was adequately answered by Tift.[47] A private letter from Asa Tift to his brother, offered in evidence, attested to the sincere devotion of the former to the Southern cause.[48]

Still to be decided was the crucial question of whether the Navy Department had acted culpably in permitting the *Mississippi* to remain at New Orleans until the actual moment of Farragut's attack. The answer to this question depended largely on the response to two further queries: first, was it the general and considered opinion at New Orleans in that fatal month of

43. A. F. Tift to Messrs. R. L. Maitland and Co., May 16, 1861 (*ibid.*, 822).
44. *O.R.*, Ser. II, Vol. I, pp. 548-49.
45. *Ibid.*, 547-48.
46. *Ibid.*, 548. In a later session of the committee there was submitted in evidence the letter of the Secretary of the Navy to the Tifts, dated August 28, 1861, explaining the conditions of the contract. Everything in the arrangement, as therein described, appeared to be to the distinct benefit of the Confederate government, and even to the financial disadvantage of the Tifts. See *ibid.*, 601; also further Mallory-Tifts correspondence submitted by Mallory to the second session of the committee, January 21, 1863 (*ibid.*, 571-608), especially the final summarizing letter of both the Tifts to Mallory from Savannah, Ga., August 26, 1862 (*ibid.*, 598-601), in which they pay the following tribute to the Secretary and to his *Mississippi* project: "You gave us all the discretion necessary and every facility which you could for the early completion of the *Mississippi*, and we will add that, notwithstanding the difficulties which we encountered, no vessel of equal magnitude and power has ever before been built in the same time, in this or any other country."
47. *Ibid.*, 549-50.                           48. *Ibid.*, 557.

April, 1862, that the enemy could pass the New Orleans forts at will; and, secondly, would the *Mississippi* really have been in a more secure position if taken upriver?

As to the ability of the Federals to run past the forts, there seems to have been, before the attack, a division of opinion, with most of the military and naval men taking the pessimistic view.[49] Governor Moore testified that he himself had felt sure that the enemy could pass the forts if the river obstructions should be broken, as they were several days before the Federals' main attack. Yet he admitted that the general public sentiment, encouraged by confident reports from some of the military authorities, had inclined to the belief that the forts would hold out.[50] This opinion was shared by Moore's aide-de-camp, Colonel Thomas C. Manning, who testified that the same view was held by "many others higher in authority than [the Tifts]."[51] The Tifts, he declared, did not think it possible for the enemy's fleet to break the line of the forts. "Hence their confident sense of security, which was a serious cause of delay."[52] Captain Sinclair declared that he had certainly been confident of completing the *Mississippi* before the Federals reached her.[53]

Conceded that the balance of opinion had been against the possibility of the holding of the forts, there arose the second question: Should the *Mississippi,* several days before the attack, have been taken upriver? On this issue Captain Sinclair was closely and vigorously questioned by Senator Foote.

Sinclair's argument was that it would have been useless to remove the *Mississippi* upriver, since she would have run into almost equal peril there. "With any force we could have put to her," he declared, ". . . the enemy would have overtaken her, even if we were 200 miles ahead of them."[54]

---

49. Captain Mitchell testified that he himself and most of the military and naval personnel with whom he discussed the matter agreed with Whittle's thesis that gunboats could pass shore batteries at will. General Lovell testified as follows: "I do not pretend to say whether the *Mississippi* could have been got away or not, but if all these officers were of opinion that these forts could be passed, I think some steps ought to have been taken in due time to secure her safety" (*ibid.,* 622).

50. *Ibid.,* 612-13.                        51. *Ibid.,* 616.
52. *Ibid.*                                  53. *Ibid.,* 510.

54. "Foote: Suppose she had been launched a week or ten days before? Sinclair: If there had been orders to that effect, I could have taken her up provided the enemy did not come up after her. Dupré: Do you know the speed with which the gunboats of the enemy travel on the Mississippi, upstream? Sinclair: I should think 8 or 10 miles an hour,—at least many of them." He added that the maximum speed at which he could have towed the *Mississippi* upstream was 3 or 4 miles an hour. Foote made a rather nasty implication that the Tifts might have been "secretly disposed to retard the work" on the *Mississippi*. But, asserted Sinclair, they showed every disposition to forward the work as much as possible. Even at night, he said, work on the ship was pushed ahead (*ibid.,* 493).

This was so, he explained, because the enemy gunboats had a speed of eight or ten miles an hour, while three or four miles an hour was the *Mississippi's* maximum while being towed upstream. "I am of the opinion," he said, "that if we had gone up the river we would have been captured. We could not possibly get her up fast enough to take her out of the enemy's way. They knew all about her. They came up to the ship before that and saw that she was in a fair way of being destroyed, and then returned. They would, I am satisfied, have followed her up the river, had we gone there; and before we could have cast the hawsers they would have captured her; nor would it be possible for us to have fired her in time."[55]

Sinclair was asked by the chair why he had delayed removing the vessel until such a late date as the twenty-fourth. "There was," he replied, "no special cause to remove her before then. We were going on rapidly with the work, and to have taken the ship away would have retarded the work a great deal. We were not aware that the enemy were coming as soon as they did come, and we deemed it best to keep her as she was and try if possible to finish her before the enemy would advance upon us."[56] Sinclair's testimony was summed up in one of his concluding sentences: "There was no place of safety within 800 miles of New Orleans . . . to which I could have carried her."[57]

Senator Foote was far from satisfied with this defense, and he pressed Sinclair hard. His aim was to force the Captain finally to admit that the Secretary of the Navy should have ordered the *Mississippi* upriver. Sinclair parried cautiously, but he was fencing with an extremely clever prosecutor.

"If you were Secretary of the Navy," urged the Senator, "as familiar as all the Secretaries of the Navy are supposed to be with the geography of the country, the depth and width of rivers, etc., with your knowledge of the fact that the enemy's gunboats were attempting to pass the forts, with the conviction on your mind that they would effect that object, would you have allowed such a ship as that to remain there until the enemy passed the forts? Would you not, with a knowledge [acquired] some time before that the attempt was [to be] made, obtain the aid of steamers to get the vessel up?"[58]

"I would," answered Sinclair, "if I thought I could have taken her up and secured her."

"If you had to act the part over again," persisted Foote, "would you not

55. *Ibid.*, 488.
57. *Ibid.*, 496.
56. *Ibid.*
58. *Ibid.*, 497.

have made the attempt to take her up to Yazoo River after you became convinced that the enemy's gunboats could have passed the forts?"

"No, sir," insisted Sinclair, "because I was perfectly satisfied that there was no place of safety for her."

But Foote was not giving up. Would not Sinclair, with his present knowledge of the suitability of the Yazoo River berth, together with his conviction that the enemy would certainly pass the forts, and his knowledge that the ship could not be finished until July 1—would not Sinclair, in view of all these considerations, have taken the *Mississippi* upriver?

"I would," said the Captain, "but I do not believe she could have been saved."[59]

Foote felt that he was getting somewhere, and he kept on going. He asked Sinclair to prove that the ship could not have been saved. "Because," said the Captain, "there was no battery for her protection at any point to which she could have been carried. If we had taken her up three or four weeks before, transferred the workshops from New Orleans to the Yazoo River, for instance, and erected batteries there, we might have saved her."[60]

Foote shifted slightly the angle of his attack. He recalled the history of the *Arkansas*. Was Captain Sinclair aware that there was a large iron foundry in Vicksburg? Captain Sinclair was not aware of the fact. If, asked Foote, the Captain had known of the existence of the foundry there, and had had his present knowledge of the Yazoo River, would he not have deemed it expedient to take the *Mississippi* up the river to some safe point where he could have completed her, a little more slowly, perhaps, than at New Orleans, but just as effectually?

Sinclair's response was, at last, an admission. "I think I would," he said.

Foote, as was evident to all, had scored. It became clear again at once, however, that the Mallory interest was very adequately represented at the investigation. The chair interrupted with a question to Sinclair: in order to have made a secure haven for the *Mississippi,* would there not have been need of a defensive battery at the spot? "Yes," said the Captain. "You did not know," pursued the chair, "of any place where there was a battery?" "No," said Sinclair. "Even now," the chair continued, "you don't know of any place where batteries are erected to which you might bring her?"[61]

But Foote was ready to counter this counter-strategy. "The Captain," he reminded the committee blandly, "said that with his knowledge of facts

59. *Ibid.*
60. *Ibid.*
61. *Ibid.,* 498.

now, to wit, that the enemy's gunboats would undoubtedly come up the river, that there was a foundry at Vicksburg which could supply all the necessary iron works for her construction, and that the Yazoo River afforded a place of safety for the vessel, he would, enlightened by experience, have taken up the vessel four weeks before to the Yazoo River."[62]

Again the chair interrupted with the objection that Senator Foote's question had been a leading one and was therefore to be ruled out. It was very obvious that the controlling group on the committee did not intend to have the Secretary of the Navy hurt.

"With all due deference to the Chair," countered Foote, "I noticed that his interrogatories to the witnesses on yesterday were essentially leading ones." The chair admitted that he might have put such questions, although in that case it was the duty of any member of the committee to have interposed. "But," continued the chair, addressing Sinclair, "I wish this thing settled. Do you know any safe place now to which you could have carried that boat?" "I do not," said the Captain, with exemplary promptness.

Foote again changed his line of attack. "What," he asked Sinclair, "do you think of the wisdom of the movement of bringing the ram *Arkansas* down the river and thence up the river to Yazoo City?" Sinclair answered that it had turned out to be a wise movement. The chair broke in with a question: "You would not have undertaken that?" "If I had had the same knowledge of the river as the captain of that vessel had I might have done so," replied Sinclair.[63]

Foote obviously felt that he had the witness on the verge of another admission damaging to the Secretary of the Navy. He kept pushing his advantage. Sinclair was insisting that he would not have taken the *Arkansas* upriver unless he had been as well acquainted with that part of the river as her actual commander had been. From that point Foote took up his questioning:

"Foote: You would not have made that an indispensable condition of removing the vessel at all?

"Sinclair: I think the two vessels [the *Arkansas* and the *Mississippi*] were very differently situated.

"Foote: If you had the same knowledge as the captain of that vessel, would you not have taken her up the river and finished her without a battery?

"Sinclair: I think I would.

62. *Ibid.,* 499.

63. *Ibid.,* p. 498.

"Foote: With the same knowledge possessed by him, and the opinion you entertained that the enemy would pass the forts, and that the boat would not be finished before the 1st of July, would you, having been thus advised by experience four weeks before the enemy did pass the ports, have taken that boat up the river, carried her to the Yazoo River, and have had her finished at some point, even though there was not a battery there, especially if you had ascertained the fact that there were large foundries at Vicksburg to furnish the necessary ironwork for her completion?

"Sinclair: [to the distinct annoyance of the majority of the committee]: I would, sir."[64]

Foote had scored again. The Mallory interest on the committee deemed it high time to enter the discussion. Senator Maxwell took over the questioning. "Would you," he asked Sinclair, "have waited before taking her from New Orleans to inquire whether there was any fleet at the mouth of the Mississippi with a view of passing the batteries?"[65]

Sinclair, rather unexpectedly and doubtless to Maxwell's slight discomfiture, responded, "No, sir," Maxwell, as determined as Foote to secure the answer that he wanted, tried again: "Do you know how long these batteries [defending New Orleans] were there?"

"I do not," answered the Captain.

"Would you have done this [i.e., taken the *Mississippi* or the *Arkansas* up the river] before there was a demonstration to pass the batteries?"

Sinclair at last gave the answer that was being so persistently angled for: "No, sir."

Maxwell followed up quickly: "Suppose, Captain Sinclair, you had been Secretary of the Navy, and had known everything which has been suggested to you by the gentleman from Tennessee [Foote], but were in constant receipt of information from those who had charge of the defenses at New Orleans, that New Orleans was safe; would you have taken her [the *Mississippi*] away, notwithstanding all that knowledge?"[66]

Sinclair's response was emphatic: "I would not."

Foote must have felt that his gains were slipping away from him. He packed all his ammunition into a final summing-up question and launched it at the Captain: "Would you, as Secretary of the Navy, taking an extended view of the whole field of operations; bound to know the whole geography of this country, both land and water; and where the proper kind of materials for constructing ships are most easy to be obtained; bound to know

64. *Ibid.*, 498-99.    65. *Ibid.*, 499.
66. *Ibid.*

the strength of the enemy which were advancing up the river; bound to know by consultation with experienced navy officers the impossibility of keeping the enemy's gunboats down the river,—would you, here in Richmond, have deemed it safe and prudent to allow that boat to remain there, the finishing of which was deemed next to impossible before the 1st of July;—would you have deemed it safe to allow her to remain there, or would you have procured all the steamboat force available and dragged her up to the Yazoo River, knowing that there was there a means of finishing her?"[67]

This was a strong and effective attack. It did not please the friends of Mallory on the committee. At once the chair objected that the question was out of order. Mr. Foote insisted that it was perfectly proper. The chair, expressing a desire to have the decision of the committee on the ruling, put the query, Shall the decision of the chair on this point stand as the judgment of the committee? The committee voted in the affirmative. Some intimation having been made by Mr. Foote in the course of the debate that it was not strictly parliamentary for the chair to participate in the examination of witnesses, the chair put the further question, whether, in the judgment of the committee, it was proper for the chair to participate in the examination of witnesses. This question also was decided in the affirmative. Mr. Foote said that he would vote for the chair's being allowed to propound interrogatories to witnesses, since the chair said that it was proper for it to do so.[68]

From this point on, the pro-Mallory part of the committee had matters pretty safely under control. To Senator Lyons' leading query, "If the *Mississippi* had been carried up the Yazoo River to Yazoo City, could she not have been pursued to that point by the boats of the enemy at any time, in the absence of a battery to protect her?" Sinclair replied, "She certainly could, as far as my knowledge of the river extends." To Lyons' second question, "Would not that be necessarily true if she drew no more water than many of the boats of the enemy?" Sinclair answered, "Certainly, it would." To a final query, "Does it not follow from the fact that boats drawing less water could follow her?" the Captain said, "It necessarily does."[69] When Foote interposed rather weakly with reference to the possibility of placing obstructions in the river to prevent such pursuit up the Yazoo River by enemy gunboats, Senator Barksdale objected that the re-

67. *Ibid.*
68. *Ibid.*
69. *Ibid.*, 500.

mark was out of order. The chair sustained the objection and announced that it was time to adjourn for lunch.[70]

Besides the charges relating specifically to the handling of the *Mississippi*, the committee investigated other accusations of a more general character which had been leveled against the Navy Department. Mr. Conrad made the following sweeping accusation: "I have had, as chairman of the Committee on Naval Affairs, my attention called to the affairs of the Navy Department. I have had a good deal of intercourse and a good many conversations with the Secretary of the Navy, and from a very early period I was impressed with the conviction that there was a want of intelligence, and especially of energy, promptitude, and forethought in the administration of that Department."[71]

Mallory, according to Conrad, had been seriously remiss in constructing and in purchasing war vessels, particularly ironclads. He had not appreciated the value of the ironclads and, when finally persuaded to build some, had been dilatory in forwarding the work.[72]

In sustaining these strictures, Conrad did not show to advantage before the committee. The pro-Mallory chair cross-questioned him closely. Was not Mr. Conrad aware that Commander Raphael Semmes had been sent to New York to purchase steam war vessels in March, 1861, and had not Mr. Conrad read Semmes's instructions? Conrad confessed to an "indistinct recollection" of Semmes's trip "somewhere to the North," but denied ever having seen the Commander's instructions. Was not Mr. Conrad aware also that Lieutenant North had been sent to the northern states to purchase steamers of war in March, 1861, and had he not seen North's instructions? Conrad answered no to both questions. Was not Mr. Conrad aware that the Navy Department had sent another agent to Canada to purchase propeller ships in May, 1861, and had he not seen this agent's instructions? "I am not aware of it," replied Conrad, in a rather surprising manner, "and do not recollect hearing of it, but it is very probable that the agent was sent. My *want of any knowledge in the matter* is owing to the fact that I was not generally in the habit of inquiring into the particulars of the Navy Department, and I do not recollect ever having seen instructions of the Department to any officer at any time or on any subject."[73] Conrad was being pushed harder and harder by the chair: "Were you not aware that the Department, from Montgomery, sent a board of officers to New Orleans on

70. *Ibid.*
72. *Ibid.*

71. *Ibid.*, 723-24.
73. *Ibid.*, 739. Italics inserted.

the 17th of March, 1861, with instructions to purchase and fit out steamers for war vessels?

"Mr. Conrad: I recollect that at one time a board of officers were sent to make arrangements at New Orleans for the purchase of vessels, but I have no recollection of the time.

"Chair: Were you not aware that the Department, immediately upon its organization, entered upon the completion of the *Fulton* at Pensacola?

"Mr. Conrad: I have no recollection on the subject.

"Chair: Were you not aware of the contracts made at Montgomery in April 1861, with Leeds and Co., of New Orleans, and with J. R. Anderson and Co., of Richmond, to make guns for New Orleans?

"Mr. Conrad: No, sir."

And so continued the rebuttal against Conrad, concluding with a reading of Mallory's letter of May 8, 1861, urging the construction of ironclads, and his report to Congress of July 18, 1861, stressing the same necessity.[74]

Other witnesses were produced to testify to the Secretary's energy and foresight in regard to the precise points on which he had been condemned by Conrad. Commander Brooke averred that Mallory had always been in favor of ironclads, and that most of the officers in the navy had been cool toward them.[75] Major William P. Williamson, Chief Engineer of the navy, attested to the Secretary's intense interest in the building of the *Mississippi*.[76]

One of the final points much stressed in the investigation was Mallory's alleged error in forbidding Commodore Hollins to bring his squadron down from Fort Pillow to reinforce the defense of New Orleans. Hollins insisted that if he had been allowed to make such a move he could have blocked Farragut's progress past the city. He declared, indeed, that he would have been able to "whip the enemy out of the river."[77]

Hollins described circumstantially how he would have done this. His gunboats, he said, were at a great advantage in going downstream. They were completely guarded with iron on their bows, and supported by forty fire boats. With this force, he believed, he could have gone below the New Orleans forts and attacked and routed the enemy's squadron. Farragut's ships were there in such numbers that they could have been thrown into inextricable confusion by such an onslaught. "I felt confident," asserted the Commodore, "that I could whip the enemy."[78]

In this declaration he was supported by two of his brother officers who

74. *Ibid.*, 740-43.
76. *Ibid.*, 638-39.
78. *Ibid.*, 474.

75. *Ibid.*, 785-86.
77. *Ibid.*, 474-76.

testified before the committee. If the Commodore had been at New Orleans with all his vessels, thought General Lovell, and if he had taken charge of the defenses afloat, it was quite possible that the result would have been a very different one from that which actually had occurred.[79] Beverly Kennon elaborated his reasons for thinking that Hollins' squadron could have saved the Gulf port. Even without the Commodore and his vessels, he declared, the Confederates had almost defeated the enemy. They had driven off seven of Farragut's ships. The great handicap was the fact that Captain Mitchell, commanding the naval defenses, had arrived only two or three days before and was not thoroughly familiar with conditions. Hollins, from his previous stay at New Orleans, was acquainted with the strategic problems and geographical difficulties. "If he had been left in command," affirmed Kennon, "I am satisfied he would have whipped the enemy out of the river. . . ."[80]

Thomas Semmes, the pro-Mallory man, kept drawing the witness out by a series of questions. If the purpose of these was to break down Hollins' position the Secretary's advocate did a rather fumbling job. It was soon evident that the more questions Semmes asked the clearer it became that Hollins, if allowed by Mallory to bring down the Fort Pillow squadron, might indeed have made a considerable difference in the issue at New Orleans.

The Commodore, at Semmes's urging, told of the telegram which he had received from the Secretary, forbidding the movement down the river. He had shown the order to Governor Moore and to some others, and had explained to them what he could do for New Orleans if he were only permitted to carry out his plan. The Governor, General Lovell, and Captain Whittle had telegraphed to the Secretary, urging him to give Hollins permission to make a dash at the enemy.

"Semmes: What was the reply?"

"Hollins: There was no reply. I waited twenty four hours for an answer, but none was received. The first intimation I received after that was a telegraphic dispatch to come on to Richmond immediately.

"Semmes: Did you come on?"

"Hollins: I did.

"Semmes: Did you see the Secretary of the Navy?"

"Hollins: I did. *I received orders to be president of the board to examine midshipmen."*

79. *Ibid.,* 624.
80. *Ibid.,* 525-26.

Semmes asked whether "this matter about your recall from the command [had been] a subject of conversation" between himself and the Secretary. Hollins said that he himself had not mentioned the subject. Had the Secretary said anything about it? "Nothing, sir," replied the Commodore, surprisingly; then, apparently as an afterthought, "I told him that if I were allowed to do as I proposed, I should have shipped the squadron." "What did he say to that?" asked Semmes. "He said nothing."[81]

Semmes's final interrogation could not have been more appropriately phrased if he had been trying to prove Hollins' case. "What finally became of your fleet [left in the Fort Pillow area by Mallory's orders]?" "It was burned, sir, at the mouth of the Yazoo River," said Hollins, drily.

The witness's examination concluded with a mild innuendo dropped by Phelan in the Mallory interest: "With reference to the supposed deficiency on the side of the enemy's fleet, you speak only of what you heard. With reference to the character of this deficiency, the officers who were in command of the fleet at the time of the combat would, of course, be much better judges of the character of this deficiency than yourself?" "I have no doubt they would," answered the Commodore.[82]

There were other charges of less moment made against the Navy Department, none of them proven. General Lovell complained of the "divided command" at New Orleans, and felt that "too much latitude had been given to the steamboat captains in charge of the river expedition."[83] James Martin, a shipbuilder of New Orleans, said that the shafts for the *Mississippi* could have been made at the city instead of at Richmond, and thus valuable time would have been saved.[84] Conrad insisted that there were more skilled shipbuilders at New Orleans besides the Tifts.[85]

The Navy Department's rebuttal to these allegations was prompt and fairly adequate.[86] It was clear that the investigation had uncovered no startling evidence of guilt on the part of the naval administration. Mallory's handling of his many difficult problems had not been without flaws; he had not done everything possible to bring success to the South; but his accusers could unearth for his discomfiture no serious proofs of remissness. In the last year of the war the final report of the committee was published and provided the Secretary with a clean bill of health that was even flamboyant in its praise.[87] This was a real tribute, even though the vindication was written largely by his friends.

81. *Ibid.*, 476. Italics inserted.      82. *Ibid.*, 480.
83. *Ibid.*, 659-60. Cf. also Lovell to Secretary Benjamin, March 6, 1862 (*ibid.*, 686).
84. *Ibid.*, 503.      85. *Ibid.*, 725-26.
86. *Ibid.*, 433-34.      87. Cf. *infra*, p. 295.

Mallory was full of hope at the end of that summer of 1862.[88] "You wish me to speak of our prospects politically," he wrote to Angela, "and I cheerfully do so, because I regard them as bright. We are stronger today than we have ever been, while our enemy is weaker. As our people have become firmly bound together for this war, those of the North have become disunited; and discord is now predominant in their counsels. Lincoln's cabinet dread a defeat, and hence their armies are everywhere retreating. We are daily expecting a battle in Tennessee and here in Virginia; and if we shall defeat Pope decidedly, the backbone of the war will be over; for the opposition to the abolition party would shear it of its strength. Disinterested and determined devotion are exhibited upon all sides of our people; and the philosophy with which men and women raised in affluence and possessed of wealth have sacrificed . . . all they had . . . is wonderful. Abroad our cause has steadily advanced and won the confidence and esteem of nations, while that of our foe has become contemptible. The work of recruiting at the North is slow and distasteful; and murmurs are heard upon all sides against the war. Lincoln has at last quailed before the fear of driving off the border states, and has declared that the negro is not an essential element of the war, but is secondary to the Union. This will bring the ultras of his party upon him, while his British friends, the abolitionists abroad, who see no prosperity or sense in the war outside of freedom to the slave, will abandon him."[89]

Yet there persisted, throughout the summer, ominous hints of what was, after all, one of the chief reasons for the final failure of the Confederacy—defective leadership on the highest levels. In his very private diary Mallory complained that the President did not consult his Cabinet concerning either plans of campaigns or military appointments. As a result, Davis was deprived of much valuable and necessary advice from his colleagues. For example, the President had sent Magruder to command in Missouri, although General Price would probably have been the better choice. But, concluded Stephen, with more charity than logic, the President doubtless took the "largest view" of things and certainly he "does all for the best."[90]

This optimistic qualification loses much of its force in the light of Randolph's resignation as Secretary of War in September because of Davis'

88. He found time to write a long letter to Governor Milton of Florida, urging that the Floridians' hospital in Richmond be placed under more centralized control (Mallory to Governor Milton, September 26, 1862 [Milton Letter Book]).

89. Mallory to Angela, August 31, 1862.

90. Mallory, Diary, part II, p. 21, June 24, 1862.

interference in the administration of that department. The fact was, Mallory admitted, that the President's familiarity with army matters "induces his desire to mingle in them all and to control them; and this desire is augmented by the fear that details may be wrongly managed, without his constant supervision."[91]

However, in handling one issue, at least, the Cabinet functioned smoothly. The President called his official advisers to a special meeting on August 1, 1862, to consider the question of retaliations. Several Federal generals, it was alleged, had countenanced atrocities against Confederate prisoners and had ordered the imprisonment of Southern civilians. Should the Confederate government retort in kind?

The Cabinet believed unanimously that retaliation was a hazardous measure, to be resorted to only on grounds of strict necessity, and to be applied with prudence. It was thought unwise to accustom the Southern people to deeds of blood perpetrated on innocent men for the sins of the guilty ones of the North who could not be reached. Retaliation should, as a general rule, stop short of provocation.[92]

On the following day the Cabinet met again, and one after another the members expressed their opinions in writing. This time the unanimity was broken by one man, who, overnight, had decided that "Federal prisoners in Southern hands should be held to answer for the barbarities threatened upon the Southern people." It was the Secretary of the Navy who had thus reversed his judgment of the preceding day. He declared that he "could not perceive the wisdom of binding ourselves to exchange all prisoners of war present and future, upon fair terms, and thus treating with our enemies upon the basis of civilized warfare, while they are waging upon us a war of desolation and extermination."

Mallory was overruled. The government, it was decided, would not adopt retaliation measures but would deliver a strong protest to the Federal commanders and to Washington. The problem was discussed again by the Cabinet two weeks later, and the Navy Secretary executed still another somersault of opinion. This time, in a divided vote, Mallory declared that "upon the score of humanity and policy both, we must do everything consistent with honor and safety to stave off a war of retaliation, and . . . all honorable efforts to do so will redound to our honor and glory."[93]

91. *Ibid.*, 28-29, September 19, 1862.
92. *Ibid.*, 22-27, for the complete discussion of this topic. Mallory's account covers the following dates: August 1, 2, 15, 16, 1862.
93. *Ibid.*, 26-27, August 16, 1862.

It is difficult to assess these chameleon views of Mallory's. In the incident, it must be confessed, he did not reveal himself at his best—a fact which his enemies would not forget to point out.

October, 1862. Report on morale from the James River submarine batteries: "The Navy generally is not getting on well here—too much jealousy, etc. Everyone wants notoriety and promotion, and I think a good many are looking out chiefly for 'No. 1.' "[94]

That situation could be handled. The Navy Secretary mounted his horse the next morning and rode down to the batteries. He had lunch with the men, threw horseshoes with them in the afternoon, then lay down for a two-hour nap in the shadow of the big guns. Late that night he cantered back to Richmond, whistling to himself softly. Officers and sailors could be handled thus, but they were not the only morale problems on the Secretary's mind.

A woman, a "dear, dear woman" of no outstanding importance in the larger story of the Civil War, was harassing dangerously the courage of a man whose importance in the war was unquestioned. Stephen was deeply hurt and "so depressed by her letters that [he] could do nothing"; but he loved her so much that he would try desperately to be patient. "I cannot argue with you, my Angela, upon your want of faith in God, your weakness, cowardice, and unpatriotism. I can only deplore them. My love for you is so unselfish, so pure and devoted . . . that you could say and do nothing to me . . . which I am not ever ready to forgive and forget. . . ."[95]

In a particularly bitter moment she had accused him of not desiring her to come to him at Richmond. "You do me injustice, Angela," he wrote. "It is pitiable that you should thus be a prey to so mean a feeling. Come to me. I want to see you, to have you with me day and night."[96]

As usual, his sense of the ridiculous enabled him at least partially to fight off his depression of mind. Angela's brother-in-law, Tim Garnett, was a never failing source of amusement. He was "unhurt and does not mean to be wounded." He was on the lookout for someone to fight in his place, but must probably pay $1,000 to secure such a substitute. Stephen advised him to retire to his home and to send his wife and baby to the army. All four parties, he felt, would profit by the exchange.[97]

94. Lieut. Hunter Davidson to Lieut. Catesby ap Jones, October 25, 1862 (*O.R.*, Ser. I, Vol. VII, p. 61).
95. Mallory to Angela, August 31, 1862.
96. *Ibid.*
97. *Ibid.*

Yarnell Garnett, another brother-in-law, spent long evenings in Stephen's lodgings, "seated with a long pipe in his mouth, puffing by jerks his smoke and his sentences between his thin compressed lips, with no more of an aperture between them than between the shells of an obstinate clam, smelling of whiskey, and with eyes glistening like those of a game cock, and his face wrinkled like that of the grandfather of Balaam's ass."[98]

Yarnell's style of talk, said Stephen, would kill a nervous man. He would speak of nothing but himself and claimed relationship with all mankind, tracing every man's "kin" back almost to Adam and Eve, to some far-off Garnett.

"Well," Yarnell would say, "I've been out to the battlefield today to look for my brother-in-law,—my brother-in-law James Moreno. My [other] brother-in-law is in the Alabama regiment, and is a brother of my wife; his name is Tim, from Pensacola. I didn't see him, but I know he wasn't killed, because I saw Norton Cerbin, a nephew of Cousin Robert Hunter's wife, who saw Tim, and he said he was sick, so he is all right. I saw another relation of ours in this fight,—Mr. Rapier, John Rapier. You know him, Stephen; you're my brother-in-law, but you never tell me anything; all I know about what's going on I find out for myself.

"I went to hunt for my cousin once removed,—Brodenax Hunter. He was there and I heard he was killed. He was the third son of my father's cousin Nancy Garnett, who married Jeemes Brodenax of Prince George. It wouldn't surprise me one bit if he was killed, for all that family were the most obstinate people in the world. His father was like a mule, nothing less than kin to a Jackass, and his mother was, if anything, more so. My nephew Nance is just so, exactly; obstinate as the devil. Cousin Robert Hunter is different,—but Yelverton, Edgar, and all that branch, they're just alike,—obstinate as mules."[99]

Stephen thought that Yarnell's wife, Pila, should come on to Richmond to hold her spouse in check. There were many animals upon whom a "tail hold" was surest, and Yarnell, he believed, was one of them. Only Pila could keep him straight. Angela was not to mention to Pila, however, that Yarnell drank at Stephen's quarters. "I am particular in this, as he is in my house, and he may get drunk when he pleases and I will not be the means of informing upon him. I must respect the rights of hospitality."[100]

98. Mallory to his wife, July 10, 1862.
99. *Ibid.*
100. *Ibid.*

Antietam came on September 16-17. Because of this setback for the South, British intervention became, in fact, less likely, although most Confederates refused to admit the unpleasant truth. At Fredericksburg, less than three months later, the Confederates struck back savagely and almost redeemed their losses. The year closed in comparative quiet. Perhaps it was sensed on both sides that 1863 would be the crisis of the war.

The Navy Department was accorded a few encouraging slaps on the back. In the Georgia Legislature Senator Ben Hill, a close friend of Mallory's, praised the latter's administration.[101] The *Richmond Enquirer* thought that the charges against the Navy Department would recoil upon their authors.[102]

But from General W. H. C. Whiting, the military commander at Wilmington, had come a complaint in mid-October which may have deserved a more respectful hearing than it actually received in some quarters. Mallory, it was charged by Whiting, was seriously weakening the defenses of the North Carolina port in order to service the commerce-raiding missions on the open sea. The General spoke as follows, not without bias, concerning the alleged strategic error: "What is it for the Navy to burn fishing smacks off New England if they lend no hand to defence of home ... ? [This is obviously unfair criticism in view of the work of the commerce raiders over the seven seas.] We have already paid for the expedition of the *Tallahassee* [formerly guarding Wilmington] with 10 or 11 of the best ships, for the 4 lost during the last ten days are due to the great increase of the [blockading] fleet brought about by that unfortunate cruise. The difficulty of getting in supplies is trebled. Both bars swarm with boats; we can't see them from shore. At what better work can this naval force be put, with or without their vessels, than operating against the enemy at our own doors?"[103]

101. Haywood J. Pearce, Jr., *Benjamin Hill: Secession and Reconstruction* (Chicago, 1928), 69.

102. September 10, 1862.

103. Major General W. H. C. Whiting to Secretary of War James A. Seddon, October 11, 1862 (*O.R.*, Ser. I, Vol. X, pp. 781-82). Whiting's protest was accorded scant sympathy by Jefferson Davis. The President's comment was as follows: "It is to be regretted that in presenting his views General Whiting should so frequently have violated the courtesy due to the naval arm of the service. The vessels referred to [by Whiting in his description of the commerce raiding operations] are not 'privateers,' and such an offense to the Navy as was committed in so calling them should have caused the return of his letter as one not entitled to a place on the files of the War Department. His strictures on the cruise of the *Tallahassee* evinced both ignorance of the events and disregard of the rights of others on whose service it was no part of his duty to report. General Bragg will enquire into the wants of the service at Wilmington, having been ordered there for that purpose before these letters were referred to me" (endorsement by Davis on letter mentioned immediately above).

# CHAPTER ELEVEN

# Vicksburg, Torpedoes, and Submarines

In the third week of January, 1863, Maggie Laurens, age sixteen, wrote from Columbia, South Carolina: "There has been considerable gaiety at Charleston for the last fortnight, parties at the different forts, and also at private houses ..., one ... given chiefly by Beauregard's aids. I hear there has been much disappointment on account of the almost exclusive use of the fancy dances, against which, you know, there is a wide spread scruple in our midst, and, in large and mixed assemblies, I think, with justice. But the little frenchmen [*sic*] on the Gen'l's staff are only pleased when whirling some poor damsel at the most furious rate. In Consequence of this, most of the girls are neglected, while the fancy dancers bear off the honors of the evening and have their heads turned in more ways than one."[1]

Although such social events at Charleston, or anywhere else in the Confederacy, were but brief diversions under a state of siege, there was no reason for the people of the South to be downhearted in the first month of 1863. Lee's victory at Fredericksburg in the preceding December had given new hope to the Army of Virginia. The new year had opened auspiciously for the Confederates with Magruder's recapture of Galveston, Texas. This was the coup which, according to report, had caused Farragut to "tear his hair."[2] The operation had been marked by excellent cooperation between the Confederate land and naval forces and was possibly the most severe

1. Maggie Laurens (granddaughter of Henry Laurens of Revolutionary fame) to Col. Chesnut, from Columbia, S. C., January 16, 1863 (Williams-Chesnut-Manning Papers, Southern Historical Collection, University of North Carolina).

2. Scharf, *History of the Confederate States Navy*, 512. In regard to this stroke at Galveston, cf. Lewis, *Farragut, First Admiral*, 148-64. Says this author: "After the Galveston affair he [Farragut] had written the Secretary that he had been compelled to withdraw four or five vessels from the Mississippi to the coast of Texas, and he begged for more ships of war to be sent as soon as possible, as he did not want to hazard an attack on Port Hudson with 'less than three ships besides the gunboats'" (*ibid.* 161-62).

blow the Federal navy had yet received.[3] That such synchronization between army and navy movements did not always prevail is evident from Mallory's complaints about the engineers' department's reluctance to afford a path for the *Richmond* through the obstructions in the James.[4]

The seizure of Fort Hindman, at Arkansas Post, by Federal gunboats and troops on January 11 was offset, to a great extent, by the news that the *Alabama* had made a sudden strike at the blockading forces at Mobile and had sunk the Federal frigate *Hatteras*. On January 15 another commerce-raiding cruiser, the *Florida,* sailed through the Mobile blockade and headed for the open sea. On the last day of the month, the Confederate gunboats *Chicora* and *Palmetto State* successfully raided the blockading fleet at Charleston, to give temporary color to the claim that the iron ring about the harbor had been broken.[5] Then, in April, came the repulse of Du Pont's monitors at the great South Carolina port.[6]

But southward down the Mississippi toward crucial Vicksburg came Grant. Working in close collaboration with the squadron under Porter, the conqueror of Fort Donelson was, with dogged persistence, hacking his way through to the great river stronghold. He had begun the effort in the preceding November from Grand Junction, along the straight overland route toward the line of the Yallabusha, but had been balked by Confederate cavalry raids on his supply line. In a further series of engagements extending from March 13 to April 5, the attempt of Federal gunboats and troops to pass southward through the Yazoo River had been defeated by a combined land and naval force. In mid-March, from the sixteenth to the twenty-fourth, another Federal effort to reach Vicksburg by a gunboat expedition through Steele's Bayou had been squelched, mainly by Confederate ships. Grant had then shifted his plan. Rejecting the strategy of the direct-line attack, he had crossed to the west bank of the Mississippi. He would bypass

3. Scharf, *op. cit.,* 512.

4. Secretary Seddon to Lieut. Gen. James Longstreet, April 7, 1863 (*O.R.A.,* Ser. I, Vol. XVIII, pp. 967-68). Cf. also General Beauregard's charges that his forces on Morris Island were being depleted by the navy's requisitions for men from the army (Beauregard to Gen. S. Cooper, September 18, 1864, enclosing "Report of Operations on Morris Island, S. C., during . . . July . . . Sept. 1863" [*ibid.,* Vol. XXVIII, part 1, p. 85]).

5. Note that this operation was carried out apparently at Beauregard's orders and under his direction (Roman, *Beauregard,* II, 56-57) In the fall of 1862 Beauregard appears to have been in actual charge of the naval defenses, including gunboat rams and torpedoes (*ibid.,* II, 47-49, 56, 57, 58).

6. A spirited and not particularly fruitful debate took place between the advocates of torpedoes and the men of the shore batteries, each party claiming for itself the chief credit for the defeat of Du Pont. Cf. Roman, *op. cit.,* II, 77-78, and Welles, *Diary,* I, 267. Also Basso, *Beauregard,* pp. 214-32; Knox, *History of the United States Navy,* pp. 264-74.

Vicksburg, recross below the fortress, and take it by coming up and around in a northeast-northwest sweep.

For the success of this tactic one factor was absolutely essential: the river must be kept open for the army's supply line, and for the re-ferrying of the army across to the east shore at some point not too far below the fortress. Naval control of the Mississippi was the key to the strategy of this decisive phase of the Vicksburg campaign. If the Confederates could close the river at or above Vicksburg, they could starve or immobilize Grant on the west shore. Ironclads, torpedoes, and channel obstructions were needed.[7]

But the Confederate navy was not up to the task. Admiral Porter ran past the Vicksburg batteries on April 16-17 and, on the twenty-second, was waiting opposite Grand Gulf with seven transports, ready to take Grant's army across. The Confederates tried their best. The land battery at Grand Gulf, fighting "over its head," on April 29, blocked the attempted ferrying operation at that point. But, with almost insolent confidence, the Federal naval and land forces moved simultaneously southward a few miles, and, by the night of the thirtieth, Grant was again on the east shore of the Mississippi at Bruinsburg with twenty-thousand men.

The story of the rest of the campaign is well known. In a swift march northward from Bruinsburg culminating in five lightning victories in six days, Grant defeated in detail the forces of Johnston and Pemberton, broke through to the heights behind Vicksburg, and began the siege which, within two months, would capture the fortress city.

In the report of the victorious General was a sentence which showed how fatal to the cause of the South had been the inability of the Confederate navy to block the Mississippi. "The Navy," declared Grant, "under Porter, was all it could be during the entire campaign. Without its assistance the campaign could not have been successfully made with twice the number of men engaged."[8]

7. Military and naval historians have remarked the frequently decisive importance of the Federal navy in determining the issue of land campaigns. In reviewing the war as a whole, says Knox, it is difficult to overestimate the worth of the services of this fighting arm. On shore the balance of military power was such, he thinks, that there was little likelihood of a decision by either side, had there been approximate equality of navies (Knox, *op. cit.,* 315; for details of the Vicksburg campaign, cf. *ibid.,* 309-11). The Sprouts point out that the Union naval forces covered the movement of the army across waters otherwise strategically impassable, and guarded the vital line of water communications to that army's ultimate source of supplies (H. and M. Sprout, *Rise of American Naval Power,* 155; cf. also: J. W. Pratt, "Naval Operations on Virginia Rivers in the Civil War," *Proc. U. S. Nav. Inst.,* XLV [February, 1919], 185 ff., Knox, *op. cit.,* ch. XXII).

8. Quoted in Henry, *Story of the Confederacy,* 172. "The [Federal] Navy assisted the Army [of Grant] in other ways than by bombarding. Large naval guns with crews to man

John C. Ropes has stressed the fact that in these operations against Vicksburg the services of the Federal navy in the field of supply were of the first importance.[9] Livermore speaks of the "essential part" taken by the navy in all the land movements of the Federals in the Mississippi area.[10] He explains how Porter had so disposed his ships that Grant could have a base at Grand Gulf below Vicksburg, from which his supplies could reach him by river and by the western shore, and from which he could communicate with Banks below; nor was there lacking to the Federal commander another depot at Haynes's Bluff, where his food and matériel and reinforcements could come directly from the North.[11] Geer also has confirmed these statements.[12]

Obviously, if the Federal navy was so important to the success of Grant's offensive against Vicksburg, it was the duty of the Confederate navy to try to block the action of the Federal squadrons on the river. What the Confederate navy might have done in the Vicksburg campaign is suggested by a dispatch from another sector later in the war. Wrote General Taylor from Harrisonburg to the commander of the Trans-Mississippi Department: "I have dispatched the War Department to the effect that I consider the crossing of any considerable body of Confederate troops impossible. Accurate observations have been made of the enemy's gunboats between Red River and Vicksburg, and from the strictness of the guard maintained no success can be anticipated."[13]

What did the Confederate navy do to break up the harmonious collaboration between the Federal land and water forces? As early as August, 1861, before the fall of Forts Henry and Donelson, Mallory had made contracts for the construction at Memphis of the ironclad rams *Tennessee* and *Arkansas*, both to be used for the defense of the Mississippi.[14] In pleading for mechanics for work on these ships, the Secretary of the Navy wrote to General Leonidas Polk at the end of December, 1861, assuring him that

them were sent on shore to operate with the besieging army. On June 6 the gunboats repelled the effort of Confederate troops in Louisiana to wreck Grant's supply line above Vicksburg at Milliken's Bend. Throughout the siege the Army and Navy under Grant and Porter cooperated like the blades of a pair of shears" (*ibid.*).

9. Ropes, *op. cit.*, I, 186.

10. Col. W. R. Livermore, *The Story of the Civil War* (2 vols.; New York, 1933), II, 330.

11. *Ibid.*

12. Geer, *Campaigns of the Civil War*, 272-75; for the Vicksburg campaign, *ibid.*, 264-82. Cf. also West, *Porter*, 213-26.

13. Lieut. Gen. R. Taylor, C.S.A., to Gen. E. K. Smith, August 18, 1864 (*O.R.*, Ser. I, Vol. XXVI, pp. 808-9).

14. Scharf, *op. cit.*, 45.

the ships were to be employed in cooperating with the movements of the army and in clearing the river of enemy squadrons.[15] In mid-March, 1862, Mallory was still urgently requesting more workers in order to finish the two ironclads. "If even one of them is completed," he said, "she will be worth more than an army of 20,000 men."[16] His strenuous efforts to get the ships launched were continued through the fall of 1862.[17]

A hint as to what even a few river vessels could have done to block the Federal naval movements on inland waters is found in a warning sent by Farragut to Secretary Welles in May 1862. The gunboats which he had left below Vicksburg, declared the Admiral, would not be able to resist the ironclad *Arkansas* if she came down to attack them.[18] The *Arkansas*, of course, was a much larger ship than those envisioned by Mallory, but it was a single vessel pitted against a squadron.

As to the potentialities of even a small fleet of gunboats for blocking an attack of a Federal land force against a river fortress, the capture of Island No. 10 might have been averted if some Confederate gunboats had been present to prevent the crossing of General Pope's army from New Madrid to the Tennessee shore. It is clear from Foote's instructions to Commander Walke, commanding the *Carondelet,* that a requisite for the safe crossing of the troops was the providing of cover by the two Federal gunboats *Carondelet* and *Pittsburg.* If these two vessels could have been driven off or knocked out of action the crossing operation would very probably have been thwarted. "It is vitally important," declared Foote, "to the capture of this place [Island No. 10] that a gunboat should be at New Madrid for the purpose of covering General Pope's army while he crosses at that point to the opposite shore. . . ."[19]

It is pertinent to ask further whether the Confederate Navy Department can justly be blamed for not having ready for the defense of Vicksburg a

15. Mallory to Maj. Gen. L. Polk, December 24, 1861 (*O.R.A.*, Ser. I, Vol. VII, p. 789).
16. Mallory to Secretary Benjamin, March 14, 1862, (*ibid.*, Vol. LII, part 2, pp. 286-87).
17. Mallory to Secretary G. W. Randolph, September 24, 1862 (*ibid.*, 357; Vol. XIX, pp. 788-89). Mallory to Capt. Samuel Barron, C.S.N., October 2, 1862 (*O.R.*, Ser. I, Vol. XXIII, pp. 703-4).
18. Farragut to Welles, May 30, 1862 (*O.R.*, Ser. I, Vol. XVIII, pp. 519-21). Cf. also Lewis, *Farragut,* 89.
19. Foote's instructions to Commander H. Walke, March 30, 1862: "You will avail yourself of the first fog or rainy night, and drift your steamer down past the batteries on the Tennessee shore and Island No. 10 until you reach New Madrid. I assign you this service, as it is vitally important to the capture of this place [Island No. 10] that a gunboat should be at New Madrid for the purpose of covering General Pope's army while he crosses at that point to the opposite shore, . . . that he may move his army up to Island No. 10, and attack the rebels in rear while we attack them in front" (Quoted in James M. Hoppin, *Foote,* 282). The whole story of the campaign against Island No. 10 is in *ibid.*, 282-93.

weapon which, on the testimony of the greatest of Confederate ordnance officers, would certainly have blocked the Mississippi. General Beauregard wrote, some years after the close of the war: "It is suggestive to think what might have been the influence on the Union cause if the Confederate practice of submarine [torpedo] warfare had been nearly as efficient at the commencement as it was at the close of the war. It is not too much to say, respecting the blockade of the Southern ports, that if not altogether broken up, it would have been rendered . . . inefficient . . . *while the command of rivers all important to the Union forces as bases of operations, would have been next to impossible.*"[20]

More creditable in the fighting record of the Confederate navy at this period was its participation in the continuing successful defense of Charleston harbor. The historian of the Confederate navy was probably not exaggerating when he declared that, "in all the history of the war upon the seaboard, the operations around Charleston easily take the first place. The progress of the siege, . . . the novel experiments in the opposition of forts to ironclad fleets, the development of heavy ordnance, the evolution of torpedo warfare in these waters, were studied with the most profound interest by the civilized world. . . ."[21] It is important to note that at Charleston it was not the Confederate naval defense that failed. Neither the harbor nor the city was ever taken by Federal attacks from the sea; Charleston fell only when Sherman's army outflanked it.

All was not harmonious, however, between the Navy Department and General Beauregard, the ranking army officer at the crucial South Carolina base. The General's criticism was directed mainly against what he claimed was the ineffectiveness of the gunboats in the harbor. The design of these boats was such, he charged, that their guns had a very limited elevation which reduced their range, under the most favorable circumstances, to only one and a half miles.[22] Another source of weakness was the ships' want of sufficient motive power for maneuvering in the face of the enemy.[23]

20. Beauregard, "Narrative by General Beauregard," *Southern Historical Society Papers,* V (January-June, 1878), 154. Italics inserted. Cf. also Lieut. Isaac N. Brown to Capt. E. D. Blake, C.S.A., from Memphis, November 1, 1861 (*O.R.A.,* Ser. I, Vol. LII, part 2, p. 194). Brown reports his progress in preparing the water defenses at Fort Pillow. He reports also that Commander M. F. Maury, while engaged in making preparations for the mining of the Mississippi River, had been ordered by the Navy Department to suspend such action and to report for special duty elsewhere.

21. Scharf, *op. cit.,* 707.

22. Maj. Gen. J. F. Gilmer to Secretary Seddon, October 4, 1863 (*O.R.A.,* Ser. I, Vol. XXVIII, part 2, p. 390); Gen. Beauregard to Gen. S. Cooper, from Charleston, July 30, 1863 (*ibid.,* 244).

23. Maj. Gen. J. F. Gilmer to Secretary Seddon, October 4, 1863 (*ibid.,* 390-91).

For this reason the naval guns, declared Beauregard, had not been brought
into action once during the first eighty-six days of the siege of Charleston.[24]
Moreover, complained the General, the gunboats were unseaworthy.[25]

In a long letter to a member of Congress, Mallory answered these strictures. He freely admitted that the gunboats were "unseaworthy," as vessels
built for harbor defense usually were. They were not expected to go to
sea, in the ordinary acceptation of the term. To have made them seaworthy
would have decreased their defensive power. Such of the enemy's monitors
as were "seaworthy" were not exposing themselves at close quarters to
Beauregard's heavy guns.[26]

In regard to Beauregard's charge that the gunboats, because of the low
elevation of their guns, could not fight the enemy at long range, Mallory re-
torted that they were never intended so to fight. They were designed and
armed to fight the enemy's ironclads, which could be successfully assailed
only at close quarters, and the range of the guns was ample for this purpose.
But, in fact, the guns of the vessels in question had the elevation which is
usually given to the port guns of cruising ships. If it was true, as General
Beauregard said, that "the enemy's ironclads are invulnerable to shots above
water beyond 800 yards," a greater range than from one and a quarter to one
and a half miles would seem to be not only uncalled for but a positive
defect, demanding, as it would, a larger opening for the gun.[27]

Beauregard had asserted that the gunboats were "incapable of resisting
the enemy's 15-inch shot at close quarters." Mallory held that the charge
was unfair. The gunboats' power of resistance to such shot was probably
greater than that of the enemy's ships, but it might well be doubted whether
any ironclad ever built was capable of resisting fifteen-inch shot at close
quarters. If the inclined shields of the Confederate gunboats were incapable
of such resistance, the shields of the enemy, being nearly vertical, were far
less resistant.[28]

Beauregard had adduced as evidence of the "total failure" of the gunboats the fact that three of them—the *Chicora, Palmetto State,* and *Charleston*—had not fired a shot in the defense of Fort Sumter during the naval
attack of April 7, 1863, nor had they fired one shot in the defense of Morris
Island and Sumter during the siege of Charleston. Mallory's answer to this

24. *Ibid.*, 391.
25. Mallory to Hon. Porcher Miles, December 19, 1863, enclosed in Miles to Beauregard,
December 30, 1863. (*Ibid.*. 594-97). For Beauregard's criticism of the gunboats, cf. *ibid.*, 503-4.
26. Mallory to Porcher Miles, *supra cit.*, 596.
27. *Ibid.*
28. *Ibid.*, 596.2.

was curt and to the point: "The fact that the ironclads did not fire a shot in defense of Fort Sumter and Morris Island, as stated, can hardly, I think, be regarded as the best proof of their total failure. The failure to fire on the occasions indicated resulted from the judgment of the commander. His ships were designed to fight the enemy's ironclads, which they could only do with fair chances of success at the close range already indicated."[29]

Another discussion took place between the Secretary of the Navy and General Beauregard with respect to a new type of vessel proposed by the latter. The General had suggested the construction of a "steamer of 400 or 500 tons, built like a blockade runner, but made shot-proof."[30] Mallory politely and in specific detail demonstrated the impracticability of such a proposal. No vessel of this character, possessing the requisite mobility, speed, invulnerability, and draught of water, he informed the General, had ever been built, or, to Mallory's knowledge, even planned. No adequate defensive armor, applicable to such a vessel, against the heavy naval ordnance then in use, had yet been devised. The question could be submitted, through the agency of Bulloch, to the best naval designers of Europe; and, if the new type could be built, the Navy Department would certainly contract for one. But the Secretary of the Navy had his grave doubts as to the possibility of securing such a ship.[31]

The story of the defense of Charleston is indeed largely the story of the success of the Confederate Torpedo Bureau. It was the torpedoes, employed in various ways, which constituted the chief barrier to the Federal ironclads that tried unavailingly for nearly four years to pierce the approaches to the crucial position. Whether sunk in the harbor or near-by rivers, or attached to swift "David" or "Diver" boats, or fastened to powerful steam

---

29. *Ibid.*, 597. Cf. Beauregard's comment on these answers of Mallory (Beauregard to Porcher Miles, January 5, 1864 [*ibid.*, 605-6]): "Your favor of the 30th ultimo, inclosing Mr. Mallory's communication to you, has been received. I have not time to read the letter at present; those notes I gave you [containing Beauregard's criticism of the gunboats] were not intended for him to read, but merely to give you information which might be useful in a discussion on the subject of these wretched gunboats. Of course, I do not suppose that Mr. Mallory can possibly admit they are worse than useless, since he is still going on with their construction. Moreover, they are to a certain extent the children of his own creation, and if he be a good father he cannot disown them or admit that they are defective, any more than the owl can admit that its young ones are ugly. But I do believe that Congress ought to interpose its authority in thus allowing Mr. Mallory, or Mr. Anybody Else, to squander our public funds in such a wanton manner, consuming time, valuable materials, and guns which might be used to a better purpose. . . ."

30. General Beauregard, "Remarks Relative to Iron-Clad Gunboats," from Charleston, November 14, 1863 (*O.R.A.*, Ser. I, Vol. XXVIII, part 2, p. 504).

31. Mallory to Porcher Miles, December 19, 1863; (*O.R.A.*, Ser. I, Vol. XXVIII, part 2, pp. 595-96).

ironclad rams, the new weapon of the Confederates made a new era in naval warfare, and caused the Federals intense concern.[32] "I believe them to constitute the most formidable of the difficulties in the way to Charleston," wrote Admiral Dahlgren in early 1864.[33] The "submarine mortar batteries" or mines, reported the head of the Confederate Torpedo Bureau, were, by the enemy's own admission, the chief reason for the failure of the Federal naval attacks against the city.[34]

The chief question concerning the defense of Charleston seems to be: Did the Navy Department do all that it could and all that it should have done in employing the torpedoes and torpedo boats?

Beauregard declared emphatically that the best protection for the harbor was the use of small but swift steamers of light draught, with very low decks and hulls ironclad several feet below the water line as well as above it. These boats were to be armed with a spar torpedo.[35] In October, 1862, he wrote to Governor Pickens concerning a plan submitted to him by Captain F. D. Lee for a "torpedo ram." This new ship, affirmed Beauregard, "would be worth several gunboats." He expressed his regret that it had not been adopted at once by the Navy Department when the plans had been submitted to the latter several months before, as Captain Lee informed him. The Captain had at that time gone to Richmond "in order to get from the Secretary of War a vessel, and other means with which to launch a spar torpedo campaign." But, Lee reported, the Secretary of War could do nothing, "and the Secretary of the Navy would not, for the reason that I was not a naval officer under his command."[36]

Now Beauregard had sent Lee again to Richmond, "after a lapse of some months," and this time had secured from the Navy Department an unfinished hull from the stocks at Charleston which he was making into a spar torpedo ship.[37] The General wrote at once to Secretary Mallory, thanking

32. Cf. John Johnson (formerly major of engineers in service of Confederate States), *The Defense of Charleston Harbor Including Fort Sumter and Adjacent Islands* (Charleston, 1890), 262-63: "To protect themselves against the engines of war and the armored vessels of the new era the Confederates were obliged to make a new era themselves, and that chiefly in the matter of harbor obstruction and torpedo defense. The iron-clad squadrons of Rear-Admirals Du Pont and Dahlgren were as effectually stopped for more than two years by fear of these as by anything else." Cf. also *ibid.*, 159: "To the close of the war the obstructions [mainly torpedoes, at Charleston] appeared to be more dreaded by the [Federal] navy than the batteries which commanded them."

33. Report of Admiral Dahlgren on the torpedoing of the *Housatonic*, report of February 19, 1864 (*O.R.*, Ser. I, Vol. XV, p. 330).

34. Brig. Gen. G. J. Rains to Secretary Seddon, November 18, 1864 (*O.R.A.*, Ser. I, Vol. XLII, part 3, p. 1219).

35. Beauregard, "Narrative by General Beauregard," 154.

36. *Ibid.*, 150.          37. *Ibid.*, 150-51.

him for the "prompt and favorable support you have given me in the desire to construct one of Captain F. D. Lee's torpedo rams."[38] It was certain, said Beauregard, "that half a dozen of these . . . , of small comparative cost, would keep this harbor clear of four times the number of the enemy's gunboats. . . ."[39] He added significantly that the same means of defense could be used for Savannah and Mobile harbors.[40]

But, five months later, Beauregard was plainly dissatisfied with the attitude of the Navy Department in the matter of the Lee torpedo boat. An agreement had been made, he said, that the State of South Carolina would cover $50,000 worth of the expenses of the project, while the Navy Department would supply, to the best of its ability, the building materials. Although the latter promise had been fulfilled to some extent, the Navy Department had not furnished the all-important iron plating, with the consequence that work on the torpedo boat had been much slowed down.

Captain Tucker, commanding the naval forces afloat at Charleston, had asserted, declared Beauregard, that the Lee invention, if completed, would be more effective as a means of defense than almost all the ironclads afloat and in construction—a belief in which the General heartily concurred. Had the torpedo boat been afloat when the enemy's ironclads had entered the harbor a few weeks previously, it was probable that only a few of them would have escaped. The War Department might well inquire into the relative value of the Lee boat and the "ironclad rams *Chicora* and *Palmetto State,* and others of the same class now building in this harbor, to the absorption of all the material and mechanical resources of this section of the country." And, in conclusion: "I do not desire to impose my views, but I feel it my duty to urge an immediate investigation, by a mixed board of competent officers, to determine whether it be best for the ends in view to continue to appropriate all the material, and employ all the mechanical labor of the country, in the construction of vessels that are forced to play so unimportant and passive a part as that which Captain Tucker, C.S.N., their commander, officially declares to me must be theirs. . . ."[41]

Whatever had been the dilatoriness of the Secretary of the Navy in this matter of the torpedo boat—and it seems that indeed he may have been at fault—he cooperated energetically with plans for two bold and carefully prepared attacks by torpedo boats in the Charleston area in the spring and

38. Beauregard to Mallory, October 31, 1862 (*O.R.,* Ser. I, Vol. XIII, p. 814).
39. Beauregard to Gov. F. W. Pickens, October 8, 1862 (*ibid.,* 811).
40. Beauregard to Mallory, October 31, 1862 (*ibid.,* 814).
41. Beauregard to General Cooper, April 22, 1863, quoted in Roman, *op. cit.,* II, 79-80. John R. Tucker also commanded the C.S.S. *Patrick Henry.*

summer of 1863. The first of these attacks was to be directed against Du Pont's monitors in the harbor. In mid-February Mallory sent detailed orders to Lieutenant William A. Webb, the officer in charge of the special expedition.

The enemy's squadron was, if possible, to be boarded. The types of vessels to be employed in the action, and the methods of preparing them, were meticulously described.[42] The boarding force was to be divided into parties of tens and twenties, each under a leader. Of these groups, one was to have iron wedges for dismantling the enemy's turrets; another would cover the enemy pilot houses with wet blankets; a third party of twenty men would throw powder down the enemy smoke stacks; a fourth group of twenty would be "provided with turpentine or camphine in glass vessels, to smash over the turret, and with an inextinguishable fire to follow it"; another party, provided with sulphuretted cartridges and the like, would watch every opening in the turrets or decks, and be ready to smoke the enemy out. These instructions were accompanied by a "rough drawing, illustrative of the design. . . ."[43]

The elaborate project was foiled when the Federal monitors slipped out of range before the expedition could get under way. A second attack on the monitors failed in August, because of a deserter who warned the senior Federal officer.[44]

It is interesting to note that in the midsummer of 1863 the army, and not the navy, appeared to be taking a conservative stand with respect to the Lee torpedo boat. Lee himself, at the very time when Mallory's subordinates were exerting themselves to launch attacks with the new vessel, wrote: "Whether this [opposition of the Army authorities to the use of the torpedo ram] grows out of prejudice to the use of the torpedo, and is a part of that opposition that showed itself in every variety of form during the progress of the work, I am not prepared to say."[45]

42. ". . . First, Row-boats and barges, of which Charleston can furnish a large number. Second, Small steamers, two or three to attack each vessel. Third, The hull of a single-decked vessel, without spars, divided into several water-tight compartments by cross bulkheads, and with decks and hatches tight, may have a deck-load of compressed cotton so placed on either side, and forward and aft, as to leave a space fore and aft in the center. A light scaffold to extend from the upper tier of cotton ten or fifteen feet over the side, and leading to the enemy's turret when alongside the ironclad, and over which it can be boarded, at the same time that boarding would be done from forward and aft. This could be made permanent or to lower at will . . ." (Scharf, *op. cit.*, 687).

43. *Ibid.*, 687-88.

44. *Ibid.*, 691-93.

45. Capt. F. D. Lee to Capt. A. N. T. Beauregard, from Charleston, July 25, 1863 (*O.R.A.*, Ser. I, Vol. XXVIII, part 2, p. 229).

Charleston was not the only beneficiary of the new means of defense. The fact that more than a hundred torpedoes were planted in the Roanoke River largely explains why, of twelve Federal vessels sent with troops to capture Fort Branch, only five returned. Of the vessels sent to take Mobile, twelve were sunk by torpedoes.[46] The disabling of the powerful Federal ships *Housatonic, New Ironsides,* and others, will be described later in these pages.[47] In 1865 the Secretary of the United States Navy reported to Congress that the navy had lost more ships during the war from Confederate torpedoes than from all other sources combined. General Rains, chief of the Confederate Torpedo Bureau, placed the total number of Federal vessels lost by torpedo attacks at fifty-eight.[48]

It is likely that the Confederate Navy Department has never received the full credit it deserves for developing this weapon. By the employment of torpedoes, it has been justly claimed, the Confederate Navy "totally revolutionized" naval warfare,[49] and "accomplished more in her several years than with all the great advancement of scientific knowledge . . . other nations have been able since to do."[50]

Opinions differ as to the part played by the Confederate Secretary of the Navy in developing the torpedo service. According to Matthew F. Maury, one of the ablest exponents of the new weapon, a whole year of argument was required before the Confederate authorities perceived the worth of torpedoes. Only after a personal demonstration which he provided in the summer of 1862 for Mallory and for the Chairman of the Committee on Naval Affairs were those two officials convinced that the new method of warfare was effective.[51] If this story is true, the Secretary of the Navy was

---

46. Brig. Gen. Rains, "Torpedoes," *Southern Historical Society Papers,* III (1877), 256.

47. Cf. *infra,* pp. 274-76, concerning *New Ironsides;* 276-79, concerning *Housatonic.*

48. Richard L. Maury, "The First Marine Torpedoes . . . ," *Southern Historical Society Papers,* XXXI (1903), 326-27.

49. *Ibid.,* 326. Cf. also, in same volume of *Southern Historical Society Papers,* p. 141 n.

50. *Ibid.,* 326.

51. "There was," says the not completely unbiased biographer of Maury, "a great prejudice against, or lack of appreciation of this undeveloped system of defence, entertained by the officials of the new Confederacy into whose hands the defence of the South had fallen. Finally, after a year had passed in futile efforts to impress the Confederate authorities with the importance, value, and economy of mining passes and channel-ways with magazines, to be sprung at will by means of the electric spark, Maury procured, in the summer of 1862, two barrels of powder from the Governor of Virginia, who was himself in favor of the plan, and prevailed on the Secretary of the Navy, and the Chairman of the Committee of Naval Affairs in the Congress . . . to go down the river and see him explode powder, by an ingenious contrivance, under water. Two magnificent jets went up; and when the two gentlemen heard the report of a barrel of powder, and saw the water pagodas rising up some hundred feet in the air, they were convinced. The next day $50,000 was placed at the service of Commander Maury . . . for mining the James River" (Diana Corbin, *A Life of Matthew Fontaine Maury,* 200).

not one of the first to recognize the importance of torpedoes, and delayed a year before accepting the enthusiastic reports of those who did realize what the grotesque but terribly destructive weapon could accomplish.

On the contrary, Hunter Davidson, one of the pioneers in the development of torpedoes, thought that "the first idea of using [them] on the Confederate side originated with . . . Mallory."[52] The Secretary of the Navy, said Davidson, "directed . . . Captain M. F. Maury . . . to make experiments with a view to their general employment, if practicable."[53] Maury, sent to Europe for further research in the field before his experiments at home were completed, was succeeded by Davidson, who, after the war, paid this tribute to the Secretary: "To the Hon. S. R. Mallory, who always believed in the success of the undertaking from the first, and ever gave me a firm hand and kind support, and materially aided me with his advice . . . I owe thanks."[54]

This last testimony appears to be nearer to the truth. Maury was a consistent carper against Mallory's policies and methods, and could scarcely be considered an objective judge of the Navy Secretary's contribution to the torpedo service. If Mallory actually did cooperate as Davidson asserted he did, the fact is all the more significant in view of the strong opposition to and distrust of the novel weapon, a distrust manifested in influential quarters. "If any one," said Davidson, "had to contend with the abuse and sneers and ridicule whilst in the performance of torpedo duty day and night, . . . he would realize that as late as the summer of 1863 some of the ablest men of the day did not regard torpedo warfare as worthy of consideration. . . ."[55]

The experiments of Maury and Davidson had begun in the spring of 1862. In the following October the Torpedo Bureau was established at Richmond under the charge of Brigadier General G. J. Rains, C.S.A, and the "Naval Submarine Battery Service," headed by Captain M. F. Maury. The first governmental grant of money for the torpedo services was made by the Congress in May, 1863—a modest $20,000 included in a general appropriation bill. Not however until the last year of the war did the legislators at Richmond award really sufficient sums to the new project. By the act of February 17, 1864, $100,000 was appropriated for the construction of submarine batteries, and by a law of June 13 of the same year $250,000 was assigned for this purpose. More was to come, but not soon enough. As

52. Hunter Davidson, C.S.N., "Electrical Torpedoes as a System of Defense," *Southern Historical Society Papers*, II (July-December, 1896), 2.
53. *Ibid.*
54. *Ibid.*, 6.
55. *Ibid.*, 5.

General Rains said: "For three years the Confederate Congress legislated on this subject, a bill passing each house alternately for an organized torpedo corps, until the third year, when it passed both houses with acclamation, and $6,000,000 was appropriated, but too late; and the delay was not shortened by the enormous appropriation."[56]

Meanwhile, torpedo stations were established at Richmond, Wilmington, Charleston, Savannah, and Mobile, with substations at other points. There was constant experimentation with various types of the new and powerful weapon. The men of the corps were sworn to secrecy and granted extraordinary privileges on account of the perilous nature of the service. Several boats engaged in laying torpedoes were destroyed with their crews in accidental explosions.

The first floating torpedoes were used in the Potomac at Aquia Creek in July, 1861. The occasion of the first employment of a submarine (submerged) torpedo was General R. E. Lee's request, after the battle of Seven Pines, that the James be blocked against the Federal ironclads.[57]

Various types of the strange and terrible weapon were used by the Confederates. There was the "spar" torpedo, a watertight cylinder of copper or other thin metal or wood, filled with fifty to a hundred pounds of powder, capped with highly sensitive percussion fuses on its conical or rounded end, the whole fixed firmly on a spar of wood or iron from thirty to thirty-five feet long projecting from the bow of a small boat and pushed through the water some feet below the surface against its object.[58] There were several kinds of river and harbor mines, some of them connected by electric wires to shore positions from which they were detonated, while others were lashed to buoys or strung between two boats and floated against enemy vessels. The main portion of the torpedo was usually some variety of cylinder, such as a boiler, a cask, or an ordinary metal can.[59]

56. Rains, *op. cit.*

57. "Soon after the battle of Seven Pines . . . General R. E. Lee . . . sent for General Rains and said to him, 'The enemy have upwards of one hundred vessels in the James River, and we think that they are about making an advance that way upon Richmond, and if there is a man in the whole Southern Confederacy that can stop them, you are the man. Will you undertake it? [Rains observed that] ironclads were invulnerable to cannon of all calibre used and were really masters of rivers and harbors; it required submarine inventions to checkmate and conquer them. So an order was issued forthwith, putting General Rains in charge of the submarine defenses, and on the James River banks, opposite Drewry's Bluff, was the first submarine torpedo made" (*ibid.*, 260).

58. John Johnson, *op. cit.*, 31. Cf. also Beauregard, "Narrative by General Beauregard," 149.

59. Cf. description of boiler-torpedo afloat off Battery Wagner. It was eighteen feet long, three feet in diameter, and contained three thousand pounds of powder (Report of Assistant

The Federals swept up the following types of mines in the James River
in the spring of 1864: "Tin cylinders in wooden cases, with long tin chim-
neys extending above the water and fitted for ventilation. In this chimney
is a piece of slow match, extending down to the magazine. These torpedoes
contain from 50 to 100 pounds of powder and are evidently intended to float
down the stream. Tin cylinders of the same size as above, to be exploded
by means of a friction primer pulled from the shore or by a vessel's wheels
or propeller getting foul of the lanyard. These torpedoes have a board float
and are suspended some 6 or 8 feet below the surface. Cylindrical tanks
with conical ends, made of half-inch boiler iron and securely riveted. These
are anchored at the bottom in the deepest water (7 and 8 fathoms), and
each has two insulated copper wires running from the center of the torpedo
through a composition plug screwed into one end and connecting with a
galvanic battery on shore, by means of which they are exploded. In the
center of the torpedo these copper wires are connected by a thread-like
platinum wire, running through a short quill filled with phosphorous and
fulminating powder. The largest one of this kind found contained about
1,950 pounds of powder, and the smallest about 1,040 pounds. "These torpedoes (galvanic)," concludes the Federal report, "are constructed with
great ingenuity and scientific skill, and when taken from the water were
in as good a state of preservation as when first put down. . . ."[60]

The most unusual, though one of the least effective, types of torpedo
was an object made to resemble as exactly as possible a piece of coal, to be
placed in the coal piles of enemy vessels. It was hoped that the deceptive
and lethal lump would, in the course of time, be shoveled into the vessel's
furnace, with the natural result.[61]

---

Engineer Charles G. De Lisle to Gen. Beauregard, May 25, 1863 [*O.R.A.,* Ser. I, Vol. XIV, pp.
950-51]); description of floating cylindrical torpedo (T. H. Eastman, Lieut. Commander,
U.S.N., to Commander Foxhall A. Parker, commanding Potomac flotilla, May 18, 1864 [*O.R.,*
Ser. I, Vol. V, pp. 432-33]); two diagrams of floating torpedoes, the first being a boiler suspended from floating casks used as buoys (*ibid.,* Vol. IV, p. 568, and Vol. XXVI, facing pp.
516, 568), report on experiments with improved galvanic "submarine batteries" or mines (Lt.
Hunter Davidson to Mallory, from C.S.S. *Torpedo,* Submarine Batteries, James River, November
18, 1862, *ibid.,* Vol. VIII, pp. 848-49.

60. Lieut. R. H. Lamson to Rear Admiral S. P. Lee, May 25, 1864 (*O.R.,* Ser. I, Vol. X, pp.
92-93).

61. Cf. T. E. Courteney (C.S.A. Torpedo Service) to Col. H. E. Clark, January 19, 1864:
"The castings have all been completed some time, and the coal is so perfect that the most
critical eye could not detect it. The President thinks them perfect . . ." (*O.R.,* Ser. I, Vol.
XXVI, p. 186). Cf. also Rear Admiral David D. Porter, General Order No. 184, March 20,
1864: "The enemy [Confederates] have adopted new inventions to destroy human life and
vessels in the shape of torpedoes, and an article resembling coal, which is to be placed in our
coal piles for the purpose of blowing the vessels up. . . . Officers will have to be careful in

The method of planting the mine fields is illustrated by the arrangement at Fort Fisher. In front of the land face of the fort, at an average distance of two hundred yards from the work and eighty feet from each other, were set twenty-four "electric" torpedoes. There were three kinds of these—twenty-inch shells, boiler-iron cylinders thirteen inches in diameter and eighteen inches long, and buoy-shaped sheet-iron vessels of about the same content as the cylinders. The system was connected with the fort by three sets of double wires, each wire apparently intended to fire five or more torpedoes.[62]

The torpedo principle was applied also on land, "On all the roads approaching the city [of Richmond]," reported a Federal officer in the fall of 1864, "torpedoes are being laid [by the Confederates] and covered with dust. Cords 400 feet long are attached to the torpedoes and men secreted in the bushes pull the cord on the approach of an enemy."[63] According to General Rains, 1,298 of these "subterra shells" had been planted on the approaches to Richmond by mid-November, 1864. The torpedoes (or land mines, to use their modern name) were protected from the effects of rain by inverted tin covers.[64]

General Rains described the rather elaborate precautions taken to protect the Confederates themselves against their own weapons. Immediately behind each mine, at a distance of three feet, was planted a small red flag on a staff three feet long to indicate the whereabouts of the destructive device. At night the flag was replaced by a dark lantern covered with red flannel. On the approach of the enemy these warning signs would, of course, be removed. In addition, long streamers laid on the ground indicated paths of safety for the Confederate troops as they threaded their way through the mine fields.[65]

The difficulties and disappointments that faced the Torpedo Bureau are revealed in the story of the attempt of the persistent officers of that depart-

---

overlooking coal barges. Guards will be placed over them at all times, and anyone found attempting to place any of these things amongst the coal will be shot on the spot. The same policy will be adopted toward those persons who are caught planting torpedoes, or floating them down, or with any of these inventions in their possession" (*ibid.*, 184).

62. C. B. Comstock (Lieut Col. and Brevet Brig. Gen., Chief Engineer, U.S.A.) to Gen. R. Delafield (Chief Engineer, U.S.A.), from Fort Fisher, January 23, 1865 (*O.R.A.*, Ser. I, Vol. XLVI, part 2, pp. 215-16).

63. Capt. John McEntee to Lieut. Col. Bowers (Asst. Adj. Gen.), October 20, 1864 (*ibid.*, Vol. XLII, part 3, p. 282).

64. Gen. Rains to Secretary Seddon, November 18, 1864 (*ibid.*, 1219).

65. *Ibid.*, 1219-20. Cf. also Gen. G. J. Rains to Secretary Seddon, October 29, 1864 (*ibid.*, 1181-82).

ment to set up a defense line in the channel between Forts Moultrie and Sumter. Attached to a shore-to-shore electrified cable were fifty torpedoes, to be exploded by any contact made with the cable by an enemy vessel. A brief trial proved that the main portion of the cable could not survive the abrasive effects of the rough channel bottom, under the action of the tide. It was therefore pulled up and reinforced with a whole new section of tougher texture.

Then the torpedoes, which were made of tin-iron, with no supporting frame inside, were found to be incapable of resisting the hydraulic pressure. They were accordingly replaced by small lager-beer barrels of thirteen-gallon capacity. For completing the insulation of the cable an india-rubber tube was absolutely necessary, but such an article existed nowhere in the Confederacy.[66] A technician from the army was assigned the task of making one. After more than two weeks of effort he confessed his inability to do the job. An assistant engineer then undertook the work and in a short time produced the needed tube.

Finally, the cable was again ready for immersion. Three unsuccessful attempts were made to lay it. During the last attempt, five hundred feet of the cumbrous line was carried by the tide one and a half miles from its original position, and the whole cable became tangled in a confused mass. The project, after consuming several weeks of time and labor, was finally abandoned.[67]

The same theater of operations witnessed at least two other laborious and abortive efforts to lay torpedoes. General Beauregard ordered a boiler-torpedo to be sunk in Ship Channel about a mile off Fort Sumter and half a mile opposite Fort Wagner. The boiler was successfully planted, but in running a cable to it the Bureau's steamer ran aground, payed out two miles of cable instead of the anticipated one mile, and snarled up the whole plan. A second effort to lay a boiler-torpedo ended with the unwieldy weapon being washed out to sea and lost.[68]

In securing the necessary materials and manufacturing the torpedoes, the Confederates encountered manifold and almost insuperable obstacles. There was neither a wire factory nor insulating material in the South, and, although an establishment for the manufacture of wire was soon created, yet, because of the blockade, it was impossible to obtain either india-rubber

66. Chas. G. De Lisle (asst. engineer) to Gen. Beauregard, from Charleston, May 25, 1863 (*ibid.*, Vol. XIV, pp. 948-49).
67. *Ibid.*, 949-50.
68. *Ibid.*, 950-52.

or gutta-percha from abroad.[69] The suggestion was actually made that the latter deficiency be supplied by the old india-rubber overshoes of Southern women.[70] Fortunately, to meet the need for wire, a windfall came in the shape of an abandoned Federal cable fished up by the Confederates from Chesapeake Bay.[71]

Ironically, the Confederates secured much of their materials for torpedoes from behind the Federal lines at St. Louis and New Orleans. The Federal provost-marshals at those points, it was reported, were likely to be very co-operative in granting permits, "and more especially to good-looking and interesting ladies."[72] The Federal aides and detectives stationed on board river packets for the precise purpose of thwarting such operations "seem to be, in general, of very easy virtue and ready to be convinced by solid arguments." It was felt that they required "fully as much surveillance as the passengers on board the vessels."[73]

Torpedoes were being constructed at secluded locations along the lower Mississippi. The informal manufactory near Black Hawk Point was typical. Demijohns loaded with powder, covered with an additional basket-like protection, and filled with tubes and floats, were made by a small detail of men working at an impromptu factory situated a few miles inland. The lethal weapons were then transported in a wagon driven by a Negro called "Old Pat" to the head of Cat Island, where they were placed in the river. Some of them were intended to float and to explode after contact with any obstacle to their progress, while others were to be anchored and detonated by means of lines connected with the shore.[74]

In this work failures that must have been heartbreaking were not infrequent. In one instance every one of a batch of twenty torpedoes proved to be useless. At once a new design was adopted by the construction detail, and eight more of the weapons were produced in a relatively short time.[75]

---

69. Diana Corbin, *op. cit.*, 199.         70. *Ibid.*, 200.

71. *Ibid.*, 200-1.

72. Report of Acting Master J. B. Devoe, U.S.N., off New Orleans, November 4, 1864 (*O.R.*, Ser. I, Vol. XXVI, pp. 709-10). Devoe reminded Capt. A. M. Pennock, U.S.N., commanding the Mississippi Squadron, that he had already reported his discovery of the transshipment of eight torpedoes, made of square chests of iron and furnished with tubes five feet in length, and with percussion attachments, from Clinton, Louisiana, four of which were destined for the river in the vicinity of Bayou Sara, and four for Tunica Bend.

73. *Ibid.*, 710.

74. Acting Master J. B. Devoe to Capt. A. M. Pennock, U.S.N., November 5, 1864 (*ibid.*, pp. 712-13).

75. *Ibid.*, 712-13. As to some of the methods of employing the torpedoes: 'Their manner of operating is to float them down or to make one fast between two skiffs at a distance of a hundred yards from each, then in the night the skiffs are floated one on each side of the boat, which brings the torpedo under the boat, when one of the men in the skiff explodes the

That the new weapon was effective cannot be denied. In May, 1864, the so-called "James River torpedo" blew up the Federal steam corvette *Commodore Jones,* sparing but 3 men out of her crew of 150.[76] According to the biographer of M. F. Maury, the engine and boilers were blown clean out of the vessel to a distance of fifty feet.[77] It was the Confederate claim that the Federals' fear of torpedoes paralyzed and rendered impotent their James River squadron during the whole of Grant's siege of Richmond.[78]

The Federal Admiral Porter confessed that, in his first attack with General Butler against Fort Fisher (gateway to Wilmington, North Carolina), it was his fear of the electrical torpedoes that kept him from entering the Cape Fear River with his gunboats. He afterward entered, found no torpedoes, and carried the place.[79] There is, however, some evidence suggesting that the fearsome weapon was not so extensively or so efficiently employed in the defense of Wilmington as might have been desired.[80]

Torpedoes, it was held by many on both sides, were the chief factors in the successful Confederate defense of Charleston. During Du Pont's attack of September 8, 1863, his leading vessel, the *Weehawken,* turned back at once on seeing torpedoes in her path.[81] The repulse of the ironclad attack of the preceding April was due, said a Northern observer, to the Confederates' submarine torpedoes.[82] Up to the close of the war, asserts the historian

---

torpedo under by means of a lanyard. [Another way of operating] is to plant them in the channel and wait for passing boats to explode them" (I. N. Early, First Lieut., commanding special scouts, giving statement of member of his command, Edward A. Harris, to Col. Myer, chief signal officer, military division of West Mississippi, from Natchez, August 30, 1864 [*ibid.,* 525]).

76. Diana Corbin, *op. cit.,* 202. Cf. also Thos. F. Wade, U.S.N., acting Vol. Lieut., late commander of *Commodore Jones,* to Secretary Gideon Welles, from U. S. naval hospital, Norfolk, May 13, 1864 (*ibid.,* Vol. X, p. 14): "While dragging for torpedoes . . . a torpedo was exploded directly under the ship with terrible effect, causing her destruction instantly, absolutely blowing the vessel to splinters."

77. Diana Corbin, *op. cit.,* 202.

78. *Ibid.,* 201, 203. A typical communication from Mallory to the head of the Torpedo Bureau, in spring of 1864: "Four monitors, the *Atlanta,* 5 gunboats, 2 ironclads, 59 transports coming up the river; also 3 rafts have passed Fort Boykin" (telegram from Mallory to Lieut. Hunter Davidson, from Richmond, May [5?], 1864 [*O.R.,* Ser. I, Vol. X, p. 11]). It is to be remarked that this evidence makes necessary a qualification of Diana Corbin's statement that the Federal flotilla on the James was "paralyzed and rendered impotent" during the whole time that Richmond was being beleaguered by Grant (cf. Diana Corbin, *op. cit.,* 203).

79. Diana Corbin, *op. cit.,* 203.

80. Gen. Rains to Secretary Seddon, from Wilmington, November 18, 1864 (*O.R.A.,* Ser. I, Vol. XLII, part 3, p. 1220): "I regret . . . that our submarine defenses of this place in Cape Fear River have not been such as desired, arising not from any fault of the commanding officer, but rather the want of proper operatives and means."

81. John Johnson, *op. cit.,* 262.

82. Richard Trussell to Rear Admiral Du Pont, from New York, April, 1863 (*O.R.,* Ser. I, Vol. XIV, p. 165). Cf. the contradiction of this view, in Roman, *op. cit.,* II, 70-72.

of the siege of Charleston, the "obstructions"—torpedoes, for the most part —appeared to be more dreaded by the Federal navy than the land batteries.[83] Rear admiral L. M. Goldsborough, the Federal commander of the North Atlantic blockading squadron, testified that it was not the forts that had for so long saved Charleston but the "obstructions," most of which were torpedoes, that were the strongest factor in the defense.[84]

But again, as in the case of the Wilmington defenses, it is not clear that the fullest potential of the torpedo weapon was utilized at Charleston. According to Johnson, fixed torpedoes were placed in the waters around the city for the first time in March, 1863, by order of General Beauregard, but there is no evidence of any having been placed between Fort Sumter and Sullivan's Island before July 10, 1863, three months after the attack by the ironclad squadron.[85]

That the Torpedo Bureau may have been the object of some jealousy in certain Confederate quarters is hinted by a debate which followed the destruction of the Federal monitor *Tecumseh* in the waters around Mobile. The first announcement of the sinking of the vessel came from one of the second lieutenants in charge of torpedo operations in the area: "The monitor *Tecumseh* struck one of our torpedoes and sunk almost instantly, carrying down with her all of her officers and crew but six. . . . Her bottom must have been almost entirely destroyed, as she went down in less than twenty-five seconds after the explosion."[86]

The Lieutenant, however, did not have the last word. His report reached the hands of Major General Dabney H. Maury, who corrected it, asserting that the *Tecumseh* had been sunk not by a torpedo but by gunfire from shore batteries. This statement, said the General, was based on the testimony of General Page.[87]

83. John Johnson, *op. cit.,* 159.

84. Goldsborough, under date of February 26, 1864, from Washington, D. C., in Exec. Doc. *Armored Vessels,* 576, quoted in Johnson, *op. cit.,* 262.

85. Johnson, *op. cit.,* 32, referring to "Capt. Gray, Report of Sec'y. of Federal Navy, 1865, p. 285." Cf. also Gen. G. J. Rains to Secretary Seddon, November 18, 1864 (*O.R.A.,* Ser. I, Vol. XLII, part 3, p. 1219): "When I left Richmond for Wilmington, in the fall of 1862, we commenced planting submarine mortar batteries in the James, and it is much to be regretted that the officer who relieved me in the submarine defenses did not continue their use, as these, the enemy report, being of a nature they could not remove, kept them out of Charleston harbor."

86. Second Lieut. F. S. Barrett to Lieut. J. T. E. Andrews, acting assistant Adjutant General, August 20, 1864 (*O.R.A.,* Ser. I, Vol. XXXIX, part 2, p. 785).

87. Endorsement by General Maury on report of Lieut. Barrett, dated September 26, 1864 (*ibid.,* 786-87). Maury followed up this endorsement with a letter to Col. Burton N. Harrison, private secretary to President Davis, on October 6, 1864, enclosing letter from Capt. J. W. Whiting of the First Alabama Field Artillery to Maury, dated October 4, 1864, from Mobile,

The Torpedo Bureau rose at once to its own defense. General Rains appealed to the report of the enemy, published in the New Orleans *Picayune* of August 9, which admitted that the vessel had been destroyed by a torpedo.[88] Mallory himself added some arguments: the suddenness of the vessels's disappearance beneath the waves could be accounted for only on the supposition that she had been struck by a torpedo; and it could not be denied that she was over the spot where the torpedoes had been placed.[89] Seddon came in with a rather evasive and diversionary observation which scarcely clarified the debate. He was gratified that "the many torpedoes used have not proved wholly unavailing." He wondered, however, why they were not more frequently effective.[90]

Further support of the Torpedo Bureau came, rather surprisingly, from a Miss Emily Lee McCleskey. "By one of those strange coincidences, doubtless under the inscrutable eye of Providence," wrote General Rains to President Davis, "whilst inditing my remarks for the inclosed, my attention was attracted to a letter unopened lying on my table from a female, a lady friend in Mobile, Ala.; and as it seems to give the best answer thereto [i.e., with regard to the sinking of the *Tecumseh*] it is forwarded for your perusal. . . ."[91]

Miss McCleskey's communication was straight to the point, and certainly gave no support to the party of General Maury. She had been greatly surprised by a statement in the *Register* that the *Tecumseh* had been sunk by guns from the fort. This was "a thing which had never been thought of before." The enemy had admitted that the vessel had been destroyed by a torpedo, and others from the fort said the same. "It really seems," concluded Miss McCleskey with some boldness, "that the prejudice which the army and navy have against torpedoes cannot be eradicated. They hate to think anything so little credited yet shall invariably do the fleet of the foe

---

attesting that the *Tecumseh* was sunk not by a torpedo but by shore batteries (*ibid.*, part 1, pp. 431-33).

88. Gen. Rains's endorsement on letter of Maury to Harrison, *supra cit.*, dated October 21, 1864 (*ibid.*, 431-32). Rains, in the same place, continued: "The enemy's report . . . states . . . that 'so rapidly [was the vessel sunk] that two acting masters who escaped from the top of the turret stepped off directly into the water.' The time of submersion determines whether shot or torpedo sunk the vessel. We have no evidence that her magazine was penetrated. How otherwise could a shot have occasioned her sinking in half a minute?"

89. Mallory's endorsement, dated October 26, 1864, on Maury-Harrison letter *supra cit.* (*ibid.*, 432).

90. Seddon's endorsement, dated August 19, 1864, on Maury-Harrison letter (*ibid.*, 433).

91. Gen. Rains to Pres. Davis, *supra cit.*, 434.

more damage than their fine fighting, but the people now have faith in torpedoes and little else."[92]

As has happened often in the history of applied science, one invention led to another and even more important one. In order to employ their "spar" torpedo more effectively, the Confederates evolved for it a new type of carriage—the submarine vessel.

Amid all the adverse criticism directed against the Confederate Navy Department in 1862-1863, it is somewhat remarkable that the South, as a whole, seemed unaware that the Department was putting into action the first submarine boat ever to engage in actual combat. The story of these first submarines is one of the finest tributes to the progressivism of the Secretary of the Navy, besides being among the great incidents of heroism in the annals of naval warfare.

At Mobile, in the summer after the capture of New Orleans, a group under Captain H. L. Hunley, C.S.N., constructed a strange vessel, a replica of a previous one that they had been forced to abandon when the Crescent City had fallen. The ship was the first combat submarine. She was ". . . built of iron, about twenty feet long, and besides a propeller at the stern, was adorned on either side by strangely shaped board metal fins."[93] She was named the *Hunley* and was taken to Charleston where, it was hoped, she would find a fruitful field for action against the blockading fleet.

On October 5, 1863, occurred one of the most sensational achievements of the Torpedo Bureau—the blow struck at the United States frigate *New Ironsides* in Charleston harbor by the Confederate submarine *David*. An account of this attack on the Federal man-of-war was given by one of the officers aboard the underwater craft. The *David* was cigar-shaped, about fifty feet long and five or six feet in diameter, and less than six feet from floor to coaming. From her bow protruded a rod about ten feet long, to the end of which was attached a torpedo. The latter could be detonated

---

92. *Ibid.*, 435. Gen. Rains also writes (*ibid.*, 434): "A person of the first respectability writes me from Mobile: 'The only serious damage done the enemy's fleet passing our forts was done by a torpedo, which sunk one of their monitors. A man who was an eye-witness of the scene told the doctor that the monitor sunk as if her bottom had been knocked entirely out. It is very, very strange that torpedoes are not relied on more by the Government, because in this war they have done the enemy more harm than our forts and Navy together.' From my own observation no smoke nor fire becomes visible from 1,500 pounds of gunpowder exploded at about thirty feet deep under water, though its effects are otherwise decided and immediate. It is no wonder, therefore, that Captain Whiting saw no more than he did. The time of submersion determines whether shot or torpedoes sunk the vessel."

93. W. A. Alexander, "Work of Submarine Boats of the C.S. Navy: Destruction of the *Housatonic*," in *Southern Historical Society Papers*, XXX (1902), 164. For a detailed description of the ship, cf. *ibid.*, 165-67.

by being rammed against a vessel while the submarine was submerged at a depth of ten or fifteen feet. The submarine's maximum speed was ten knots.[94]

Early in the evening of October 5, 1863, the *David*, with a crew of four men, left the wharf at Charleston and proceeded down the main ship channel, passing unobserved through the entire enemy fleet until she arrived opposite the *New Ironsides* at 8:30 P.M. Lieutenant W. T. Glassell, commanding, kept the submarine standing off for thirty minutes while he waited for the flood tide to make. At 9:00 P.M., "everything being favorable and every one in favor of the attack," the *David* headed for the *New Ironsides*.[95]

At a distance of fifty yards they were challenged by the stern lookout of the big frigate. Glassell answered with a shot from his double-barreled gun which mortally wounded the alert Yankee. Two minutes later they struck the *New Ironsides* at full speed under the starboard quarter, detonating the torpedo about six and a half feet under her bottom.[96] The explosion brought down upon the *David* a great column of water which nearly capsized the frail craft.

With her fires doused and her engines disabled by the shock of ramming the frigate, the little submarine was deserted by all her crew except Walker Cannon, the pilot. Lieutenant Glassell and James Sullivan, the fireman, swam off in the direction of the enemy's vessels and were picked up by the Yankees. Tomb, after leaping overboard, returned to the foundering *David*, finally started up the engines again, and, with the aid of the pilot, ran the

94. Dahlgren, *Diary*, under "Tuesday Oct. 6, [1863?]," (*O. R.*, Ser. I, Vol. XV, p. 19). For a description of the difference between the striking method employed by the navigators of the *David* and that used by Lieutenant George E. Dixon, commanding the *Hunley*, cf. *infra*, n. 96.

95. Report of acting first assistant engineer James Tomb, October 6, 1863 (*O.R.*, Ser. I, Vol. XV, p. 20).

96. The submarine was kept on the surface as the strike was made, the torpedo on its spar having been lowered under water just before the impact. The reason for this tactic was later explained by Tomb in his criticism of an alternative method used by another submarine commander: "Should she attempt to use a torpedo as Lieutenant Dixon [in the *Hunley*] intended, by submerging the boat and striking from below, the level of the torpedo would be above his own boat, and as she had little buoyancy and no power [since the *Hunley* was run without steam propulsion, but entirely by hand-operated cranks], the chances were the suction caused by the water passing into the sinking ship would prevent her [the submarine's] rising to the surface, beside the possibility of . . . being disabled" ("Notes from papers of first assistant engineer Jas. H. Tomb, C.S.N., regarding the submarine torpedo boat [*Hunley*]," from Charleston, January, 1864[5?] [*ibid.*, 334-35]). The danger pointed out by Tomb with reference to the *Hunley* should not have been as acutely present in the case of the *David*, since the latter, by means of its superior power, might have been expected to get clear of the water that would rush into the struck ship's aperture. It might be observed, however, that the *David*, after striking the *Ironsides*, just barely avoided being swamped.

gauntlet of gunfire from the whole Federal squadron to get the submarine safely back home.[97] While the *New Ironsides* had not been sunk, her injuries were serious enough to incapacitate her for several months.[98]

An important testimony to the effectiveness of the new Confederate torpedo boats came from the Federal Admiral John Dahlgren. "It seems to me," he admitted, speaking of the attack on the *New Ironsides*, "that nothing could have been more successful as a first effort, and it will place the torpedo among certain offensive means."[99] The *David's* was, he thought, the best form of torpedo which had ever come to his notice.[100] He felt that the "secrecy, rapidity of movement, control of direction, and precise explosion" indicated that the torpedo, so employed, was a "means of certain warfare." He urged the Federal authorities to begin the construction of similar torpedo boats—"we can make them faster than [the enemy] can."[101] His sole qualification of this praise was his opinion that the torpedo boats were dangerous only in smooth water and at slack tide.[102] The Confederates, he surmised at the beginning of 1864, had ten *Davids* in course of construction at Charleston, as well as the somewhat differently planned *Diver*.[103]

In the winter of 1863 began the saga of the *Hunley,* crude but true predecessor of the great undersea war vessels of today. Lieutenant John Payne, C.S.N., volunteered with eight men to take the boat out on her first attack. They had scarcely got aboard when the craft, swamped by a swell, sank

97. Report of Tombs, October 6, 1863 (*ibid.,* 20-21).

98. Report of Admiral John Dahlgren, November 19, 1863, enclosing report of Captain S. C. Rowan, commanding *New Ironsides,* and that of Theodore H. Bishop, carpenter of *New Ironsides* (*ibid.,* 16-18).

99. Dahlgren, *Diary,* "Tuesday, Oct. 6, [1863]" (*ibid.,* 19).

100. Report of Admiral Dahlgren on attack on *New Ironsides* by *David,* dated October 7, 1863 (*ibid.,* 11).

101. *Ibid.,* 13-14. For a further description of the *David* and her sister-ship *American Diver,* cf. testimony secured from examination of deserters, January 7, 1864 (*ibid.,* 228-9). For a diagram of the *David,* cf. *ibid.,* 15. For a diagram of the *Hunley,* cf. *ibid.,* facing 338. For another description of the *David* by a Federal officer, see *ibid.,* Vol. IX, p. 601. Also another report of Admiral Dahlgren on the Confederate torpedo boats, *ibid.,* Vol. XV, pp. 238-9. Concerning the sinking of the *Housatonic* by Dixon and his torpedo boat, see *ibid.,* 334-5. Report of First Assistant Engineer Jas. H. Tomb on abortive attempts to torpedo the *Memphis* in the North Edisto, with the torpedo boat *David,* is in *ibid.,* 358-9; cf. also the reasons given by F. D. Lee, chief of engineers, for this failure (*ibid.,* 358).

102. "Report of Rear-Admiral Dahlgren . . . regarding the Confederate *Davids* and the *Diver*," dated January 13, 1864 (*ibid.,* 238-39).

103. Cf. *ibid.,* 238: "The action . . . of the *Diver* is different [from that of the *David*], as it is intended to submerge completely, get under the bottom, attach the torpedo, haul off, and pull trigger. So far the trials have been unlucky, having drowned three crews of 17 men in all. Still she does dive, as one of the deserters saw her pass twice under the bottom of the vessel he was in, and once under the *Charleston*. The *Diver* can also be used as a *David,* so that there are really three of these machines ready to operate."

suddenly, drowning the trapped crew with the exception of Payne. The boat was raised; Payne and eight more men at once volunteered to go out again. Another swell came and the ship sank. This time six of the crew were lost. Payne and two others escaped. Again the boat was raised and, with a new crew of volunteers, another attempt was made. These brave men met the same fate as the others, and this time there were no survivors.[104]

Once more the treacherous *Hunley* was hauled up from the bottom of the harbor. Once more the volunteers stepped forward. Two engineers, George Dixon and William Alexander, both of the twenty-first Alabama Artillery Regiment, were put in charge of the ship. Reluctantly, General Beauregard gave them permission to make another try against the Federal ships in the harbor and outside the bar. Alexander has told the story of the careful preparations they made for their expedition. After a short spell of practice in the river they were ordered to moor the boat off Battery Marshall, on Sullivan's Island. The nearest vessel, which they understood to be the United States frigate *Wabash,* was about twelve miles off, and was intended to be their objective.

"In comparatively smooth water and light current the *Hunley* could make four miles an hour, but in rough water the speed was much slower. It was winter, therefore necessary that we go out with the ebb and come in with the flood tide, a fair wind, and dark moon. This latter was essential to our success, as our experience had demonstrated the necessity of occasionally coming to the surface, slightly lifting the hatch-cover, and letting in a little air. On several occasions we came to the surface for air, opened the cover, and heard the men in the Federal picket boats talking and singing.

"Our daily routine, whenever possible, was about as follows: Leave Mount Pleasant [their quarters] about 1 P.M., walk seven miles to Battery Marshall on the beach (this exposed us to fire, but it was the best walking), take the boat out and practice the crew for two hours in the Back bay. Dixon and myself would then stretch out on the beach with the compass between us and get the bearing of the nearest vessel as she took her position for the night; ship up the torpedo on the boom, and, when dark, go out, steering for the vessel; proceed until the condition of the men, sea, tide, wind, moon, and daylight compelled our return to the dock; unship the torpedo, put it under guard at Battery Marshall, walk back to quarters at Mount Pleasant, and cook breakfast.

"During the months of November and December, 1863, through January and the early part of February, 1864, the wind held contrary, making it

104. Alexander, *op. cit.,* 167-68.

difficult, with our limited power, to make much headway. During this time we went out on an average of four nights a week; but on account of the weather, and considering the physical condition of the men to propel the boat back again, often, after going out six or seven miles, we would have to return. This was always a task, and many times it taxed our utmost exertions to keep from drifting out to sea, daylight often breaking while we were yet in range [of the enemy]. This experience, also our desire to know, in case we struck a vessel (circumstances required our keeping below the surface), suggested that while in safe water we make the experiment to find out how long it was possible to stay under water without coming to the surface for air, and not injure the crew. It was agreed by all hands, to sink and let the boat rest on the bottom, in the Back bay, off Battery Marshall, each man to make equal physical exertion in turning the propeller. It was also agreed that if any one in the boat felt that he must come to the surface for air, and he gave the word 'up,' we would at once bring the boat to the surface.

"It was usual, when we were practicing in the bay, that the banks would be lined with soldiers. One evening, after alternately diving and rising many times, Dixon and myself and several of the crew compared watches, noted the time, and sank for the test.

"In twenty-five minutes after I had closed the after man-head and excluded the outer air the candle would not burn. Dixon forward and myself aft, turned on the propeller cranks as hard as we could. In comparing our individual experiences afterwards, the experience of one was found to have been the experience of all. Each man had determined that he would not be the first to say 'up.' Not a word was said, except the occasional, 'How is it?' between Dixon and myself, until it was as the voice of one man, the word 'up' came from all nine. We started the pumps, but I soon realized that my pump was not throwing. From experience I guessed the cause of the failure, took off the cap of the pump, lifted the valve, and drew out some seaweed that had choked it.

"During all the time it took to do this the boat was considerably by the stern. Thick darkness prevailed. All hands had already endured what they thought was the utmost limit. Some of the crew almost lost control of themselves. . . . We soon had the boat to the surface and the man-head opened. Fresh air! What an experience! . . . We had been on the bottom two hours and thirty-five minutes. . . . We . . . went over early next morning to the city [Charleston] and reported to General Beauregard the facts of the affair. [The report had already spread that the crew was lost.] They were all very glad to see us."[105]

On February 17, 1864, two and a half miles off Charleston bar, the *Hunley* torpedoed and sank the great Federal frigate *Housatonic*. The submarine herself was carried down to the bottom with the wreck, and every man of the Confederate crew was lost.[106]

The Confederate torpedoes did more than destroy ships. They compelled the Federals to divert large forces of men and matériel from other important duties in order to attempt to neutralize the devastating effects of the new weapon. General Rains was gratified that the torpedo campaign on the James had caused the enemy to watch the river banks with thousands of their soldiers who might otherwise have been employed against Lee.[107]

The Federal force assigned to mine-sweeping duties on the James in the spring of 1864 was listed as follows: the *Tritonia*, the *Stepping Stones*, the *Delaware*, eleven armed cutters from the various vessels, and 175 sailors, marines, and soldiers employed as skirmishers and pickets to drive back the small bodies of Confederates along the left bank so that the boats could safely pursue their search.[108] Before the Federals dared to attack through the torpedo-sown channel between Fort Esperanza and the bar at Pass Cavallo, in the lower Mississippi area, they sent for reinforcements.[109]

The effectiveness of the torpedoes raised the question of whether the Confederate Navy Department failed to utilize with sufficient vigor their

105. *Ibid.*, 170-72.

106. *Ibid.*, 174: "The *Housatonic* was a new vessel on the station, and anchored closer in than the *Wabash* or others. On this night the wind had lulled, with but little sea on, and although it was moonlight, Dixon, who had been waiting so long for a change of wind, took the risk of the moonlight and went out. The lookout on the ship saw him when he came to the surface for his final observation before striking her. He [Dixon] of course, not knowing that the ship had slipped her chain and was backing down upon him, then sank the boat a few feet, steered for the stern of the ship and struck with the torpedo. The momentum of the two vessels brought them together unexpectedly. The stern of the ship *Housatonic* was blown off entirely. The momentum carried the torpedo boat into the wreck, Dixon and all his men, unable to extricate themselves, sinking with it." Cf. also, for the contest between the *Hunley* and the *Housatonic*, William E. Beard, "The Log of the C. S. Submarine," *United States Naval Institute Proceedings*, XLII, 1545-57; and General Beauregard's account of the *Hunley's* sinking of the *Housatonic*, *Southern Historical Society Papers*, V, 152-54.

107. Brig. Gen. Rains to Secretary Seddon, from Torpedo Bureau, Richmond, November 18, 1864 (*O.R.A.*, Ser. I, Vol. XLII, part 3, p. 1219). Cf. also the exchange of letters between Secretary Welles and Capt. A. H. Kilty, commanding U.S.S. *Roanoke*, at Point Lookout, Md. (*O.R.*, Ser. I, Vol. V, pp. 500-1).

108. Lieut. R. H. Lamson to Rear Admiral S. P. Lee, May 25, 1864 (*ibid.*, Vol. X, pp. 92-93).

109. D. Bradbury (Captain, U.S.A.), to Col. Jas. Duff, from Victoria, January 9, 1864 (*O.R.A.*, Ser. I, Vol. XXXIV, part 2, pp. 854-55).

destructive power. Could a large fleet of torpedo boats like the *David* have struck a decisive series of blows at the Federals? There were many on both sides who seemed to think so. John B. Read pleaded for support of his plan (a development of that of M. F. Maury) of arming small active steamers with torpedoes for destroying the enemy's ships-of-war. His project was, he said, warmly approved by the Governor of South Carolina. He was sure that the tactic if put into execution, would raise the siege of Charleston, and claimed that seven naval officers agreed with him on this point.[110]

General Beauregard proposed a variation of the Read plan: "It is stated that a proper-sized steamer, 400 or 500 tons, built like a blockade runner, but made shot-proof and armed with one of Lee's repeating submarine torpedo apparatus, could be built in about three months' working time in England for the sum of about $250,000. I venture to say that with one of those vessels here the blockade of Charleston could be raised in less than one week, and the army of Gillmore captured very shortly afterwards. Half a dozen of these steamers would raise the blockade of our Atlantic and Gulf coasts, and enable us to recover the navigation of the Mississippi River. Indeed, a few years hence we will ask ourselves in astonishment how it was that with such a great discovery, offering such magnificent results, we never applied it to any useful purpose in this contest. . . . It is evident, according to Lord John Russell's own views, that those steamers can be constructed in England as shot-proof, unarmed blockade runners, without incurring the risk of being seized by the English government."[111]

That this type of strategy might indeed have succeeded is at least suggested by the fears expressed by Admiral Dahlgren in the face of only a handful of *Davids*. "The blockade is important," he declared in early 1864, "but the safety of the ironclads much more so."[112] His reaction to the sinking of the *Housatonic* by a torpedo boat was as follows: "The Department will readily perceive the consequences likely to result from this event; the whole line of blockade will be infested with these cheap, convenient, and

110. John B. Read to Governor Luke Milledge Bonham of South Carolina, August 12, 1863 (*ibid.,* Vol. XXVIII, part 2, p. 277). A contemporary observer wrote with respect to the Franco-Prussian war: "The mines and small coast defense vessels which had proved so effective in the Crimean and American wars had sealed the mouths of the German rivers against naval attack" (Theodore Ropp, "Continental Doctrines of Sea Power," in *Makers of Modern Strategy,* ed. Edward Mead Earle [Princeton, N. J., 1944], 446).

111. Beauregard, "Remarks . . . relative to ironclad gunboats," from Charleston, November 14, 1863 (*O.R.,* Ser. I, Vol. XV, p. 695). Cf. also Mallory's adverse criticism of Beauregard's statement (Mallory to Porcher Miles, December 19, 1863 [*ibid.,* 699-700]).

112. Dahlgren to Commodore S. C. Rowan, February 5, 1864 (*ibid.,* 273).

formidable defenses, and we must guard every point. The measures for prevention may not be so obvious."[113]

In estimating the potentialities of the torpedo boats, however, it is necessary to consider the strength of the defense devised by the North against them. If that defense was powerful enough to reduce to a reasonable minimum the Federal losses from torpedo boat attacks, then the force of the arguments for such plans as those of Maury and Read is considerably lessened. To what extent had the Federals perfected their counteraction against the formidable *Davids* and *Divers?*

In the early spring of 1864 Admiral Dahlgren declared in a report to Secretary Welles: "With an increased number of steam tugs and some torpedo boats like these of the rebels [which he could certainly acquire] I should feel no apprehension whatever from this base [*sic*] style of rebel warfare."[114] By August of the same year the Admiral was confident that he had developed a practically infallible defense against torpedoes for his ships.[115] In November, 1864, General Rains was forced to admit that "many abortive attempts to destroy their shipping [in the James] . . . have rendered them so watchful that I almost despair of accomplishing anything that way now, with the obstructions in the river and guards to their vessels."[116] The Federal commanders at Savannah[117] and Wilmington[118] reported successes in rendering the torpedoes harmless by means of various devices.

Indeed it might be argued that the Confederate torpedo program backfired, since the Federals proved themselves apt imitators. The following special order was issued by Rear Admiral Porter to the James River Squadron: "Anyone who has a large boat will have her rigged with a spar and a torpedo. . . . I am confident there is pluck enough in this squadron to make a dash with their boats rigged with torpedoes. The officers and men will be instructed in the use of them."[119]

113. Report of Dahlgren on the sinking of the *Housatonic,* dated February 19, 1864 (*ibid.,* 329).

114. Report of April 6, 1864 (*ibid.,* 394).

115. Dahlgren to Lieutenant Commander T. Scott Fillebrown, U.S.N., commanding U. S. ironclad *Passaic,* August 15, 1864 (*ibid.,* 628).

116. Brig. Gen. G. J. Rains to Secretary Seddon, November 18, 1864 (*O.R.A.,* Ser. I, Vol. XLII, part 3, p. 1219).

117. Lieut. J. P. Bankhead to Commander John Rodgers, U.S.N., February 19, 1862 (*O.R.,* Ser. I, Vol. XII, p. 504). The following methods were used with success by the Federals: producing harmless explosions of the floating torpedoes by means of hand grapnels; cutting the torpedo wires; shooting rifle balls into the torpedoes.

118. Rear Admiral David D. Porter to Secretary Welles, from Cape Fear River, February 22, 1865 (*ibid.,* 45).

119. Special Order of Rear Admiral Porter to James River Squadron, February 25, 1865 (*ibid.,* Vol. XII, 52). Cf. also S. P. Lee to Secretary Welles, June 1, 1864 (*ibid.,* Vol. X, p.

Some interesting scruples with regard to the use of torpedoes arose in the minds of some of the Confederate leaders. General Rains had placed land mines behind the rear guard forces near Richmond. This method of defense was prohibited by General Longstreet, who did "not recognize it as a proper or effective method of war."[120] Rains vigorously protested. Were not land mines, he argued, as "moral" as ambuscades, masked batteries, and other such methods of surprise? The enemy, he had learned, had intended to blow up Fort Magruder at Yorktown. If such devices for wholesale killing were proper, why should not smaller mines be allowed? "Must we accord to them alone," he asked, "the privilege of using against us the vast supplies of gunpowder, for which they have raked the world by [means of] advantages derived from a navy much of which properly belongs to us?"[121] Rains's reasoning was supported by Major General D. H. Hill, who declared succinctly, "In my opinion, all means of destroying our brutal enemies are lawful and proper."[122]

This case of conscience was submitted to Secretary of War G. W. Randolph, who delivered the following opinion: "Whether shells planted in roads or parapets are contrary to the usages of war depends upon the purpose with which they are used. It is not admissible in civilized warfare to take life with no other object than the destruction of life. Hence it is inadmissible to shoot sentinels and pickets, because nothing is attained by the destruction of life. It would be admissible, however, to shoot a general, because you not only take life but deprive an army of its head. It is ad-

---

111): "I send by express a specimen of the copper torpedoes used by the rebels in James River. The plan of its construction is excellent, and I request that the Department will furnish me with a number of the same description . . . with fuzes such as were found on board the *Atlanta*."

120. Asst. Adj. Gen. G. Moxley Sorrel to Brig. Gen. Rains, from H. Q. of Second Corps, Dept. of North Virginia, May 11, 1862 (*O.R.A.*, Ser. I, Vol. XI, part 3, p. 509).

121. Endorsement of Gen. Rains to foregoing letter of Gen. Sorrell (*ibid.*, 509-10).

122. Endorsement of Gen. D. H. Hill to same letter (*ibid.*, 510). Cf. the contrary spirit evinced by Secretary Seddon with respect to attack by means of "submarine apparatus" against merchantmen or passenger vessels: "In my judgment, only ships of war and transports carrying troops, munitions of war, or supplies to armed forces are legitimate objects of the attacks contemplated. Passenger ships or those in ordinary commerce should not in general be assailed in so destructive a way, as the main aim of legitimate war in such cases is to capture, not destroy. Only in very exceptional cases, where some special cause for destruction existed and would morally justify, should such fatal agencies be employed against passenger or commercial vessels" (Endorsement of Seddon to letter of Uriel Wright to President Davis, August 11, 1864 [*ibid.*, Ser. IV, Vol. III, p. 581]. The plan referred to by Seddon was that of marine engineer C. Williams. It consisted of "shipping on board of the enemy's vessels and into depots of supplies incendiary apparatus or torpedoes, to set fire or explode at a given time. . . ." (Williams to President Davis, August [?], 1864 [*ibid.*, 581-83]). The Uriel Wright referred to above was Major Wright, who served for some time under Major General Earl Van Dorn.

missible to plant shells in a parapet to repel an assault, or in a road to check pursuit, because the object is to save the work in one case and the army in the other. It is not admissible to plant shells merely to destroy life and without other design than that of depriving your enemy of a few men, without materially injuring him. It is admissible to plant torpedoes in a river or harbor, because they drive off blockading or attacking fleets. As Generals Rains and Longstreet differ in this matter, the inferior in rank should give way, or, if he prefers it, he may be assigned to the river defenses, where such things are clearly admissible."[123]

The delicate moral sense of the Confederates was further troubled by a charge made by General McClellan. The rebels, declared the Federal leader, had been guilty of "the most murderous and barbarous conduct near Yorktown in placing torpedoes within abandoned works near wells and springs, and near flag staffs, magazines, and telegraph offices, and in carpet-bags, barrels of flour and such like." Some four or five men had been killed and perhaps a dozen wounded by these "barbarous" methods.[124]

Major General D. H. Hill was at once ordered by his superiors to ascertain whether there was any truth in McClellan's assertion. When Hill, in turn, questioned Rains, the latter replied with a long and somewhat bitter statement. He knew nothing about torpedoes being placed in wells, carpetbags, and so forth, as his command had been the first to leave Yorktown. But he doubted the military usefulness of such devices and assumed therefore that the torpedoes had not been so placed. He had indeed employed land mines as part of the defenses of Yorktown. But at the time he did so he was, with a total force of 9,300 men, facing an attacking army 100,000 men strong. Again at Williamsburg in a desperate crisis, he had used four land mines. And what, in the meanwhile, had the enemy done? They had bombed the civilians, women, and children of Yorktown during a whole month—"fiendish acts, unknown among civilized nations."[125]

Toward the end of the war, General W. T. Sherman laid down his views concerning the use of torpedoes (land mines) on land. "General [Steedman]: As the question may arise, and you have a right to the support of my authority, I now decide that the use of the torpedo is justifiable in war in advance of an army, so as to make his advance up a river or over a road more dangerous and difficult. But after the adversary has gained the coun-

123. *Ibid.*, Ser. IV, Vol. III, p. 510.
124. Extract from report of Gen. McClellan, enclosure in letter of Asst. Adj. Gen. A. P. Mason, C.S.A., to Maj. Gen. D. H. Hill, May 12, 1862 (*ibid.*, Ser. I, Vol. XI, part 3, p. 511).
125. Rains to General D. H. Hill, May 14, 1862 (*ibid.*, 516-17).

try by fair and warlike means, then the case entirely changes. The use of torpedoes in blowing up our cars and the road after they are in our possession, is simply malicious. It cannot alter the great problem, but simply makes trouble. Now, if torpedoes are found in the possession of an enemy, to our rear, you may cause them to be put on the ground and tested by wagon-loads of prisoners, or, if need be, citizens implicated in their use. In like manner, if a torpedo is suspected on any part of the road, order the point to be tested by a car-load of prisoners, or citizens implicated, drawn by a long rope. Of course an enemy cannot complain of his own traps."[126]

Torpedoes and submarines were part of the more spectacular side of the Navy Department's achievements. Perhaps of equal importance was a reform accomplished by Mallory in May, 1863, with no fanfare or theatrical color. Congress, at the insistence of the Secretary of the Navy, and in accord with principles that he had upheld strenuously for eight years in the United States Senate, enacted a law creating the "Provisional Navy."[127] The aim of the measure, as explained later by Raphael Semmes, was, ". . . without interfering with the rank of the officers in the Regular Navy, to cull out from the navy list younger and more active men, and put them in the Provisional Navy, with increased rank."[128] The Secretary was thus enabled to accomplish his object of bringing forward younger officers for active service without wounding the feelings of the older officers, since the latter were not superseded *in the Regular Navy* by their juniors. The distinction was indeed thin, but it was enough to save the pride of the ancients. The whole maneuver was not a poor piece of diplomacy, and it was certainly apt personnel management and reform; it was also in keeping with Mallory's basic postulate that a navy, in order to be active, must be manned by active officers.

Mallory's insistence on order and regularity in naval administration is evidenced by his cold response to an offer made by some persons who were desirous of initiating—for a share of the prize money—guerilla tactics on the western rivers. These men with their ships hoped to act as a unit practically independent of the Confederate navy, yet, according to their proposal, they would be rewarded by the government for capturing or destroying any enemy merchantmen or vessels of war. The Secretary's unenthusiastic reception of the proposition stressed the necessity of strict subordination of

126. Gen. W. T. Sherman to Maj. Gen. J. B. Steedman, June 23, 1864 (*ibid.*, Vol. XXXVIII, part 4, p. 579).
127. Cf. *supra*, pp. 70-83.
128. Semmes, *Service Afloat*, 368-69.

all naval personnel to the office at Richmond, and pointed to the desirability of formal enrollment in the navy.[129]

Another advance in the all-important task of creating a competent officer group was the establishment of the Confederate Naval Academy in March, 1863. The rules and regulations of this training school for midshipmen reveal the high qualifications required of the applicants. Any of the following physical disabilities would bar a young man from the academy: "muscular tenuity; glandular sweatings; chronic cutaneous affections; severe injuries of the bones of the head; convulsions; fistula lachrymalis; deafness, copious discharge from the ears; impaired or inadequate efficiency of one or both of the superior extremities, on account of fractures, contractions of a joint, extenuation, a deformity; an unnatural excurvature or incurvature of the spine; impaired or inadequate efficiency of one or both of the inferior extremities, on account of varicose veins, fractures, flatness, lameness, contraction, unequal length, bunyons, overlying or supernumerary toes." Candidates must be over fourteen and under eighteen years of age. They must be of good moral character. They must be able to read and write well, and must be conversant with the elementary operations of arithmetic.[130] One of the first young men to be enrolled in the institution was Mallory's son Buddy.[131]

Not only was it necessary, for purposes of exact administration, to maintain a close liaison between the Navy Department and its ships at sea, but precautions of secrecy also had to be observed. Mallory instructed his commanders to send their reports in partial code. To the officer in charge of the *Florida* he wrote: "For the purpose of communicating with your Government you will proceed as follows: Obtain at Mobile [where the *Florida* was then anchored] two uniform copies of any small lexicon or dictionary, one to be retained by you and the other to be sent to the Department. Whenever in your letters or dispatches a word is used which may betray what you desire to conceal, instead of using that word write the numbers, in figures within brackets, of the page where it is to be found, and also the number of the word on the page, counting from the top."[132]

129. Mallory to Colonel E. C. Cabell, C.S.A., September 10, 1863 (*O.R.A.*, Ser. I, Vol. XXII, part 2, pp. 1001-2).

130. Circular: Extract from Regulations of Navy School (photostat), issued by Confederate Navy Department, December 15, 1863 (Duke University Archives, Durham, N. C.).

131. Roster of Midshipmen Enrolled in Naval Academy, 1863 (Virginia State Library Archives, Richmond, Va.).

132. Mallory to Lieut. Com. John N. Maffitt, commanding steam sloop *Florida*, October 25, 1862 (*O.R.*, Ser. I, Vol. I, p. 762). Cf. also Commander R. Semmes to Mallory, from New Orleans, June 16, 1861 (*ibid.*, 615-16). Semmes reports his compliance with a similar instruc-

Mallory's enthusiasm for daring projects had not noticeably cooled. Early in 1863 he received from Lieutenant William Murdaugh a proposal embodying a great deal of the spectacular and some sound possibilities. Murdaugh wished to make a naval raid on the northern lakes and wrest from the enemy control of those important waters. His rather complex plan involved the purchase of a two-hundred-ton steamer in Canada, the capture of the U. S. S. *Michigan* in Lake Erie, and the burning of the shipping at Buffalo and Chicago. A degree of rather naïve cooperation would also be demanded of the Canadian authorities.

The Lieutenant explained in minute and enthusiastic detail. The party was to leave the Confederacy at the earliest possible day, the commanding officer to be furnished with a letter of credit for $100,000, "although it is not presumed that more than half of this amount will be expended."[133] After buying a vessel through an agent in Canada, he would assemble a crew of fifty men for the ostensible purpose of mining operations on Lake Superior. The true object of the expedition was not to be made known to the men until the vessel was clear of the Canadian coast, when strong inducement for making the attempt was to be held out to them in the shape of extra pay. Those not willing to engage in the project would be returned to the Canadian shore; those who were eager to "go along" would be shipped into the Confederate service. The crew would be armed with cutlasses and revolvers and the vessel would be provided with a number of small iron buoys to be used as torpedoes for the destruction of canal locks. There must also be on board plenty of spirits of turpentine and incendiary materials for rapid work in starting fires.

The first point to be aimed at was Erie, Pennsylvania, the arrival there to be so timed as to make it about 1:00 A.M. The vessel was to be laid along-

---

tion sent to him by Mallory. For an example of how this order was carried out, see Lieut. J. N. Barney, commanding C.S.S. *Harriet Lane,* to Mallory, from Galveston Bay, March 19, 1863 (*ibid.,* Vol. XX, p. 805): "In my last of 9th by Lieutenant Warley I reported that General Magruder proposed to (177)-2-16- the (216)-1-15 - (113)-3-85- in (29)-3-36-(23)-3-29. I am officially informed that (163)-1-34- will prevent (85)-3-14- from (115)-1-7-. As my previous suggestions are thus defeated, I presume the (262)-3-22 will not be kept in (54)-2-33, (215)-2-26 being entirely useless. I beg leave respectfully to suggest that being so near (149)-1-30-a (156)-1-8- the (163)-3-40 might be (213)-2-21- (10)-1-21-. A dispatch sent by army pony express via Alexandria will reach me most expeditiously. P.S. What shall be done with the (150)-3-12- sent from Richmond in case the above suggestion is carried out? Some might, if practicable, be sent (10)-1-12-. N.B. The second or middle figure indicates the column, 1st, 2nd, or 3rd." To what extent the Federal code-breakers were foiled by this somewhat transparent stratagem is a matter of considerable doubt.

133. Lieut. Murdaugh to Mallory, from C.S.S. *Beaufort,* Richmond, February 7, 1863 (*ibid.,* Vol. II, p. 828).

side the U.S.S. *Michigan,* which was to be carried by boarding with as little noise as possible. If the operation could be effected secretly, the two vessels would then leave the harbor and proceed toward the Welland Canal, with a view to getting through into Lake Ontario before the news of the capture reached the Canadians, who ". . . might interpose objections . . . should the object of . . . [the] voyage be apparent." If, on the other hand, the capture could not be made secretly, then the work of burning every particle of Federal property afloat should be immediately commenced.

Once arrived in Lake Ontario, the raiding vessel would have a fine field, but the most important part of her work would be to destroy the aqueduct of the Erie Canal, which crossed the Genesee River at Rochester, seven miles from the lake. The locks of a branch of this canal at Oswego were also to be demolished. If a passage through the Welland Canal should be refused by the Canadians, both vessels were to operate in Lakes Erie, Huron, and Michigan.

In Lake Erie, Buffalo would be the first point to be visited, and the fleet of trading vessels in its harbor and the locks of the great Erie Canal would be destroyed. The next stop would be Tonawanda, which would also be destroyed. Then the ships would coast along the southern shore of the lake, smash the locks of the four canals leading to the Ohio River, enter into Lake Michigan, and set a course for Chicago. At Chicago—"burn the shipping and destroy the locks of the Illinois and Michigan Canal, connecting Lake Michigan and the Mississippi River." Then "turn northward, through Lake Huron, and finally run the vessel aground in Georgian Bay." Only four officers would be required for the expedition.[134]

The scheme, according to Murdaugh, was approved by the Navy Department and, after some argument, endorsed by the President and the Cabinet; and he was given $100,000 to cover the costs of the expedition.[135] Then, just when all was ready for the start, Davis became over-cautious. The President said that he thought the project practicable and almost sure of success, but that it would raise such a storm about the violation of the neutrality laws that England would be forced to halt the building of some Confederate ironclads in her yards and would take rigid action against the

134. *Ibid.,* 828-29.

135. Lieutenant R. D. Minor said that "it was only after repeated efforts that the Government was induced to take any active part in promoting the expedition, *though Mr. Mallory . . . was in favor of it from the inception of the plan. . . .*" (Minor to Admiral Buchanan, from Richmond, February 2, 1864 [*ibid.,* 823; italics inserted]). Lieutenant Minor was to be an assistant to Murdaugh in the proposed expedition, and was actually in charge of the one next to be proposed. Cf. *infra,* p. 288.

Confederate government everywhere. "So," grieved Murdaugh, "the thing fell through and with it my great chance. About a year afterwards, when many attempts had been made from Canada, and when the Yankees were long since on the qui vive, an expedition was sent in a large steamer with a flourish of trumpets, and of course the commander could do nothing and had to return. This is a specimen of how the Navy was treated and how it was managed."[136]

Although the main project was thus thwarted, another similar and even bolder plan was formulated, this time, apparently, by the War Department. About two thousand Confederate prisoners of war, all officers, had recently been moved to a prison camp on Johnson's Island, in Lake Erie. It was proposed to rescue these men, by means of "the old St. Nicholas game," as Lieutenant R. D. Minor described it.[137] A body of picked men would go on board one of the lake steamers at Windsor, opposite Detroit, seize the vessel in mid-lake, then run her into Johnson's Island, capture the place, and take off the prisoners.

Mallory, on Minor's testimony, cooperated satisfactorily with the plan, although, says the latter, there was an "unaccountable" delay of "nearly a month" before the Secretary of the Navy put him in command of the expedition and gave him $111,000, partly in gold, for expenses.[138] After a series of adventures this stratagem, too, met with failure, because of the disloyalty of a Canadian whom the Confederates had thought to be trustworthy.[139]

During this period there were the usual difficulties in getting money from the Treasury Department. In mid-January, Mallory complained to Memminger that, instead of a badly needed assignment of actual currency, he had sent to the Navy Department some of the notorious 8 per cent bonds, the proceeds of the sale of which were to be placed to the credit of Bulloch in England. Mallory regretted that he could not concur with Memminger's views in this matter. What he needed was funds in the shape of cold cash—"The operations of this Department must suffer in consequence of the bond arrangement and I will submit the question as to the disposition of these bonds to the President." The transfer to navy agents abroad of cotton certificates to the amount of $1,500,000, at the current rate of exchange, would actually make the charge upon the Navy Department $4,000,000![140]

136. *Ibid.*, 829-30.    137. *Ibid.*, 824-25, 823.
138. *Ibid.*, 823-24.    139. *Ibid.*, 824-28.
140. Mallory to Memminger, January 12, 1863 (Treasury Department Records, National Archives).

In early June Mallory wrote to Memminger that he had just received the following telegram from the officer William F. Lynch, C.S.N., at Wilmington, North Carolina: "Mechanics on *Raleigh* refuse to work until paid. Borrowed five thousand dollars for present emergency. Please send funds." The Secretary of the Treasury was reminded in the same communication that on May 20 a requisition had been made for $151,000 in favor of the navy paymaster engaged in the construction of gunboats at Wilmington.[141]

In an effort to solve his own and the Treasury Department's difficulties, Mallory offered to Memminger a constructive suggestion. Since the Treasury Department was unable to supply the money appropriated by Congress for the navy, to be spent abroad, could not cotton certificates be issued to the Navy Department for cotton to be delivered within a stated time after the war, the price to be fixed in the certificate? Mallory knew, he said, a party who would deliver ships and supplies in return for such certificates.[142]

In answer to Memminger's objection that the treasury was without the means to purchase and to pay for cotton to meet these certificates, Mallory suggested that, in view of the present circumstances of the country, and "the necessity for funds abroad to build up and provide a navy, the use of certificates or scrip in advance of such purchase be not demanded." To the further objection that the sale of such scrip by Navy Department agents in the open market would depreciate the scrip's value, he answered that the scrip's value could be determined by a sale in the open market, judiciously made; or the scrip might be retained in the hands of the Treasury Department's agents and sold by them in response to calls from the Navy Department.[143]

"The wants of the Naval Service," urged the Navy Secretary, "for . . . supplies of all kinds are . . . urgent, and the great importance of building and providing ships abroad for the Naval Service [is] evident. . . ." It was his earnest conviction that the "safety, honor, and interests of the country demand a navy, that the opportunity to build, arm, and equip a navy abroad within a brief period is now presented, and that money alone is wanting to accomplish this great object."[144]

This suggestion was not received cordially by the harassed gentleman who was trying with no little ineptitude to shore up the tottering structure

141. Mallory to Memminger, June 8, 1863 (*ibid.*).
142. Mallory to Memminger, July 25, 1863 (*ibid.*).
143. *Ibid.*
144. *Ibid.*

of Confederate finance. Mallory continued until the end of the war to protest unavailingly against the nonfulfillment of his requisitions.[145]

Not all of the Navy Department's difficulties stemmed from financial circumstances. Urgently, throughout the year 1863, Mallory pleaded for more men to fill up the crews of vessels and to supply the navy's various workshops. The ships at Mobile and at Charleston, he wrote in July, 1863, had not enough men to fight their own guns, nor men to spare for any enterprise against the enemy. Recruits could not be obtained by voluntary enlistment, and there was no conscription for the naval service. If Flag Officer Tucker had a few hundred seamen, such as could be found in the army and such as had applied for service in the navy, he could organize, by means of torpedo parties, a strong means of attack in Charleston harbor.[146]

On May 1, 1863, Congress had approved a law providing that "all persons serving in the land forces of the Confederate States who shall desire to be transferred to the naval service, and whose transfer as seamen or ordinary seamen shall be applied for by the Secretary of the Navy, shall be transferred from the land to the naval service. . . ." This law, said Mallory, had not been observed. He had requested the transfer from the army to the naval service of about six hundred seamen and ordinary seamen, all of whom had applied to the Navy Department for service in the navy. Not one of these men had been transferred.

Secretary Seddon had laid down the rule that "seamen should be selected and application made for them from the armies with which the vessels to be manned are cooperating, or from conscripts to be assigned." He had added the explanation that ". . . distant commanders, not appreciating the exigency for seamen, naturally present every obstacle to the transfer of their tried soldiers." Mallory replied that he could recognize no other rule in applications for transfers than that prescribed by the imperative terms of the law. He was aware of the necessity of making the transfers in such a way as would be least detrimental to the army, and he was perfectly willing to confer with Secretary Seddon on this point. Indeed, the suggestion as to taking men from the armies with which the vessels needing the men are cooperating had been anticipated. The important fact, in Mallory's eyes, was the ever-increasing and alarming shortage in naval personnel. In any

145. Cf. proposal of Toombs to reconstruct the dilapidated Confederate finances, Phillips, *Toombs*, 249.

146. Mallory to President Davis, July 24, 1863 (*O.R.A.*, Ser. IV, Vol. II, pp. 662-63).

assessment of the Navy Department's successes and failures, this fact must be given due weight.[147]

The old plague of the intermixture of the army and navy administrations, with consequent clashes between naval and military authorities, was at this time evident in the Galveston theater of operations. It may be, as has been suggested previously, that it is difficult to overestimate the degree to which such vagueness of administrative limits between the two services was an embarrassment to the Confederate war effort.

General Magruder, through Secretary of War Seddon, had tried to secure the appointment of an army officer to the command of the captured *Harriet Lane*.[148] Mallory had very curtly rebuffed the request: "The appointment of a citizen to a post-captaincy over the heads of nine-tenths of the naval officers, as recommended by General Magruder, could only be justified in my judgment by considerations which the case he cites does not present, even could it be done legally, which it cannot."[149]

In March the navy had apparently transferred the *Harriet Lane* to the War Department.[150] But the commander of the vessel, Lieutenant J. N. Barney, while taking orders from General Magruder, regarded himself as being subject also to the instructions of the Navy Department.[151] He did not feel "authorized to adopt any plan or to make any alteration in the ship"—as indeed he had been ordered to do by Magruder—without sanction from the Secretary of the Navy.[152] To heighten the confusion, Commander W. W. Hunter, with his men, was detached from army service and assigned to the *Harriet Lane* by orders from the Navy Department.[153] It is no wonder if Barney, Magruder, Hunter, and Mallory himself were puzzled as to who had first authority over the *Harriet Lane*.

147. Mallory to Secretary Seddon, August 11, 1863 (*ibid.*, 705-6).

148. General Magruder to Secretary Seddon, from Galveston, January 6, 1863 (*ibid.*, Ser. I, Vol. XV, pp. 931-32).

149. Mallory to President Davis, January 24, 1863 (*ibid.*, 959).

150. Mallory to Secretary Seddon, March 31, 1863 (*ibid.*, 1030).

151. J. N. Barney to Brig. Gen. W. R. Scurry, April 4, 1863 (*O.R.*, Ser. I, Vol. XX, pp. 808-9); cf. also Barney to Scurry, April 21, 1863 (*ibid.*, 817).

152. Barney to Scurry, April 4, 1863 (*ibid.*, 808-9).

153. W. W. Hunter to Mallory, from Trinity River, Polk Co., Texas, April 15, 1863 (*ibid.*, 814). Cf. also, concerning administrative confusion: "Special Orders No. 150: Headquarters District of Texas, New Mexico, and Arizona; Houston, June 4, 1863; XIV. Major Leon Smith, commander of the vessels on the coast, will at once cause all the gunboats now lying in these waters to be prepared for immediate action and directed to proceed to Galveston Bay for immediate use in defending Galveston. By command of Major-General Magruder" (*ibid.*, 829). Also Magruder to Brig. Gen. W. R. Boggs, chief of staff, from Houston, June 25, 1863 (*ibid.*, 831). In the same sense, E. Kirby Smith, Lieut. Gen., to Gen. S. Cooper, Adj. Gen., from Shreveport, June 29, 1863 (*ibid.*, 832-33).

The breaking down and confusion of administrative lines between land and naval forces was strikingly illustrated in what was, nevertheless, a successful engagement. In late February, 1863, the Federal ironclad steamer *Indianola* was met in battle near Vicksburg and captured by the Confederate steamers *Queen of the West* and *Webb*. The operation as a whole was under the direction of a major of the army, but the two Confederate vessels were commanded by naval officers.[154]

Whatever his faults and whatever his achievements, one thing was certain: the Secretary of the Navy, in some quarters, was not giving satisfaction. It was not only Du Pont's frigates that were booming in the summer of 1863, as was made clear by a typical blast from the *Richmond Examiner*, evoked by the news of the misfortune suffered by the *Atlanta*. The circumstances of the capture of the vessel, mourned the editor, were particularly shameful. Only nine shots were fired before she struck her flag. The Yankees received her in almost perfect condition, and would doubtless use her against the South. Nor had the Confederacy reason to be proud of the manner in which the commander of the *Atlanta* had conducted himself. "After making a brief address to his crew of Georgians, in which he advised them to be resigned, [he] fainted away on his quarter-deck."[155]

This magnificent ship, continued the editor, had been virtually built for the enemy. It had gone the way of all Mr. Mallory's ironclads. Indeed their way had been from bad to worse. Hitherto they had only been burnt or blown up within a few weeks of their completion. Now they had learned the trick of dropping into the enemy's hands as soon as they had left port.

The *Examiner* then proceeded to become even more personal in its remarks. "If," it declared, "history lacked proof that there is such a thing as an evil fortune, a bad luck attendant on all the steps of particular men, the chapter of *Mallory* will hereafter furnish them those proofs, to confirm the conviction of the greatest minds . . . upon that point. So long as Mallory reigns, all that he touches—quamvis Pontica pinus, Sylvae filius nobilis— will explode or sink. Never yet has he turned out of hand one good thing. The curse is on him, not on the Confederate sea-flag, as the exploits of the

154. Maj. Gen. Richard Taylor, commanding District of Western Louisiana, to Gen. S. Cooper, from Vicksburg, February 25, 1863 (*O.R.A.*, Ser. I, Vol. XXIV, part 1, pp. 361-62). Cf. also Lieut. Col. Fred. B. Brand, commanding, in report to Lieut. Gen. Pemberton, February 25, 1863 (*ibid.*, 362-63).

155. *Richmond Examiner*, July 1, 1863. Cf. also *Charleston Mercury*, August 11, 1863, condemning Davis for "thrusting away ability and character, and keeping dependants of favor like Mallory and Benjamin, and Northrop, and Myers about him."

*Alabama, Florida, Tacony,* which he did not make, furnish a daily and glorious evidence."[156]

This was clearly exaggerated and unfair, and it was not difficult to find a rebuttal. But many people in the South were in a mood to subscribe to such strictures. Nor was it the press only that manifested a critical tone. In the Confederate Congress nerves were frayed, and bitter observations were made against the Davis administration. It was charged that many government clerks were receiving salaries higher than that of General Robert E. Lee.[157] According to Senator Foote, Lucius B. Northrop, the Commissary-General of Subsistence, "had been a curse to the country. Though he had injured the country more than the enemy, he was retained in office. He was a pepper doctor from South Carolina, and he looks more like a vegetarian than any man he [Foote] ever saw. Northrop should be dragged from his position. Northrop would bring disgrace upon any government."[158]

One significant fact, however, emerges from a thorough study of the proceedings of this irritable Congress. Amid all the recriminations, there is not a single word of censure directed against the Navy Department or its Secretary. This is all the more remarkable when it is remembered that Foote, hitherto one of Mallory's chief critics, continued to be extremely vocal in his attacks against the Davis administration as a whole. The navy and its needs are occasionally, though not frequently, mentioned, but never is the navy blamed. While it would be unwarranted to make too much of the fact, it is reasonable to suppose, nevertheless, that the reason for this absence of complaints against Mallory was the general realization that the Navy Department was doing just about all that it could be expected to do.[159]

It is clear now that the turning point of the war came sometime in 1863. After the reverses at Gettysburg and at Vicksburg in midsummer, the Confederate armies never regained their former strength and morale. With the fall of Port Hudson on July 8, the last remaining Confederate stronghold on the Mississippi was gone. The year closed with the costly breakdown of the Confederate campaign in Tennessee. The heavy losses sustained by the Southern forces in the fighting at Chickamauga (September 19-20), Lookout Mountain, and Missionary Ridge (November 23-25) were far more

156. *Richmond Examiner,* July 1, 1863.

157. Proceedings of the Confederate Congress, 1st Congress, 4th Session, December 28, 1863 (Douglas Southall Freeman Transcripts, by special permission of Dr. Freeman).

158. *Ibid.,* December 9, 1863.

159. A considerable portion of the Southern press, however, continued to criticize adversely both the Navy Department and the Administration as a whole.

than the South could ever repair. The blockade was remorselessly tightening. Charleston, Wilmington, and Mobile were the only seaboard points of importance left in Confederate hands.

For the Navy Department the year had brought a keen disappointment with regard to its program for shipbuilding in foreign ports. Mallory, a few months after the close of the war, analyzed the reasons for the failure of Bulloch's earnest efforts. The plans of the Confederate government for obtaining fighting ships from Europe, he insisted, were well devised, but they met with determined opposition. The depredations of the *Alabama* and the *Florida,* both built by the Lairds at Birkenhead, had brought down upon the British government the "concentrated indignation of the United States."[160] In the face of the outcries of the American press, the heated charges against Britain voiced in the American Congress, and the remonstrances of Mr. Charles Francis Adams, John Bull, "though with evident reluctance," was compelled to choose between offending the United States or the Southern Confederacy. They were both capital customers, but he had to decide, and he did it in his characteristic way, which Mallory thus describes: "The portly old sea-dog jammed his hat down upon his head, thrust his hands into his pockets, expanded his chest, puffed out his cheeks, dilated his eyes, turned red in the face, and with well-simulated passion swore roundly at the 'so-called Confederate Government', and turned Mr. Mason out in the cold. Lord John Russell adroitly patted him [John Bull] on the back, and kept the dogged old fellow in this humor by telling him to go ahead and seize all rams and all other suspicious water animals, and that though the foreign enlistment act would not justify it, he would appeal to Parliament to make a law to suit the case."[161]

There was, however, thought Mallory, an interesting difference in the attitudes of England and France. "It is but fair to say . . . that while the results of the action of the British and French governments upon the subject were the same to the Confederacy, their conduct was widely and characteristically different. While John Bull put his foot squarely down and said to the 'so-called Confederate Government', 'Don't come here to get any more ships and kick up a row; damn me, I'll not stand for it!', France, the government of the emperor sans peur and sans reproche, fair and false to both sides, exhibited about as much good faith and sincerity as might be expected from any professional Jeremy Didler."[162]

160. Mallory, Diary, reprinted in *McClure's Magazine,* XVI (November, 1900-April, 1901) 106.

161. *Ibid.*                    162. *Ibid.,* 106-7.

# CHAPTER TWELVE

*1864*

Representative Barksdale, of the Joint Committee of the two Houses of Congress appointed to investigate the management of the Navy Department, submitted a report which was laid on the table and ordered to be printed. In the third year of the war, it was the official verdict on Mallory's administration. It concluded with these words: "Taking into consideration the poverty of our means and the formidable power and boundless resources of our enemy at the beginning of this war, our people have no sufficient cause for shame or discouragement in the operations of our Navy. What has been and is being done to resist the enemy on the waters of our rivers and on the sea, should inspire confidence, and excite strong hope that our Navy will yet prove an efficient and worthy ally of our noble armies in achieving our independence. It has already won the admiration and applause of neutral nations, for its gallant and glorious achievements; and, if we should succeed in getting into the service the war vessels completed and in progress of construction, the Committee believes that our naval triumphs will yet rival the brilliant and heroic achievements of our land forces."[1]

Dupré and Foote submitted a minority report far less favorable to Mallory's administration,[2] and vigorous adverse criticism of the Navy Department from other quarters had by no means ceased; but there were many who echoed the final verdict of the Investigating Committee.[3]

1. *Proceedings of the Confederate Congress,* 1st Cong., 4th Sess., February 17, 1864 (Freeman Transcripts).

2. *Journal of Congress* (House), VI, 848, 851 (February 17, 1864). For further complaints against the naval administration, cf. Roman, *Beauregard,* II, 417-18. The purchase of supplies in Europe by the Navy Department, claims this author, was begun too late; consequently the fruits of these delayed purchases were insignificant—"Most of the wholly insufficient supply of arms that was obtained came through the private enterprise of merchants shipping at their own risk, and were sold to the Government." It is also asserted by Roman that the Navy Department permitted the blockade to grow in strength, although, he believes, the cotton-purchase plan would have broken the iron ring if that plan had been tried early enough. (The arguments against the cotton-purchase plan have been noted, *supra,* pp. 145-46, 151-52.)

3. Cf. *De Bow's Review,* XXXIV, 1864, 102 ff. Cf. also the following typical later judg-

From Benjamin Hill—who, it must be remembered, was a close friend of Mallory's—came the ringing declaration that ". . . no portion of the government has been managed with more industry, under the disadvantages to which it has been subjected, than the naval."[4] It was pointed out by this supporter of the naval administration that much of the work and policy of that department had been, of necessity, kept secret from the public. The people, or, rather, "some persons," condemned because they did not know all the facts, and the Secretary had to submit in silence, because to defend would be to expose and damage the public service.

When the war began, Hill recalled, nothing was expected of the navy, in view of the admitted deficiency of Confederate resources. But, while the country had been resting satisfied that little could be done on the water, the navy had been at work, and suddenly the country was awakened, the world was awakened, by the "grandest naval achievement in all history." Like Minerva, full grown and full armed at her birth, the ironclad *Virginia* leaped into life, and in a day taught the world a lesson in naval warfare, the wonder of which mythology had never imagined nor centuries of science discovered. At once, hundreds of sea-monsters, long terrible on the waters, were shown to be worthless. Nautical science was conning her rules anew, and every nation was revising her designs for naval construction, now that the South had opened a new path.

The necessities which had required the destruction of such vessels as the *Virginia* and *Mississippi* were great misfortunes to the South; but the misfortunes were great in precise proportion as the works were powerful. If the *Virginia* and the *Mississippi* had not been constructed, the South would not have known how immense was their loss. Those who produced these ships could not have been dull or idle. Regrets for losses that had been caused by the necessities of the condition of the South as a naval power could not justify Southerners in blaming those who had done so much to improve that condition. The magnitude of the losses was realized only by reason of the splendor of the successes. Impartial history would do justice to the Confederate Navy Department—"while in this respect of

ments. H. J. Eckenrode, *Jefferson Davis, President of the South* (New York, 1923), 126, says: "The Confederate navy was the creation of genius." Also, from the same author: "The South showed wonderful resourcefulness on the water, and some of the credit certainly attaches to Mallory. . . . The Southerners launched the first workable submarine and blew up the first ship sunk by a torpedo. In fact, they made the torpedo an instrument of marine warfare. This is a very creditable list of achievements" (*ibid.*, 349-50).

4. Speech of Benjamin Hill before the Georgia Assembly, December 11, 1862, quoted by Benjamin Hill, Jr., in *Senator Benjamin H. Hill, of Georgia, His Life. Writings, and Speeches* (Atlanta, 1891), 257.

naval warfare we have not done what all desired, yet all candid minds must confess we have done far more than any in the beginning antici-pated."[5]

More reserved was the opinion of a Confederate naval officer in 1864 in regard to the accomplishments and future possibilities of the navy. Lieuten-ant Minor confided to his friend Commander Catesby ap R. Jones that it was difficult to see how a sufficiency of officers could be secured for the new ironclads. He hinted at a drop in morale in the service. Officers, he said, did not seem to be interested in promotion. Everybody appeared to be looking forward to an early peace for the creation of a navy, forgetting that war was the time to build up for the service a love which would make the navy popular in peacetime. He was beginning to fear that the oppor-tunity for creating a powerful naval force had passed. He regretted the fact, for, as he declared, "we have the elements of a splendid navy in the Confederacy, and it only requires zeal, pluck and dash to bring it to the surface."[6]

To the same Catesby ap R. Jones, Admiral Buchanan described the de-ficiencies in naval personnel at Mobile: "No captain has yet been ordered to the *Tennessee*, and I have but two young, inexperienced lieutenants; no midshipmen, and but two green master's mates; Phillips, the doctor; a young, inexperienced paymaster; an inexperienced master, appointed from civil life for the war."[7]

It is clear that the navy was not receiving the replacements which it urgently required and that, in its efforts to recruit, it was getting very little cooperation from the army. The situation was aggravated for the navy by the conscript law of February 17, 1864, which placed in the army all white male residents of the Confederate States between the ages of seventeen and fifty. The "transfer" law of May 1, 1863, was, says Scharf, "in practice . . . almost entirely disregarded."[8] If it was true, as charged, that Mallory had not placed enough gunboats on the James in the early part of 1864,[9] the above facts might be adduced as a partial excuse.

5. *Ibid.*, 257-58.

6. Lieut. R. D. Minor to Comm. Catesby ap R. Jones, from Richmond (unofficial), March 23, 1864 (*O.R.*, Ser. I, Vol. IX, p. 807).

7. Rear Admiral Franklin Buchanan to Commander Catesby ap R. Jones, from Mobile, Janu-ary 30, 1864 (*ibid.*, Vol. XXI, p. 871-72). In the same sense, Buchanan to Jones, from Mobile, May 7, 1864 (*ibid.*, 896-97).

8. *History of the Confederate States Navy*, 40.

9. Maj. Gen. Geo. E. Pickett, to Sec'y. Seddon, from Petersburg, January 25, 1864 (*O.R.A.*, Ser. I, Vol. XXXIII, p. 1122). The last sentence in this letter indicates the high value of naval cooperation with land forces: "If the two gunboats were below the obstructions, as promised by the Secretary of the Navy, it would be worth 5,000 men to us."

On the record, the Navy and the Navy Department, in the early spring of 1864, were by no means lacking in vigor and in achievement. Mallory was requesting funds for the building in Europe of six or eight more large steamers for blockade running. Memminger's response was not encouraging, although he expressed his willingness to do his best in the matter.[10] An unexpected and very welcome gift to the Navy Department came in the form of $30,000 from the ladies of Charleston, for the building of a gunboat to be called the "Ladies' Gunboat."[11] The army was persuaded to transfer 1,200 of its men to the sister branch of the service, "in order to man efficiently . . . the vessels of the Navy."[12] Naval officers proceeded to the headquarters of each army corps for the purpose of selecting the men so to be transferred.[13]

The accomplishments of the ordnance department alone merit praise not as yet sufficiently accorded. It has been said that this department's development of banded and rifled guns was the most important improvement made in Confederate ordnance during the war.[14] The Secretary of the Navy went further: "The reports of the enemy's naval officers commanding ironclad ships concur with the results of our own experiments in showing that the heavy naval rifles are the most effective ordnance yet used against these vessels."[15]

The meticulous care displayed by the ordnance directors in manufacturing guns and powder, and the constant experimentation that was carried on to improve the results, is indicated in the exchanges between the foundries and powder works and the commanders of vessels.

10. Memminger to Mallory, March 22, 1864 (Thian Collection, Part IV, pp. 608-9; Duke University).

11. Mallory to Memminger, April 16, 1864 (Treasury Department Records, National Archives).

12. S. Cooper (Adjutant and Inspector General, acting for Secretary of War) to Gen. R. E. Lee, from Richmond, March 22, 1864 (O.R., Ser. I, Vol. IX, p. 805).

13. Ibid.

14. Parker, Recollections of a Naval Officer, 207. For a brief but very valuable history of the founding and activities of the Ordnance Department, cf. Josiah Gorgas, "Extracts from my notes written chiefly after the close of the war," reprinted in Claude E. Fuller and Richard D. Steuart, Firearms of the Confederacy: The Shoulder Arms, Pistols and Revolvers of the Confederate Soldier, Including the Regular United States Models, the Imported Arms and Those Manufactured within the Confederacy (Huntington, W. Va., 1944), 112-31. The editor of Army Ordnance, reprinting Gorgas' "Extracts" in that periodical's issue of January-February, 1936, comments: "It is doubtful whether there is a more valuable ordnance paper in existence (112). He feels that ". . . the object lesson it teaches contains great current significance. . . ." (ibid.). Cf. also Journal of Confederate Congress, I, 753-4, February 4, 1862: Senator Conrad moved that Congress proceed to the consideration of a bill passed by the Congress and returned with the President's veto; the purpose of said bill was to "encourage the manufacture of gunpowder, saltpeter, and small arms within the Confederate States."

15. Mallory to President Davis, July 1, 1864 (O.R.A., Ser. IV, Vol. III, p. 521).

Lieutenant D. P. McCorkle, at the Atlanta naval ordnance works, gave a lecture to Commander Jones of the Selma foundry, concerning the difficulties involved in tailoring big guns to fit ironclads. The size of gun requested by the commander of the *Nashville,* said McCorkle, would be unsuitable for that vessel, for, "the angle of shield [of the ship] being 29 degrees, and the woodwork being 4 feet 11 inches, . . . the gun would not clear the port." In addition to the woodwork, continued McCorkle, the vessel was sheathed with six inches of iron. It would not avail to lengthen the gun five inches, as had been suggested, for "there are two bow guns of the *Nashville,* each shifting into two ports, one port for each, right astern, and one right abeam; in fighting both sides, there is not room for the two chassis, if the gun should be made longer." McCorkle favored cutting away the woodwork instead of lengthening the gun.[16]

After supplying the guns, the ordnance experts kept careful watch over their performance. "Will you please request General Maury," wrote Commander Jones at the Selma works to Admiral Buchanan, "to have a record kept of the number of times that the VII-inch has been fired, with the charge and elevation?" Jones strongly counseled that the gun not be fired at great elevations, except when absolutely necessary, as such handling would strain the weapon very much.[17]

Repeated experiments were made to improve the effectiveness of ordnance products. The superintendent of the naval powder works at Columbia, South Carolina, informed Commander Jones that there was no doubt the coarser grained powder had formerly been prepared too hard. There had been a change made in this respect since the preceding November, and, a few days since, there had been forwarded to Admiral Buchanan samples of a powder of a different size, made under a pressure of 150 tons, and also samples of some made under pressure of 90 tons. The pressure originally

16. Lieut. D. P. McCorkle, from naval ordnance works, Atlanta, to Commander C. ap R. Jones, January 25, 1864 (*O.R.,* Ser. I, Vol. XXI, pp. 869-70).

17. Jones to Buchanan, from Selma, March 1, 1864 (*ibid.,* 879-80). A typical despatch of the Ordnance Bureau to a naval commander: "Your letters of the 28th ultimo and 1st instant have been received. Every pound of powder that could be procured has been sent to Norfolk for the *Virginia.* This office expects, however, to get enough in a few days to send you 50 rounds for each of your rifled guns, and also the quantity you require for the VIII and X inch guns. The cylinders for the rifled guns went to the *Patrick Henry* by mistake. As they are now there, it would be better to retain them and fill them on board. But if that plan is not practicable, and there is no place on shore convenient for the purpose, you can send them back to Richmond. The powder and filled cylinders will be probably sent to you this week" (Geo. Minor, commander in charge of Ordnance Bureau, to Commander John R. Tucker, commanding *Patrick Henry,* March 4, 1862 (*ibid.,* Vol. VI, p. 780).

used was 250 tons. Buchanan, on completing his tests of this new powder, would inform Jones of the results.[18]

Jones himself sent to a naval commander a succinct report of experiments with powder: "In proving a rifled and banded VII-inch with 16 pounds of powder and 111 pounds ratchet sabot service bolt, I found more of the powder was unconsumed and the recoil less than with the unbanded smoothbore with 14 pounds and 120-pound bolt, the powder being Nos. 8 and 9, penetration 30 feet."[19]

The ordnance department operated under unusual difficulties. "The metal with which we are furnished for guns," complained the head of the Selma works, "differs so much that the test gun is no guide to us. We have just commenced to cast again, but the iron differs from any that we have had before. We therefore cannot tell how it will turn out. . . ."[20] Again the same official reported: "I had intended to have sent to you [Admiral Buchanan] two VII-inch guns by the boat today, but she refused to take them, alleging that it would be dangerous. If possible, please have orders given to the boats to take the guns whenever we are ready to ship them."[21]

In the winter of 1864 Lieutenant McCorkle was obliged, because of "the imminent approach of the enemy's forces," to pick up all the machinery of his Atlanta factory and transfer it to Augusta.[22] At almost any moment the workmen in the ordnance foundries were subject to call to military duty, with consequent serious interruption of ordnance production.[23] Not infrequently whole factories were destroyed by the enemy.[24]

The report of the chief of the Nitre and Mining Bureau exhibits the obstacles faced by the Confederate services of supply, as well as the dogged

18. P. Baudery Garesché, Superintendent, naval powder works, Columbia, S. C., to Jones, at Selma, February 9, 1864 (*ibid.*, Vol. XXI, p. 876).

19. Jones to Lieut. J. R. Eggleston, C.S.N., at Mobile, from Selma, February 11, 1864 (*ibid.*, 877).

20. Jones to Buchanan, April 12, 1864 (*ibid.*, 892).

21. February 16, 1864 (*ibid.*, 878).

22. John M. Brooke (Commander in charge of Office of Ordnance and Hydrography) to Mallory, November 4, 1864, in *Report of the Secretary of the Navy, 1864,* 43-44 (Rare Books Division, Library of Congress).

23. *Ibid.*, 44-45. Cf. also Message of the President communicating, *Report of the Secretary of the Navy,* February 7, 1865 (Rare Books Division, Library of Congress): "The force of mechanics required by this Department will depend much upon the movements of the enemy. If our works shall be exempt from interruption, a much larger force than estimated for can be very usefully employed. All our white mechanics and workmen are under military organization, armed and equipped for service, and are frequently called into active service."

24. H. Ashton Ramsay, chief engineer, in charge of Charlotte ordnance works, to Commander John M. Brooke, chief of Bureau of Ordnance and Hydrography, May 5, 1864 (*O.R.A.,* Ser. IV, Vol. III, pp. 521-22, enclosed in letter of Mallory to President Davis, July 1, 1864 [*ibid.*, 520-23]).

determination with which these obstacles were met: "It will be noted that the Virginia furnaces have been worked with all the interruptions of war, —from the actual presence of the enemy to the impressment of supplies by our own forces. In Alabama the government furnaces have been worked in an abundant country, and almost with peace regularity.

"From enclosed tabulated statement 'A,' concerning the furnaces named Lucy Salina and California: 'These furnaces were worked conjointly, and with many interruptions, the [working] force being driven off during Hunter's raid. Serious difficulties were also experienced from seizure of furnace supplies by the [presumably Confederate] cavalry.' Concerning the furnace named Westham in Virginia: 'Worked as a military necessity. Iron particularly adapted to manufacture of rifle shell. Ore and limestone brought 180 miles by canal to the furnace.'

"From tabulated statement 'B':
'Names of Proprietors of Furnaces Operated in 1864:

| *Contractors:* | *Remarks:* |
| --- | --- |
| D. and H. Forrer, Shenandoah Iron Works, Virginia | Interrupted by enrolling officer; |
| Lewis, Crawford & Co., Mount Vernon Furnace, Virginia | Destroyed by enemy; |
| D. and H. Forrer, Elizabeth [works], Va | Destroyed by enemy, but rebuilt; |
| J. D. & A. Brooks, Mount Tory [works], Va | Destroyed by enemy, but rebuilt; |
| Scott & Welford, Catherine [works], Va | Destroyed by enemy, but rebuilt; |
| J. R. Anderson & Co., Columbia, Va | Destroyed by enemy, but rebuilt; |
| " Grace, Va | Destroyed by enemy, but rebuilt; |
| " Cloverdale, Va | Destroyed by enemy, but rebuilt; |
| " Catawba, Va | Destroyed by enemy, but rebuilt; |
| Victoria Mining & Mfgring Co., Victoria, Va | Destroyed by enemy, but rebuilt.' "[25] |

25. Report of Chief of Nitre and Mining Bureau (Col. I. M. St. John) to Hon. Jas. A. Seddon, Secretary of War, January 31, 1865 (Rare Books Division, Library of Congress).

Outweighing all other difficulties, perhaps, was the ever prevailing short-age of workmen. At the Charlotte factory, where much of the heavy forg-ing for the war vessels was done, many of the most important tools were idle a large part of the time for want of mechanics to operate them. Vitally needed ships and railroad locomotives could not be built or repaired until more men were sent to Charlotte. The following replacements were needed before this factory could begin to function at even a minimum basis of productivity: seven machinists, eight blacksmiths, eight gun-carriage ma-kers, two blockmakers, one pattern maker, one coppersmith, and two molders.[26]

In May, 1864, Lieutenant McCorkle, in charge of the works at Atlanta, had three molders, four machinists, and one blacksmith. He required, for ordinary work, nine molders, five blacksmiths, and eleven machinists. For the past four months he had been unable to forge the wrought-iron bolts for the Brooke gun. Wrought-iron bolts, he warned, would be an important item in the defense of Mobile. Nearly all his lathes were idle for want of hands. Army officers who were unwilling to loan workmen to ordnance works did not seem to be aware that each rifle shell had to be turned in a lathe. McCorkle put his grievances bluntly: "I have asked for details [from the Army] until I am tired; and even those conscripts who are unwillingly detailed to the works are accompanied by so many orders and so many papers (the orders are changed once a week) that a clerk is constantly em-ployed to try and keep their papers correct. It would appear that officers employed in manufacturing ordnance are not deemed patriotic by the Con-script Bureau, as they seem to think that an officer who asks for a detail of a man to do Government work is doing something wrong. They require so many descriptive lists of him, so many certificates, that it is absolutely appalling. I think with the additional number of mechanics mentioned above, detailed for [the duration of] the war, I could prepare six times (or more) as much ammunition and ordnance stores as I do now."[27]

Jones at Selma insisted that he could, if supplied with a reasonable num-ber of mechanics, roll all the iron that was needed by the navy and produce a gun a day. But lack of help had kept his rolling mill completely idle.[28]

26. H. Ashton Ramsay, chief engineer, in charge of Charlotte ordnance works, to Com-mander John M. Brooke, chief, Bureau of Ordnance and Hydrography, May 5, 1864 (*O.R.A.*, Ser. IV, Vol. III, pp. 521-22, enclosed in letter of Mallory to President Davis, July 1, 1864 [*ibid.*, 520-23]).

27. McCorkle to Capt. J. M. Brooke, May 7, 1864 (*ibid.*, 522).

28. Mallory to President Davis, July 1, 1864 (*O.R.A.*, Ser. IV, Vol. III, p. 523) The Secre-tary of the Navy, in his *Report* for 1864, asked that mechanics be enlisted into the navy instead

Shortly before, the same official had taken a small dig at the Secretary of the Navy: "Without more blacksmiths we cannot finish the guns faster. . . . I find it useless to represent these things at Richmond. It produces no effect."[29]

Added to all these embarrassments for the Ordnance Bureau, there were, not infrequently, workmen's strikes. In mid-July, 1864, the operations of Buchanan's squadron were seriously incommoded when all his mechanics refused to work because of an order which added an hour to their daily stint.[30] The resourceful Lieutenant McCorkle, when faced by a similar crisis at Selma, proposed a rather drastic remedy: "My men have all struck for $10 a day, because Governor Brown, the miserable devil, has given that price to the men in State road shops. My plan is to have all the men enlisted (or rather shipped) in the Navy, furnish them with provisions and clothing at cost. As soon as a conscript comes into the naval works let him be transferred instead of detailed (shipped or conscripted for the war), and let them be drilled for the defense of the place. . . . If they misbehave, send them on board ship."[31]

General Josiah Gorgas, in the spring of 1864, summarized, with pardonable pride, the work done by the Ordnance Bureau.[32] Since he had taken charge of the department three years before, he had "succeeded beyond [his] utmost expectations."[33] Although it had once been the worst supplied of

---

of merely detailed from the army to the various naval works (*Report of the Secretary of the Navy, 1864*, 7-8).

29. Jones to Buchanan, May 9, 1864 (*O.R.,* Ser. I, Vol. XXI, p. 897). The Navy Department's task in securing more mechanics was not lightened by an order of the War Department, issued in mid-April 1864, which deprived of "deferred status" (relative to army draft) those workers engaged in navy projects (Circular No. 16, War Department, Bureau of Conscription, April 15, 1864 [*O.R.A.,* Ser. IV, Vol. III, p. 305.]).

30. Buchanan to Jones, from Mobile, July 13, 1864 (*O.R.,* Ser. I, Vol. XXI, p. 906).

31. McCorkle to Commander Jones, from Selma, January 25, 1864 (*ibid.,* 870). The following is an example of the method used (not with complete success) by the navy in an effort to man its vital manufacturing plants: Commander A. B. Fairfax, C.S.N. to Secretary Seddon, from Selma, February 19, 1863: "The services of the following named persons, to be detailed from the Army, are required on the part of the Navy Department in the establishment purchased by the Government of Colin[?] I. McRae." There follow the names of H. W. Lee, clerk of the paymaster of the Montgomery Blues, of the 3rd Alabama regiment, then stationed at Drewry's Bluff, and Harry Herbert, private, of Anderson's Division, a stone mason. "If it can be granted, I desire, also, authority to apply directly to Commandants of Military Districts, for the detail of such men as are required for work under my command from time to time" (National Archives, Washington, D. C.).

32. Cf. the rather unfair estimate of Gorgas presented by J. B. Jones: "Information from the Western army indicates that only about one shell in twenty, furnished by Col. Gorgas, will explode. This reminds me of the doubts expressed by Gen. Cobb of the fitness of Col. G. for his position" (*Rebel War Clerk's Diary,* II, 92).

33. Journal of Gen. Gorgas, 133, quoted in Charles H. Wesley, *The Collapse of the Confederacy* (Washington, D. C., 1922), 389.

the bureaus of the War Department, it was in this regard now the best. Large arsenals had been organized at Richmond, Fayetteville, Augusta, Columbus, Macon, Atlanta, and other points, and smaller ones at Danville, Lynchburg, and Montgomery, besides other establishments elsewhere. A "superb" powder mill had been built at Augusta. Lead smelting works had been set up at Petersburg and turned over to the Nitre and Mining Bureau. There was a cannon foundry at Macon for heavy guns, and there were bronze factories at Macon, Columbus, and Augusta; a foundry for shot and shell at Salisbury, North Carolina; a large shop for leather work at Clarksville, Virginia; a manufactory of carbines; a rifle factory at Asheville, transferred to Columbia, South Carolina; a new and very large armory at Macon, including a pistol factory; and another pistol factory at Columbus, Georgia.[34]

In the light of the foregoing, the tribute paid by the artillery expert of the Confederacy is not unexpected: "No department of our government deserves more credit than our Ordnance Bureau in Richmond under Josiah Gorgas, for its success in supplying the enormous amount of ordnance material consumed during the war. Although always economical of ammunition, yet we never lost any action from the lack of it."[35]

Schwab is rather deprecatory of the accomplishments of the Ordnance Bureau in producing small arms. He doubts the statement of the Chief of Ordnance that more than 14,000 of this class of weapon had been manufactured, and that the public armories could turn out over 2,000, and the private armories over 1,500, per month. He thinks it fair to assume that small arms were not manufactured at that rate, and that most of the establishments were given up, or were destroyed by the advancing Federal troops. Only one factory, he believes, was manufacturing these arms as

34. *Ibid.* Cf. also the testimony of Schwab, *op. cit.,* 269-70: "Heavy ordnance was more extensively manufactured in the South [than were small arms]. Foundries and similar ironworks at least attempted to turn out cannon, and those in Augusta and Columbus were still in operation in 1863. We hear of plans to establish smelting works, and of some rolling mills; but fuel and ore were too scarce to come into general use, though iron mines in South Carolina and coal mines in Alabama and North Carolina are mentioned."

35. Edward P. Alexander, *Military Memoirs of a Confederate: A Critical Narrative* (New York, Scribner's 1907), 54. Cf. also the following example of Confederate ingenuity in ordnance manufacture: "Thomas Dwyer, who came to Charlotte [navy yard] with the navy yard men, invented a machine for turning a perfect sphere, a cannon ball or shell. It was the first successful invention of its kind and was used in the Charlotte navy yard. This valuable invention was confiscated by the United States government and put into use in the United States navy yards, no credit or remuneration ever being given to the Southern inventor" (Violet G. Alexander, "The Confederate States Navy Yard at Charlotte, N. C., 1862-1865," *Charlotte News,* June 5, 1910. This article includes a history of the navy yard related by its first head, H. Ashton Ramsay).

late as the spring of 1863.[36] The same author's claim that there were few gunpowder plants in operation after 1863,[37] has been challenged by other investigators.[38]

Another achievement of Mallory's Department was the ropewalk at Petersburg, erected to manufacture cordage for the use of the Navy. The production from this works proved adequate not only for its primary purpose, but also for meeting large requisitions from various branches of the army, from coal mines, and from railroad and canal companies. Established as a fresh venture soon after the outbreak of war, by the end of 1864 it had paid off all expenses and even yielded a considerable net profit. Experiments in the manufacture of cotton rope as a substitute for hemp cordage were carried through with great success. The amount of rope made from April 1, 1863, to September 30, 1864, was 163,665 pounds. Of this the army took 50,212 pounds, the navy 84,259 pounds, while 21,898 pounds were delivered to other parties. Late in 1864, as the Federal forces closed in on Petersburg, the walk was moved farther south.[39]

So, as 1864 wore on, the Confederate navy was not without its achievements. A minor but welcome success was won in mid-April when the Confederate ironclad ram *Albemarle,* supported by a land force, retook Plymouth, North Carolina.[40] By early May the Federal Red River expedition under Nathaniel Banks had been pushed back to New Orleans. The James River squadron was forcing the Federal ironclads to stay in that river for the purpose of protecting Grant's communications. It was the James River squadron, therefore, that was keeping the ironclads away from other Southern ports. A Federal squadron of far superior numbers refused a challenge to battle from three Confederate ironclad rams and a Davidson torpedo boat.[41] In early May the Federal gunboat *Commodore Jones* was

36. Schwab, *Confederate States of America,* 269. Schwab cites the following in confirmation of his statement: *Charleston Courier,* June 18, 1861, January 18, 1862; *Charleston Mercury,* March 3, 1862; *Petersburg Express,* April 14, 1862; *Richmond Examiner,* May 13, 1863.

37. Schwab, *op. cit.,* 271.

38. Wesley, *op. cit.,* 388-89. Wesley says of Schwab's claim: "The above table [in Wesley, *op. cit.,* 388] and the subsequent statement by General Gorgas [quoted in *ibid.,* 389, from Gorgas' Journal, 133] definitely refutes this statement."

39. S. S. Lee (Captain in charge of Office of Orders and Detail) to Mallory, October 21, 1864, in *Report of the Secretary of the Navy, 1864.* Concerning the removal of the ropewalk, see House of Representatives [Bill] No. 277, December 13, 1864 (Rare Books Division, Library of Congress. Mallory asked for an appropriation of $75,000 for this purpose ("Estimate for the removal and erection of the Naval Rope-Walk," Rare Books Division, Library of Congress).

40. The later loss of the *Albemarle* might have been averted, hints Emma Maffit (no advocate of Mallory's) if Mallory's orders that she should attack had not been blocked by the army (Emma Maffitt, *op. cit.,* 338-39).

41. Scharf, *op. cit.,* 733-35.

blown up in the James by an electric torpedo, with a loss of 75 out of a crew of 120.[42]

The navy was apparently cooperating smoothly with the land forces in the James River area. Close contact was being maintained between Navy Department headquarters and the army commanders,[43] and naval units in the river were lending effective aid in blocking crossings of enemy troops.[44] Below Bishop's [Landing?] an ironclad and a gunboat were protecting General Pickett's left.[45] Movements of enemy land forces near Fort Harrison were being harassed by naval gunfire.[46]

The services of the navy extended to the provision of emergency supplies for the army. Pressed by General R. E. Lee, Mallory promised to build some badly needed railroad cars for the former at navy-engaged plants.[47] A shortage in the army's food stocks was remedied by the transfer to the War Department of 1,500 barrels of salt pork and beef from navy stores.[48]

A temporary break in this rapport between the two services occurred in late May, when the engineer bureau objected to opening a path in the river obstructions in order to let the *Richmond* pass through.[49]    The disagreement was ultimately solved, but Mallory charged that the delay in facilitating the *Richmond's* movements prevented the vessel from striking a crippling blow at the enemy.[50]

The great key points, Charleston, Wilmington, Savannah, and Mobile,

42. *Ibid.*, 731-32.
43. Cf. the following exchanges. Mallory to Maj. George H. Terrett at Drewry's Bluff, May 9, 1864 (*O.R.A.*, Ser. I, Vol. XXXVI, part 2, p. 977): "How is the condition of affairs? Is the enemy in sight?"  G. H. Terrett to Mallory, May 9, 1864, *ibid.*: "Orders just received from General Barton to get in readiness to meet the enemy immediately. It is reported that the enemy are within 2 miles of the trenches, and advancing slowly and in force." Same to same, May 9, 1864, *ibid.*: "There has been quite a heavy fight in the direction of Port Walthall. My command is in position in the trenches [at Drewry's Bluff] and everything is in readiness. I will keep you informed of the occurrence of anything important."
44. Gen. R. E. Lee to Seddon, from headquarters, Army of Northern Virginia, September 26, 1864 (*O.R.A.*, Ser. I, Vol. XLII, part 2, p. 1290).
45. J. K. Mitchell (flag officer, commanding James River squadron) September 30, 1864 (*ibid.*, 1290-91).
46. *Ibid.*, 1290.
47. Gen. R. E. Lee to Secretary Seddon, April 19, 1864 (*ibid.*, Vol. XXXIII, p. 1294).
48. President Davis to Gen. R. E. Lee, December 15, 1864 (*ibid.*, Vol. LI, part 2, supplement, p. 1054).
49. Mallory to Secretary Seddon, May 24, 1864 (*ibid.*, Vol. XXXVI, part 3, pp. 829-30).
50. *Ibid.*, 830. There was another example of a clash between departments of the Confederate service when the Confederate diplomatic representative at Havana balked Mallory's [?] plan to capture the *Roanoke*. See Charles J. Helm to Hon. J. P. Benjamin, from Havana, August 17, 1864, dispatch no. 30 (Pickett Papers, Vol. K, no. 48). Cf. also same to same, October 20, 1864, dispatch no. 32, recounting strange details of the capture of the *Roanoke* (*ibid.*).

were still holding out, largely and perhaps mainly because of the navy's efficient torpedo service and the shore batteries manned partly by naval personnel. Farragut himself later in the year testified to the strength of the Confederate naval defenses at Wilmington. He could employ successfully, he explained, only his lighter vessels within either of the harbors at Wilmington, and nearly all of these vessels were badly in need of repairs.[51] "And," he warned the Federal Navy Department, "if the [Confederate] ironclad the [Federal Naval] Department speaks of as being 'in the river in commission' at Wilmington, is half as formidable as the *Tennessee,* she ought to destroy as many of the light gunboats as would float on its surface. The main dependence therefore will be upon light-draft monitors. . . ."[52]

The Confederate naval positions at Wilmington were so well established, admitted Secretary Welles to Farragut, that the harbor and city could be taken only with the aid of the army: "The Department, like yourself, appreciates the great difficulties that present themselves against a purely naval operation against Wilmington, and it is only in cooperation with the army that the movement is [to be] made. Could the capture of the place or the closing of the port have been effected by a purely naval attack, the work would long since have been effected. But as at Mobile, and more essential than there, we have been compelled to wait the movements of the military."[53]

Farragut elaborated further on what was to him the distressing ability of the Confederate Navy to defend Wilmington against any exclusively naval attack that might be mounted. He regarded as highly imprudent any naval movement against the harbor without the cooperation of the army.[54] In view of this testimony, it would seem that the Confederate Navy was not doing a poor job at Wilmington. The situation at Mobile was, from the Confederate standpoint, more dubious.

It is not surprising that a more sanguine view of Confederate prospects for ultimate victory was entertained at this time by some European observers. Lord Russell was quoted as declaring that the North could not overcome the South, and that the Northern people were becoming aware of that fact.

51. Farragut to Secretary Welles, confidential report from flagship *Hartford,* Mobile Bay, September 22, 1864 (*O.R.,* Ser. I, Vol. XXI, pp. 655-56). Farragut reported again from Mobile Bay on October 19: "Nearly every vessel in the fleet will have to undergo most extensive repairs within the next three or four months; in truth, not half of them are fit to keep the sea now" (*ibid.,* 692). This suggests that previous Federal victories had not been without cost.

52. Farragut to Welles, September 22, 1864 (*ibid.,* 656).

53. Welles to Farragut, October 1, 1864 (*ibid.,* 669).

54. Farragut to Welles, from flagship *Hartford,* Mobile Bay, October 18. 1864 (*ibid.,* 690-92).

Disraeli, it was said, was meditating a parliamentary resolution favorable to the South if General Lee should be successful in his defense of Richmond.[55]

The year's first important setbacks for the Confederate Navy occurred in February and May, with the failure of two successive attempts to recapture New Bern, North Carolina. On the second of these tries, the C. S. S. *Albemarle* attacked a whole Federal squadron in Roanoke River, but the gallant effort did not affect the final result. The omens were not good, but the navy was still doggedly fighting and hoping. On the day of the second rebuff at New Bern, the Government commissioned a new commerce-raiding cruiser, the famous *Georgia*.

The feelings of some of the "official ladies" with regard to the war at this time were revealed in a letter written from Richmond by Angela Mallory to her bosom friend Mrs. Clement Claiborne Clay, whose husband had recently been dispatched on a secret mission to Canada.[56] Angela sympathized with her friend's sense of bereavement: "I know what the feeling is, to be left alone, for no matter whom I have with me, I feel all alone if my husband is absent. Oh! the tears that I have shed at being left! I am certain had they been collected they would float the whole Confederate Navy."[57]

Mrs. Clay must seek her consolation in frequent prayer to God that He might give her the faith to believe that her separation from her husband was for the good of their bleeding country. "I have the most implicit faith in prayer, and when we meet again . . . I will tell you my experience, and I know you will think that I have good reasons for my faith." If Clay should succeed in his mission, "and by so doing will be the means of bringing about an honorable peace," would not his wife feel that she was the most fortunate woman in the Confederacy? Mrs. Clay must visit the Mallorys soon again, and Angela would try to cheer her, or at least distract her thoughts from the sad subject by telling her of the Mallory troubles and tribulations.[58]

55. James Mason to Secretary Benjamin, from London, June 9, 1864, dispatch no 9, quoted in Virginia Mason, *The Public Life and Diplomatic Correspondence of James M. Mason* (Roanoke, 1903), 500-1.

56. It was hoped by the Confederate authorities that Clay might be able to secure from the Canadian government both diplomatic support and financial aid. He was to attempt also a closer *rapprochement* with the "Northern Democrats." For details of the purpose and ultimate failure of this mission, cf. John W. Headley, *Confederate Operations in Canada and New York* (New York, 1906), 211-31; George C. Gorham, *Life and Public Services of Edwin M. Stanton* (2 vols.; Boston, 1899), II, 143-56.

57. Angela to Mrs. Clay, from Richmond, May 6, 1864 (Clay Papers, Duke University).
58. *Ibid.*

The war, of course, was filling everybody's life at Richmond. On the preceding night Angela had been greatly disturbed by the information reported to her husband that several Yankee gunboats and numerous transports were coming up the river and were within fifteen miles of Drewry's Bluff. Mallory had at once gone off to look after his boats and men, and had not returned home until very late. By that time Angela was so sleepy that she could not ask him a question, and had learned nothing about the details of the scare until the next morning.

She had gone recently with Mrs. Yulee to visit City Point. They had a fairly pleasant day, but the sight of the "poor sick men" (Federals) who were exchanged made her feel so bad, and she was so saddened by the thought that "people who a short time since were as one should now be willing to destroy each other," that she rather regretted having gone.

She felt very uneasy over the determination displayed by the Yankees in their drive to reach Richmond—"not that I believe they will, but I suppose I will have to go away; I dread it so much that I think of it all the time."

Poor Mrs. Davis! Her bereavement—she had just lost her son, killed in a fall from a porch—had been very great. She used to call him her black-eyed boy, and seemed to love him more than her other children. "He was a beautiful boy, and his parents' loss has been his gain, for he is now where the rumors of Wars never enter. Oh, if I could only be there, too, with all those who are dear to me!"

Strangely enough, they were still holding tea parties in Richmond. Angela had lately attended one, but had been forced to decline an invitation to another. "From all I hear about it, we did not miss much, as her [the hostess'] company did not all come until after ten o'clock, and her Tea was kept waiting for those who were absent until they came. I would not be surprised if some of the company wished they had peanuts and suet when they went home."

In conclusion, Angela urged her friend to come soon, "and then we will console each other and if we can get nothing else to eat we can always find peanuts and suet." She also had plenty of ham, "so we can't starve for some time." Mrs. Clay should not trouble herself about sending boots for Ruby, for whom a pair was being made in Richmond.[59]

Whatever the efforts of the South to think hopefully, events were slowly gathering toward a crisis. In early May came the bloody Battle of the Wild-

59. *Ibid.*

erness (May 5 to 7), and, from May 8 to May 18, the fight at Spottsylvania Court House. As June opened, Lee's army repulsed a vicious Federal attack at Cold Harbor (June 1 to 3). Grant shifted his immediate objective from Richmond to Petersburg, and, on June 14, began his crossing to the south side of the James. Meanwhile, May 5 to May 9, Sherman had begun his march to Atlanta, and on May 9 opened the Kennesaw Mountain period of that campaign. The two Union armies were closing in carefully and deliberately on their adversary. The siege of Petersburg, which was to last until April 2, 1865, began on June 12.

There was certainly no tone of depression in Mallory's private letters at this period. He wrote to Mrs. Clay at the beginning of June to inform her that he was sending by a trusted emissary the goods she had ordered from Nassau. He listed the precious articles that had been successfully transported through the blockade: "One lady's umbrella, 1 doz. Gents' Hkfs. [handkerchiefs], 2 prr. gaiterboots. . . ." He was happy to report that her bale of cotton, for European sale, was safely on its way. He would, as soon as possible, send her an account of its proceeds, which would constitute her foreign bank to be drawn upon at pleasure through him.[60]

"We all miss you, my whole household," he assured her, "as I think everybody must do whenever you leave them; and all send their love to you except myself, who hate you cordially. Angela is not well, and I still keep her on hand, but ready to move. Please present my kindest regards to your Sunbeam of a sister, whom Heaven, in pity, has bestowed upon one man only to prevent her from being the death of men."[61]

Another letter to the same correspondent was a mixture of affectionate playfulness, family news, and some rather encouraging comments on politics. "Why don't you come?" he complained. "Don't you know that I have lots of good things to say to you and to make for you? And that clever and lovable women, who can inspire happiness by permitting others to contribute to their pleasures, have no right to close their eyes upon their duty and their friends at once? In spite of Col. Clay's ipse dixit that you would not come, Angela and I have been daily believing that you would; and now that Sherman's barbarians are in unpleasant proximity to Macon, why not come to the front, where security, sympathy, mint juleps and brandy

60. Mrs. Clay's cotton did not reach Europe, but was captured en route. The Secretary forwarded to her the report of the misfortune, with the following note: "Inclosed you will see the fate of your first attempt at consignments of cotton. This will justify another turn of hatred's screw upon the Yankeys" Mallory to Mrs. Clay, November 13, 1864 [Clay Papers, Duke University].

61. Mallory to Mrs. Clay, June 1, 1864 (*ibid.*).

smashes, an admiring audience, the freshest gossip and the most unselfish regard, all combine with the boom and flash of the guns to welcome your coming? Angela requests me to say all this and more in her behalf, but I beg you to receive it as exclusively my own."[62]

Mallory thought that the correspondence between Mrs. Clay's husband and James P. Holcombe, on the one side, and Horace Greeley, on the other, was doing good service. The parties, fragments, and cliques and individuals in the North who desired peace, but differed only in regard to the means of securing it, would now learn that with Lincoln at the head of affairs no peace was possible; while the faint hearts, "our weak brothers in North Carolina and Georgia," who had "clamored so loudly that peace negotiations should be made by us," could not fail to see that "at present peace with Lincoln means degradation."[63]

He was optimistic about Clay's mission to Canada.[64] His concluding sentence was typical: "Please present my profound admiration and sincere regard to your fair sister, who, if not the lost Pleïade, is at least a Heavenly body."[65] The airy tone of this epistle is all the more unexpected, when we recall that ten days previously the *Alabama* had been sunk by the *Kearsarge* off Cherbourg. The news had probably not reached Mallory as yet.

Sometime in this summer of 1864—the exact date is uncertain—the Secretary of the Navy participated personally in a military engagement. Postmaster-General Reagan, Mallory's partner in the adventure, has told the story in his *Memoirs*.[66]

One morning cannon firing was heard to the northwest of Richmond. The fact was unexpected and puzzling, since there had been no reports of Federal movements into that sector. The reaction of the two members of Jefferson Davis' Cabinet was prompt and decisive: "As we had no troops

62. Mallory to Mrs. Clay, August 1, 1864 (*ibid.*)

63. *Ibid.* James P. Holcombe served in the first Confederate Congress as a representative in the lower house from Virginia.

64. Some wild and sinister charges were made against Clay in connection with his mission to Canada. Cf. J. Holt to Secretary Stanton, December 6, 1865 (*O.R.A.,* Ser. II, Vol. VIII, pp. 855-61): "During the summer, fall, and winter of 1864 this rebel was a resident in Canada as one of the accredited agents of the so-called Confederate Government, and, in connection and most intimate association with Jacob Thompson, Cleary, Sanders and others . . . was . . . engaged in maturing treasonable enterprises, in violation of the laws and usages of civilized war" (*ibid.,* 1856). And, the most serious charge of all: "As to his connection with the introduction of pestilence: Prominent among the deeds of infamy . . . with which the name of Clay . . . is connected . . . is the plot for the destruction of the lives of our soldiers and citizens by means of the introduction into the country of clothing infected with virulent contagious diseases" (*ibid.,* 589). This claim of Holt's was never proved.

65. Mallory to Mrs. Clay, August 1, 1864 (Clay Papers).

66. Reagan, *Memoirs,* 182-83.

there, Secretary Mallory and I got our horses and galloped out to where the noise was," reported Reagan. On reaching the old and now unoccupied line of Confederate entrenchments, they beheld Colonel Lyon, one of Richmond's most prominent citizens, riding along the front and gesticulating as if giving orders. They asked him what he was doing. "Commanding the forces," he responded. "Reagan, you command the right; Mallory, you the left; and I will take the center." The mimicry was undertaken in all earnestness. "We rode up and down the line of intrenchments for some time, as if giving directions to men, with the shells cracking over us, until the firing ceased." The attacking party—a regiment of cavalry and some pieces of light artillery—was completely fooled by the three-man show, and soon retired.[67]

Charleston, Wilmington, Savannah, and Mobile—the last ports left to the Confederates on the Atlantic and Gulf coasts! The first three were still under the stars and bars, but there was disaster shaping up at Mobile.

The blunt fact was that the navy's defenses were, from the necessities of the situation, spread too thin. In order to protect Charleston and Wilmington, the Confederate naval effort had to be less elaborate at the Gulf port. This was the dilemma. Mallory had the harbor approaches at Mobile well sown with torpedoes; he had the great ironclad ram *Tennessee* straddling the channel; but to these defenses he could add but three more ships of moderate size and gun power. Accordingly, in early August, Mobile harbor was breached despite the torpedoes which Farragut swore at but respected, and despite the *Tennessee* whose power so won the Federal Admiral's admiration.

Adverse criticism of the Navy Department's preparations at Mobile had not been wanting during the weeks before the attack. The movements of the *Tennessee,* it was charged, had been too slow and not sufficiently secretive. Iron had been wasted, it was said also, in building gunboats that proved to be totally inefficient. If the same iron had been applied to the ships in process of construction on the Tombigbee, those ships would have been ready and able to repel Farragut when he appeared in Mobile Bay. The efforts that were made to fit out the *Nashville* were useless, since the ship was a failure.[68]

Despite these and other recriminations, Mallory's report of the battle

67. *Ibid.* The gentleman referred to by Reagan as "Lyon" may have been James Lyons, the prominent Richmond citizen and lawyer, whose sister married John A. Wise.

68. Commander Richard L. Page to his nephew, Commander Catesby ap R. Jones, from Fort Morgan, Mobile, June 26, 1864 (*O.R.,* Ser. I, Vol. XXI, pp. 903-4).

was almost defiant: "On the 5th of August . . . a formidable fleet of the enemy, consisting of eighteen ships, including four ironclads, mounting 199 guns and manned by 2700 men, under Admiral Farragut, crossed the Mobile bar, when they were vigorously attacked by the forts and by our small squadron, under Admiral Buchanan. This force consisted of the steam sloops *Morgan* and *Gaines,* each carrying 6 guns, the *Selma,* 4 guns, and the ironclad ram *Tennessee,* 6 guns; in all, 22 guns and 470 men. Naval history records few contests between forces so unequal in ships, guns, and men, and but few in which the weaker party displayed equal heroism."[69]

At the first news of the defeat he had written: "Against the overwhelming forces brought to bear upon our little squadron defeat seems to have been inevitable; but the bearing of our officers and men has snatched credit even from defeat. The triumph of the enemy leaves the honor of our service untarnished."[70]

Admiral Buchanan suggested another and perhaps more ominous reason for the disaster: "I seriously felt the want of experienced officers during the action. All were young and inexperienced, and many had but little familiarity with naval duties, having been appointed from civil life within the year."[71] General Robert E. Lee, gazing anxiously northward from the entrenchments around Petersburg, might have expressed, *mutatis mutandis,* the same sentiments.

Some important lessons, Mallory felt, could be learned from the engagement. It was, he pointed out, "the first in which the modern and improved means of naval warfare, offensive and defensive, [had] been tested." The enemy's ships, among the finest afloat, were armed with nine-, ten-, eleven-, and fifteen-inch guns, whose projectiles varied in weight from 84 to 428 pounds. Their broadsides, the heaviest known, were discharged upon the *Tennessee* at distances ranging from three to thirty yards, and three of their heaviest ships, fitted as rams, ran into her repeatedly at full speed. The massive strength of the frame and the sloping armor of the ship resisted these assaults. Only one shot reached or made any impression upon the woodwork of the shield, and this did not go through it. On the sixth of August, the day after the battle, Admiral Farragut ordered a board of

69. Report of the Secretary of the Navy on the battle of Mobile Bay, dated November 5, 1864 (*ibid.,* 599-600).

70. Mallory to Lieut. J. W. Bennett, commanding P.N.C.S. *Mobile,* August 23, 1864 (*ibid.,* 591).

71. Report of Admiral James Buchanan to Mallory on the battle of Mobile Bay, from U. S. Naval Hospital, Pensacola, August 25, 1864 (*ibid.,* 577). Cf. also Lewis, *Farragut,* 221-96; Wilson, *Ironclads,* I, 114-34.

four naval officers to examine and report the condition of the *Tennessee,* and the official report of this board, made on the thirteenth of August, after detailing the specific injuries sustained by the ship, said "The *Tennessee* is in a state to do good service now." The resistance offered by inclined armor to the heaviest ordnance ever used upon the sea was here fully tested at short ranges, and the result, so far as was known, showed the superiority of this arrangement over similar armor upon vertical planes. Confederate naval officers, constructors, and engineers, concluded the Secretary of the Navy, should not fail to avail themselves of the instruction offered by this engagement.[72]

The critics of the government were becoming increasingly vocal. Josiah Gorgas wrote in his journal despondently: "There is a sentiment of hopelessness abroad—a feeling that all our sacrifices tend to nothing, . . . in short that there is no leadership. It must be confessed that we are badly off for leaders both in the council and in the field."[73]

Gorgas did not single out the Secretary of the Navy for condemnation, but there were others who did. A recurring question, involving doubts as to the prudence of Navy Department policy, related to the disposition of the large cruisers. The issue was aired thoroughly in an exchange of correspondence between Richmond and General Whiting, one of the army commanders at Wilmington.

The cruisers *Tennessee* and *Chickamauga* had been removed from their defense stations within the harbor at Wilmington and sent to sea on a commerce-destroying mission. Whiting protested that this dealt a two-fold blow to his defense operations: it deprived him of the two vessels' officers, men, and guns, which he imperatively needed for the protection of the harbor; and it induced the enemy to tighten its blockade of the port. With the departure of these vessels there was no proper naval force afloat to defend Wilmington, nor a sufficient number of gunners to serve the rips batteries. Also, as a consequence of the *Tallahassee's* withdrawal, the Federal blockading fleet had been doubled.[74] Furthermore, the ship's commander, before

---

72. Mallory, Report on the battle of Mobile Bay, dated November 5, 1864 (*loc. cit.*).

73. Josiah Gorgas, Journal, 1864-1878, typescript copy, University of North Carolina Archives, 14-15, n. d. He continues: "Lee is about all we have and what public confidence is left rallies around him, and he, it seems to me, fights without much heart in the cause. I do him wrong, perhaps, but I doubt if he believes we will or can succeed in this struggle. The President has, alas, lost almost every vestige of the public confidence. He has undoubtedly done much, perhaps irreparable wrong, by adhering to the wrong men."

74. Maj. Gen. W. H. C. Whiting to Mallory, September 27, 1864 (*O.R.A.,* Ser. I, Vol. XLII, part 2, p. 1297). Whiting continued his complaints in a communication addressed to General R. E. Lee, which said that at the very moment when the ironclad *Raleigh* had been destroyed

leaving, compelled several of the blockade runners to supply him with hard coal from their own holds; the subsequent use of soft coal, which produced dense black smoke, revealed the positions of the blockade runners to the enemy and resulted in the loss of seven of the ships.[75]

Whiting claimed that Generals R. E. Lee and Beauregard, as well as the chief officers of the Navy, agreed with him in this matter.[76] Certainly General Lee had endorsed one of Whiting's burning protests with the following observation: "If the naval boats and officers required for the defense of Wilmington can be efficiently used for that purpose, I think they had better be so applied. The loss of Wilmington to us would weigh more than the destruction of the enemy's coasters."[77] And General Braxton Bragg wrote to the President from Wilmington toward the end of October, 1864: "The naval expedition should not sail until the question of the attack here is decided. Its presence in the harbor may become of vital importance; its operations at sea can be but secondary at best."[78]

Three months later, Whiting's argument was reiterated with equal vigor by Governor Vance, who protested that the Navy Department, in order to fuel the *Tallahassee,* had taken, without the authorization of the government of North Carolina, coals belonging to the state's steamer *Advance.* Mallory denied—possibly with some casuistry—that the seizure of the coal had been a violation of the rights of the *Advance.*[79] The broader significance of the

and the ironclad *North Carolina* rendered useless, when the port was being gravely threatened and the enemy's fleet doubled, an expedition was sent off, taking away officers, men, guns, and ships, all of which were needed urgently for the defense of Wilmington (September 26, 1864 [*ibid.,* 1294]).

75. Whiting to Mallory, October 6, 1864 (*O.R.,* Ser. I, Vol. X, p. 75).

76. Whiting to Mallory, September 27, 1864 (*O.R.A.,* Ser. I, Vol. XLII, part 2, p. 1297).

77. Lee's endorsement on letter of Whiting to Lee, September 26, 1864 (*ibid.,* 1295).

78. General Bragg to President Davis, October 22, 1864 (*ibid.,* part 3, p. 1160).

79. Cf. Vance to Mallory, February 9, 1865: "Nor do I care to argue the 'question of fact' so gravely made upon me, involving only a quibble as to whether coal in the possession of my agent was in my possession. The distinction between that kind of possession which is required to support an indictment for larceny and that required to sustain an action of trespass *vi et armis* might be learnedly discanted upon here. ... But though such is my susceptibility to reason that I may be induced to forego an argument on the question of the possession of my agent being my possession, I confess I am not quite ready to admit that the possession of A. B. abstractly considered is not the possession of A. B., or that other remarkable proposition that the legal and undisputed possession of an article affords not 'the slightest claim' of property. And yet such doctrine I understand you to advance when acknowledging that Power, Lowe & Co. were part owners of the steamer *Advance,* that your agents took one hundred and sixty-nine tons of coal from them, and yet you assert that not one particle of coal was taken from the steamer *Advance,* nor one pound impressed to which the State or any of the joint owners of that steamer had the slightest claim! From Moses to Captain Pinkney, who *did* have any claim to that coal? Who *was* its owner?" (North Carolina Department of Archives and History, Raleigh, N. C., courtesy of Professor Frontis W. Johnston).

dispute, however, lay in the Governor's criticism of the Navy Department's general policy of giving priority to the commerce-raiding program. The enemy's recent attack against Wilmington, complained Vance, had been due directly to the withdrawal of the *Tallahassee* from that harbor. The needs of North Carolina were being neglected in favor of the Department's commerce-raiding plans.[80]

The case for the Navy Department's policy was presented vigorously by President Davis. In a communication to General Bragg the Chief Executive pointed out that the naval vessels in the harbor could avail nothing against a land attack and very little against an attack by vessels of war. Far from reducing the rigors of the blockade, the presence of Confederate cruisers in the harbor would induce the Federals to increase their efforts to seal up Wilmington; while, on the other hand, the departure of the cruisers for operations at sea would probably draw off in pursuit the most effective vessels of the blockading fleet.[81]

That Generals Lee and Beauregard were in favor of an opposite strategy, the President was not convinced.[82] The question was whether or not the Confederate Navy should cease from the effort to harass and weaken the enemy by the destruction of his commerce. To hold the *Tallahassee* and *Chickamauga* in Wilmington harbor would be, in effect, to seal up the port and actually aid the enemy in maintaining the blockade. Furthermore, these two ships, not having been constructed as ships of war, could render little if any service in defending Wilmington. By going to sea, on the contrary, they could be extremely useful both in injuring enemy commerce and in weakening the blockade. "One object in sending out the cruisers has been to weaken the efficiency of the blockade by drawing off the fastest vessels of the [Federal] squadron in pursuit of them, at a time when valuable cargoes were expected to arrive, a result in which the expectation of the Government has not been disappointed."[83]

The records proved, declared Davis, that since the last cruise of the *Tallahassee* and the *Chickamauga* a larger number of steamers had succeeded in entering Southern ports than ever before during the same period of time. "Our only hope of peace," the President concluded, "beyond the achievements of our noble armies in the field, must lie in making the burden

80. Governor Z. B. Vance to Mallory, from Raleigh, N. C., January 3, 1865 (*ibid.*). Also February 9, 1865 (*ibid.*).
81. Davis to Bragg, October 24, 1864 (*O.R.A.*, Ser. I, Vol. LI, part 2, supplement, p. 1048).
82. Davis to Samuel J. Person, at Raleigh, December 15, 1864 (*ibid.*, Vol. XLII, part 3, pp. 1273-74). Person was a member of the legislature of North Carolina.
83. *Ibid.*, 1274.

of the war oppressive to the people of the North. Under such a policy [of withholding the cruisers from commerce raiding] ... how is the [Northern] shipping interest to be made to feel those burdens? Or is it to be left in undisturbed security to wield all its wealth, power, and influence for our destruction?"[84]

Mallory himself was led to answer the charge made by Governor Vance that the captures effected by the cruisers out of Wilmington were merely "a few insignificant smacks." The Secretary felt that "so strange an error of fact and one so unjust to the officers and men of these cruisers, could only have found a place in [the Governor's] message from want of information upon the subject, and that its correction would promptly follow a presentation of the facts." He invited the Governor's attention to the list of captures—forty-six in all, including nineteen square-rigged vessels. He regretted that while the Governor's "derisive reference" to a "few insignificant smacks" was being circulated throughout the country, the correction of that statement, in the face of the facts, should have escaped His Excellency's attention.[85]

With such opposing arguments the debate continued, and, to a degree, it still continues today. A fair verdict would seem to be that the commerce-raiding strategy was, in the light of all the circumstances, basically sound, but the navy may have erred in believing that such a strategy relieved the government of the necessity of providing more and more gunboats and other types of small war vessels for purposes of harbor defense. It must be added, however, that modern experts such as the Sprouts have substantially agreed with Mallory's theory that Confederate command of the open sea would be an effective means not only of breaking the blockade but also of protecting the Southern seacoast.[86]

It is important to remember, when trying to judge Mallory's cruiser policy by means of testimony emanating from Wilmington, that a very unfriendly feeling existed between Whiting and Lynch, the naval commander at the port. In March, 1864, the two officers were actually threatening to use violence against each other.[87] It is, then, at least possible that Whiting's

84. *Ibid.*, 1274-75.
85. Mallory to Governor Vance, January 28, 1865 (North Carolina Department of Archives and History).
86. Cf. Sprout, *Rise of American Naval Power*, 160; "Command of the open sea was enabling the Union Navy to blockade Southern ports. The inability of the South to contest that command frustrated not only their efforts to break up the blockade, but also to prevent Union forces from occupying one strategic shore point after another."
87. Cf. Whiting-Lynch-Seddon correspondence, *O.R.A.*, Ser. I, Vol. XXXIII, pp. 1219-29.

strictures on the employment of the cruisers were somewhat colored by his personal dislike for Lynch.[88]

Indeed, the old difficulty of conflicts between army and navy commands was rearing its ominous head at other points besides Wilmington. There was trouble in this respect in March, 1864, at Galveston,[89] while General Beauregard was complaining that the naval force at Mobile was substantially a part of the local defenses, and should be under one—military—head.[90] A conflict existed, he said, between the land and naval commanders as to a torpedo-boat. The former ordered it into active service; the latter refused to obey. "What," asked the General, "must be done?"[91]

Secretary Seddon sent the complaint to Mallory with the rather plaintive query, "Cannot harmony between the two branches of the service be secured with respect to this boat? If the navy objects to using it, and volunteers from the army are anxious to test it, may not the liberty be allowed?"[92] Mallory replied that he knew nothing of the boat referred to, and had heard nothing of the alleged want of harmony in the matter. He would refer the subject of the boat to the naval commander in the theater, "with appropriate suggestions looking to the public interest."[93]

In at least one instance the charge of noncooperation could be leveled also by the navy against the army. A project of Mallory's which appears to

88. Note however the following evidences of cooperation of the Navy Department with the land command at Wilmington. Mallory, in a letter to Seddon, April 27, 1863 (*ibid.*, I, Vol. XVIII, p. 1023), encloses two letters: (a) Whiting to Seddon, April 21, 1863 (*ibid.*, 1024): "Please to ask the Secretary of the Navy if he will lend me the armament of the *Raleigh,* especially the Brooke rifles, until she is ready to use them." (b) Mallory to Whiting, April 25, 1863 (*ibid.*, 1024), assuring Whiting that he will grant the request as soon as the guns are ready.

89. Cf. *O.R.*, Ser. I, Vol. XXI, pp. 887-89.

90. Beauregard to Gen. S. Cooper (Adjutant and Inspector General), from Charleston, December 26, 1864 (*O.R.A.*, Ser. I, Vol. XLV, part 2, p. 735).

91. *Ibid.*

92. Endorsement of Seddon to letter of Beauregard *supra cit.*, Seddon's endorsement dated December 27, 1864 (*ibid.*, 735).

93. Endorsement of Mallory on same letter of Beauregard, Mallory's endorsement dated December 29, 1864 (*ibid.*, 736). The torpedo boat in question was commanded by Lieutenant [?] Halligan, who seems to have been seized with acute timidity in regard to his duties. Wrote Major General Dabney H. Maury to President Davis from Mobile on January 13, 1865: "Halligan, with torpedo and boat, will not attack enemy; has been transferred by Commodore Farrand. Please have him and boat placed under my orders, with authority to me to place an officer of the army or navy in command, that the enemy may be attacked at once. The boat is said to be the best of the kind. Halligan and five or six men have now been for months exempt from service on account of her. There has never been so good an opportunity for a torpedo boat to operate as is afforded by the fleet off Mobile" (*ibid.*, 781). Maury had written to Seddon on December 4, 1864: "Halligan, recently appointed lieutenant, has not yet used his torpedo boat; I do not believe he ever will" (*ibid.*, 649).

have been both practicable and useful was blocked in the summer of 1864 by army officers at Plymouth, North Carolina.

The Navy Secretary wished to have the ironclad steamer *Albemarle* attack the Federal fleet in Plymouth Sound. The worth of the plan was admitted by the Federal commander at New Bern. ". . . If they [the *Albemarle* and two other ironclads which it was thought were under construction] can succeed in coming into the Sounds together, we have no naval force to cope with them."[94] But the military authorities at Plymouth were unwilling to forego the protection which, they felt, was being provided by the *Albemarle* so long as she remained near the shore; and they spiked Mallory's plan for launching her on an offensive. They were unmoved by the Secretary's stiff observation that "she [the *Albemarle*] was not designed to act as a floating battery merely, and while her loss must not be lightly hazarded, the question of when to attack the enemy must be left to the judgment of the naval officer in command, deciding in view of the relations she bears to the defense of North Carolina."[95] And so, says Scharf,[96] "from the 24th of May to the 27th of October [when she was torpedoed at her mooring][97] the *Albemarle* lay in inglorious inactivity at Plymouth. . . ."

A rather interesting negotiation was carried on between Mallory and the Federal Secretary of the Navy in the late summer and early fall of 1864, with regard to a proposed large-scale exchange of prisoners. The business was not pursued without some misunderstandings on all sides.

Secretary Welles announced that he had made to the Confederate government an offer to exchange some naval prisoners, and that the offer had been declined by Secretary Mallory. The latter promptly denied having received any such proposition, and asserted that the Confederate authorities had proposed to "exchange mutually all naval officers and men" and that "no notice whatever has been taken of this proposition." In response to another offer of Mr. Fox to exchange some prisoners, Mallory replied that he accepted this proposition "as embracing the exchange of all our naval

94. Brig. Gen. I. N. Palmer, commanding military district of North Carolina, to Major R. S. Davis, July 19, 1864 (*ibid.*, Ser. I Vol. XL, part 3, p. 343).

95. Endorsement of Mallory to letter of Brig. Gen. L. S. Baker, commanding 2nd district, department of North Carolina and South Virginia, to Captain J. M. Otey, July 8, 1864, Mallory's endorsement dated July 30, 1864 and addressed to Secretary Seddon (*ibid.*, 753). Cf. also Brig. Gen. L. S. Baker to Secretary Seddon, July 8, 1864, enclosing letter of Col. Geo. Wortham, commanding post at Plymouth, to Captain J. C. McRae, assistant adjutant-general, July 2, 1864 (*ibid.*, 751-53).

96. *Op. cit.*, 412.

97. *Ibid.*, 413-14.

officers."[98] Welles accepted this offer, understanding that it comprised "all the naval prisoners including marines that are now held in the North."[99]

At this point everything appeared to be settled, but the negotiations were abruptly halted by a letter of Secretary Stanton to Major General Butler, dated October 5, 1864: "Your telegram of yesterday was my first information of the contemplated exchange of naval prisoners. On inquiry it appears that there has been direct communication by the Secretary of the Navy with Mr. Mallory and an arrangement for an exchange between them. This was unknown to the President and myself until today. He has directed the exchange to be adverted [sic, for averted], and directing the correspondence to be forwarded to General Grant with authority [to Grant] to stop the proceeding, or let it go on under your supervision and in accordance with the principles hitherto maintained in your correspondence with Mr. Ould, according as General Grant may think proper."[100]

The exchange as originally agreed on by Mallory and Welles was ultimately effected; but the Federal Secretary of the Navy had been given a sharp rap on the knuckles for assuming somewhat too much authority.[101]

On September 2, 1864, Atlanta fell. A letter from Mallory to Mrs. Clay showed him, somewhat surprisingly, to be far from crushed by this serious loss. He had made the arrangements for Mrs. Clay's journey to Canada to rejoin her husband.[102] He regretted that he had not been able to send her

98. Mallory to Welles, August 20, 1864 (*O.R.A.*, Ser. II, Vol. VII, pp. 661-62).

99. Welles to Mallory, September 9, 1864 (*ibid.*, 790). Cf. also Welles to Rear Admiral Dahlgren, September 24, 1864 (*ibid.*, 867-69).

100. *Ibid.*, 924-25.

101. From Welles's account in his *Diary*, II, 168-72, it would seem that the chief objection to the negotiations stemmed from jealousy of the Federal War Department toward the Navy Department. Stanton is represented by Welles as being the chief blocker of the plan, while Lincoln apparently was willing to go along with it. Stanton objected that the Confederate government did not wish to include Negro prisoners in the exchanges, and that the Confederates would insist on returning Negroes to their masters. Welles denied the first of these charges, and declared that it was none of the North's business even if the second charge was correct. Says Welles (*ibid.*, 170-71): "He [Stanton] thought I ought not to write the Confederate Secretary of the Navy, recognizing him as Secretary. As regarded Mallory, I told him [Stanton] I had carefully avoided giving him a title,—that I had written to the Hon. Mr. Mallory. . . ." Cf. also Richard Sedgewick West, *Gideon Welles, Lincoln's Navy Department* (New York, 1943).

102. Mallory to Mrs. Clay, September 27, 1864 (Clay Papers, Duke University). That chivalry was apparently not dead from the rigors of war is clear from a dispatch of a Confederate officer at Galveston to the Federal commander of the naval forces off that port: "The parties to whom a passage has been accorded shall be promptly notified of your kindness. I have also been requested by a Mrs. Dugard and a Mrs. Duval to apply to you for the same indulgence [of a passage through the Federal lines], and have consented to do so with the distinct understanding that parties so leaving will not be permitted to return within our lines. It is proper that I should inform you that our authorities are not disposed to abuse a flag of truce or trespass [sic] upon your courtesy by aiding anyone to leave under such cir-

in a public vessel, but he had no blockade runners under his control. She must be sure to avoid Bermuda and Nassau, for the yellow fever still was raging at those places, and was embracing newcomers at the very beach; "and knowing that nothing on earth would ever fail to embrace you that had the power of doing so, and having [had] a painful experience of his warm and glowing nature, I am anxious that you shall keep out of his way."

He told her his heart admonished him that, in her departure at this dark hour of their country, the severance of a "loved link of a long cherished chain" was impending. Like a boy restraining by bonds the flight of his first bird, since he knows that if it goes away he may never see it again, "I would like thus to control you, and feel that wherever your flight might be, you could but drag a greater length of chain." He assured her that he would attend to her requests and would be always happy to serve in any way herself or her noble husband.[103]

He and Angela had been greatly comforted by Mr. Clay's message assuring them that their daughter Maggie at Bridgeport was safe and well. No doubt the "Abolition vampires" were watching her movements. Could Mrs. Clay drop her a line, telling her about her parents, and where she might see Mrs. Clay? "Your letters will probably be opened if they go through the Bridgeport P. O., and if you could have them personally delivered it would be judicious. Ask her *particularly* to advise me by a *safe hand* whether certain funds in the hands of a party in N. York are secure."[104]

The letter ended on a playfully romantic note: "If your Sunbeam of a sister, whose smile steals over the hearts of all men as the whisperings of harps soothe the sadness of the sorrowful, will permit me to occupy a corner of her heart, not in squatter sovereignty, but as a tenant at will, until your return, I think she would get an occupant who, though he could not hope to leave the premises better than he found them, would endeavour to do no damage while in possession; and would furthermore promise, upon a notice to quit, to leave as soon as he could. I confess that I fear that every corner is already occupied, and that my hopes of obtaining a place rest upon vacancies to be created by her withdrawal from Macon. But be pleased to let her know that I stand ready as a pre-emptor to move in." In

cumstances who may design to return. I am at all times, however, ready to aid unfortunate non-combatants to rejoin their natural protectors, and will either receive or forward them, whenever the consent of the United States naval authorities has been previously obtained" (Brig. Gen. J. M. Hawes, C.S.A. to Capt. Geo. F. Simmons, December 5, 1864 [*O.R.,* Ser. I, Vol. XXI, p. 931]).

103. Mallory to Mrs. Clay, September 27, 1864 (Clay Papers).
104. *Ibid.* Italics in original.

the very last sentence there was a swift and startling change to a sober note: "In the hope, and the fear of its failure, of seeing you soon, with our country independent and free. . . ."[105]

To Mallory's enemies, and some of his friends, his gaiety amid dark events was an indication of light-headedness, of insensibility to the misfortunes of the Confederacy, and the result of a failure to realize the ominous meaning of the recurring reverses of the South. It is more probable, however, that his cheerful small talk was no sign of weakness, but the light bantering of a fighter who, for the moment, deliberately relaxes, in order to keep on fighting even what seems to be a losing battle.

The autumn of 1864 was a succession of setbacks for the Confederates. Nevertheless the Secretary of the Navy, in the face of Early's failures in the Valley,[106] the sinking of the cruiser *Florida* off Brazil,[107] and the loss of the ram *Albemarle*,[108] could write to his favorite correspondent one of his chattiest and gayest epistles. He told Mrs. Clay that he could scarcely resist the temptation to gossip through pages of response to her recent charming note; but having only a moment to listen to the whisperings of his heart he wrote to say that he and Angela were looking forward with pleasure to the promised visit of herself and husband. On that occasion he would omit no effort to make for her some mint juleps with his own hands.

He was happy to learn that Mr. Clay did not venture his journey to Canada in the *North Heath,* and he hoped that Clay would select a ship with more liquid sounds in her name, and one less suggestive of being left out in the cold, when he left Canada for Dixie. Clay's long report on public matters had just been received, and Mallory concurred with every word of it.

The enemy was "pegging away" at Richmond, the flash of his guns being visible from the Mallory piazza. The Yankees' approach had been very slow, but they had taken no steps backward and were inching toward the capital surely and methodically, like gophers. They would continue their advance unless the Confederate forces, by hard fighting, could drive them back.[109]

The rest of the letter presented reflections on the death and character of Mrs. Greenhow, the Confederacy's most renowned female spy. Mallory had been shocked at her tragic passing away—"Poor lady! What a bathos

105. *Ibid.*
106. E.g., at the fourth battle of Winchester, September 19, and at Fisher's Hill, September 22.
107. On October 7.
108. At Plymouth, North Carolina, October 27, by a Federal torpedo attack.
109. Mallory to Mrs. Clay, October 28, 1864 (Clay Papers).

from the climax of an Ambassadress's position must she have found three
fathoms of water! With destitution upon her lips, and a bag of gold around
her neck carrying her to the bottom, she presented as great a contradiction
in death as she had ever done in life."[110] As "illustrative of her devotion
and religious zeal," he recounted the following anecdote: "When your little
cousin was married at Wain's Hotel, Mr. Clay and I left the Senate at three
P.M. to join you, and we found you the centre of a joyous gathering, in
which dancing, talking, cake and wine were to be had for the asking. At
one of the passageway doors stood this poor lady; and as her face wore a
comical expression of mingled sherry, piety, and humor, I asked her to
tell me the thoughts she had. She gently with a single glance directed my
attention to Bishop D., standing close on her left, and said to me in Spanish
that he was squeezing her hand. This was the first and only time I ever
saw this warm-hearted divine, but the circumstance made him a fixture in
my mind.[111]

Mrs. Greenhow, thought Mallory, was a clever woman, much more
clever than was ever admitted by her associates. She started, early in life,
into the great world, and found in it many wild beasts; but only one of the
latter did she consider worthy of special attention, and thereafter she hunted
man with that resistless zeal and unfailing instinct which made Gordan
Cumming so successful with elephants. She was equally at home with
ministers of state or their doorkeepers, with the leaders and with the led;
and she had a shaft in her quiver for every defense which the game might
attempt, a shaft to which the game was sure to succumb. If, like Gordan
Cumming, she had displayed the fruits of her bow and her spear, her collection would have been far more rare and interesting than was his mu-
seum of tiger, leopard, and lion skins. What scalps she might have shown!
Seward, like a great beast or bear, proved, in her regard, an exception to the
conduct of his sex generally. He put her in prison and treated her rudely
and harshly, and this, Mallory declared, was the great sin for which Seward
should never be forgiven.[112]

A report from Mallory to the President toward the end of this year indicates both the accomplishments and difficulties of the Navy Department.
At Mobile there was under construction a large ironclad side-wheel steamer,
but it had not yet been completed for want of iron. Two light-draft,
double-propeller ironclad steamers, mounting four guns each, were also

110. Mrs. Greenhow died by accidental drowning while performing an espionage mission.
111. Mallory to Mrs. Clay, October 28, 1864, *supra cit.*
112. *Ibid.*

being built at the same place, but the iron armor to complete these vessels was not available. On the Tombigbee another large ironclad was in progress, but the armor was wanting. "It will be seen," stated the Secretary of the Navy, not without reason, "that everything has been done to get up an ironclad fleet of vessels which could possibly be done under the circumstances, but in consequence of the loss of our iron and coal regions, with the rolling mill at Atlanta, our supply of iron has been very limited. The mills at Richmond are capable of rolling any quantity, but the material is not on hand, and the amount now necessary to complete vessels already built would be equal to 4230 tons. . . ." The complete roster of ships just completed or in process of building was as follows: at Richmond, two vessels; at Wilmington, one vessel; at Charleston, two vessels; at Savannah, two vessels; at Columbus, one vessel; at Mobile, three vessels; on the Tombigbee, one vessel.[113]

The Navy Department could claim at least part of the credit for the achievements of one of the most remarkable of the Confederacy's services of supply, the Bureau of Nitre and Mining.[114] The report of Colonel I. M. St. John, the chief of this bureau, told a story of persistence, efficiency, and scientific research under fire which has seldom been equalled. During the past year, St. John wrote in his report of October, 1864, the events of the war had borne with special severity upon the mining service. Ten large iron furnaces in Virginia, all but three in Tennessee, all in Georgia, and four in Alabama had been burned or lost, and with them many forges, foundries, and rolling-mills.[115] The Ducktown copper mines were still under hostile occupation. Important nitre works in Virginia, Georgia, and upper Alabama had been repeatedly destroyed, and workmen killed or captured. The effort of the bureau had consequently been one of incessant reconstruction as well as production.

All the accessible works destroyed had been rebuilt at government cost, and several of the larger furnaces were either in or about to resume blast. The construction of smelting furnaces for copper and lead had been commenced in more interior localities, since the Petersburg works had finally

13. "Report of Vessels Now in Course of Construction," by John L. Porter, Chief Constructor, C.S.N., to Secretary Mallory, November 1, 1864, forwarded by Mallory to President Davis (*O.R.,* Ser. I, Vol. XXI, p. 600).

114. Cf. passage from the report of Colonel I. M. St. John, chief of the bureau to Secretary Seddon, October 1, 1864: ". . . It is my duty to acknowledge the co-operation of naval officers in many important points connected with the mining service" (*O.R.A.,* Ser. IV, Vol. III, p. 695).

115. Cf. *ibid.:* "For iron, the Secretary of the Navy has on several occasions after the loss of important iron works, waived his own requisitions, on the appeal of the Bureau."

come under fire. In connection with the construction of these works, examinations of interior ore beds had been persistently continued with a view to obtaining valuable mineral information. Notwithstanding all difficulties, military and financial, the more important requisitions of the army for nitre and for the metals and minerals which the bureau was supposed to supply had been promptly met, and, for the Navy, all requisitions for nitre and nearly all those for metals and coal.

The home production of nitre had progressed more favorably than had been expected. Increased results from the better training of workmen had offset losses from acts of the enemy. This domestic production had until recently exceeded importations. In the nitriaries the accumulation of nitrous material had gone so far that the bureau's experts were using part of the supply in experiments in the fertilization of fields. In this line, laboratory analyses and practical tests already were indicating general results proportionally (when time was considered) in advance of the French nitriaries as recorded by Dumas and Barruel. It had been the aim of the bureau to "work to the last our natural deposits (as distinct from artificial nitrates), at times even within the enemy's lines," and to examine carefully for new deposits in every possible locality. In North Carolina this experimental work had been attended with a success altogether unlooked for by scientific men.[116]

The military organization of the nitre workmen had been attended with gratifying results. Assembled rapidly on call, they went into action on their own ground and with home instincts fresh upon them, and under these influences they had invariably done well. The danger over, they returned to their work generally unaffected by camp habits; and, "clothing and feeding each one himself, soon again returns each his quota of nitre. . . ."[117]

The results accomplished by the Navy's Office of Medicine and Surgery are worth attention. At the end of 1864, this office declared that, ". . . by the operations of the [medical] purveyor's department, an ample supply of medicines, instruments and every thing to meet the wants of the sick, has been furnished up to the present time . . . ," although it was feared that the relentless tightening of the blockade would cause a scarcity of these indispensable articles.[118]

116. Cf. "Nitre Exhibit A," accompanying St. John's report, *ibid.*, 698.

117. St. John to Seddon, *ibid.*, 697. Cf. Mallory's orders for a search for new deposits of coal and ore: Mallory to Secretary G. W. Randolph, October 25, 1862 (*O.R.A.*, Ser. IV, Vol. II, p. 143).

118. "Report of Office of Medicine and Surgery, Nov. 1, 1864," in *Report of the Secretary of the Navy, 1864*, 46-49 (Rare Books Division, Library of Congress).

All the naval hospitals had been well provided with clean and comfortable bedding, blankets, furniture, crockery, and so forth, for the relief of the sick. This had been effected at a very moderate expense, by taking advantage of auction sales at which articles were procured at 200 per cent less than they could have been bought for in the wholesale establishments in Richmond. By the employment of an upholsterer to remodel and renovate the beds, much expense also had been saved.[119]

The great peril was in the reduced numbers of the personnel of the department. The corps of surgeons had been reduced from the original number of twenty-three to twenty-two by the death of Surgeon D. S. Green. The number of surgeons on duty was by no means adequate to the wants of the service, and there were several places where one surgeon was trying to fill the place of several. There was need also of another medical officer to assist in the general management of the department, which was, in 1864, mostly under the charge of newly appointed assistant surgeons. Of the latter, however, the chief of the department said that they had shown a "competency not to be expected from inexperienced young men, just commencing their professional career."[120]

The department's assets, including cash and materials of all sorts, were at the time of the last annual report, $36,339.11. Receipts in cash and materials during the past year had been $271,341.88.[121]

The report of the Office of Provisions and Clothing, rendered in October, 1864, was also of a decidedly encouraging nature, and a tribute to the prudent management displayed by that department.

There was in the storehouse at Rocketts a supply of bread and flour for eight months, beef and pork for six months, rice and beans for six months, sugar and molasses for five months, and tea and coffee for eight months from the following November. There were also three hundred barrels of flour in transit to Richmond, and two hundred in the mills of the city and a short distance from it.

The commissary department of the army was indebted for wheat loaned to it by the navy, equal to six hundred and twenty barrels of flour. The supply on hand in naval storehouses was sufficient to last until a new crop of wheat would be harvested. There was very nearly a six months' supply of bread and meat and the other principal parts of the ration on hand at

119. *Ibid.* Cf. the unfavorable description of the army medical service presented by Bradlee, *op. cit.*, 48-49.
120. "Report of Office of Medicine and Surgery, Nov. 1, 1864," *loc. cit.*
121. *Ibid.*

the naval station at Mobile, and a four months' supply at Savannah. At Charleston there was nearly sixty days' supply, and the same amount at Wilmington. The navy agent at Augusta, Georgia, had a sufficient amount of stores on hand to increase the supply at the two last-named stations to make each of them self-sufficient for four months.

At the general storehouse at Charlotte, North Carolina, there were on hand, on the first of September, seven hundred barrels of beef and pork, and since that time there had been received at Charleston and Wilmington six hundred barrels more, which were being forwarded to Charlotte. There were also in the general storehouse one hundred thousand pounds of coffee, thirty thousand pounds of sugar, and one thousand pounds of tea, with fifty barrels of beans and other component parts of the ration. In the storehouse at Albany, Georgia, there were over eight hundred barrels of beef. The flouring mill and bakery established there by the navy was in successful operation. It was turning out some five to six thousand pounds of hard bread daily, which could be increased by skillful workmen to probably eight thousand pounds per day, sufficient for the navy.

The cloth imported from Europe was being made up as rapidly as possible, and would be sufficient to furnish each man in the navy with one suit. If the consignments of clothing from abroad could be successfully brought through the blockade, there would be an ample supply for a year.

An arrangement had been made with the commissary general of the army to supply the navy with flour, beef, pork, rice, and beans, since the navy had been having difficulty in securing provisions from the farmers, who, by law, were obliged to give to the army supply officers preferential treatment in the matter of purchases. The report urged that application be made to Congress for an amendment of the "tithe" law so that the navy would be included in the benefit and also be allowed to purchase provisions from the "bonded" farmers.

The Office of Provisions and Clothing was very much concerned with the necessity of a further tightening up of its administration. Accounts should be opened with each paymaster and assistant paymaster and the office, that the latter might have an intelligent understanding of matters under its supervision. Also, two or three more clerks—there was only one in 1862—should be appointed for the more efficient management of this important department of supply. The measure was deemed all the more urgent since "all of the assistant paymasters have but little experience, and it will require a constant supervision of their monthly and quarterly returns to prevent much loss to the government. . . ."[122]

The Navy Department's "flouring mill" at Albany, Georgia, was the occasion for a reprimand from Congress. The House of Representatives resolved "that the President . . . be requested to inform this House under and by what authority the Secretary of the Navy has contracted with Nelson Tift and others for the erection of a flouring mill in the city of Albany, Georgia; the terms of the contract, if any, under which said mill has been erected . . . ; also, what estate, if any, the Government has acquired in the land on which said mill has been located, the extent of the same, and the amount contracted to be paid therefor."

To this request the Secretary of the Navy responded: "This Department has not contracted with Nelson Tift, or others, for the erection of a flouring mill in the city of Albany, Georgia. To supply the Navy at Mobile, Selma, Savannah, and Charleston, this Department has purchased machinery and established a flour and grist mill and bakery at Albany, which is in operation under the charge of Nelson Tift, Assistant Paymaster in the Navy. The land occupied by the mill and bakery consists of one lot, one hundred by two hundred feet; one lot, two hundred by two hundred and ten feet; one lot, one hundred by two hundred feet. The lease, under which this property is held for the Confederate States, stipulates that no rent is to be paid for it during the war, and that after the war the property may be held, at the pleasure of the Confederate States, at a rent to be fixed by the Secretary of the Navy, or his successor in office."[123]

In connection with its services of supply, the Navy Department became involved in the states' rights dispute which in 1864 was so seriously hampering the Confederate war effort.

Congress had passed a law declaring the right of the Confederate government to one half of the cargo space of all seagoing vessels, private or state-owned. Accordingly, the Navy Department asserted its claim to one half of the carrying capacity of the privately owned steamer *Hansa*, about to sail from Wilmington. The reply of the fiery Governor Zebulon Vance was immediate: "Is it possible that such an unblushing outrage is intended by the Government? I have no comment to make on such a proceeding further than that I will fire the ship before I will agree to it."[124]

122. "Report of the Office of Provisions and Clothing," 1864, in *Report of the Secretary of the Navy, 1864, supra cit.*

123. President Davis to the House of Representatives, January 4, 1865, enclosing letter of Mallory to Davis, dated December 21, 1864 (Rare Book Division, Library of Congress).

124. Z. B. Vance to Hon. J. A. Seddon, from Raleigh, March 8, 1864 (*O.R.A.*, Ser. I, Vol. LI, part 2, supplement, pp. 828-29).

Secretary Seddon, to whom Vance had addressed his protest, transmitted it to Mallory with the endorsement: "Respectfully referred to the Hon. Secretary of the Navy to exhibit the spirit in which it is feared the new regulations may be met by parties interested, backed, unfortunately, in some cases, by the Governors of States."[125] There were rather strong reasons for believing that Vance had a personal financial interest in the blockade-running operations of the *Hansa*.

Mallory returned the letter to Seddon with this tart comment: "The times are strangely out of joint when a uniform regulation made by the President in direct conformity with an act of Congress to aid the country in its great struggle is denounced by a Governor of a State as an 'unblushing outrage.' The 'notice' in question [requesting the cargo space] was given to the agent of the steamer *Hansa*. What is the precise interest of North Carolina in this vessel is not stated."[126] The contentions of the Navy Department were upheld by the Congress and ultimately enforced;[127] but the problem of states' rights did not cease to plague the Confederate war effort.[128]

A controversy between the Navy Department and the State of South Carolina deserves close study because of the thorough airing of the constitutional bases of Confederate government-state relations that it evoked.

The Navy Department was erecting a distillery in South Carolina for the sole purpose of manufacturing whiskey for the use of the navy. The Governor of the state demanded the cessation of the work on the grounds that the laws of South Carolina prohibited the establishment of distilleries. Mallory proposed to Attorney-General George Davis the question of the

125. Endorsement of Seddon to *ibid.*, endorsement dated March 12, 1864. In a letter addressed to President Davis, under date of December 30, 1863, Vance had recommended the undertaking of negotiations for peace, suggesting that if the offer should be rejected the insult would strengthen the war spirit of the South! (Clement Dowd, *Life of Zebulon B. Vance* [Charlotte, N. C., 1897], 88). For further details concerning conflicts over the government's claim of space in blockade runners, cf. Frank L. Owsley, *State Rights in the Confederacy* (Chicago, 1925), 128-49.

126. Endorsement of Mallory on letter of Vance to Seddon *supra cit.* (Mallory's endorsement has no date).

127. Cf. Schwab, *op. cit.*, 258.

128. For a full discussion of the conflicts between the Confederate government and the states in the matter of conscription, see Albert B. Moore, *Conscription and Conflict in the Confederacy* (New York, 1924), 12-26, 52-113, 162-90, 228-304; Schwab, *op. cit.*, 193-202, 196-98; Owsley, *op. cit.*, 205-18. Owsley inclines to accept the statement of the enrolling officer in Georgia that in 1864 there were more men between eighteen and forty-five years of age staying at home than had gone from the state into the Confederate service during the war (*ibid.*, 208, based on *O.R.A.*, Ser. IV. Vol. III, p. 75). Says the same author: "After 1861 it became more a question of men than arms. Arms aplenty were available to equip 600,000 men. But by this time the states had placed in local organizations most of the surplus manpower willing to fight. It is probable that over 100,000 men were thus held in state service in the spring of 1862" (Owsley, *op. cit.*, 273).

rights of the state in such a matter. Davis upheld the Navy Department's constitutional power to set up the distillery, despite the Governor's protests. This view, said the Attorney-General, was based on the decision of his predecessor, Judge Wade Keyes, in a similar case decided a few months before.[129]

Keyes's discussion of the relative powers of the Confederate and state governments was an unusually able and striking expression of at least one current of Southern constitutional law. The decision was perhaps even more remarkable for the heavy borrowings it made from the Marshall-Story-Webster theory of the federal relation. The undoubted truth, said Judge Keyes, that sovereignty resided only in the people of each state did not preclude the possession of supreme power by the central government with regard to some of its acts. For the people of each state joined with the peoples of all the other states to confer on the central government exclusively all the powers necessary for securing the good of the peoples of all the states. Therefore, whenever the central government was exercising one of these powers, the central government was supreme with respect to the governments of the states.[130]

The central government was not superior to the government of a state in any matter over which the people of that state never gave the central government competence; but in regard to a matter over which the people of a state *did* originally give the central government power, the latter government was superior to the state government. This superiority of jurisdiction had its whole source in the character of the original grant of power made by the people of each state.[131]

---

129. Attorney-General ad interim Judge Wade Keyes to Secretary Seddon, December 18, 1863 (*O.R.A.*, Ser. IV, Vol. III, pp. 876-79). Concerning another distillery conflict, see Schwab, *op. cit.*, 217. The North Carolina legislature called on Governor Vance to suppress the government-operated distillery at Salisbury. Cf. also *Raleigh Progress*, November 28, 1864.

130. For a defense of the constitutional supremacy of the central government with respect to the states, cf. the speech of Benjamin H. Hill before the General Assembly of Georgia, December 11, 1862, quoted in full in Benjamin H. Hill, Jr., *Senator Benjamin H. Hill of Georgia*, 252-72. An analysis of this speech is in Haywood J. Pearce, *Benjamin H. Hill, Secession and Reconstruction*, 67-74. It is interesting to note that the Governor of Florida assumed what was for the period an exceptional attitude. Says Albert Moore (*op. cit.*, 253-54): "Governor Milton's encomium of the President and his Cabinet was as strange a soliloquy in a wilderness of doubt and misgiving. He was happy to report to the [Florida] legislature that 'the President . . . and the distinguished gentlemen, the heads of the different departments who compose his Cabinet have consistently acknowledged the right of the States whenever their attention has been invited to interference with them. Nevertheless, in a few instances insurmountable obstacles have prevented a compliance with applications, the justice and propriety of which were not disputed.' This was a unique bit of gubernatorial charity in the lower South at that time."

131. From opinion of Judge Keyes, *supra cit.*, 876-77. The Judge stated: "Certain powers

Judge Keyes, speaking remarkably like John Marshall, declared that some of the difficulties in keeping straight the central government-state relationship might be seen in *McCulloch* vs. *Maryland*, *Osborn* vs. *Bank of the United States*, the License and Passenger cases, and the writings of John Taylor of Caroline. As for the particular case that he was considering—a contract made by the Confederate government with a citizen of Virginia for the purpose of providing whiskey for the army—the making of such a contract was within the competence of the Confederate government even in the face of a state law which prohibited that kind of an agreement. Continuing in the strain of John Marshall he asserted: . . . "The Confederate Government has the express power 'to support armies'; . . . any means may be used which are 'necessary and proper' to obtain supplies for that support; . . . a contract with a citizen of a State is a means of obtaining them, and . . . it is a means both necessary and proper; . . . a State has not the power to forbid the fulfillment of a contract which the Confederate Government has the power to make. . . ."[132]

In deciding the case of the Navy Department's distillery, Attorney-Gen-

---

were delegated to the Confederate Government, and certain powers intrusted to the State government. It was not intended that either government should be a check or an obstacle to the legitimate action of the other; and hence it was declared that powers not delegated were reserved; and it was provided that the legitimate action of the Confederate Government should be the supreme law of the land. But neither government can act directly upon the other, except in certain judicial cases. They are distinct and independent governments, acting separately, but acting upon the same persons and the same things. Both are governments of powers limited in number, and in some cases at least limited in extent. Thus the power of the Confederate Government to raise armies cannot be so exercised as to destroy the State government by the conscription of officers necessary to its [the State's] existence; nor under the power to lay and collect taxes can Congress tax a state house, or a county jail, or the income of a State. So a State government, though its power of taxation be unlimited by express words, cannot tax the amount of customs received by the Confederate collector at a seaport town within the limits of the State, nor the dock-yards, nor the foundries, nor the amount of direct taxes in the hands of a tax collector of the Confederate Government." In contrast, cf. the following statement of Governor Joseph E. Brown, of Georgia: "I regret to say that you have fallen into the error, now so common among Confederate officers, that the States derive their powers, and the people of the States their rights and privileges, from the will of the Congress; when in fact Congress and the Confederate Government derive all the powers they possess from the delegation of the respective States. The fundamental error into which you have fallen is in assuming that Congress, and not the State legislatures, have jurisdiction over State officers, and that the acts of Congress, when in conflict with the Constitution, are the 'laws of the country'" (Brown to Maj. Gen. Howell Cobb, from Milledgeville, May 5, 1864 [*O.R.A.*, Ser. IV, Vol. III, p. 381]). For a severe criticism of Brown's states' rights theory, cf. Louise B. Hill, *Governor Brown and the Confederacy* (private edition distributed by the Joint University Libraries, Nashville, 1938; Ph.D. thesis at Vanderbilt University), 52-54. For a defense, not altogether convincing, of Brown's theories see Herbert Fielder, *A Sketch of the Life and Times of Joseph E. Brown* (Springfield, Mass., 1883), 258-86, 309, 318-54, 355-97.

132. Opinion of Judge Keyes, *supra cit.*, 879.

eral Davis was merely applying the foregoing doctrine. "The States by their own voluntary consent," he observed, "have made the Constitution of the Confederate States their supreme law, before which all other laws must yield. That Constitution empowers Congress 'to provide and maintain a navy.' A State cannot prevent Congress from providing a navy by prohibiting the building of ships. . . . Neither can it prevent the maintenance of a navy already provided for by prohibiting the procurement of the necessary supplies."[133] It would be difficult to distinguish this theory from that of the Webster-Marshall-Story tradition.[134]

A bitter comment on the attitude of some of the state governments was made by Jefferson Davis at the end of this year: ". . . the difficulties with which this Government has to contend in opposing with its limited resources the devastating tide of invasion which the power of our enemy is pouring upon us would be great enough under any circumstances and with the most united and harmonious action of our whole people. But those

133. Davis to Mallory, March 7, 1864 (*O.R.A.,* Ser. IV, Vol. III, pp. 879-80). Cf. also note 130, p. 330.

134. Later in this same year, Davis rendered a similar decision in favor of the War Department. An act of Congress of June 14, 1864, authorized the Surgeon-General or Commissary-General to establish distilleries for the manufacture of spirituous liquors for the army and hospitals. Under the authority of this act the Surgeon-General set up a distillery at Buchanan, Virginia, for the purpose of distilling liquors exclusively for the army and hospitals. The circuit court of Botetourt County, under the aegis of a law of Virginia which prohibited distillation, issued an attachment ordering the sheriff to seize and take into his possession the distillery, grain, and all the material belonging to the government, and instituted a criminal prosecution against the officer who was managing the distillery for the government. Davis' opinion in this case was as follows: "Virginia, in common with her sister States, has accepted the Constitution of the Confederate States as her supreme law, which displaces and overrules all other conflicting laws. That Constitution confers upon Congress in the fullest and broadest terms the power 'to raise and support armies.' Of what avail is this power if it can be so easily rendered nugatory by State legislation? If the Legislatures of the States can prohibit and prevent any one of the steps necessary in the process of raising and supporting armies, they may prohibit and prevent them all. If they can prohibit the manufacture by the Government of hospital supplies, they can prohibit the manufacture of powder, arms, and all the munitions of war, and the enlistment of men, and so the whole war power of the Confederate Government would be prostrate at the feet of the State Legislatures. In regard to the course to be pursued by the Government, . . . as a conflict of force with the authorities of a State ought only to be resorted to in a case of extreme emergency, if ever, there is but one remedy left, and that is to defend the suits in the court below, and, if necessary, take them by appeal to the highest tribunal of the State. I have every confidence that they will be adjudicated by that tribunal with a due regard to the constitutional rights of the Confederate States, as well as to those of the State of Virginia. As the Surgeon-General intimates that delay may be injurious, and as the Legislature of Virginia is so soon to assemble, I respectfully suggest that the matter be laid before the Governor, with a request that he will call it to the attention of the Legislature, and thus give them an occasion, of which I doubt not they will readily avail themselves, so to modify their legislation as not to interfere with the exercise of the just powers of the Confederate States" (Attorney-General Davis to the Secretary of War, November 30, 1864 [*O.R.A.,* Ser. IV, Vol. III, pp. 875-76]).

difficulties have been materially increased by the persistent interference of
some of the State authorities—legislative, executive, and judicial—hindering
the action of this Government, obstructing the execution of its laws, de-
nouncing its necessary policy, impairing its hold upon the confidence of the
people, and dealing with it rather as if it were the public enemy than the
Government which they themselves had established for the common defense
and which was their only hope for safety from the untold horrors of Yankee
despotism."[135]

One of the last orders issued by the Secretary of the Navy in 1864 was
sent to the commanding officer at Savannah: "In the present aspect of affairs
at Savannah, the Department takes it for granted that you will use every
possible effort to beat back the enemy. Should the city fall, however, you
must save your vessels. The Savannah, Isondiga, and Macon, at least, should
be saved. Charleston, Wilmington, and Georgetown are open to them. It
would seem that the Savannah and your other gunboats, keeping well together, might fight their way into Charleston at night, if they could not do
better. Under any circumstances, it is better for the vessels, for the Navy,
for our cause and country, that these vessels should fall in the conflict of
battle, taking all the risks of defeat and triumph, than that they should be
tamely surrendered to the enemy or destroyed by their own officers. If fall
they must, let them show neither weakness of submission nor of self-destruc-
tion, but inflict a blow that will relieve defeat from discredit."[136]

This was written on the day after Hood's army had been broken at
Nashville, and four days before Savannah fell.[137]

135. President Davis to Hon. Samuel J. Person, December 15, 1864 (O.R.A., Ser. I, Vol.
XLII, part 3, p. 1275). Davis had said in his message to Congress, January 12, 1863: "Our
Government, born of the spirit of freedom and of the equality and independence of the States,
could not have survived a selfish or jealous disposition, making each only careful of its own
interest or safety. The fate of the Confederacy . . . depends upon the harmony, energy, and
unity of the States. It especially devolves upon you . . . to cultivate fraternity, and to sustain
in the people a just confidence in the Government of their choice. To that confidence and to
the unity and self-sacrificing patriotism [is due our success]" (ibid., Ser. IV, Vol. II, p. 349).

136. S. S. Lee, for Secretary of the Navy, to W. W. Hunter, from Richmond, December
17, 1864 (O.R., Ser. I, Vol. XVI, p. 481).

137. In this fall of 1864 Mallory was seeking an appropriation for the erection of additional
buildings at Drewry's Bluff for the accommodation of the acting midshipmen ("Estimate of
the amount required for the erection of additional buildings at Drewry's Bluff for the accommodation of Acting Midshipmen," Rare Books Division, Library of Congress). The amount
required was $6,000.

# CHAPTER THIRTEEN

# ... And 1865

After New Year's Day, 1865, it was clear that the Confederacy was breaking up fast.[1] In swift and terrible succession came the final blows. Charleston and Wilmington fell within five days of each other as Sherman's army closed in on the rear.[2] Lee's position before Richmond was becoming more and more untenable. Nevertheless, on the fifth day of January the Secretary of the Navy submitted the following report to President Davis:

"I have the honor to submit the following data . . . upon the general condition of the country. The means at the command of this Department for supplying munitions of war:

"*The Selma (Ala.) foundry*: The capacity of this establishment is large; and would enable it to supply per week seven heavy guns, of calibres varying from [?] to 11 inches, ranging in weight from 11,000 to 24,000 pounds each, and five field pieces, with all the projectiles for the same, and projectiles also for the general service of the Navy. It is now delivering two heavy guns and one field piece per week, but no projectiles, the discrepancy between its capacity and its product being due to the want of skilled labor.

"*The Naval Ordnance Works, Charlotte, N. C.*: This establishment manufactures shells, and wrought iron and cast shot. Worked to its full capacity it could supply the Navy and shore batteries in charge of the Navy. The heaviest forgings in the Confederacy are also done here and much ma-

---

1. It is not surprising that the popularity of the Cabinet continued to decline. Cf. the following entry in the *Diary of the Rebel War Clerk for January 21, 1865*: "The *Examiner* this morning says very positively that Mr. Secretary Seddon has resigned. Not a word about Messrs. Benjamin and Mallory—yet. The recent action of Congress is certainly a vote of censure with great unanimity" (J. B. Jones, *op. cit.*, II, 393). For other criticisms of the Cabinet at this time, see *ibid.*, II, 415, 421, 422. Cf. also *Raleigh Progress*, February 4, 11, 1865.

2. Cf. the eloquent appeal of the women of Charleston just before the city fell: "We implore, as the greatest boon, fight for Charleston! At every point, fight for every inch, and if our men must die, let them die amid the blazing ruins of our homes" (*Charleston Mercury*, January 24, 1865).

chinery manufactured. It is now worked to about one half of its capacity only for the want of mechanics.

"*Naval Ordnance Works, Richmond, Va.*: Ordnance equipments of every description are manufactured and heavy guns are banded here. The capacity is sufficient for all naval wants in the waters of Virginia, and to meet a large demand from the Army, but for want of skilled labor only one half of its capacity is developed.

"*Naval Ordnance Works at Atlanta, Ga.*: The machinery of this establishment was removed to Augusta, Ga., upon the fall of Atlanta, and from Augusta upon the approach of the enemy to Fayetteville, N. C. It will soon be in operation with a capacity to employ one hundred mechanics in the production of all ordnance equipments and projectiles.

"*Naval Powder Works, Columbia, S. C.*: This establishment is worked to its full capacity and makes 20,000 pounds of powder per month with ten experts. In the course of a few weeks the capacity will be doubled by the addition of new machinery and five more experts. The supply of crude material, iron nitre, etc., etc., concerned in these works, is shown by the returns of the nitre and mining Bureau.

"*Means of supplying transportation*: Of the three kinds of transportation employed in the public service, viz., railroad, field and water transportation, the means of this Department enable it to supply but little. We have repaired locomotives and built cars as far as our limited force of experts permitted. With additional mechanics our shops could render very important service in this respect, and we might construct transport vessels when required.

"*Means of supplying subsistence*: We have ample means of supplying all the subsistence required by the Navy, and of accumulating supplies for occasional aid to the Army. We rely upon open purchases and upon importations. We have a packing establishment for beef and pork, and grist and flour mills and bakery in successful operation at Albany, Ga."[3]

3. Mallory to President Davis, January 5, 1865 (Davis Papers, Duke University). Cf. also Mallory to President Davis, February 7, 1865, indicating the number of men required by the various bureaus of the Navy Department: for construction and repairs of vessels: 330 white men, 280 Negroes; for ordnance: 532 white men, 541 Negroes; for construction and repairs of steam machinery: 143 white men, 136 Negroes; for Medical Department: 52 white men, 56 Negroes; for Provisions and Clothing Office: 25 white men, 130 Negroes. "The force of mechanics required by this Department," said the Secretary, "will depend much upon the movements of the enemy. If our works shall be exempt from interruption, a much larger force than estimated for can be very usefully employed. All our white mechanics and workmen are under military organization, armed and equipped for service, and are frequently called into active service" (Rare Books Division, Library of Congress).

So the report went on while, on every front, the land and naval forces of the Confederacy were reeling to the finish. The Navy Department was dying hard. Fort Fisher, the key of Wilmington, fell on January 15.[4] On the next day, Mallory pressed Flag Officer Mitchell to strike a blow at the enemy at City Point. Defeat for the Federals there would force Grant's withdrawal, he thought, from the Petersburg line.[5] Mitchell delayed. Four days later came another message to him from Mallory: "Though still very ill, my anxiety about your proposed movement constrains me to write thus to you. I have just sent a dispatch informing you that I expect you to start tomorrow. I do this because convinced that the enemy must learn your design and may defeat it, and because I regard the service which I am so solicitous about as of the utmost interest to our cause. You have an opportunity, I am convinced, rarely presented to a naval officer, and one which may lead to the most glorious results to your country. I deplore that you did not start immediately after the freshet, and have deplored the loss of every day since."[6]

The "service" which Mallory was urging so earnestly on his subordinate had been planned shortly before, in a conference with General R. E. Lee. It was hoped that Mitchell's squadron could pass down the James, disperse the Federal fleet at City Point, destroy Grant's base of supplies there, and thus relieve the military pressure on Petersburg and Richmond. The attempt failed.[7] On February 18, the day after the evacuation of Charleston, Semmes was put in charge of the now demoralized James River squadron, and the navy's chief object became a successful retreat.[8]

Mallory was still fighting, but he must have known that the end was very near. As late as March 7 he was desperately pressing the Treasury Department for funds to keep the mechanics working at the Peedee, S. C., navy yard.[9] A week later he was demanding coin shipments for his dis-

4. Regarding the fall of Fort Fisher. cf. West, *Porter*, 276-86; Wilson, *Ironclads*, I, 135-42; E. P. Alexander, *Military Memoirs*, 582-84.

5. Mallory to Mitchell, January 16, 1865 (*O.R.*, Ser. I, Vol. XI, 797-98).

6. Mallory to Mitchell, January 21, 1865 (*ibid.*, 803).

7. For details, cf. Scharf, *History of the Confederate States Navy*, 739 ff.

8. *Ibid.*, 744-49. A tragic episode at this time was the torpedo boat attempt, foiled by the treason of a member of the party (Scharf, *op. cit.*, 742-44, from W. F. Shippey, C.S.N., "A Leaf from my Log-Book," in *Southern Historical Society Papers*, XII (1884), 416-21).

9. Mallory to Secretary George A. Trenholm, March 7, 1865 (Treasury Department Records, National Archives). One of the last gasps of the Navy Department was the following message sent by Mallory to the Secretary of War: "Of course no subsistence should be sent off so long as we can hold the city [Richmond], and I was not aware that Paymaster Semple . . . contemplated doing so. I have directed him to keep them here. I regret that we cannot turn over further subsistence to the Commissary-General. Our mechanics, who are entitled to subsistence from the Army, are receiving nothing and are nearly in a state of starvation, while

bursing agents "so that they can purchase necessary supplies and pay mechanics."[10] But by the night of the first of April he knew that the game was up. On the next day he wrote to Semmes the momentous order: "General Lee advises the Government to withdraw from this city, and the officers will leave this evening accordingly. General Lee withdraws his lines towards Danville this night; and ... upon you is devolved the duty of destroying your ships this night, and with all the forces under your command joining General Lee. Let your people be rationed as far as possible for the march and armed and equipped for duty in the field."[11]

"The 2nd of April, 1865," wrote Mallory in his diary a few months later, "though a clear, beautiful day in Richmond, will ever be remembered as the darkest in her history. The temperature wooed the people abroad, a pleasant air swept the foliage and flowers of the Capitol grounds, the sun beamed upon its bronze group of conscript fathers ... and the church bells pealed their invitations. . . . The old city had never, during the war, worn an aspect more serene and quiet; and yet at that very moment the hours of the Confederacy ... were being numbered. . . ."[12]

Rumor spoke of a new battle around Petersburg, but nothing definite was known of Lee's situation, save that it was growing hourly more desperate. At eleven o'clock that morning President Davis was attending services at St. Paul's church. Those near his pew scrutinized his face anxiously for some sign of good or bad news. But his expression, says Mallory, "varied not from that cold, stern sadness which four years of harassing mental labor had stamped upon it; ... the cold, calm eyes, the sunken cheek, the compressed lip, were all as impenetrable as an iron mask."[13] Yet Davis' heart was agonized, and his brain sorely perplexed by Lee's dispatches of the early morning, telling of Grant's overwhelming charge through his center, of heavy Confederate losses, and of the impossibility of regrouping the defense lines.

A messenger from the War Department entered the church, went directly to the President's pew, and whispered a few words in his ear. All eyes followed Davis as he rose and left the edifice. Not a line of his face,

---

our supplies do not admit of meeting their wants" (Mallory to Secretary of War John C. Breckinridge, March 23, 1865 [O.R.A., Ser. I, Vol. XLVI, part 3, p. 1336]).

10. Mallory to Trenholm, March 14, 1865 (Treasury Department Records).

11. Mallory to Semmes, April 2, 1865 (O.R., Ser. I, Vol. XII, p. 191).

12. Mallory, Diary, a section reprinted in McClure's Magazine, XVI (November, 1900-April, 1901), under title of "The Last Days of the Confederate Government," 100.

13. Ibid.

however, hinted at the news he had just received: new and heavier losses by Lee, and the General's advice that the capital be evacuated at once.

The Cabinet was hastily summoned. The members did their best to conceal their agitation. "Mr. Benjamin," remarked Mallory, "having completed his plain and unexceptionable toilet, and scanned the latest foreign papers, pursued his way from his residence . . . to the State Department, with his usual happy, jaunty air; his pleasant smile, his mild Havana, and the very twirl of his slender, gold-headed cane contributing to give, to casual observers, expression to that careless confidence of the last man outside the ark, who assured Noah of his belief that 'it would not be such a h—— of a shower, after all.'" But the friends of the debonair Secretary of State saw through his pretense and caught the distress in his eyes.

Davis, "in a few words, calmly, solemnly," informed the Cabinet of the late news from Lee and ordered the immediate withdrawal of the government from Richmond. Less than an hour later the boxes of official records and papers were on their way to the depot, and the President and his Cabinet were preparing to follow.

There was, affirmed Mallory later, no noise, no confusion, no undue excitement in the city. People gathered in groups to gaze sadly, silently, on the closing scenes of the tragedy. "Women . . . clad in deepest black, for all Virginia's daughters mourned the loss of kindred in the war, . . . wept in the streets. . . ."[14]

At eleven P.M. the President and his party took their seats in the train that was to carry the last Confederate government to Danville and points farther south.[15] "The train moved in gloomy silence over the James River. A commanding view of the river front of the city was thus afforded, and

14. *Ibid.,* 100-2.

15. A description of Richmond a few days later, by an eye-witness: "The city was a sad sight. Every house was alight and open and the women and children generally crying on the steps or standing silent on the corners of the streets. Stragglers soon commenced to break open stores and the guards to fire on them—they sometimes to return it all over Main Street. Mitchel & Tyler—nearly every store on Main Street was plundered. Several men were killed and wounded. The government stores were thrown open and thousands of hideous Irish and Dutch and negroes, men, women, and children crowded them, carrying off bacon, corn, butter, saddles, harness and every variety of army store. I stood for some time near the Danville Depot which was crowded with property of every kind which could not be carried away. Some thousand or more blankets were among them. It is growing too dark to write and I must hurry to a close. The scene was one never to be forgotten; many fires and some explosions lighted the whole city, and . . . the Iron Clads were blown up with the most tremendous report I have ever heard." (E. P. Alexander to his wife, from Richmond, April 9, 1865 [Alexander Papers, Southern Historical Collection, University of North Carolina]). For details of the flight of the Confederate Cabinet, cf. A. J. Hanna, *Flight Into Oblivion* (Richmond, 1938).

as the fugitives receded from its flickering lights, many and sad were the commentaries they made upon the Confederate cause." Mallory, in recalling that night, thought of his own special cause for grief: "The James River squadron, with its ironclads, which had lain like chained and sulky bulldogs under the command of . . . Semmes, to prevent the ascent of the enemy's ships, would . . . 'go up' before morning, the order having already been given; and the naval operations of the Confederacy east of the Mississippi would cease."

Mallory has left some vivid portraits of his companions as they rode southward in that inglorious retreat. John Reagan, the Postmaster-General, plain, honest, and great hearted, "silent and sombre, his eyes as bright and glistening as beads, but evidently seeing nothing around them, now whittling a stick down to the little end of nothing without ever reaching a satisfactory point, . . . sat chewing and ruminating in evident perplexity." Secretary of the Treasury Trenholm, "as usual with men of his practical sense and knowledge of the fitness of things, . . . was provided with abundant supplies for the inner man," including some "inexhaustible" hampers of "Old Peach," all of which he shared generously with his companions. Benjamin's "Epicurean philosophy" and hope and good humor refused to desert him. He rallied his associates over their mournful faces as he munched a sandwich with great relish, "and, with a never-give-up-the-ship sort of air, referred to other great national causes which had been redeemed from far gloomier reverses than ours."[16]

The party reached Danville in the late afternoon of April 3. "A large number of the people of the town were assembled at the depot as the train entered it, and the President was cordially greeted; but there was that in the cheers which told as much of sorrow as of joy."[17] For five days Davis was to wait here in anxious expectancy of further news from Lee. On the afternoon of the ninth a courier arrived from the Army of Virginia with the grim tidings: a few hours before, Lee had surrendered at Appomattox.

The information "fell upon the ears of all like a fire-bell in the night." The President received the blow at about four o'clock in his improvised office, where several members of his Cabinet and staff were assembled. They "carefully scanned the message as it passed from hand to hand, looked at each other gravely and mutely, and for some moments a silence, more eloquent of great disaster than words could have been, prevailed."[18] That night at eleven o'clock the remnants of the Confederate government started

16. Mallory, Diary, reprint *supra cit.,* 105.
17. *Ibid.*                                   18. *Ibid.,* 107.

southward for Greensboro. Arriving there a few hours later, they received their first rebuff from their own people. Latchstrings were "pulled in" against the President, his Cabinet, and his staff. The citizens of the town did not desire to compromise themselves with the members of a beaten regime. The official party set up quarters in a railroad car.[19]

During the one-week stay at Greensboro they adapted themselves remarkably well to their unwonted lodgings and fare. Mallory took pleasure in describing later their mode of existence: "Here was the astute Minister of Justice, a grave and most exemplary gentleman, with a piece of half-broiled 'middling' in one hand and a hoe-cake in the other, his face beaming unmistakable evidence of the condition of the bacon. There was the clever Secretary of State busily dividing his attention between a bucket of dried apples and a haversack of hard-boiled eggs. Here was a Postmaster-General sternly and energetically running his bowie knife through a ham as if it were the chief business of life; and there was the Secretary of the Navy courteously swallowing his coffee scalding hot that he might not keep the venerable Adjutant-General waiting too long for the coveted tin cup! All personal discomforts were not only borne with cheerful philosophy, but were made the constant texts for merry comment, quaint anecdotes, or curious story. State sovereignty, secession, . . . and other . . . recurring and fruitful themes of discussion, gave place to the more pressing and practical questions of dinner or no dinner, and how, when, and where it was to be had, and to schemes and devices for enabling a man of six feet to sleep upon a car seat four feet long."[20]

On the night of the fifteenth of April, in Jefferson Davis' room at Greensboro, a conference took place between the President and his two generals, "Joe" Johnston and Beauregard, who had been summoned there for the purpose. Davis asked their opinion of the present state of the affairs of the Confederacy. The Generals' response was brief and to the point: further military resistance was hopeless; terms should be asked of Sherman as they had been asked of Grant. The President, after a slight pause, said to Johnston: "Well, sir, you can adopt this course, though I confess I am not sanguine as to ultimate results."[21]

On the next day the Confederate government continued its tedious and somewhat aimless progress southward. Davis still clung to some last shreds of hope of further resistance on the part of the deeper South, but his optimism evoked no sympathy from his companions. Their route lay through

19. *Ibid.*                                      20. *Ibid.*, 239.
21. *Ibid.*, 240.

Jamestown, High Point, Lexington, Salisbury, and Charlotte, where they heard the news of the assassination of Lincoln. "I expressed my deep regret," says Mallory, "and, among other views, my conviction of Mr. Lincoln's moderation, his sense of justice, and my apprehension that the South would be accused of instigating his death. To this Mr. Davis replied sadly: 'I certainly have no special regard for Mr. Lincoln; but there are a great many men of whose end I would much rather have heard than his. I fear it will be disastrous to our people, and I regret it deeply.' "[22]

At Charlotte, Davis received the propositions agreed on by Johnston and Sherman and, after consulting with his Cabinet, approved them.

Mallory's peace proposals were expressed in a letter to Davis dated April 24, 1865, from Charlotte. He felt that the Johnston-Sherman agreement should be accepted for the following reasons: 1) it provided for the restoration of the several States of the Confederacy to the old union; 2) it preserved the integrity of the States' governments; 3) it guaranteed the security and rights of the people of the states; and 4) it granted a general amnesty for participation in the war.

He admitted that "the great object of our struggle is hopeless." Nine-tenths of the Southern people, weary of the war and desiring only peace, would subscribe to the propositions of Johnston and Sherman. Such an admission has been forced upon him by "the vast army of deserters and absentees from ... military service during the past twelve months, the unwillingness of the people to enter the armies, . . . the present utter demoralization of our troops."

He did not believe that it would be possible to organize, arm and equip and bring into action east of the Mississippi fifteen thousand men within the next sixty days. A guerrilla warfare might be carried on for a time, but would be, in the last analysis, useless.

The seaboard and the ports being in the enemy's hands, the Confederacy could not rely upon supplies of arms and other munitions of war from abroad, and the means of producing them at home, already limited, were daily decreasing. The loss of Selma and of Columbus, where much valuable machinery for the manufacture of ordnance and ordnance stores had been collected, had been fatal.

The Confederate currency was nearly worthless and would become utterly so with further military disasters.

The President, under the Constitution, could not dissolve the Confed-

22. *Ibid.*

eracy and remit the States composing it to the government of the United States. But the Confederacy was conquered; its days were numbered; Virginia was lost to it, and North Carolina must soon follow; and state after state under the hostile tread of the enemy, must re-enter the old union.

"The occasion," concluded Mallory, "the emergency, the dire necessities and misfortunes of the country, the vast interests at stake, were never contemplated by those who framed the Constitution. They are all outside of it; and in the dissolution of the Confederacy and the wreck of all their hopes, the States and the people will turn to you whose antecedents and present position and powers constitute you, more than any other living man the guardian of their honor and their interests, and will expect you not to stand upon constitutional limitations but to assume and exercise all powers which to you may seem necessary and proper to shield them from useless war and to save from the wreck of the country all that may [be] practicable of honor, life and property."[23]

On April 24, however, Johnston's army was informed that the convention had been refused by the Federal government, and that hostilities would be reopened within twenty-four hours. After receiving this news, Davis and his party resumed their dolorous march southward. The day of the Confederacy, they must have realized at last, had come to a close.

At Washington, Georgia, Mallory handed to his chief a brief note of resignation dated from Abbeville, Georgia, May 2, 1865. "The misfortunes of our country," he wrote, "have deprived me of the honor and opportunity longer to serve her, and the hour has approached when I can no longer be useful to you personally. Cheerfully would I follow you and share whatever fate may befall you, could I hope thereby in any degree to contribute to your safety or happiness. The dependent condition of a helpless family prevents my departure from the country, and under these circumstances it is proper that I should request you to accept my resignation as Secretary of the Navy.

"In thus terminating our official relations, language fails to give expression to my sense of your patriotic devotion to our common country, or to the grateful promptings of my heart for the kindness, consideration, and courtesy which you have extended to my humble efforts to serve her. May God watch over and protect you; and may the smiles of Heaven be upon the Pathway of yourself and your loved ones."[24]

23. Dunbar Rowland, *Jefferson Davis, Constitutionalist*, VI, 574-76. Cf. also the Confederate Cabinet's proposals for peace, submitted to Davis at Charlotte, April 17, 1865 (*ibid.*, 568-69).
24. *Ibid.*, 586.

In accepting the resignation, Davis wrote: "Yours of the 2nd inst., tendering your resignation has been duly considered, and under the circumstances I feel bound to accept it.

"It is with deep regret that I contemplate this separation. One of the members of my first cabinet, we have passed together through all the trials of the war and the not less embarrassing trials to which the Congress has of late subjected the Executive. Your minute knowledge of naval affairs and your counsel upon all important measures have been to the Administration a most valuable support. For the zeal, ability and integrity with which you have so long and so constantly labored, permit one who had the best opportunity to judge, to offer testimonial and in the name of our country and its sacred cause to return thanks. I will ever gratefully remember your uniform kindness and unwavering friendship to myself; and will fervently pray for your welfare and happiness in whatever position you may hereafter be placed."[25]

Thus Mallory took leave of Jefferson Davis and started for Atlanta and La Grange, where Angela and the children were staying. There he "resolved to await the action of the [United States] government." A few days later, at the little Georgia town, he was arrested.[26]

The last comment of the Secretary of the Navy in this part of his diary was brief but full of restrained emotion: "There never was a cause which more thoroughly united a population than that of the Confederacy. Tears frequently streamed down the faces of the people as Mr. Davis passed and bowed to them, and all hearts overflow with sympathy for him."[27]

25. *Ibid.*, 586-87.
26. *Ibid.*, 247-48.
27. *Ibid.*, 248. In regard to the arrest of Mallory and Hill, cf. Hill, Jr., *Benjamin Hill*, 46.

# CHAPTER FOURTEEN

# Fort Lafayette

THEY WERE TAKING STEPHEN MALLORY to prison. Up from La Grange, by easy stages through Nashville and along the Western route, two Federal officers escorted northward the former Confederate Navy Secretary and his fellow-prisoners, Benjamin Hill and General Howell Cobb.[1] The Yankee guard made it as easy as possible for the captured and defeated men. They were furnished with a carriage, were given frequent rest periods, and were, generally, treated with what Mallory described as "great civility."[2]

From one of the stopping points Stephen wrote to his wife encouragingly. All things considered, he told her, he was hopeful. Exile had for him no terrors, and exile, he felt, was the most that they could do against him. He urged Angela and the children to go to Maggie's home at Bridgeport as soon as possible. Angela was to examine his papers and was to destroy all those of a political nature, although he thought he had none that were worth destroying. She was to sell their Pensacola house at once, even on credit, if well secured.[3]

Two days later he scribbled in pencil another brief note to her: "I am quite well, and write this upon my knees at the foot of a tree."[4]

On May 28 they reached Chattanooga, where he talked with a Confederate officer who had seen Angela in Atlanta a few days before. Husband and wife had missed each other there by only a few hours. How he regretted his captors' determination to hurry him on! "Your affection for me

1. Hill was a Georgia politician of the second rank but of respectable reputation among his political associates. He was a close friend of Mallory. General Cobb, also of Georgia, had been speaker of the House of Representatives in 1849, had been elected Governor of Georgia in 1851, and had been made Secretary of the Treasury in 1857. He was a strong secessionist, and served in the Confederate Army as a brigadier general and, finally, major general. He was not favorably disposed to the administration of Jefferson Davis.
2. Mallory to his wife, from Allantor, May 25, 1865.
3. *Ibid.*
4. Mallory to his wife, from Resaca, May 27, 1865.

is so sacred," he wrote to Angela that night, ". . . that . . . I feel a pride in you that enables me to bear up bravely. . . ." His journey so far, he assured her, had been as pleasant as under the circumstances it could have been.[5]

The rest of the letter was a blend of admonitions regarding her safety, and miscellaneous chat. She should try to sell his horse, either at La Grange or at Atlanta, where, he had heard, the Yankees were eager to buy thoroughbreds. She was to go to Bridgeport, he repeated, without delay. Their friends could tell her when railroad travel would be open through Augusta, Richmond, and Washington. If possible, she was to secure as a chaperon some "Federal officer who is a gentleman." He hoped that their servants would remain faithful. As long as his wife's love burned warm and bright, while she bore her trials after the example set by her Savior—"here's a sight for those who love, and a smile for those who hate; and whatever sky's above, here's a heart for any fate."

He had seen by the papers that Mrs. Clay and Mrs. Davis, while en route northward with their husbands, had been very bitter and sarcastic toward the Yankees, and had been returned south. There was no truth in the story of President Davis' feminine disguise when he had been arrested. A thousand kisses to his darling Ruby, and love to noble Buddy and to dear Attie![6]

Meanwhile, a new and pregnant act of a greater drama was opening—the period of American history misnamed the Era of Reconstruction. A revolution—or, as the South regarded it, a movement for national independence—had been crushed. But the essential task, the reorganization of a society, North and South, that had been shaken to its roots, was yet to be achieved. As Mallory and his companions were being escorted northward, the first moves in the political program which was, for better or for worse, to remake America were getting under way.

The Freedmen's Bureau of the War Department had been created on March 3, 1865. It was a military administration for the protection of the Negro in his new constitutional rights, and for the economic relief of all the needy, black and white, of the South. It was frequently despotic in its actions, and it was used as a party tool by the Radical Republicans, but it undoubtedly did immense good in fulfilling its primary functions of alleviating desperate want and of throwing the shield of legal guardianship around the freed Negro.[7]

5. Mallory to his wife, from Chattanooga, May 28, 1865.
6. *Ibid.*
7. Cf., regarding the Reconstruction period: J. G. Randall, *Civil War and Reconstruction* (Boston, 1937), 689-846; Charles E. Chadsey, *The Struggle Between President Johnson and*

By early May, the presidential reconstruction program of Andrew Johnson was proceeding with relative smoothness. Provisional governors were being appointed in all the former Confederate states where they had not already been established by Lincoln. Under these governors, constitutional conventions were being called and new frames of government established, with legal rights accorded to the freedmen. The beaten people of the South were cooperating with good grace. The "Black Codes," soon to be the object of violent Radical attack, were defended by Southerners—not with totally convincing logic—as merely necessary provisions made by the new state legislatures for the maintenance of law and order under the new conditions.

On Sunday, June 4, the prisoners reached Fort Lafayette, where Stephen and Hill were placed in the same cell. Shortly afterward the two men were locked in separate compartments. On his first day of solitary confinement Stephen wrote to his wife that he and Hill regarded their separation as a bitter addition to the rigors of imprisonment, but that both their rooms were airy, clean, and sufficiently spacious for moderate exercise. The beds were clean, straw mattresses, and the food, though plain, was abundant and wholesome. He was permitted on that first day to walk for exercise, for an hour or two, alone, on the parade ground of the fort.

It was inconceivable, he wrote again to his wife, how much consolation he derived from the reflection that no prisoner or other unfortunate ever in the past had applied to him for aid without receiving it. Seeing now how small acts of kindness from others lightened the prisoner's weary burden, he could well understand to what extent his own acts of mercy in favor of prisoners and distressed persons must have been appreciated by them.[8]

He was confident that he would not be detained in prison for any great length of time. When it was understood that his entire career in Congress had been marked by adhesion to the Union; that he had taken the most earnest stand in favor of compromise even after Florida seceded, and by telegraphing advice to Chase not to attack Fort Pickens had brought down upon himself the bitter rebuke of his own people; that he had resigned his office as Navy Secretary on hearing of Johnston's surrender, and had sought only to return to his state as a private citizen, in order to aid as far as he could in restoring that state to the Union; that he wished to take the oath of allegiance and to pass the rest of his days in quiet—when all these facts

*Congress Over Reconstruction* (New York, 1897); Paul S. Peirce, *The Freedmen's Bureau: A Chapter in the History of Reconstruction* (Iowa City, Iowa, 1904); E. Merton Coulter, *The South During Reconstruction, 1865-1877* (Baton Rouge, La., 1947).

8. Mallory to his wife, June 7, 1865.

were understood, he was confident, his release on parole or on some other terms would be granted. To Angela's affection and "zeal in the proper quarters" he looked for a proper presentation of his case. She knew the names of many who would be ready to aid her in this work. Let God watch over and protect his noble wife and his children and servants! To His goodness and mercy must they all look.[9]

This letter was followed a few days later by another to Angela. He could not "keep from paper," he told her, "the whisperings of a heart from which you are never absent, though I greatly fear that the distance and the obstacles which separate us may permit not an echo of them to reach you."[10]

Although his imprisonment, he said, was robbed of many of its rude aspects no less by the uniform attention bestowed upon his health and comfort than by the humanity and courtesy which the officers ever mingled with the vigorous discharge of their duties, it was to him "but one remove from death."[11] Constrained separation from those who filled up his world and who formed his only source of happiness in it, separation from his wife and children, was a vulture at his heart. Could he but be assured of their welfare, he could possess his soul in patience, and regard the "rusting away" of his life in prison as but a preparation for that union with them which he hoped for in the next life. But, he said, he knew too well his Angela's nature not to be convinced that life to her would be a weary road so long as she was kept apart from him.

But he desired her to keep up her courage. He was sure that his case, properly presented, would receive the favorable consideration of President Johnson. He asked her to constitute herself his representative in high quarters, and was sure that her love and courage, aided by the counsels of prudent friends, would know no such word as failure. This was somewhat over-optimistic. The President, on May 29, had issued his amnesty proclamation, but had excluded from its benefits all civil, military, and naval officers of the Confederacy.

So many of his previous political ideas, he admitted, had changed. As a slaveholder he recognized that the institution was gone forever, and he was prepared to conform to the new situation. He wanted no political station, nor did he care to cast another vote. He wished to pass the rest of his days

9. *Ibid.*
10. Mallory to his wife, June 12, 1865.
11. *Ibid.* Mallory's diary certainly refutes the charge made by Benjamin Hill, Jr., to the effect that "They [Mallory and Hill] were not allowed to have any communication, and were treated with great indignity and unkindness by the officials" (Hill, Jr., *Benjamin Hill,* 46).

in the walks of private life. He even desired to see at Washington a "strong government." He had observed and thought much during the late struggle, and had surrendered many ideas of government and individual rights as being Utopian. Quite in accord with the sentiments prevailing at the moment on the national scene were these feelings, as the new governments were being set up in the Southern states by the President with the loyal concurrence of Southern men.

His affections came near to overwhelming him. "Oh, if I could but see you for an hour! Kiss our little ones for me. Tell my noble boy Buddy that I long ardently to see him. And tell my servants that I count upon their good faith until we meet. God grant that I may be able to do something for them to start them fairly in their new life."[12]

The prisoner gradually adapted himself, as well as he could, to his difficult surroundings. He played chess with himself, read from the books which, apparently, were supplied to him abundantly from the fort library, and occasionally was permitted to talk with Hill in one or the other of their cells. One day they passed a pleasant hour in comparing the Catholic and Protestant versions of the New Testament. He was much troubled by the gout, which, he felt, was aggravated by the dampness of the prison. He had spells of dizziness, and spent whole days in bed. He was frequently visited by the officers in charge of the prisoners, and found them courteous and thoughtful for his comfort.

His chief thoughts were of his loved ones at home. He was worried at not having had any recent letters from Maggie: "What can be the reason," he wrote in his diary, "that I have recd. no letter from my dear daughter since her note of the 4th inst.? May God grant that no misfortune has occurred to her!"[13]

The pain of separation from Angela and the children was made to seem more keen by an event which occurred in mid-July. He and Hill had, apparently, been put back in the same compartment. One day Brevet Brigadier General Burke, commandant of the fort, came to them to notify Hill that he was released. "He is gone," Mallory wrote in his diary that night, "and I am here alone. My trust is in God. I rejoiced at his release, but feel my isolation bitterly. God bless him; he will soon embrace his dear wife and children."[14]

At this time there was lying on President Johnson's desk at the White

12. Mallory to his wife, June 12, 1865.
13. Mallory, Diary, part II, pp. 2-3, July 17, 1865.
14. Ibid., 3, July 7, 1865.

House the most important of the letters written by Mallory from Fort Lafayette. Less than three weeks after his incarceration the former Secretary of the Confederate Navy had addressed to the Chief Executive a formal plea for pardon. The communication constituted a review and defense of Mallory's entire political career up to that moment, and stated his present attitude toward the Federal government.

The fact is that Mallory and some of the other Southern political prisoners were, at this time, in some danger of undergoing severe punishment. "If embittered Northern politicians could have worked their will," says William Watson Davis, "Mallory, Yulee, and probably Allison would have been tried and executed for treason."[15] The opinion of Mallory held by the Federal Judge-Advocate-General was: "His administration of a department of the rebel Confederacy whose only business, in the absence of a navy, was simply the authorization and direction of a general system of piracy, has rendered his agency in conducting the rebellion more conspicuous and his name more odious than that of his former colleague Yulee."[16]

In his letter to the Chief Executive, Mallory explained that he was respectfully petitioning for a pardon and for the restoration to himself of the rights of a citizen of the United States. He was anxious to do all that was necessary in order to take the oath of allegiance and, in good faith, to assume, maintain, and observe all the duties of a citizen of the United States. While unwilling to advert to others whose antecedents or present positions might be analogous to his own, or to suggest comparisons between relative claims to executive clemency or consideration, he deemed it proper to state frankly some circumstances of his case.[17]

He was now, he wrote, over fifty years of age; and, from his entry into politics, he had never been guilty of any disloyalty to the Union. He had loved the Union. Never had he in any way conspired against it.

When Florida, by a convention of her people, had formally seceded, he had, at the command of that convention, withdrawn from the Senate and retired to private pursuits. That was, he averred, the most painful act of his life.

He had consistently believed that secession, whatever its theoretical justification, was unwise. The South, he had held, could best procure redress of her grievances by remaining within the Union. Hence, in the dark days

15. *The Civil War and Reconstruction in Florida* (New York, 1913), 336.
16. J. Holt to Secretary Stanton, November 23, 1865 (*O.R.A.,* Ser. II, Vol. VIII, p. 865)
17. Mallory to President Johnson, from Fort Lafayette, June 21, 1865 (Mallory Letterbook, Library of Congress)

of 1860 to 1861, he had looked first to the Committee of Thirteen appointed by the Senate to consider means of adjusting the sectional difficulties; and secondly, he had hoped for some compromise based on love of the Union and the fraternal feeling which, he had believed, still prevailed in the country.

When the Committee of Thirteen had failed to effect grounds of concord—and it was Mallory's view that the failure was due not to the difficulties of the task but to the lack of organization of the body—and after South Carolina had seceded, he had persisted in his hope that the dread arbitrament of blood would be averted; and to this end he had exhausted every argument and effort in his power.

Learning with astonishment and grief, at Washington, that armed bands of Alabamians and Floridians had assembled at Pensacola in order to attack Fort Pickens, and viewing such a proceeding with horror, since it would have destroyed all hope of peace and reconciliation, he had addressed by telegraph the commanding officer of the proposed expedition, and thus prevented a fatal calamity. For thus interfering, as well as for his opposition to disunion, he endured the bitter hostility of some of the leading men of his state.[18]

He had already returned to Pensacola when, upon the organization of the provisional Confederate government, he received from President Davis a request to come to Montgomery. At the "urgent and repeated" plea of Davis he had accepted the office of Secretary of the Navy. In February, 1862, when the government was reorganized, he had tried to resign the post, but the President had refused to release him.

Though opposed to disunion, he had nevertheless regarded the commands of his state as decisive of his path of duty, and he had followed where she led. She had repeatedly honored him by her confidence and favor, far beyond his merits; and he had accepted her trusts and confidence with full knowledge of her claims to state sovereignty. "I will not further advert to the Confederacy," he continued, "than to say that, in my judgment, it contained the fruitful elements of its own destruction; and that now, recognizing its death as the will of Almighty God, I regard and accept His dispensation as decisive of the questions of Slavery and Secession.

"Your large views and patriotic labours for the organization of the Southern States and their restoration to the union as States entitle you to the gratitude which a generous people will not fail to evince. If permitted I

18. Cf. *supra*, pp. 124-29.

would, as would many others whose positions are similar to mine, be glad to aid, so far as a private citizen by precept and example might, in conforming the course of my State to her new status under the policy which you so wisely adopted."

He concluded the letter with a categorical denial of the charge that he had ever treated Federal prisoners cruelly.[19]

Shortly afterward a follow-up communication was sent by Mallory to Secretary Seward. He apologized to Seward for thus troubling him, but said, "I trust . . . to that generous kindness which misfortune ever meets at your hands, for my apology." Imprisonment, in consequence of the "utter ruin of my private affairs and the helpless condition of my family," seemed worse than death.[20]

He had carefully read such expositions of the President's policy as had reached him, and accepted it in its entirety—continued union of all the States, abolition of slavery, and so forth. He desired to do all in his power to make that program effective. As a slaveholder he had already taken measures to place his servants in positions where they could make themselves not only independent but useful. "I feel assured," he continued, "that your review of the revolution, its causes and consequences, no less than the men engaged in it, has convinced you that your course toward Southern men must, to a large extent, be determined rather by what they may justly be expected to do in the future than by what they have done in the past. The dead must bury its dead. New ideas must underlie new laws and institutions at the South, and these must be the work of time, intelligence, and mutual confidence and labour; and those who will in good faith become workers in the new field of the President's policy should, I think, be set at work."

The sufferings of the Southern people, he ventured to suggest, could not be defeated and allayed by mere words. His desire to serve them in the difficult days of reconstruction, was most ardent. "All my sympathies are with them, for with them I and mine must live and die."

He regarded it as the duty of every Southern man to recognize at once the supremacy of the United States and to conform his private and public conduct to the President's policy. He looked upon every man who sought further to agitate secession or slavery as an enemy of the public peace.

"These views," he concluded, ". . . convince me that I can do good service in my State, and that the President can have no desire to keep me here. I

19. Mallory to President Johnson, June 21, 1865, *supra. cit.*
20. Mallory to Hon. W. R. Seward, July 1, 1865 (Mallory Letterbook).

would feel very grateful to you for your interposition in my behalf, and know that you would find in my future course nothing to induce you to regret it."[21]

This plea was being addressed, although Mallory did not know it, to an administration which was fast losing its control of the government. The Radical Republicans in Congress, led by Sumner, Stevens, Fessenden, and others, were carefully organizing their campaign to supersede the moderate policy of Johnson by a ruthless "punitive" program against the South. Their views were well expressed by one of Sumner's correspondents, who declared that to let the South back into the Union would be a "cruel cruel breach of faith and honor to the Freedmen,"[22] and by another who expressed his opinion that the readmission of the Southern states with or without Negro suffrage would be a serious blunder; a "probationary system," he said, was "indispensable."[23]

Mallory received word on July 19 that his wife and children had arrived safely at Maggie's home in Bridgeport. It was the twenty-seventh anniversary of his marriage. "I return my heartfelt thanks to Almighty God," he wrote to Angela immediately, "for the safety and welfare of yourself and my children, a matter of far greater interest to me than anything affecting my own person can possibly be."[24]

The letter announcing her arrival at Bridgeport had, he told her, awakened all his dormant philosophy, and enabled him to say with defiant cheerfulness, "Let fate do her worst, there are relics of joy, bright dreams of the past which she cannot destroy." There was not in prison walls or bars, nor in all earthly ills, power enough to rob him of the twenty-seven years of happiness with all their precious memories—those "crushed yet fragrant flowers"—which began on their wedding day.

He told her that he had requested from General Joseph Hooker, second in command at the prison, permission for herself and the children to visit Fort Lafayette. General Hooker, he was confident, would grant the request, as he was of the old army and was known to be generous to the fallen and defeated.[25]

Nor was the Federal commander the only one who was to be petitioned

21. *Ibid.*

22. Judge J. C. Underwood, from Alexandria, Va., to Sumner, July 17, 1865, quoted in E. Merton Coulter, *op. cit.*, 41, n. 52.

23. Thomas I. Durant, from New Orleans, to Sumner, October 1, 1865, quoted in *ibid.*

24. Mallory to Angela, July 19, 1865.

25. Mallory to Angela, July 20, 1865.

for a favor. Stephen proposed to Angela a plan that had been for some time past forming in his mind. He asked her to call personally on the President and Mr. Seward, with a plea for his pardon. With both of these men, he said, his relations had ever been kind and cordial. She needed no introduction to either, for messengers in behalf of justice and mercy were, he was sure, always admitted by them. Angela could, "in her own frank manner," satisfy the President and Seward of the correctness of the conclusions to which he had already called their attention, and ask for his release. Seward had already written to him two letters, in one of which he had kindly promised to bring his case to the President's attention.[26]

Marvin had been made provisional governor of Florida, and he well knew whether or not Stephen's services could aid the government in the state. Angela should try to see the Judge before the latter left for the South. And Angela's intercession with the President, thought Stephen, was absolutely essential.[27]

Stephen's current "sentiments, purposes, and views" were further elaborated in this same letter. State sovereignty, and the consequent right of secession by a number of states as a remedy for political wrongs deemed irreparable by any other means, were the doctrinal foundations of the "revolution"; and those principles, he believed, were older than the Constitution, co-existent with that document, and cherished as a rule of faith by leading men of the South from Jefferson to Calhoun. But a large majority of the states and overwhelming majorities of the people had decided against the theory, no less by cartridge boxes than by ballot boxes; so that the right of secession was "laid as effectively as Father O'Leary ever laid a ghost."

Stephen accepted frankly and without qualification that verdict of the people. Butler, he added, might ridicule the practice of "teaching religion orthodox by Apostolic blows and knocks,"[28] but they would ever be applied to sustain the orthodoxy of political as well as of religious faith. As to slavery, he would not restore it if he could. His only aim with regard to his own twenty-five or thirty black servants was to see them settled in some honest pursuit suitable for their support. (At about this time, incidentally, Mallory's friend John Reagan was urging his fellow-Texans to concede the franchise to the black man, and to submit willingly to Republican policy.)[29]

26. *Ibid.*
27. *Ibid.*
28. Cf. Samuel Butler's *Hudibras,* part I, canto I, line 199: "And prove their doctrine orthodox By apostolic blows and knocks."
29. Reagan's letter to the people of Texas, written from his prison at Fort Warren, Boston, August 11, 1865, reprinted in Reagan's *Memoirs,* 286-95; original in *Executive Correspondence*

He closed this letter in his usual playful and affectionate tone. Angela must not permit her mind to be disturbed by apprehensions of his suffering, nor by any incident of his imprisonment beyond that of their separation. The officers of the fort were all gentlemen of high tone, and he had been granted every indulgence consistent with the rules of the prison, and all the consideration he could justly expect. In fact, his captors commanded his gratitude, and he would never forget their uniform urbanity and courtesy, despite all the restraints upon him.

He was very lonely, of course; but then he had more time to think of her. He was very silent, of course; but then he should have all the more to say to her. His walking was restricted to very narrow limits, of course; but then he looked forward to such pleasant walks with her. And thus she could easily see that all his clouds had silver linings, and that she peeped out from under every one of them. He trusted that she would find his reasoning more satisfactory than did the Chief Clerk of the India House that of Charles Lamb, who, when rebuked for inattention to the duties of his desk, with the remark, "Mr. Lamb, you come to your desk too late in the morning, sir!" replied, "Yes, but you see, Mr. Clerk, I go home so early in the afternoon."[30]

In a postscript he suggested that she might persuade Marvin to accompany her to the White House. The President, in carrying out his reconstruction policy, must necessarily look more to what a man was to be and to do in the future rather than what the man had done in the past. But "I am ready to be judged by either rule." He said that he had been desirous of taking the Sacrament, and had written to Archbishop McCloskey of New York to find out whether a priest could visit him. The Archbishop had written to Washington for such permission. "I would prefer an American or Irish priest; strange that I can not surmount my repugnance to Germans or Frenchmen."[31]

On July 21, he wrote to ask Angela "to purchase for me a pair of plain steel framed light spectacles. Strange to say, mine are getting too old for me; but then, you know, I have had them a long time. To guide your purchase it is unnecessary to say how old I am getting. I differ so widely from some who are considered wise in their generation, that I feel sometimes as

---

(Executive Archives, Austin, Tex.). Cf. also Charles W. Ramsdell, *Reconstruction in Texas* (New York, 1910), 87-88, for summary of this letter. Cf. also Reagan's letter to the Governor, from near Palestine (Reagan's home), *Memoirs*, 301, summarized in Ramsdell, *op. cit.*, 120.

30. Mallory to Angela, July 20, 1865.

31. *Ibid.*

if I were but now attaining the years of discretion; and you will be quite safe to put me down as of a 'certain age.' I must trust their selection to your own eyes, for I have seen rather more clearly with them than I have with my own; and I doubt not that had I more frequently looked through your glasses, I would not now have to complain of some troublesome spectacles."[32]

His long hours of solitude had induced also more weighty thoughts on political matters. Believing as he did in a superintending, overruling Providence, he accepted the defeat of the Confederacy as the will of Almighty God. This once admitted, it was easy to see other reasons of a more natural character which foredoomed the Southern effort to failure. "Had independence been secured, the Confederacy would not, in my judgment, have held together more than three or four years. Voltaire says that the most inscrutable of God's ways is the circumstance of His placing so many incapables at the heads of governments. And surely among us we had so many of the 'rule or ruin' type who would rather rule in hell than serve in heaven, so many theorists and abstractionists, so many prejudiced and obstinate yet feeble politicians, so many, as Dr. Johnson says, 'with the nodality of the oak without its strength, and the contortions of the Sybil without her inspiration,' that I can truly see independence as leading to anarchy and then to despotism. The President, from the peculiarity of his intellectual character, adhered to it [the hope of Southern independence] as the ivy does to the wall,—until the wall is ruined,—and then adheres to it to sustain and fall with it."[33]

The brightest sunbeams that found their way into Stephen's cell were the occasional letters from his "darling Ruby." He told her, one day during the second month of his imprisonment, that her recent epistle had given him as much pleasure as anything that had happened since he had been "at this fashionable resort."[34] He passed some high compliments on her epistolary style, and, for her further improvement in the art, added some instructions which, considering the fact that Ruby was only ten years old, were of a rather ponderous character.

He also gave her some much more serious advice. Ruby and her brothers were to avoid entertaining any unkind feelings against little Northern boys and girls, who were always to be treated gracefully and gently. "We are no longer at war; we are all one people now, and your duty to your country, to yourselves, and to God requires you to banish all ill feelings towards

32. Mallory to Angela, July 21, 1865.
33. Mallory to Angela, July 21, 1865.
34. Mallory to Ruby, July 22, 1865.

them if you should have any."[35] All contentions and wrangles about North and South were to be avoided. His children must remember that "no wrongs that are ever likely to be inflicted upon them politically are worth the sacrifice of one single life to rectify."[36]

In view of such an attitude on the part of the conquered, there was an excellent prospect that the sectional breach would be healed, not only politically but by a real union of sentiment. At this time the provisional governors seemed to be doing their best to win the good will of the South. Said Governor Hamilton in his proclamation to the people of Texas: "The Government of the United States seeks not . . . to humiliate the people of the South. It but asks them to be friends rather than enemies."[37]

In the seventh week of his imprisonment Stephen had the joy of receiving a visit from Angela and the children, including Maggie. "Oh, how glad I was to see her and them!" he wrote in his diary the next day. "And yet," he added, "their presence made me feel so sad that but for an extraordinary exertion to appear cheerful I must have looked down when they left me. I find that in my excitement of mind, I omitted a great many matters which I desired to converse about with Angela."[38]

On the following day he hastened to write to Ruby that the visit had been so brief that he had no time for even one of the thousand things he wished to say to her, one of which was that she must commit to memory the "Prologue" by Oliver Wendell Holmes. She could obtain the poem in Holmes's works; in the Boston edition of 1862 the desired piece could be found on page 308, beginning, "A Prologue! Well, of course, the ladies know." She was merely to memorize it, and to make no attempt to recite it or to use gestures until the two of them had rehearsed it together. There followed a long exhortation on the utility of taking careful notes from her readings, so as to provide herself with sparkling and apt commonplaces for conversation.

He assured her that she was, "as a tailor might say, 'cut out' for a talker."[39] Yet, while extolling the art of conversation, he added some pertinent qualifications. Silence, too, had its virtues. It was a wonderfully defensive armor, and very little harm had ever come from wearing it. For a woman, he thought, it was more difficult to learn how and when to be

35. *Ibid.*
36. Mallory to Ruby, July 22, 1865.
37. *Annual Cyclopedia*, 1865, 11-12.
38. Mallory, Diary, part II, p. 4 (July 25, 1865)
39. Mallory to Ruby, July 26, 1865.

silent than when and how to talk. A bright, clever, cultivated woman, confronted under pleasant circumstances with stupid or inferior men, finds it difficult to play second fiddle; and so she talks, and sparkles, and shines, is luminous and witty. She never learns to become a listener until she finds that "the great herd of men will flock like crows around her as long as she is unarmed, but are off at the first sight of a weapon, and will tell all the other crows how she is armed."[40]

Of course her father desired that Ruby should be a good talker. But "I would have you talk like Tokay wine, superior to all other wines and greatly prized by the best judges; or like precious stones, very rare and brilliant, and whose value everybody is ready to admit; or like a faithful mirror, which ever responds truthfully to whatever is presented."[41] She must speak only when she has something to say, and then she must say it "with the most charming manner and in the most appropriate language."[42] It requires courage to be perfectly truthful; and hence, he thought, men are, as a general rule, more truthful than women.

The last lines of the letter to Ruby revived old echoes: "But, my dear little Ruby, if you will conform in all respects to the example of your mother I will never ask of you anything beyond. Come and see me soon."[43]

That Mallory had no regrets for his past political actions, and that he was hopeful for the future of the country, and ready to play an energetic part as a citizen in the new era was made manifest in a long letter of early August to his friend Zachariah Chandler.[44]

Chandler had promised to forward the prisoner's cause at Washington. In expressing his thanks for this favor, Mallory reminded his friend that, "should my presence be for any purpose required by the government, it can be as well secured by my parole as by my continued imprisonment." He added, characteristically, "For, come what may, I must abide with my people." His present position, he continued, could readily have been avoided. Means and opportunity for leaving the country after the surrender had been at his command. But he saw the South lying bleeding and prostrate; and, although he would not be understood as reflecting upon those who enter-

40. *Ibid.*                                    41. *Ibid.*
42. *Ibid.*

43. *Ibid.* A brief note to his son Buddy at this time contained an instruction of another kind: "Your signature to this letter [sent by Buddy to his father on July 19 in collaboration with sister Maggie] is 'Stephen Mallory'. Why do you ignore the 'R'? Unless you have some sufficient reason,—and I cannot think of any,—you must retain it; just because it is a part of your name, and next, out of respect to your Irish Grandfather Stephen Russell who was, 'take him all in all', a rare man in his day" (Mallory to Buddy, July 28, 1865).

44. Cf. *supra*, p. 69, n. 23.

tained or acted upon opposite views, he had not been able to find in the temptations of ease and security, nor in the fear of personal consequences, a justification for abandoning his homeland in its darkest hour.

He was confident that the Southern people were ready and willing to recognize and to conform to their new status. This view he based on his knowledge of the views Southern leaders expressed during the six months preceding the fall of Richmond, when defeat was already seen to be probable.

While in some sections of the South a spirit of defiant anarchy was said to prevail, the people in many other localities were quiet, orderly, and industrious, working their farms with hired Negro labor, without difficulty, manfully making the most of the situation. Where disorders existed, they were due often to small local feuds among the Southern people themselves. There was no doubt, Mallory declared, that the South would enjoy a "thorough pacification" and a revival of her prosperity.

But time was necessary. The wounds and heart burnings of the war could not be ignored by a people whose every hearthstone had been visited by death, while the monuments of their subjugation were still before their eyes. But, while the war's sad memories might be recalled by a small minority to foster agitation or to promote strife, they would stimulate her sons generally to bind up her wounds and to restore peace within the Union to a brave and proud people.

In regard to the problem of the Negro, Mallory was optimistic. He believed that God had decreed "not only that the Negro should dwell amongst us, but also that he should be free." All schemes for getting rid of the black man in this country had always seemed to Mallory to be impracticable. If any such plan were now suggested, he would regard it as inconsistent with the interests of both North and South. No true friend of the Negro would desire to remove him. The Southern people, under fair and just laws, would find in him a most desirable agricultural free laborer. The Southerner had no prejudice against the Negro, as time would show. The Southerner's interest lay in keeping the black man in the country, and in making him as useful to it as possible. This interest would, in time, render easy the removal of the obstacles in the way of the Negro's progressive usefulness, now that the great stumbling block, slavery, had been laid aside. Free Negroes, Mallory pointed out, had been themselves slaveholders and real property holders in Florida ever since the acquisition of the territory from Spain; and these freedmen had ever been regarded as good law-abiding people.

As a qualification of these views regarding the Negro, Mallory would probably at this time have approved the statement of the Florida Convention of 1865: "The people of the State of Florida, in general Convention assembled, do ordain and declare, that while we recognize the freedom of the colored race, and are desirous of extending to them full protection, . . . We declare it the unalterable sentiment of this Convention that the laws of the States shall be made and executed by white men."[45]

The most significant paragraph of Mallory's letter to Chandler is the concluding one: "I concur in all you say of the power developed by the North, a power that finds no parallel in history; and I am sure that you were not prepared for the resources and strength manifested by the South. It may be that, in His inscrutable wisdom, the God of Battles, in decreeing that, as a people, we are one and indissoluble, presented as a warning to mankind the tremendous power of the Separate Sections. Evidences are abundant that the warning has been taken. May it constitute an enduring bond of peace on Earth to men of good will."[46]

In the summer of 1865 Mallory had an opportunity to display, in practical form, his loyalty to the Union. The raiding cruiser *Shenandoah,* commanded by James Waddell of North Carolina, was still, four months after the formal termination of hostilities, operating against Federal commerce in the southwest Pacific. His isolation from the seat of political events in America had kept Waddell ignorant of the fact that the war was over; and he could hardly be blamed for refusing to believe the assurances offered to him by the outraged officers of Federal merchantmen which he was still energetically seizing.

It was, of course, at Mallory's order that the *Shenandoah* had been dispatched on her mission, and he knew the vessel's itinerary and capabilities. Actuated by a "desire to do what I can to stop this more than useless destruction of property," he penned a note to Brigadier General Martin Burke, commandant of Fort Lafayette, with a constructive suggestion. The speed of the *Shenandoah,* he informed Burke, was such that the heavier armed vessels now searching for her would have small chance of success. The surest means of catching up with her would be to use a light, fast, propeller-driven ship, provided with the necessary information and credentials to convince Waddell that his mission was over. To facilitate the task of the Federal Navy Department Mallory wrote out from memory the planned course of the Confederate raider: starting from the Cape of Good Hope

45. *Florida Convention Journal,* 1865, 81.
46. Mallory to Chandler, August 4, 1865 (Mallory Letterbook).

she was to have steered nearly a due east course to Australia, looking in at Sydney, thence northward along the east shores of New Guinea, in the track of whalemen, visiting the Louisiade Archipelago, the Moluccas, and onward via Loo Choo to Japan, and thence to the Okhotsk Sea. Once apprised of the true state of political affairs, Commander Waddell would be only too glad to cease his depredations.[47]

Ruby was very much in her father's mind. He sent her a long letter in the first week of that long sultry August at Fort Lafayette.

Her letters, he assured her, gave him deep pleasure. And, as one of the sources of purest enjoyment to which she must look forward in life was her ability to contribute to the happiness of others, she must continue to write to him. He reminded her that she enjoyed an advantage over him in the matter of letter writing. She had so many fruitful subjects on which to elaborate—her delightful Bridgeport home, her music lessons, her companions, walks, rides, dances, and plays. Her father, on the contrary, was forced to "sit here like a solitary spider in his corner, and spin out for myself the threads of all the fabricks I weave for you."[48]

His mention of the spider suggested another admonition which, characteristically, he immediately subjoined: she and Attie were to read a little book called the *Natural History of the Spider*. There was no insect nor animal which at the same time so wonderfully exhibited the goodness of God in adjusting its instincts to its destiny, and displayed also so many habits and traits worthy of imitation. Ruby could not but be charmed with the female spider's domestic economy and housekeeping. Like most very tidy ladies she was just a bit of a "fuss maker." When she once put her parlor in order she did not permit Mr. Spider to "lie around loose" on her carpet or furniture, or make any litter; and she enforced her wishes upon these points with something just as painful as a broomstick. But she made up for a quick temper by being the most loving, courageous, industrious, and ingenious wife in the world. Ruby must read the book.[49]

She was to work hard, he warned her, at her music lessons, under her skilled teacher, Miss Thorpe. When she had learned some pieces, he too would master them, and "we will play together, just as Mag and I used to do, 'in the days when we went gipsying, long, long ago.' "

Distance was not necessarily a bar to their loving intimacy. "I sit here by the hour all alone, and let my thoughts wander to Bridgeport, and so

47. Mallory to Brig. Gen. Burke, September 19, 1865 (Mallory Letterbook).
48. Mallory to Ruby, August 3, 1865.
49. *Ibid.*

intense are they that many a time when you are playing with your little nephew, or are with Miss Thorpe taking a lesson, I am there alongside of you, and I cannot make myself heard. You must act, however, just as if I were looking on all the time. Read and romp, and practice and pray, my dear Ruby, and let each bring you something useful and new. Kick up your heels and get good health and when we meet again we will have many interesting things in store for each other."

The letter closed with a gentle rap at Attie: "Can you tell me why Attila does not write to me? I know, of course, that he must be very busy, for all people who have nothing to do, are; but he might, I think, devote one day in the week, if necessary, to his correspondence."[50]

It was to Angela, however, that he revealed his deepest feelings as he sat in his lonely cell. "Your letter of the 16th", he wrote to her, ". . . came to me . . . There is an undertone of sadness about your little note, my dear wife,—what an artist might call depth of shadow,—which I would gladly change. The brightest and most inspiring pictures may develop sombre traits when placed in an uncongenial atmosphere; and you may be assured that prison walls demand, for the comfort of those whom they surround, the modern French school of art rather than the Salvator Rosa style, and that all shadows are deepened by falling upon them."[51]

Angela was apparently in need of some cheering and strengthening advice, and he strove to give it to her: "Neither my mood nor my situation qualify me much as comforter, but I think that you who have the consolations of our Holy Faith at hand, and who daily commune with God and the B. Virgin, must see that your present is not without its 'silver lining', and that cheerful, calm submission to the trials of our fleeting hour is a duty no less commanded by Heaven than by the dignity of our nature. I am not precisely upon a bed of roses, though it is a far better one than many a better man has had; but, believing that one of the strongest proofs of manhood, no less than one of the greatest gifts of God, is the power to rise upon mind over matter, above and beyond the 'slings and arrows of outrageous fortune,' I shall fear God and nothing else, and preserve a heart for any fate."[52]

In a postscript he termed this letter "stiff and stilted . . . ; I've done my best today to come out of the shadow, to see nothing but sunlight, to raise up heart,—and this is all the result."[53]

50. *Ibid.*
51. Mallory to Angela, August 21, 1865.
52. *Ibid.*                                    53. *Ibid.*

Summer was changing into fall. The President's reconstruction program was nearly completed. By the end of the year new constitutions and new governments would have been set up in all the former states of the Confederacy except Texas. Johnson was applying Lincoln's policy of moderation, and the South was beginning to hope and to live again. "I am satisfied," wrote General Grant to the President at this time, "that the mass of thinking people in the South accept the situation of affairs in good faith."[54]

But Congress, dominated by the Radicals, would assemble in early December, and the fortunes of the South would take a sharp turn for the worse. Johnson's brief period of comparative supremacy was fast waning as the leaves began to turn in late September.

The mornings at Fort Layfayette were cooler and decidedly damper now, and nightfall came sooner. Stephen confided more and more of his feelings to his diary. He said he had no heart to jot down the daily lapse of time in "this depressing confinement, which, but for the kind attention, the devotion and love of my dear wife would depress me beyond my powers of endurance. She, God bless and preserve her, comes here, and her interest at once disperses gloom and puts to flight all my preying and harrowing cares. Oh God Eternal, Father of all, and thou, Jesus, Saviour of the world, grant me gracefully and implicitly to submit myself humbly to thy dispensations, and to look upon them as justly due to my transgressions. I beseech Thee to pardon my sins, and to grant me grace to attain life with Thee. Watch over me, oh blessed spirit, assigned by God to attend upon my walk in life, and admonish me continually of my sins that my thoughts and words may not turn me aside from the path that leads to God. And Thou, oh Blessed Trinity, Father, Son, and Holy Ghost, I implore Thee to watch over and protect my wife and children, to guide them by Thy Holy precepts, to the end that they and I may enjoy bliss eternal with Thee. Amen."[55]

He read continually from such books as he had been able to procure, and daily he played chess with himself. On Monday, September 11, he recorded that he had been unwell for several days past and had taken twenty grains of "blue mass." The mind, he observed with forced cheerfulness, was always improved by the effects of this medicine, and was enabled to pray better. He was able to eat "scarcely anything." His only meal was breakfast, which consisted of a single piece of toast and a cup of tea.[56]

54. S. E. Morison and H. S. Commager, *The Growth of the American Republic* (2 vols; New York, 1937-40, II, 36).
55. Mallory, Diary, part II, p. 4 (October 10, 1865).
56. *Ibid.*, 7 (September 11, 1865).

On one of the first days of September he had an important conversation with an important visitor—Secretary of War Stanton, at Fort Lafayette on a tour of inspection. As the two men faced each other across the small rough table of Mallory's cell, they must have gone back in memory to a day fourteen years before, when Stanton, as legal advocate for David Yulee, and Mallory as attorney for himself had debated each other on the floor of Congress with the senatorship of Florida as the stake. The situation was indeed changed in this September of 1865, and no longer did they stand up to each other as political equals.

Gravely and not unkindly Stanton listened while the former Secretary of the Confederate Navy explained "frankly" his position on politics, his "views of the revolution, . . . [his] desire to take the oath of allegiance, to obtain pardon, . . . [and to] assume . . . all the duties . . . of a citizen of the U. States." Afterwards, recalling the interview, Mallory had his moments of doubt: "I regret now that I had this conversation with him, because I find in my mind the renewal in force of a belief which had nearly faded out, that he is prejudiced against me for and on account of his association as Counsel with Mr. Yulee, in opposition to my right to a seat in the U. S. Senate. I hope I do him injustice, and that he is guided in his high office only by a sense of justice and a fear of God; but nous verrons."[57]

The visits that brought him real consolation were those of his wife. "Whenever Angela comes," says his diary, "I feel a better man, and am more hopeful of my future, my distant future. She prays for me, and I feel the benefit of them [her prayers]. God give me strength and grace, and self control, never to say an unkind or inconsiderate word to her; for no wife can be more worthy of a husband's devoted affection."[58]

He read much from the New Testament, and meditated long on what he had read. "How simple and sublime," he wrote, "is the whole story of God upon earth, and by what natural and appropriate means are the great truths of salvation communicated to men. Infidelity, instead of accepting the simplicity of the means as an evidence of the sublimity of the truths of the great dispensation, cavils at them as opposed to truth."[59]

His concern for his dear ones was becoming more and more acute. On September 19 he penned a note to the commandant of the fort, asking permission to confer privately and confidentially with his wife and children

57. *Ibid.*, 7-8 (September 11, 1865).
58. *Ibid.*, 11 (September 15, 1865). Shortly after this time Angela went to Washington to plead personally with the President in her husband's behalf.
59. *Ibid.*, 12. September 17, 1865.

on their next visit. Hitherto a guard had remained in Mallory's cell as long as Angela and the children were present. "The unfortunate condition of my wife and children," he wrote, "impoverished and rendered dependent by the rebellion, is, of course, inexpressibly aggravated by my imprisonment. We mutually feel that they never before so urgently required my counsels and advice; and hence I respectfully pray that they may be allowed to visit and confer with me without the restraint which the presence of others imposes. They are innocent sufferers by my course in the rebellion, which never met my wife's approval. I beg that you will not regard me as inconsiderate, or as ungrateful for the kindness and courtesy which has so greatly ameliorated my confinement here, in making this request. I seek in good faith only permission to confer with my wife and children in relation to themselves and their future."[60]

The request was granted, and, when Angela and Buddy visited the prison a few days later, for the first time they were allowed to talk to Mallory without the presence of a guard.

As the weeks dragged on, the task of keeping up his spirits became increasingly difficult. "I have been much disturbed," he wrote on September 25, ". . . by a strange sensation, never before felt, of oppression, and, at the same time, of hollowness in my breast, accompanied by idle apprehensions of coming evils which I could not dispel. Not having eaten meat for some time, but living chiefly upon bread, may, perhaps, account for it. Have studied Spanish every day, and read several novels. . . . Read some in Thomas a Kempis. . . . Oh! Great God of the Universe! . . . have mercy upon me. I implore thee for mercy upon my cherished wife and my darling children; and that they may have grace to live and die in such manner as may bring them to Eternal Life."[61]

His desolation of spirit persisted. "26 Sept. Tues. Never before have I experienced the restlessness and distress that I now feel; and cut off from the counsels of others who might, perhaps, inform me of its cause, I am at a loss to account for these sensations. It is becoming difficult for me to adhere to any line of thought, or to fix my mind upon anything. I sometimes think that this condition of my mind may be the result of my abstinence from meat."[62]

He was continually distressed by anxiety for his wife and children. "My noble, pure souled Angela, my beloved Buddy and Attie and my dar-

60. Mallory to Brig. Gen. Martin Burke, September 19, 1865 (Mallory Letterbook).
61. Mallory, Diary, part II, pp. 13-14 (September 25, 1865).
62. Ibid., 14.

ling little Ruby! May God, in his infinite mercy, watch over them and shield them from harm, fill their hearts with obedience to him and love for mankind, and save their souls. I have done for them as well as I could, and my love for them is indescribable. My children have in them every element of goodness, and will, by God's grace, make good citizens."[63]

Remorse—whether reasonable or not—added to his depression. "In my present state of mind," he confessed, "how wretchedly frivolous seem all causes from which I have felt annoyance at my wife; whose affection, candor, truth and devotion to me, her children, and her duties, and relations as wife and mother, I have never had the slightest doubt of, or cause for doubt. But my heart, in condemning my conduct, tells me that if I loved her less I would have, at such times, been less hasty and inconsiderate. May God forgive me for all my harshness towards her, for she has merited from me nothing but love and kindness."[64]

By the end of September Mallory had not yet received any response to his letter addressed to the President, and he was much distressed at the apparent coldness displayed by the Chief Executive. Furthermore, Angela's interview with Johnson had been unsatisfactory. The President had listened to her appeal politely, but had made no promises and had taken no action in behalf of her husband. Finally, Mallory wrote a second note to the White House: "Mr. President: Permit me to throw myself upon your generous kindness. Hearing nothing of my petition to you of the 21 of June last I feared that I failed in the statement of my case.

"You are merciful and forbearing; and I am sure you would not inflict one pang upon any human heart but from a high sense of duty. Let me assure you therefore that . . . your efforts to raise up the South has my hearty thanks, and I pray you to release me that I may share the benefits they confer upon our people.

"If I seem importunate, Mr. President, I implore you to attribute it to my distress. I have been four months a prisoner; I am impoverished and ruined; my wife and children, helpless and dependent, are to me a constant source of mental anguish. Her anxiety led her to your presence in my behalf recently, but she had not the power to say to you what filled her heart.

"I recognize fully your policy for the restoration of harmony to a united people, and I will pledge my good faith to aid it to the extent of my power. . . ."[65]

63. Ibid., 14-15 (September 26, 1865).
64. Ibid., 15 (September 26, 1865)
65. Mallory to President Johnson, September 27, 1865 (Mallory Letterbook).

It was indeed true that at this time Andrew Johnson was preoccupied with other problems besides that of Mallory's status. In a little more than two months, Congress, led by his enemies, would reconvene. The event would mark, the President knew, a full-scale onslaught against his whole Reconstruction policy.

Early in October a new and crushing blow came to Mallory. Angela, on her way to visit her husband, was injured in a railroad accident and taken back to Bridgeport in a serious, though not critical, condition. "My dear Wife," he wrote on the evening of October 3, "Your note apprising me of your condition has this moment reached me and has added a feeling of sorrow almost unbearable to my sadness. I looked for your visit today until long past the time for you to come, not knowing how seriously hurt you were. Is it not sad, my noble wife, that I cannot go to you? To me this is the most depressing event of my life. I have ever been ready to lay it down for you, and to enable me now to go to you and serve you there could hardly be a condition prescribed that I would not assent to. But for a source of consolation to which I would not now be able to appeal but for your watchful affection I would this night despair. God grant that you may be speedily restored. God bless you."[66]

On the following day he declared to her that she was not for an instant absent from his mind. Nothing could make him forget the picture of her suffering, and he unable to fly to her to pillow her dear head in his arms! He could not imagine, he confided to her, how other men with fewer resources, less schooled in philosophy, and without religious faith (which, he confessed again, he owed to her devotion) could live under such a sorrow as this. His reliance upon God and upon his own soul, he admitted, was being sorely taxed. But "the great thought that Heaven can only be gained by bearing, as God exemplified, those crosses which are the lot of humanity . . . has a calming and soul subduing effect."[67]

He refused to despair. God would restore her to health. If she would but keep her spirits up and get well, he will promise to be as cheerful as in the old happy days of their courtship. "There is a good time coming, my noble wife, for all whose souls are right; and as I can only be subdued through you, I am confident of sharing in its blessings if you will but lead on with a heart for any fate."[68]

66. Mallory to Angela, October 3, 1865.
67. Mallory to Angela, October 4, 1865.
68. *Ibid.*

To Angela he had to write cheerfully. She must not guess the crucifixion of spirit revealed in his diary. "Oh my God!" he wrote in those secret pages, "I feel this heavy misfortune. Enable me to overcome my murmuring and wretched spirit, and to regard this as a cross which tries my soul for its sanctification. Lord Jesus, grant that she may be speedily restored, and that her heart may be cheered and purified by love of Thee. Walking this lonely cell to and fro, as I have seen wild beasts do in their cages, a thousand images of man's inhumanity to man crowd upon me and sicken me with life. Wrote twice to her. Her note of the 2nd gave me a terrible shock, and my condition of health does not enable me to resist much."[69]

His personal sorrows did not, however, completely extinguish his interest in political events. On October 5 he wrote to Governor Marvin a letter warmly approving the progressive sentiments of the latter's recent speech on reconstruction and the Negro problem. Marvin had recommended immediate extension of full civil rights to the Negro. This policy, said Mallory enthusiastically, was "far in advance of public opinion, as truth ever is," and he felt that the "wisdom, justice, and expediency of your views must speedily and firmly lodge them in the minds of judicious men in spite of every thing which the ghosts of the past may plead. . . ." Marvin's "wise and frank treatment" of the other political maladies of the Southern states also deserved commendation. Political Bourbons, Mallory declared, who could neither learn nor forget anything, might seek remedies in nostrums of the past; what was needed was precisely such programs as Marvin's, "of the living, progressive, common sense school . . . which . . . will sweep from the patient all the drugs, lotions, and plasters which political empirics would apply and get him upon his legs at once."[70]

Mallory took the opportunity to develop further his own views in regard to the Negro, who, he pointed out, had become a free man by the fiat of Almighty God. The South must take him as he was, and make the most of him. His progressive enlightenment and improvement in all that enabled man to do his duty toward God and society were demanded no less by the eternal principles of justice than by the plainest dictates of Southern interest. Opinions might differ as to the capacity of the black man for improvement, but every Southerner would admit that there were some Negroes whose

69. Mallory, Diary, part II, p. 15 (October 5, 1865).
70. Mallory to Marvin, October 3, 1865 (Mallory Letterbook). Cf. also Mallory's comment in his diary with regard to this part of Marvin's speech: "We must cut loose from the past and make a long stride in advance of former ideas" (Mallory, Diary, part II, p. 16 [October 5, 1865]).

good sense, good morals, and intelligence were quite equal to the judicious exercise and enjoyment of the rights of a free man. The attainment of the mass of former slaves to a condition pre-eminently superior to that of their progenitors in spite of the lions which Southern views had placed in their paths was sufficient answer to many a ream of foolscap argument against the Negro's capabilities.[71]

To his beloved Buddy, Mallory spoke of politics in a more comprehensive and philosophical manner. "Let me conjure you, my dear Son, never to draw sword or raise your hand against the Government or constituted authorities of your country, the United States of America. Its cause may possibly be wrong,—but judge not so harshly of this as to find justification in raising your arm against it. Act openly, frankly, honorably, towards it; and ever, in the fear and love of God, maintain . . . your rights under its flag. . . . Such have been my sentiments through life."[72]

He confided to his son his somber estimate of the meaning and effects of the war which had just concluded. Before the recent struggle, he declared, Americans had gloried in the possession of such inalienable and indestructible rights as "individual liberty," "freedom of the press," and the "consent of the governed." The war had, at least as far as the Southern states were concerned, abolished the exercise of those rights. The Southern states were being treated as conquered provinces under military law. The whole people of the South were at the uncontrolled command of the executive. This showed "how rapidly men drift when once they grasp irresponsible power."[73] The character of all power in government is aggressive, he said, with a constant tendency to augment itself; the history of our government provided no exception to this rule.[74]

During the war the Federal government had violated flagrantly the basic liberties of the people of the North, and now it was suppressing with even greater violence the rights of the citizens of the South. "It is impossible that such a course of events should not radically change the theory, the practice and the whole character of the Government, which will no longer be regarded as a Confederation of willing, sovereign states,—no longer be thought of as the creature or agent of the independent states, existing by their will, authority, and consent, but as a national, supreme government, existing by its own right, with right and power as well against the states, all or one, as

71. Mallory to Marvin, October 3, 1865 (Mallory Letterbook).
72. Mallory, Diary, part II, p. 12, letter to Buddy, September 27, 1865.
73. *Ibid.*, 9-10.
74. *Ibid.*, 10.

against individuals or foreign nations, to maintain itself, and to enforce obedience to its authority."[75]

One hope for American liberties Mallory saw: if the President should succeed in his program of "bringing the South back [to the Union] as States," these Southern states would be a "check on radicalism in every form." The people of the South were naturally conservative; they would conserve the basic rights of Americans as against all despotic tendencies of the central government. The state governments, maintained in their proper degree of vigor, were the necessary safeguards of American democracy.[76]

These are strong words in favor of Jeffersonian decentralization. Yet the essentially balanced character of Mallory's political thinking was revealed in his qualifying sentence: "Perhaps the changes coming and to come are required and will be well for us. I certainly look upon a reasonably strong government with more favor now than ever before."[77]

The duty of the men of the South was "to do all they can to restore their States to the Union at the earliest possible moment. The South, having lost, . . . must abide the consequences, and under God's holy laws and grace, so act as best to recover from disaster."[78]

Some much more personal admonitions were addressed to Buddy by his father: "Cling to your religion, my son, . . . as the sheet anchor of life here and to come. Never permit yourself to . . . question its great truths, or mysteries. Faith must save you or nothing can; and faith implies mystery. The rationalist who believes only what he can understand . . . has led away the ardent minds of youth from the days of the Grecian philosophers. . . . He cannot be a Christian."[79]

Buddy should partake regularly of Holy Communion. "I frankly say to you,—and not without regret and humiliation,—that I too long neglected this, and that I did not give you the proper example. Learn by my present feeling . . . to do your duty. Before I left Richmond I visited the Confessional, made a clean breast of it to the Almighty God, and partook of the B. Sacrament at Charlotte and at Atlanta. You have ever had the example of your mother, to whose noble, wife-like devotion I owe my own confession and Communion, after years of neglect."[80]

Buddy should "cultivate the society of elevated minds, and particularly of high toned Catholic ladies."[81] Although disavowing any sentiments of

75. *Ibid.*, 11.
76. *Ibid.*, 11-12.
77. *Ibid.*, 12.
78. *Ibid.*
79. *Ibid.*, 14.
80. *Ibid.*, 16.
81. *Ibid.*, 18.

bigotry, Mallory insisted on the special charm and virtue accruing to the Catholic woman because of her religion: "There is that in the faith and worship of Catholic women which inevitably refines them, subdues and controls them, and gives a softness and a womanly delicacy, charity, and kindness to their thoughts and manners, which is reflected upon and is beneficial to their associates. The peculiar and beautiful relations which the mother of God holds towards woman tend to give that refinement, frankness and truth that is so generally found to distinguish Catholic ladies. The immediate interposition of the B. Virgin in behalf of her afflicted daughters is the fountain of infinite consolation and holy peace to those who invoke it,—and is one of the holiest and most attractive features of Catholic doctrine."[82]

Should Buddy ever decide to marry (which, incidentally, he did not), he must not let accident determine his choice, ". . . but say to yourself in advance, while judgment and not devotion or affection to woman guides you, what you regard as indispensable in your choice. First, see that the family of the woman upon whom your hope of Earthly happiness is to depend, is respectable; by which term I mean, honest, truthful, and moral. Next, make up your mind to marry none but a Catholic, and let this be a sine qua non. She should be a practical Catholic, accustomed to commune in prayer with her God at least twice every day, and to look to Him for consolation and guidance under all trials."[83]

Between two hearts ever so loving and closely united in marriage, however pure and honest their intentions, however generous and unselfish their mutual relations, there would come "temporary coldness and chill blasts, misrepresentations, misinterpretations of words or looks, and harsh things lightly spoken."[84] Under such circumstances, "however wrong you may be, however hasty or harsh or selfish or unfeeling may have been your looks, or words, or conduct, towards her whom you really love, your heart will yearn for reconciliation while your temper, vanity, or pride will stand in the way. A practical Catholic heart in such moments . . . will not permit you to continue wrong; God will guide her affection right, and with words of deep devotion, gentleness, and, if necessary, self humiliation, she will calm your thoughts, win you back to reason and to yourself, enable you to look upon your conduct like a just and true man, . . . and win you nearer to God and to herself."[85]

82. *Ibid.*, 18, 23.     83. *Ibid.*, 22.
84. *Ibid.*, 22-23.
85. *Ibid.*, 23. It is interesting to speculate how much of this is autobiographical.

Buddy was not encouraged by his father to enter politics. "Political life, my dear boy, brings with it neither wealth nor quiet, and its distinctions are not worth the pursuit even of the most successful. The rising man on the political ladder, however truthfully and nobly he may advance, does so ever over the heads of the carping and envious, whose number increases with every round that he gains; and the higher he goes the more does he enlarge the circle of his enemies: Measurably, this may be the case in some other pursuits, but in none so much as in politics."[86]

Soon there came a more hopeful report from Angela, and, to add comfort, a surprise visit from Maggie and Buddy, who "shone in upon his dark room as suddenly and pleasantly as unlooked-for Sunbeams,"[87] and brought further good news about their mother's condition. The rise in Stephen's spirits was evident in his next letter. Of course he was vastly relieved, he told her. Her escape was, he thought, miraculous. "Had not your habits of active outdoor exercise made you as sure footed as a *Dear*—I was going to say *Cat!*—your attempt to visit me would have had a very lame conclusion. Most women thus subjected to the rough and tumble treatment of our railroads would have come down, as the boys say, lumpus, and broken every fragile thing about them into smithereens; whereas you seem to have subsided, if not precisely like a snow flake, yet as gently as it is possible for any hundred and forty pounds to gravitate to earth."[88]

He prayed her not to move or to attempt to see him until all danger of injury should have passed away. Although her visits "leave a sort of aureole in my room and strip imprisonment of every pang," he preferred that they should be still more like those of the angels if they were to be made at the expense of her prompt recovery. She would be glad to know that he had quite recovered from his last attack. "Reynolds' Specific" had put the enemy to the right about, even though it had left the patient's stomach and brain as confused as were those of honest Sancho after he had been tossed in a blanket.[89]

In the days of his young manhood at Key West, little had Stephen dreamed that his sedulous note-taking habit would prove to be such a consolation during a period when it was his fate to endure a painful exile. His prison diary was one of his chief comforts, after prayer and the visits of his loved ones, and it is the best transcript of his feelings and thoughts. During the last months of his imprisonment, the entries lengthened out:

86. *Ibid.*, 13.       87. Mallory to Angela, October 14, 1865.
88. *Ibid.*
89. *Ibid.*

"20 Oct., 1865. Yesterday I expected to see my noble wife; but recd. her note of the 17 telling me that she was unable to walk. What a bitter disappointment! I had risen very early, animated by the idea of seeing her, and through the morning prepared a pleasant surprise in the way of a lunch, and was greatly cheered by my confidence of seeing her at one o'clock. When her note was read I felt wretchedly, not so much at missing the happiness I anticipated, but by reflecting upon the painful cause of her detention. Had it not been for me she might not have been injured. Am I then to be charged with her suffering? Am I not the sole cause of it? I feel that I am; and a species of guilt seems constantly weighing upon me as I see her upon her bed of suffering.

"Oh God, Great First Cause and Father and Author of all, and Thou Oh Blessed Son, Saviour of men, give to her that peace of mind, that resignation, that spirit of reliance upon Thy Will and laws which will enable her to look above and beyond the things, the sufferings of Earth, and to dwell upon her life eternal. Blessed Virgin, Mother of My Saviour, purest of women born, throw around her and my children thy gracious protection, fill their minds with the love of Thee and of God's Holy Will, shield them from every harm, and guide them and me to a future with Thee and the Angels."[90]

The apparent change in the attitude toward him of General Burke, commandant of the fort, was another source of distress for the prisoner. Formerly the General had been wont to drop in on Mallory and spend a few moments in casual chatting. Of late these visits had ceased. Nor had Mallory been allowed his usual hour's walk outside the prison walls. His pain at what seemed to be the newly assumed coldness of his captors was somewhat lightened by a surprise visit from his dear friend John Reagan, just paroled from Fort Warren. For two hours they conversed together, with an officer present throughout. "I do not know," commented Mallory, "that we had anything to discuss which we desired to do privately."[91]

A few hours after Reagan had left, a letter arrived from Angela. The doctor had told her that she might not be able to walk for two months yet. Into Stephen's diary that night went another prayer for her: "Great God of the Universe, and Thou Oh Gracious Saviour, watch over and protect her. Inspire her soul with resignation and a practical unswerving reliance upon Thy mercy and an ardent love of Thee. Give her Thy protection, I pray Thee, O Blessed Virgin. Be with, and cheer her. Let her not despond

90. Mallory, Diary, part II, October 20, 1865.
91. *Ibid.,* October 23, 1865.

nor deem her lot too heavy to bear, but inspire her with cheerful hope and confidence in the love and protection of God here and hereafter."[92]

With the approach of Christmas Mallory's mental and physical sufferings seemed to increase: "Dec. 4. Low spirits and constant efforts to avoid yielding to them have kept me from recovering during the past month. If I should yield for a single day I fear that I would lie down and not get up again alive."[93] One night he had a strange dream which, in his distracted state, continued to disturb him in retrospect: "I was walking with my wife, when, a few steps in advance, upon the ground, a black snake about eight inches long ran ahead and for some time kept at the same distance, while it gradually increased in length to a foot or more. As I gained upon it, it ascended a tree beyond my reach, becoming gradually about three feet long; and when I came to the tree it threw itself, mouth open, vigorously, upon a black cat (the one about the fort here) which was passing beneath, seized the cat by the head, and then commenced a most savage and determined fight between snake and cat, the snake having the cat by the head and holding on. I awakened before it was over."[94]

Whether or not the dream had any significance, there were indeed reasons for Mallory and for the South as a whole, as well as for Andrew Johnson, to be depressed at this time. On December 4 the Radical Congress had opened its sessions. Its mood was manifested at once by its refusal to allow the clerk of the House to read at the roll call the names of the members-elect from the reconstructed states.

On December 6 Mallory wrote in his diary: "Am I to be released or not? Patience, fortitude, resignation, manhood befriend me! Suffered much pain for days back. But I must not complain."[95]

He put down in writing also his argument against the proposed trial of some of the Southern leaders—notably Jefferson Davis—on the charge of treason. American constitutionalists, instructed by the excesses of European despots, had, he recalled, narrowed the definition of treason. In the American tradition the charge was never to be made without serious, weighty, and indisputable proof. For other reasons, too, prosecution of

92. *Ibid.*
93, *Ibid.*, December 5, 1865.
94. *Ibid.*
95. *Ibid.*, December 6, 1865. According to William A. Dunning, *Reconstruction Political and Economic, 1865-1867* (New York, 1907), 22-23, the chances that Mallory would be kept in prison much longer or indicted for treason were very slim. This author believes that such punishment would have been permitted neither by Northern public opinion nor by constitutional lawyers.

Southerners was both unjust and unnecessary. The South, in seceding from and warring against the Federal government, had been acting on a theory of the Union which, until 1865, had been admitted by many Americans of wisdom and of high prestige. But the question of the nature of the Union had been decided definitively, not by argument but by the arbitrament of arms; and in that decision the South was perfectly willing to acquiesce. Why, then, inflict a double defeat on Southern men by forcing them to face a treason charge? "Surely a decision of law against secession is not wanted for the North. If needed to operate any where it must be at the South; and what effect will any decision [of law] produce there? The South acquiesces in the results of the battle field; acquiesces in good faith and will conform in good faith to the theory of the 'National Government' instead of the 'Federal Government,' and never again attempt secession. All the arguments that any Court can produce will fall upon unheeding ears at the South."[96]

For a long time Mallory had suspected that his chances for release were not improving. There was the apparent cooling of the relations of the officers of the fort toward him. His emissaries at Washington had for the past few weeks been strangely silent. There was still no response to his two letters to the President. His fears were confirmed early in December, 1865, when he received word that Secretary Stanton was urging his immediate trial for treason.

In this crisis, Angela rose to the occasion. At about the same time that the bad news was received, she had been able at last to leave her bed. Within a few days' time she had visited Fort Lafayette, to assure her husband that she was leaving for Washington that night, to plead his cause again with President Johnson.

Her loyalty touched him deeply, and he greatly needed the comfort that such loyalty brought to him. He poured his heart out in a long entry in his diary. He could not understand why he alone of all the members of the Confederate Cabinet should be submitted to trial. For the sake of his wife and children he would do anything that an honorable man might do in order to avert a judicial proceeding which, he was convinced, would be a mockery. But his trial seemed inevitable; and he was too familiar with such state tribunals not to know that, under existing circumstances, a trial would be but a certain and easy formula for conviction. For what he was

96. Mallory, diary, part II, December 6, 1865.

to be tried, he knew not. More suffering, he foresaw, perhaps death, awaited him.[97]

"May God give me strength to meet the cross as becomes a Christian, and a Southern gentleman." The lines were written firmly and with a sort of flourish in his diary. "Let me examine my conscience," he continued; "do I stand self-condemned? Certainly not. I am unconscious of ever having wronged a human being save my dear wife, and she has forgiven me. I have pursued an honest, honorable life, doing in my sphere all the good I could, violating no man's rights and sympathizing with the wrongs and misfortunes of my fellows. I do not wish to praise myself, for I am a weak, erring mortal. But I have sought to live justly, soberly, honestly, towards all men. Why then am I specially singled out for punishment? Alas, without intending it I have made enemies, and though I feel them to be enemies, I know not why or wherefore they are. But they persecute me most persistently. May God forgive them."[98]

He knew that he must keep bitterness from his thoughts. "Knowing that to love others as ourselves, and to forgive those who injure us, is a precept that lies at the foundation of our salvation, I have earnestly prayed for grace and strength to do so, and I believe I have eradicated from my heart all animosity toward any fellow being."[99]

For several days there came no word from Angela in Washington. He was tormented by the thought of what she must be enduring there. At the

97. *Ibid.*, 34 (December 14, 1865).
98. *Ibid.*
99. *Ibid.*, 35. Mallory's gloom would not have been alleviated if he had known of Stanton's attitude toward him at this time. Says Welles, under date of December 12, 1865: "Not a very long session of the Cabinet. Some conversation in regard to the Rebel leaders led me to inquire whether it might not be best to parole Mallory, who has written me personally. He offers to make disclosures and assist in reestablishing Union feeling. Stanton objected; says Judge Holt advises his trial, etc." (Welles, *Diary*, II, 395-96). Early in the following January, Stanton wrote to President Johnson: "Mallory is imprisoned, charged with treason, and with organizing and setting on foot piratical expeditions against the United States commerce and marine on the high seas" (Stanton to Johnson, January 4, 1866 [*O.R.A.*, Ser. II, Vol. VIII, p. 844]). Cf. also the following from Robert McN. McElroy, *Jefferson Davis, the Real and the Unreal* (2 vols.; New York, 1937), II, 552-53: "On December 26 [1865] O'Conor wrote to Mason: '. . . About ten days ago Mr. Stanton himself assured a friend of Mr. Mallory's that that gentleman would be tried for treason in a civil court "within thirty days". . . . It is a suggestive fact that after murdering poor Wirz by military commission, they should first try their newly-to-be-constituted courts upon a subordinate officer before venturing to strike at "the head of the rebellion". It indicates the character of the men who conduct the assassination bureau at Washington.' " Charles O'Conor was at this time one of the most brilliant lawyers in the country. He was a pro-slavery "Northern Democrat" and was senior counsel for Jefferson Davis in the latter's trial. Henry Wirz had been in charge of the Confederate prison at Andersonville and was accused of brutality toward Northern prisoners. Mason is Senator J. M. Mason of Virginia, of *Trent* fame.

same time he was able to write to Buddy, now a student at Georgetown College, a letter in the old style. He reminded his son that "no institution can educate a youth; all that it can do is to afford the necessary means and encouragement for the youth to educate himself; he himself must climb, nor hope for more than judicious boosting at opportune moments."[101] The chief function of a college was to teach men how to study, what to study, and what not to study, and the last was by no means the least important. "I am a notable example," wrote Mallory, ". . . of loss of time by the study of trash."

Buddy should work hard at his Latin and mathematics, those "dumb bells and the beef and pudding of the mind." The art of conversation was also to be cultivated: "A well stored mind, like a full jug, may be poured out in an enlivening, even pleasant flow, or in that gurgling 'fits and starts' style which makes one wish that it would soon empty itself." And the student must, furthermore, act diplomatically and tactfully toward his professors, even though they might be "uncompanionable, arrogant, harsh, or otherwise unpleasant in manner."[101]

Stephen was solicitous above all that Buddy should attend to his religious duties. Youth, he reminded his son, could give no more convincing proof of high tone, honor, and true nobility of soul, than by communing with God "after the forms of our holy Church." Buddy must plod on in his work. He was to expect much uphill struggle, but, "courage, courage, courage, and you will succeed."[102]

Christmas and New Year's Day came and went, and still there was no favorable news from Angela in Washington. It was painful to think of her there, an innocent lamb among cold, hard politicians. "Straightforward, truthful, and honest as light itself, she knows not the meaning, practically, of the word *policy;* and proud and independent, she is unprepared for the atmosphere of assumed superiority. How her feelings and patience must be tried!"[103]

Once more he penned in his intimate journal a tribute to Angela: "Whatever may be my fate, I cannot be deprived of the happiness she has shed upon my life. In thinking over the events of my life, and sometimes reflecting in what respects a different course from the one pursued might have served me, I invariably arrive at the conclusion that few men have

100. Mallory to Buddy, December 28, 1865.
101. *Ibid.*
102. *Ibid.*
103. Mallory, diary, part II, 26 (January 18, 1866).

been happier, that I have nothing to complain of, and that my wife has been the key and corner stone of it all. I pray for her night and day."[104]

Despite his efforts to raise his spirits, he was having a hard, bitter fight against despair. On the nineteenth of January he wrote: "My mind becomes despondent, and more than usual efforts to avoid surrendering it to gloom are constantly required. Six hours' sleep, a very low diet, and constant occupation in reading and writing are my resources, beyond morning and evening prayer. I am subject to strange mental distractions at prayers, and frequently impose upon myself the duty of repeating the prayers several times to get rid of them and to concentrate my thoughts. I am constantly disquieted, too, as to my salvation. How can I know that God has forgiven or will forgive my sins and save my soul? I have faith in the Great Sacrifice of my God Jesus and the salvation of all men; and I am honestly endeavoring so to act, think, and live as to bring myself within his merciful scheme of forgiveness. But how supremely happy would I be could I feel, firmly feel, that my salvation is certain, and that my noble wife and children are to meet me and be with me in happiness beyond the grave, with my father, mother, and all connected with me."[105]

Interest in the political scene continued to be a healthful distraction for the prisoner. He noted with approval that Congress had passed the Negro suffrage bill for the District of Columbia. "So important is an early admission of our states to Congress, and so disastrous to them is every month's delay, that I would, had I the power, confer the elective franchise today upon negroes, with certain qualifications."[106] The attitude exhibited by the Southern people was, he thought, admirable. They were, as a body, quiet, silent, resigned, and patient, because they were really anxious for peace, and for the restoration of their rights in the Union. But he feared that the ordeals to which they were being subjected, the constant irritations surrounding them, if continued for another year, would drive them, in most of the states, into acts of madness which would be held up as reasons for the further postponement of their reconstruction.

This was his sober comment on the state of the Union as 1866 began: "When I calmly survey the condition of public sentiment and the condition and increase of the country now with their condition in 1826, just forty years ago, and the wonderful innovations made in that time upon what were held to be the rights of the states and the true principles of our government, I confess my fears for republicanism.

104. *Ibid.*      105. *Ibid.*, 27-28.
106. *Ibid.*, 28 (January 19, 1866).

"With a Union composed of a few compact states, and a limited population, it was easy to preserve the sovereignty of the states and to repress the tendency of the Central government, the agent of the states, to encroach upon their rights and powers. But the difficulty of doing so increases with the growth of the country, the increase of area, population, Federal patronage, which place in the Executive hands a large standing Army and Navy and more offices and pensions to bestow than the Crown of England during the same term.

"So greatly do I apprehend disastrous changes that as an American citizen today I would compromise upon a Government as just and stable as that of Britain. God preserve our Country, I pray, and may my fears prove unfounded. A paper constitution is a very good thing usually so long as it lasts as intended by its framers; but it is necessarily open to construction; hence to change, and to such construction as to destroy its good and develop its bad features. As the country and people for whom it was written change, the paper constitution must change to suit them; and *construction,* not amendment, quietly affects, undermines, and destroys it.

"The popular will of three millions of people, spread over thirteen sparsely settled states could be wisely considered and represented; but this popular will, when the population comes to be thirty millions, and the states forty, covering a half a continent, must, in times of high political excitement, formed by sectional jealousies, local schemes for power, combinations and demagogues, becomes the most tyrannical form in which the power of man can be exercised."[107]

A note arrived from Angela on January 24. She had utterly failed in her mission of mercy and was returning to Bridgeport the next week. She visited her husband immediately on her return from the unsuccessful journey and found him suffering acutely from gout and a violent attack of palpitation of the heart. "It makes my soul sink within me," she wrote to Mrs. Clay a few days later, "when I see my husband languishing in a prison and I can not help him out. He suffers all the excruciating torments that no other disease but the one he has can inflict, without a word of complaint; and the consequence is that those around him who do not know him believe that he does not suffer much; but I who for seventeen years witnessed the great sufferings which he undergoes know that he can not bear it much longer."[108]

107. *Ibid.*
108. Angela to Mrs. Caroline Tunstall Clay, from Bridgeport, February 7, 1866 (Clay Papers, Duke University).

On this visit she consoled him by relating how the President, although unable at the moment to grant her request, had received her kindly, and urged her to remember that God "is our only hope and therefore we must trust Him and carry our crosses with patience, hope, and confidence." These words, she said, were "words indeed of comfort to me."[109]

But she was deeply concerned about her husband's health. "I would not be surprised if some morning when Gen. Burke goes into Mr. M's room to see that he has not escaped, if he finds nothing but his body there, for his soul can not be detained by earthly prisons."[110]

Clay had just lost his mother, and Angela's message to him is a revealing expression of her own feelings at this time. "Tell him," she wrote, "not to give way to feelings of sadness, for this world is a place where our souls are prepared and refined by sorrow and cares, to make us acceptable to our heavenly father."[111]

Even in this darkest hour, however, there were forces of which Mallory was ignorant working for his release. Governor Marvin had made a strong representation in favor of his former law clerk. Seward and Stanton had finally risen above all littleness and rancor and forwarded his case with the President, who had really never desired to punish him. And Angela's visit to Washington had not been entirely without effect. On the tenth day of March, 1866, the former Confederate Navy Secretary left Fort Lafayette on partial parole, but actually a free man.

Only a few weeks before, the bitter struggle between the President and Congress had begun in earnest with Johnson's veto of the first Freedmen's Bureau Bill. On the issue of that struggle depended much of Stephen Mallory's future fortunes.

109. *Ibid.*
110. *Ibid.*
111. *Ibid.*

# CHAPTER FIFTEEN

# A New Beginning

$\mathbf{M}$ALLORY WAS ORDERED to remain in Connecticut until granted permission to move southward. He went immediately to Maggie's home at Bridgeport, where Angela, Attie, and Ruby were still staying. One of his first acts, after the joyous reunion, was to write to his loyal friend John Reagan. He was, he informed Reagan, remaining temporarily at Bridgeport, "very quietly watching the movements of events and calculating possibilities. He was delighted to learn that Reagan was comfortably settled again on his farm, and wished the former Postmaster-General "that prosperity . . . and that peace and happiness in your daily life which your pure life and unselfish devotion to principle so eminently merit."[1]

As for himself, he reported, Florida was beckoning, but he was still undecided as to how he could earn a living and support his family. He was financially ruined. When he had been arrested his sole possessions were his saddle horse and his watch.[2] A few months before, in a letter to another intimate friend, he had said that he accepted poverty "as the badge of honor," and that he was quite willing to work for his rations. A lawyer's profession, he felt, would be unremunerative for some time to come, and, without capital, other avenues of profit could not readily be opened. Another obstacle to his practice of law was the test oath, which, in effect, excluded Southern attorneys from all Federal courts. The failure of the Supreme Court to decide on the constitutionality of this oath was, he thought, a "sad commentary upon the times and manners."[3]

With regard to political prospects he had very definite views, already formed while he had been cooped up in Fort Lafayette. Florida, he thought, and, to a greater or less extent, every other Southern state, would be terribly

1. Mallory to Hon. John Reagan, from Bridgeport, April 11, 1866 (Mallory Letterbook).
2. *Ibid.*
3. Mallory to General J. E. Johnson, from Fort Lafayette, November 2, 1865 (Mallory Letterbook).

retarded in recovering from the desolation of war by the policy which Congress was pursuing. (The Civil Rights Bill, which forbade the states to discriminate between citizens on the grounds of race or color, had been passed a few weeks before, over the President's veto.) If there was any hope of future prosperity for the South, such hope must not rest on the Republican Party, which was then governing the country, but could be fulfilled only in defiance of that party.[4]

"We mistake ... the character of this party," he declared, "for I observe that our papers are constantly speaking of a 'radical party' as an element or branch of Republicanism; whereas, in my judgment, radical party and republican party are convertible terms; the radicals are the large, ruling, governing mass [of the party], and the Doolittles, Dixons, ... who split off upon any measure whatever, and walk not squarely in the traces, will be surely left behind, and will find no resting place, no affiliations, no 'habitation' or 'name' outside of the Democratic party."[5]

The Democrats, Mallory felt, were recovering ground and exhibiting vitality on all sides. If the President continued to pursue his course unaltered, they would soon be a power in public affairs. In Connecticut, at the recent gubernatorial election, the Democrats had a majority of some seven thousand to overcome. They had reduced it to five hundred, and, had the President written word to indicate his preference between the opposing candidates, the state would have gone decidedly Democratic.[6]

Party lines throughout New England were more unyielding, and more proscriptive than Mallory had ever known or heard of elsewhere, and were as strictly observed in all business relations as they were in churches, religious societies, and social life, into all of which they had thrust cleavages. In the little town of Bridgeport, even the Episcopalian church, generally conservative, had split on political lines; and the "Church of the Holy Copperheads"—as its Republican brothers in the faith called it—contained not a single Republican worshiper.[7]

"Outside of the Democratic party," complained Mallory, "no Southern man or woman finds a friend in New England, but every Democrat talks and acts like a friend. The Republicans hate us with an intensity which

4. *Ibid.*
5. *Ibid.* James Rood Doolittle was a United States Senator for Wisconsin, 1857-1869. He had been a delegate to the peace convention of 1861. His "regularity" was questioned by some thoroughgoing Republicans. Archibald Dixon was United States Senator for Kentucky from December 20, 1852, to March 3, 1855, filling out the unexpired term of the deceased Henry Clay. During the war he was an advocate of peace, and in 1863 was a delegate to the peace convention held at Frankfort, Kentucky.
6. *Ibid.*                                    7. *Ibid.*

finds no parallel in animal life; and the thorough enforcement of Mr. Stevens' plan of utter disfranchisement and confiscation at the South would fail to satisfy their thirst for vengeance, which stops at nothing short of blood. (I speak of the masses; of course there are exceptions, and I refer with great pleasure to the kind course which Senator Wilson, Horace Greeley and others pursued towards myself.) Depend upon it, my friend, that the South is to be kept out of Congress until she grants negro suffrage, or until all laws necessary for perpetuating Republican power shall have been passed; and that we cannot hope for much before the next presidential election."[8]

To Mrs. Clay also he wrote about many things, beginning with his release "upon a parole which requires me to remain in this State and abide the further orders of the Government." He was deeply concerned about her husband, who was still in prison. He saw no reason why Clay should be discriminated against in this way, when so many others who had labored in the Confederate cause had already been granted their freedom. A struggle for power, he correctly surmised, was occurring between the President and Congress, and this was preventing the former from assuming towards Clay the merciful course which he really wished to adopt. "But the restoration of civil law throughout our country opens a way which his [Clay's] friends may very properly take, and to which I am persuaded the Government would not object. . . ."[9]

Angela, he reported, had not yet fully recovered from her railroad accident. He feared "that her dancing [would] be seriously interrupted by it for some time to come." Ruby and Attie were well, and Buddy was at Georgetown College—"if you could give him a smile and a word of good cheer sometimes, I know they would prove powerful and pleasing stimulants to his progress."[10]

Of the future he said: "I am persuaded that our States and people are to be prosperous, despite the portentous clouds which are now around us; and that the day is not far distant when, 'regenerated and disenthralled', you and your incomparable lord with other congenial spirits will smile at fate and look back to the paths we are now treading with more of pride than of sorrow. Give my love to Clay, God bless him. What would I not give to be able to serve him!"[11]

8. *Ibid.* Senator Henry Wilson entered the Senate in 1855 as a representative from New Hampshire. He was a strong abolitionist.
9. Mallory to Mrs. Virginia C. T. Clay, April 8, 1866 (Clay Papers, Duke University).
10. *Ibid.*
11. *Ibid.*

But Clay, happily, was to be not much longer in need of help. Two weeks later Mallory sent an exuberant message: "Hon. C. C. Clay: Ten thousand thanks to God, my Dear friend, for your release. May he punish with rigorous justice upon the spawn of Puritanism your unjustifiable and most cruel incarceration. My wife and I if gout and indescribables would permit us to dance at all, would dance with joy today at the news of your release. Love to your good wife, God bless her bright spirit and noble heart; and may we meet in Florida, one acre of whose barrens I would not give for all N. England."[12]

Stephen Mallory had left prison walls, but he still had many personal problems to solve. He had not as yet received his formal pardon, but was still on indefinite parole. The war had meant for him heavy financial losses. His house at Pensacola was half ruined from its wartime occupancy by Federal officers. His law practice was destroyed. His land investments in Missouri were in danger because of his precarious legal status as a paroled prisoner. His health had been seriously impaired by the strain of the war and especially by the months at Fort Lafayette.

He could not prolong indefinitely his stay with Maggie and her husband, so in late May of 1866 he determined on a course of action. Leaving Angela and Ruby at Bridgeport for the time, he and Attie would return to the South to the old associations and scenes, and there he would try to reestablish his fortunes. He must seek an interview at Washington with the President and the Secretary of War, to thank them for his release and to request permission to go to Florida.

Mallory and his son arrived in the national capital early in June and were greeted, to his pleasant surprise, by many old Southern friends. One of these, Dick Mead, apparently another former suitor of Angela's, was already manifesting his rapid recovery of morale by vigorously pressing on Congress a personal claim for indemnity. "Before this prodigal Congress," wrote Mallory to Angela, "his chances . . . are better than ever . . . His nose is sharper, his visage more a la Quixote, his tone more melancholy and his voice more complaining and husky than when under the inspiration of love and whiskey, he invited you to 'come o'er the sea, maiden, with me', and you fondly listened to a lover 'half seas over.' "[13]

The former Confederate Navy Secretary's interviews with the President and the Secretary of War apparently went off smoothly, although Mallory's account is disappointingly brief. "In my last," he wrote to Angela, "I re-

12. Mallory to Hon. C. C. Clay, April 23, 1866 (Clay Papers, Duke University).
13. Mallory to Angela, from Cedar Hill, June 22, 1866.

ferred to my interview with Mr. Stanton and the President as satisfactory, but did not give you the details. 'Mr. Stanton, I am on my way to Florida upon my parole to proceed there; and I call upon you this morning to thank you for your courtesy to my daughter,[14] and next to inquire whether it will be consistent with your views that I shall return for my family in the fall?' 'Oh certainly, come whenever you choose'. 'Thank you, sir, good morning'. 'Good morning, sir'. Such was our brief interview . . . With the President I remained from a half to three quarters of an hour; and upon telling him of what Mr. Stanton said he remarked: 'Oh certainly, come and go when you like'; and he seemed disposed to be cordial and friendly."[15]

Moving on to Richmond, Mallory found there the warmest of welcomes from a host of friends. Everyone, he wrote to Angela, was disappointed to find that she and Ruby were not with him, and all inquired most affectionately after her, sounding her praises in a strain most grateful to his feelings. But Richmond, he felt, offered him no business openings, although he admitted that he would have liked to stay there for a few years at least. The city was making a brave effort to rebuild its damaged sections. "Large and elegant brick stores are rapidly going up in the burnt portions of the city, and Wall Street is taking a large interest in all improvements, for there is but little money here." The feeling against the Radicals was intense, especially among the Southern women.[16] The Federal officers and soldiers, so far as he could learn, were behaving civilly towards the people. There was no social intercourse, however, between the Richmond ladies and the wives of Yankees, officers or men. Mrs. Craven,[17] wife of the author of the book on Jefferson Davis, was the only Federal lady whom he had heard of as having been "received" by the Richmond ladies.[18] Attie was delighted with everything, and was with a crowd of his old playmates ten minutes after he arrived. He was a good traveler, with an excellent sense of humor.[19]

Ruby, too, must have her letter from the South. Stephen told her about her numerous little Richmond friends, all of whom sent their love. There were also many ladies and gentlemen who were asking for "darling Ruby."

14. Maggie had seen Stanton on behalf of her father.
15. Mallory to Angela, from Cedar Hill, June 22, 1866.
16. Mallory to Angela, from Richmond, June 15, 1866.
17. Her husband was Dr. (Col.) John J. Craven, attending physician of Jefferson Davis during the latter's imprisonment. Dr. Craven, with the aid of his daughter, wrote the *Prison Life of Jefferson Davis* (New York, 1866).
18. Mallory to Angela, from Richmond, June 29, 1866.
19. Mallory to Angela, from Richmond, June 15, 1866.

"You cannot imagine, my dear child, how much I was gratified by their praises of you, because I know that they love you for your love, obedience, and kindness to your mother and for your general good conduct; be gentle and kind to all, be just and truthful towards God and man, and you will continue to command the love of your friends."[20]

He recounted how he had "walked to the old hill where we lived, and every thing seemed just as we left it." He visited the cemetery and found all the graves of the Confederate soldiers covered with flowers. General Stuart's grave had an arch and bower of evergreens eight feet high over it, and it was said that every Southern woman and child who could possibly be there had assisted in this labor of love. Thirty thousand people had attended his funeral, and flowers had been sent from all parts of the country by car loads.[21]

The devoted father could not forego a few more admonitions: "I hope, my dear Ruby, that you will study, day by day, to serve and help your mother, and to be obedient and loving to her in all things. She requires and deserves all your affection. I hope, too, that you will read, as I requested you, and improve yourself. You must write to me every Saturday regularly, and however irksome this may prove at first, you will find it an easy task after a few efforts. If any of the little Yankey girls treat you politely, you can reciprocate; but do not seek their acquaintance, or place yourself purposely in their way. God bless you, my dear child."[22]

Mallory made another brief trip to Washington in order to confer with some of his intimate friends regarding his Missouri lands, the securing of his formal pardon, and other business matters.[23] He drew up a memorial to the President, requesting protection for person and property until pardoned. His advisers felt that they could obtain for him the necessary legal instruments that would enjoin all proceedings against his lands and other holdings.[24]

He then proceeded farther southward, reaching Cedar Hill, Georgia, in late June. From this place he wrote to Angela some descriptions of the South in process of rehabilitation. Some of the people of the region were despondent over their future prospects. Others were adapting themselves cheerfully, or at least resignedly, to the new conditions, and were already achieving financial recovery.[25]

20. *Ibid.*                                    21. *Ibid.*
22. *Ibid.*
23. Mallory to Angela, from Cedar Hill, June 22, 1866.
24. *Ibid.*                                    25. *Ibid.*

The Negroes were apparently behaving better than they had before they were liberated; but they were beginning to realize that now, because they were free, they must work harder, while their cares and responsibilities had increased, and their opportunities for enjoyments had decreased. They were no less respectful and subservient to their employers than they had been toward their masters. They worked more industriously because they were now obliged to work or to starve. Some of them, for the first time in their lives, were beginning to feel what want meant. The first Negro beggars Mallory had ever seen he had met in Richmond a few days previously. Many old servants who had long been a charge on the generosity of their masters were now homeless and without food.[26]

Amid more serious concerns, there was time for Mallory to indulge in a few relaxations. One day he rode over to visit his friend Major Dosuell [?] to inspect the latter's racing stock. Over a julep of the Major's best manufacture, they discussed nothing but race horses for an hour or more. The famous "Planet" was the pride of the Dosuell stable. "After winning more running races than any horse in America he is now without a visible blemish."[27]

A week later Mallory was back in Richmond. A news item in a recent letter from Angela had caused him some disappointment. "You speak of having Buddie with you, which surprises me, as I had inferred that you preferred that he should not go to Bridgeport, where he has no suitable associates, and can have none. I do not desire him to be subjected to the cool hatred of the rising generation there, and I know that you do not. In Bridgeport he would be thrown much with young men who drink whiskey and play billiards, accomplishments which he might readily acquire. If therefore he visits you, don't permit him to stay there beyond two or three days."[28]

26. *Ibid.* Cf. the following description of the difference between Northern and Southern methods of treating the Negro: "One of the best women I ever knew, a lecturer and missionary to her race [Negro], said to me once: 'Some of these [Northern] people call me 'Miss', and ask me to sit down in their grand parlors in satin chairs while they tell me how well off my people are. Your kind [Southern people] says, 'You, Susan Jones! You're just wet through, tramping the streets; go straight downstairs to my kitchen and get dry and have your dinner . . .'" (Mrs. Burton Harrison, *Recollections Grave and Gay* [New York, 1912], 142-43).

27. Mallory to Angela, from Cedar Hill, June 22, 1866. This sportsman host of Mallory's is probably Major J. T. Doswell, of Fredericksburg, Virginia. During the war he was an aide to Major General T. H. Holmes. Mallory's slurring of the "w" in the name has made the identification difficult and uncertain.

28. Mallory to Angela, from Richmond, June 29, 1866. On Mallory's last trip to Washington, he had spent a day with Buddy. "He went everywhere with me, and I presented him,

But it was high time for him to be moving toward Florida. Although he had a momentary thought of buying a small farm near Richmond, and practicing law at the same time, he saw no way of raising the requisite money, and so rejected the idea.[29] He would push on, therefore, to Petersburg and points farther south. But an attack of gout forced him to delay his departure for a few days, and gave him an opportunity to send off another note to Angela in which he observed: "I am happy to reflect that your admirers, so far as they manifest themselves to me, are of your own sex; for, notwithstanding my exemption from jealousy, I am not sure but that my attention, if not my surprise, and uneasiness, would be aroused, to hear all these pleasant things which greet me, from the lips of men. Dr. Haxall, Judge Lyons and father, and other gentlemen, are careful to temper their expletives of admiration, to praise you in abstract, general terms, and particularly to refer to your judgment and skill as a housekeeper and hostess; but I can see that they fear to make me uncomfortable by echoing the compliments of the other sex."[30]

Early in the first week of July he and Attie were on the southward road again. Soon they reached La Grange, Georgia, where they stayed at the home of their dear friends, the Hills.[31] From this temporary stopping point went two long letters to Bridgeport. The first was to Angela:

"I am in my bed room, wrapped in a charitable night shirt, writing by a kerosene lamp to the one woman of all this world who has ever controlled my heart, and soul and life. (May every blessing which God in his mercy can bestow, be hers.)

"In your last letter, to which the beginning of this refers, you speak of being very unhappy. I doubt not that your physical condition may depress your spirits, and predispose you to regard the present and future despondingly. But if you will fearlessly look at your situation, and properly estimate the goodness and mercy of God towards you, as proved in part by the health and affection and characters of your husband and your children, and their unswerving devotion to you, you will, I feel assured, even from so

---

with a great deal of pride, to all friends who saw me. He has greatly improved, and is a fine fellow in all respects. I gave him $20 to pay his expenses to any point he may go to during vacation. He promised to write [to his mother] more frequently. His right thumb was badly injured some time ago in playing base ball, at which he is among the college 'nine' experts; but it is now well" (Mallory to Angela, from Cedar Hill, June 22, 1866). Buddy used the twenty dollars to travel to Bridgeport.

29. Mallory to Angela, from Richmond, June 29, 1866.

30. Mallory to Angela, from Richmond, July 1, 1866. Concerning the Haxalls, cf. *supra*, p. 384 concerning Judge Lyons, cf. *supra*, pp. 177, 312.

31. Cf. *supra*, p. 344.

partial a view of your blessings, regard yourself as not altogether wretched. How priceless would these blessings alone seem to you were you deprived of them, and how ready would you be to acknowledge that with them life under any circumstances would be happy! Depend upon it, my noble good wife, that you are *not* unhappy, that you do not deserve to be unhappy, and that your husband and children, of whose affections you are the light and life and center, are resolved that you shall not be unhappy. For you to be wretched *now*, when I have awakened to a life and its holy connections for which you have so long prayed in my behalf, is almost enough to induce a doubt of its value.

"You indulge, I see, a fear that Mrs. Bishop's [Maggie's] friends may be kept away from visiting her by your presence. For heaven's sake don't let this apprehension disturb you for a moment. The more such people are kept away from her the better. There is some good in all classes of people, but the Republican ignorant women and men seem to me the least meritorious, if not the most despicable white people I have ever met with; and I trust that you will not allow yourself to think or care for what they *say*, or *do*, or *think*, any more than you would for the opinions or conduct of so many penitentiary convicts; and that you will ignore their existence. To converse about them even is to give them confidence. If you return a visit to them, you confer an honor upon them. They are an inferior people to us in all respects, and they have cruelly wronged us; and if, under these circumstances, we are so placed as to render intercourse with them expedient, we must feel that we are condescending much to do so."[32]

On the same day he wrote to Ruby: "Miss Ruby Mallory. My darling Ruby:

"My last letter to you was from Richmond, and since its date I have been whirled along at twenty miles an hour, 'through tangled juniper, beds of reeds, and many a place where the serpent feeds', in Va., North and South Carolina and Georgia, and now find myself at midnight, in my bed room at Mrs. Hill's house, again chatting with you, just as we chatted, you and I alone before going to bed, and while your mother said her extra prayers.

"Emilia [Hill] was sadly disappointed at not seeing you with me, for she loves you dearly, and had planned many schemes for fun and frolick with you. Her doll house is a large dry goods packing box, just such as you once had; and here her several dolls have their several suits [*sic*] of rooms, their library and kitchen; the latter supplied with a real cooking stove, and

32. Mallory to Angela, from La Grange, July 6, 1866.

with all the means for preparing meals for an extensive family. She has taken dancing lessons, dances beautifully, and loves it dearly.

"I hope you will see Cicero [Hill] who . . . has gone North. He is a fine, manly fellow, with all the courage, truth, and generosity of our noble Southern boys. I have suggested to Mrs. Hill to send him to Georgetown College, and doubt not that Mr. Hill would do so, were he aware of the advantages offered by this institution.

"As soon as we reached the house Attie started, with Charley [Hill], for the pond, and realized all the pleasures of a swim, of which he had been constantly thinking as we journeyed over the dusty roads. I have taken a look at our old house and grounds, from the street, and wandered over Mrs. Hill's garden, which is not only lovely, but which just now is bearing cart loads of Cape Jasamine and roses and other sweet flowers.

"I hope, my dear daughter, that you continue to improve and industriously practice with your music; that you read the books I advised, and that in all things you love and obey your dear Mother, who is, and ought to be, more cherished by us than is life itself.

"Your mother, in her last letter, referred to a party you attended at Mrs. Carr's,[33] and to a chap with whom you were pleased, or, maybe, she said that he was pleased with you. I trust that you will never allow yourself to make the slightest advance towards the acquaintance of any Republican in Bridgeport. While I am grateful to Mrs. Carr for her kindness to you, and while I desire you to conduct yourself towards all . . . as a well bred SOUTHERN lady, I am unwilling for you to have any intimacies or any other than a formal intercourse with them. We are as different from them as oil is from water, and we can no more mingle harmoniously together than can an african 'tom-tom' and an Aeolian harp. You are superior to ninety-nine in any hundred of them; superior in all respects,—in heart, soul, mind, life, and character, and in the love and estimation of noble Southern friends. Do not be lavish of conversation with them, and, above all, do not recite for any but your friends, and only when your Mother desires you, and never hesitate when she requires it.

"I send you a song which you must learn to recite, so that you can do so for your friends in Richmond; and as I cannot be with you, I have appended notes for your direction, which you must carefully observe, and recite it for your mother alone, and take her advice and criticism. It demands great expression and feeling; if you can draw tears from your hearers you may know that you have sung it nearly right.

33. Mrs Carr, of Bridgeport, has not been identified.

"God bless you and keep you, my dear child, and remember always that whenever you may feel unhappy at any of the little ills of life, you have what no time or misfortune can deprive you, the love of your affectionate "Father."[34]

The travelers left La Grange on July 16 and arrived at Montgomery on that same night. Once more they were greeted by a host of friends.[35] Mallory had some interesting news to report about their former domestic slaves: "Attie and I have just returned from a visit to Jack, Nancy, and Willie, who are boarding with a negro family on the outskirts of the town, and who are all sick. Jack was in bed with a low, tenacious, intermittent fever, and had just been bled to restore him to consciousness, for he was so raving mad as to require several men to hold him. Nancy has an infant girl, two weeks old, the image and color of Jack; and, in addition to the loss of her upper teeth, which changes her appearance greatly, she is as thin as a crane, and has two large lumps, one over each eye, from neuralgia. . . . Jack has made nothing and is in debt; but he has had several offers . . . which he has deferred accepting, preferring to live with us if we want him. He is now too sick to make any arrangements for himself. Nancy has but one desire in life, and this is to return to Pensacola where Bob and Adeline[36] are living. She folded her arms around Attie, and with tears in her eyes kept calling him 'poor little Attie,' 'my dear little tilla'. She inquired earnestly all about you and Ruby and Maggie and Hy.[37] Attie will go back to see them this evening, to carry to Nancy the articles which Mag sent her."[38]

The final leg of the journey was made from Montgomery to Pensacola in twenty-two hours.[39] They left Montgomery in the evening, reached Pollard at seven o'clock next morning, took a mule team at once for Milton, arrived there at 2:00 P.M., went on board the tugboat that was waiting there, and landed at Pensacola at 6:30 P.M. that same day. "By the sage arrangements of the road, we left [Montgomery] too early to get supper, reached and left Pollard too early for breakfast, and arrived and left Milton too late for dinner; and the consequent fast of twenty four hours made Attie as cross as an old maid without her accustomed tea, and gave me an intense head ache."[40]

34. Mallory to Ruby, from La Grange, July 6, 1866.
35. Mallory to Angela, from Montgomery, July 17, 1866.
36. Her daughter and son-in-law.
37. "Hy" was Henry Bishop, Maggie's husband.
38. Mallory to Angela, from Montgomery, July 17, 1866.
39. *Ibid.*
40. Mallory to Angela, from Pensacola, July 19, 1866.

Angela's large and interesting family, led by her father, were on hand to meet them as they disembarked at the Pensacola wharf. Everybody inquired most solicitously for Angela. The two travelers were escorted to their temporary quarters at the Morenos', and—"here am I, at half past twelve, in this little cocked hat of a room, chatting with my darling wife over my first day in Pensacola."[41]

Stephen's old sense of humor enlivened this letter. He repeated Mr. Moreno's description of one of his Negro slaves: "You don't want to believe he's de wus fellow you ever see for mis-che-vus, and he's quick as lightning, —jes like Angela; and he don't gon to be 'fraid of notting, too, jes like her."

Of Angela's sister Maria, he wrote: "Mary's face has lengthened in proportion to her years; and she has contracted a most demonstrative and comical habit of *butting* her smiles at you somewhat in the style of Malley's Billy [goat], when rearing upon his hind legs, and adjusting his head to its fiercest expression. Every time she shakes her head, like the shake of a deer's tail, enables me to tell just what is coming and to dodge; for her smile has as little of mirth or pleasure in it as the opening and shutting of a mouse-trap."[42]

But Stephen was obliged to occupy himself in more serious activities than observing the idiosyncrasies of those around him. He had returned to Pensacola in order to start anew his professional career and to make his damaged house habitable again for his family. The latter task consumed most of his time and energy during the next few months.

The Mallory mansion, used as a headquarters by Federal officers during the war, was in need of extensive repairs.[43] It was still standing, but, inside and out, it had suffered much. Most of the furniture was gone, and the

41. *Ibid.*

42. *Ibid.* "Your father continues . . . very kind and attentive to Attie and me . . . and he has even sung some five hundred French and Spanish songs for me, all of which bear a marvellous resemblance to each other . . ." (Mallory to Angela, July 29, 1866).

43. The associate editor of the *Waterbury American* (n.d.) was quoted by the *St. Augustine Examiner* as follows: "During the war we remember to have visited Pensacola, and according to our recollections it was the most desolate and deserted of Southern cities. At the time to which we refer the residence of the 'Confederate Secretary' was used as headquarters, and from our recollection we should think his 'place of residence' needed 'reconstructing' " (*Examiner*, February 2, 1867). The house was occupied by Col. (later Brig. Gen. by brevet in the Volunteer Forces) Wilson, commander of the celebrated New York Zouaves. Wilson was termed variously the "notorious Col. Wilson" and the "most maligned colonel in the U.S. service" (Gouverneur Morris, *The History of a Volunteer Regiment* [New York, 1891] 82). The Zouaves have been described as "the hardest boiled outfit of gunmen that ever happened." They were towed behind a steamer all the way from New York to Pensacola, during which voyage they threatened to wipe from the face of the earth another group of Federal soldiers who were accompanying them (Clubbs, *Life of Stephen Russell Mallory*).

rooms were filled with debris of various sorts. Walls and ceilings were damaged and, in some places, broken through.

A few days after his arrival, Stephen, with the enthusiastic aid of Attie and the less whole-hearted help of some hired men, began the work of rehabilitation.

"But for constant hard work," he informed Angela, "I would soon get into a train of low spirits, but, as it is, I am in bed by nine every night, sleep well, and preserve my health amidst general sickness. Upon looking at everything around me I think we have ample reason to thank a merciful God for all His goodness to us; and yet it requires an effort for me to recognize this, and to appear at all cheerful. Wages here are very high, and negroes will not stay with their late owners, and all are unwilling to hire themselves by the month."[44]

As yet, he said, he had not decided how he was to support his family. If he stayed at Pensacola he would, of course, practice law, but he realized that he must have another business besides. "I can work, and work hard at anything I may undertake, and, with industry and integrity, will not starve."[45] He had written to Henry Bishop about business matters generally and had suggested the possibility of their purchasing jointly at sheriff's sale the rights and charter of the Central Wharf Company at Pensacola. The income was, he thought, very tempting for the money involved. The railroad people were sanguine that they could complete the road southward to

44. Mallory to Angela, August 18, 1866. Southerners reacted variously to the defeat and to the new conditions consequent on the defeat. For example: Geo. A. Trenholm to Hon. W. W. Keyes, former Attorney-General of the Confederacy, from Charleston, June 4, 1865: "Peace is firmly reestablished. I have lately traversed large districts of the interior and I never saw, in any country, any people more orderly or more earnest in their determination to accept with patience the losses and disappointments of the present, or more resolved to perform in good faith and sincerity the obligations placed upon them for the future" (Trenholm Papers, Library of Congress). Willie Alexander to his brother, General E. P. Alexander, from Petersburg, October 12, 1865: "It makes me very, very sad, Genl, as I sit down in my store, and see the Yankees go riding by; to compare our situation now, to what it was one year ago; it is a hard fate to submit to, and one that is more to be deplored when we see how ready and willing the southern people were to return to the U.S. Government. This is a terrible decree of providence which I can neither appreciate or understand. I fear our future will be a dark one, but still have a lingering hope that something will turn up which will accrue to our good. Pres. Davis is still at Fort Monroe, the Yankees are treating him now with more kindness, having placed him in more comfortable quarters, and allowing him to take exercise. His fate is a sad one and I fear deserves more sympathy than the Southern people are willing to give him. Gen., since the surrender I have come to the conclusion that our people are not at all what we imagined them to be. The conduct of the nation has been dastardly in the extreme in regard to their chief especially. The ex-rebels are all going to work; that is, all who can get employment" (Alexander Papers, University of North Carolina Southern Collection).

45. Mallory to Angela, August 18, 1866.

Pensacola, and this would greatly brighten business prospects in West Florida. He was unwilling to embark in any doubtful venture, however, and preferred to "wait and look on for awhile." If he could sell his house and Angela's lands at Pensacola, the money, invested in United States stocks, would provide ample support for the family and would set his mind at ease.[46]

Work on the house continued steadily but slowly. Angela's renovated dwelling would not be ready for her until November, at the earliest.[47] All the carpenters had been laid up with yellow fever. He was distressed at the "drawings, and pencillings, and illustrations of Yankey brutality" on the walls of Angela's room. Attie was working "like a galley slave every day, besides going crabbing early in the morning."[48]

Angela was told not to complain at not hearing from him more often. Although he blamed himself somewhat for his apparent neglect of her, she must believe his assurance that writing to her was his greatest joy. But unremitting toil and consequent fatigue so stole upon his time and disposition to write that even this pleasure was readily procrastinated.[49]

For her enjoyment he described his daily schedule. Attie and he slept together in one of Mr. Moreno's garret rooms. Their mattress "comes up to all that the penitential office could require as to hardness, and the pieces of old matting upon the floor harbour a set of sprightly and attentive fleas." He rose at seven o'clock to give his little sister-in-law Corinne her lessons in grammar, arithmetic, and writing, "a labor equaled only by that of sawing wood upon a hot day; for a more thoroughly inert and unappreciative mind I have never met."[50]

He could not forbear a more extended description of Corinne's intellectual capacity. She was not only lazy to a degree rarely found in a girl of her age, but she was altogether indifferent as to whether she knew anything or not. Her replies recalled the stories one read about absurd answers in school examinations. She had been for over a month endeavoring to learn the difference between the genders. " 'What gender is mother, Corinne?' 'What gender is mother?' (She thus repeats every question I ask.) 'Mother is masculine because he is a female.' 'What gender is father?' 'Father is feminine because she's masculine.' She delights in the neuter gender, and

---

46. *Ibid.* From the same letter: "Dr. Scott and wife are still preaching here, and we have a priest in Father Gibbon, an Irishman of the stamp of Father Sinnott. Efforts are being made to build a church, and in the meantime we meet in a temporary affair. I went to Confession and took the Sacrament when Bishop Quinlan was here. . . ."

47. Mallory to Angela, August 21, 1866.    48. Mallory to Angela, August 18, 1866.
49. Mallory to Angela, August 28, 1866.    50. *Ibid.*

assigns it to all her relations pretty equally; and only to my stern remonstrances does she yield her Uncle, Aunt, Parent, and sister, any claims to what she calls 'he' and 'she' gender. But I persevere, for my pride as a teacher is involved, and having in my time taught dogs, monkeys, parrots, and Indians, I think I may possibly teach her something."[51]

He breakfasted with Attie soon after eight, and by nine he had ridden double with Attie, on Mr. Moreno's old horse, over to the house. Within five minutes afterward they were both at work, fencing, whitewashing, scrubbing paint, and aiding the carpenters and plasterers, now on the roof, now in the cellar. They labored unceasingly until one o'clock when they rode home, changed their underclothes, dined at two, and then returned to the house at three, where they worked until dark. In the hottest days of August they had worked "unflenchingly" and had not been ill a moment. Attie's message to his mother was, "Tell Ma that she must not be anxious about me, for I take care of myself, and, so far from being sick, I was never better in my life." Attie, Stephen confided, was of more service to his father than any man could possibly be, and was growing smarter every day.[52]

By seven o'clock Stephen had again changed his clothes, had sat with Angela's father in the latter's favorite corner of the piazza, had sipped coffee with him at eight, and, at nine, had gone to bed, "sadly fatigued." Attie and he would then lie on their bed in the dark and have lessons in grammar and arithmetic. In these studies Attie was making capital progress. The repairs and renovations, Stephen was happy to report, were succeeding even beyond his hopes, and, "by reason of my constant attention and labor," all was being done with economy.[53]

His excuses for not writing more frequently were, it seems, not satisfactory to Angela, and once more he was called on to soothe her into better humor. He announced that he was writing "under great pain from gout." He was further distressed by the non-arrival of the door locks which he had asked Angela to secure from the dealer in Bridgeport. He felt sure that the directions sent by him concerning the locks were clear. "You should have expected that a man of common sense who had studied the most complicated of all locks as long as I did, and mastered it in defiance of all your opposition, should be able to comprehend any ordinary bolt or ward."[54]

He had thought that his previous account of his daily employments

51. *Ibid.*
52. *Ibid.*
53. *Ibid.*
54. Mallory to Angela, September 3, 1866.

would have explained to her satisfaction why he could not write to her more often. But, as she was determined to listen to no excuse for silence, and insisted, "with Shylock pertinacity," upon her bond, he would write to her henceforth morning and evening, enclosing a lock of his hair with the doctor's certificate that he was free from all febrile symptoms, and giving to her a minute description, so far as he could foresee, of his actions until the next day.

She was to be assured that Attie and he were well, though somewhat thinner; he was down to 168 pounds, "among the 'light weights.'" He then furnished her with an elaborate report of the daily round at Pensacola: "We . . . rise at 7 A.M., teach Corinne until eight; breakfast upon batter cakes and hominy—the hominy unsifted, I think, though upon this point I am not quite positive—with coffee; reach my house by nine; hammer, chop, saw, scrub, whitewash, lay bricks, mix mortar, hold the ends of boards for carpenters to saw; and thus labor, from the roof to the cellar, flooding the inner man with libations of cold water; return to your father's at one P.M., change all my clothes,—no, this not quite accurate, for of one kind of garments (red belts) I have but one; dine at two upon gumbo, in which I always put viniger [sic], the pepper not being the agil which you most approve, but a confounded (excuse the expletive, but the subject is exciting) little oblong semispherical or rather semi-cylindrical thing, which bears the same relation to the agil that a goatee bears to a goat.

"After the gumbo, upon the final disposal of which my plate is changed for one of shallower depth, I usually continue inactive and meditative for a minute or two, during which brief space memory runs off to my darling wife and 'the days when we went gipsying'; and I ask myself whether, under all the circumstances, she would approve of my affirmative or negative answer to the question from [Mr. Moreno], 'What for you don't eat nattin'?'; and I help myself in accordance with what fancy deems that approval or disapproval would be.

"Three o'clock finds me again with carpenters, gardeners, masons or whitewashers' tools; and at seven I return, again to change my clothing, my belt this time being taken off and hung up in front of the dormer window to dry; the dormer window being thus used because the only others in the room are two very small square holes which do not admit much air. At eight we have batter cakes and coffee, of which batter cakes Attie usually eats a dozen; and at nine our recumbent recitations are renewed."[55]

55. *Ibid.*

"My dreams, . . . though not what they should be in all respects, possess doubtless, in your anxious state of mind, considerable interest for you, to whom they always refer. If a dream of a lovely or interesting woman, whatever the face may be, it gradually slips and slides into those charming lineaments which have so long warmed my heart and guided my way; and thus in dreams as in wakeful hours, whatever may be the enchantment of realities or fancies,—'I hear a voice they cannot hear, A voice that bids me stay; I see a hand they cannot see, That beckons me away.'

"Thus, my charming wife, whose hold upon my heart like the chain upon the fettered prisoner teaches me that 'Where'er I rove, whatever realms I see, My heart responsive fondly turns to thee, To thee, Silveria, turns with ceaseless pain and drags at each remove a lengthening chain.' (I must apologize—and I do so in parenthesis, as my remark is of general application) that my attempts to alter and improve Goldsmith's feeling lines, though not triumphant, are quite as successful as can be expected. He wrote under the inspiration of strong Madeira, while my halting lines tremble under the toleration of gout.

"But not, as Mr. Snagsby says, to put too fine a point upon the matter,— 'You see, Mrs. Snagsby, how the affair stands,' and how my duty, my promises and love to my cara sposa are 'cabin'd, cribbed, confined,' by the necessity of complying with the holy mandate to 'put my house in order.' Be patient, then, my good wife; and although this mandate to your all enduring, long suffering, never complaining, meek and gentle nature is as unnecessary as would have been a command to Sancho to be wise or to Quixote to be heroic, yet I still say it (at this distance) and I say it boldly! Be patient, and doubt not my disposition to correspond with you to your heart's content."[56]

He concluded with some cheering news about the progress of the repairs. All the rooms of their house were now as clean and as white as ever; all the roofs were tight, all sashes and glazing were completed, all blinds and doors hung, all fences and cross-fences up, and scrubbing was in progress. The masons had been paid off with $350. The carpenters were still at work; and Stephen would see to it that they followed Angela's very explicit directions regarding the reconstruction of her kitchen. "We are lucky, very lucky, to get our house even in the order it was. Thousands are mourning over the loss of everything."[57]

56. *Ibid*. For Mr. Snagsby, cf. Dickens' *Bleak House*.
57. *Ibid*.

Soon Angela and Ruby would be able to come down to take possession of their renovated house. One of the last of Stephen's letters to reach his wife before she left Bridgeport contained a few items of special interest. She had asked him how the people of Pensacola were treating him, and whether they were holding anything against him for his alleged weakness of behavior in the Pickens episode. He allayed her fears. They were treating him kindly, "as much as their condition and nature permit." At a recent public meeting on railroad matters they called on him to speak, and cheered him heartily. Angela's father and his third wife had been more than kind to Stephen and to Attie. But Mr. Moreno was feeling sore, very sore, at Angela's silence toward him. A gossipy letter in Spanish from her would do him much good. He had lost all his pure English through the imposed silence of the war years, and spoke now in a style which Stephen said defied description.[58]

Toward the end of September Mallory sent Angela her traveling directions. The house was at last finished, and he wanted her and Ruby to come down at once.[59]

So he and Angela began again their life at Pensacola. It was no slight struggle to get back on his feet financially. He had a great need of ready cash. He sought to liquidate as much as possible of his properties in stocks and lands, and was forced to part with some of the latter at a heavy loss.[60] He opened a law office in partnership with Judge Maxwell.[61] The extent of his handicaps is suggested by his letter to a New York book exchange to which he sent his entire library: "Please do the best you can with them for me in exchanging them for law books, my law library having been annihilated in our late war."[62]

There was also another rather unexpected economic problem which he did not fail to face. Most of his former slaves had elected to stay with him in their new status of freedom. It very soon became evident that they could

58. Mallory to Angela, September 15, 1866.
59. Mallory to Angela, September 28, 1866.
60. Says Clubbs, *op. cit.,* 316: "The correspondence of the ex-Secretary upon his return to Pensacola is filled with pathos. He is in the financial dilemma in which he must realize on any salable asset." In a letter to Rector and Snizer, of St. Louis, Mallory expressed his willingness to sell some of his Missouri lands at one dollar an acre, "though this is considerably less than the first cost of the land many years ago" (March 12, 1867). He also wrote to his brokers in New York, instructing them to dispose of some of his A.C. stock (Mallory to Filor and Wood, from Pensacola, February 13, 1867).
61. Augustus E. Maxwell had represented Florida in the House of Representatives (cf. *supra,* pp. 90-91), had served in the Confederate Senate, and had been a member of the Naval Investigating Committee of the Confederate Congress (cf. *supra,* p. 231).
62. Mallory to Lloyd Book Exchange, of New York City, from Pensacola, January 6, 1867.

not support themselves even on the generous wages he accorded them. Their new gift of liberty had not taught them to be provident, industrious, and alert to the tricks of those who were everywhere seeking to impose on them and to defraud them. He found himself, therefore, forced by what he regarded as a humanitarian obligation to feed them. Some of his orders for foodstuffs show the extent of his self-imposed burden. As Clubbs says, it would be difficult for a family of five to dispose of the following typical requisition sent by Mallory to a dealer in New York: ½ barrel of family beef; one tub of butter; ½ barrel of grits or hominy; 2 barrels of best family flour; ½ barrel of white crushed sugar.[63]

It was not Mallory's intention to dissociate himself entirely from politics. From his prison cell at Fort Lafayette he had written to Judge Marvin that he wished earnestly to assist, by every means in his power, the political and economic regeneration of his state within the Federal Union. He was not a defeatist or a sulker. The Confederacy had lost; and each Southern State, he believed, should accept the defeat gracefully and exert her whole strength to rebuild herself as a useful member of the Union.

By the early spring of 1867 it was becoming clear that sharp political conflict was shaping up in Florida, and throughout the South. The moderate reconstruction program of President Johnson was being superseded by a congressional policy frankly designed to keep the former Confederate states in political bondage. As a means to this end, the Negro was to be given the electoral franchise and equality of civil rights. At once the South, not without reason, saw the specter of the "black peril." The first Reconstruction Act, the so-called "Military Bill," became Federal law on March 2, 1867.[64] On March 23 of the same year, the Supplementary Reconstruction Law was enacted by Congress.[65]

In the preceding July, the Republican leaders had blocked the seating of Florida's representatives in the Senate.[66] Less than five months later, the Florida Assembly had refused to approve the Fourteenth Amendment. "We will not bring as a peace offering," declared that body, "the conclusive evidence of our own self-created degradation."[67]

63. Mallory to Benner, Brown and Pinkey, at New York, from Pensacola, January 6, 1867. Cf. a similar order to Mr. A. D. Grieff, at New Orleans, from Pensacola, March 11, 1867: ". . . 12 hams; 1 barrel of best family flour; 3 bags of corn; 1 dozen sweet oil; 1 barrel best Irish potatoes." The three letters referred to in footnote 60 and in this footnote are from Clubbs, *op. cit.* 317. Miss Clubbs's observation is from the same page of her work.

64. William Watson Davis, *The Civil War and Reconstruction in Florida* (New York, 1913), 446-47.

65. *Ibid.*, 447.                    66. *Ibid.*, 429.

67. *Ibid.*, 437.

The former Confederate Navy Secretary was given an opportunity to state his political views at a large meeting attended by both races at Pensacola, on March 28, 1867.

After being "loudly and repeatedly called upon," he briefly adverted to the prostrate condition of the state under the recent legislation of Congress and counseled submission in good faith. There was, he declared, no degradation in the submission of a gallant people when further resistance would be madness.

He then addressed himself to the Negro problem. In the South, where Negroes constituted nearly half the population, the ballot—qualified or otherwise—was a natural consequence of their freedom, a result which would not follow their freedom in the Northern states, where in point of numbers they were unimportant. Since the Negro was entitled to vote, it was in the interest of the state that he should be educated and enlightened and made to comprehend the priceless value of the ballot and the importance to himself and to the state of its judicious use.

"The prosperity of the State," he declared, "must depend upon the virtue and intelligence of her people, and no wise man will hesitate to do all in his power to elevate and improve the character and condition of the colored race, between whom and the Southern people an indestructible bond of sympathy, based upon a thousand happy memories, exists. Let us fully and frankly acknowledge, as well by deeds as by words, their equality with us, before the law, and regard it as no less just to ourselves and to them than to our State and her best interests to aid in their education, elevation, and enjoyment of all the rights which follow their new condition."[68]

He then earnestly addressed the colored people present, pointing out to them that henceforth they and the white men must tread the same onward path, and that the political and economic interests of whites and blacks were inseparably blended. He counseled them against secret political societies, as well as against any organizations for party purposes based on race or color; these, he warned, were destructive of the interests of blacks and whites alike. The Negro was being met and treated with in a spirit of manly frankness by his former master and by the Southern people generally;

68. *St. Augustine Examiner*, April 20, 1867, quoting the *Pensacola Observer*, n.d. Cf. also Davis, *op. cit.*, II, 456. The speech, says Davis, *loc. cit.*, was reprinted in the *Floridian*, April 9, 1867, and in the *New York Herald*, April 8, 1867. He refers also to the *Pensacola Observer*, March 30, 1867. Cf. also Mallory's urgings that his Florida friends should support the Federal government and that they should submit to the changes that were being effected by that government (Mallory to Charles E. Dyke, editor of the *Floridian*, November 1, 1865, reprinted in *New York Daily News*, n.d., 1865 [Townsend Library, Columbia University]).

societies such as those described were organized only by designing men in order to abuse the Negro's confidence for selfish ends.

He advised the Negro to seek the best advice possible as to the political questions at issue and as to the merits of candidates, and to cast his vote accordingly. He pointed out that with their liberty the Negroes assumed the responsibility of supporting themselves and their families.[69] He closed the speech with a moving exhortation to both races: "They [the Negroes] must come out of the shade, come out in the pure open air, before the light of heaven, and be free men before God, and exercise the judgment He gave them and be no slaves as before. That day is past and gone. The light of freedom shines the same on the black man as on the white man. It was the white man's interest to protect the black man, and the black man's interest to make friends of the white man, and to vote for the best man."[70]

These were indeed large and statesmanlike sentiments, in the best tradition of the sound reconstructionists. And, at this time, in early 1867, the voice of the former Secretary of the Confederate Navy was not alone in urging submission to the new order.[71] But neither the moderate Democrats as a whole, nor Mallory himself, were able to continue this policy of restraint and cooperation.[72] The program of the Radical Republicans was going ahead too ruthlessly for the self-respect of the Southern people. The Reconstruction Acts of 1867 and 1868 and the consequent setting up of new governments in the conquered states; the establishment of Negro suffrage; and the frequently, though not consistently, despotic administration of the Reconstruction legislation convinced the white South that the Republican North was set on keeping the former Confederate states in a condition of vassalage.

69. *St. Augustine Examiner*, April 20, 1867.

70. *Semi-Weekly Floridian*, April 9, 1867. Cf. the observation of Davis, *op. cit.*, II, 456, on this election of April 1, 1867, at Pensacola: "The Conservative ticket carried the election. Thereupon a mob of negroes threatened disturbance. This was a good beginning for Conservatives, but it was a dangerous beginning and proved to be about the first and last Conservative victory under military rule."

71. The *New York Times* testified to the enlightened statesmanship of the South. "With regard especially to the question of the blacks," said this journal, "the action of the Southern Legislatures has been, in almost every instance, humane and liberal to a very high degree" (quoted, n.d., in the *Semi-Weekly Floridian*, January 11, 1867).

72. Cf. John R. Ficklen, *History of Reconstruction in Louisiana Through 1868* (Baltimore, 1910), 187-89. For a condemnation of the Reconstruction Acts from a constitutional standpoint, see John W. Burgess, *Reconstruction and the Constitution, 1866-1876* (New York, 1902), 113-15. Cf. the following accounts, by contemporary observers, regarding Reconstruction conditions in the South: Edward King, *The Great South . . .* (Hartford, 1875); Charles Nordhoff, *The Cotton States in the Spring and Summer of 1875* (New York, 1876); Whitelaw Reid, *After the War: A Southern Tour, May 1, 1865, to May 1, 1866* (New York, 1866); Robert Somers, *The Southern States Since the War, 1870-1871* (London, 1871).

As Dunning has remarked, there were many reasons for a feeling in the South in 1867 that had no parallel in 1865. Military rule displacing civil governments that had worked with satisfactory efficiency for a year was a different thing from military rule that expressed merely the temporary dominion of a conqueror at the close of a long war. The Southerners felt that the policy of Congress had no real cause except the purpose of Radical politicians to prolong and extend their party power by means of Negro suffrage. This and this alone, the South felt, was the purpose for which major generals had been empowered to remodel the state governments at their will, to exercise, through general orders, executive, legislative, and judicial functions, and to compel the white people to recognize the blacks as their equals wherever the stern word of military command could reach.[73]

By early 1868 Mallory was taking a not inconsiderable part in the counter-attack of the Southern Democrats against "Republican Radicalism." He was apparently writing the leading editorials for an aggressive Democratic paper named the *West Florida Commercial,* of Pensacola. This journal, said the more powerful *Tallahassee Sentinel,* "is an able, bold, and influential organ. It is generally supposed that its leading editorials are written by the Hon. S. R. Mallory. They bear the impress of a mind of more than ordinary calibre."[74]

These writings of Mallory supply the best indications of his political views during the period of Reconstruction, and they represent, perhaps, his most important contribution to the political activity of the era. Before we sample them, however, the problem of authorship must be briefly discussed.

It is only by means of indirect evidence that Mallory's responsibility for the editorials can be determined. They are all unsigned, but that he wrote them is beyond reasonable doubt. The following are the chief reasons substantiating this view.

Besides the fact that the general literary style of the articles tallies with

73. William A. Dunning, *Reconstruction, Political and Economic, 1865-1877* (New York, 1907), 110-11. "It was as inconceivable to the southerners," says Dunning, "that rational men of the North should seriously approve of negro suffrage *per se* as it had been in 1860 to the northerners that rational men of the South should approve of secession *per se.* Hence, in the one case as in the other, a craving for political power was assumed to be the only explanation of an otherwise unintelligible proceeding" (*ibid.,* 111). For a moderate discussion of the Negro suffrage question, cf. Howard K. Beale, *The Critical Year: A Study of Andrew Johnson and Reconstruction* (New York, 1930), 173-95.

74. *The Tallahassee Sentinel,* March 12, 1868. It is interesting to note the opposite attitude maintained by Mallory's friend Benjamin Hill, who advocated complete submission to the Reconstruction program, even in regard to its planks respecting the Negro (Pearce, *Hill,* 201-15).

that of the other writings of the former Navy Secretary,[75] a remark of the *Commercial's* editor with regard to one of them implies strongly that Mallory was the author. "An interesting article in the present number," says the editor in the issue of December 20, 1867, ". . . evinces a knowledge of certain events connected with the Confederate Executive, which could scarcely belong to any other than a member of the Cabinet." By a process of elimination, Mallory would seem to be the only Cabinet member who had the opportunity to write for the *Commercial*.

A further rather persuasive indication of Mallory's authorship is an interesting repetition which occurs in one of his paragraphs. In an editorial stressing the point that the Negro, when freed from the guardianship of the white man, inevitably degenerates in character, the former Navy Secretary wrote: ". . . just as those useful grains and fruits, which man's cultivation through laborious successive stages has redeemed and developed from their repulsive character, return to their original types when his care and cultivation are withdrawn, has the negro, when unrestrained, returned to the condition of savage nature from which the superior race has improved him."[76]

In a speech on the Cuban question, delivered in the United States Senate on February 25, 1859, Mallory had said: ". . . just as there are certain grains and fruits which the industry of man has redeemed, by careful culture, from their original and savage nature—from some wild grass or bitter nut—which, if withdrawn from his care, will relapse back to their original type; just so does the African in these colonies [the West Indian colonies of Great Britain], when left to himself, relapse back stage by stage to the original barbarism of his fathers."[77]

The two main themes of Mallory's contributions to the *Commercial* were uncompromising opposition to Negro suffrage and bitter recrimination against what he regarded as the despotism of the congressional Reconstruction program. It is to be noted that the first of these represents a marked change of attitude on Mallory's part since the early part of the preceding year.[78]

In a relatively moderate utterance voiced in the late fall of 1867, Mallory complained that ". . . to the descendants of the slaves held by Washington

75. Cf., for instance, his frequent use of the phrase "nous verrons"; *Commercial,* January 17, 20, 28, February 27, August 27, 1868. The only existing copies of this rare journal are in the Boston Athenaeum.

76. *West Florida Commercial,* December 20, 1867.

77. 35 Cong., 2 Sess., February 25, 1859 (*Cong. Globe,* 1330). Cf. *supra,* p. 108.

78. Cf. *supra,* pp. 399-400.

is being transferred supremacy over his descendants; and this, by the descendants of the men whom he led to battle in vindication of a common cause of freedom. In an age of revolutions, this is one of the greatest. . . ."[79]

Negro suffrage, he warned the Radicals, had formed no part of the Republican creed of Lincoln; and when the first congressional Reconstruction Act was passed, no provision for Negro suffrage was dreamed of. But "Radicalism seeks to engraft it upon the dogmas of the party in defiance of the thousands who, with . . . influential Republican leaders, concur with the President in opposition to it."[80]

He had a brief moment of optimism in early 1868, when he observed that, although the aspect of public affairs at Washington was painful to behold, yet it evinced the "elastic strength and recuperative power of a government resting directly upon the will of the people." A similar situation in any other country could result only in bloodshed, "whereas Congress and the President wage a war of Messages, Bills, Vetoes, Votes, Rejections, Removals, Appointments, Opinions, and Speeches, Executive, Sensational, and post-prandial, and other 'paper pellets of the brain' which, though neither dull and pointless, pierce no hearts, lop off no heads."[81]

But he soon began to launch out in dead earnest against the Radicals, who finally inspired him with real fear. They had, he charged, by enfranchising the Negroes, "made voters of the ignorant, the vicious, the brutal."[82] They had given the benighted Negro the right to vote and the power to rule, while at the same time they admit his unfitness for either by

79. *West Florida Commercial*, November 25, 1867.
80. *Ibid.*, January 8, 1868. Cf., concerning labor problems involving Negroes, outgoing Governor Marvin's address, December 20, 1865, quoted in Walter L. Fleming, *Documentary History of Reconstruction, Political, Military, Social, Religious, Educational, and Industrial, 1865 to the Present Time* (2 vols.; Cleveland, 1906), I, 255-57. For evidence of fairness of the laws of Florida in 1865 regulating labor contracts for Negroes, see *Acts and Resolutions of General Assembly of Florida, 1865-1866*, p. 32, January 12, 1866. Negro politician John Wallace defended the Black Codes in *Carpetbag Rule in Florida* . . . (Jacksonville, Fla., 1888) 35. Regarding laws concerning freedmen in Florida, see Edward McPherson, *The Political History of the United States of America During the Period of Reconstruction* (Washington, D. C., 1875), 38-41.
81. *West Florida Commercial*, January 20, 1868.
82. *Ibid.*, December 13, 1867. Cf., concerning the deceits practiced on Negro freedmen in the matter of land "sales," Wallace, *op. cit.*, 39. Also, in *ibid.*, 38, see the weird story of Negro "congressman" Joseph Oats. Wallace thus describes the methods by which the Radicals trained the Negroes for citizenship: "After finishing the arithmetic lesson [in the school] they must next go through the catechism. 'Who is the 'Publican Government of the State of Florida?' Answer—'Governor Starns.' 'Who made him Governor?' Answer—'The colored people.' 'Who is trying to get him out of his seat?' Answer—'The Democrats, . . . and some white and black Liberal Republicans.' 'What should the colored people do with the men who is [*sic*] trying to get Governor Starns out of his seat?' Answer—'They should kill them'" (*ibid.*, 326).

directing, controlling, and sustaining him in his new relations by means of the Freedmen's Bureau, the bayonet of the soldier, and the disenfranchisement of the citizen.[83] The keynote of the struggle was, he declared, "that this is a white man's government, and that the ascendancy of the white race must and shall be maintained."[84]

The Negro enfranchisement provision of the new Florida "congressional" constitution aroused Mallory's deepest indignation. That there were, he declared, colored men in Florida who were capable of rightly using the ballot, colored men of intelligence, integrity, and character, everyone knew; and had this constitution, in giving suffrage to the Negro, limited it to men of this type, either by a property or educational qualification or by some such restriction, no word of opposition would have come from the whites of Florida. But "a thousand brutal and ignorant Negroes, ignorant of language, law, and letters; ignorant of the principles of freedom, of government, of public justice; ignorant of their own and of the antecedents of men and of races; ignorance which is as the shadow of intellectual death, and which appreciates liberty only as license; a thousand of such poor benighted creatures may balance the votes of a thousand patriots, philosophers, and sages upon any or upon all the intricate questions of public policy, . . . and one more negro would govern them. We have seen them, under Radical rule, driven to the polls like sheep to a pen, and made to hand in a ballot without the faintest comprehension of what the proceeding meant."[85]

The Negro was not allowed to vote, Mallory pointed out, in fifteen Northern states. In New York every male citizen voted, but colored voters were required to own $250 worth of taxable property.[86] "If we must submit to despotism," he pleaded, "and a choice of despots be left us, let the sword be in the hands of our own race. Let it not be said that this degrading device was riveted upon our gallant little State by her own children."[87]

83. *West Florida Commercial*, December 13, 1867.
84. *Ibid.*, February 25, 1868. This was the editorial called by the *Tallahassee Sentinel* "one of the most forcible of these editorials" (March 12, 1868).
85. *West Florida Commercial*, March 24, 1868. Cf., concerning the conventions and constitutions of 1867-68, Dunning, *op. cit.*, 110-23. Concerning the constitution of Florida adopted by the convention on February 25, 1868, and ratified on May 6, 1868, see McPherson, *op. cit.*, 328-29. Cf. Ficken, *op. cit.*, 193, concerning the question of holding a constitutional convention for Louisiana and choosing delegates for it. Says Ficklen, *loc. cit.*: "The negroes, who never before in Louisiana had been legally entitled to vote, came out in large numbers, but the white citizens generally abstained from voting, with the forlorn hope that this action would defeat the plans of the Republicans, which required the majority of the registered voters to vote. In this they were disappointed. The registered voters amounted to 127,639, of whom 82,907 were blacks. The vote for the convention was 75,083, with only 4006 against it."
86. *West Florida Commercial*, March 24, 1868.
87. *Ibid.*, March 21, 1868.

It was Mallory's charge that the Radicals were rapidly changing the American Republic into a despotism. Under our system of checks and balances, he argued, the assumption, by any one of the three departments of the government, of duties pertaining to either of the others reversed the character of the system and brought tyranny. Such a revolution, he believed, was being effected—in the most dangerous manner, not suddenly, but gradually, so as to veil the insidious intent.[88]

He denied the theory that that government is best which is best administered, although many patriotic men, he declared, were, under pressure from the Radicals, falling back on that pernicious idea. Uniformity, predictability, and constancy in government were the essential requirements— "the capricious mutations of a political oligarchy are what men dread."[89]

In the Radicals' attack on the Supreme Court he saw one of the great perils to the Republic. It was reported that the Reconstruction Committee was seeking to prohibit the court from the exercise of appellate jurisdiction in any case arising under the Reconstruction Acts. This was an even more direct assault on the American principle of judicial review than was the other Radical proposal which would require the concurrence of two thirds of the justices of the high court for the nullification of a congressional enactment.[90]

In his typical "grand" style, Mallory summed up the situation as he saw it in February, 1868: "As those who approach the great Niagara, and mark, with bated breath, the rising roar of its mighty waters, feel that a point must soon be reached where return is impossible and destruction inevitable, and thenceforth carefully scan every step of the perilous advance, so have thoughtful men marked with rising apprehension the nation's approach to that political vortex beyond whose dark and mighty turmoil nothing can be seen or known. Like some staunch ship, struggling against a sweeping current, the Constitution is steadily losing ground, steadily drifting towards that fatal abyss of the sword, within which the voices of reason, law, and religion and humanity are hushed by the clash of arms. And as, from the grand old ship's fatal and precipitous plunge, a shattered spar or mangled corpse may alone reach the surface of the troubled waters, to announce her fate, so from out the dark and stormy sea of the sword, who can tell what

88. *Ibid.,* January 22, 1868. Cf. also, from *ibid.,* January 28, 1868: "The most dangerous usurpations of authority are not those which boldly ride over or set aside existing laws or institutions, but such as, while asserting veneration for the law, so construe as to abrogate it, or make it the instrument of its own destruction; and this is the case here. Nous verrons."
89. *Ibid.,* January 22, 1868.
90. *Ibid.,* January 28 and 22, 1868.

vestige of the Constitution may float above the common ruin? Able pilots have pointed out the old beacons and landmarks and warned us of our rapid drift, as, one by one, they have disappeared."[91]

He made much of the argument that "despotism" exercised against the South would ultimately bring into subjection the North as well. Of necessity, the Southern states would not suffer alone. "The same hand which thrusts into them the poisoned poniard, will drive it through to others when the passion moves it. The present victims disposed of, new ones must be found. . . . There can be no rest for the hand of a . . . despot."[92]

By the subjugation of the Southern states, he believed, the character of the American government had been radically altered, its federative form lost in centralization. One had but to consult the teachings of history to discover how rapid was the transition from the government of a congress to the government of a tyrant.[93] With such a vast central power at its head, the democratic form of government would certainly perish. Mallory summarized, again in the rotund style: "What the ancients said of the avenging gods, that they were shod with wool, is true of these ideas of Congressional domination and high centralization of government. They have come upon us softly, and we stand in their presence. The most insidious and dangerous idea is that the majority governs; insidious because in apparent harmony with the American system, and dangerous because where any one, or two, or ten, or ten thousand men can do what they have the will to do, there is no liberty. Arbitrary power does not become less so because it is the combined power of many. The usurpation of power by the Congress of the United States, by setting aside the checks and balances of the Constitution, simplifies the government and leads thereby to despotism."[94]

The approach of the presidential election of 1868 brought new hope to Mallory, as to the whole South. In an editorial of August 27, 1868, the former Navy Secretary proclaimed confidently that the Conservative Democrats, under the leadership of Seymour and Blair, were as good as elected. The people of Florida were being called "revolutionists," and the charge was true. But "theirs is not a revolution by arms, by force, by resistance to law, by invasion of private or public rights, or by disturbance of the public peace; theirs is the revolution of sentiment, of opinion, of judgment, a revolution to be wrought not by . . . [arms], but by the stern, silent, inevitable ballot in the hands of freemen. Nous verrons!"

91. *Ibid.*, February 11, 1868.       92. *Ibid.*, January 30, 1868.
93. *Ibid.*, February 27, 1868.       94. *Ibid.*, March 3, 1868.

At a meeting of the Seymour and Blair clubs at Milton, Mallory gave a speech which was summarized in the *Commercial*. He "feelingly described" in this address the surrender of Lee at Appomattox Court House, the fraternization between the soldiers of both sides, the good feeling of the commanders, and the general expectation of the country that the conquerors would be just, and even magnanimous. He elaborated on the confidence felt by Southern men at that time that the victors would be governed by their persistent declarations made so often during the war, declarations that the war was not waged for conquest, nor for the abridging of the rights of the states, but for the preservation of the Union under the Constitution, with the rights of all the states intact and with the representatives and senators of the Southern states returned to the halls of Congress.

He then recalled the manner in which the Radical Party, false to its professions, had repudiated its promises and had added other conditions to reconstruction; how the Southern people had acceded to those conditions and had repudiated their debt, abolished slavery, and done everything else that they had been ordered to do. Then had come the Reconstruction Acts, and the infamous men who crowded the offices and legislative halls of the state, and called themselves the government of Florida, and overburdened the people with taxes in order to pay for the vast extravagance of that so-called government. He assured his listeners that the election of Seymour and Blair would be a return to government under the Constitution, with economy in the administration and the speedy payment of the public debt.[95]

The election of 1868 was lost by the Democrats, although they put up a very creditable fight.[96] In one of his most pungent editorials some months later, Mallory described what he felt was the state of the nation.

It was the clearly expressed judgment of the founders of the country, he declared, that our form of government would never survive the destruction of the rights of the states and the consolidation of power at Washington. That the rights of the states had been subverted, and those states, in their capacity as sovereigns, made subject to the dictation of Congress, was

---

95. *West Florida Commercial,* September 8, 1868, letter of "Escambia" to the editor.

96. The *West Florida Commercial,* however, scored the "indifference" of the voters of Florida (December 15, 19, 1868). Cf. the following opinion of a close student of the election of 1868: "Considering everything, the Democrats did remarkably well. The party was reorganized while under fire, and succeeded in polling a majority of the white voters of the country. Furthermore, the Democrats had forced their opponents to put aside their statesmen, actively identified with Republican doctrines, and nominate the military hero of the war. These facts indicate the vitality of the underlying principles of the Democracy, and the existence of widespread discontent with the Radical Republican program" (Charles H. Coleman, *The Election of 1868: The Democratic Effort to Regain Control* [New York, 1933], 377).

beyond dispute. When a state is ordered, as three states were then being ordered, to pass a constitutional amendment as a condition precedent to its enjoyment of the rights of a sovereign state, and when this is done in the face of a Supreme Court decision which affirmed that these rights can never be lost, and that the rights of the states are beyond the reach of Congressional legislation, it was too late to talk about Union.[97]

"The fact is," Mallory asserted, "the destruction and disruption of the United States Government, as one of States possessing independent sovereignty, has been accomplished, and a consolidated empire built upon its ruins."[98] As a proof of this statement, he quoted from a remarkable journal called *The Imperialist,* which had begun publication in New York City: "We believe Democracy to be a failure. Though theoretically plausible, in its practical workings it has been found totally inadequate to the wants of the American people. We believe . . . that an Imperial Government can alone secure and protect the rights of national creditors. We believe . . . in short, that Democracy means lawlessness, corruption, insecurity to person and property, robbing of the public creditors, and civil war, and that the Empire means law, order, security, public faith and peace."

The murders and plunders of the French radical revolutionists, Mallory reminded his readers, and the excesses and military usurpations of the rump and long parliaments in England, were followed by the dictatorship of Cromwell and by the establishment of an empire. Who could say that in the case of the American Republic history would not repeat herself once more? Who would say, in view of the changes, revolutions, and startling modifications of the organic laws, both state and national, that *this* would not come next?

The barriers interposed by the founders of the American government to prevent the consolidation necessary to the exercise of kingly power had been swept away in the name of democracy, the people's rights, and universal suffrage—the old, old story—and now, "when the temple is swept and garnished, why shall not the legitimate occupant of such a chamber enter and take possession?"[98]

There was but one remedy, declared Mallory, and if this remedy

97. *West Florida Commercial,* April 23, 1869, "The Empire." Mallory is here apparently referring to the Supreme Court opinion in *Texas* vs. *White,* pronounced in this same April, 1869. His interpretation of the opinion seems to be not completely accurate. While the court decided that a state could never be out of the Union, and hence could never lose its basic rights, the court declared also that the power to reconstruct the state governments resided primarily in the Congress and not primarily in the President.

98. *Ibid.*

failed, all was lost. "The government," he declared, "must be turned back upon its course, and made to resume its original position. If this is not done, and that speedily, the child may be living who will shout, 'Long live the Emperor,' on Pennsylvania Avenue." He was not referring, he assured his readers, to the subject of slavery, but to the Constitution and to the doctrine of states' rights, as these existed before the war. No proposition for the re-enslavement of the Negro would be entertained by any party or faction North or South.[99]

Amid his preoccupations with business and public life, Stephen Mallory found time for pleasant correspondence with old friends.

James H. Rochelle, a former Confederate naval officer, had written to him, urging that somebody write a history of the Confederate navy, and suggesting that Mallory himself might attempt the work. Stephen approved the general idea, but, "in regard to my own labors in this direction, they must be deferred, if ever entered upon, for an unknown or indefinite future; my present condition demanding every hour which I can wring from disease, to support those dependent upon me, at the labors of my profession. Much, by far the largest and most important of the data important for such a work was destroyed, upon and soon after the evacuation of Richmond; and personal recollection must be relied upon, always a most unsatisfactory authority in matters touching the relative claims, merits, etc. . . . of men or military operations,—to make up history."[100]

Mallory expressed his satisfaction that George Cary Eggleston, at that time editor of the *Mobile Tribune,* was preparing such a naval history. "In reply to a letter from him . . . I tendered to him all the information and aid at my command. . . ."[101] This letter to Rochelle contained one of Mallory's last defenses of his work during the war years: "I am satisfied that, with the means at our control, and in view of the overwhelming force of the enemy at the outset of the struggle, our little navy accomplished more than could have been looked or hoped for; and if I have ever felt any surprise connected with its operations, it was that we accomplished so much. Our Navy alone kept that of the U. S. from reaching Richmond by the

99. *Ibid.*

100. Mallory to James Henry Rochelle, from Pensacola, May 21, 1867 (Rochelle Papers, Duke University). Rochelle himself wrote a rather indifferent *Life of Rear Admiral John Randolph Tucker,* under whom he had served. It was published in Washington in 1903.

101. *Ibid.* George Cary Eggleston (1839-1911) was a Hoosier journalist and novelist. He is best known for his novel *Evelyn Byrd* and his *Recollections of a Varied Life,* published in 1904 and 1910, respectively. His *History of the Confederate War* (2 vols., 1910) cannot be considered a contribution to American historiography.

James River, and from reaching Savannah and Charleston; and yet, not ten men in ten thousand of the country know or appreciate these facts."[102]

A postscript gives a further glimpse of Mallory's life at this time: "I am just out of a sick bed, which must be my apology for treating upon a sub-ject which interests me deeply. I am here practicing law. It is touch and go to make a living however."[103]

Mallory's last extant letters are those he wrote from Pensacola to Attila, who was pursuing, with varying success, his studies in the college depart-ment of Georgetown University. These communications reveal not only a great deal about the boy's character, but much also of his father's heart and mind as the end of his life drew near.

On October 3, 1868, Stephen wrote to his son "with little hope of amus-ing [him], as I am in pain today." Attie might possibly detect "some of the features of old gout in these lines."[104] After reporting such items as the running away of Jeff, one of the Mallory horses, and the accidental death, by hanging, of Vixen the dog, the father let his feelings speak a little: "Your room I went into yesterday, for the first time since you left us; for I disliked to go into it. The sight of your pictures, rifle, trunk, bed, desk, table, books and all, just as you left it, gave me a feeling of sadness and made me more than usually realize your absence. But I rejoice, my dear boy, that you are getting an education, and I am confident that you properly appreciate your opportunities to do so, and that you have talents to make education of great value."[105]

Attie seems to have acquired the idea that his love for study was being doubted by his father. Stephen sought to dispel the discouraging belief by expressing his complete confidence in his son's industry and capacity for learning: "I have ever said since you left us that I knew that you would

102. *Ibid.*

103. *Ibid.*—Cf. also Raphael Semmes to Mallory, from Mobile, May 15, 1868: "My dear sir: I have received your letter of the 6th instant, and am obliged to you for the interest you have manifested in my literary undertaking *Service Afloat.* . . . Your suggestions as to mixing up with the main narrative personal memoirs of the mess table, sketches of forecastle life, etc., are valuable, and I had already resolved to pursue this course to a limited extent. Unfor-tunately for me, in this respect, I was the Commander, and therefore, as you know, more or less isolated socially from the rest of my officers. I not only lack the materials, but, I fear, the Marryatt [*sic*] capacity for this portion of the work. Still, I will try my hand at it occa-sionally. I am much obliged to Mrs. Mallory and yourself for your kind invitation to visit you at Pensacola, but I fear I shall not have the requisite leisure. I have sent you a copy of the *Mobile Sunday Times* of the 10th inst., containing the 9th chapter of my book, in which I speak of yourself, and I trust that you will find that my recollection of our interview corre-sponds with your own" (Mallory-Kennedy Collection).

104. Mallory to Attila, October 3, 1868.

105. *Ibid.*

study and that your talents and your judgment were far superior to those of any nine boys out of ten that I meet." The core of the letter was this passage: "You must exert every faculty, my dear boy, to profit by your college course. There is one idea that you should not lose sight of; and it is, that your companions and people generally will expect more from you than from others, from the fact that you are the son of S. R. Mallory. The world, my dear boy, takes for granted that a man who has succeeded in climbing life's ladder as high as I have, above the heads of his fellows, must necessarily be more clever or able than they, and they naturally expect his children to manifest something of the same character, and are apt, on this account, to expect too much of them and to do them less than justice. In this respect the world often makes two mistakes: first, in over estimating the sire, and attributing to talent what may have been the result of accident; and next in denying the real merit of the son because he may not reach their imaginary standard. But, for your own sake, it may be well to imagine that brains as well as luck helped me, and endeavor to meet the world's expectations." Then in a brief postscript, "Your Mother sends you Four dollars enclosed."[106]

A report of Attie's scholastic progress, some months later, evoked from his father a mixture of encouragement and mild correction: "I have just rec'd. . . . your report from the College, and I congratulate you on the general result of your numbers. Improvement is quite evident; but as the report says, 'Attila is a little inattentive and talkative in Mathematics,' and still gives you '9,' I infer that if you had been more attentive and less 'cheeky,' you would have received 10, or the highest mark of knowledge in your class. I suppose you must find mathematics—by which I infer the report to refer only to algebra—vastly amusing, though, for the life of me, I could never see much to laugh at in the study."[107]

Attie was exhorted to remember his promising abilities and the college opportunities which his father never had enjoyed. "Any failure of a son of mine," Stephen wrote, "would mortify me to the grave."[108] Then follows the sober instruction: "Fix your eyes upon the first honors of the College, and never cease to struggle for them. Aim not only at success, but at triumph; at being not only ahead of all others, but so far ahead that you may stand in a class by yourself. Work will do this. Nine tenths of all you may hear about genius and talent, if by these terms is meant a faculty for learning

106. *Ibid.*
107. Mallory to Attila, July 18, 1869.
108. *Ibid.*

without labor, you may discard as bosh. Genius is industry, talent is labor, success is work. Go ahead, therefore, and never cease incessant labor until the incoming Democrat of the White House shall present you a B.A. with the first rewards of Georgetown, in my presence! Remember, my dear son, that as you conduct yourself now, you will walk and live hereafter. Be honest, frank, manly, and truthful as day. Be kind and gentle with women and aged people, and polite to all, and scorn rudeness, vulgarity and bad manners as you would some foul disease." The proper conclusion is not wanting: "I enclose $5 which I happen to have. If you have no use for it you can eat soft shell crab for my benefit."[109]

Attie's epistolary style was not without flaws. Stephen sent him a few directions: "Observe, my dear Attie, how this note is begun, and conform to this manner in your letters. After 'Pensacola' there is a comma, and after 'Fla.' a period, as there also is after the '/69,' which is, as you see, abbreviated. Then, after 'Attila F. Mallory,' a comma comes, and a period after the 'Va.,' which is the abbreviation for Virginia;[110] and a semi-colon follows the address 'My Dear Boy'; all these details may seem trivial, but they are essential to correctness, and are demanded by the grammatical construction of our language."[111]

Spelling and the correct choice of words were, apparently, giving the young student considerable difficulty. "Now, my dear boy," wrote Stephen, "in all my readings of standard writers, I have never met with either the expressions or the orthography which you some times adopt; and, for example, I do not remember to have seen the positive of 'most' spelled 'mutch.' True, you may find authority for your practice in 'Dutch,' but the phlegmatic sour Crouters are never accurate to a 't.' There are several other words in familiar use by you, whose orthography you have enlarged; and though, if the question of which is best, yours or Johnson's method, were an open one, I might stand by you, upon the principle of standing by one's friends, yet, in the present state of the language, I can hardly do so."[112]

May 11, 1870, was Attie's birthday. "Your good mother," wrote Stephen, "told me last evening that this day is the anniversary of your birth; and, in conveying this information, she both laughed and cried over recollections which your wonderful career awakened. But tears and smiles were

109. Ibid.
110. It is not clear why Mallory was using "Virginia" as a part of the address of his letter to his son at Georgetown College.
111. Mallory to Attila, August 24, 1869.
112. Ibid

equally the result of an affection which consumes her heart for her children; for she but wept with pleasure at the prospect of seeing you this summer."[113]

A year later a crisis had arisen in Attie's academic life. His father met the situation with a rather surprising equanimity and hopefulness for his son's future: "Your letter addressed to me at Key West, relative to your aversion to Georgetown College, and expressive of an earnest wish to leave it, was received by me there. I did not reply to it because my time was engrossed by matters that could not be so conveniently postponed; but I did not doubt the correctness of your judgment of your scholastic progress, and was assured by its tone that Georgetown college is not your special affinity, and that justice to you and to the institution demanded a separation, if not a divorce, *a vinculo matrimonii.* I trust, my Dr. Boy,—you see you're a capital boy,—that you will bear with the infirmities of the old Alma Mater until the next vacation, when you can shake the dust of her time honored walks from your feet, steel your heart against her bread pudding and humanities, tear your affections from honors and rewards which you assuredly decline, and return home.[114]

"Your last report,—gratifying in all other details,—does not specially commend your efforts in algebra. I begin to think that you are not entirely in love with mathematics; but you may console yourself with the reflection that a mathematical is the driest, most unappreciative, barren, and unattractive of minds, and that men of the highest order of genius have not excelled in this branch of learning. Newton, La Place [*sic*], Herschel, and a few others have done something at star gazing and Skedaddling about after eclipses, transits, comets, and Meteors; but, after all, we may ask, cui bono?, and question whether the Braminical [*sic*] theory that the earth stands upon the back of an elephant, or the Naturalistic idea that it stands upon a rock, and that rock upon another, all the way down, are not equally simple and satisfactory?"[115]

If Attie was determined to leave college, he must become a merchant. "In sober earnest, my dear boy, you will, in my judgment, succeed as a merchant, and will accumulate, keep, and use money as an honest man, and spend it like a Christian gentleman. You have what cannot always be learned, and what I have no more taste for than you have for astronomy: you have the ability to keep money.[116]

113. Mallory to Attila, May 11, 1870.
114. Mallory to Attila, March 29, 1868.
115. *Ibid.*
116. *Ibid.*

The all-important thing was that the possibility of failure should be ruled out of the boy's calculations. "There must be no such word as *fail!* Rather . . . live and die in an honest effort, worthy of a man, tugging away at fortune even if she present nothing better to your grasp than the pigtail of the 'Heathen Chinee.' "[117]

In this same letter Stephen informed his son that Ruby had left for Paris, where, during the next few years, she would attend the school of the Sisters of the Sacred Heart and, in her father's words, "will become frenchified and a lady of the world."[118] He could hardly bring himself to part with her for such a long period, but he wanted her to have the best possible education. Nothing, he felt, could be too good for Ruby.

The spring and summer of 1871 passed. For Stephen Mallory the sands were running out. During the following mild Florida winter his gout troubled him even more than usual, and he was increasingly anxious about his heart. Ruby was still in Paris, and he missed her greatly. But another spring was coming, and he was always cheered by the spring. And Ruby would be home again next August or September. In a letter to Attie—his last surviving letter—he made what was for him an unwonted confession: "I am quite sick."[119] He wrote the words on the sixth anniversary of his assignment to a cell at Fort Lafayette.

In September, 1872, Ruby was back from Paris. No more was she "little Ruby," but an accomplished and very sweet and gracious, lady of the world. Stephen listened to her for hours as she told her parents about her stay in Europe. We may imagine him looking lovingly at her and at Angela, and perhaps musing to himself that the love of his dear ones had meant most in his life.

On the morning of the eleventh of November, 1873, Stephen played chess in his room, by himself, as he used to do at Fort Lafayette. Angela sat with him for awhile, and noted his listlessness. Twelve years ago, on the same date, he had been studying the reports of the fall of Port Royal. That night he fell grievously ill. They were all there with him, except Attie. He died early on the morning of the twelfth.

His will was a simple document, and it expressed much of his life and character. It read, in part, as follows: "In the Name of God, Amen! I, Stephen R. Mallory . . . do make this my last will and testament, to wit: I do give and bequeath unto my darling wife, Angela S. Mallory, her heirs,

117. *Ibid.*
118. *Ibid.*
119. Mallory to Attila, June 7, 1872.

executors, and administrators, all my real and personal estate, and all property and effects whatsoever. This I do as a mark of Confidence in her character, and her affection for myself and her children; and as an evidence of my boundless love for her, no less than as an act of justice to her devotion and duty as wife and Mother."[120]

120. From original in Escambia County Court House, Pensacola, Fla.

# *Critical Bibliography*

*Manuscript Collections.* The core of the documentation of this study consists of Stephen R. Mallory's unpublished papers, divided into three main classes.

There is, in the first place, his Diary and Letter Book, covering parts of the first two years of his Confederate period, the period of his imprisonment after the war, and, in the form of a long letter to his son, the salient details of his boyhood and young manhood at Key West. Nowhere else are the inner attitudes and character of the man revealed more clearly than in these private recordings, most of them written in 1865-1866 from his prison cell at Fort Lafayette, New York. The original Diary and Letter Book is in the Southern Historical Collection of the University of North Carolina, Chapel Hill, N. C. It has been used by courtesy of Dr. J. G. de Roulhac Hamilton, curator of the Southern Historical Collection and Professor of History at that institution.

Also of high value to the author has been the collection of more than a hundred of Mallory's personal letters, most of them addressed to his wife and children. These letters are in the possession of three of Mallory's surviving descendants, Mrs. Thomas Kennedy, Mr. Thomas Kennedy, Jr., and Miss Cora Mallory, residents of Pensacola, Florida. Without the cooperation, so cordially and generously extended, of these three custodians of the Mallory literary remains, this biography could not have been adequately written.

Finally, many other letters from and to Mallory, other of his writings, or documents affording direct or indirect evidence of his activities were found in several other collections, particularly the following:

United States Treasury Department Records, in the National Archives, Washington, D. C., referring mostly to Mallory's period as Collector of Customs at Key West.

Miscellaneous Letters to the [United States] Navy Department, in the National Archives, referring chiefly to Mallory's activities as chairman of the Committee on Naval Affairs of the United States Senate.

Admiralty Records of the United States District Court, Southern District of Florida, Key West, for Mallory's activities as a pleader in wreckage and salvage cases.

Deed Records in the Monroe County Court House, Key West, for evidences of Mallory's prominence as a landowner and man of business at Key West.

Minute Book of the Circuit Court, Escambia County Court House, Pensacola, for evidence of Mallory's postwar legal activities at Pensacola; and the Records of Cases pleaded before the Supreme Court of Florida, State Capitol, Tallahassee, for his briefs read before that body. Also at the Capitol are several dossiers of cases participated in by Mallory.

Clement Claiborne Clay Papers, Duke University, Durham, N C., for some important personal letters of Mallory to Mrs. Clay, and for two letters of Mrs. Mallory to the same correspondent. As indicative of the attitude of Mallory at a time of acute crisis (1864) these communications are of very great value. The letters of Mrs. Mallory are the only ones from her pen which still survive, and they are of high importance for an insight into a deeper phase of her character.

One important letter of Mallory in the James H. Rochelle Papers, Duke University, expressing Mallory's final judgment on his own work as Navy Secretary of the Confederacy.

Several wartime letters from Mallory to Governor John Milton of Florida in the John C. Milton Collection and William H. Milton Collection, both in the Florida Historical Society Library, St. Augustine, Fla.; and, in the same collections, some letters of Mallory to Milton concerning Indian troubles in the fifties.

Four letters from the wartime correspondence between Mallory and Governor Zebulon B. Vance of North Carolina concerning the respective jurisdictions of the Confederate government and the states. These letters are in the Z. B. Vance Collection, North Carolina Department of Archives and History, Raleigh, N. C., and were kindly supplied in photostat to the author by Professor Frontis W. Johnston, of the Department of History, Davidson College, Davidson, N. C.

Some letters of Mallory and other Southern senators in the Simon Gratz Autograph Collection, Pennsylvania Historical Society, Philadelphia, relating to the "Pickens Truce." Also, in the James Buchanan Papers, Pennsylvania Historical Society, a letter from President Buchanan offering to Mallory the post of ambassador to Madrid, and Mallory's reply to this offer.

An important letter of Mallory concerning the general political situation in December, 1860, addressed to James Hammond, in the James Hammond Papers, Library of Congress.

Three letters from the Mallory-Vance correspondence (already referred to), supplied in photostat by the Henry E. Huntington Library and Art Gallery, San Marino, Calif.

Correspondence of Mallory with the commandant of Fort Jefferson in the late fifties, relative to the wages of slaves at the fort, from the Journal and Letterbook of Fort Jefferson, Federal Writers' Transcripts, Key West, by courtesy of Judge Enrique Esquinaldo, of Key West. This correspondence is important as revealing Mallory's favoring of the interests of the middle-class monied interests of Key West.

An important communication of Mallory to President Davis, dated January 5, 1865, describing the resources of the Confederate Navy Department at that time, in the Jefferson Davis Papers, Duke University.

Mallory's Last Will and Testament, in Escambia County Court House, Pensacola, Fla.

For Mallory's relations with the United States Naval Retiring Board of the fifties, and for favorable and unfavorable criticism of the Board, the following collections in the Library of Congress were used: Hamilton Fish Papers, Hannibal Hamlin Papers, J. M. Clayton Papers, G. B. Crittenden Papers, and—most important of all—the Matthew Fontaine Maury Papers. Maury was bitterly critical of Mallory and of the Naval Retiring Board, and his opinions, because of his personal involvements with the Board, must be weighed with great care. The most balanced estimates of the virtues and defects of the Board were, in the author's opinion, those of Hamilton Fish.

Some letters in the Drew Collection, Pennsylvania Historical Society, threw light on the practice of flogging in the United States Navy of the fifties. For naval affairs generally in the fifties the Henry A. Wise Papers in the Library of Congress were helpful. The W. P. Fessenden Papers in the Library of Congress were valuable concerning the slavery question and in regard to the building of navy yards by the United States government in the fifties and the contrast between sections of the country in this matter.

For various aspects of Southern and Northern feeling during, before, and after the war, the Williams-Manning-Chesnut Papers in the Southern Historical Collection of the University of North Carolina were rewarding.

For sectional views in the critical year 1860, the William Porcher Miles Papers, in the same collection, were important. The E. P. Alexander Papers, also in the Southern Collection of the University of North Carolina, contain an illuminating tribute to the work of the Confederate Ordnance Department by a master artillerist of the Confederacy. The same collection was useful also for indications of Southern feeling during and after the war.

The following manuscript material was used in relation to Confederate naval organization and naval activities and administration:

Confederate [Virginia Volunteer] Navy: Organization and Reorganization of, "VN 1861-1865," in National Archives.

Pickett Papers, Library of Congress, particularly useful for details of blockade running.

Drew Collection, Pennsylvania Historical Society, concerning naval appointments in the Confederacy.

Roster of Midshipmen Enrolled in [Confederate] Naval Academy, 1863, Virginia State Library, Richmond, Va.

Circular: Extract from the Regulations of Navy School, issued by Navy Department, December 15, 1863 (photostat), Duke University.

Josiah Gorgas, Journal, 1864-1878, typescript copy, in the Southern Collection, University of North Carolina, for activities and organization of the Ordnance Department.

A letter from Commander A. B. Fairfax, C.S.N., to Secretary Seddon, from Selma, February 19, 1863, in Naval Records, National Archives, concerning transfer of men from the army to the Ordnance Bureau of the navy.

Estimate for the removal and erection of naval ropewalk, Rare Books Division, Library of Congress; an incident of naval administration indicating the special difficulties under which Mallory labored.

Letter Books of the Mallory Steamship Line, Key West Office, concerning activities of the Tift Brothers, naval constructors for the Confederacy, in April-June, 1861, at Key West; indications that the Tifts were not averse to dealing with both sides.

For details of organization and administration of the Confederate Navy, the transcripts of the Proceedings of the Confederate Congress, 1 Cong., 4 Session, prepared under the direction of Dr. Douglas Southall Freeman, were useful. The transcripts were read by special permission of Dr. Freeman.

*Governmental Publications and Other Documentary Collections.* For Mallory's speeches and debates in the United States Senate the *Congressional*

*Globe* was the chief source. Concerning the dispute over Mallory's election to the Senate in 1850: *Documents relating to the disputed election of 1850,* in the P. K. Yonge Library of Florida History, University of Florida, Gainesville, Fla. (To the rich scholarship and gracious courtesy of Mr. Julien C. Yonge, curator of this library, the author is deeply indebted for many suggestions regarding documentary materials.) Also, with respect to this disputed election: *Reply of Mr. Mallory, of Florida, to the supplemental argument of Mr. Yulee, claiming his seat in the Senate of the United States,* in Rare Books Division, Library of Congress.

In regard to naval reform and naval development in the fifties: *United States Statutes at Large* [1855-1858]; *United States Navy Registers, 1853-1860; Annual Report of the Secretary of the* [United States] *Navy,* 1858, concerning the necessity of building small gunboats of shallow draft instead of large ships of war.

The chief source of information regarding the administration, organization, and activities of the Confederate Navy is the monumental *Official Records of the Union and Confederate Navies in the War of the Rebellion* (30 vols.; Washington, D. C.: The Navy Department, 1894-1922); and *The War of the Rebellion: A Compilation of the Official Records of the Union and Confederate Armies* (128 vols.; Washington, D. C.: The Department of War, 1880-1901). These beautifully edited sets constitute a rich mine of data which has never been fully tapped by scholars. The detailed index renders easy the use of the volumes for specific searches. A defect of the work is the absence of references to the present location of the documents. The defect is not serious however, since the transcripts can be trusted. Numerous monographs on the military and naval history of the Civil War are latent in this superb collection.

For further details of the organization and administration of the Confederate navy, the following published documentary material was highly useful: *Regulations for the Navy of the Confederate States* (Richmond, 1862); *Confederate States Navy Registers, 1861-1865; Reports of the* [Confederate] *Secretary of the Navy, 1861-1865; Register of the Commissioned and Warrant Officers of the Navy of the Confederate States to January 1, 1864; General Orders and Circulars of the Confederate Navy; Instructions for the Guidance of the Medical Officers of the Navy of the Confederate States* (Richmond, 1864); *Report of the Office of Medicine and Surgery,* November 1, 1864, in *Report of the Secretary of the Navy, 1864.* All of the above are in the Library of Congress, Rare Books Division. Also, in the same repository, *Ordnance Instructions for the Confederate States Navy . . .* (London, 1864). For relations of the Navy Department with the Treasury Department, *Correspondence with the Treasury Department of the Confederate States of America, 1861-1865,* compiled under the direction of Brevet Major General E. D. Townsend, by Raphael P. Thian, Chief Clerk, Adjutant General's Office (5 vols.; Washington, D. C., 1880). A rare set of these volumes is in the Duke University Library.

For details of the organization and administration of the Confederate government in general: *An Official Guide of the Confederate Government from 1861 to 1865 at Richmond* (Richmond, n.d.); *Journal of the Congress of the Confederate States, 1861-1865,* reprinted at Washington in 1904 as *Senate Document No. 234,* 58 Cong., 2 Sess.; Dunbar Rowland (ed.), *Jefferson Davis, Constitutionalist: His Letters, Papers, and Speeches* (10 vols.; Jackson, Miss., 1923); James D. Richardson (ed.), *A Compilation of the Messages and Papers of the Confederacy* (2 vols.; Nashville, Tenn., 1906).

Concerning Reconstruction legislation in Florida under "Presidential" rule, and particularly for evidence of the moderate character of the Florida "Black Code": *Acts and Resolutions of the General Assembly of Florida, 1865-1866,* under date of January 12, 1866. Also, for early Reconstruction legislation in the State, *Florida Convention Journal,* 1865.

*Newspapers and Periodicals.* For Mallory's general Florida background the volumes of the *Florida Historical Society Quarterly* were used freely. For his Key West background, and for light thrown on his character as a young man at Key West, the only surviving volume of copies of the *Key West Enquirer* was indispensable. Mallory was a regular contributor to this paper, which had a brief existence from 1834 to 1836. He wrote for it several light essays, some romantic verse (probably inspired by his future wife), a few letters on Key West politics, and a defense of the wrecking industry of Key West. As a mirror of his mind at the period of his young manhood, the *Key West Enquirer* occupies high rank. The author was permitted by Mrs. Hollis Moseley Cooley of Miami to use the volume while it was still in her possession. She has since donated it to the P. K. Yonge Library of Florida History.

Two items in another rare newspaper, the *Key West Gazette,* were informative with regard to general political attitudes at the island town in 1831. The *Gazette* volume, when read by the author, was in the possession of Mrs. Cooley, but it is at present in the P. K. Yonge Library.

For an interesting description of the physical appearance of Key West in 1852, the *Florida Republican* (Jacksonville) was helpful, under date of May 27, 1852.

Descriptions of the activities of the wreckers at Key West were provided by *Hunt's Merchants' Magazine* for April, 1842, and January, 1852, and also by an article in the *St. Augustine Examiner* for March 24, 1860.

Mallory acted as the Key West correspondent of the *New York Tribune*. He wrote for that journal's issues of November 1 and November 6, 1846, a description of the destructive hurricane of that year.

The *Florida News,* September 8, 1858, discusses Mallory's participation in the legal dispute between the Franciscans at St. Augustine and the United States government.

For Florida politics in the fifties, with special reference to Mallory and West Florida, the two Pensacola papers, the *Gazette* and the *Observer,* are full of information. However, both journals are violently biased against Mallory and hence must be used with care. The *Florida Sentinel* was the mouthpiece of the Whigs and, while usually maintaining a rather suspicious attitude toward Mallory, accorded him, in the main, fair treatment. The *Florida Republican, Florida News,* and *St. Augustine Examiner* were generally favorable toward Mallory. The *Floridian and Journal* of Tallahassee, edited by Charles Dyke, appears to be the most objective of the Florida journals of the period. For an account of Mallory's activities in Florida in the presidential campaign of 1860, the *Weekly East Floridian,* August 9, 1860, was helpful.

For social and political Washington of the fifties, the following items were useful: *New York Herald,* February 12, 1855, describing a typical "official" ball; *ibid.,* February 9, 1854, describing the attendance of ladies at Senate sessions; *ibid.,* February 14, 22, 1854, and February 15, 1855, for unfavorable comments on Washington society by New Yorkers; *ibid.,* March 21, 23, 1856, describing spring fashions in Washington; *ibid.,* May 5, 1854, for a strong adverse criticism of the Pierce administration. This newspaper was also consistently helpful for comments and information regarding naval reform activities of the period. The *Washington Union,* March 19, 1853, contained a sharp disapproval of the rules of procedure of the Naval Retiring Board. The *National Republican,* January 23, 1861, commented acidly on Mallory's farewell speech in the Senate.

The *National Intelligencer,* May 18, 1854, discussed the alleged "plot" of Southern senators to precipitate a war with Spain in order to acquire

Cuba for the expansion of slavery. The *Natchez Courier* and the *Mississippi Free Trader* supported the radical Southern position in 1860 with regard to the expansion of slavery into the Territories. The *Charleston Mercury,* edited by the somewhat splenetic Rhett, took a jaundiced view of the Southern politicians of 1860-1861. The *New Orleans Delta,* January 19, 1861, assumed a similar position to that of the *Charleston Mercury,* though with more restraint.

For the significance of the naval reform efforts of the fifties, see the article by Charles O. Paullin, "A Half Century of Naval Administration in America, 1861-1911," *United States Naval Institute Proceedings,* Vol. XXXIX.

The Confederate Navy Department—and the Confederate Government as a whole—sustained a rather surprising amount of hostile criticism from the Southern press. Among the most vocal of these critics were the *Richmond Examiner* and the *Charleston Mercury.* The shafts directed against Mallory and his department by the two journals were intemperate and partisan, but they were indicative of what numerous intemperate and partisan people in the South were saying, and are therefore of historical value. The *Richmond Enquirer* was the "administration" journal, and usually supported Mallory. When it did not do so, its adverse criticism was, of course, particularly significant. The *St. Augustine Examiner* seems to have maintained for the most part a creditable degree of objectivity. Its occasional disapproval of Confederate navy policies is therefore of some weight.

Mallory's administration never fully succeeded in pleasing the *New Orleans Bulletin,* the *Norfolk Day Book,* the *New Orleans Bee,* the *New Orleans True Delta,* the *Atlanta Confederacy,* the *Montgomery Advertiser,* and the *Savannah Republican.* The *Georgia Constitutionalist* showed signs that it was trying to be fair to the Navy Secretary.

The following specific items were of special value for this study: *Richmond Whig,* October 11, 1861, for a well-reasoned adverse criticism of Secretary Memminger's financial policy. The *Whig's* judgments usually were moderate and fair. *Southern Confederacy,* January 31, 1862, complimentary to the Navy Department for its provisioning of Fort Pulaski. *Raleigh Progress,* February 4, 11, 20, 1865, for bitter criticism of the Confederate Cabinet. *De Bow's Review,* XXXIV (1864), concurring with the findings of the majority of the Naval Investigation Committee. *Asheville Times,* August 22, 1926, supporting claims of Commander G. G. Williamson as the original planner of the *Virginia. Mercantile Weekly Report,* of Havana,

Cuba, 1862, for a record of blockade running at Havana. *Galaxy,* April 1867, concerning blockade running.

For Mallory's participation in Reconstruction politics in Florida, the *Pensacola Observer,* March 30, 1867, and *passim,* and the *Semi-Weekly Floridian,* through 1867, were found to be useful. The strong Reconstruction editorials of the (Pensacola) *West Florida Commercial,* 1867-1868, were, many of them, written by Mallory, as explained in the text of this study. On Reconstruction politics in Florida generally, the *Tallahassee Sentinel* is probably the best informant and commentator.

A document of prime importance is the estimate of Mallory's character given by his aged widow in an interview printed in the *New Orleans Times-Picayune* for January 12, 1898.

*Reminiscent Works and Autobiographies.* The best descriptions of the general social and political atmosphere of Washington of the fifties are contained in the memoirs of some of the "official ladies." The present study has drawn heavily on four of these memoirs: Mrs. Clement Claiborne Clay, *A Belle of the Fifties,* ed. Ada Sterling (New York, 1904); Mrs. Burton Harrison, *Recollections Grave and Gay* (New York, 1912); Mary W. Windle, *Life in Washington and Life Here and There* (Philadelphia, 1859); Mary C. Ames, *Ten Years in Washington: Life and Scenes in the National Capital as a Woman Sees Them* (Hartford, Conn., 1875). For an eye-witness' account of the personalities in the Senate of the fifties, nothing better could be asked for than the small volume of Christian Eckloff, *Memoirs of a Senate Page, 1855-1859,* ed. P. Melbourne (New York, 1909).

Other works useful for recreating the Washington of this period are the following: Harriet Beecher Stowe, *Men of Our Times* ... (Hartford, 1868); G. W. Curtis, *The Potiphar Papers* (New York, 1860); James C. Dobbin, *Portrait of Eminent Americans Now Living* (New York, 1853-54); Henry S. Foote, *Casket of Reminiscences* (Washington, D. C., 1874); Rufus R. Wilson, *Washington, the Capital City and Its Part in the Making of the Nation* (2 vols.; Philadelphia, 1902); Frederic Bancroft, *The Life of William H. Seward* (2 vols.; New York, 1900); George F. Milton, *The Eve of Conflict: Stephen A. Douglas and the Needless War* (Boston, 1934); Roy F. Nichols, *Franklin Pierce: Young Hickory of the Granite Hills* (Philadelphia, 1939); Elizabeth F. Ellet, *Queens of American Society* (New York, 1867).

The American Civil War is not remarkable for having occasioned the production of many works of reminiscence. The typical veteran of the conflict wrote of his experiences weightily but not well. Eye-witnesses' reports, however, cannot be completely ignored; and some of the Civil War personal accounts are very revealing.

For the purposes of this study, *The Rise and Fall of the Confederate Government,* by Jefferson Davis (2 vols.; New York, 1881), was useful for its cordial praise of Mallory's conduct of his Department, and for some details regarding naval affairs of the Confederacy. The diary of J. B. Jones, *A Rebel War Clerk's Diary at the Confederate States Capital,* ed. Harold Swiggett (2 vols.; New York, 1935) is chatty and often gossipy, always interesting, and not always free from personal bias. Jones did not particularly like Mallory. The *Diary of Gideon Welles,* ed. John J. Morse, Jr. (3 vols.; Boston, 1911) is solid when not pedestrian, and is surprisingly fair to Mallory. Raphael Semmes's *Memoirs of Service Afloat, During the War Between the States* (New York, 1893) is a sea story as fresh and clean cut as the silhouette of the *Alabama* against a sinking sun, and an indispensable aid to an understanding of the achievements of the commerce-raiding cruisers. James Bulloch's *The Secret Service of the Confederate States in Europe,* (2 vols.; New York, 1884), a straightforward account of the chief Confederate negotiator for ships in Europe, was useful also for its account of Bulloch's first interview with Mallory. The small volume entitled *The Supplies for the Confederate Army: How They Were Obtained in Europe and How Paid For* (Boston, 1904), by Caleb Huse, one of the Confederate buyers, is important because it was written by Huse, but he could have made a much better book from his experiences. The *Memoirs* of Mallory's friend, John Reagan (New York, 1906), are disappointing because Reagan writes so well on the subjects which he selects that we wish he had not omitted the treatment of so many other topics of importance. *The End of an Era* (Boston, 1889), by John S. Wise, is one of the best of the Confederate reminiscences and contains some helpful information with regard to naval activities. William H. Parker's *Recollections of a Naval Officer 1841-1865* (New York, 1883) has some good material on the coastal and river operations of the war. *The Naval History of the Civil War* (New York, 1886), by Admiral David D. Porter, the naval collaborator of Grant, is spotty, but indispensable for the river campaigns of 1862 and 1863. Edward P. Alexander's *Military Memoirs of a Confederate: A Critical Narrative* (New York, 1907) was helpful for this study because of the Confederate artillery expert's comments on the administration of the Ordnance Bureau. For the general atmosphere of wartime Richmond, an important source was Mrs. Sallie A.

B. Putnam's *Richmond During the War; Four Years of Personal Observation* (New York, 1867). A series of anonymous sketches in the *New York Citizen,* 1867-1868, while cynical in appraising the Confederate government, contains some excellent character sketches of the heads of the Confederate departments, including Mallory.

For Reconstruction conditions, the following contemporary accounts were used with profit: John Wallace, *Carpetbag Rule in Florida* (Jacksonville, 1888). Wallace was a Negro freedman whose judgments on Reconstruction policies are marked by notable moderation and soundness. Edward King, *The Great South* . . . (Hartford, 1875). Charles Nordhoff, *The Cotton States in the Spring and Summer of 1875* (New York, 1876). Whitelaw Reid, *After the War: A Southern Tour, May 1, 1865 to May 1, 1866* (New York, 1866). Robert Somers, *The Southern States Since the War, 1870-1871* (London, 1871).

*Biographies.* The author is especially indebted to the scholarly Master's thesis, unpublished, The Life of Stephen Russell Mallory the Elder, by Miss Occie Clubbs of Pensacola. The thesis was written for the University of Florida, Gainesville, Florida, and was completed in 1936.

Of the many standard works valuable for details of social and political Washington of 1850-1861, the following were most frequently used by the author: Frederic Bancroft, *The Life of William H Seward* (2 vols.; New York, 1900); Roy F. Nichols, *Franklin Pierce: Young Hickory of the Granite Hills* (Philadelphia, 1939); George F. Milton, *The Eve of Conflict: Stephen A. Douglas and the Needless War* (Boston, 1934). James B. Ranck, *Albert Gallatin Brown, Radical Southern Nationalist* (New York, 1937) and Wilmer C. Harris, *Public Life of Zachariah Chandler* (Michigan Historical Commission, 1917) were important for the purposes of this study because of the relations of Mallory with Brown and Chandler.

*The Life of John Ericsson* (New York, 1911), by William C. Church, was valuable for details of the early development of plans for ironclads. Mallory was a warm supporter of Ericsson. With regard to Dahlgren's ordnance innovations, forwarded by Mallory as chairman of the Naval Affairs Committee, the *Memoir of John A. Dahlgren,* by Madeleine Vinton Dahlgren (Boston, 1882) was helpful.

One of the severest critics of the Naval Retiring Board of the fifties was Matthew Fontaine Maury, the famed oceanographer, who was cashiered by the Board in 1855. The biography of Maury by his daughter is, understandably, quite uncomplimentary to the Board; it is also a valuable statement of the grounds of opposition to the Board—Diana Fontaine Maury Corbin, *A Life of Matthew Fontaine Maury* (London, 1888). A more recent biography of Maury by Jacquelin A. Caskie, *Life and Letters of . . . Maury* (Richmond, 1928), adds very little to Mrs. Corbin's work.

It seems safe to say that, as of 1954, no member of the Confederate Cabinet, with the exception of Davis and Benjamin, had found his definitive biographer. Robert Meade's *Judah P. Benjamin, Confederate Statesman* (New York, 1943) was satisfying and extremely helpful because of Mallory's intimate association with Benjamin. The short biographical sketches by Burton Hendrick—*Statesmen of the Lost Cause: Jefferson Davis and His Cabinet* (New York, 1939) and Rembert W. Patrick—*Jefferson Davis and His Cabinet* (Baton Rouge, La., 1944) were more useful to the author than the formal and longer works on the Cabinet members.

In the author's opinion, the best all-round biography of Jefferson Davis is Robert McN. McElroy's *Jefferson Davis, the Real and Unreal* (New York, 1937). Armistead C. Gordon, *Jefferson Davis* (New York, 1918), and Elisabeth Cutting, *Jefferson Davis, Political Soldier* (New York, 1930), were most helpful to the author in his efforts to understand the character of the Confederate President. Frank H. Alfriend, *The Life of Jefferson Davis* (Philadelphia, 1868), is frankly a panegyrist of Davis, and Edward A. Pollard, *A Life of Jefferson Davis* (Chicago, 1869), is too bitter an opponent of the President to be trusted. H. J. Eckenrode, *Jefferson Davis, President of the South* (New York, 1923), and W. E. Dodd, *Jefferson Davis* (Philadelphia, 1907), were read, with no notable profit for this study. Morris Schaff, *Jefferson Davis, His Life and Personality* (Boston, 1922), was helpful on one important point—the refutation of the charges of cruelty practiced by the Confederate government against Northern prisoners. Eron Rowland's *Varina Howell, Wife of Jefferson Davis* (2 vols.; New York, 1931) is not only the definitive biography of the Confederate First Lady but supplies also much of value regarding the character and attitudes of her husband, and is excellent in its treatment of the social life of official circles in Montgomery and Richmond.

The following books present forcibly the anti-administration and states' rights position in the Confederacy: Percy S. Flippen, *Herschal V. Johnson of Georgia, State Rights Unionist* (Richmond, 1931); Louis B. Pendleton, *Alexander H. Stephens* (Philadelphia, 1908); Rudolph von Abele, *Alexander H. Stephens* (New York, 1946); Clement Dowd, *Life of Zebulon B.*

*Vance* (Charlotte, N. C., 1897); Herbert Fielder, *A Sketch of the Life and Times of Joseph E. Brown* (Springfield, Mass., 1883). A severe criticism of Brown's states' rights theories is presented by Louise B. Hill in her *Governor Brown and the Confederacy* (Nashville, 1938; private edition).

*The Life and Times of C. G. Memminger,* by Henry D. Capers (Richmond, 1893) was important for this study because of Mallory's necessarily close relations with the Confederate Treasury Department. This is not the definitive work on Memminger. U. B. Phillips' *The Life of Robert Toombs* (New York, 1913) was used in this study only for a discussion of Toombs's powerful arguments against the Naval Retiring Board of the prewar period.

For Confederate diplomatic operations abroad, the following work was used once: Virginia Mason, *The Public Life and Diplomatic Correspondence of James M. Mason* (Roanoke, Va., 1903).

Three competent biographies of great Union naval leaders were consistently helpful to the author: Richard S. West, Jr., *The Second Admiral: A Life of David Dixon Porter, 1813-1891* (New York, 1937); Charles L. Lewis, *David Glasgow Farragut, Our First Admiral* (Annapolis, Md., 1943); and James M. Hoppin, *Life of Andrew Hull Foote, Rear Admiral United States Navy* (New York, 1874).

General Beauregard and Mallory had many disagreements as to the conduct of the war. For the Beauregard points of view the two following works are important: Alfred Roman, *The Military Operations of General Beauregard in the War Between the States, 1861 to 1865* (New York, 1884) and Hamilton Basso, *Beauregard, the Great Creole* (New York, 1933). The former is well documented; the latter is largely a partisan and somewhat sentimental defense of the General.

A highly partisan biography, inimical to Mallory, is Mrs. Emma Maffitt's *Life and Services of John Newland Maffitt* (New York, 1906).

Two biographies of Stanton are useful with regard to the attitude of the Union Secretary of War toward Mallory's imprisonment and final pardon: Frank A. Flower, *Edwin McMasters Stanton, the Autocrat of the Rebellion, Emancipation, and Reconstruction* (New York, 1905); and George C. Gorham, *Life and Public Services of Edwin M. Stanton* (2 vols.; Boston, 1899).

*General and Special Histories.* For Mallory's Key West background the following books were found to be most useful: Walter C. Maloney, *A Sketch of the History of Key West, Florida* (Newark, N. J., 1876); and Jefferson

B. Browne, *Key West, the Old and the New* (St. Augustine, Fla., 1912). These two authors lived in Key West in the generation immediately following that of Mallory, and their volumes therefore partake of the nature of primary works. An unpublished manuscript history of Key West by an old resident, Marie L. Cappick, Island Pageant: A History of Key West (Key West, 1935), was graciously put at the author's disposal by Miss Cappick, and proved to be of high value for this study. Also useful were the following: *Florida, A Guide to the Southernmost State* (Federal Writers' Project; New York, 1939); *Key West, Florida: Photogravures,* ed. H. Crain (1896), containing a photogravure of the Mallory home; Ernest Hemingway, *To Have and Have Not* (London, 1937), for general atmosphere of Key West; and William Marvin, *A Treatise on the Law of Wreck and Salvage* (Boston, 1858), for details of the methods of judicial control of the wrecking industry. Mallory was active as a lawyer in this field.

For Florida background in general the following works were used: Caroline M. Brevard, *A History of Florida from the Treaty of 1763 to Our Times* (2 vols.; Deland, Fla., 1924); Rowland H. Rerick, *Memoirs of Florida, Embracing a General History of the Province, Territory, and State . . . ,* ed. Francis P. Fleming (2 vols.; Atlanta, Ga., 1902); Kathryn T. Abbey, *Florida, Land of Change* (Chapel Hill, N. C., 1941); W. T. Cash, *The Story of Florida* (4 vols.; New York, 1938); Alfred J. Hanna, *Flight Into Oblivion* (Richmond, 1938). The last volume is excellent also for its treatment of the last days of the remnants of the Confederate Cabinet in retreat.

For prewar political alignments and political activities in Florida, William Watson Davis, *The Civil War and Reconstruction in Florida* (New York, 1913), was basic.

For Mallory's Moravian period at school at Nazareth, Pennsylvania, two books were indispensable: Levine T. Reichel, *The Early History of the Church of the United Brethren (Unitas Fratrum) . . .* (Nazareth, Pa., 1888); and *The Whitefield House on the Euphrata Property at Nazareth, Pennsylvania, 1740-1914* (Bethlehem, Pa., 1914).

Avery Craven's *The Repressible Conflict, 1830-1861* (Baton Rouge, La., 1939) was useful as an interpretation of Northern and Southern feeling on the eve of the war. James C. Dobbin's *Portraits of Eminent Americans Now Living* (New York, 1853-54) and Elizabeth F. Ellet's *Queens of American Society* (New York, 1867) provided intimate contemporary sketches of personalities of social and political Washington of the prewar decade. For social life of the same period at the capital city, Rufus R. Wilson's *Washington, The Capital City and Its Part in the Making of the Nation* (2 vols.; Philadelphia, 1902) was read with profit by the author. For the slavery debate of the fifties, the *Rise and Fall of the Slave Power in America* (3 vols.; Boston, 1872-77) cannot be ignored.

In regard to the efforts through 1853-1860 to develop the United States Navy, the following standard works were frequently consulted: Frank M. Bennett, *The Steam Navy of the United States: A History of the Growth of the Steam Vessel of War in the United States Navy* (Pittsburgh, 1896); Dudley W. Knox, *A History of the United States Navy* (New York, 1936); H. W. Wilson, *Ironclads in Action: A Sketch of Naval Warfare from 1855 to 1895* . . . (London, 1896); James P. Baxter, *Introduction of the Ironclad Warship* (Cambridge, Mass., 1933); Harold and Margaret Sprout, *The Rise of American Naval Power, 1776-1918* (Princeton, N. J., 1939).

For details of social life and general atmosphere of official circles at Montgomery and Richmond, Eron Rowland's *Varina Howell, Wife of Jefferson Davis* (2 vols.; New York, 1931) was more illuminating than any other work. Also useful was the volume by Francis B. Simkins and James W. Patton, *The Women of the Confederacy* (Richmond and New York, 1936) and an article by R. B. Rhett, "The Confederate Government at Montgomery," in *Battles and Leaders of the Civil War* (4 vols.; New York, 1884-87). On this phase of the Confederate story the reminiscences and biographies already mentioned were, of course, also sources of information.

In regard to the organization and administration of the Confederate Navy Department the following special and general works were consulted freely: Charles A. Vanfelson, *The Little Red Book or Department Directory, for the Use of the Public in the Confederate States of America* (Richmond, 1861); Vanfelson was one of the messengers in the Navy Department at Richmond, and his small book gives a good broad description of the physical layout of the Navy Department at the capital, and several helpful details regarding the organizational setup. J. T. Scharf, *History of the Confederate States Navy* . . . (New York, 1887); this is still the best all-round history of the Confederate Navy, although it leaves much to be desired. Francis B. Bradlee, *Blockade Running During the Civil War and the Effect of Land and Water Transportation on the Confederacy* (Salem, Mass., 1925); Bradlee has compiled some very accurate and thrilling accounts of specific instances of blockade running, and has added some stimulating essays on the land and water transportation problems of the Confederacy. William M. Robinson, Jr., *The Confederate Privateers* (New Haven, 1928), the standard monograph on the subject. Ben La Bree (ed.), *The Confederate Soldier in the Civil War, 1861-1865* (Louisville, Ky., 1897), valuable for the purposes of this study because of its sketch of Confederate naval history by Admiral Franklin Buchanan and other naval leaders of the South. W. J. Tenney, *The Military and Naval History of the Rebellion in the United States* (New York, 1865) lacks objectivity and scientific treatment, but is useful for its description of the financial difficulties of the Confederacy. Samuel B. Thompson, *Confederate Purchasing Operations Abroad* (Chapel Hill, N. C., 1935) is informative and soundly critical. Herbert H. Todd, *The Building of the Confederate States Navy in Europe* (Nashville, Tenn., 1941) is brief, but deserving of a place in this list. John Johnson (formerly major of engineers in the Confederacy), *The Defence of Charleston Harbor, Including Fort Sumter and Adjacent Islands* (Charleston, 1890) threw much light on the activities of the Torpedo Bureau. Claude E. Fuller and Richard D. Steuart, *Firearms of the Confederacy* . . . (Huntington, West Va., 1944) was useful for it reprint of Josiah Gorgas' excellent history of the founding and organization and work of the Ordnance Department. Charles H. Wesley, *The Collapse of the Confederacy* (Washington, D. C., 1922) contains several extracts from Gorgas' *Journal*. Gorgas was the first chief of the Confederate Ordnance Department.

The following general military and naval histories were used with profit: Matthew F. Steele, *American Campaigns* (2 vols.; Washington, D. C., 1922); this, in the opinion of the present author, is the most authoritative and most compendious of the military and naval histories of the Civil War. Almost equally useful was *The Story of the Civil War* (2 vols.; New York, 1933) by John C. Ropes, and the continuation of the same work by Col. W. R. Livermore (2 vols.; New York, 1933). Walter Geer's *Campaigns of the Civil War* (New York, 1926) is also a competent military and naval history, though not as complete as that of Ropes and Livermore. Allan Westcott has edited the volume entitled *American Sea Power Since 1775* (Philadelphia, 1947), useful with regard to the operations of the ironclads in the Civil War and the commerce-raiding cruisers. The Sprouts' volume on the *Rise of American Naval Power,* mentioned above, has a brief but illuminating survey of Confederate naval strategy. Also Burton Hendrick's *Statesmen of the Lost Cause* and Rembert Patrick's *Jefferson Davis and His Cabinet,* both cited above, contain excellent interpretations of Confederate naval strategy in the chapters devoted to Mallory.

Of the general histories of the Civil War, the most useful for this study was *The Story of the Confederacy* (New York, 1943) by Robert S. Henry. (Douglas Freeman has referred to this work as the book to which historians of the Civil War must always return.) John C. Schwab's *The Confederate States of America, 1861-1865, a Financial and Industrial History of the South During the Civil War* (New York, 1901), fulfills completely the professions implicit in its title. E. A. Pollard's *Southern History of the War* (2 vols.; New York, 1866) is strongly prejudiced against the Davis administration, and hence not completely reliable. Edward McPherson's *The Political History of the United States During the Great Rebellion* (Washington, D. C., 1864) is still valuable. J. G. Randall's *Civil War and Reconstruction* (Boston, 1937) was, of course, used by the author with great profit. Clifford Dowdey's *Experiment in Rebellion* (New York, 1947), deficient in many respects, was, however, very useful for its account of the intimate relations between Mallory and Benjamin. The *Southern Historical Society Papers, passim,* were frequent and rich aids to the author.

On the following special topics there were some books of particular value. For the attempts of the Confederate government to raise an opposition to the United States via Canada and New York: John W. Headley, *Confederate Operations in Canada and New York* (New York, 1906). In regard to "states rights" conflicts in the Confederacy: Frank L. Owsley, *State Rights in the Confederacy* (Chicago, 1925); Albert B. Moore, *Conscription and Conflict in the Confederacy* (New York, 1924); S. D. Brummer, "Judicial Interpretation of the Confederate Constitution," in *Studies in Southern History and Politics* (New York, 1914). Probably the definitive work on judicial interpretation of the Confederate Constitution: William M. Robinson, *Justice in Grey: A History of the Judicial System of the Confederate States of America* (Cambridge, Mass., 1941). Also useful in its restricted field of study is John A. Crago, Contemporary Confederate Criticism of President Davis (unpublished Master's thesis, University of Florida, 1940).

For the politics of the Reconstruction era, the following works were found to be most helpful: J. G. Randall, *Civil War and Reconstruction,* mentioned above; Walter L. Fleming, *Documentary History of Reconstruction* . . . (2 vols.; Cleveland, 1906); E. Merton Coulter, *The South During Reconstruction, 1865-1877* (Baton Rouge, La., 1947); Edward McPherson, *The Political History of the United States of America During the Period of Reconstruction* (Washington, D. C., 1875); W. A. Dunning,

*Reconstruction Political and Economic, 1865-1877* (New York, 1907); John W. Burgess, *Reconstruction and the Constitution, 1866-1876* (New York, 1902).

For Reconstruction conditions in Florida, William Watson Davis' *The Civil War and Reconstruction in Florida* (New York, 1913) was a constant guide to the author.

For special phases of Reconstruction the following works were used: Charles E. Chadsey, *The Struggle Between President Johnson and Congress Over Reconstruction* (New York, 1897); Paul S. Peirce, *The Freedmen's Bureau: A Chapter in the History of Reconstruction* (Iowa City, Iowa, 1904); Howard K. Beale, *The Critical Year: A Study of Andrew Johnson and Reconstruction* (New York, 1930), including one of the most moderate and most objective discussions of the Negro suffrage question; Charles H. Coleman, *The Election of 1868: The Democratic Effort to Regain Control* (New York, 1933). (Mallory campaigned vigorously in favor of Seymour and Blair in this election.)

Charles W. Ramsdell, *Reconstruction in Texas* (New York, 1910) was useful for its description of the Reconstruction position of Mallory's friend John Reagan. John R. Ficklen, *History of Reconstruction in Louisiana Through 1868* (Baltimore, 1910) was helpful with regard to Negro suffrage problems common to the lower South.

# Index

# Date Due

| | | | |
|---|---|---|---|
| M 4393905 | | | |
| 11-27-44 | | | |
| | | | |
| | | | |
| | | | |
| | | | |
| | | | |
| | | | |
| | | | |
| | | | |
| | | | |
| | | | |
| | | | |
| | | | |
| | | | |
| | | | |
| | | | |